Exam 70-441: *Pro: Designing Database Solutions by Using Microsoft® SQL Serve*

MW01254334

Objective

Designing Database Testing and Code Management Procedures (1.0)	
Design a unit test plan for a database. ■ Assess which components should be unit tested. ■ Design tests for query performance. ■ Design tests for data consistency. ■ Design tests for application security. ■ Design tests for system resources utilization. ■ Design tests to ensure code coverage.	■ Chapter 10, Lesson 1 ■ Chapter 10, Lesson 2 ■ Chapter 10, Lesson 3 ■ Chapter 10, Lesson 4 ■ Chapter 10, Lesson 5 ■ Chapter 10, Lesson 6
Create a performance baseline and benchmarking strategy for a database. ■ Establish performance objectives and capacity planning. ■ Create a strategy for measuring performance changes. ■ Create a plan for responding to performance changes. ■ Create a plan for tracking benchmark statistics over time.	■ Chapter 11, Lesson 1 ■ Chapter 11, Lesson 2 ■ Chapter 11, Lesson 3 ■ Chapter 11, Lesson 4
Create a plan for deploying a database. ■ Select a deployment technique. ■ Design scripts to deploy the database as part of application setup. ■ Design database change scripts to apply application patches. ■ Design scripts to upgrade database data and objects.	■ Chapter 12, Lesson 1 ■ Chapter 12, Lesson 2 ■ Chapter 12, Lesson 2 ■ Chapter 12, Lesson 2
Control changes to source code. ■ Set file permissions. ■ Set and retrieve version information. ■ Detect differences between versions. ■ Encrypt source code. ■ Mark groups of objects, assign version numbers to them, and devise a method to track changes.	■ Chapter 13, Lesson 2 ■ Chapter 13, Lesson 3 ■ Chapter 13, Lesson 4 ■ Chapter 13, Lesson 5 ■ Chapter 13, Lesson 6
Designing an Application Solution for SQL Server 2005 (2.0)	
Select and design SQL Server services to support business needs. ■ Select the appropriate services to use to support business needs. ■ Design a SQL Web services solution. ■ Design a Notification Services solution to notify users. ■ Design a Service Broker solution for asynchronous database applications. ■ Design a Microsoft Distributed Transaction Coordinator (MS DTC) solution for distributed transactions. ■ Design a Reporting Services solution. ■ Design an Integration Services solution. ■ Design a SQL Server core service solution. ■ Design a SQL Server Agent solution. ■ Design a DatabaseMail solution.	■ Chapter 1, Lesson 1 ■ Chapter 1, Lesson 3 ■ Chapter 1, Lesson 4 ■ Chapter 1, Lesson 3 ■ Chapter 1, Lesson 3 ■ Chapter 1, Lesson 4 ■ Chapter 1, Lesson 3 ■ Chapter 1, Lesson 2 ■ Chapter 1, Lesson 2 ■ Chapter 1, Lesson 2
Design a logical database. ■ Design a normalized database. ■ Optimize the database design by denormalizing. ■ Design data flow architecture. ■ Optimize queries by creating indexes. ■ Design table width. ■ Design index-to-table-size ratio.	■ Chapter 2, Lesson 2 ■ Chapter 2, Lesson 3 ■ Chapter 2, Lesson 4 ■ Chapter 4, Lesson 1 ■ Chapter 4, Lesson 2 ■ Chapter 4, Lesson 2
Design an application solution to support security. ■ Design and implement application security. ■ Design the database to enable auditing. ■ Design objects to manage user access. ■ Design data-level security that uses encryption.	■ Chapter 8, Lesson 1 ■ Chapter 8, Lesson 2 ■ Chapter 9, Lesson 4 ■ Chapter 8, Lesson 2
Design an application solution that uses appropriate database technologies and techniques. ■ Design a solution for storage of XML data in the database. ■ Choose appropriate languages. ■ Design a solution for scalability. ■ Design interoperability with external systems. ■ Develop aggregation strategies.	■ Chapter 5, Lesson 1 ■ Chapter 5, Lesson 2 ■ Chapter 5, Lesson 3 ■ Chapter 5, Lesson 4 ■ Chapter 5, Lesson 5

Note: Exam objectives are subject to change at any time without prior notice and at Microsoft's sole discretion. Please visit the Microsoft Learning Certification Web site (*www.microsoft.com/learning/mcp/*) for the most current listing of exam objectives.

Design an application solution that supports reporting. ■ Design a snapshot strategy. ■ Design the schema. ■ Design the data transformation. ■ Design indexes for reporting. ■ Choose programmatic interfaces. ■ Evaluate use of reporting services. ■ Decide which data access method to use.	■ Chapter 15, Lesson 2 ■ Chapter 15, Lesson 2 ■ Chapter 15, Lesson 2 ■ Chapter 15, Lesson 2 ■ Chapter 15, Lesson 3 ■ Chapter 15, Lesson 1 ■ Chapter 15, Lesson 2
Design data distribution. ■ Design a DatabaseMail solution for distributing data. ■ Design SQL Server Agent alerts. ■ Specify a Web services solution for distributing data. ■ Specify a Reporting Services solution for distributing data. ■ Specify a Notification Services solution for distributing data.	■ Chapter 14, Lesson 1 ■ Chapter 14, Lesson 2 ■ Chapter 14, Lesson 3 ■ Chapter 14, Lesson 4 ■ Chapter 14, Lesson 5

Designing Database Objects (3.0)

Design objects that define data. ■ Design user-defined data types. ■ Design tables that use advanced features. ■ Design indexes. ■ Specify indexed views to meet business requirements.	■ Chapter 3, Lesson 2 ■ Chapter 2, Lesson 5 ■ Chapter 4, Lesson 3 ■ Chapter 4, Lesson 4
Design objects that retrieve data. ■ Design views. ■ Design user-defined functions. ■ Design stored procedures.	■ Chapter 6, Lesson 1 ■ Chapter 6, Lesson 3 ■ Chapter 6, Lesson 2
Design objects that extend the functionality of a server. ■ Design scalar user-defined functions to extend the functionality of the server. ■ Design CLR user-defined aggregates. ■ Design stored procedures to extend the functionality of the server.	■ Chapter 7, Lesson 2 ■ Chapter 7, Lesson 4 ■ Chapter 7, Lesson 1
Design objects that perform actions. ■ Design DML triggers. ■ Design DDL triggers. ■ Design WMI triggers. ■ Design Service Broker applications. ■ Design stored procedures to perform actions.	■ Chapter 7, Lesson 3 ■ Chapter 7, Lesson 3 ■ Chapter 14, Lesson 2 ■ Chapter 1, Lesson 1 ■ Chapter 7, Lesson 4

Designing a Database (4.0)

Design attributes. ■ Decide whether to persist an attribute. ■ Specify domain integrity by creating attribute constraints. ■ Choose appropriate column data types and sizes.	■ Chapter 3, Lessons 4 and 5 ■ Chapter 3, Lesson 4 ■ Chapter 3, Lesson 1
Design entities. ■ Define entities. ■ Define entity integrity. ■ Normalize tables to reduce data redundancy. ■ Establish the appropriate level of denormalization.	■ Chapter 3, Lessons 3 and 4 ■ Chapter 3, Lessons 3 and 4 ■ Chapter 2, Lesson 2 ■ Chapter 2, Lesson 3
Design entity relationships (ER). ■ Specify ER for referential integrity. ■ Specify foreign keys. ■ Create programmable objects to maintain referential integrity.	■ Chapter 3, Lesson 3 ■ Chapter 3, Lesson 3 ■ Chapter 3, Lesson 5
Design database security. ■ Define database access requirements. ■ Specify database object security permissions. ■ Define schemas to manage object ownership. ■ Specify database objects that will be used to maintain security. ■ Design an execution context strategy.	■ Chapter 9, Lesson 1 ■ Chapter 9, Lesson 3 ■ Chapter 9, Lesson 2 ■ Chapter 9, Lesson 4 ■ Chapter 9, Lesson 5

Developing Applications That Use SQL Server Support Services (5.0)

Develop applications that use Reporting Services. ■ Specify subscription models, testing reports, error handling, and server impact. ■ Design reports. ■ Specify data source configuration. ■ Optimize reports.	■ Chapter 15, Lesson 3 ■ Chapter 15, Lesson 3 ■ Chapter 15, Lesson 4 ■ Chapter 15, Lesson 4
Develop applications for Notification Services. ■ Create Notification Services configuration and application files. ■ Configure Notification Services instances. ■ Define Notification Services events and event providers. ■ Configure the Notification Services generator. ■ Configure the Notification Services distributor. ■ Test the Notification Services application. ■ Create subscriptions. ■ Optimize Notification Services.	■ Chapter 16, Lesson 1 ■ Chapter 16, Lesson 1 ■ Chapter 16, Lesson 2 ■ Chapter 16, Lesson 3 ■ Chapter 16, Lesson 3 ■ Chapter 16, Lesson 4 ■ Chapter 16, Lesson 5 ■ Chapter 16, Lesson 6
Develop packages for Integration Services. ■ Select an appropriate Integration Services technology or strategy. ■ Create Integration Services packages. ■ Test Integration Services packages.	■ Chapter 17, Lesson 3 ■ Chapter 17, Lesson 1 ■ Chapter 17, Lesson 2

Microsoft

MCITP Self-Paced Training Kit (Exam 70-441): Designing Database Solutions by Using Microsoft® SQL Server™ 2005

Dejan Sarka, Adolfo Wiernik,
Javier Loria, and Andy Leonard
of Solid Quality Mentors

PUBLISHED BY
Microsoft Press
A Division of Microsoft Corporation
One Microsoft Way
Redmond, Washington 98052-6399

Library of Congress Control Number: 2007931455

Printed and bound in the United States of America.

1 2 3 4 5 6 7 8 9 QWT 2 1 0 9 8 7

Distributed in Canada by H.B. Fenn and Company Ltd.

A CIP catalogue record for this book is available from the British Library.

Microsoft Press books are available through booksellers and distributors worldwide. For further information about international editions, contact your local Microsoft Corporation office or contact Microsoft Press International directly at fax (425) 936-7329. Visit our Web site at www.microsoft.com/mspress. Send comments to tkinput@microsoft.com.

Microsoft, Microsoft Press, Active Directory, ActiveX, Excel, FrontPage, InfoPath, Microsoft Dynamics, MSDN, Natural, OneNote, Outlook, PowerPoint, SharePoint, SQL Server, Visio, Visual Basic, Visual C#, Visual C++, Visual SourceSafe, Visual Studio, Windows, Windows Server, and Windows Vista are either registered trademarks or trademarks of Microsoft Corporation in the United States and/or other countries. Other product and company names mentioned herein may be the trademarks of their respective owners.

The example companies, organizations, products, domain names, e-mail addresses, logos, people, places, and events depicted herein are fictitious. No association with any real company, organization, product, domain name, e-mail address, logo, person, place, or event is intended or should be inferred.

Acquisitions Editor: Ken Jones
Developmental Editor: Karen Szall
Project Editor: Maria Gargiulo
Editorial Production: nSight, Inc.

Body Part No. X13-92845

About the Authors

Dejan Sarka

Dejan Sarka, mentor and director of Adriatic operations for Solid Quality Mentors, develops database and business intelligence applications and spends the rest of his time training and mentoring. He is a frequent speaker at top international conferences including TechEd, SqlDevCon, and PASS, as well as regional Microsoft events such as the NT Conference, the biggest Microsoft conference in Central and Eastern Europe. Dejan founded the Slovenian SQL Server and .NET Users Group. As a guest author, he has contributed to *Inside Microsoft SQL Server 2005: T-SQL Querying* (Microsoft Press, 2006) and *Inside Microsoft SQL Server 2005: T-SQL Programming* (Microsoft Press, 2006). Dejan has also developed two courses for Solid Quality Mentors: Data Modeling Essentials and Data Mining with SQL Server 2005.

Adolfo Wiernik

Adolfo Wiernik, a mentor and director of operations in Latin America for Solid Quality Mentors, is passionate about service orientation, design patterns, and integrating the .NET platform with SQL Server to generate new services and businesses. He worked as lead architect at the Microsoft .NET Center Central America and at the Microsoft Technology Center in Tel Aviv, Israel. Founder and organizer of the Costa Rica .NET User Group, Adolfo was recognized by Microsoft as an influencer in Central America and received the Best Regional Director Latin America 2004 award. He coauthored *Microsoft SQL Server 2005: Database Essentials Step by Step* (Microsoft Press, 2006), *Microsoft SQL Server 2005: Applied Techniques Step by Step* (Microsoft Press, 2006), and *MCTS Self-Paced Training Kit (Exam 70-431): Microsoft SQL Server 2005– Implementation and Maintenance* (Microsoft Press, 2006) and served as the subject matter expert for Microsoft Learning Clinic 2783, *Designing the Data Tier for Microsoft SQL Server 2005*. Adolfo is a regular speaker at local and international industry events.

Javier Loria

Javier Loria, a Solid Quality Mentors mentor based in Costa Rica, began his professional career in 1992 as a software developer and system engineer. His career evolved rapidly to include training, especially in the XML and OLAP worlds, and he has trained customers across Latin America. Javier currently spends most of his time as a software architect and business intelligence architect, assisting Latin American clients. Named a SQL Server MVP in 2001 Javier is also an MCT, MCSE, MCSD, MCDBA, and MCAD. He co-wrote Microsoft Course 2782: *Designing Microsoft SQL Server 2005 Databases*; *MCTS Self-Paced Training Kit (Exam 70-431): Microsoft SQL Server 2005–Implementation and Maintenance* (Microsoft Press, 2006); and *Microsoft SQL Server 2005: Database Essentials Step by Step* (Microsoft Press, 2006).

Andy Leonard

Andy Leonard, a mentor for Solid Quality Mentors, is a SQL Server database developer, MVP, and engineer, as well as the founder and manager of *VSTeamSystemCentral.com*, a community dedicated to Visual Studio Team System and Team Foundation Server users. Andy's experience includes database development using SQL Server 6.5, 7.0, 2000, and 2005; data warehouse development using SQL Server 2000 and SQL Server 2005; Web application architecture and development with Visual Basic .Net, ASP, and ASP.NET; SQL Server Integration Services (SSIS); and test-driven database development. Andy is also a trainer and author.

Francisco A. González

Francisco A. González is a Solid Quality Mentors data platform architect based in Spain and works in the integration and business intelligence (BI) fields. He earned his master's degree in computer science at the University of Murcia, Spain, and at Kennesaw State University in Georgia. His master's project was an automatic support answerer that used BizTalk Server and SQL Server BI technologies. Now, he combines his work with Solid Quality Mentors with the subject of his PhD thesis: systems integration and business processes. Francisco is an MCT and MCP in BizTalk Server and SQL Server and presented a session on ETL at Microsoft's first Business Intelligence conference in Seattle, Washington.

Jesús López

Jesús López, a mentor for Solid Quality Mentors, focuses on developing database and .NET applications, teaching SQL Server and .NET courses, and mentoring clients in areas ranging from SQL Server optimization to security design. A Visual Basic MVP for three years, Jesús has presented at several conferences for his MVP colleagues in Spain and participated in webcasts and conferences in Latin America and Spain. Before working for Solid Quality Mentors, he worked for the Spanish Air Force as a database architect and solutions developer, as an independent instructor for MOC courses, and as an independent consultant.

Contents at a Glance

Table of Contents

What do you think of this book? We want to hear from you!

Microsoft is interested in hearing your feedback so we can continually improve our books and learning resources for you. To participate in a brief online survey, please visit:

www.microsoft.com/learning/booksurvey/

5 Using Appropriate Database Technologies and Techniques for Your Application. 125

6 Designing Objects That Retrieve Data. 151

7   Designing Objects That Extend Server Functionality **185**

14   Designing for Data Distribution 417

What do you think of this book? We want to hear from you!

Microsoft is interested in hearing your feedback so we can continually improve our books and learning resources for you. To participate in a brief online survey, please visit:

www.microsoft.com/learning/booksurvey/

Introduction

This training kit is designed for software developers who plan to take Microsoft Certified IT Professional (MCITP) Exam 70-441: Designing Database Solutions by Using Microsoft SQL Server 2005. The primary objective of this exam is to certify that developers and database administrators know how to design efficient database solutions for Microsoft SQL Server 2005. We assume that before you begin using this kit, you have spent at least three years doing dedicated database work. This work should include writing Transact-SQL (T-SQL) queries, implementing programming objects, optimizing databases, and designing and implementing databases on conceptual, logical, and physical levels. The Preparation Guide for Exam 70-441 is available at *http://www.microsoft.com/learning/exams/70-441.mspx*.

The labs in this training kit will use SQL Server 2005 Enterprise Edition, and a 180-day evaluation edition is included on the companion DVD. If you do not have access to this software, you can download a 180-day trial of SQL Server 2005 through *http://www.microsoft.com/sql/downloads/trial-software.mspx*. You can also consider purchasing SQL Server 2005 Development Edition, which contains all required features.

By using this training kit, you will learn how to do the following:

- Design database testing and code management procedures.
- Design an application solution for SQL Server 2005.
- Design database objects.
- Design a database.
- Develop applications that use SQL Server support services.

Hardware Requirements

We recommend that you use a test workstation, test server, or staging server to complete the exercises in each practice. However, it would be beneficial for you to have access to production-ready data in your organization. If you need to set up a workstation to complete the practice exercises, the following are the minimum system requirements:

- Personal computer with a 600 MHz Pentium III–compatible or faster processor
- 512 MB of RAM or more (1 GB or higher recommended)
- 350 MB of free hard disk space for the SQL installation
- 450 MB of additional free hard disk space if you plan to install SQL Server Books Online and sample databases

- 3 GB of additional free hard disk space for Microsoft Visual Studio 2005
- CD-ROM drive or DVD-ROM drive
- Super VGA (1,024 x 768) or higher-resolution video adapter and monitor
- Keyboard and Microsoft mouse or compatible pointing device

Software Requirements

Note that you will need SQL Server 2005 and, in some cases, Visual Studio 2005 to complete the labs included with each chapter. Although these products can be installed on a production server, you are not recommended to do so. Instead, install these products and execute the labs in each chapter on a single development computer. The following software is required to complete the practice exercises.

- One of the following operating systems:
  - Microsoft Windows Server 2003, Standard Edition SP1
  - Windows Server 2003, Enterprise Edition SP1
  - Windows Server 2003, Datacenter Edition SP1
  - Microsoft Windows XP Professional SP2
  - Windows Vista Business
  - Windows Vista Ultimate
  - Windows Vista Enterprise
- SQL Server 2005. For instructions on downloading and installing SQL Server 2005 Enterprise Edition, see the "Installing SQL Server" section of this Introduction.
- SQL Server 2005 Samples and SQL Server Client Tools.
- Visual Studio 2005. A 90-day evaluation edition of Visual Studio 2005 Professional Edition is available for download from the MSDN Web site at *http://msdn2.microsoft .com/en-us/vstudio/bb188238.aspx*. You can also use Visual Studio 2005 Express Edition, Microsoft Visual Basic 2005 Express Edition, or Microsoft Visual C# 2005 Express Edition. You can download Visual Studio Express editions from *http:// msdn.microsoft.com/vstudio/express*. Ideally, you should also have access to Microsoft Visual Studio 2005 Team Foundation Server. A trial version can be downloaded from *http://www.microsoft.com/downloads/details.aspx?FamilyID=d5c12289-f4e4-49a9- 9235-ab2f6d4ca097&DisplayLang=en*.

NOTE Install Visual Studio 2005 Service Pack 1, Service Pack 1 Update, and SQL Server 2005 Service Pack 2 for Windows Vista

If you are running Windows Vista, it is recommended that you download and install Visual Studio 2005 Service Pack 1 (SP1) and Visual Studio 2005 Service Pack 1 Update for Windows Vista. Visual Studio 2005 SP1 is available for download from *http://www.microsoft.com/downloads/details.aspx?familyid=bb4a75ab-e2d4-4c96-b39d-37baf6b5b1dc&displaylang=en.* (This download is good for Visual Studio 2005 Standard Edition, Professional Edition, and Team Edition). Visual Studio Express Editions SP1 is available for download from *http://www.microsoft.com/downloads/details.aspx?familyid=7B0B0339-613A-46E6-AB4D-080D4D4A8C4E&displaylang=en.*

Visual Studio 2005 Service Pack 1 Update for Windows Vista for all editions of Visual Studio can be downloaded from *http://www.microsoft.com/downloads/details.aspx?familyid=90e2942d-3ad1-4873-a2ee-4acc0aace5b6&displaylang=en.*

You can also view the Visual Studio 2005 update for Vista release notes at *http://support .microsoft.com/kb/929470.*

For Windows Vista, you also need SQL Server 2005 Service Pack 2. You can download SQL Server 2005 SP2 from *http://technet.microsoft.com/en-us/sqlserver/bb426877.aspx.*

- The *AdventureWorks* database, available as a separate download with the SQL Server 2005 samples from *http://www.microsoft.com/downloads/details.aspx?FamilyID=e719ecf7-9f46-4312-af89-6ad8702e4e6e&DisplayLang=en.*

- Microsoft Office Visio or, if you do not have Office 2007, Visio 2007 Viewer, available for download from *http://www.microsoft.com/downloads/details.aspx?FamilyID=d88e4542-b174-4198-ae31-6884e9edd524&DisplayLang=en.*

- If you do not have Microsoft Office 2007, you can use Office 2007 data connectivity components to access Office files. You will use Microsoft Excel files in some labs. You can download Office 2007 data connectivity components from *http://www.microsoft.com/downloads/details.aspx?familyid=7554F536-8C28-4598-9B72-EF94E038C891&displaylang=en.*

- Microsoft Internet Explorer 6.0 SP1 or later.

- Internet Information Services (IIS) 5.0 or later.

- Internet Information Services (IIS) 5.0 or later with Simple Mail Transport Protocol (SMTP) virtual server installed.

Installing SQL Server 2005

SQL Server 2005 Enterprise Edition is required to run some of the code samples provided in this book. A 180-day evaluation edition is available on the companion DVD. Alternatively, to download and install a free 180-day evaluation edition of SQL Server 2005 Enterprise Edition, perform the following steps:

1. Browse to *http://www.microsoft.com/sql/downloads/trial-software.mspx* and click the Download SQL Server 2005 link.

    You will need to complete a registration form that requires you to have a .NET passport account.

2. Read and follow the instructions on the download page to download the SQL Server 2005 Enterprise Evaluation Edition. Locate the correct download file for your environment.

3. Once the install executable has been downloaded to your local machine, execute the downloaded file (SQLEVAL.EXE) and click Run to extract the setup files to your local development computer.

4. Browse to the location to which you extracted the setup files. Execute Setup.exe from the Servers folder to begin the installation process.

5. Select I Accept The Licensing Terms And Conditions and click Next.

6. Click Install from the Installing Prerequisites dialog box. Once complete, click Next to continue.

7. The installation will then perform a system configuration check. From the Welcome dialog box, click Next to begin the installation.

8. Once the System Configuration Check is complete, click Next.

9. Type name and company information in the Registration Information dialog box and click Next to continue.

10. Click Next to accept the defaults from the Feature Selection dialog box.

11. Click Next and accept the defaults from the Instance Name dialog box.

12. Click Next and accept the defaults from the Logon Information dialog box.

13. Click Next and accept the defaults from the Error And Usage Report Settings dialog box.

14. Click Install from the Ready To Install dialog box and wait for the installation to complete.

15. You will also have to download and install the *AdventureWorks* database, which is referenced in some of the chapter labs.

Installing Visual Studio 2005

Visual Studio 2005 Professional Edition is required to run some of the code samples provided in this book. To download and install a free 90-day evaluation edition of Visual Studio 2005 Professional Edition, perform these steps:

1. Browse to *http://msdn2.microsoft.com/en-us/vstudio/bb188238.aspx* and click the Download link for the Visual Studio 2005 Professional 90-day trial. You will need to complete a registration form that requires you to have a .NET passport account.

2. Read and follow the instructions on the download page to download the Visual Studio 2005 Evaluation Edition. Locate the correct download file for your environment.

3. Once the ISO image file has been downloaded to your local computer, copy it to a blank DVD-R, which will result in an exact copy of the installation media. Even though this copy is fully functional, the license is valid for only 90 days.

4. Once copied to a DVD-R, you can browse to the DVD drive and begin the installation by executing the Setup.exe file.

5. Click Install Visual Studio 2005. The installation will begin by copying required setup files to a temporary directory. When it is complete, click Next to continue the installation.

6. Select the I Accept The Licensing Terms And Conditions check box and click Next to continue the installation.

7. Click Install from the Select Features To Install dialog box and accept the default installation. Once complete, click Next to continue.

    The installation will take several minutes to complete, and the time will vary, depending on the speed of your development computer.

Installing the AdventureWorks Database

You can download and install a sample database for Adventure Works, a fictional retailer that is referenced in some of the labs in this book. To install the sample database, perform the following steps:

1. Browse to *http://www.microsoft.com/downloads/details.aspx?FamilyID=e719ecf7-9f46-4312-af89-6ad8702e4e6e&DisplayLang=en*.

2. Select the appropriate download for your computer system (x86, x64 or IA64) and follow the instructions on the download page to run the Case-Insensitive Collation DB installation package (AdventureWorksDBCI.msi).

3. Once the installation package has finished downloading, double-click the executable file and click Run to execute the Installer.

4. Click Next from the Welcome dialog box.

5. Click the I Accept The Terms In The License Agreement and click Next from the License dialog box.

6. Click Next and accept the defaults in the Destination Folder dialog box.

7. Click Install from the Ready To Install dialog box.

8. Click Finish on the Wizard Completed page.

Case Scenarios and the 70-441 Exam

All 200 practice test questions included on the companion CD are based on case scenarios and assess the understanding of the information presented. Each case scenario describes a fictitious company that has an existing IT structure and is facing increasing needs or having problems and asks the exam candidate to decide on solutions. Each case scenario is self-contained, describing both business and technical details, both of which you need to analyze.

To understand case scenarios and questions based on case scenarios, it is recommended that the exam candidate read through each case scenario and the questions for this scenario quickly for the first time, to identify the major challenges of the fictitious company. Before answering each question, read the business and technical requirements details that relate to that specific question. Read the scenarios and the questions thoroughly to absorb all the relevant information.

Case Scenario Structure

Each case scenario begins by describing the background of a fictitious company, including a brief company overview, a detailed description of the existing environment, and plans for changes. This background information also includes problems that the company is currently facing. Because this exam involves designing a SQL Server solution, only the relevant technical details are included in case scenarios. You should focus on business problems in case scenarios; however, do not neglect technical details when they are provided.

After you understand the company's background, move to the business and technical requirements in the case scenario. Business requirements should drive your solution design. Technical requirements involve details about security, performance, data integrity, versioning, and other requests that your solution has to satisfy.

Using the CD and DVD

A companion CD and an evaluation software DVD are included with this training kit. The companion CD contains the following:

- **Practice tests**   You can practice for the 70-441 certification exam by using tests created from a pool of 200 realistic exam questions. These questions give you many different practice exams to ensure that you're prepared to take the real thing.
- **Practice Files**   Many chapters in this book include samples with T-SQL and .NET code, Visio, Excel, and other files associated with the practice exercises at the end of every lesson. For each exercise, a complete solution is provided for your review. To install the practice files on your hard disk, run Setup.exe in the Practice_Files folder on the companion CD. The default installation folder is \My Documents\Microsoft Press\MCITP Self-Paced Training Kit Exam 70-441.

■ **An eBook** An electronic version (eBook) of this book is included for times when you don't want to carry the printed book with you. The eBook is in Portable Document Format (PDF), and you can view it by using Adobe Acrobat or Adobe Acrobat Reader, available from *http://www.adobe.com.*

The evaluation software DVD contains a 180-day evaluation edition of SQL Server 2005 Enterprise Edition, needed to run the practice files in this book.

How to Install the Practice Tests

To install the practice test software from the companion CD on your hard disk, perform the following steps:

1. Insert the companion CD into your CD drive and accept the license agreement. A CD menu appears.

IMPORTANT   If the CD menu doesn't appear

If the CD menu or the license agreement doesn't appear, AutoRun might be disabled on your computer. Refer to the Readme.txt file on the CD-ROM for alternative installation instructions.

---

2. Click the Practice Tests item and follow the instructions on the screen.

How to Use the Practice Tests

To start the practice test software, follow these steps:

1. Click Start, select All Programs, and choose Microsoft Press Training Kit Exam Prep.

    A window appears that shows all the Microsoft Press training kit exam prep suites installed on your computer.

2. Double-click the practice test that you want to use.

Practice Test Options

When you start a practice test, you choose whether to take the test in Certification Mode, Study Mode, or Custom Mode.

■ **Certification Mode** Closely resembles the experience of taking a certification exam. The test has a set number of questions, it's timed, and you can't pause and restart the timer.

■ **Study Mode** Creates an untimed test in which you can review the correct answers and the explanations after you answer each question.

■ **Custom Mode** Gives you full control over the test options so that you can customize them as you like. You can click OK to accept the defaults, or you can customize the number of questions you want, how the practice test software works, which exam objectives you want the questions to relate to, and whether you want your lesson review to be timed. If you're retaking a test, you can select whether you want to see all the questions again or only those questions you missed or didn't answer.

In all modes, the user interface you see when taking the test is essentially the same but with different options enabled or disabled, depending on the mode.

After you click OK, your practice test starts.

■ To take the test, answer the questions and use the Next, Previous, and Go To buttons to move from question to question.

■ After you answer an individual question, if you want to see which answers are correct—along with an explanation of each correct answer—click Explanation.

■ If you'd rather wait until the end of the test to see how you did, answer all the questions, and then click Score Test. You'll see a summary of the exam objectives you chose and the percentage of questions you answered correctly overall and per objective. You can print a copy of your test, review your answers, or retake the test.

When you review your answer to an individual practice test question, a References section lists where in the training kit you can find the information that relates to that question and provides links to other sources of information. After you click Test Results to score your entire practice test, you can click the Learning Plan tab to see a list of references for every objective.

How to Uninstall the Practice Tests

To uninstall the practice test software for a training kit, use the Add Or Remove Programs option in Windows Control Panel.

Microsoft Certified Professional Program

The Microsoft certifications provide the best method to prove your command of current Microsoft products and technologies. The exams and corresponding certifications are developed to validate your mastery of critical competencies as you design and develop, or implement and support, solutions with Microsoft products and technologies. Computer professionals who become Microsoft certified are recognized as experts and are sought after industry-wide. Certification brings a variety of benefits to the individual and to employers and organizations.

IMPORTANT   All the Microsoft certifications

For a full list of Microsoft certifications, go to *http://www.microsoft.com/learning/mcp/default.asp.*

Technical Support

Every effort has been made to ensure the accuracy of this book and the contents of the companion CD. If you have comments, questions, or ideas regarding this book or the companion CD, please send them to Microsoft Press by using either of the following methods:

E-mail: tkinput@microsoft.com

Postal Mail:

Microsoft Press
Attn: MCITP Self-Paced Training Kit (Exam 70-441): Designing Database Solutions by Using Microsoft SQL Server 2005 *Editor*
One Microsoft Way
Redmond, WA 98052–6399

For additional support information regarding this book and the CD-ROM (including answers to commonly asked questions about installation and use), visit the Microsoft Press Technical Support Web site at *http:/www.microsoft.com/learning/support/books.* To connect directly to the Microsoft Knowledge Base and enter a query, visit *http://support.microsoft.com/search.* For support information regarding Microsoft software, please visit *http://support.microsoft.com.*

Evaluation Edition Software Support

The 180-day evaluation edition provided with this training kit is not the full retail product and is provided only for the purposes of training and evaluation. Microsoft and Microsoft Technical Support do not support this evaluation edition.

Information about any issues relating to the use of this evaluation edition with this training kit is posted to the Support section of the Microsoft Press Web site at *http://www.microsoft.com /learning/support/books.* For information about ordering the full version of any Microsoft software, please call Microsoft Sales at (800) 426-9400 or visit the Microsoft Web site at *http:// www.microsoft.com.*

Chapter 1
Selecting and Designing SQL Server Services to Support Business Needs

Microsoft SQL Server 2005 is far more than a relational database management system (RDBMS). Providing multiple services, tools, and components, SQL Server 2005 is a comprehensive platform for enterprise applications. When developing modern applications, a key success factor is selecting the appropriate services to support business needs. To make the best use of SQL Server 2005 services, you must understand their capabilities and limitations and how they fit into the complete SQL Server architecture.

In this first chapter, you will get an overview of the services and components included in the SQL Server 2005 platform, from the database engine's core services to mail and replication components as well as advanced notification, reporting, and analysis services. You will see how these services and components fit into an enterprise solution, and you will explore important considerations for their usage.

Exam objectives in this chapter:

- Select and design SQL Server services to support business needs.
    - Select the appropriate services to use to support business needs.
    - Design a SQL Web services solution.
    - Design a Notification Services solution to notify users.
    - Design a Service Broker solution for asynchronous database applications.
    - Design a Microsoft Distributed Transaction Coordinator (MS DTC) solution for distributed transactions.
    - Design a Reporting Services solution.
    - Design an Integration Services solution.
    - Design a SQL Server core service solution.
    - Design a SQL Server Agent solution.
    - Design a DatabaseMail solution.
- Design objects that perform actions.
    - Design Service Broker applications.

Before You Begin

To complete the lessons in this chapter, you must have:

- A general understanding of multi-tiered, asynchronous, and service-oriented architectures.
- A general understanding of the relational model and relational database systems.
- A general understanding of business intelligence.
- Knowledge of Transact-SQL language elements.

Lesson 1: Selecting the Appropriate Services

Estimated lesson time: 20 minutes

SQL Server supports online transactional processing (OLTP), data warehousing (DW), and e-commerce applications. It also supports a variety of business intelligence (BI) applications, including data integration, reporting, online analytical processing (OLAP), and data mining solutions. By thoroughly understanding the SQL Server architecture, you can select the correct component or service for a specific business problem. Figure 1-1 illustrates the components of SQL Server 2005.

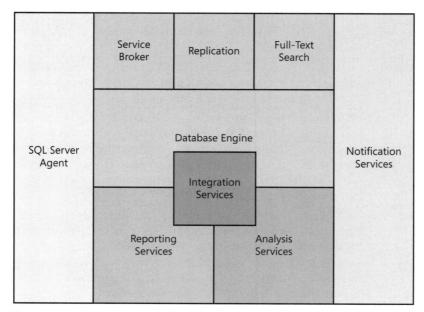

Figure 1-1   SQL Server 2005 components

Table 1-1 briefly describes each of these components.

Table 1-1   Describing SQL Server 2005 Components

Component	Description
Database Engine	The database engine comprises the core services of SQL Server and is responsible for storing, processing, and securing data. You use the database engine to create relational databases for OLTP data and to build data warehouses for BI applications. In SQL Server 2005, the engine includes many new features, including common language runtime (CLR) integration and support for extensible Markup Language (XML) and Web services.

Table 1-1   Describing SQL Server 2005 Components

Component	Description
Service Broker	Service Broker extends the database engine's capabilities by providing native support for queuing and messaging applications. You can use Service Broker to build reliable asynchronous applications easily within a single database or a single instance as well as asynchronous applications in a distributed environment.
Replication	You use replication to copy data and database objects between distributed databases. With its set of replication technologies, SQL Server synchronizes and maintains consistency between databases.
Full-Text Search	Full-Text Search (FTS) enables you to run full-text queries against character data in your SQL Server tables. FTS enables fast indexing for keyword-based queries that can include words and phrases or multiple forms of words and phrases.
SQL Server Agent	SQL Server Agent is a database administration tool for scheduling and executing regular jobs such as database backups and integrity checks for configuring alerts and for sending messages to operators.
Integration Services	SQL Server Integration Services (SSIS)—the platform's extraction, transformation, and loading (ETL) platform—handles data integration and transformation. With Integration Services, you can extract data from a variety of sources, including XML data files, flat files, and relational data sources, and then load the data into different destinations while performing transformations in real time.
Reporting Services	SQL Server Reporting Services (SSRS) is a server-based platform for managing reports from relational and multidimensional data sources. Users can view reports in different formats and subscribe to reports by using a variety of delivery channels. In addition, with Reporting Services, developers can prepare a semantic model of a database, and end users can then use this report model to build ad hoc reports themselves.
Analysis Services	SQL Server Analysis Services delivers OLAP and data mining functionality for BI applications. Analysis Services supports multidimensional structures with detail and aggregated data from multiple sources in a single unified logical model. It also provides rich metadata that supports additional calculations, Key Performance Indicators (KPIs), translations, actions, and different perspectives for flexible data analysis. In addition, Analysis Services provides a variety of data mining models that support all the most popular data mining algorithms.
Notification Services	Notification Services enables you to develop applications that generate and send notifications to subscribers based on specified events or on a schedule. You can send notifications, which can be richly formatted, to many different devices.

Practice: Selecting the Appropriate Services to Support Business Needs

In this practice, you will perform the conceptual exercise of choosing the appropriate technology.

Exam Tip   When answering an exam question with more than one correct answer, be aware that it is not always possible to determine all correct answers directly from the question. Sometimes you have to think carefully about what additional services you need for a real-life solution.

▶ **Exercise: Use an Appropriate Technology**

In this conceptual exercise, you will select appropriate SQL Server 2005 services for an analytical system.

> You are designing an analytical system. Your system has to include a data warehouse, three OLAP cubes, and two data mining models. Which SQL Server 2005 services would you use for these tasks? Remember to consider using services that might not be mentioned but that you would use in a real-life solution.
>
> **Suggested Answer**
>
> For the data warehouse, you should use the database engine. A data warehouse is typically stored on a RDBMS. For OLAP cubes and data mining models, use Analysis Services. You should also anticipate usage of Integration Services for the ETL tasks.

Quick Check

1. Which component would you use to create asynchronous distributed applications?
2. How could you enable end users to create ad hoc reports themselves?
3. Which of the following features are new in SQL Server 2005? (Choose all that apply.)
   - A. CLR integration
   - B. Full-Text Search
   - C. SQL Server Agent
   - D. Service Broker
   - E. Replication

Quick Check Answers

1. You can use Service Broker for asynchronous, distributed, and loosely coupled applications.
2. Reporting Services report models enable end users to create reports by themselves.
3. The correct answers are A and D. CLR integration and Service Broker are new in SQL Server 2005; Full-Text Search, SQL Server Agent, and replication are also part of SQL Server 2000, although they are enhanced in SQL Server 2005.

Lesson 2: Evaluating Core, SQL Server Agent, and Database Mail Solutions

Estimated lesson time: 25 minutes

SQL Server 2005 introduces many database-engine enhancements that make it even easier for you to write efficient code. This lesson helps you evaluate the use of core engine improvements such as the new Transact-SQL (T-SQL) elements, XML data support, and CLR integration. In addition, the lesson covers considerations for using SQL Server Agent and Database Mail.

Transact-SQL Enhancements

SQL Server 2005 substantially extends the functionality of the T-SQL language. The most important new features include:

- Common table expressions (CTEs).
- Ranking functions.
- New large object (LOB) and XML data types.
- Statement operators.
- Structured exception handling.
- DDL triggers and event notifications.

A *CTE* is a temporary result set stored during the execution of a SELECT, INSERT, UPDATE, or DELETE statement. You can use CTEs instead of derived tables (subqueries in a FROM clause) or instead of views and table-valued functions to simplify coding logic and improve performance. Unlike the case with derived tables, you declare CTEs before the main SELECT statement in the new WITH clause, and CTEs are available immediately after the declaration in the main query or in following CTEs. You can reference a CTE multiple times, for example, to join it to itself in the main query. If you wanted to use a derived table for the same purpose, you would have to declare it twice, which could lead to a suboptimal execution plan. In addition, you can easily write a recursive query by using a recursive CTE to retrieve hierarchical data.

Ranking functions return positional information about rows in a result set. They can return a ranking value for each row in a partition or in the entire result set. SQL Server 2005 includes four ranking functions: *ROW_NUMBER*, *RANK*, *DENSE_RANK*, and *NTILE*.

In SQL Server 2000, *varchar*, *nvarchar*, and *varbinary* data types stored up to 8,000 bytes of data. For large text, Unicode text, and pictures, you had to use text, ntext, and image types. However, working with these large object types was somewhat awkward because only a limited number of system functions support these types. In SQL Server 2005, the database engine now supports a MAX length specification for the *varchar*, *nvarchar*, and *varbinary* data types.

When you specify MAX, the data types can store the same size data as *text*, *ntext*, and *image* types (up to 2 gigabytes) but process the same way as when they store shorter strings. This technology provides a unified LOB programming model.

IMPORTANT   Deprecated types

Microsoft intends to drop support for the *text*, *ntext*, and *image* data types in upcoming releases of SQL Server. For this reason, Microsoft recommends that you stop using these data types.

The new *XML* data type is a natural choice for storing XML documents and fragments in a database. You can validate XML values against an XML schema from a pre-defined XML schema collection. By using the XQuery language, you can query XML data, and, with SQL Server extensions to XQuery, you can modify XML data. You can use the *XML* data type as you would any other data type; therefore, you can store XML instances in columns, variables, or stored procedure parameters.

The new statement operators in SQL Server 2005 are:

- *OUTPUT*, which enables you to retrieve the original and/or new rows affected by a data-modification operator and store them in a table or table variable.
- *APPLY*, which you use in the FROM clause to invoke a table-valued function for each row returned by an outer-table expression or query.
- *PIVOT* and *UNPIVOT* operators, which enable you to transform column values of a rowset into columns and vice versa. You can use *PIVOT* for cross-tabulation reports. *UNPIVOT* performs the opposite operation by rotating columns of a rowset into column values.
- *TOP(expression)*, an enhanced *TOP* operator. In earlier versions of SQL Server, you could use only an integer constant as a TOP parameter; if you needed to use an expression as a parameter value, you had to generate dynamic SQL.

Error handling is much easier in SQL Server 2005. You now have a structured exception-handling mechanism through the new TRY . . . CATCH construct. You do not need to test the @@error after each statement; instead, you can handle the errors that can occur in a block of T-SQL code at run time in a uniform way by using TRY . . . CATCH logic.

SQL Server 2005 is not limited to data-modification language (DML) triggers anymore. Now, you can create a trigger on any data-definition language (DDL) event as well. The DDL triggers fire when a user executes DDL statements such as CREATE, ALTER, or DROP. You can use them to prevent dangerous DDL operations or to audit operations performed by developers.

For auditing DDL operations, event notifications provide an asynchronous alternative to DDL triggers. Event notifications send information about T-SQL DDL statements and SQL Trace events to a Service Broker service. The event notifications execute asynchronously after the operation ends.

Considerations for Using CLR Integration

Developers often need to extend the functionality of T-SQL database applications to interact better with the operating system and environment. Before SQL Server 2005, you could enrich T-SQL by using extended stored procedures and Component Object Model (COM) classes. However, a malfunctioning extended stored procedure could compromise the database engine or even stop the SQL Server service. SQL Server now features integration with the CLR component of the Microsoft .NET Framework. This CLR integration gives developers a rich programming model, the power of the .NET Framework library, improved safety and security compared to extended procedures, improved performance in some situations compared to T-SQL, and streamlined development through the standardized Microsoft Visual Studio .NET environment.

Using .NET languages such as Microsoft Visual Basic and Microsoft Visual C#, you can write programmatic objects for SQL Server databases. You can still write some programmatic objects in T-SQL. Table 1-2 lists which objects you can write in .NET CLR languages and which you can write in T-SQL.

Table 1-2   Programmatic Objects and Languages

Object	CLR Languages	Transact-SQL
Stored procedure	X	X
User-defined function	X	X
Trigger	X	X
User-defined aggregate	X	
User-defined data type	X	

Using CLR objects can still pose a security risk if a database administrator (DBA) does not know what the objects do and has no knowledge of Code Access Security (CAS) in .NET. When SQL Server 2005 is installed, the integrated CLR is disabled by default, and a DBA must enable it explicitly by using the *sp_configure* system stored procedure. Let's look at some other points you should evaluate when considering using CLR objects.

CLR objects do not rely on external dependencies. For CLR objects, the complete assemblies are stored in a database—unlike COM objects and extended stored procedures, which rely on external libraries. Therefore, CLR objects run in the same process as the database engine, which ensures better performance and safety compared to running an additional process for COM objects and extended procedures. In addition, the CLR carefully manages its own objects to prevent compromising the database engine, unless you explicitly configure the CLR to bypass the safety features.

You can control the resources that CLR objects can access by using CAS. CAS can be complicated, but in SQL Server, the CAS permissions are grouped into three sets—SAFE, EXTERNAL_ACCESS, and UNSAFE—which enables effective administration. By granting the EXTERNAL _ACCESS or even UNSAFE permission set to an assembly, you are potentially bypassing the built-in security features of the CLR. Not all .NET Framework classes are available for use inside SQL Server because some classes, such as windowing classes, are not appropriate for server-side use.

SQL Server versions earlier than 2005 do not support the CLR, so if you need to maintain backward compatibility, you cannot use the integrated CLR. You also need to pay special attention to code performance when developing CLR objects. If a developer builds a problem into a user-defined data type, a DBA can do nothing to improve the performance in production.

Using the integrated CLR is appropriate in the following scenarios:

- **Extending functionality**   You cannot write user-defined aggregates or user-defined data types (except simple aliases) in T-SQL.
- **Accessing external resources**   If you need to access external resources such as Web services, the file system, the Windows event logs, or network resources from SQL Server, you should use the CLR. However, you need to understand how to use CAS before allowing the CLR code to access external resources.
- **Performing complex processing**   The managed code of the CLR performs much better than T-SQL for CPU-intensive functions and procedures that feature complex logic.
- **Replacing extended stored procedures**   Use the CLR in place of extended procedures unless you must maintain backward compatibility.

Here are scenarios in which you should use T-SQL instead of the CLR:

- **Querying the database**   T-SQL is designed specifically for direct data access and manipulation, and it excels in performing database operations.
- **Performing row-by-row processing**   You might consider using CLR code instead of T-SQL cursors. However, T-SQL set-based operations, such as updating a set of rows, perform magnitudes better than row operations, even if you write them in one of the .NET languages.
- **Availability of T-SQL functions, operators, and expressions**   If T-SQL offers an available function, operator, or expression, you should not rewrite the functionality in the CLR. For example, for expanding hierarchies, use CTEs; for calculating averages, use the T-SQL *AVG* function.

Using SQL Server Agent

SQL Server Agent is a Microsoft Windows service that you can use for scheduling the execution of regular administrative tasks and routine maintenance operations. You can also use it for automated administration—for the programmed response to predictable administrative responsibilities or server events. Note that SQL Server Agent is disabled by default during the SQL Server installation; you can enable it by using the Configuration Manager or the Surface

Area Configuration tool. SQL Server Agent can notify an operator if a predictable event occurred or a scheduled job finished; you should make good use of this capability.

SQL Server Agent provides valuable functionality for the following tasks:

- **Performing regular maintenance operations**   All production databases should have a regular backup plan, for example. Other important regular maintenance operations include reorganizing or rebuilding indexes and checking the integrity of databases.
- **Performing regular business tasks**   In many businesses, DBAs have to perform regular processes on specific schedules. These processes can include ETL, end-of-period consolidation, and other resource-intensive operations that you need to execute during the peak hours. You can use SQL Server Agent jobs to schedule these processes to execute on a recurring basis at a specified time.
- **Responding to alerts**   SQL Server Agent responds to a recognized alert by notifying an operator or executing a scheduled job. You can set up alerts on SQL Server error messages written in the Windows Event Log, on SQL Server performance conditions, or on Windows Management Instrumentation (WMI) events.

In earlier SQL Server versions, SQL Server Agent could execute T-SQL, command prompt, ActiveX, and replication steps. In addition to those tasks, in SQL Server 2005, SQL Server Agent can execute SQL Server Analysis Services command and query steps and Integration Services package steps.

Using Database Mail

Although earlier versions of SQL Server were limited to Messaging Application Programming Interface (MAPI) components for sending e-mail, SQL Server 2005 introduces Database Mail, which uses the standard Simple Mail Transfer Protocol (SMTP) to send e-mail.

IMPORTANT   SQL Mail is deprecated

SQL Server provides SQL Mail (the MAPI messaging component) for backward compatibility only. Microsoft will remove this feature in a future release of SQL Server.

The following Database Mail characteristics make a strong case for using the component:

- **Reliability**   The component that delivers mail runs in a separate process outside SQL Server. SQL Server will queue messages even if the external process fails. You can specify more than one SMTP server to use and thus have failover accounts. Database Mail is fully supported on a Windows cluster.
- **Scalability**   Database Mail delivers messages in a background asynchronous process using Service Broker queues. You can define multiple mail profiles within a SQL Server instance, and each profile can have multiple failover accounts. Database Mail is supported on 64-bit versions of SQL Server; SQL Mail is not.

Lesson 3: Using Advanced Services

Estimated lesson time: 25 minutes

The database engine in SQL Server 2005 provides various advanced services that you can include in your applications. In this lesson, you will gather core information about SQL Server Web services, Service Broker, replication, and distributed transactions. With this information, you will be able to determine when to use these advanced services.

SQL Server Web Services

The native protocol for accessing a database in SQL Server is Tabular Data Stream (TDS). TDS is a proprietary protocol for Windows-based clients, which commonly also use Microsoft Data Access Components (MDAC). You install the MDAC stack on client computers. However, Web-based clients need a more open communications protocol.

In SQL Server 2000 and earlier versions, you can achieve Web-based access to SQL Server through SQLXML 3.0, which is a middle-tier component, but you also have to use Microsoft Internet Information Services (IIS). The SQL Server 2005 database engine provides native XML Web services by using established open standards. These standards include Hypertext Transfer Protocol (HTTP), a core and platform-neutral protocol behind the Web; Simple Object Access Protocol (SOAP), which defines how to use XML and HTTP to access services, objects, and servers regardless of operating system; and Web Services Definition Language (WSDL), an XML document format you can use to describe Web-based services. Figure 1-2 illustrates the two environments for Web-based access to SQL Server: through SQLXML 3.0, MDAC, and TDS, or through the native Web services in SQL Server 2005.

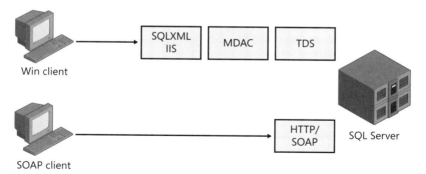

Figure 1-2   Alternatives for Web-based access to SQL Server 2005

In SQL Server 2005, HTTP endpoints serve as the gateway through which HTTP-based clients can query the server. After you establish an HTTP endpoint, you can expose stored procedures and user-defined functions as Web methods. A Web service is a collection of Web methods that you design to use together. SQL Server can also consume Web services, but you have to design the consumer procedures by using a .NET language and CLR integration.

HTTP endpoints use the SOAP open protocol, which provides interoperability. If your clients use an operating system other than Windows, using HTTP endpoints is your obvious choice. HTTP endpoints use the http.sys kernel mode driver, which provides better performance than IIS-based solutions. However, HTTP endpoints do not scale out because they use the database engine directly. Consider security issues with HTTP endpoints also. You should not expose your database to the Internet directly; if you must provide access to your database over the Internet, use other technologies that include the middle tier, such as ASP.NET Web services.

IMPORTANT   HTTP listener

HTTP support requires the HTTP listener, called the http.sys driver, which is available only on operating systems Microsoft Windows Server 2003 and Windows XP Service Pack 2 or later.

Here are some scenarios in which you should consider using HTTP endpoints:

- **Providing reports for internal use**   You can easily create stored procedures to retrieve data and expose it through HTTP endpoints. Then, internal users can connect to the URL of the HTTP endpoint and use a Web browser to display the data.
- **Using XML**   If your applications can process data as XML, you can use an HTTP endpoint to exchange data in XML format instead of in relational format.
- **Using Service-Oriented Architecture (SOA)**   Many modern applications use SOA, and HTTP endpoints conform to the SOA.

You should not use SQL Server native Web services in the following situations:

- **Using the Windows 2000 operating system**   HTTP endpoints are supported for Windows Server 2003 and Windows XP Service Pack 2 (SP2) or later operating systems only.
- **Performing real-time transaction processing**   HTTP endpoints do not perform as well as connecting to SQL Server by using TDS and ADO.NET, for example. Therefore, you should not use HTTP endpoints when you need fast, mission-critical response times.
- **Using LOBs**   When you serialize large object (LOB) data in XML format, you can consume significant processing power. Transporting this data can require a lot of network bandwidth.
- **Using middle-tier business logic**   You can accommodate the demands of large-scale business logic better by using middle-tier components.

Using Service Broker

Many modern applications can benefit from asynchronous processing. SQL Server Service Broker is a new technology in SQL Server 2005 that helps you build reliable, scalable, and loosely coupled distributed applications. Service Broker also provides messaging between

SQL Server 2005 instances. Server Broker is a SQL Server alternative to Microsoft Messaging Queue (MSMQ) service.

Traditional messaging systems such as MSMQ store messages in memory or in their own message store. However, Service Broker stores messages in hidden tables inside a database. This database integration prevents inconsistency between a database and a message store. Messages are backed up when you back up the database. You secure Service Broker objects as you do any other database object. In addition, database integration of Service Broker, which can handle messages up to 2 GB in size, enables automatic resource management by the SQL Server database engine. Service Broker messages are automatically involved in transaction management.

One of Service Broker's most useful features is automatic activation. Service Broker activation starts a new queue reader (for example, a stored procedure) when there is work for the queue reader to perform. For activation outside the database, Service Broker generates an activation event. However, Service Broker cannot deliver messages between heterogeneous systems; in such cases, you will need to use another system, such as MSMQ.

Appropriate scenarios for SQL Server Broker usage include:

- **Scaling out** You can divide the workload among multiple SQL Server instances or implement asynchronous processing within a single instance to shorten interactive response time. For example, you can process triggers asynchronously. A trigger can queue a message instead of processing some commands; the program that implements the service performs the work in a separate transaction. Another example is large-scale batch processing. You can store the data to be processed in a Service Broker queue and process it periodically by using a program that reads from the queue.
- **Improving reliability and availability** In a distributed system, you can improve reliability and availability by using Service Broker. If one of the servers in a distributed system fails, Service Broker can send messages to a working server, and the application can continue processing.
- **Consolidating data for client applications** You can have an application consolidate data from multiple databases onto a single screen. You can send requests from an application to different services in parallel. When the services respond, your application can collect the responses and display the results.
- **Auditing** Event notifications use the Service Broker infrastructure for asynchronous processing of various events. You can use event notifications to implement asynchronous auditing, which has less impact on the database engine than synchronous auditing solutions, such as solutions that use DDL triggers.
- **Maintaining cached data** SQL Server 2005 can also send query notifications. Query notifications inform an application that maintains data in its own cache that the cached data is outdated so that the application can refresh its cache. An application has to subscribe to query notifications by using ADO.NET classes. Again, SQL Server uses the Service Broker infrastructure to enable query notifications.

Replication Enhancements

SQL Server replication is a well-known technology for implementing low-overhead distributed solutions. You can use replication to improve availability and scalability. SQL Server 2005 provides many replication enhancements, including enhancements in replication security and performance. The most important enhancements include:

- **Peer-to-peer topology** You can view this topology as an asynchronous distributed application. All nodes in a peer-to-peer topology are peers. Each node publishes and subscribes to the same schema and data, although the same row can be changed at only one location at a time. The peer-to-peer topology is best suited for server environments requiring high availability and read scalability.

- **Schema changes** You can now replicate DDL operations easily. You do not need to use special stored procedures for adding and dropping columns, and schema changes are no longer limited to adding and dropping columns.

- **Heterogeneous replication** In SQL Server 2005, Oracle publishers beginning with version 8.0.5 are supported out of the box. In addition, you can use Oracle and IBM DB2 as push subscribers of transactional and snapshot replication.

- **Replicating over the Internet** With merge replication, you can synchronize sites over the Web by using the Hypertext Transfer Protocol Secure (HTTPS) protocol. HTTPS merge replication supports SQL Server Mobile Edition subscribers as well. If you need to implement transactional replication over the Web, you can use a virtual private network (VPN) connection to SQL Server.

SQL Server 2005 still supports snapshot, transactional, and merge replication. *Snapshot replication* is most appropriate when data changes are substantial but infrequent. Snapshot replication is also commonly used for initialization of other types of replication. Consider using *transactional replication* when you want to propagate the changes from publishers to subscribers with low latency. Transactional replication supports updating subscribers; however, because updating conflicts can occur, use subscribers that make only occasional changes. Consider using *merge replication* when you want to enable multiple subscribers to update the same data and propagate those changes to the publisher and to other subscribers. Subscribers can be offline most of the time; they need connection to the publisher only when they are merging the data. With merge data, conflicts might occur when users update the same data at more than one node; you have to be prepared to detect and solve these conflicts.

Implementing Distributed Transactions

A distributed transaction updates data on two or more computers in a network. Database management systems such as SQL Server that are included in a transaction are called *resource managers*. Management of the transaction between the resource managers is the duty of a server component called the *transaction manager*. Each computer involved in a distributed transaction has a local transaction manager, and those transaction managers interact with other transaction managers.

An application manages a distributed transaction in a similar manner to how it manages a local transaction; at the end of the transaction, the application has to decide whether to commit or roll back the transaction. The transaction manager controls the distributed commit to minimize the risk that some resource managers might successfully commit while others roll back the transaction because of a network or other failure. The transaction manager safeguards the transaction by using a two-phase commit. The two phases are called *prepare* and *commit*. During both phases, the transaction manager communicates with resource managers. If any resource manager reports a failure to prepare, the transaction manager sends a rollback command to each resource manager and indicates the failure of the commit to the application.

The MSDTC is a service you use as a distributed transaction manager for the Windows platforms. In a distributed environment with SQL Server instances, you must consider whether to manage distributed transactions through T-SQL or through the database application programming interface (API). If you use T-SQL distributed transactions, you need only the following few T-SQL statements to control the transactions:

- Statements that start a distributed transaction. You can start the distributed transaction in the following ways:
    - ❏ You can start an explicit distributed transaction by using the BEGIN DISTRIBUTED TRANSACTION statement.
    - ❏ Inside a local transaction, you can execute a distributed query.
    - ❏ You can use the SET REMOTE_PROC_TRANSACTIONS ON statement and then call a remote stored procedure.
- Statements that perform distributed queries against linked servers or that execute remote procedure calls against remote servers.
- Standard statements that complete the transaction (COMMIT TRANSACTION, COMMIT WORK, ROLLBACK TRANSACTION, or ROLLBACK WORK).

Database interfaces (APIs) that support distributed transactions include ADO.NET, ODBC, OLE DB, ADO, and even DB Library. However, when you use the .NET Framework 2.0 Data Provider for SQL Server (SqlClient) with SQL Server 2005, you get promotable transactions. Promotable transactions optimize distributed transactions by deferring the creation of a distributed transaction until you need it. If only one resource manager is required, no distributed transaction occurs.

Note that if you use immediate updating subscribers with transactional replication, you use distributed transactions as well. When you update the data at a subscriber, the changes are propagated immediately to the publisher using the two-phase commit. If you use queued updating subscribers, the changes are stored in a queue and then applied asynchronously at the publisher.

Practice: Using Advanced Database Engine Features

In this practice, you will perform the conceptual exercise of selecting the best SQL Server 2005 Database Engine service or feature.

▶ **Exercise: Use the Appropriate Technology**

In this exercise, decide which advanced database engine feature to use to solve a business problem.

1. You want to offload your production system, so you decide to use an additional SQL Server instance for reporting. You want to have a copy of the data on the reporting server available with low latency. Which technology would you use?

2. You need to make your data available to your domain users while they are traveling. They need to create simple reports from the latest data. What can you do to help them?

Suggested Answers

1. You should use transactional replication to make a copy of the data available on the reporting server. Distributed transactions do not help you in a scenario like this; whether you query the data on the reporting server via distributed transactions or local transactions, you are still adding to the server load. Service Broker is not appropriate because you need only a copy of the data; you do not need any further processing on the reporting server. In addition, you would have to change your applications to use either distributed transactions or Service Broker. Setting up a transactional replication solution in this case is only an administrative task.

2. You can implement HTTP endpoints to make the data that users need available to them through stored procedures exposed as Web methods. You have known (domain) users only, so this is not a security risk because you can control the exposure of HTTP endpoints.

Quick Check

1. In your company, sales representatives need to start visiting customers directly, instead of having just phone communication. They will use laptop computers to insert new data during or right after the visit. They want to continue using the existing sales application. However, their laptop computers will be disconnected most of the time. Which of the following technologies would you use?

   A. Service Broker

   B. Transactional replication

   C. Distributed transactions

   D. Merge replication

2. Can you consume query notifications inside a T-SQL stored procedure?

Quick Check Answers

1. The correct answer is D, merge replication. You can install SQL Server Express edition and create a copy of the sales database on their laptop computers. You can install sales the application as well. Then you can replicate only the tables they need to update. Your main production server would become the publisher, and all laptop computers would become subscribers. They can connect to the central server in the evening and merge the data. Distributed transactions do not help you in a scenario like this; for distributed transactions, they would need a constant connection. Service Broker is not appropriate because this would be a more complicated solution that would involve application changes. Setting up a merge replication solution in this case is only an administrative task. Transactional replication is not appropriate because you would have to use updating subscribers, and for updates from subscribers, transactional replication uses distributed transactions.

2. No, you cannot consume query notifications with T-SQL; you need a .NET application for this task.

Lesson 4: Evaluating Other Services

Estimated lesson time: 20 minutes

Besides the database engine, SQL Server 2005 includes other services that enable you to create enterprise applications, as discussed in Lesson 1, "Selecting the Appropriate Services to Support Business Needs." In this lesson, you will get an overview of considerations for using SQL Server 2005 Notification Services, Reporting Services, Analysis Services, and Integration Services. Chapter 15, "Designing Applications That Support Reporting and Use Reporting Services," Chapter 16, "Developing Applications for Notification Services," and Chapter 17, "Developing Packages for Integration Services," provide in-depth coverage of designing solutions using Reporting Services, Notification Services, and Integration Services, respectively. Designing for Analysis Services, a BI component, is beyond the scope of this book. To learn more about business intelligence components in SQL Server 2005, refer to the Microsoft Business Intelligence Web site at *http://www.microsoft.com/bi/*.

Notification Services

Communication is a key element in modern applications. Sometimes you need an alerting application and an event-based notification system to communicate with your customers, employees, and even computers. Notification Services is a programming framework for creating applications that generate and send notifications as well as a platform for hosting those applications. A Notification Services application manages subscriptions, collects events, generates notifications, and then renders and distributes the notifications by using external delivery services, including SMTP. Using Notification Services, which provides many elements for building notification applications out of the box, you can reduce development time. Here are some considerations for deciding whether to implement a Notification Services solution:

- **Data**   A Notification Services application stores its data in SQL Server databases. Therefore, you can control the access to the data and optimize performance of the Notification Services databases as you do for other databases.

- **Events**   Notification Services supports three standard event providers: File System Watcher, which is triggered when an XML file is added to a watched folder; SQL Server Event Provider, which uses a T-SQL query to get the data from a SQL Server database and then uses stored procedures to create events based on this data; and Analysis Services Event Provider, which uses a multidimensional expressions (MDX) query to gather data from an Analysis Services cube and submits the data as events to an application. In addition, you can develop custom event providers. Notification Services applications use rules for generating notifications based on events. You can focus on the definition of the rules instead of on the implementation details.

- **Scalability**   Notification Services applications use set-oriented techniques for processing to support a large number of subscribers. In addition, Notification Services can scale out and run on different SQL Server instances. In addition to standard notification-by-notification formatting and delivery, you can use digest delivery and multicast delivery. You use digest delivery to group multiple notifications in a single message for an individual subscriber. You use multicast delivery to format a notification only once and then send it to multiple subscribers.

- **Formatting**   Notification Services includes a standard Extensible Stylesheet Language Transformations (XSLT) content formatter. It works with one XSLT file for each device type and locale. You can also develop custom content formatters.

- **Delivery**   Notification Services applications do not deliver messages; instead, they use delivery channels. A delivery channel packages the notifications appropriately for its protocol and sends them to the delivery services. Standard delivery channels include the SMTP protocol, the extensible HTTP protocol, and the File protocol. You can develop additional delivery channels.

- **Tracking and retrying**   Notification Services retains notification delivery information. For each type of notification, you can configure a retry schedule.

- **Processing**   Notification Services is appropriate for sending notifications asynchronously; it is not useful for asynchronous processing. For asynchronous processing scenarios, you should use Service Broker.

Reporting Services

As the need to extract information from data grows, database administrators and developers face increasing pressure to provide ever more reporting and analysis features in their business applications. SQL Server Reporting Services helps you create, organize, and manage reports efficiently and securely. In addition, Reporting Services can hold one or more snapshots of the data. These snapshots can lower the demand on the production systems from reporting queries, but they also might introduce another problem: Reports from the snapshots might not show the latest data. You can access the report over a local network or over the Internet; you can use different rendering formats, including HTML, XML, PDF, and Microsoft Office Excel; and you can even use different delivery mechanisms. In a pull delivery scenario, end users can request reports from a local portal. If a portal does not exist yet, they can use Report Manager, a Web-based report access and management tool shipped with Reporting Services. In a push delivery scenario, you can deliver reports through e-mail, files on a shared folder, or through a custom delivery channel.

Scenarios for using Reporting Services include business reporting, ad hoc reporting, reports embedded in applications or intranet portals, and Internet reporting. If you use snapshots of data, consider how old the data can become before losing its usefulness. You can also generate the reports on a specific schedule, for example, during off-peak hours. When implementing a Reporting Services solution, consider the following issues:

- Reporting Services has its own security model, independent of SQL Server security.
- Queries from reports put additional burden on your database. You might want to separate the production and the reporting databases, for example, by using a copy of the production database (managed with replication) for reporting.
- Snapshots of data need additional disk space in Reporting Services databases.
- You can scale out Reporting Services by having several Reporting Services instances share the same Reporting Services database.
- You can create reports from relational sources, XML, SAP, Integration Services, and Analysis Services OLAP cubes and through ODBC drivers and OLE DB providers. Reports from OLAP cubes are typically extremely fast.

End users typically create ad hoc reports. However, end users do not want to write queries because they do not know query languages such as T-SQL and MDX or the database schema. Besides that, users need the data described in terms of entities and attributes, using business terms they understand. They also do not want to spend too much time on report layout or on working with a complex tool such as Microsoft Business Intelligence Development Studio (BIDS) Report Designer. You can solve these problems by implementing report models.

A *report model* is a semantic layer of metadata stored in the Reporting Services database that describes the data from a business point of view, adding properties that enable the quick and easy authoring of reports. A report model is not something an end user would prepare. When you complete the model, you can deploy it to your report server as you would deploy a report, and your analysts can then start writing their own ad hoc reports by using the Report Builder, a light development tool that ships with Reporting Services.

Analysis Services

Reporting Services, even with its report models, does not solve all the reporting problems businesses face today. Report Builder still requires advanced users, and the reports might still run against the production database, putting further processing burden on it. The analysis process is too slow. Although end users can change the reports by themselves, they still have to move back to the development environment (Report Builder or even Visual Studio) whenever they want to change the structure of a report, such as changing the attribute that defines the columns for a pivot table. Running a report might be too slow as well, and the number of the reports can quickly grow into the hundreds.

Beyond adding managed reports to your analysis arsenal, you can create a SQL Server Analysis Services solution to give users online analytical processing (OLAP) and data mining capabilities. With OLAP, the end user can change the view (the report) online inside a client tool without having to go back to the report development environment, and the server will respond with lightning speed. Therefore, OLAP means both changing and running reports in real time.

The two pillars of an OLAP system are the *star schema* and *aggregations*. If you want to change the pivot table inside your client in real time, your client tool must know the database schema in advance. The tool needs to guide you through selecting the appropriate attributes to use for groupings (rows and columns in a pivot table) and the attributes to use for summarizing data. The typical relational schema is too complicated and does not give enough information to the client tool. An OLAP client tool instead uses the star schema to create the user interface in real time and enables simple reporting for end users. Figure 1-3 shows a typical star schema, prepared for sales analysis; notice that its structure resembles a star, hence its name.

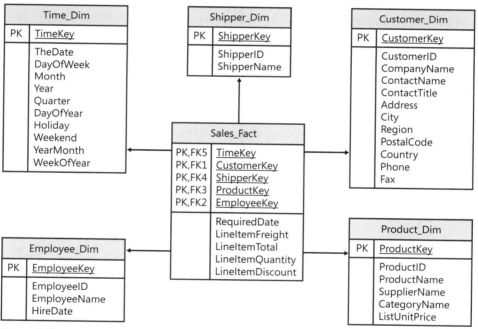

Figure 1-3 A star schema

You cannot change the schema of the production database; thus, to create an Analysis Services OLAP solution, you must create redundant data. Typically, you create several star schemas, each one covering a different business process, in a relational database called a *data warehouse*. A data warehouse contains cleansed data, collected over time, and merged from multiple production sources. Cleansing the data might include correcting invalid data on a source, presenting data consistently among different sources (for example, you might have gender represented in one source with the numbers 1 and 2 and, in other sources, with the letters F and M), removing duplicate rows, and similar tasks. From the data warehouse, you create

OLAP cubes inside Analysis Services. OLAP cubes are based on star schemas; because you browse them like you would navigate through a multidimensional hypercube, they are called cubes. Analysis Services databases are optimized for browsing. In an Analysis Services database, you prepare aggregates commonly used for the reporting, such as sales total, in advance.

Traditionally, OLAP cubes have had quite poor metadata. They just inherited star schemas from a data warehouse. In SQL Server 2005, Analysis Services databases feature much richer metadata—providing even more metadata than in a SQL Server database. Therefore, you can model a database from either the SQL Server database engine or Analysis Services. Because you can start your database modeling from either component, Analysis Services 2005 introduces the new term Unified Dimensional Model (UDM) instead of OLAP cube.

In OLAP cubes, through star schemas, you are still preparing a model in advance. Although end users can change the view online, they cannot find complex patterns and rules. This is the territory of data mining. Data mining is a set of mathematical methods that do not suppose any model in advance; they search for a model in the data. Data mining includes many different algorithms.

UDM (OLAP) and data mining solutions are clearly valuable for analysis, but consider the following issues as you evaluate your system design options:

- Preparing a consolidated data warehouse takes a lot of time and effort.
- You get plenty of redundant data in data warehouse and Analysis Services databases.
- Maintaining a data warehouse, OLAP cubes, and data mining models is additional administrative work.
- You administer Analysis Services databases separately from SQL Server databases. You need to set up security for the Analysis Services databases, back them up, and monitor and occasionally optimize their performance.
- Especially for data mining, you need a lot of knowledge in your company. Developers of data mining solutions should understand your business thoroughly, and your business analysts should understand the different data mining algorithms you can choose to implement.

Exam Tip   How do you decide when it is time to invest in a data warehousing and OLAP solution rather than using a reporting solution, which is typically much easier to implement? Besides the lightning speed and freedom of analyses you get with OLAP, the key point is that in a data warehouse, you collect data over space and time. If you need historical data, consolidated from multiple sources, then a simple reporting solution is not the correct solution.

Integration Services

SQL Server Integration Services is a platform that enables you to build data integration solutions. You typically use Integration Services to extract, transform, and load data into data warehouses.

When working with Integration Services, a unit of execution is called a package. A *package* is an organized collection of connections, control flow, data flows, event handlers, variables, and configurations. A package can execute complex ETL tasks, including merging data from heterogeneous sources, populating a data warehouse, performing simple and intelligent data cleansing, and standardizing data.

Exam Tip   There is a plethora of possibilities for disseminating the data in SQL Server 2005. Make sure you understand the strengths and weaknesses of each possibility.

When evaluating whether to use Integration Services, consider the following:

- **Automation**   A SQL Server Agent job step can execute an Integration Services package.
- **Merging**   An Integration Services package can merge data from heterogeneous sources, including relational databases, flat files, OLAP cubes, XML files, and Web services.
- **Performance**   Integration Services packages are very efficient. After you read the data from a source, you perform a series of transformations in memory buffers and write the data to a destination only once. You do not need to stage the data in temporary or permanent tables. Nevertheless, be careful not to overstress production servers when you read and write large amounts of data or perform complex transformations on a production server.
- **Scale out**   Integration Services packages execute as a client application. You can easily scale out the execution of packages to multiple computers. In addition, you can write transformed data from a single package to multiple destinations in parallel without having to reread or stage the data.
- **Transformations**   Integration Services packages support complex transformations. You can add derived data, get additional data or check existing data with lookups from reference tables, perform fuzzy lookups when you do not have exact matches in reference tables, and add your own transformations through a Visual Basic .NET script or through a custom transformation component.
- **Intelligence**   You can use Integration Services packages for intelligent data cleansing. You achieve intelligence in cleansing through data mining transformations when you check the data for outliers against an existing data mining model.
- **Security**   You can store Integration Services packages in SQL Server (in the *msdb* database) or in the file system. You have to secure the packages through pre-defined Integration Services roles and NTFS permissions or SQL Server permissions, depending on the storage you use. In addition, encrypt sensitive information, such as connection strings, inside a package. You can also digitally sign a package.

Practice: Using Other Services

In this practice, you will perform the conceptual exercise of selecting the best additional SQL Server 2005 service.

▶ **Exercise: Use the Appropriate Service and Feature**

In this exercise, decide which additional service shipped with SQL Server 2005 you would use for a business intelligence solution.

The sales department of your company needs to analyze the sales data. They are checking whether there are any problems with sales of any category of products, of any specific group of customers, or of any sales channel. If they find a problem, they have to investigate until they find whether the product, customer, or sales channel is problematic. They have to perform many different analyses in quite a short time. What can you do to help them?

Suggested Answer

This is a typical problem for Analysis Services UDM cubes. The analyses the sales department is performing start with aggregated data such as product categories, and they have to investigate to the base data. They have to perform numerous analyses in a short time. You should prepare UDM cubes and give the analysts OLAP client tools such as Office Excel.

Quick Check

1. Your users complain that when they need a new report, they have to wait three days for it. Some of them already started to create their own reports using Excel. However, these reports are not available to their colleagues. What can you do to mitigate their problems?
2. You find out that the reports your advanced users want to create would occasionally use two different data sources, and the data from those sources is not standardized. What can you do?

Quick Check Answers

1. You can deploy a Reporting Services solution. You can prepare report models to help the advanced users (users who are already using Excel) use Report Builder to create reports. Then, those users can deploy the reports to a company portal and make them available to colleagues.
2. You can create a third, consolidated database and populate it by using an Integration Services package that reads the data from both sources and then merges and standardizes the data.

Case Scenario: Select SQL Server Services to Support Business Needs

You are a database developer for a small company that distributes products from a single supplier to known customers. Currently, you transfer product data from your supplier to your database overnight. You have a fast and reliable link to your supplier, and your business application accesses the transferred and local data through stored procedures. Your business application is outsourced, so any modifications cost a lot of money and take a significant amount of time, neither of which your company can afford. However, your company has all the latest Microsoft software available.

Once a month, you send reports that include five years of payment history to your customers. At the end of the month, you create a staging database that contains the history data, and your reports run against this staging database. Preparing the staging database takes 10 hours. However, more and more customers have asked for fast access to their payment history over the Internet anytime and anywhere. Then one day, your supplier makes multiple changes to some products throughout the day, and you realize that your day-old data is not current enough anymore. Your supplier has implemented a Web service that uses Web methods to expose the latest data about the products, and you start thinking about the possibilities.

1. How can you enable your customers to see their payment history over the Internet?
2. How can you incorporate the data from the supplier's online database so that you always have the latest product information?

Chapter Summary

- SQL Server 2005 is more than just a relational database management system; it is a comprehensive platform for building enterprise applications.
- The database engine is not limited to the Transact-SQL language and relational data anymore, although SQL Server 2005 features powerful enhancements to these traditional features. Through new CLR and XML integration, you can work with object-oriented languages and XML data.
- With SQL Server 2005, you have many ways to work with distributed data, including distributed queries, replication, and Integration Services. In addition, you can distribute processing synchronously and asynchronously by using distributed transactions and Service Broker.
- SQL Server 2005 is a complete business intelligence platform, providing Reporting Services for classical reports, Analysis Services for OLAP and data mining analysis, and Integration Services for ETL processes.

Chapter 2
Designing a Logical Database

Databases are central to information systems, and a structure called a *data model*–also known as a *schema*–specifies a database. Changes in this structure can have a radical and expensive impact on the programs that use it. Therefore, it is important to think through your database design thoroughly in advance and develop a design that will satisfy business needs, perform adequately, behave predictably, and enable extensibility and data reusability.

In this chapter, you will learn how to design a normalized database to support online transactional processing (OLTP) applications and how to denormalize the design to support business intelligence (BI) applications. You will also see how to plan the data flow, how to use advanced table features such as supertype and subtype tables, and how to model hierarchies.

Exam objectives in this chapter:
- Design a logical database.
  - ❏ Design a normalized database.
  - ❏ Optimize the database design by denormalizing.
  - ❏ Design data flow architecture.
- Design objects that define data.
  - ❏ Design tables that use advanced features.

Before You Begin

To complete the lessons in this chapter, you must have:

- Knowledge of the Transact-SQL data definition language (DDL) elements.
- The SQL Server 2005 *AdventureWorks* and *AdventureWorksDW* sample databases installed. Sample databases are available with SQL Server 2005 Enterprise Edition but are not a part of the default installation. Alternatively, you can install sample databases from *http://msdn2.microsoft.com/en-us/library/ms143739.aspx*.

- Microsoft Visual Studio 2005 or Microsoft Visual C# 2005 Express Edition installed. You can download Visual C# 2005 Express Edition for free from *http://msdn.microsoft.com/vstudio/express/*. (Optionally, you can have Microsoft Visual Studio Team System or Microsoft Visual Studio Team Edition for Database Professionals installed.) You can find more information about these products at *http://msdn2.microsoft.com/en-us/teamsystem/aa718803.aspx*.

- Microsoft Office Visio or Visio 2007 Viewer, available as a free download from *http://www.microsoft.com/downloads/details.aspx?FamilyID=d88e4542-b174-4198-ae31-6884e9edd524&DisplayLang=en*.

Lesson 1: Systematically Approaching Design Stages

Estimated lesson time: 20 minutes

A database and an application together provide a comprehensive picture of a real-world system. Data modeling is a structure design process. Often, you can move forward with data modeling in parallel with functional design. You explore your choices by using analysis, abstraction, experience, heuristics, and creativity. There are always many candidate solutions; to find the best one, you have to approach the design systematically. Developing a data model is an iterative process: you develop a model, check it with domain experts, and refine the model. When your model is prepared, it can serve as an effective communication tool between domain experts and developers.

The most important data model is the relational model, which represents data in the form of two-dimensional tables consisting of rows and columns. This model is a simple, yet rigorously defined, concept of how users perceive data. Each table represents a real-world entity (person, place, thing, or event) about which you collect information. In mathematics, the relational model is based on set theory; mathematically, each table represents a set. Edgar F. Codd of IBM contrived the relational model in 1969, explaining a relational database as a collection of tables. The organization of data into relational tables is the logical view of the database. The way the database software physically stores the data on a computer disk system is the internal view of the database; it differs from product to product.

In the planning phase, according to the Microsoft Solutions Framework (MSF) process model, you deal with three distinguishable data-modeling phases. Each phase yields a phase schema. The three phases, schemas, and methods you use in a specific phase are as follows:

- **Conceptual phase**   As a database designer, in this phase, you collect all business requirements and rules in cooperation with business domain experts. You create a conceptual schema by using the object role modeling (ORM) method. An ORM diagram documents a business problem. You can also use the entity relationship (ER) method in this phase, especially the Integration Definition for Information Modeling (IDEF1X) method, although it is a less expressive method than ORM and does not allow the diagramming of all possible business rules. Alternatively, you could use Unified Modeling Language (UML), although this language suits application design better than database design.
- **Logical phase**   During the logical phase, you represent data that is already grouped logically in entities by adding attributes and relationships between entities. ER diagrams document this relational design. The most-used ER models are the Extended ER model and the IDEF1X model, both supported by Microsoft Office Visio.

■ **Physical phase**   You implement the relational model physically, in a database on a relational database management system (RDBMS) such as Microsoft SQL Server. No matter which method you use for implementation (automatically via a tool or manually), you have to prepare DDL statements for creating database objects in a language that your RDBMS understands.

In addition to these phases, when you are modeling a database, you can start with another schema, called the external schema, that usually comes from the application design process but that can be a good starting point for data modeling. The external schema shows how your system will be used. A common way to show the external schema is by using UML Use Case diagrams. Table 2-1 shows all four stages in a condensed format.

Table 2-1   Data Modeling Stages

	External Phase	**Conceptual Phase**	**Logical Phase**	**Physical Phase**
Focus	Analyze business needs, verify UI and reporting needs	Capture business requirements	Document relational design	Implement relational design
Roles involved	Domain expert, application designer	Domain expert, database designer	Database designer	Database designer, developer
Methodology	UML	ORM	ER	DDL

Key Steps and Best Practices for Data Modeling

The first step in developing a data model is identifying requirements. You must communicate with domain experts, key stakeholders, and even end users to gather all the information you need. You can help yourself by using UML Use Case diagrams, if they already exist, and existing reports. You can then create a conceptual model, which documents all business requirements and rules as facts. From the conceptual model, you create a logical model. Alternatively, you can create a logical model directly, without the conceptual model. In either case, check the conceptual or logical model with domain experts and refine it as needed. Iterate through the model at least a couple of times.

From the logical model, you create a physical model. The design process is not finished here, though. Next, you refine the physical model according to security, performance, auditing, availability, and scalability needs. Finally, you build a prototype to test the database design.

For smaller projects, you can skip some of these steps. However, for larger projects, you should implement all of these steps, including creating a conceptual model. Here are additional best practices for data modeling:

- **Be especially careful with the scope of the project.**   Many projects fail because the scope is not well defined. Alternatively, many developers use scope expansion as an excuse for their bad work. Your customers simply cannot know everything they need in advance. Even if they did know everything they needed today, you have to consider that business changes quickly. Therefore, you must be prepared for several iterations during the design process. Three iterations in refining the model is normal; more iterations than that usually means the scope was not well defined, or the customer requested features that should be part of a different project.
- **Choose the appropriate methodology.**   ER diagrams are an informal standard for the database part of documenting a project, so the ER method should be one of your selected methodologies. In addition, ORM, which is more expressive than the ER model, is useful for presenting complex rules.
- **Use a professional database-modeling tool.**   Tools such as Visio for Enterprise Architects enable forward engineering—creating a logical model from a conceptual model and then creating a physical model from the logical model. Make sure you are familiar with the tool before you start your design.
- **Include your physical model, the DDL scripts, in a source control system.**   You can use Visual Studio Team System for source control.
- **Start with a strict relational model, but be prepared to make some compromises to satisfy business needs.**   For example, usually you have to denormalize some data to achieve satisfactory performance. (You will learn about denormalization in Lesson 3, "Optimizing the Database Design by Denormalizing.") Document such compromises thoroughly.
- **Use free models as a starting point.**   You can find free models in books and on the Web. Check existing models if you upgrade an application. An upgraded application must provide all the features of the old application; otherwise, users will not be satisfied.

Object Role Modeling and the Conceptual Model

In our natural, speaking language, we use statements of fact or, in logic, propositions about entities of interest asserted to be true. For example, it is a fact that Lubor Kollar was employed by Tailspin Toys on March 19, 2004. The idea behind ORM is that you simply write down all the facts. The tool then converts those facts to a conceptual ORM diagram and produces logical and physical diagrams out of that ORM diagram. ORM pictures the world in terms of objects that play roles. Data elements are not combined into tables a priori. Descriptions of data-element relationships serve as input to a table-building algorithm. ORM thereby incorporates normalization into the methodology. (You will learn about normalization in the next lesson.)

ORM verbalizes the relevant data as elementary facts. It uses no attributes; attributes are facts related to entities. In ORM, you distinguish between two types of objects. An *entity* object is the one you can uniquely identify; however, you cannot write down a concrete value of the object unless you use values of attributes of the object. ORM represents entity objects as named ellipses. The *Value* object is a scalar attribute, which enables you to write down any concrete value the object can take. In ORM, you represent a value object as a dotted or dashed ellipse (~ attribute). Relationships between objects (that is, roles the objects play) are represented by lines and subdivided boxes that establish connections. For example, in the following paragraph, you have a collection of facts you gathered through an interview with a domain expert.

> *The system you are developing must support sales. Customers send orders. Each order can contain multiple products, and a single product can appear on multiple orders. A customer orders a product in a quantity with or without a discount. A single customer presumably and hopefully sends multiple orders. Each product has a name, a unit of measurement, and a price. For each customer, you need to collect the customer's name, address, and tax number. Tax numbers are unique. An order always has a date and a known customer. You must provide a way to identify customers, products, and orders.*

Figure 2-1 shows the ORM model for the facts in the preceding paragraph.

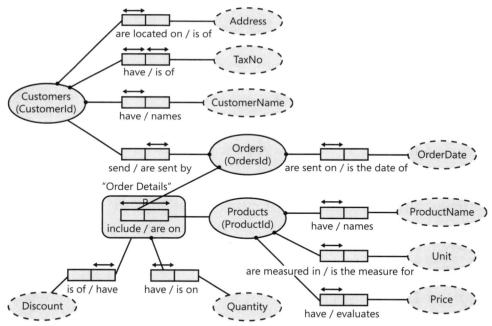

Figure 2-1   ORM model that supports the sales application

When you create an ORM model, follow the Conceptual Schema Design Procedure (CSDP). If you follow the procedure exactly, ORM guarantees a fully normalized model. (You will learn about normalization in Lesson 2, "Designing a Normalized Database.") The seven steps of the CSDP are:

1. Transform familiar information examples into elementary facts, and apply quality checks.
2. Draw the fact types, and apply a population check (that is, write down examples) for each fact.
3. Check for entity types that should be combined, and note any arithmetic derivation.
4. Add uniqueness constraints, and check arity of fact types. *Arity* means how many objects are involved in the proposition. Typical facts are binary; they involve two objects. You can also have unary, ternary, and quaternary facts. You must check whether you can decompose facts of larger arity to more elementary facts.
5. Add mandatory role constraints, and check for logical derivations.
6. Add value, set comparison, and subtype constraints.
7. Add other constraints, and perform final checks.

Entity Relationship and the Logical Model

The ER model is a top-down approach to data modeling, supported by a widely used diagramming convention. An entity is a thing that you can distinctly identify and that is of business interest; an entity in an ER model has three properties:

- You can uniquely identify each representation of an entity.
- Each representation of an entity plays an important role in the system it lives in. (It has to have a reason to be there.)
- You can describe each representation of an entity by using one or more attributes (data elements such as name, age, and quantity).

You classify entities into different entity sets. An entity set is a set of entity instances (occurrences) of the same type. Entity sets, therefore, are not always disjoint. (A company employee can belong to the employees and managers sets.) A database consists of a collection of entity sets; it also includes information about relationships between the entity sets.

Relationships are associations between entities. A relation is a subset of the cross products of the entity sets involved in the relationship. Each entity set in a relationship has a role or a function that the entity plays in the relationship. For example, person has the role of *employee* in the relationship *works for company*; company has the role of *employer*. The degree of a relationship is the number of entities associated in the relationship. Binary associations can be classified according to cardinality (one-to-one, one-to-many, many-to-many) and optionality (mandatory or optional).

Entities are the objects of interest, so you must have some information about them that is of interest. Each entity instance is described by a set of *attributes* that define its qualities, characteristics, or properties and the values of the attributes. For each attribute, there are a number of legal or permitted values. These sets of legal values are value sets or domains of that attribute. Relationships can also have relevant information about them.

Because you represent entities by the values of their attribute set, the set of attribute values must be different for each entity instance. A group of attributes (or possibly one attribute) used for identifying entities in an entity set is called an entity key. Similarly, each relationship instance in a relationship set needs to be identified. The identification is always based on the primary keys of the entity sets involved in the relationship set. Sometimes you cannot uniquely identify the entities in an entity set by the values of their own attributes; such entities, which require a relationship to be identified, are called *weak entities*. We call normal entities strong or regular entities.

There is no single graphical representation of an ER model. However, all ER diagrams look similar. Entities are diagrammed as rectangles. Attributes can be diagrammed as ovals attached to the rectangle that they belong to, or they can be listed inside the rectangle or even listed separately. Relationships can be diagrammed as diamonds or shown as connecting lines. They can show cardinality and optionality, either explicitly with numbers or with crow's feet symbols.

Figure 2-2 shows an IDEF1X ER model, on the left, and an Extended ER model, on the right, for the same sales database in the ORM lesson example.

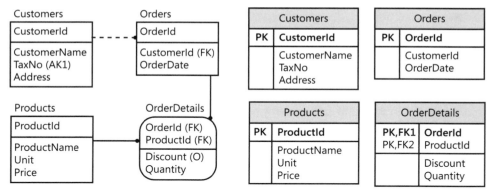

Figure 2-2   IDEF1X and Extended ER models that support the sales application

When you are doing ER modeling directly (not from an ORM source model), you must study the description of the business problem. You start with entities, identifying nouns. Then you find relationships, identifying verbs. You look for typical verbs such as "is," which leads to investigation of the hierarchical structure (you will learn about supertypes and subtypes in Lesson 5, "Supertypes and Subtypes"), or "has" and other verbs, which lead to investigation of the relational structure. You then allocate attributes to entities, identifying adjectives. You identify primary and foreign keys, and, for foreign key associations, you identify cardinality and optionality. Your product is an ER model; however, you need to analyze the ER attributes—forgetting the attributes leads to missed entities.

On the Companion Disc   You will find all the models for this chapter on the companion CD in the C:\My Documents\Microsoft Press\TK70-441\Chapter02\Practice folder.

Practice: Opening Models

In this practice, you will examine ORM and ER models.

▶ **Exercise: Open and Examine Models**

In this exercise, you check whether it is possible to reconstruct statements that describe a business problem from a conceptual and a logical database model.

1. On the companion CD, navigate to the C:\My Documents\Microsoft Press\TK70-441\Chapter02\Practice folder, and open the Ch02_Sales_ORM.bmp file. Check the facts and how they are diagrammed.

2. Open the Ch02_Sales_IDEF1XER.vsd and Ch02_Sales_ExtendedER.vsd files. Try to recreate the original propositions from the example.

Quick Check

You have to prepare a database model to support an application for managing projects. You collect the following information: each project has a single customer, each project can have many activities, and each project can have many employees assigned to it. In addition, you want to follow the time spent (in hours) on projects by specific employees and by activity for each day. Using this information, answer the following questions:

1. List the entities you can find from the description of the problem.
2. What is the cardinality of the relationship between projects and activities?

Quick Check Answers

1. You should find the following entities: projects, customers, activities, employees as strong entities, and project details as a weak entity.
2. The relationship between projects and activities is many-to-many.

Lesson 2: Designing a Normalized Database

Estimated lesson time: 25 minutes

Tables representing propositions about entities of one type (that is, representing a single set) are fully normalized. Correct and complete mapping of a conceptual ORM model to a logical model yields fully normalized tables. Properly designed entities in an ER model lead to fully normalized tables as well. However, both ORM and ER modeling start with the business description of a problem; it is possible to miss some dependencies between entities and leave some tables denormalized. Of course, there could also be a bug in the tool that produces the DDL script from the ORM and ER models. However, any denormalization can lead to update anomalies. Data integrity and consistency are fundamental for databases. Remember that a database holds propositions, and propositions are facts. If propositions are not true, they are not facts; they are falsehoods. You need a logical method that yields a fully normalized database.

Normalization is the process of redesigning the model to unbundle any overlapping entities. The process involves decomposition; however, decomposition cannot yield a loss of information. You perform the decomposition by applying a linear progression of rules called normal forms. Normalization eliminates redundancy and incompleteness. Note the part that designers frequently overlook: normalization eliminates incompleteness, not just redundancy. Many normal forms (NFs) are defined; the first six are called first NF, second NF, third NF, Boyce-Codd NF, fourth NF, and fifth NF. If a database is in fifth NF, the database is fully normalized. Only the first three NFs are important; usually, if a database is in third NF, it is in fifth NF as well. You should understand the normalization form and use it to perform a final check of your database design, checking the model you created by using other methods.

First Normal Form

Imagine a table such as the one that Table 2-2 shows. The table holds information about sales. In this case, only the OrderId column is part of the primary key.

Table 2-2   Table Before First NF

OrderId	CustomerId	OrderDate	Items
1	1	2006.10.22	Nt Nuts q=5, Bo Bolts q=10
2	1	2006.10.24	Sc Screws q=12
3	2	2006.09.15	Nt Nuts q=3, Sc Screws q=3
4	3	2006.10.22	Bo Bolts q=5

With a design like this, you can have the following anomalies:

- **Insert**   How do you insert a customer without an order?
- **Update**   If item Bo is renamed, how do you perform an update?
- **Delete**   If order 3 is deleted, the data for customer 2 is lost.
- **Select**   How do you calculate the total quantity of bolts?

Note that only update and select anomalies deal with redundancy: they are problematic because the table contains redundant data. Insert and delete anomalies deal with incompleteness of the model. The rule for first NF is, "A table is in first normal form if all columns are atomic." This means there can be no multi-valued columns—columns that would hold a collection such as an array or another table. First NF is somewhat redundant with the definition of a relational table or of a relation. A table is a relation if it fulfills the following conditions:

- **Values are atomic.**   The columns in a relational table are not a repeating group or arrays.
- **Columns are of the same kind.**   All values in a column come from the same domain.
- **Rows are unique.**   There is at least one column or set of columns, the values of which uniquely identify each row in the table.
- **The order of columns is insignificant.**   You can share the same table without worrying about table organization.
- **The sequence of rows is insignificant.**   A relational table can be retrieved in a different order and sequence.
- **Each column must have a unique name.**   This is required because the order of columns is not significant.

You can see in the example in Table 2-2 that the last column is multi-valued; it holds an array of items. Before starting with decomposition, let us briefly review the textual notation of a relational table. Remember the earlier example proposition, "Lubor Kollar was employed by Tailspin Toys on March 19, 2004." In a general form, you can write "Employee with (Name) was employed by (Company) on (EmploymentDate)." This generalized form of a proposition is a *predicate*. Terms in parentheses are value placeholders (entity attributes). A predicate defines the structure of a table. You can write the structure briefly as:

```
Employees(EmpId, EmployeeName, CompanyId, EmploymentDate)
```

Underlined columns form the primary key. Actually, they form a candidate key, and a table can have multiple candidate keys. You could underline all candidate keys and double underline the primary key.

You decompose the table shown in Table 2-2 on the Items column. Every item leads to a new row, and every atomic piece of data of a single item (ProductId, ProductName, Quantity) leads to a new column. After the decomposition, you have multiple rows for a single order; therefore, you have to expand the primary key. You can compose the new primary key from the OrderId and ProductId columns. However, suppose you can allow multiple products on a single order, each time with a different discount, for example. Thus, you cannot use ProductId as part of the primary key. However, you can add the *ItemId* attribute and use it as a part of the new primary key. A decomposed table in first normal form would look like this:

```
Orders(OrderId, CustomerId, OrderDate, ItemId, ProductId, Quantity,
ProductName)
```

Before moving to second NF, you have to understand a common misconception about first NF. You might have heard or read that you should not have a repeating group of columns. However, this advice is incorrect; repeating groups means you should not have a repeating group (that is, a collection) in a single column. For example, imagine this table:

```
Employees(EmployeeId, EmployeeName, Child1, Child2)
```

This table is perfectly in first NF. This design has a built-in constraint, allowing only employees who have two children. If you do not allow unknown (NULL) values for the *Child1* and *Child2* attributes, then you allow employees with exactly two children. This kind of constraint is not typical for business; nevertheless, it is a constraint built into the model, which is in first NF. Such constraints are rare, and a repeating group of columns typically represents a hidden collection. Take care not to decompose such groups automatically before checking whether this is a special constraint.

Second Normal Form

After achieving first NF, the decomposed table from Table 2-2 looks like Table 2-3.

Table 2-3   Table in First NF

OrderId	CustomerId	OrderDate	ItemID	ProductId	Quantity	ProductName
1	1	2006.10.22	1	Nt	5	Nuts
1	1	2006.10.22	2	Bo	10	Bolts
2	1	2006.10.24	1	Sc	12	Screws
3	2	2006.09.15	1	Nt	3	Nuts
3	2	2006.09.15	2	Sc	3	Screws

You still have the following anomalies:

- **Insert** How do you insert a customer without an order?
- **Update** If customer 1 changes the order date for order 1, how do you perform the update? (In many places, possible inconsistencies could exist.)
- **Delete** If you delete order 3, the data for customer 2 is lost.

To achieve second NF, a table must be in first NF, and every non-key column must be fully functionally dependent on the entire primary key. This means that no column can depend on part of the primary key only. In the example in Table 2-3, you know the customer and the order date if you know the value of the OrderId column; you do not need to know anything about ProductId, which is part of the primary key. The CustomerId and OrderDate columns depend on part of the primary key only—OrderId. To achieve second NF, you need to decompose the table into two tables:

```
Orders(OrderId, CustomerId, OrderDate)
OrderDetails(OrderId, ItemId, ProductId, Quantity, ProductName)
```

In the Orders table, you leave attributes that depend on OrderId only; then you introduce a new table, OrderDetails, to hold the other attributes. When achieving first NF, you are converting values from a multi-valued attribute to rows and changing the primary key; for second and all other NFs, you decompose tables into more tables. Second NF deals with relationships between columns that are part of a key and other columns.

After decomposing to multiple tables, you must have some common value that enables you to join the tables in queries; otherwise, you would lose some information. The decomposition has to be lossless. Of course, you need relationships between tables. A relationship is an association between two or more tables. Relationships are expressed in the data values of the primary and foreign keys. A primary key is a column or columns in a table whose values uniquely identify each row in the table. A foreign key is a column or columns whose values are the same as the primary key of another table—in other words, a copy of the primary key from another relational table. The relationship is made between two relational tables by matching the values of the foreign key with the values of the primary key.

Third Normal Form

After achieving second NF, the decomposed tables from Table 2-3 look like the tables in Table 2-4 and Table 2-5. Note that in the Orders table (Table 2-4), another attribute, CustomerName, is added to show that normalization violations can appear in any table.

Table 2-4 Orders Table in Second NF

OrderId	CustomerId	CustomerName	OrderDate
1	1	Tailspin Toys	2006.10.22
2	1	Tailspin Toys	2006.10.24
3	2	Wingtip Toys	2006.09.15

Table 2-5 OrderDetails Table in Second NF

OrderId	ItemId	ProductId	Quantity	ProductName
1	1	Nt	5	Nuts
1	2	Bo	10	Bolts
2	1	Sc	12	Screws

Table 2-5   OrderDetails Table in Second NF

OrderId	ItemId	ProductId	Quantity	ProductName
3	1	Nt	3	Nuts
3	2	Sc	3	Screws

Second NF solves the update anomaly (if customer 1 changes the order date for order 1); however, you still have the following anomalies:

- **Insert**   How do you insert a customer without an order?
- **Delete**   If you delete order 3, the data for customer 2 is lost.

To achieve third NF, a table must be in second NF, and every non-key column must be non-transitively dependent on the primary key. For example, in Table 2-4, from OrderId, you can find CustomerId; then from CustomerId, you can get transitively to the *CustomerName* attribute value. Similarly, in Table 2-5, you can get transitively to ProductName through ProductId from OrderId and ItemId. If you think of the rule for third NF from the non-key attributes point of view, it simply means you should have no functional dependencies between non-key columns. Non-key columns must depend on keys only. In the examples in Table 2-4 and Table 2-5, CustomerName depends on CustomerId, and ProductName depends on ProductId. Thus, to achieve third NF, you must create new tables for dependencies between non-key columns:

```
Customers(CustomerId, CustomerName)
Orders(OrderId, CustomerId, OrderDate)
Products(ProductId, ProductName)
OrderDetails(OrderId, ItemId, ProductId, Quantity)
```

This schema is free from all the update anomalies you had before normalization. However, it is not free from all update anomalies. For example, the schema itself cannot prevent you from inserting an unreasonable order date. (You will learn more about additional constraints in Chapter 3, "Designing a Physical Database.") Note that this schema is also essentially the same (except for a couple of attributes omitted for the sake of brevity) as you received by using the ORM and ER approach. As mentioned earlier, use normalization for final checking and refining of your model.

Practice: Normalizing the Database

You are developing a database model that will support an application for managing projects (as in the Quick Check in Lesson 1, "Systematically Approaching Design Stages"). You collect the following information: each project has a single customer, each project can have many activities, and each project can have many employees assigned to it. You want to follow time spent (in hours) on projects by specific employee by activity for each day. Your initial design is:

```
Projects(ProjectId, ProjectName, CustomerId, CustomerName,
    Activities(Activity1Id, Activity1Name, …, ActivityNId,
    ActivityNName), Employees(Employee1Id, Employee1Name, …,
    EmployeeNId, EmployeeNName), WorkDate, TimeSpent)
```

▶ **Exercise 1: Achieve the First Normal Form**

In this exercise, you will bring this model to first NF. To achieve first NF, you need to eliminate all attributes that are collections.

1. Check the Activities part of the table. Is this a collection?
2. Check the Employees part of the table. Is this a collection?

    Your model should look like this:

```
Projects(ProjectId, ItemId, ProjectName, CustomerId, CustomerName,
    ActivityId, ActivityName, EmployeeId, EmployeeName, WorkDate,
    TimeSpent)
```

▶ **Exercise 2: Achieve the Second Normal Form**

In this exercise, you will bring this model to second NF. To achieve second NF, you must make sure your model does not contain attributes that depend on only part of the primary key.

1. The complete primary key in the table you created in Exercise 1, "Achieve the First Normal Form," consists of ProjectId and ItemId.
2. Do you really need both columns to find CustomerId and CustomerName associated with a project?

    Your model should look like this:

```
Projects(ProjectId, ProjectName, CustomerId, CustomerName)
    ProjectDetails(ProjectId, ItemId, ActivityId, ActivityName,
    EmployeeId, EmployeeName, WorkDate, TimeSpent)
```

▶ **Exercise 3: Achieve the Third Normal Form**

In this exercise, you will bring this model to third NF. To achieve third NF, you need to look at dependencies between non-key attributes.

1. Is there any dependency between CustomerId and CustomerName?
2. Is there any dependency between ActivityId and ActivityName?
3. Is there any dependency between EmployeeId and EmployeeName?

    Your model should now look like this:

```
Projects(ProjectId, ProjectName, CustomerId)
    ProjectDetails(ProjectId, ItemId, ActivityId, EmployeeId,
    WorkDate, TimeSpent)
Customers(CustomerId, CustomerName)
Activities(ActivityId, ActivityName)
Employees(EmployeeId, EmployeeName)
```

> **Exam Tip**   Be sure to understand the difference between second and third normal forms.

Quick Check

1. What is the difference between second and third NFs?
2. Why would you normalize a database?

Quick Check Answers

1. Second NF deals with dependencies between non-key and key columns. Third NF deals with internal dependencies between pairs of non-key columns.
2. You normalize a database to prevent anomalies by eliminating redundancy and incompleteness.

Lesson 3: Optimizing the Database Design by Denormalizing

Estimated lesson time: 20 minutes

You implement normalization with a specific purpose: to maintain data integrity. However, in a real-life project, you typically have to bring back some data redundancy either for performance reasons or to maintain a history.

A fully normalized schema shows current state only. For example, in an invoicing application that is in a fully normalized design, you keep a customer's address only in the Customers table. Suppose that a customer moves and you update that customer's address with the new one. A few days later, the same customer reports that he accidentally lost some printed invoices during the move and asks you to print copies of lost invoices. It would be impossible to print exact copies of the invoices if you do not maintain some history about the customer's address. You can solve this problem by maintaining a copy of customer address information on the invoice date in the Invoices table. Similarly, customers can change their name, so you also need to maintain a copy of customer names as part of the invoice data in the Invoices table.

During the normalization process, you decompose tables into more tables. The more tables you have, the more joins you have to perform in your queries, and joins have a negative impact on performance. To help, you can replicate a foreign key from the first child table to the second one. Take the invoicing system example again. Say you have an Employees parent table, and you add the EmployeeId column to the Customers table to serve as the foreign key because every customer has an account manager. Now, your typical queries must find invoices together with customer account manager data, requiring you to join three tables—Invoices, Customers, and Employees. However, if you replicate the EmployeeId column in the Invoices table, you can achieve the same goal and satisfy the same query by joining only the Invoices and Employees tables.

The best way to boost performance in a normalized system is to use derived data. For example, before creating an invoice item, you must check whether a product is in stock. You can always calculate levels and states from events, but what if you had to aggregate all the events for the current year just to tell a customer the product he or she wants to buy is out of stock? The customer would probably never return. You can solve this problem by maintaining total quantity in stock in a column in the Products table and by maintaining a separate ProductsInWarehouses table that holds the quantity of products in stock in your warehouses (if you have multiple warehouses).

Finally, you might have many queries that aggregate sales across customers. In a fully normalized system, you would have to aggregate all invoice details for a single customer multiple times. You can greatly improve performance by maintaining the year-to-date sales summary in a column in the Customers table. Figure 2-3 shows ER diagrams of the invoicing database before normalization, and Figure 2-4 shows ER diagrams after denormalization.

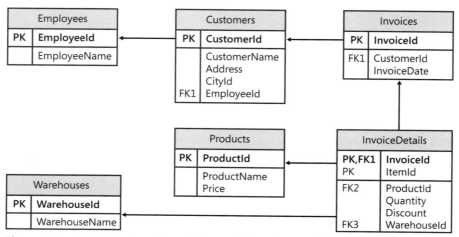

Figure 2-3   Part of the invoicing database before denormalization

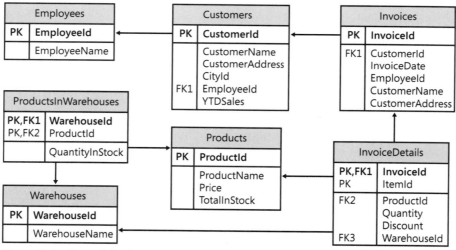

Figure 2-4   Part of the invoicing database after denormalization

Still, denormalization brings the danger of update anomalies back to the database. Therefore, you have to do it deliberately. You should document any denormalization thoroughly. To make sure your application correctly maintains denormalized data, you need to use transactions appropriately. A transaction is the smallest unit of work that must either complete entirely or not at all. For example, in the Invoices system, a transaction might mean an insertion to a table such as InvoiceDetails, which must be followed immediately by an update of the derived-level column TotalInStock in the Product table or a StockLevel column in the ProductsIn-Warehouses table, depending where you maintain the stock level information. If one of those actions fails, the entire transaction is rolled back to ensure data consistency. An even better choice for maintaining denormalized data, however, is to leave that task to the RDBMS. You can do this by introducing data manipulation language (DML) triggers. A RDBMS fires a trigger automatically as part of a transaction. In the invoices example, a DML trigger for insert, update, and delete on the InvoiceDetails table can maintain the TotalInStock column and the ProductsInWarehouses table. In addition, you should have procedures in place to rebuild the derived data from scratch. You can always rebuild this data from events tables in case of inconsistency between the sum of events and states.

IMPORTANT   Maintain denormalized data in transactions

After a denormalization, you have to make sure to maintain the denormalized data in transactions. For example, you have to correct the stock level any time you sell a product in a single transaction.

For reports and analysis, a better practice than maintaining aggregate information in an OLTP database is to introduce a data warehouse, which is based on a somewhat denormalized multidimensional model and a Microsoft Online Analytical Processing (OLAP) system. An OLAP database management system typically takes care of the aggregations for you.

Practice: Denormalizing the Database

In the previous practice, you prepared a fully normalized model for the Projects database. In this practice, you will denormalize this model to improve performance. Your current design is:

```
Projects(ProjectId, ProjectName, CustomerId)
    ProjectDetails(ProjectId, ItemId, ActivityId, EmployeeId,
    WorkDate, TimeSpent)
    Customers(CustomerId, CustomerName)
    Activities(ActivityId, ActivityName)
    Employees(EmployeeId, EmployeeName)
```

▶ **Exercise 1: Denormalize to Maintain History**

In this exercise, you will perform the denormalization to maintain history.

> Your company requires your system to maintain a customer's name from the time that you started a project for a customer. A customer can later change the name. How would you achieve this requirement?
>
> **Suggested Answer**
>
> In the Customers table, you maintain the current name only. Therefore, you have to add the customer name to the Projects table.

In addition, it is always a good practice to have the information about the date when the name was valid. Therefore, you should add the start date in the Projects table as well. Note that you would probably already have the start date of a project in a real-life design.

Your improved design should look similar to the following. (The denormalized attributes are StartDate and CustomerName.)

```
Projects(ProjectId, ProjectName, CustomerID, StartDate, CustomerName)
```

▶ **Exercise 2: Denormalize for Performance**

In this exercise, you will perform the denormalization to improve performance.

You have performance problems with a report that calculates total time spent on a project. Because you are tracking multiple projects, you run this report multiple times a day. How would you improve report performance?

Suggested Answer

The problem is that you have to aggregate project detail rows, in which you have the information about time spent or each activity on a project. You have to add a column to hold the total time spent in the Projects table.

Your improved design should look similar to the following. (Denormalized attribute that you should add in this exercise is TotalTimeSpent.)

```
Projects(ProjectId, ProjectName, CustomerId, StartDate,
    CustomerName, TotalTimeSpent)
```

Quick Check

1. What are some benefits of denormalization?
2. What problems can you encounter when you decide to introduce some denormalization into your model?

Quick Check Answers

1. Some benefits of denormalization are improved performance, the need for fewer joins, and the ability to maintain history information.
2. When you denormalize a database, you can encounter problems with data consistency, especially with aggregated data, which must be updated for any single event.

Lesson 4: Designing the Data Flow Architecture

Estimated lesson time: 10 minutes

When you design a database, consider data flow. Prepare your data model and document possible data flow before you start the physical implementation of any databases. Data flow includes flow from the database to the middle tier and clients, flow to copies of data, and flow for archiving purposes.

Data Flow for OLTP Applications

In OLTP applications, the application typically uses data-access components such as ADO.NET to maintain the flow of data from a database to the middle tier or clients. However, as a data modeler, you must be prepared for multiple copies of data that can exist at the same time. For example, an application can implement a disconnected model in which it brings data to the client and then disconnects, only to reconnect later to make changes to that data. However, in the meantime, another user might have accessed that same data, making his or her changes. With multiple copies of data, you can expect update conflicts. Thus, you need to have a solution for resolving conflicts when the same piece of data is updated independently in multiple places.

One solution is to store a copy of the data in application cache. For example, you can use the ADO.NET *DataSet* object and persist part of the data about a client. An application can cache the data in other objects, such as any of the .NET collections, as well. An application is responsible for resolving update conflicts that stem from its own cache. However, a distributed application could need a copy of a database stored in relational format in a RDBMS on a disconnected client. Merge replication is the mechanism in SQL Server for such needs. Merge replication comes with plenty of built-in conflict-resolving procedures, and you can add your own. In any case, you must document the resolution process thoroughly, including details about the resolving algorithm. In addition, if you use merge replication, you should have a plan for merging data. You perform merging between a single subscriber and a publisher at a time. With hundreds of subscribers, you could get in trouble with your time window for merging if you do not give your merge process plenty of time. Remember that in the same time window, you usually have to accomplish other maintenance tasks, such as backups, as well.

Many OLTP applications perform intensive work on a small part of the data only. Stale data is more or less read-only, used just for queries. This old data has a different maintenance plan; for example, you do not need to check the integrity of your database with DBCC CHECKDB on old data as often as on current data, which undergoes heavy modification activity. You can speed up maintenance of the current data by moving the old data to an archive. You can implement the archive in multiple ways:

- An application can perform the archiving at the end of a period—such as at the end of a fiscal year.
- You can use a data warehouse.
- You can create archive tables in a different filegroup of the OLTP database or even in a different database.
- In SQL Server 2005, you can partition a table and create archive partitions in separate filegroups. You will learn more about table partitioning in Chapter 3, "Designing a Physical Database."

Data Flow for Business Intelligence Applications

Data flow for OLTP applications typically does not involve transformations. For BI applications, just copying the data makes less sense. It is more valuable to do some data preparation in advance so that the data can serve better for analysis. For example, in a data warehouse, you use a multidimensional data model that includes merged and cleansed data. In addition, even simple reports on the same structure as it is in the OLTP database can benefit from copies of data. With copies of data, you can improve performance because you implement load balancing and diminish locking contention. Plan the data flow for BI applications in advance. Again, for extracting, transforming, and loading (ETL) data, you typically have a limited time window during off-peak hours.

SQL Server 2005 comes with many methods for data distribution and transformation that you can use for BI applications.

- **Snapshot isolation**   With this isolation level, SQL Server uses the *tempdb* system database to maintain the version of a row just before it is updated. SQL Server drops the old rows immediately after no connection uses them anymore. With snapshot-isolation levels, readers do not block writers, so you diminish locking contention. However, you have to devote special attention to *tempdb*.
- **Database snapshots**   You can use these read-only snapshots of a source database as the source for reports, reducing locking contention. You must create and drop database snapshots, preferably with the help of SQL Server Agent scheduled jobs.
- **Transactional replication**   This type of replication is especially useful when you need a copy of the data in a different server with low latency. Although you can improve the replication with your own procedures that can do some data transformation, replication is more suited for maintaining copies of data.
- **SQL Server Reporting Services**   Reporting Services can keep its own snapshots of data. You can prepare these snapshots in advance, before end users start to execute reports. Note that you must consider Reporting Services security; it has its own security model.
- **SQL Server Integration Services**   This tool is especially useful for complex transformations and for merging data from multiple sources. SQL Server Integration Services (SSIS)

is a perfect tool for maintaining data warehouses. However, you cannot achieve low latency with SSIS; typically, you load a data warehouse in off-peak hours.

- **SQL Server Analysis Services**   Analysis Services can pull data directly from the source database. For OLAP applications, you typically have to transform and merge data; therefore, in most cases, you would choose to create a data warehouse and use SSIS for the ETL process.

- **Additional tools**   SQL Server 2005 provides other tools you can use for data flow to BI applications, even though they are not primarily designed for that purpose. For example, to create a copy of data for BI applications, you could use the Copy Database Wizard, snapshot replication, backup and restore, log shipping, and detaching and attaching a database.

No matter which method you select, you must plan your data flow during the data-modeling phase of your project and document it thoroughly.

Quick Check

1. Which is the best method for maintaining data flow?
2. What problems can you expect when you have multiple copies of updateable data at a time?

Quick Check Answers

1. There is no simple answer to this question. When you investigate which method would be best for your environment, consider your latency requirements, your need for transformations, security issues, tool availability, existing knowledge in your company, transactional consistency, and more.
2. You should be prepared for update conflicts.

Lesson 5: Supertypes and Subtypes

Estimated lesson time: 20 minutes

In this final lesson, you learn about supertypes and subtypes. Many times, you have a hierarchy in your data, but you do not know the number of hierarchy levels in advance. Let's look at how to model this kind of problem.

Supertypes and Subtypes

Two entities are of distinct types if they have no attributes in common. It is possible for entities to have both common and distinct attributes. If they have a common identifier (that is, a common primary key), they have a special supertype-subtype relationship: they are neither distinct nor the same. You use supertypes and subtypes to represent different levels of entity generalization. Normalization and denormalization are about breaking down and assembling. Supertyping and subtyping are about generalization and specialization. Think of normalization as widening and subtyping as deepening. When you analyze your business problem, the verb *is* usually leads to a supertype/subtype relationship. For example, a company is a customer, and a person is a customer as well. Obviously, companies and persons have something in common.

In the companies/persons example, you started with a bottom-up approach. You can continue this generalization further. For example, both customers and suppliers are partners. You could also start from the top and discover specializations. The question is where to stop with this process. It is easy to find where to stop when you use the top-down approach: specialization makes sense only if subtypes have additional attributes. With the bottom-up approach, you could finish with just a few entities—for example, with subjects, objects, and events. Theoretically, you should stop when you reach abstract objects, objects that do not exist in the real world. For example, a computer table is a table, and a table is furniture; however, when you come to a store, you do not order "a piece of furniture." Still, sometimes it is good to have a supertype just to share common identification (that is, a common primary key). This enables you to gather all the information for a supertype for advanced analysis. A practical approach is to stop when you have a problem naming the supertype. If you cannot name it quickly, probably nobody would need to perform analysis on that supertype.

If you overlooked supertypes and subtypes when you analyzed your business problem or if you are working on refining an existing model, you can still identify them from the existing model. A huge table with sparse known values and many *NULL* values is a candidate for specialization. Check whether those unknown values are really unknown or whether they are simply meaningless for some rows. If they are meaningless, you can get rid of them when you introduce subtypes. Using the bottom-up approach from an existing model is possible only if the model stays with a naming convention; otherwise, you have to re-analyze the business problem. Tables that have many columns with similar or even the same names probably need a supertype table.

Modeling Hierarchies

A business problem can introduce something that, from a business perspective, is a called a hierarchy. For example, an employee organizational chart is a hierarchy. A bill of materials is another hierarchy. From a mathematical point of view, hierarchies are actually graphs and trees. In graph theory, a graph is a set of nodes (also called points or vertices) connected by links (called lines or edges). In a graph, you can arrive at a node through different paths. You can travel in any direction. Links can have different weights. Paths can make cycles. A tree is a special kind of graph in which any two nodes are connected by exactly one path. A forest is a graph in which any two nodes are connected by at most one path; a forest is, of course, a set of trees. An employee hierarchy is usually a tree, and a bill of materials is a directed, acyclic graph.

You can model a tree or a forest by using a single table that contains two columns connected by a foreign key. Figure 2-5 shows the Employees table with a hierarchy modeled. A manager is also an employee, so there is a row for each manager in the table. Each employee has a unique EmployeeId. Employees also have managers; this structure is modeled through the ManagerId column. A foreign key connecting the Employees table to itself uses EmployeeId as the parent and ManagerId as the child column. A single manager, who is an employee, can manage multiple employees. You can denote the highest-ranking employee by using a *ManagerId* value of unknown (NULL) or one that is the same as the *EmployeeId* value.

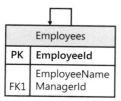

Figure 2-5 Employees table with hierarchy—a tree

For modeling a graph, you need two tables. Figure 2-6 shows a model for bill of materials. You need a table for parts (materials, semi-products, products) and a separate one for bill of materials, which joins parts into assemblies. The BillOfMaterials table has a primary key made up of the PartId and AssemblyId columns; both are parts, so you have two foreign keys from the BillOfMaterials table to the Parts table.

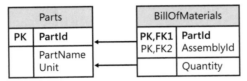

Figure 2-6   Parts and BillOfMaterials tables with hierarchy—a graph

To present the data to end users, you have to resolve the hierarchies. In previous versions of SQL Server, this was a tedious job. You needed a loop to resolve a hierarchy, implemented either through a WHILE construct or with recursion. In SQL Server 2005, you can use recursive common table expressions (CTEs) to resolve hierarchies. CTEs also perform better than loops.

Practice: Supertypes, Subtypes, and Hierarchies

You have a fully normalized model (as before the denormalization practice) for your database that supports project management applications. You discover that the business has expanded to offer support and training services, and you need to include these services in your database design. Support and training are services similar to projects, and each service can have its own hierarchy. For example, a project can be part of a bigger project, which can include training and support. Your current design is:

```
Projects(ProjectId, ProjectName, CustomerId, StartDate, CustomerName, TotalTimeSpent)
ProjectDetails(ProjectId, ItemId, ActivityId, EmployeeId,
    WorkDate, TimeSpent)
Customers(CustomerId, CustomerName)
Activities(ActivityId, ActivityName)
Employees(EmployeeId, EmployeeName)
```

▶ **Exercise 1: Find Supertypes and Subtypes**

In this exercise, you need to find supertypes and subtypes.

1. Find supertypes and subtypes.

   Services are the supertypes of projects.

2. You have to change all references to the projects to services. Change the name of the Projects and ProjectDetails tables to Services and ServiceDetails. Change the names of the *ProjectId* and *ProjectName* attributes to *ServiceId* and *ServiceName*.

3. Add the service type to distinguish between services. You should add a lookup table for different service types.

   Your improved design should look like the following.

```
Services(ServiceId, ServiceName, ServiceTypeId, CustomerId,
    StartDate, CustomerName, TotalTimeSpent)
ServiceTypes(ServiceTypeId, TypeName)
```

```
ServiceDetails(ServiceId, ItemId, ActivityId, EmployeeId,
    WorkDate, TimeSpent)
```

This design might surprise you; you might have expected explicit subtype tables for projects, training, and support. However, in the business problem description, there is no information about specific attributes for each service type. Introducing subtype tables would just complicate the design; all you need is a column that shows service type. This is an example of subtypes hidden, or stored implicitly, in a supertype; if there is no additional information about subtypes, they collapse to a single status attribute of a supertype.

IMPORTANT   Find supertypes in the conceptual design stage

If your database was already in production, then you could not change the names of the tables and columns so easily. Changing the names would probably lead to changes in your application as well. Therefore, it is very important to find supertypes in advance, in the conceptual design stage.

▶ **Exercise 2: Find Hierarchies**

In this exercise, you need to find hierarchies.

1. You need to model the hierarchy (tree) of the services.

   What you need is a column for the identification of the parent service.

2. In addition, add a foreign key between the ServiceId and ParentServiceId columns.

   Your improved design should look similar to this:

```
Services(ServiceId, ServiceName, ServiceTypeId, ParentServiceId,
    CustomerId, StartDate, CustomerName, TotalTimeSpent)
```

IMPORTANT   Remember foreign keys

In this brief notation, the foreign key is not explicitly shown. However, you should not forget about it.

Quick Check

1. How do supertypes and subtypes differ from graphs and trees?
2. How would you model a road system?

Quick Check Answers

1. Supertypes and subtypes show hierarchy in the structure; graphs and trees show hierarchy in the data.
2. You should model a road system as a graph with cities as nodes.

Case Scenario: Design a Logical Database

Tailspin Toys needs reports about outstanding debts. However, some of its customers are its suppliers as well. The company needs to see how much Tailspin Toys owes a partner as well as how much a partner owes Tailspin Toys. Currently, the company has two separate tables: Customers and Suppliers. In addition, its daily maintenance operations take too much time to perform in the off-peak operations window. The organization keeps all invoice history in two tables: Invoices and InvoiceDetails. Tailspin Toys updates its data for the current fiscal year only; all other data is just for analysis.

1. How can you generate a report that shows the complete picture of operations with a partner?

2. How can you speed up daily maintenance tasks so that they complete within the available window?

Chapter Summary

- When you design a database, you should do it as a formal process.
- For conceptual modeling, use ORM.
- ER models are standard for the logical level. ER diagrams are usually part of the application documentation.
- Check your model by using normalization.
- Denormalize for performance and history. Denormalize deliberately and thoroughly document your denormalization changes.
- Plan your data flow at design time.
- Take special care to find supertypes and subtypes during the design process; retrofitting an existing database to accommodate missed supertype and subtype relationships can be difficult.
- When talking about hierarchies, be sure to distinguish between graphs and trees and model each type appropriately.

Chapter 3
Designing a Physical Database

In Chapter 2, "Designing a Logical Database," you learned how to design the data model on the conceptual and logical levels. Now, it is time to move forward and design the database on the physical level. In this chapter, you will learn how to select appropriate data types, including data types you create (that is, user-defined data types—UDDTs). Then, you will learn how to create tables and add computed columns to attributes that you defined at the logical level. You might sometimes even decide to persist and index a computed column. By now, you should realize the importance of constraints, but you will also learn how to implement entity, referential, and domain integrity as well as business rules by using constraints and triggers.

Exam objectives in this chapter:
- Design objects that define data.
  - Design user-defined data types.
- Design attributes.
  - Decide whether to persist an attribute.
  - Specify domain integrity by creating attribute constraints.
  - Choose appropriate column data types and sizes.
- Design entities.
  - Define entities.
  - Define entity integrity.
- Design entity relationships (ER).
  - Specify ER for referential integrity.
  - Specify foreign keys.
  - Create programmable objects to maintain referential integrity.

Before You Begin

To complete the lessons in this chapter, you must have:

- Knowledge of the Transact-SQL data-definition language (DDL) elements.

- The Microsoft SQL Server 2005 *AdventureWorks* and *AdventureWorksDW* sample databases installed. Sample databases are available with SQL Server 2005 Enterprise edition but are not a part of the default installation. Alternatively, you can install the sample databases from *http://msdn2.microsoft.com/en-us/library/ms143739.aspx.*

- Microsoft Visual Studio 2005 or Microsoft Visual Basic or C# .NET 2005 Express edition installed. You can download Visual Studio Express editions for free from *http://msdn.microsoft.com/vstudio/express/.* (Optionally, you can have Microsoft Visual Studio Team System or Microsoft Visual Studio Team edition for Database Professionals installed.) You can find more information about these products at *http://msdn2.microsoft.com/en-us/teamsystem/aa718803.aspx.*

IMPORTANT **Practices in this chapter build upon each other**

Beginning with Lesson 2, "Designing User-Defined Data Types," the lesson practices build upon each other; to move to the next practice, you need to finish the previous one.

Lesson 1: Choosing Column Data Types and Sizes

Estimated lesson time: 20 minutes

Every attribute you model at a logical level has a domain of possible values. You express domains as data types on the physical level. Domains comprise the things we can talk about. For example, if we are talking about cars, we do not talk about flying. Logically, domains include all possible integrity constraints. However, implementing all possible constraints in data types on the physical level would be difficult because you probably would have to create hundreds of data types. In addition, you would have huge problems if some constraints changed. Users of your data types would also then have to learn how to use all the constraints. Therefore, having some common, defined data types that you can use immediately is usually best. The tradeoff here is that defined types implement basic constraints only; you must use other mechanisms to implement additional constraints.

All database management systems and programming languages come with a set of built-in data types. If you studied the models in the previous chapter that were created using Microsoft Visio for Enterprise Architects, you might have noticed that attributes already have data types. It is a good practice to think of data types in advance, when you design a database on a conceptual level. In Visio, you can use so-called portable or physical data types. Physical data types should match the destination database system. The examples in Chapter 2 use SQL Server 2005 physical data types.

System Data Types

You should always thoroughly understand what physical data types your system provides and their limitations. In addition, you have to detect whether your data is strictly structured, semi-structured, or unstructured. Structured data has a rigid form. Entities with structured data typically have a well-defined schema, which does not change much over time. Tables that represent structured entities have columns with system data types that occupy a mostly known amount of storage. Semi-structured data has an internal structure; however, this structure changes over time, can be quite complex, and can occupy a lot of space. Unstructured data can be literally anything: images, long texts, movies, and so on. SQL Server 2005 provides system data types for all kinds of data.

Numeric System Data Types

Numeric data types can store integers or decimal values. They can store an exact representation of a number or an extremely close approximation of the value. In business applications, you should typically use data types that store exact values. However, approximate data types can store much larger values than fixed data types. Table 3-1 shows a condensed overview of numeric data types, their limitations (that is, the range of values they accept), whether they are approximate or exact, and the space they consume in bytes.

Table 3-1   Numeric Data Types

Type	Range	Exact	Storage
Bit	0 to 1	Yes	Up to 8-bit columns in 1 byte (for instance, 10-bit columns use 2 bytes)
Tinyint	0 to 255	Yes	1 byte
Smallint	-2^{15} to 2^{15}-1	Yes	2 bytes
Int	-2^{31} to 2^{31}-1	Yes	4 bytes
Bigint	-2^{63} to 2^{63}-1	Yes	8 bytes
Numeric and Decimal	-10^{38} to 10^{38}, depending on precision (p) and scale (s)	Yes	p 1 to 9: 5 bytes; p 10 to 19: 9 bytes; p 20 to 28: 13 bytes; p 29 to 38: 17 bytes[*]
Smallmoney	-214,748.3648 to 214,748.3647	Yes	4 bytes
Money	-922,337,203,685,477.5808 to 922,337,203,685,477.5807	Yes	8 bytes
Real	-3.40E + 38 to -1.18E-38, 0 and 1.18E-38 to 3.40E + 38	No	4 bytes
Float(n)	-1.79E+308 to -2.23E-308, 0 and 2.23E-308 to 1.79E+308	No	Depending on value (n) n 1 to 24: 4 bytes; n 25 to 53: 8 bytes

* With SQL Server 2005 Service Pack 2 (SP2) Enterprise Edition, you can define variable storage for numeric and decimal data types.

String Data Types

String data types can store non-Unicode and Unicode strings. Non-Unicode strings have fixed collation; you can use the database's default collation or specify a different collation for each column separately. With non-Unicode strings, every character occupies a single byte. In Unicode data types, you can store strings with different collations in different rows of a single column. As always, however, nothing is cost-free: with Unicode types, every character occupies two bytes. In addition, string data types can occupy a fixed or variable number of bytes. Variable string data types occupy an additional two bytes of storage for a hidden in-row pointer to the location of the column in a row. Large data types have their own section later in this lesson. SQL Server 2005 string data types for small strings are:

- **Char(n)**   A non-Unicode data type with fixed length. For example, if you define Char(10), all values will occupy exactly 10 bytes, even if they are shorter. You can define the number n in a range from 1 to 8,000; thus, you can store up to 8,000 characters in this type.
- **Varchar(n)**   A non-Unicode data type with variable-length storage. You can define the number n in a range from 1 to 8,000; thus, you can store up to 8,000 characters in this type.
- **Nchar(n)**   A fixed-length Unicode data type. You can define the number n in a range from 1 to 4,000; thus, you can store up to 4,000 characters in this type, which will occupy up to 8,000 bytes.
- **Nvarchar(n)**   A variable-length Unicode data type. You can define the number n in a range from 1 to 4,000; thus, you can store up to 4,000 characters in this type, which will occupy up to 8,000 bytes.

Binary Strings

Binary data types do not have any constraint on the domain of possible values that you can store, except for the length. There are two small binary data types: *binary(n)* and *varbinary(n)*. As with small string data types, you can specify the number n in a range from 1 to 8,000.

Datetime Data Types

SQL Server 2005 still does not support separate *Date* and *Time* date types. In both data types that support dates and times, you always get both date and time. This makes working with dates and times more difficult. SQL Server has many built-in datetime functions for handling date and time data. See SQL Server 2005 Books Online: Date and Time Functions (Transact-SQL) at *http://msdn2.microsoft.com/en-us/library/ms186724.aspx* for a list of those functions. The two datetime data types in SQL Server are:

- **Smalldatetime**   You can store dates from January 1, 1900, through June 6, 2079, in a column of this data type, with one-minute accuracy. The *smalldatetime* data type occupies 4 bytes of storage.
- **Datetime**   You can store dates from January 1, 1753, through December 31, 9999, in a column of this data type, with 3.33-millisecond accuracy. The *datetime* data type occupies 8 bytes of storage.

Exam Tip   Be sure you know the datetime functions in SQL Server 2005.

Large Data Types

Large data types can store up to 2 gigabytes (GB)—up to 2^{31}-1 bytes—of data. Large data types are appropriate for unstructured data. There are two kinds (three kinds, if you count the *XML* data type in this category) of large data types: old and new. Old types existed in previous versions of SQL Server and are primitive in terms what you can do with them. Most string functions do not work with them, for example. New SQL Server 2005 types support all string functions.

The old large data types are:

- **Text**   This variable-length non-Unicode data type has a maximum length of 2^{31}-1 (2,147,483,647) characters.
- **Ntext**   This variable-length Unicode data type has a maximum length of 2^{30}-1 (1,073,741,823) characters.
- **Image**   This variable-length binary data type can hold from 0 through 2^{31}-1 (2,147,483,647) bytes.

SQL Server 2005 introduces a new length specifier for the *varchar*, *nvarchar*, and *varbinary* data types. The *max* specifier expands the storage capabilities of these data types up to 2^{31}-1 (2,147,483,647) bytes. These new data types have many advantages over the old ones. Besides supporting more functions, the new data types enable you to declare variables, which you cannot do with the old types. In AFTER triggers, you can reference the new large data type columns in the Inserted and Deleted tables. The UPDATE statement supports chunked update with the new *Write* method when you use the large data types. Microsoft even plans to discontinue support of old large data types in future versions of SQL Server.

Besides string functions, you can create full-text indexes on large and small string data types. With full-text indexes, you get additional full-text search predicates, which expand the functionality of string data types.

XML Data Type

The new *XML* data type stores Unicode strings in XML format. XML is a worldwide standard for storing semi-structured data. XML, which is always Unicode, is also the de facto standard for exchanging data between applications. You could store XML as simple text by using the *nvarchar(MAX)* type. However, plaintext representation means you have no knowledge of the structure built into an XML document. You could decompose the text, store it in multiple relational tables, and use relational technologies to manipulate the data. However, relational structures are quite static and are not easy to change. The *XML* data type in SQL Server 2005 attaches functionality to the type that can support a wide variety of XML technologies. For example, you can validate values of an *XML* data type column (XML documents and fragments) against an XML schema collection, which can include multiple XSD schemas. XML validated against a schema is called *typed XML*.

There are many good examples of when to use the *XML* data type, such as the following:

- If the structure is volatile but you still need to validate the data against some pre-defined structure, the *XML* data type is your choice.

- XML is hierarchically organized, so you might find it easier to store hierarchies in the XML type compared to using the adjacency model (presented in Chapter 2) and common table expressions (CTEs).

- The *XML* data type works well if you need to modify or retrieve parts of the data based on its structure. Remember that XML is a large data type. Because the *XML* data type supports the XQuery language for traversing XML nodes and properties through various methods for browsing and updating the XML document, modifying and retrieving data is much more efficient than with other large data types.

- Besides full-text indexes, the *XML* data type supports specific XML indexes.

- You can use the *XML* data type for a variable. For example, you can pass an array as a parameter to a stored procedure with the help of the *XML* data type.

Other Data Types

Other data types in SQL Server include types you cannot easily classify in the groups introduced so far. Here are brief descriptions of those other data types:

- **Sql_variant** This type stores values of various SQL Server 2005–supported data types except *text*, *ntext*, *image*, *timestamp*, and *sql_variant* types. A column of type *sql_variant* might contain rows of different data types; however, before performing operations on *sql_variant* values, you must cast the value to the base data type. The *sql_variant* type can occupy up to 8,016 bytes.

- **Timestamp and its synonym, rowversion** SQL Server automatically generates unique binary numbers within a database for a column of this data type. A new value is generated for every insert or update of a row. Use timestamp for version-stamping table rows, to determine whether any value in the row has changed since the last time you read it. Storage is 8 bytes.

- **Uniqueidentifier** This is a 16-byte global unique identifier (GUID). You can generate the value with the *NEWID* or *NEWSEQUENTIALID* functions.

- **Table** This is a special data type that you can use to store a temporary result set for later processing; typically, you would use it for a set of rows returned as the result set of a table-valued function. You cannot use this data type for columns of a table; you can use it for variables and functions only.

- **Cursor** This is a data type for variables or stored procedure OUTPUT parameters that contain a reference to a cursor; you can use it to pass cursors from one procedure to another. Because you should generally not use cursors in your T-SQL code in applications anyway, your usage of this data type should be limited.

IMPORTANT   **Generating duplicate timestamps**

You can generate duplicate timestamp values by using a SELECT INTO statement in which a time-stamp column is in the SELECT list. You should not use timestamp columns when you are copying existing data.

Best Practices for Data Types and Sizes

The first and very basic best practice for data types is to use the smallest possible data types that can hold the range of values you need. Bigger data types can mean wasted space and, thus, reduced performance of your database. However, you should also anticipate growth of your database. If you know, for example, that you are going to run out of possible values of the *int* data type in six months, select the *bigint* type at the beginning.

Exam Tip   The initial preference should be to use smaller data types.

Use fixed-string data types for strings that do not vary much in length or for very short strings. (Remember the two bytes of overhead that variable data types require.) Larger strings often vary considerably in length; therefore, variable-length data types are more appropriate. If you need to support multilanguage applications, you should use Unicode data types. However, if your database is very large and you know that all values of a column will have the same collation, you should use a non-Unicode data type so that you avoid the storage and performance overhead of storing two bytes for a single character.

If you need to support dates beyond the range of built-in datetime data types, or if you need better accuracy, you have to use numeric data types and create your own date and time logic in your application or create common language runtime (CLR) user-defined data types, which are described in Lesson 2, "Designing User-Defined Data Types." For example, if you need one-millisecond accuracy, you can store the time in a *bigint* column where the integer value means the number of milliseconds from 24:00. In addition, never forget that you have the time part in your datetime columns, even if you work only with dates.

In addition, be careful not to overuse the *XML* data type. It is so easy to say that your schema is volatile; however, often that simply means you did not spend enough time analyzing your business problem, so you missed the schema behind it. It is harder to implement constraints on an *XML* data type column than on multiple separate columns of smaller data types, and you already know that constraints are crucial for data integrity.

If backward compatibility is not an issue, choose the new *varchar(MAX)*, *nvarchar(MAX)*, and *varbinary(MAX)* data types over the old *text*, *ntext*, and *image* data types. Last, avoid using the *sql_variant* data type. Strong typing is one of the most important pillars of building reliable applications.

Practice: Choosing Appropriate Data Types

In this practice, you will strengthen your mastery of system data types by answering a few questions.

▶ **Exercise: Choose the Best Data Type**

In this exercise, you select the appropriate data type or answer general questions about data types.

1. Which data types are appropriate for unstructured data?
2. Which data types would you use for storing exact numbers?
3. Can you list the data types that you cannot use in table definitions?
4. What is the maximum number of bytes you can store in a single column? Which data types support this maximum?

Quick Check

You are creating a table and must make several decisions based on the information in the following questions.

1. You must store three-character abbreviations of month names. Which data type would you use?
    A. *Varchar(3)*
    B. *Char(3)*
    C. *Real*
    D. *Nvarchar(MAX)*
2. You have to support a multilanguage application. Which data types can help you?
3. You have to store large numeric values; however, they can be approximate. Which data type would you use?

Quick Check Answers
1. The correct answer is B: you should use *char(3)* in this case.
2. You have to use Unicode data types—*nchar(n)*, *nvarchar(n)*, and *nvarchar(MAX)*. You should avoid using *ntext*, which is deprecated.
3. You would use the *float* data type.

Lesson 2: Designing User-Defined Data Types

Estimated lesson time: 30 minutes

In SQL Server 2000 and earlier, you can create UDDTs. However, these types are just aliases for existing system data types. In SQL Server 2005, you can create full-fledged user-defined types (UDTs) by using CLR code. Let's look at how to create T-SQL aliases and then see how to use CLR code to define UDTs.

IMPORTANT   CREATE TYPE vs. T-SQL aliases

Using the sp_addtype system stored procedure to create T-SQL aliases is deprecated and will be removed from future SQL Server versions. Use the *CREATE TYPE* command instead.

T-SQL Aliases (UDDTs)

T-SQL aliases do not really bring anything new to a database; you can always use native system types instead. However, these aliases are a nice way to standardize data types for attributes that appear in many tables. For example, you have attributes for addresses in multiple entities, such as Customers, Employees, and Warehouses. You want to be sure that the address line attributes are always *nvarchar(50)* and not once *char(30)* and other times *nvarchar(70)*. You can force standard types by creating a T-SQL alias, as the following code example shows:

```
CREATE TYPE StandardAddress
  FROM nvarchar(50) NULL;
GO
```

You can then use this type for all addresses. As you can see, you can also specify whether the type allows unknown (*NULL*) values. You could define some basic constraints for the type as well by binding a *Default* or a *Rule* to the type. However, defaults and rules as independent objects are deprecated in favor of constraints, so you should not use this feature.

Exam Tip   On the exam, do not select answers that use deprecated features if another answer uses the new syntax (unless you are asked to choose all possible correct answers). Although the deprecated feature might be a correct answer for SQL Server 2005 and previous versions of the database management system, it will not be available for future versions.

CLR User-Defined Types (UDTs)

When we are describing a business problem, we implicitly use domains. In fact, you can describe any business problems with relations (as relational tables) and domains. Domains comprise the things we can talk about; relations comprise the truths we utter about those things. Domains and relations are necessary and sufficient—logically, we do not need anything else. According to the book *Practical Issues in Database Management* by Fabian Pascal (Addison-Wesley Professional, 2000), a domain consists of the following:

- A name.
- One or more named possible representations:
  - ❑ One is physically stored.
  - ❑ At least one is declared to the users.
- Type constraints.
- A set of operators permissible on the type's values.

Domains constrain possible values of an attribute through a set of permissible operations and through specific type constraints. Actually, in domains, you could implement every constraint you need except one. The only additional constraint you need is the one that helps you uniquely identify every entity instance in an entity set—that is, every row in a table—namely, a *primary key*. If every constraint on the relation is a logical consequence of the definition of keys and domains, then the relation is in *domain-key* normal form (DKNF). This is the ultimate normal form; a relation in DKNF is free of all modification anomalies. However, there is no simple algorithm to produce DKNF; you have to implement it programmatically through your own data types.

Putting all constraints in a data type seems attractive at first glance. After all, you get a database that is free from all anomalies. However, having too many constraints in a data type is not practical. First, you do not know who the user of your data type is going to be or whether the constraints are going to be acceptable for all possible users. Second, constraints change over time. If a constraint is volatile, the most painful change process possible is if the constraint is built into the data type. Imagine what Microsoft changing the definition of the *integer* data type would mean for millions of databases and applications around the world.

This short theoretical introduction should give you the basic idea underlying best practices for using CLR types: the KISS principle ("Keep It Simple, Simon!"). However, logical reasons are not the only reasons to stick with the KISS principle. Another problem for potential users of your data type is that they have to learn what operations your type supports, what these operations do, and how to call them. For standard data types, you know the answers from previous experience or school or because the operations are standard or even defined in mathematics. For example, you know that you can add, subtract, and multiply integers; however, division is not defined on the integer domain. Remember the *datetime* data type? Because it is a little more complex and not standard, you immediately have more problems and need to have additional knowledge when you work with it. Finally, if your data type code is not efficient, you cannot improve performance later when you design and tune a database that uses this type.

To make this a bit easier to understand, Microsoft subscribed standard names and parameters for a couple of basic operations for CLR data types. A data type needs at least a selector and a mutator operation if you want to make it useful. In addition, a data type for relational databases must know how to deal with unknown values. When you create a CLR data type, you create a *structure* or a *class* in the .NET code. The names of the prescribed operations are *ToString* and *Parse*, implemented as methods, and *Null* and *IsNull*, implemented as properties. If you create your code with Visual Studio 2005 Professional edition or later, you can use a SQL Server Project template for CLR objects, which provides prebuilt code for the prescribed operations. Otherwise, you need to create an empty Class Library project and carefully create the methods and properties manually.

The following code shows an example of a data type for e-mail addresses. To make the example more understandable, the data type has implemented only the prescribed operations. In addition, because the type uses reference objects (.NET strings) and not just value objects, you have to implement your own binary serialization (serializing means persisting in object-oriented programming—or OOP—terminology) by implementing the *IBinarySerialize* interface, which has *Read* and *Write* methods. If your type would use value types only, such as integers, SQL Server would know how to serialize it automatically. You define the serialization method by attributes in the beginning of the type definition. From the code, you can see that the *Parse* method accepts a string as parameter, and the *ToString* method returns a string; this is the default way of updating and retrieving values from CLR UDTs—through strings. Finally, notice in the *Parse* method that the input string is validated against a regular expression. If the regular expression is 100 percent correct and allows valid e-mail addresses only, then in a column of this data type, no one can insert anything but a valid e-mail address.

```csharp
//C#
using System;
using System.Data;
using System.Data.SqlClient;
using System.Data.SqlTypes;
using Microsoft.SqlServer.Server;
using System.Text;
using System.Text.RegularExpressions;
using System.IO;

[Serializable]
[Microsoft.SqlServer.Server.SqlUserDefinedType(Format.UserDefined,
MaxByteSize = 8000)]
public struct EmailCS : INullable, IBinarySerialize
{
    // Regular expression used to parse values that are of the form
somebody@somecompany.domain
    private static readonly Regex RegExParser
        = new Regex(@"^([\w-]+\.)*?[\w-]+@[\w-]+\.([\w-]+\.)*?[\w]+$",
                RegexOptions.CultureInvariant);

    // Internal member for the e-mail address
    private StringBuilder parsedemail;
    // Internal member to show whether the value is null
```

```csharp
    private bool m_Null;

    // Constructor for a known value
    public EmailCS(string value)
     {
          this.parsedemail = new StringBuilder();
          this.parsedemail.Append(value);
          this.m_Null = false;
     }

    // Default selector method
    public override string ToString()
     {
 return this.parsedemail.ToString();
     }

    // Handling Null values
    public bool IsNull
    {
         get
         {
              return m_Null;
         }
    }

    public static EmailCS Null
    {
         get
         {
              EmailCS h = new EmailCS();
              h.m_Null = true;
              return h;
         }
    }

    // Default mutator method
    public static EmailCS Parse(SqlString s)
    {
         if (s.IsNull)
              return Null;

         // Check whether the input value is matching the regex pattern
         string value = s.ToString();
         Match m = RegExParser.Match(value);
         // If the input value is not in correct format or is too long,
         // throw an exception
         if (!m.Success || value.Length > 4000)
              throw new ArgumentException(
                   "Invalid format for e-mail address. "
                   + "Format is somebody@somecompany.domain, "
+ "length has to be max. 4000 characters.");

         // Everything ok
```

```
        EmailCS u = new EmailCS(value);
        return u;
    }

    // User-defined serialization
    public void Read(BinaryReader r)
    {
        parsedemail = new StringBuilder(r.ReadString());
    }

    public void Write(BinaryWriter w)
    {
        w.Write(this.parsedemail.ToString());
    }
}
```

On the Companion Disc   This chapter includes many code examples. You will find all the code on the companion CD in the C:\My Documents\Microsoft Press\TK70-441\Chapter03\folder.

From Visual Studio, you can deploy assemblies in a database and create data types and other CRL objects directly. However, in production, a database administrator controls the deployment by using T-SQL, a procedure you will see how to perform in the practice at the end of this lesson.

Best Practices for User-Defined Data Types

For T-SQL aliases, the best practice is clear: use them to standardize data types for repeating attributes in your company. For CLR data types, the most important best practice is to keep them simple.

In addition, when you create a CLR data type for a production environment, you have to watch for many more problems than the ones that the preceding e-mail example shows. How does your type sort? How does it compare values? These are important questions. You do not want to surprise your users when they use your type in WHERE, JOIN, or ORDER BY clauses. In addition, because the default input and output of your data type are strings, you have to ensure that your type works in all possible collations. Note that you must call the default output method (*ToString*) explicitly; otherwise, you get the value returned as a binary stream. This is an optimization. You put the burden of deserialization on the client application, which must know how to perfect it. (It must know the definition of the UDT through a reference in a project.) Also, be aware of limitations of CLR types: user-defined serialization is limited to 8,000 bytes in SQL Server 2005.

Practice: Creating User-Defined Data Types

In this practice, you will create a T-SQL alias and two CLR UDTs and use them for a variable. You can use them for tables as well, which you'll see in the practice for Lesson 3, "Defining Entities and Entity and Referential Integrity."

IMPORTANT Remaining practices build upon each other

For the remaining practices in this chapter, you need to prepare a database and turn on CLR integration. In addition, you have to copy the assemblies from the companion CD to your local hard drive. Finally, because the remaining practices in this chapter build on each other, please do not delete your work after you finish a practice exercise.

▶ **Exercise 1: Setup**

In this first exercise, you prepare the infrastructure for the practice by installing the companion CD and creating a new practice database.

1. Install the complete companion CD on your computer and browse to C:\My Documents\Microsoft Press\TK70-441\Chapter03\Sql folder to find the suggested CLR solution. (Alternatively, you can copy the CLR solutions with source and compiled code for this chapter to your local hard drive.)

2. In SQL Server Management Studio (SSMS), in a new query window, create a database for this chapter and turn on the CLR integration by using T-SQL code. (Alternatively, you could turn on CLR integration by using the Surface Area Configuration tool.) Your code should look like this:

```
USE master;
GO
EXEC sp_configure 'clr enabled', 1;
RECONFIGURE;
GO
IF DB_ID(N'TK441Ch03') IS NULL
    CREATE DATABASE TK441Ch03;
GO
```

3. Click Execute from the SQL Editor toolbar.

▶ **Exercise 2: Create T-SQL Aliases**

Create a type to standardize all addresses. Your type should allow a maximum of 50 characters. You do not know in which country it is going to be used, so you need to be prepared to accept any collation. Finally, an address is not always required, so you need to allow unknown values. In the query window, your code should look like this:

```
USE TK441Ch03;
GO
CREATE TYPE StandardAddress
```

```
     FROM nvarchar(50) NULL;
   GO
```

▶ **Exercise 3: Create CLR UDTs**

Now you need to import assemblies to your database and create CLR UDTs. As a database administrator (DBA), you need to perfect these tasks by using T-SQL.

1. Import both Visual Basic and C# assemblies. Use the SAFE permission set.

   In the query window, your code should look like this:

   ```
   USE TK441Ch03;
   GO
   CREATE ASSEMBLY Ch03CS
   FROM 'C:\My Documents\Microsoft Press\TK70-441\Chapter03\Ch03CS\bin\Debug\Ch03CS.dll'
   WITH PERMISSION_SET = SAFE;
   GO
   CREATE ASSEMBLY Ch03VB
   FROM 'C:\My Documents\Microsoft Press\TK70-441\Chapter03\Ch03VB\bin\Ch03VB.dll'
   WITH PERMISSION_SET = SAFE;
   GO
   ```

2. Now, create the data types by using code that looks like this:

   ```
   CREATE TYPE dbo.EmailCS
   EXTERNAL NAME Ch03CS.EmailCS;
   GO
   CREATE TYPE dbo.EmailVB
   EXTERNAL NAME Ch03VB.EmailVB;
   GO
   ```

▶ **Exercise 4: Test the CLR UDTs**

Finally, test how your CLR UDTs work. Test both Visual Basic and C# UDTs. There is no special need to test the T-SQL alias, but you are welcome to do it as well. Test the data types for regular, unknown, wrong, and too-long values. The following code example shows tests for the C# type only.

1. Test for an unknown value:

   ```
   DECLARE @myemail EmailCS;
   SET @myemail = NULL;
   SELECT @myemail;
   GO
   ```

2. Test for a wrong value:

   ```
   DECLARE @myemail EmailCS;
   SET @myemail = N'wrong#address';
   GO
   ```

3. Test for a value that is too long:

   ```
   DECLARE @myemail EmailCS;
   SET @myemail = REPLICATE(N'a',4000)+N'@a.com'
   GO
   ```

4. Test for a correct value:

```
DECLARE @myemail EmailCS;
SET @myemail = N'dsarka@solidq.com'
SELECT @myemail, @myemail.ToString();
GO
```

Quick Check

1. Why would you use a CLR user-defined type?
2. How would you create a T-SQL alias? Select the correct answer.
    A. EXEC sp_create type
    B. EXEC sp_addtype
    C. CREATE TABLE t1 (c1 WITH TYPE)
    D. CREATE TYPE

Quick Check Answers

1. Besides standardization, one of the most important reasons to use a CLR UDT would be constraints. If a constraint is extremely important and not volatile, you might decide to implement it in a CLR data type. In addition, you might want to create CLR data types to alleviate T-SQL or Microsoft .NET programming for standard problems. For example, you could create a data type *Point*, which could already have built-in knowledge of how to calculate geometrical distance between two points in a multidimensional space.
2. The correct answer is D. You would use CREATE TYPE to create a T-SQL alias.

Lesson 3: Defining Entities and Entity and Referential Integrity

Estimated lesson time: 30 minutes

After you've selected your conceptual and logical design and data types (and created them, if you need user-defined data types), it is time to create tables. Designing tools such as Office Visio feature forward engineering, so you can create a database and database objects directly from the tool. However, you can also simply create a script and then move from design to such development tools as Visual Studio Team System for Database Professionals. Probably the better practice is to move to development tools because they enable version control, development of a whole application rather than just the database part of it, creation of test data and unit test procedures, and more. You should still use design tools for documentation of your application and database. This lesson assumes that you are going to switch from graphical tools to T-SQL code. You will learn how to design and create entities, design entity and referential integrity, and use special types of columns.

Designing and Creating Entities

You already designed entities on the logical level. So what is left to design on the physical level? In an ideal world, the physical level should be just an implementation of the logical level. However, when you get to the physical level, you have to deal with concrete products and their strengths and weaknesses. To make your database perform well, you need to understand the database management system you are working with and refine your logical design.

SQL Server stores data in a fundamental unit called a *page*, which has a fixed size of 8 kilobytes (KB). SQL Server reads and writes whole pages. For space management, SQL Server uses *extents*. An extent consists of eight physically contiguous pages, so it has a fixed size of 64 KB. SQL Server maintains two types of extents: mixed and uniform. Up to eight objects can share a mixed extent. Each object can own one or more pages in the extent. However, only one object can own a uniform extent. For a new table or index, SQL Server allocates pages from mixed extents. When the table or index reaches the size of eight pages, SQL Server switches to use uniform extents for further allocations. If you create an index on an existing table that has enough rows to generate eight pages in the index, all allocations to the index are in uniform extents.

SQL Server allocates table and index rows on pages. A row typically cannot span multiple pages. Because SQL Server stores some internal metadata on pages as well, the actual maximum size of a row is 8,060 bytes. However, SQL Server 2005 relaxes this restriction for tables with *varchar*, *nvarchar*, *varbinary*, *sql_variant*, or CLR UDT columns. The length of each column is still a maximum 8,000 bytes; the combined width, however, can exceed the 8,060-byte limit. In SQL Server 2000, you can define a table with variable columns that together exceed 8,060 bytes in metadata; however, when you try to insert a row that would exceed 8,060 bytes, you get an error. SQL Server 2005 does not return an error; instead, it stores the variable-length data that exceeds 8,060 bytes in additional row-overflow data pages.

SQL Server stores large value types—*varchar(MAX)*, *nvarchar(MAX)*, *varbinary(MAX)*, and *XML*—and large object (LOB) data types (*text*, *ntext*, and *image*) in separate pages and stores only a 16-byte pointer in the data row to indicate where SQL Server can find the actual data. However, if the values are small, you can store them or at least part of them in data rows. You control this behavior by using two options in the sp_tableoption system stored procedure: the *large value types out of row* option for large value types and the *text in row* option for large object types.

IMPORTANT *Text in row* option

The *text in row* option is deprecated and will be removed in a future version of SQL Server. Store large data by using the *varchar(MAX)*, *nvarchar(MAX)*, or *varbinary(MAX)* data types.

This short introduction to internal storage should help you design your entities. Be careful about row length. You can store more, shorter rows (versus long rows) in a single page. If SQL Server has to read fewer pages for the same number of rows, you get better performance. Variable-length columns typically enable you to use the 8-KB page space better. However, if the columns together exceed 8,060 bytes and SQL Server stores them in row-overflow units, your application might take a performance hit. Working with large objects is typically slower than working with in-row data; nevertheless, you can speed up processing by storing smaller LOBs in rows. For more internal data-storage details, see the book *Inside Microsoft SQL Server 2005: The Storage Engine* by Kalen Delaney (Microsoft Press, 2006).

With this information, you are ready to create tables for your database. You create tables by using the *CREATE TABLE T-SQL* command. The complete syntax of the command is quite complex; part of it is shown here to give you the overall impression of everything you must define for your tables. For the complete syntax, see SQL Server Books Online: CREATE TABLE (Transact-SQL) at *http://msdn2.microsoft.com/en-us/library/ms174979.aspx*.

```
CREATE TABLE
    [ database_name . [ schema_name ] . | schema_name . ] table_name
        ( { <column_definition> | <computed_column_definition> }
        [ <table_constraint> ] [ ,...n ] )
    [ ON { partition_scheme_name ( partition_column_name ) | filegroup
        | "default" } ]
    [ { TEXTIMAGE_ON { filegroup | "default" } ]
[ ; ]

<column_definition> ::=
column_name <data_type>
    [ COLLATE collation_name ]
```

```
    [ NULL | NOT NULL ]
    [
        [ CONSTRAINT constraint_name ] DEFAULT constant_expression ]
      | [ IDENTITY [ ( seed , increment ) ] [ NOT FOR REPLICATION ] ]
    ]
    [ ROWGUIDCOL ] [ <column_constraint> [ ...n ] ]
<data type> ::=
[ type_schema_name . ] type_name
    [ ( precision [ , scale ] | max |
        [ { CONTENT | DOCUMENT } ] xml_schema_collection ) ]
...
```

You can see that in a single statement, you can define columns and their data types and nul-lability, computed columns, all kinds of constraints, and more. However, in your real project code, keep the base table definition relatively simple and not too cluttered. For example, you can define columns with their data types and nullability in the CREATE TABLE statement only and then add constraints later by using separate ALTER TABLE statements. For data types, you can use your user-defined data types just as you use system data types.

Entity Integrity

Tables represent sets. By definition, sets consist of unique elements. Therefore, you need some-thing to identify each row of a table uniquely. This is what entity integrity is about—uniquely identifying rows in a table. You identify a row by its key value. You can have one or more col-umns or combinations of columns that identify each row uniquely. Therefore, you can have multiple candidate keys. You select one of them for your primary identifying schema and call it the primary key. SQL Server has two constraints for entity integrity: the *Unique* constraint for candidate keys and the *Primary Key* constraint for primary keys. You can have multiple *Unique* constraints and one *Primary Key* constraint per table.

Theoretically, every table should have a primary key. However, database management systems do not strictly enforce the *Primary Key* constraint. The only reason for this is purely practical. Imagine you need to import data from a text file. If you had a *Primary Key* constraint for your table, you would have to cleanse the data in your text file before the import. Cleansing text files is much less practical than cleansing data in a SQL Server table. Nevertheless, in production, all your tables should have a primary key.

A primary key has two required properties—uniqueness and applicability—and two desired properties: stability and minimality. If you want to track changes for an entity over time, as you do in data warehousing scenarios, stability becomes a required and not just a desired property. For best performance, your primary key should be as minimal as possible.

In many books and forums, you can find an old discussion about which type of key is better: *natural* or *surrogate*. A natural key has a logical relationship with other attributes of an entity. A surrogate key is the one a designer creates and adds to the attributes of an entity. Typically, a surrogate key is a simple sequential number. However, this discussion does not make much sense. You cannot strictly distinguish between natural and surrogate keys. For example, is a social security ID (SSID) natural or surrogate? Somebody invented it, and this person was just as natural as the current designer of a database is. A better definition of natural keys is that "a key is natural if the attribute it represents is used for identification independently of the database." Nevertheless, do not worry too much about this distinction. If you have something unique, applicable, stable, and short in your table, use it. If not, add a sequential number for the primary reference schema, and you will have all required and desired properties for your primary key.

The required applicability property of a primary key means that all values must be known. SQL Server enforces this rule by prohibiting columns that allow *NULL* values from participating in *Primary Key* constraints. You can create *Unique* constraints on nullable columns; however, for *Unique* constraints, all *NULL* values are the same value. For example, if you create a *Unique* constraint on a single nullable column, you can insert only a single row with a *NULL* value in that column. Additional rows with a *NULL* value in that column would yield a *Unique* constraint violation.

Physically, *Primary Key* and *Unique* constraints create unique indexes. A *Primary Key* constraint creates a clustered index by default, and a *Unique* constraint creates a nonclustered index by default. You will learn more about indexes in the next chapter; for now, just use the defaults.

Referential Integrity

As you learned in Chapter 2, you implement relationships between entities by using foreign keys. A foreign key is a column or columns whose values are the same as the primary key of another table—in other words, a copy of the primary key from another relational table. SQL Server helps you enforce rules for the relationships with the *Foreign Key* constraint.

There are four standard ANSI rules for enforcing relationships between entities; each rule implements four sub-rules. Two sub-rules deal with the primary (parent) table, and two deal with the secondary (child) table. The two sub-rules for the child table are immutable:

- You cannot insert a row in the child table if there is no related row in the parent table.
- You cannot update the foreign key column or columns in the child table in a way that would leave them without a related row in the parent table.

The two sub-rules for the primary table differ based on standard rules for referential integrity. The four standard rules and the implementation of sub-rules are:

- No Action rule
    - You cannot delete a row in the primary table if it has related rows in the child table.
    - You cannot update the primary key column or columns in the primary table if they have related rows in the child table that would become orphaned.
- Cascade rule
    - If you delete a row in the primary table, you have to delete all related rows in the child table.
    - If you update a primary key in the parent table, you have to update foreign keys in all related tables to the same new value.
- Set Null rule
    - If you delete a row in the primary table, you have to set to unknown (*NULL*) value all foreign keys of related rows.
    - If you update a primary key in the parent table, you have to set to unknown (*NULL*) value all foreign keys of related rows.
- Set Default rule
    - If you delete a row in the primary table, you have to set to a pre-defined default value all foreign keys of related rows.
    - If you update a primary key in the parent table, you have to set to a pre-defined default value all foreign keys of related rows.

In short, whatever you do, you should never leave rows in the child table orphaned. The *Foreign Key* constraint in SQL Server 2005 enables you to implement all four rules. However, you should typically use only the No Action rule. The Cascade rule is useful for cascade deletes only, in case you want to implement a strong relationship between the parent and the child tables, a relationship in which the child table rows make no sense without parent rows. For example, order-line details cannot exist without an order; therefore, if you delete an order, you should delete all of its line items. If you use cascade updates, it means your primary key in the parent table is not stable, and this is not a good practice. The Set Null and Set Default rules are useful for maintaining history of the child table; however, if you maintain history in a data warehouse, you do not need these rules.

A *Foreign Key* constraint must reference a *Primary Key* or *Unique* constraint. A *Foreign Key* constraint can refer to the table itself. This way, you can model graphs, trees, and hierarchies, as you saw in Chapter 2.

Special Attributes

You already know the special *timestamp* (and its synonym, *rowversion*) and *uniqueidentifier* data types. You can use two additional special types of attributes in your table design: columns with the Identity property and computed columns.

Identity Columns

Simple sequential numbers are very practical for a primary key. Because they are so commonly used, SQL Server has an automatic mechanism for assigning sequential numbers. You mark a column for auto-numbering by adding the Identity property to it when you create a table. SQL Server treats identity values in a way similar to variables—they are not part of a transaction. If a transaction is rolled back, the identity value is not rolled back but instead is used by SQL Server; the next insert gets the next sequential value, and you get a gap in the sequence. In addition, SQL Server does not reuse automatically deleted identity values; again, you can get gaps in your sequence.

Exam Tip   Do not forget that with the Identity property, you can get gaps in your sequences.

If you want to fill the gaps manually, you have to use the *SET IDENTITY_INSERT* command to turn the manual identity insert to ON. Then, you can insert explicit values in the identity column. In addition, SQL Server has several functions that help you work with identity values:

- The *IDENT_SEED* function returns the seed (the initial) value.
- The *IDENT_INCR* function returns the increment value you specified during the creation of the identity column.
- You can use the *IDENTITY* function (do not mix it with the Identity property) in a SELECT statement with an INTO clause to insert an identity column into a new table.
- The *IDENTITY_SCOPE* function returns the last identity value inserted into an identity column in the same scope (that is, in the same module, such as stored procedure, trigger, function, or batch).
- The *IDENT_CURRENT* function returns the last identity value generated for a specified table or view in any session and any scope.
- The *@@IDENTITY* function returns the last identity value inserted, regardless of the scope of the table.

With the *DBCC CHECKIDENT* command, you can check the current identity value for the specified table and change the identity value. You can also use *DBCC CHECKIDENT* to set a new seed value manually for the identity column.

Computed Columns

You can define a column as an expression that can use other columns in the same table. This is a computed column. The expression can use other noncomputed columns, constants, functions, variables, and any combination of these connected by one or more operators. You cannot use a subquery in the expression. Computed columns can make writing queries easier and more standardized. Computed columns are virtual columns unless you explicitly specify you want to materialize them. To store a computed column physically, use the *PERSISTED* keyword in the CREATE TABLE and ALTER TABLE statements. SQL Server updates the value of computed columns when any columns are part of their calculation change. If you define a computed column as persisted, you can create an index on a computed column that is deterministic but not precise. If a computed column references a CLR function, the database engine cannot verify whether the function is truly deterministic. In this case, you can persist the computed column and then create indexes on it. (You will learn more about indexes in Chapter 4, "Designing a Database for Performance.") Persist a computed column if users frequently use it. You should index it if the users use it for search expressions, for ordering, or for joining. However, consider the extra space the persisted computed column takes and how frequently you update the values of this column.

Practice: Defining Entities and Entity and Referential Integrity

In this practice, you will start with just part of the CREATE TABLE syntax to create a table with column definitions only. Then you will refine your table by adding *Primary Key* and *Foreign Key* constraints and a computed column.

IMPORTANT   Practices build upon each other

To work successfully with this practice, you need to have finished the practices from the previous lesson.

▶ **Exercise 1: Create a Simple Table**

In this exercise, you will create a table by using system-supplied data types and the user-defined data types that you created in the Lesson 2 practice, "Creating User-Defined Data Types."

1. Create an Employees table. At this time, you need an identification for each employee, an identification for each employee's manager, employee first and last name, two lines for an address, company and private e-mail addresses, and a column for education level. (You will store integer values from 1 to 5 in this column.)

2. Use a standardized data type for address lines and *EmailCS* and *EmailVB* data types for e-mail addresses.

3. Do not allow unknown values for the identification column, first and last name, education level ID, and company e-mail. In a new query window, your code should look like this:

```
USE TK441Ch03;
GO
CREATE TABLE dbo.Employees
(EmployeeId int NOT NULL,
 ManagerId int NULL,
 FirstName nvarchar(30) NOT NULL,
 LastName nvarchar(30) NOT NULL,
 AddressLine1 StandardAddress NULL,
 AddressLine2 StandardAddress NULL,
 CompanyEmail EmailCS NOT NULL,
 PrivateEmail EmailVB NULL,
 EducationLevelId tinyint NOT NULL);
GO
```

▶ **Exercise 2: Entity Integrity**

In this exercise, you need to alter the Employees table from Exercise 1, "Create a Simple Table," to add a *Primary Key* and a *Unique* constraint.

1. In the Employees table, the EmployeeId must be the primary reference schema. Implement this rule by using a *Primary Key* constraint. In a new query window, your code should look like this:

```
USE TK441Ch03;
GO
ALTER TABLE dbo.Employees
 ADD CONSTRAINT PK_Employees PRIMARY KEY (EmployeeId);
 GO
```

2. In addition, the company e-mail address must also be unique. Try to enforce this rule by using a *Unique* constraint. In a new query window, your code should look like this:

```
ALTER TABLE dbo.Employees
 ADD CONSTRAINT UC_Employees_CompanyMail UNIQUE (CompanyEmail);
 GO
```

However, this code should raise an error, number 1919: "Column 'CompanyEmail' in table 'Employees' is of a type that is invalid for use as a key column in an index." The problem is with your *EmailCS* user-defined data type. Because it is created in a very simplified way, it does not tell SQL Server that the serialized representation of the value is byte ordered. (Use the *IsByteOrdered* attribute in the definition of your data type.) SQL Server cannot create an index on this column because it cannot determine the correct order. This example shows you again that working with CLR user-defined types can be complex. You will solve this problem later in this chapter in a different way.

▶ **Exercise 3: Design a Foreign Key and Identity and Computed Columns**

In this exercise, you will use the Identity property to generate identification values for the EmployeeId column of the Employees table automatically. You will then create a computed column to compute the bonus percentage based on the education of an employee. Finally, you need to denote the manager–employee hierarchy in your Employees table. Do not forget to re-create the *Primary Key* constraint as well.

1. Use the Identity property for your EmployeeId column. Note that you cannot change the Identity property by using the ALTER TABLE statement; you must drop and re-create the table. Plan your identity values carefully.

2. Add a computed column to calculate an employee's bonus percentage based on his or her education level. The bonus formula is five percent additional pay for each education level higher than level 1. (That is, for level 1, you get 0 percent; for level 2, you get 5 percent; for level 3, you get 10 percent; and so on.) Do not persist the computed column.

3. Create the *Foreign Key* constraint between the ManagerId and EmployeeId columns. Do not forget to re-create the *Primary Key* constraint first because the *Foreign Key* constraint must reference it. Your complete code should look like this:

```
USE TK441Ch03;
GO
DROP TABLE dbo.Employees;
GO
CREATE TABLE dbo.Employees
(EmployeeId int IDENTITY NOT NULL,
 ManagerId int NULL,
 FirstName nvarchar(30) NOT NULL,
 LastName nvarchar(30) NOT NULL,
 AddressLine1 StandardAddress NULL,
 AddressLine2 StandardAddress NULL,
 CompanyEmail EmailCS NOT NULL,
 PrivateEmail EmailVB NULL,
 EducationLevel tinyint NOT NULL,
 BonusPct AS (EducationLevel-1)*5
);
GO
-- Recreate the Primary Key
ALTER TABLE dbo.Employees
 ADD CONSTRAINT PK_Employees PRIMARY KEY (EmployeeId);
GO
-- Adding a Foreign key constraint
ALTER TABLE dbo.Employees
 ADD CONSTRAINT FK_Employees_MgrEmployee FOREIGN KEY (ManagerId)
   REFERENCES dbo.Employees (EmployeeId);
GO
```

Quick Check

1. In the table defined with the following code, can you define a *Primary Key* constraint?

```
CREATE TABLE dbo.Mytable
(id int NULL,
 name nvarchar(30) NULL);
```

2. What kind of entity integrity constraint could you define?
3. If you use only fixed-length data types in your table definition, can a row span more than 8,060 bytes?

Quick Check Answers

1. All columns in the table are nullable, so you cannot define a *Primary Key* constraint on this table.
2. You could use a *Unique* constraint on the ID column, for example.
3. No, a row cannot span more than 8,060 bytes if you use only fixed-length data types in your table definition.

Lesson 4: Defining Domain Integrity and Business Rules

Estimated lesson time: 25 minutes

Data integrity does not end with entity- and referential-integrity rules. You must also limit your attribute values to values from only specific domains, and you need to make them comply with more or less advanced business rules. You already learned how to limit the domain of possible values by using CLR UDTs. However, you also learned that working with CLR UDTs can get quite complicated. In this lesson, you will learn how to implement domain integrity and business rules with the help of *Check* and *Default* constraints.

Default Constraints

Default constraints are not real constraints because they do not constrain anything. However, they help you insert correct values when you do not specify explicit values. In this way, they help you maintain domain integrity, so you could count them in the set of constraints.

Default constraints are applicable for INSERT statements only. You can have a single *Default* constraint per column. You can use system-supplied values for the defaults with the help of system functions. If a column does not allow unknown values and does not have a *Default* constraint definition, you must explicitly specify a value for the column, or you will get an error when inserting a row. If you specify an explicit value for a column, this value is inserted. If you want to insert the default value explicitly, you can use the *DEFAULT* keyword as the value placeholder. To insert default values in all columns, you can use the DEFAULT VALUES clause of the INSERT statement. Note that in this case, all columns must either have a *Default* constraint assigned or allow *NULL* values.

Use *Default* constraints when you have a column with an obvious and frequent default value. You can use a *Default* constraint for a column that does not allow *NULL* values and if you have an application (probably a legacy application) that does not insert values in this column explicitly.

Check Constraints

A *Check* constraint restricts the domain of possible values for a column. SQL Server enforces *Check* constraints for every INSERT and UPDATE statement. You can have multiple *Check* constraints defined on a single column; a value in the column has to adhere to all of them. You cannot create a *Check* constraint on *timestamp/rowversion*, *text*, *ntext*, or *image* columns.

A *Check* constraint can be any logical expression that returns true or false. The syntax of a *Check* constraint expression is similar to expressions you use in the WHERE clause. However, a *Check* constraint cannot contain subqueries. If you need a subquery in a *Check* constraint, you can create a scalar user-defined function (UDF) that returns a Boolean value, depending on evaluation of a subquery in the body of the function.

Check constraints can be as simple as checking a range of values. For example, in the Employees table from the practices in this chapter, you could use a simple *Check* constraint to limit the possible values for the EducationLevel column to a range of 1 to 5:

```
ALTER TABLE dbo.Employees
 ADD CONSTRAINT CK_Employees_EducationLevel
  CHECK (EducationLevel BETWEEN 1 AND 5);
```

The question is what to do when you do not know the allowed range in advance or when you add values to the allowed range dynamically. In addition, the number of values in this range could be very large, up to countable infinity. It would not be very practical to modify the *Check* constraint whenever a new possible value appears. You can use lookup tables in such cases. Lookup tables typically consist of only two columns: a column that identifies each row (and thus every allowed value in a domain) and a column that gives the name to the value. The identification column is the primary key of the lookup table. In the original entity, the entity for which you are designing the constraint, you hold only the identification column as the foreign key. You add the *Foreign Key* constraint to enforce the range-integrity rule automatically.

Check constraints as a domain-integrity mechanism overlap a bit with CLR user-defined types (UDTs). The e-mail CLR C# and Visual Basic UDTs enforce proper e-mail addresses with the help of a regular expression evaluated in the *Parse* method of the type. Besides other problems with the CLR UDT that you have already seen, there is another issue. The UDT code is not reusable (unless you consider copying and pasting the code as reusing the code). Evaluations against regular expressions are common needs for character strings in a database. Unfortunately, T-SQL does not support regular expressions natively. This is where CLR integration can show its strength. You can easily create a CLR function that validates an input string against a regular expression.

```
//C#
using System;
using System.Data;
using System.Data.SqlClient;
using System.Data.SqlTypes;
using Microsoft.SqlServer.Server;
using System.Text.RegularExpressions;

public partial class CLRFunctions
{
    // Validate input string against regular expression
     [SqlFunction(IsDeterministic = true, DataAccess = DataAccessKind.None)]
    public static SqlBoolean RegExMatchCS
         (SqlString inpStr, SqlString regExStr)
    {
         if (inpStr.IsNull || regExStr.IsNull)
              return SqlBoolean.Null;
```

```
      else
            return (SqlBoolean)Regex.IsMatch(
                  inpStr.Value, regExStr.Value,
                  RegexOptions.CultureInvariant);}
};
```

On the Companion Disc   This chapter includes many code examples. You will find all the code from this chapter on the companion CD in the C:\My Documents\Microsoft Press\TK70-441 \Chapter03\folder.

You can see that CLR functions are public static (shared in Visual Basic) methods of a public class in the CLR code. If you want to learn more about writing CLR code for use inside SQL Server, see *Inside Microsoft SQL Server 2005: T-SQL Programming* by Itzik Ben-Gan, Dejan Sarka, and Roger Wolter (Microsoft Press, 2006).

With the help of this CLR function, you can now change your e-mail addresses to use native *varchar* or *nvarchar* data types, and you can validate the e-mail addresses against a regular expression by using a *Check* constraint that uses this function. You will do so in the following practice.

Practice: Implementing Domain Integrity

In this practice, you will use various domain-integrity techniques.

IMPORTANT   Practices build upon each other

To work successfully with this practice, you need to have finished the practices from Lessons 2 and 3.

▶ **Exercise 1: Create a Lookup Table**

In this exercise, you will create a lookup table for the education-level attribute. You will use this table in the following exercise to limit the possible values the education-level attribute can accept by using a *Foreign Key* constraint.

Create the EducationLevels lookup table. It should have only two columns: one for the ID and one for the name of the education level. Insert five rows for five possible levels: Partial High School, High School, Partial College, Bachelors, and Graduate Degree. Your code should look like this:

```
USE TK441Ch03;
GO
CREATE TABLE dbo.EducationLevels
(EducationLevelId tinyint NOT NULL PRIMARY KEY,
 EducationLevelName nvarchar(20) NOT NULL);
GO
```

```
INSERT INTO dbo.EducationLevels(EducationLevelId, EducationLevelName)
 VALUES(1,N'Partial High School');
INSERT INTO dbo.EducationLevels(EducationLevelId, EducationLevelName)
 VALUES(2,N'High School');
INSERT INTO dbo.EducationLevels(EducationLevelId, EducationLevelName)
 VALUES(3,N'Partial College');
INSERT INTO dbo.EducationLevels(EducationLevelId, EducationLevelName)
 VALUES(4,N'Bachelors');
INSERT INTO dbo.EducationLevels(EducationLevelId, EducationLevelName)
 VALUES(5,N'Graduate Degree');
GO
```

▶ Exercise 2: Domain Integrity, Part 1

In this exercise, you will use the lookup table to limit the possible values in the education-level attribute. You will add a *Default* constraint to this attribute: the default education level should be Partial High School. You will re-create the Employees table without CLR UDTs.

1. Re-create the Employees table. Use the *nvarchar(100)* data type for the e-mail addresses. Add a *Default* constraint for the education-level attribute in the CREATE TABLE statement. Your code should look like this:

```
DROP TABLE dbo.Employees;
GO
CREATE TABLE dbo.Employees
(EmployeeId int IDENTITY NOT NULL,
 ManagerId int NULL,
 FirstName nvarchar(30) NOT NULL,
 LastName nvarchar(30) NOT NULL,
 AddressLine1 StandardAddress NULL,
 AddressLine2 StandardAddress NULL,
 CompanyEmail nvarchar(100) NOT NULL,
 PrivateEmail nvarchar(100) NULL,
 EducationLevelId tinyint NOT NULL DEFAULT 1,
 BonusPct AS (EducationLevelId-1)*5
);
GO
```

2. Add a *Foreign Key* constraint to limit the possible values of the EducationLevelId column of the Employees table. Do not forget to add the *Primary Key* and the other *Foreign Key* (the one for the hierarchy) constraints:

```
ALTER TABLE dbo.Employees
 ADD CONSTRAINT FK_Employees_EducationLevel FOREIGN KEY (EducationLevelId)
   REFERENCES dbo.EducationLevels (EducationLevelId);
GO
-- Recreate the Primary Key
ALTER TABLE dbo.Employees
 ADD CONSTRAINT PK_Employees PRIMARY KEY (EmployeeId);
GO
-- Recreate the hierarchy Foreign key
ALTER TABLE dbo.Employees
```

```
ADD CONSTRAINT FK_Employees_MgrEmployee FOREIGN KEY (ManagerId)
  REFERENCES dbo.Employees (EmployeeId);
GO
```

▶ **Exercise 3: Domain Integrity, Part 2**

In this exercise, you will use the CLR functions inside *Check* constraints to validate e-mail addresses against a regular expression. Finally, try to add the *Unique* constraint on the company e-mail address.

1. Create the C# and Visual Basic functions. You should already have assemblies imported in the database. If you have not performed this task yet, see the "User-Defined Data Types" practice in Lesson 2. Your code for cataloging the CLR functions should be:

```
CREATE FUNCTION dbo.RegExMatchCS
  (@inpstr AS NVARCHAR(MAX), @regexstr AS NVARCHAR(MAX))
RETURNS BIT
EXTERNAL NAME Ch03CS.CLRFunctions.RegExMatchCS;
GO
-- Create the VB CLR function
CREATE FUNCTION dbo.RegExMatchVB
  (@inpstr AS NVARCHAR(MAX), @regexstr AS NVARCHAR(MAX))
RETURNS BIT
EXTERNAL NAME Ch03VB.CLRFunctions.RegExMatchVB;
GO
```

2. Use the C# function for the company e-mail address *Check* constraint and the Visual Basic function for the personal e-mail address constraint:

```
ALTER TABLE dbo.Employees
 ADD CONSTRAINT CK_Employees_CompanyEmail
  CHECK (dbo.RegExMatchCS(CompanyEmail,
         N'^([\w-]+\.)*?[\w-]+@[\w-]+\.([\w-]+\.)*?[\w]+$')
        = CAST(1 AS bit));
GO
ALTER TABLE dbo.Employees
 ADD CONSTRAINT CK_Employees_PrivateEmail
  CHECK (dbo.RegExMatchVB(PrivateEmail,
         N'^([\w-]+\.)*?[\w-]+@[\w-]+\.([\w-]+\.)*?[\w]+$')
        = CAST(1 AS bit));
GO
```

3. Now when you have e-mail addresses in columns that use the system *nvarchar* data type, you can try to add the *Unique* constraint on the company e-mail address attribute. This time, you should succeed.

```
ALTER TABLE dbo.Employees
 ADD CONSTRAINT UC_Employees_CompanyMail UNIQUE (CompanyEmail);
GO
```

Quick Check

1. In the preceding practice, you used a *Foreign Key* constraint to implement domain integrity. Could you use a *Check* constraint to implement referential integrity?
2. Can you temporarily disable a constraint?

Quick Check Answers

1. Yes, you could use a *Check* constraint to implement referential integrity. You would have to create a Boolean scalar UDF that would query the parent table with a search parameter and return true if a single row in the parent table is found. Then you would have to add a *Check* constraint to the child table. In the *Check* constraint, you would need to create an expression, which would call the UDF, using the foreign key column as a parameter and evaluate to true if the UDF returns true. However, creating a simple *Foreign Key* constraint would be much simpler and more effective.

2. Yes, you can temporarily disable *Check* and *Foreign Key* constraints to avoid checking existing data when you add a constraint or to improve performance when you run large batch jobs.

Lesson 5: Creating Programmable Objects to Maintain Integrity

Estimated lesson time: 25 minutes

Sometimes business rules are too complex to implement by using constraints. In addition, constraints cannot span a database boundary. You cannot have, for example, a parent table in one database and a child table in another with a *Foreign Key* constraint between them. In such cases, you must implement your constraints through program code. You can write this code in the middle tier, called the data-access layer. However, the closer the constraints are to the data, the harder it is to circumvent them. You can program the constraints in SQL Server stored procedures. However, an application could still bypass stored procedures. You have another option: put your constraints in data-modification language (DML) triggers.

DML triggers are a special kind of stored procedure. SQL Server executes them automatically instead of or after a DML statement. Previous versions of SQL Server support only DML triggers; SQL Server 2005 also supports DDL triggers. You will learn more about stored procedures in Chapter 6, "Designing Objects That Retrieve Data," and more about DDL triggers in Chapter 7, "Designing Objects That Extend Server Functionality and Perform Actions." In this lesson, you will learn how you can use DDL triggers to enforce data integrity.

DML Triggers

SQL Server supports two categories of DML triggers:

- AFTER triggers fire after an INSERT, UPDATE, or DELETE statement.
- INSTEAD OF triggers execute instead of an INSERT, UPDATE, or DELETE statement.

A trigger is always part of the same transaction as the statement that caused a trigger to fire. You can roll back the transaction from the trigger body if you encounter a business-rule violation. In the body of a trigger, you can reference columns of other tables and, thus, enforce more complex rules than with *Check* constraints. In the body of a trigger, you have access to the state before the modification through a special temporary Deleted table and to the state after the modification through a special temporary Inserted table. Triggers can also cascade changes to other tables. However, constraints typically perform better; if you can implement the same rule with a constraint, you should use a constraint.

It is crucial to understand the order of integrity checks:

1. INSTEAD OF triggers fire instead of the actual statement.
2. *Default* constraints are applied.
3. Nullability is checked.

4. *Foreign Key* constraints are enforced.
5. *Primary Key* and *Unique* constraints are checked.
6. AFTER triggers fire.

All integrity checks, but AFTER triggers are checked before the actual modification takes place. That is why you have to roll back a transaction in the body of a trigger explicitly if a rule is violated. It is a good practice to inform the client application with an error message if a rollback occurs. You can raise ad hoc errors, some system errors, and custom error messages. You can add custom error messages by using the sp_addmessage system stored procedure. If you perform some corrective action in the body of a trigger and thus execute another data modification statement, you should use structured exception handling (by the TRY . . . CATCH structure) to catch exceptions your corrective action might produce.

Exam Tip   Be sure to understand the implications of the order of the integrity check on performance.

You can define a DML trigger for INSERT, UPDATE, and DELETE actions. You can define one trigger per action, or you can define a single trigger for multiple actions. You can define a single INSTEAD OF trigger per action and multiple AFTER triggers per action.

The primary purpose of INSTEAD OF triggers is to enable views that would not be updateable to support updates. If a view is defined on multiple base tables, inserts, updates, and deletes cannot reference more than one base table. However, you can bypass this limitation with INSTEAD OF triggers. They fire in place of the triggering action. In the body of the trigger, you have to reprogram data modification actions to reference a single base table per DML statement. In the body of an INSTEAD OF trigger, you have access to the Inserted and Deleted tables as well. You can also use INSTEAD OF triggers for efficient batch updates; you can let a part of the batch succeed and reject the other part, logging the rejected part.

You can program triggers in T-SQL or CLR code. A trigger can perform nearly any action you can imagine. There is a short list of disallowed T_SQL commands in a trigger:

- *CREATE, ALTER,* and *DROP DATABASE*
- *RESTORE DATABASE* and *RESTORE LOG*
- *RECONFIGURE*

Additionally, you cannot use the following T-SQL commands in the body of a DML trigger when used against the table or view that is the target of the triggering action:

- *CREATE, ALTER,* and *DROP INDEX*
- *DBCC DBREINDEX*
- *DROP TABLE*

- *ALTER PARTITION FUNCTION*
- *ALTER TABLE* to add, modify, or drop columns; to switch partitions; and to add or drop *Primary Key* and *Unique* constraints

A trigger can call a stored procedure. Be careful when you design a trigger and consider performance implications. If you design a performance problem into a trigger, you slow down all data modification actions. Be aware that a data modification action can modify a single row or multiple rows; your triggers should be prepared for both possibilities. You can improve performance of an UPDATE trigger if you check the columns updated and fire it only if a user updated specific columns. You can check which columns were updated by using an IF UPDATE() clause or the *COLUMNS_UPDATED* function.

A trigger can perform a data modification action on another table; because this table can have some DML triggers defined as well, you get *nested* triggers. Nesting triggers is enabled by default; you can disable it for a complete instance by using the sp_configure stored procedure on the server level. You can nest triggers up to 32 levels in depth. If you exceed this depth, SQL Server rolls back the complete transaction. You can use the *@@NESTLEVEL* system function to check the level of nesting in the body of a trigger. When you have nested triggers, you might encounter a situation in which you would fire the same trigger again directly or indirectly. This would be a *recursive* trigger. Recursive triggers are disabled by default. You can enable them on the database level by using the *ALTER DATABASE* command.

Trigger Security

Triggers execute under the context of the user who calls the trigger (that is, the user who executed the original statement that caused the trigger to fire by default). Be aware of the possibility of malicious code in the body of a trigger. For example, in the body of a trigger, an attacker could add a GRANT statement to gain elevated privileges. If such a malicious trigger fires in the context of a privileged user such as dbo, the execution of the GRANT statement succeeds, and the attacker gets permissions. Check the code of the triggers in your databases regularly. You can get information about all triggers on your database by querying the sys.triggers and sys.server_triggers catalog views:

```
SELECT type, name, parent_class_desc FROM sys.triggers
UNION
SELECT type, name, parent_class_desc FROM sys.server_triggers;
```

You can check the code of a trigger by querying the sys.sql_modules catalog view. You can also disable execution of selected dangerous triggers or even execution of all triggers on a database or server.

Practice: Creating DML Triggers and Testing Data Integrity

In this chapter's final practice, you will create an AFTER DML trigger. You will also test all the data-integrity checks you implemented throughout the practices in this chapter.

IMPORTANT   **Practices build upon each other**

To work successfully with this practice, you need to have finished the practices from Lessons 2 through 4.

▶ **Exercise 1: Create a DML Trigger**

In this exercise, you create a DML trigger.

Part of the Tailspin Toys mission statement is to promote education. The company policy is to disallow the employment of more than two employees with a partial high school education at the same time. In this exercise, you have to implement this rule. You can enforce the rule by using a trigger that counts the number of rows that have the lowest education levels in the EducationLevelID column (one). The code should look like this:

```
CREATE TRIGGER EmployeesEducationLevel
 ON dbo.Employees
AFTER INSERT, UPDATE
AS
IF (SELECT COUNT(EducationLevelId)
      FROM dbo.Employees
      WHERE EducationLevelId = 1) > 2
 BEGIN
  RAISERROR ('Maximally two employees with Partial High School are allowed!', 16, 10);
  ROLLBACK TRANSACTION;
 END;
GO
```

▶ **Exercise 2: Test Data Integrity**

Now that you have all data integrity checks in place, it is time to test them.

1. Insert a valid manager:

```
INSERT INTO dbo.Employees
(ManagerId,
 FirstName,
 LastName,
 AddressLine1,
 AddressLine2,
 CompanyEmail,
 PrivateEmail,
 EducationLevelId)
VALUES
(NULL,
 N'Lubor',
 N'Kollar',
 N'Lubor''s Address line 1',
```

```
    N'Lubor''s Address line 2',
    N'lubor@tailspintoys.com',
    N'lubor@adventure-works.com',
    5);
```

2. Test the *Default* constraint by inserting a valid employee without specifying the EducationLevelId column:

```
INSERT INTO dbo.Employees
(ManagerId,
 FirstName,
 LastName,
 AddressLine1,
 AddressLine2,
 CompanyEmail,
 PrivateEmail)
VALUES
(1,
 N'Janko',
 N'Cajhen',
 N'Janko''s Address line 1',
 N'Janko''s Address line 2',
 N'janko@tailspintoys.com',
 N'janko@adventure-works.com');
GO
```

3. Insert a valid employee. Specify the default education level explicitly:

```
INSERT INTO dbo.Employees
(ManagerId,
 FirstName,
 LastName,
 AddressLine1,
 AddressLine2,
 CompanyEmail,
 PrivateEmail,
 EducationLevelId)
VALUES
(1,
 N'Barbara',
 N'Sankovic',
 N'Barbara''s Address line 1',
 N'Barbara''s Address line 2',
 N'barbara@tailspintoys.com',
 N'barbara@adventure-works.com',
 1);
```

4. Check the trigger. Try to insert a third employee with the lowest education level:

```
INSERT INTO dbo.Employees
(ManagerId,
 FirstName,
 LastName,
 AddressLine1,
 AddressLine2,
```

```
CompanyEmail,
PrivateEmail,
EducationLevelId)
VALUES
(1,
N'Rick',
N'Byham',
N'Rick''s Address line 1',
N'Rick''s Address line 2',
N'rick@tailspintoys.com',
N'rick@adventure-works.com',
1);
```

5. Check the *Foreign Key* constraint of the education-level attribute. Try to update the EducationLevelId to a value that does not exist in the lookup table:

```
UPDATE dbo.Employees
   SET EducationLevelId = 6
 WHERE EmployeeId = 2;
```

6. Check the *ring* constraint, the *Foreign Key* constraint that implements hierarchy. Try to update the ManagerId column to a nonexistent manager:

```
UPDATE dbo.Employees
   SET ManagerId = -1
 WHERE EmployeeId = 2;
```

7. Test the e-mail *Check* constraint by trying to update the company e-mail address to a non-valid value:

```
UPDATE dbo.Employees
   SET CompanyEmail = N'janko#cajhen'
 WHERE EmployeeId = 2;
```

8. Test *data type* constraint. Try to update the company e-mail address to a too-long value:

```
UPDATE dbo.Employees
   SET CompanyEmail = REPLICATE(N'a',99)+N'@a.com'
 WHERE EmployeeId = 2;
```

9. Check the *Unique* constraint on the company e-mail address attribute by trying to update an address to a duplicate value:

```
UPDATE dbo.Employees
   SET CompanyEmail = N'janko@tailspintoys.com'
 WHERE EmployeeId = 3;
```

10. Finally, check the data. Be sure to check the bonus-percentage attribute computed column to see whether the computed value is correct:

```
SELECT EmployeeId,
       ManagerId,
       FirstName,
       LastName,
       AddressLine1,
       AddressLine2,
```

```
        CompanyEmail,
        PrivateEmail,
        BonusPct
   FROM dbo.Employees;
GO
```

▶ **Exercise 3: Clean Up**

Finally, clean up your SQL Server.

Cleanup code:

```
USE master;
DROP DATABASE TK441Ch03;
GO
EXEC sp_configure 'clr enabled', 0;
RECONFIGURE;
GO
```

Quick Check

1. How could you make a view updateable?
2. How can you enforce cross-database referential integrity?

Quick Check Answers

1. You can use INSTEAD OF triggers to make a view updateable.
2. You can use programmable objects, such as DML triggers, to enforce cross-database referential integrity.

Case Scenario: Design a Physical Database

Tailspin Toys has a table that holds information about its partners. In the same table, Tailspin Toys inserts departments of companies, subsidiaries, and enterprises. The company would like to track the hierarchy of its partners, but the number of levels in the hierarchy of its partners is not known in advance. In addition, some rows in the Partners table have a known tax ID. Tax ID is not applicable for departments, and for some partners that are suppliers only, Tailspin Toys does not know the tax ID. The company would like to ensure that known tax IDs are unique. Given these goals, answer the following questions:

1. How can you implement a partner hierarchy?
2. How can you enforce uniqueness for known tax IDs?

Chapter Summary

- You start the physical design of a database by choosing appropriate data types for your entity attributes.
- You can standardize your design by using T-SQL user-defined data types (UDDTs).
- You can achieve the ultimate domain-key normal form (DKNF) by using CLR user-defined types (UDTs).
- Programming a broadly useful CLR type is not an easy task.
- In your database, implement entity, referential, and domain integrity by using constraints.
- If you cannot use constraints to implement integrity and business rules, you can use DML triggers.

Chapter 4
Designing a Database for Performance

After you create a physical database, you need to prepare it to achieve the performance that your applications and end users need. Although maintaining performance is an ongoing task, and many database administrators (DBAs) perform this task regularly, you should understand indexing and partitioning strategies so that you can deliver an acceptable solution and minimize future work and dissatisfaction. In this chapter, you will learn how to design efficient indexes that optimize query performance and how to create a partitioning strategy.

Exam objectives in this chapter:
- Design a logical database.
    - ❑ Optimize queries by creating indexes.
    - ❑ Design table width.
    - ❑ Design index-to-table-size ratio.
- Design objects that define data.
    - ❑ Design indexes.
    - ❑ Specify indexed views to meet business requirements.

Before You Begin

To complete the lessons in this chapter, you must have:

- A good understanding of logical and physical database design.
- Knowledge of Microsoft SQL Server database objects.
- Knowledge of the Transact-SQL (T-SQL) language.
- The SQL Server 2005 *AdventureWorks* and *AdventureWorksDW* sample databases installed. Sample databases are available with SQL Server 2005 Enterprise edition but are not a part of the default installation. Alternatively, you can install the sample databases from *http://msdn2.microsoft.com/en-us/library/ms143739.aspx.*
- SQL Server 2005 Enterprise edition, Enterprise Evaluation edition, or Developer edition. With other editions, you will not be able to check how the query optimizer uses an indexed view even though you do not reference the view explicitly in a query.

IMPORTANT   Practices in this chapter build upon each other

Beginning with Lesson 2, "Designing Indexes," the lesson practices build upon each other; to move to the next practice, you need to finish the previous one.

Lesson 1: Optimizing Queries by Creating Indexes

Estimated lesson time: 20 minutes

Imagine you are searching for a word in a book. You go to the index, where you can easily find the pages on which the word you are searching for appears because the words in an index are sorted alphabetically. You can turn to those pages and read everything associated with the searched word. However, what would happen if the book did not have an index? You would have to read the book from the beginning, page by page, to find all occurrences of the word you are looking for.

The same logic applies to SQL Server when it searches for a value of an attribute. If you index that attribute, SQL Server can perform an index seek; if not, SQL Server must read all pages. In SQL Server terminology, reading all pages is called a *table scan*. Indexes are the most important tool that a database developer or administrator can use to improve performance.

The Basics of Optimizing Queries

Searching for a single value of an attribute is not the only way that SQL Server can benefit from indexes. However, you cannot optimize all types of queries. For example, a query such as the following cannot be optimized at all.

```
SELECT * FROM table
```

With this query, you are asking SQL Server to read the complete table, and doing a table scan is the most efficient method for completing this task. Remember that you can never improve performance by using database tools such as indexes as much as you can spoil the performance in your application with poorly written code. In addition, if your T-SQL queries are inside stored procedures (that is, if your application uses stored procedures), you can improve the queries without having to recompile and redeploy the complete application. As long as the results from the procedures are the results the application is expecting, you can alter the code of the procedures as you want.

Exam Tip   Do not forget that stored procedures can also help you optimize database performance. You can improve queries inside procedures without redeploying the application.

Following is a list of types of queries and query parts that can benefit from indexes. (Because the query optimizer in SQL Server is arguably the most complex part of SQL Server, and it is always being improved, this list is probably not exhaustive, but it provides general guidelines for indexing.)

- Exact searches for the value of an attribute in the WHERE predicate (for example, WHERE PrimaryKeyColumn = value). Note that these kinds of queries are not only typical for SELECT statements, they are frequent for UPDATE and DELETE statements as well.

- Exact searches for the value of an attribute compared to a list of possible values (such as the WHERE predicate with the *IN* operator).

- Approximate string searches that use the *LIKE* operator, especially searches for matching rows that start with a specific character string such as "xyz%."

- Range searches in the WHERE predicate such as searches that use the *BETWEEN* operator.

- Queries that join multiple tables such as queries that use the *JOIN* or *APPLY* operators.

- Queries that return sorted row sets by using ORDER BY. Sorting a huge row set without an index is a highly inefficient operation.

- Simple aggregate queries such as queries that use the *MAX* aggregate function.

- Grouped aggregate queries that use *GROUP BY* or *PIVOT* operators.

- *Primary Key* and *Unique* constraint checks. Note that *Primary Key* and *Unique* constraints physically create unique indexes.

- *Foreign Key* constraint checks. If you delete or update a row in the parent table, SQL Server must check whether the row has associated rows in a child table.

- The SELECT part of a query, which can benefit from indexes as well. If you have an explicit column list in the SELECT part of a query, SQL Server considers covering a query with nonclustered indexes. You will learn more about types of indexes and covered queries in Lesson 2.

You can see that many types of queries can benefit from indexes. Thus, you might be tempted to index all possible attributes. However, SQL Server has to maintain all the indexes you create. So the more indexes you have, the slower the updates are. Consider the typical usage of your data when you design indexes. You can use SQL Server Profiler to capture queries from the production system and then analyze the Profiler traces to find typical patterns of your data usage.

Maintaining Statistics

Imagine again that you are searching for a word in a book. If the word appears frequently on many pages—that is, if the word is dense in the book—going back to the index for each page that the searched word appears on and then going to that page is less efficient than reading the entire book. Again, the same is true for SQL Server searches. If the value you are searching for is dense, a table scan is more efficient than an index seek. The important thing to consider is the density of the searched values. If the index is unique or nearly unique, it is very selective, and SQL Server is probably using it a lot.

Exam Tip   Remember that density is a term connected with searched values, and selectivity is a term connected with indexes.

SQL Server must decide in advance which indexes it should use when it executes a query. Therefore, SQL Server must know before the search the density of searched values and the selectivity of the indexes. Statistical pages provide this information to the query optimizer. SQL Server collects statistics about individual columns (single-column statistics) or sets of columns (multicolumn statistics). SQL Server can collect the statistics automatically, or you can force the collection manually by using CREATE STATISTICS and UPDATE STATISTICS T-SQL statements. In addition, you can manually update all existing statistics in a database by using the sp_updatestats system stored procedure.

Automatically gathering statistical information is the default for SQL Server 2005; you can disable it for a specific database by using the ALTER DATABASE statement. However, it is a best practice to let SQL Server collect the statistics automatically and add or update statistics manually only in specific cases when automatic gathering, which works with samples of data, is not precise enough. If statistical information is old, SQL Server might decide to use a table scan instead of an index seek because the query optimizer cannot be sure that the statistics are still valid. Therefore, if you know you have an index, you know your query is not poorly written, and SQL Server still does not use the index, you should first check the statistics for problems.

Practice: Selecting Columns to Index

In this conceptual practice, you must determine the appropriate columns to index to improve the given queries.

▶ **Exercise 1: Select Columns to Index**

1. Which columns would you index to improve performance of the following query?

   ```
   SELECT ColumnA, SUM(ColumnB)
   FROM schema.table
   GROUP BY ColumnA
   ```

2. Which columns would you index to improve performance of the following query?

   ```
   UPDATE schema.table SET ColumnA = value
   WHERE PrimaryKeyColumn = value
   ```

3. Which columns would you index to improve performance of the following query?

   ```
   SELECT ColumnA, ColumnB
   FROM schema.table
   ORDER BY ColumnB
   ```

Suggested Answers

1. This query would benefit from an index on ColumnA.

2. This query would benefit from an index on PrimaryKeyColumn. Any other indexes would deteriorate performance of this query.

3. This query would benefit from an index on ColumnB. In addition, if the index would be a nonclustered index, you could include ColumnA in the index to cover the query with the index. This would improve the performance even more.

Quick Check

1. What is the prerequisite for efficient indexing?

2. How many indexes do you need on a database?

Quick Check Answers

1. The prerequisite for efficient indexing is efficient queries.

2. It is impossible to answer such a general question without thorough knowledge of data-usage patterns, which you can determine by using SQL Server Profile to trace operations.

Lesson 2: Designing Indexes

Estimated lesson time: 30 minutes

Now that you have reviewed the basics of query optimization, you are ready to delve deeper into designing indexes. In this lesson, you will learn more about different types of indexes and the most important guidelines for index design.

Clustered and Nonclustered Indexes

A table without a clustered index is stored as a heap. It has a single partition by default. If a table has multiple partitions, each partition has a heap structure. Special system pages called *Index Allocation Map* (IAM) pages point to data pages used by the heap of a table. SQL Server uses IAM pages for reading the data from a heap. Because IAM pages define the sequence of reads, SQL Server returns data unordered unless you specify the ORDER BY clause in your query.

SQL Server organizes indexes in balanced trees (B-trees). The structure resembles an inverse tree. Each page in the tree is called a *node*; the top node is the *root* node. The bottom-level nodes are *leaf* nodes. Between the root node and the leaf nodes, an index can have multiple *intermediate* levels. SQL Server starts all index searches from the root node, then traverses through intermediate-level nodes, and finishes a search in an index in a leaf node. On a leaf-node page, all the index key values and pointers to data pages are in a nonclustered index, and all the data is in a clustered index. (You will learn more about clustered and nonclustered indexes in a moment.) Root and intermediate-level node pages contain pointers to index pages. The search is quicker if there is less disk input/output (IO)—that is, if SQL Server has to read fewer pages. You can immediately conclude that an index is more effective if it has fewer intermediate levels. Fewer intermediate levels means the key of the index must be short.

There are two main types of indexes: clustered and nonclustered. If a table is *clustered* (that is, if it has a clustered index), the logical order of rows and pages is based on the index. The clustered index includes data pages—in other words, the clustered index is the table itself. Therefore, you can have only one clustered index per table. When you create a clustered index, the physical order is similar or the same as the logical order. However, there is still no guarantee of the order of the rows returned unless you specify the ORDER BY clause in your query. For example, SQL Server might start reading data pages somewhere in the middle of the table if the physical disk head is currently there. In addition, over time the physical order of rows and pages can become less and less aligned with the logical order as SQL Server allocates new pages wherever free space in a database is available. This is known as *logical fragmentation* of an index. You can eliminate logical fragmentation by re-creating the index, rebuilding it, or reorganizing it. For more information about managing index fragmentation, see the description of the *ALTER INDEX* command in SQL Server 2005 Books Online at *http://technet.microsoft.com/en-us/sqlserver/bb428874.aspx.*

Exam Tip   Using the ORDER BY clause is the only guaranteed way to have SQL Server return a row set in a specific order.

You can have up to 249 nonclustered indexes on a table. A *nonclustered index* has the same B-tree structure as a clustered index. However, the data rows are not sorted in the order of the nonclustered index. In addition, leaf-level pages are index pages, not data pages. Leaf-level pages include key values and pointers to rows. If you build a nonclustered index on a heap, the pointer is the row ID. SQL Server maintains row IDs internally; they are not exposed to queries. If you build a nonclustered index on a clustered table, the pointer is the clustered index key.

This structure might seem a bit less efficient for data retrieval because to find a specific row, after SQL Server traverses all levels of the nonclustered index, it must traverse all levels of the clustered index as well. However, the index structure is typically very flat, so this performance price is quite low. On the other hand, unless you change the clustered key, SQL Server does not have to update nonclustered indexes if a row moves because of table update or maintenance. If index keys are long, you have fewer rows on leaf-node pages. Thus, you need more leaf-node pages, which in turn results in more intermediate levels, which makes indexing less efficient. Having a short key is especially important for clustered indexes because the key appears on leaf pages of all nonclustered indexes.

Unique and Composite Indexes

When you create an index, you can specify it as *unique*, meaning that the values of the key are unique. Unique indexes reject non-unique values when you insert or update the data, thus working as constraints. However, you should use constraints to constrain something, and use indexes only to boost performance. After all, *Primary Key* and *Unique* constraints are physically implemented with unique indexes. A clustered index is always unique internally, even if you create it on a non-unique column. Suppose you have, for example, a simple table such as the one that Table 4-1 shows:

Table 4-1   Simple Table

ID	LastName
17	Kollar
34	Kollar
2	Cajhen

The values in the ID column are unique, while the values in the LastName column are not. You could create a clustered index on the LastName column and a nonclustered index on the ID column. The leaf level of the nonclustered index would look like Table 4-2.

Table 4-2   Leaf Node of a Nonclustered Index on the ID Column

Key	ClusteredKey
2	Cajhen
17	Kollar
34	Kollar

Now imagine that you are searching for ID 17. You get the LastName Kollar. You then go to the clustered index, and you get two rows; however, because the ID is unique, you should be able to find the exact row you are looking for. That is why SQL Server always creates a clustered index as unique internally by adding a sequential number to the duplicate values. Therefore, the leaf node of the nonclustered index from the example would really look like Table 4-3.

Table 4-3   The Real Leaf Node of a Nonclustered Index on the ID Column

Key	ClusteredKey
2	Cajhen
17	Kollar
34	Kollar0001

Adding this information to identify rows uniquely in a clustered index widens the clustered key and, thus, makes all indexes less effective. Therefore, it is a good practice to create clustered indexes on unique columns. The SQL Server defaults are not that bad after all, right? The *Primary Key* constraint creates a clustered index by default.

You are not limited to a single column for an index key. You can create indexes with composite keys defined on multiple columns. You can have up to 16 columns in a composite key; however, altogether, the key cannot exceed 900 bytes. Use composite indexes to support queries that use multiple columns in their search arguments, to support GROUP BY columns, and to reduce the number of indexes you need to maintain. However, you should have the most selective column first for quick searches of single rows or small row sets. Indexes with composite keys are less efficient in searches but better for covered queries. In addition, to create covering indexes without affecting the key, you can include columns on the leaf-level nodes of an index in SQL Server 2005.

Indexes with Included Columns

An index is covering a query if SQL Server finds all information the query needs in an index. In this case, SQL Server does not have to traverse to data pages to fulfill the query requirements.

Such a query is a covered query. Clustered indexes cannot be covering indexes because they include data pages. Because you typically have shorter rows on leaf nodes of a nonclustered index compared to rows on data pages, SQL Server has to read fewer pages to return the same amount of rows. Thus, covered queries can be more effective. In SQL Server 2005, you can include one or more columns on the leaf-level nodes of a nonclustered index to cover queries.

Theoretically, you could include all non-key columns in an index. This would make no sense; reading from this index would be no faster than reading from data pages, whether data pages are organized as a heap or as a clustered index. Therefore, carefully and deliberately choose which columns to include in an index. If you want to cover a frequent query, and you need one more column to cover it, include it in an index. However, check the performance of other queries because the index could become less effective due to wider rows on the leaf nodes.

The included columns do not count in the 16-column and 900-byte limits. You need at least one key column for an index, and you can have up to 1,023 non-key (included) columns. With included columns, you can have more covering indexes, while you still maintain small and efficient keys.

XML and Full-Text Indexes

XML data type columns can contain up to 2 gigabytes (GB) of data. Shredding this amount of data for a single column of each row when executing a query can be quite inefficient. To make queries more efficient, you can index an XML column by using *XML indexes*. XML indexes are new in SQL Server 2005, as is the *XML* data type. (You will learn more about XML indexes in Chapter 5, "Using Database Technologies and Techniques for Your Application," which covers guidelines for working with XML data.)

In addition to regular SQL Server indexes, you can define special full-text indexes on character data. A *full-text index* is a token-based functional index. SQL Server does not maintain full-text indexes; the Microsoft Full-Text Engine for SQL Server (MSFTESQL) service maintains them. The structure of a full-text index is not a B-tree. MSFTESQL builds an inverted, stacked, compressed index structure based on individual tokens from the text you are indexing. When you have full-text indexes, you can use the additional T-SQL full-text predicates CONTAINS and FREETEXT as well as the CONTAINSTABLE and FREETEXT table table-valued functions in your queries. Full-text indexes and full-text searches are beyond the scope of this book; to learn more about them, see the "Full-Text Search Concepts" chapter in SQL Server 2005 Books Online at *http://msdn2.microsoft.com/en-us/library/ms142547.aspx*.

Creating Indexes

You create indexes explicitly by using the CREATE INDEX statement or implicitly through constraints by using the CREATE TABLE or ALTER TABLE statement. By default, you create, drop, and alter indexes in offline mode. This means that SQL Server holds exclusive locks on the underlying data and associated indexes during the index data-definition language (DDL) operations. In SQL Server 2005, you can perform DDL operations on indexes in online mode. If you use the ONLINE option when you create an index, SQL Server allows concurrent user access to the underlying heap or clustered index data and any associated nonclustered indexes during the index creation. The same is true for altering and dropping an index. However, these online operations do not come free. During online index operations, SQL Server uses the snapshot isolation framework and, thus, puts a lot of burden on the *tempdb* database. In addition, online index operations are limited to SQL Server 2005 Enterprise edition only.

When you create indexes, follow these guidelines:

- Create the clustered index first. If you create nonclustered indexes on a heap and then later create a clustered index, SQL Server has to re-create all nonclustered indexes.
- Create a clustered index on a single small and unique column if possible. Update the columns of a clustered index infrequently, if at all.
- Consider supporting range queries with clustered indexes. Do not forget that even range queries can be more efficient with nonclustered indexes if the nonclustered indexes cover the query.
- Clustered indexes are very efficient in supporting ORDER BY and GROUP BY queries.
- Most of the time, you should create an index on Foreign Key columns. Do not forget that the *Foreign Key* constraint does not create an index as *Primary Key* and *Unique* constraints do.
- Nonclustered indexes are especially efficient for queries that return small or singleton row sets.
- Nonclustered indexes can cover queries. You can add included columns to improve query covering.
- If you perform online index operations, be prepared for this operation to take longer than an offline one. In addition, monitor your *tempdb* database for space and performance.
- Index DDL operations can cause the transaction log to fill up quickly. To make sure that SQL Server can roll back the index operation, you cannot truncate the transaction log until SQL Server completes the index operation; however, you can back up the log during the index operation. Take care to have enough space in the transaction log when you perform index operations.

Practice: Designing Indexes

IMPORTANT Remaining practices build upon each other

Beginning with this practice, the practices in this chapter build upon each other. You should not delete your work after you finish this practice.

In this practice, you will create different indexes on a table and check different execution plans you get for the same query.

On the Companion Disc This chapter includes many code examples. You will find all the code from this chapter on the companion CD in the C:\My Documents\Microsoft Press\TK70-441 \Chapter04\Sql folder.

▶ **Exercise 1: Create the Infrastructure and a Clustered Index**

To prepare the infrastructure for this practice, you first need to create a test database and a populated table. In addition, you will test the clustered index.

1. Create a test database and a test table based on the Person.Contact table from the *AdventureWorks* database. Include ContactId, Title, FirstName, LastName, Suffix, Email-Address, and Phone columns. Populate the table with the data from the Person.Contact table. Your code should look like this:

```
IF DB_ID(N'TK441Ch04') IS NULL
    CREATE DATABASE TK441Ch04;
GO
-- Create a populated table
USE TK441Ch04;
GO
CREATE TABLE dbo.MyContacts
(ContactId int NOT NULL,
 Title nvarchar(16) NULL,
 FirstName nvarchar(100) NOT NULL,
 LastName nvarchar(100) NOT NULL,
 Suffix nvarchar(200) NULL,
 EmailAddress nvarchar(100) NULL,
 Phone nvarchar(50) NULL);
GO
INSERT INTO dbo.MyContacts
SELECT ContactId, Title,
       FirstName, LastName,
       Suffix, EmailAddress,
       Phone
  FROM AdventureWorks.Person.Contact;
GO
```

2. In SQL Server Management Studio (SSMS), turn on the actual execution plan. Search for the contact with ContactId equal to 1,350. Retrieve the ContactId, FirstName, and Last-Name columns. Check the execution plan. You should see a *Table Scan* operator. Your query should look like this:

```
SELECT ContactId,
       FirstName, LastName
  FROM dbo.MyContacts
 WHERE ContactId = 1350;
GO
```

3. Create a unique clustered index on the ContactId column. Repeat the query from the previous task and check the execution plan. You should see a *Clustered Index Seek* operator. Your *INDEX-CREATION* command should look like this:

```
CREATE UNIQUE CLUSTERED INDEX CL_Mycontacts_ContactId
 ON dbo.MyContacts(ContactId);
GO
```

4. Try to insert a duplicate row. The unique index should reject the action. Your *INSERT* command should look like this:

```
INSERT INTO dbo.MyContacts
(ContactId, Title,
 FirstName, LastName,
 Suffix, EmailAddress,
 Phone)
VALUES
(1350, 'Mr',
 'Janko', 'Cajhen',
 NULL, 'janko@tailspintoys.com',
 '398-555-0132' );
GO
```

▶ **Exercise 2: Create a Nonclustered Index**

Now you will add a nonclustered index to your table and check the query execution plan without and with an index.

1. Search for the contact with LastName Guzik. You should get a *Clustered Index Scan* operator in the execution plan. Your code should look like this:

```
SELECT ContactId,
       FirstName, LastName
  FROM dbo.MyContacts
 WHERE LastName = 'Guzik';
GO
```

2. Create a nonclustered index on the LastName column. Search for the contact with Last-Name Guzik again. This time in the execution plan, you should get an *Index Seek* operator for the nonclustered index seek and a *Key Lookup* operator for the lookup in the clustered index for actual data pages. Your index-creation code should look like this:

```
CREATE NONCLUSTERED INDEX NCL_Mycontacts_LastName
ON dbo.MyContacts(LastName);
GO
```

▶ **Exercise 3: Include a Column in a Nonclustered Index**

In this practice, you include a column in the leaf-level nodes of a nonclustered index.

Re-create a nonclustered index on the LastName column; this time, include the First-Name column in the index. Search for the contact with LastName Guzik. You should get an *Index Seek* operator in the execution plan. This means that SQL Server found all data needed for the query in the nonclustered index. Your index re-creation and query code should look like this:

```
DROP INDEX dbo.MyContacts.NCL_Mycontacts_LastName;
GO
CREATE NONCLUSTERED INDEX NCL_Mycontacts_LastName
 ON dbo.MyContacts(LastName)
 INCLUDE(FirstName);
GO
-- Repeat the contact Guzik query
SELECT ContactId,
       FirstName, LastName
  FROM dbo.MyContacts
 WHERE LastName = 'Guzik';
GO
```

Quick Check

1. Which of the queries from the preceding practice was the most effective?
2. Your nonclustered index with an included column had LastName as the key column and FirstName as the included column. However, the query used the ContactId column in the SELECT list as well. Why could this query be covered with the nonclustered index?

Quick Check Answers

1. The last query, the covered query, was the most efficient because it used the least amount of disk IO.
2. The ContactId column is the key of the clustered index. The key of the clustered index appears on leaf-level nodes of all nonclustered indexes. That is why the nonclustered index was able to cover the query.

Lesson 3: Specifying Indexed Views

Estimated lesson time: 25 minutes

You already know that you can specify a computed column when you create a table. The computed column is a virtual column. However, you can index this column and thus materialize it—if you meet some prerequisites. The problem is that when you index a computed column, SQL Server must maintain this index the same way it has to maintain other indexes. To find the value it has to update, SQL Server has to have a deterministic and precise path to that value. The following prerequisites ensure that SQL Server is able to update the index on a computed column.

Views are, in their simplest appearance, just a saved and named SELECT statement and represent a virtual table. You can use them in place of tables. Views do not have data by default and are thus virtual objects as well. Similarly, as you can index a computed column, you can index and materialize a view. However, you have to meet even more strict prerequisites to index a view. You will learn more about views in Chapter 6, "Designing Objects That Retrieve Data." In this lesson, you will learn how to index a computed column and a view.

Indexing a Computed Column

If you want to index a computed column, you have to meet the following prerequisites:

- **Ownership requirements** All functions referenced in an expression of a computed table must have the same owner as the owner of the table where the computed column is.
- **Determinism requirements** The computed column expression must be deterministic (that is, must return the same result for the same input). An expression is deterministic if:
  - ❑ All functions used in the expression are deterministic and precise. For example, the *SQRT* built-in function is always deterministic, and GETDATE is always non-deterministic.
  - ❑ All columns in the expression come from the same table.
  - ❑ The expression does not use data from multiple rows. Therefore, if you use an aggregate function in the expression, the expression is nondeterministic.
  - ❑ The expression has no system or user data access.
  - ❑ If you use a common language runtime (CLR) function in the expression, the expression still has to be deterministic, and the compute column has to be marked as PERSISTED when you create the table.

- **Precision requirements**   The expression must be precise. It is precise if you do not use the float or real data types in the definition of the expression and if the expression does not return a float or real data type.

  You can create an index on a computed column with a deterministic but imprecise expression if you mark the column as PERSISTED.
- **Data type requirements**   You cannot index a computed column for which the expression returns *text*, *ntext*, or *image* data types.
- **SET option requirements**   You must have correct SET options for your connection when you create the index. The correct options are:
  - ❑ NUMERIC_ROUNDABORT must be set to OFF.
  - ❑ ANSI_NULLS, ANSI_PADDING, ANSI_WARNINGS, ARITHABORT, CONCAT _NULL_YIELDS_NULL, and QUOTED_IDENTIFIER options must be set to ON.

Indexing a View

The SELECT statement in the view definition can be quite complex. For example, it can involve multiple joins or aggregates. If you reference such a view in multiple queries, your database performance could be less than satisfactory. You can improve the performance by creating a clustered index on the view. This way, you materialize the view, and SQL Server maintains the index as any other index. In addition, in Enterprise edition, SQL Server can use the indexed view even if you do not reference it directly in your queries. Therefore, you might improve the performance of existing queries without changing the application's code.

Indexed views are not so useful if you have write-intensive applications because SQL Server must maintain them as it does any other index. In addition, if you do not use aggregate queries or queries with multiple joins, the performance benefit is minor.

To be able to create an index on the view, you have to meet the following prerequisites:

- You have to create the view with the SCHEMABINDING option. This option prevents changes to the structure of the underlying tables unless you drop the view.
- Even if you use a user-defined function in a view, you have to create the function with the SCHEMABINDING option.
- The ANSI_NULLS and QUOTED_IDENTIFIER options must have been set to ON when you create the view.
- When you create the underlying tables, the tables you reference in your view, the ANSI_NULLS option must have been set to ON.
- The view must reference base tables only.
- All tables referenced by the view must be in the same database as the view.

- All base tables must have the same owner as the view.
- You have to reference all objects with two-part names.
- All functions used in the view definition must be deterministic.
- If the view definition uses an aggregate function, the SELECT list must also include COUNT_BIG (*).
- If you use CLR functions in the view definition, they have to meet the following prerequisites:
  - ❑ CLR functions cannot be part of the key of the clustered index.
  - ❑ CLR functions and methods of CLR user-defined types used in the view definition must have the DETERMINISTIC and the PRECISE properties set to TRUE, the DATA ACCESS property to NO SQL, and the EXTERNAL ACCESS property to NO.
- The SELECT statement in the view definition cannot contain:
  - ❑ An asterisk in the column definition. (That is, you cannot use SELECT * FROM.)
  - ❑ A derived table, a common table expression (CTE), or subqueries.
  - ❑ Rowset functions (such as *OPENQUERY*).
  - ❑ *UNION, EXCEPT,* or *INTERSECT* operators.
  - ❑ Outer or self joins.
  - ❑ A TOP clause.
  - ❑ An ORDER BY clause.
  - ❑ A *DISTINCT* keyword.
  - ❑ A *COUNT* aggregate function. *COUNT_BIG(*)* is allowed.
  - ❑ The *AVG, MAX, MIN, STDEV, STDEVP, VAR*, or *VARP* aggregate functions or a CLR user-defined aggregate function.
  - ❑ A *SUM* function that references a nullable expression.
  - ❑ The OVER clause, which includes ranking or aggregate window functions.
  - ❑ The full-text predicates CONTAINS or FREETEXT.
  - ❑ A COMPUTE or COMPUTE BY clause.
  - ❑ The *CROSS APPLY* or *OUTER APPLY* operator.
  - ❑ The *PIVOT* or *UNPIVOT* operator.
  - ❑ Table hints and join hints.
  - ❑ Direct references to XQuery expressions. However, you can use XQuery expressions in a user-defined function (UDF) used in the view definition.
- If GROUP BY is specified, the view SELECT list must contain a *COUNT_BIG(*)* expression, and the view definition cannot specify HAVING, CUBE, or ROLLUP.
- You cannot include *text, ntext,* or *image* columns in the view.

In addition, when you are creating the index, you have to meet the following prerequisites:

- SET option requirements: you need to have correct SET options for your connection when you create the index. The correct options are the same as they are if you want to create an index on a computed column:
  - ❑ NUMERIC_ROUNDABORT must be set to OFF.
  - ❑ ANSI_NULLS, ANSI_PADDING, ANSI_WARNINGS, ARITHABORT, CONCAT _NULL_YIELDS_NULL, and QUOTED_IDENTIFIER options must be set to ON.
  - ❑ The IGNORE_DUP_KEY option must be set to OFF.
- If your SELECT statement in the view definition specifies a GROUP BY clause, the key of the unique clustered index can reference only columns specified in the GROUP BY clause.
- Imprecise expressions can be part of the key column of an indexed view unless an imprecise expression forms the value of an index key column and references a stored column in a base table underlying the view. This column can be a regular stored column or a persisted computed column.
- You must be the owner of the view you are indexing.

You might think that indexed views are too much trouble because of this long list of prerequisites. Nevertheless, you do not have to worry too much about the SET options if you leave the defaults intact. In addition, the query optimizer is quite smart, and it can calculate the average from the view if you use *SUM* and *COUNT_BIG* aggregate functions. Many decision-support queries can benefit greatly from indexed views. The following practice shows you that it is not so difficult to deal with indexed views.

Practice: Specifying Indexed Views

IMPORTANT   Practices build upon each other

To work successfully with this practice, you need to have finished the practice from Lesson 2, "Designing Indexes."

This practice will help you understand that indexing a view is not that difficult. Be sure to have the actual execution plan available.

▶ **Exercise 1: Build the Base Query**

You have to prepare statistics on the Title column in the dbo.MyContacts table. You are interested in how many titles are NULL and how many are NOT NULL in your table.

Prepare the query. The query is not your typical basic query because you have to use the CASE expression. In the query, use the *COUNT_BIG(*)* function—instead of *COUNT(*)*—because you are going to use the same query for the view. In the execution plan, you should get a *Clustered Index Scan* of the dbo.MyContacts table. Your query should look like this:

```
USE TK441Ch04;
GO
SELECT CASE
        WHEN Title IS NULL THEN 0
        WHEN Title IS NOT NULL THEN 1
        END AS TitleNum,
        COUNT_BIG(*) AS TitleStatistics
   FROM dbo.MyContacts
GROUP BY CASE
          WHEN Title IS NULL THEN 0
          WHEN Title IS NOT NULL THEN 1
          END;
GO
```

▶ **Exercise 2: Create an Indexed View**

Create and index a view based on the query in Exercise 1, "Build the Base Query." Then test it.

1. Create the view by using the following code:

```
CREATE VIEW dbo.TitleStats
WITH SCHEMABINDING
AS
SELECT CASE
        WHEN Title IS NULL THEN 0
        WHEN Title IS NOT NULL THEN 1
        END AS TitleNum,
        COUNT_BIG(*) AS TitleStatistics
   FROM dbo.MyContacts
GROUP BY CASE
          WHEN Title IS NULL THEN 0
          WHEN Title IS NOT NULL THEN 1
          END;
GO
```

2. Index the view by using the CREATE UNIQUE CLUSTERED INDEX statement:

```
CREATE UNIQUE CLUSTERED INDEX TitleStats_TitleNum
    ON dbo.TitleStats(TitleNum);
GO
```

3. Test your indexed view. If you are using SQL Server 2005 Enterprise edition, Enterprise Evaluation edition, or Developer edition, you can execute the same query you used in Exercise 1, and SQL Server should use the view. You should get a *Clustered Index Scan* operator operating on the view, even though the query references the base table. If you do not have any of the editions mentioned, you can still reference the view in your queries directly and thus make queries more effective.

Quick Check

1. You have a query that groups data. Groups are based on a very selective column, which means you get nearly as many groups as there are base rows. Would this query benefit from an indexed view?

2. You have a view that joins customers, orders, and order details base tables. Based on this view, you create another view that aggregates order details amounts per customer. Can you index the second view, the one that aggregates data?

Quick Check Answers

1. No, a query such as this would not benefit much from an indexed view.

2. No, a view has to reference base tables only if you want to index it.

Lesson 4: Partitioning a Table

Estimated lesson time: 20 minutes

In your application, you might need to access a huge table. The data in the table is likely to be used in many different ways. For example, you might need to insert single rows as well as do some bulk inserts. To achieve minimally logged bulk insert, your table should have no rows or indexes, and you should use the Bulk_Logged or Simple recovery model for the database. Unfortunately, most of the tables already have data and indexes. However, there might be logic in your business application that partitions the data in the table horizontally.

In SQL Server 2000 and earlier versions, you can create multiple tables and then refer to the complete data through a view that unites rows from all base tables. This is called a *partitioned view*. If the base tables are located in multiple instances of SQL Server, even on multiple boxes, this would be a *distributed partitioned view*. In SQL Server 2005, you can still perform partitioning this way. However, SQL Server 2005 introduces a new feature called *table partitioning*. With table partitioning, you can have multiple physical partitions of a single table, stored on multiple filegroups of the same database. In the application, you refer to the table as if it were not partitioned because you refer to it by its logical name.

IMPORTANT **Partitioned views deprecated**

Because of table partitioning, partitioned views in a single database are deprecated.

Understanding Table Partitioning

To implement table partitioning, you have to prepare a couple of new objects in advance. Namely, you have to prepare a *partition function* and a *partition scheme*. A partition function serves as a guideline for the rows; it defines how the rows are mapped to partitions based on the values of partitioning columns. A partition scheme maps each partition specified by the partition function to a filegroup.

The partitioning column determines how a table is partitioned. The *partition* function separates data in ranges of values of the partitioned column. In SQL Server 2005, you can have up to 1,000 partitions per table. You do not have to have a filegroup for each partition; through a partition scheme, you can map multiple or even all partitions to a single filegroup.

Table partitioning is especially useful for sliding-windows scenarios, which are very common for data warehouses. For example, you might need to bulk load new data by the end of each month and then delete or move to the archive the oldest month's data. You can switch partitions from one table to another table if certain conditions are met. You can bulk insert new data to an empty table, turn on minimally logged bulk insert, and then switch the data of this table to a single partition of the partitioned table by using the ALTER TABLE statement. Similarly, you can switch the oldest partition of the partitioned table to an empty table and then use the *TRUNCATE TABLE* command to clear the old data efficiently.

Table partitioning can also improve join performance in some scenarios. If you have an equi-join between two partitioned tables, their partitioning columns are the same as the columns on which you perform the join, and the tables use the same partition function, then the query optimizer can perform the join between the partitions themselves.

Using Aligned Indexes

If you do not specify a separate partition scheme when you create an index on a partitioned table, SQL Server automatically partitions the index by using the same partition scheme and partitioning column you used for the table partitioning. Such an index is called an *aligned* index. Aligning indexes are especially useful in sliding-windows scenarios. With aligned indexes, switching partitions is only a metadata operation. In addition, you can support joins efficiently between partitions of two collocated partition tables with aligned indexes.

You can design index partitioning independently of table partitioning so the indexes are not aligned. This strategy could be useful if the base table is not partitioned, or your table participates in collocated joins with multiple tables. When you partition a unique index, you must have the partitioning column among the columns used in the index key.

Exam Tip   Opt for aligned indexes unless you have a good reason for a different decision.

Switching Partitions

Switching partitions is a very efficient operation for moving blocks of data. However, you must meet the following prerequisites:

- **General requirements**   If you are adding a table as a partition to an existing partitioned table or moving a partition from one partitioned table to another, you must create the receiving partition in advance, and it must be empty. If you are reassigning a partition to form one nonpartitioned table, you must create the table in advance that is receiving the partition, and it must be empty. If you want to switch a partition from one table to another, you have to partition both tables on the same column.
- **Structure requirements**   In short, both the source and the target table of the partition switching must have the same structure.
- **Constraint requirements**   You have to take care that you switch the data in a single partition of the target table. For example, if you are adding a nonpartitioned table as a partition to an existing partitioned table, you must have a *Check* constraint defined on the column of the source table that corresponds to the partition key of the target table. The *Check* constraints must ensure that all the data from the source table fits into a single partition of the destination table.

■ **Index requirements**   Indexes on both source and destination tables have to be aligned with the tables.

Practice: Partitioning a Table

IMPORTANT   Practices build upon each other

To work successfully with this practice, you should have finished the practice from Lesson 3, "Specifying Indexed Views."

In this practice, you will implement table partitioning on the dbo.MyContacts table that you created in Exercise 1 of the Lesson 2 practice "Designing Indexes." You will create two additional tables with the same schema and then switch partitions between the original and these two new tables.

▶ **Exercise 1: Prepare the Infrastructure**

First, you have to create a partition function, a partition scheme, and two new tables.

1. Prepare a partition function that will partition a table based on the ContactId integer column. The function should split the data into three partitions: ContactId <= 10,000; ContactId > 10,000 and <= 20,000; and ContactId > 20,000. Note the special syntax for the partition function. Your code should look like this:

    ```
    USE TK441Ch04;
    GO
    CREATE PARTITION FUNCTION pf_ContactId (int)
    AS RANGE RIGHT
    FOR VALUES (10000, 20000);
    GO
    ```

2. Prepare a partition scheme that will map all partitions to a single, Primary filegroup. Your code should look like this:

    ```
    CREATE PARTITION SCHEME ps_ContactId
    AS PARTITION pf_ContactId
    ALL TO ([PRIMARY]);
    GO
    ```

3. Create two tables, one for old contacts and one for new contacts. Make sure you have a *Check* constraint in the table for the new contacts that ensures that all of the data for this table can be mapped to the last partition of the original contacts table. Insert a row in the new contacts table. Your code should look like this:

    ```
    CREATE TABLE dbo.OldContacts
    (ContactId int NOT NULL,
     Title nvarchar(16) NULL,
     FirstName nvarchar(100) NOT NULL,
     LastName nvarchar(100) NOT NULL,
     Suffix nvarchar(200) NULL,
    ```

```
 EmailAddress nvarchar(100) NULL,
 Phone nvarchar(50) NULL);
GO
CREATE TABLE dbo.NewContacts
(ContactId int NOT NULL CHECK (ContactId > 20000),
 Title nvarchar(16) NULL,
 FirstName nvarchar(100) NOT NULL,
 LastName nvarchar(100) NOT NULL,
 Suffix nvarchar(200) NULL,
 EmailAddress nvarchar(100) NULL,
 Phone nvarchar(50) NULL);
GO
INSERT INTO dbo.NewContacts
(ContactId, Title,
 FirstName, LastName,
 Suffix, EmailAddress,
 Phone)
VALUES
(20001, 'Mr',
 'Janko', 'Cajhen',
 NULL, 'janko@tailspintoys.com',
 '398-555-0132' );
GO
```

▶ **Exercise 2: Re-Create and Partition the Original Table and Switch Partitions**

Now you will re-create and partition the original contacts table. Then, you will switch a partition from this table to the old contacts table and switch the data from the new contacts table in a partition of the original table. Note that you will have to drop the schema-bound indexed view from the previous exercise first.

1. Drop the indexed view you created in Exercise 2 of the Lesson 3 practice "Specifying Indexed Views." Re-create the dbo.MyContacts table. Create it on the partitioning scheme you created in the previous exercise. Insert the data:

```
DROP VIEW dbo.TitleStats;
GO
DROP TABLE dbo.MyContacts;
GO
CREATE TABLE dbo.MyContacts
(ContactId int NOT NULL,
 Title nvarchar(16) NULL,
 FirstName nvarchar(100) NOT NULL,
 LastName nvarchar(100) NOT NULL,
 Suffix nvarchar(200) NULL,
 EmailAddress nvarchar(100) NULL,
 Phone nvarchar(50) NULL)
ON ps_ContactId(ContactId);
GO
INSERT INTO dbo.MyContacts
SELECT ContactId, Title,
       FirstName, LastName,
       Suffix, EmailAddress,
```

```
        Phone
   FROM AdventureWorks.Person.Contact;
GO
```

2. Check how the data is partitioned by using the *$PARTITION* function:

```
SELECT ContactId,
       $PARTITION.pf_ContactId(ContactId) AS PartitionNo
  FROM dbo.MyContacts
ORDER BY ContactId;
GO
```

3. Switch the first partition to the old contacts table:

```
ALTER TABLE dbo.MyContacts SWITCH PARTITION 1 TO dbo.OldContacts;
GO
```

4. Switch the data from the new contacts table to the third partition of the partitioned contacts table:

```
ALTER TABLE dbo.NewContacts SWITCH TO dbo.MyContacts PARTITION 3
GO
```

5. Recheck the partitions of the partitioned table, the data in the new contacts table, and the data in the old contacts table:

```
SELECT ContactId,
       $PARTITION.pf_ContactId(ContactId) AS PartitionNo
  FROM dbo.MyContacts
ORDER BY ContactId;
SELECT ContactId
  FROM dbo.OldContacts;
SELECT ContactId
  FROM dbo.NewContacts;
GO
```

6. Clean up your SQL Server installation:

```
USE master;
DROP DATABASE TK441Ch04;
GO
```

Quick Check

1. Why do you need a *Check* constraint on a nonpartitioned table if you want to switch the data from this table to a partition of a partitioned table?
2. Can you use table partitioning across instances of SQL Server?

Quick Check Answers

1. A *Check* constraint guarantees that all data from the nonpartitioned table fits into a single partition of the partitioned table.
2. No, you can partition a table in one database of one instance of SQL Server only.

Case Scenario: Design a Database for Performance

Users of the Tailspin Toys database complain that their regular reports, which aggregate sales data based on EmployeeId, perform too slowly. You are using SQL Server 2005 Enterprise edition. However, you cannot change the legacy application to redirect the aggregate queries to an aggregate table. In addition, your end users do not understand why the query that retrieves employee details (that is, EmployeeId, EmployeeName, and social security ID [SSID] columns from the Employees table) performs so poorly. You research the indexes and discover that you have a clustered Primary Key on the EmployeeId column and a nonclustered index on the EmployeeName column.

1.   How can you improve the performance of the aggregate query?
2.   How can you improve the performance of the employee-details query?

Chapter Summary

■   Indexes are the most efficient database tool for improving performance.
■   For poorly written queries, indexes do not help.
■   Take special care when you choose the key of a clustered index.
■   You can cover more queries with included columns in nonclustered indexes.
■   Indexed views can improve performance of aggregate queries and of queries that use multiple joins.
■   For large tables, consider partitioning.

Chapter 5

Using Appropriate Database Technologies and Techniques for Your Application

The relational model is appropriate for business applications because it enforces data integrity. This enforcement comes through data types, the database schema, constraints, and programmatic code. However, constraints have a drawback as well—they constrain. That is their purpose. Sometimes, however, you need a bit more relaxed schema. This chapter begins its coverage of using appropriate database technologies and techniques for your application needs by showing you how to use XML inside a database properly and efficiently. This chapter also discusses when to use common language runtime (CLR) languages inside a database and when Transact-SQL (T-SQL) code is more appropriate.

In addition, you never know how large your database is going to grow, so you need to design for scalability. Scalability can act as a synonym for performance in the database world, so this training kit discusses it throughout. In this chapter, you will get a general overview of scalability with some small concrete examples. Another consideration when deciding which technologies and techniques are appropriate for your application solution is how your database is going to communicate with the outer world. There are many techniques for interoperability, including distributed queries, replication, and Microsoft SQL Server Integration Services (SSIS). In this chapter, you will get an overview of different interoperability methods, and you will focus on query notifications in the related practice. Finally, this chapter reviews different aggregation techniques.

Exam objectives in this chapter:

- Design an application solution that uses appropriate database technologies and techniques:
    - Design a solution for storage of XML data in the database.
    - Choose appropriate languages.
    - Design a solution for scalability.
    - Design interoperability with external systems.
    - Develop aggregation strategies.

Before You Begin

To complete the lessons in this chapter, you must have:

- Knowledge of Microsoft SQL Server database objects.
- Knowledge of the Transact-SQL language.
- The SQL Server 2005 *AdventureWorks* and *AdventureWorksDW* sample databases installed. Sample databases are available with SQL Server 2005 Enterprise edition but are not a part of the default installation. Alternatively, you can install sample databases from *http://msdn2.microsoft.com/en-us/library/ms143739.aspx*.
- Microsoft Office 2007 data connectivity components installed. If you do not have Office 2007, you can download Office 2007 data connectivity components from *http://www.microsoft.com/downloads/details.aspx?familyid=7554F536-8C28-4598-9B72-EF94E038C891&displaylang=en/*.

Lesson 1: Using XML Data in Databases

Estimated lesson time: 30 minutes

XML technology is incredibly popular among developers. Some database developers and administrators have concerns about the widespread use of XML, but many application developers complain that the relational model is constraining, so they prefer the open possibilities they have with XML. It is true that the relational model constrains. Nevertheless, this constraining has its purpose: it enforces data integrity, which is crucial for databases, especially if you are talking about databases that support online transactional processing (OLTP) business applications. This database, the OLTP database, is where the data is collected in the enterprise. If the data is not correct at this point, no application or business intelligence (BI) system can help you. Relational databases are the heart of modern IT systems. You can implement some constraints, such as schema validation, for XML as well; however, constraints enforced in a relational database can be more complex and are usually easier to implement. As in a relational database management system (RDBMS), the constraints are typically more ready to implement. Therefore, the concerns about XML technologies are reasonable.

Be aware of potential data integrity problems; opt to use XML in your database deliberately. Whenever you need constraints to enforce business rules, the relational schema is the answer. However, one big problem with the relational schema is the evolution of the schema. Typically, a schema change is quite expensive, even meaning, often, having to upgrade an application. If the schema is changing frequently, a slightly more relaxed model, such as the XML model, combined with or in the relational model, can be the correct answer. However, do not forget that often when it seems the schema is constantly changing, it simply means that the problem analysis was not done correctly at design time. You can find a plethora of examples of inappropriate use of XML in relational databases. For example, you can find instances in which customers have a relational table, and their orders are stored in an XML column in the Customers table. However, the schema of the orders is very well known (you can even define design patterns for sales documents), and the constraints are very important because you are dealing with money here!

XML Data Type Usage

You just looked at the customers–orders example of when using XML is not appropriate. Imagine now a different example. Suppose you have to support a retail store with tens, if not hundreds of thousands, of different products on shelves. You can group these products in categories. All products have some common attributes such as product ID, name, unit of measure, and price. However, some attributes change from group to group. For example, for fruit juices, you should store the percentage of Recommended Daily Allowance (RDA) of vitamins. For mobile phones, you are interested in whether customers have a digital camera. If you had to worry about only those two categories, you could simply model subtypes. However, you can have tens of categories, and you might need to add a new category at any time. Using subtypes, you would quickly reach a very complex model, which would be hard to maintain. Many applications like to use a special Entity-Attribute-Value (EAV) table approach in situations such as this. However, the EAV approach has a big disadvantage: it can be quite complex to implement even simple constraints, such as attaching a correct attribute to the right article, without using triggers. You could end up storing in your database a predicate such as, "My orange juice has a digital camera." Another solution might be using a CLR user-defined type (UDT) for storing a collection of category attributes. However, this would not be a standard solution, and, depending on your UDT, it might get quite complex to retrieve separate scalar values from it. In short, this situation is a good candidate for using the *XML* data type. With the *XML* data type, new in SQL Server 2005, you get a reasonable compromise for all your goals:

- You get a quite open and dynamic schema.
- You have a standard solution. (XML is standard.)
- You can implement simple constraints, such as schema validation, without using programmatic code.

There are some other viable options for storing XML inside a database. These options include sparse data, hierarchical data, and data with inherent order. In addition, if you already have XML data stored in files in the file system, you could benefit from automatic validation by storing this data in SQL Server. SQL Server 2005 also supports XML indexes, so browsing your XML data could be faster in SQL Server than in the file system.

You might also decide to shred your XML data in relational tables by using scalar columns. Consider shredding your XML data if you need constraints that you cannot implement in an XML schema. Also, shred your XML data if you plan to reuse it for analysis. Standard BI systems, including reporting and online analytical processing (OLAP) systems, typically cannot perform analyses on XML data directly. Finally, you might want to persist your application objects by using XML instead of binary serialization, thus gaining the ability to query the objects by using a standard language (XQuery) without having to de-serialize them first.

XML Indexes

The *XML* data type is a binary large object (BLOB), meaning it can store up to 2 gigabytes (GB) of data. In most cases, your XML values should be small to keep up the performance of your database. For large XML values, you might consider using XML indexes. XML indexes can be especially useful if you query your XML data with XQuery often, and you are retrieving only small parts from large XML values. As with any other indexes, consider the price of maintaining XML indexes as you consider your design strategy.

The first index you create on an XML column is the *Primary* XML index. The Primary XML index indexes all tags, values, and paths for the XML instances of an XML column. For you to be able to create this index, your base table must have a clustered primary key. After you have the Primary XML index, you can add three types of secondary XML indexes: *Path*, *Property*, and *Value*. If your queries typically search for a path in your XML instances, the Path secondary XML index might be a good option. The *exist() XML* data type method, for example, uses path expressions. The Property XML index clusters paths within XML instances, so it is appropriate for scenarios in which you search for multiple values from your XML instances. If you are commonly searching for values in your XML instances without knowing the element or attribute names that contain those values, consider using a Value secondary XML index. Finally, you can use full-text indexes on XML columns as well. However, full-text indexes do not know anything about XML semantics, so it is probably more efficient to use XML indexes instead.

Exam Tip   For XML data type columns, you need to have a valid, considered reason to use full-text indexes rather than XML indexes.

Practice: Using XML Data in a Database

In this practice, you will learn how to use the *XML* data type to build a dynamic database schema.

On the Companion Disc   This chapter includes many code examples. You will find all the code from this chapter on the companion CD in the C:\My Documents\Microsoft Press\TK70-441 \Chapter05\Sql folder.

▶ **Exercise 1: Prepare the XML Schema Collection**

1. Start by creating a new database for practices in this chapter:

```
USE master;
GO
IF DB_ID(N'TK441Ch05') IS NULL
    CREATE DATABASE TK441Ch05;
GO
```

2. Your task in this practice is to create an XML schema collection of simple schemas for mobile phones and fruit juices, with each schema allowing a single element only. (The HasCamera bit flag for mobile phones and the RDA integer for fruit juices.) You do not have to type XSD documents manually; you can help yourself with the new FOR XML. XMLSCHEMA('target namespace URI') option. Therefore, you can create empty tables and use SELECT . . . FOR XML to get the schema you need. Just as you can create an XML schema collection from a variable, you can store results from your SELECT . . . FOR XML statements in a variable and create a schema collection from the variable. Finally, drop the auxiliary tables. Your code should look like this:

```
USE TK441Ch05;
GO
-- Auxiliary tables:
CREATE TABLE dbo.MobilePhones
(HasCamera bit NOT NULL);
GO
CREATE TABLE dbo.FruitJuices
(RDA int NOT NULL);
GO
-- Create the schema collection.
-- Store the schemas in a variable and create the collection.
-- Note the XMLSCHEMA('target namespace') part.
DECLARE @mySchema nvarchar(max);
SET @mySchema = N'';
SET @mySchema = @mySchema +
 (SELECT *
    FROM dbo.MobilePhones
  FOR XML AUTO, ELEMENTS, XMLSCHEMA('MobilePhones'));
SET @mySchema = @mySchema +
 (SELECT *
    FROM dbo.FruitJuices
  FOR XML AUTO, ELEMENTS, XMLSCHEMA('FruitJuices'));
SELECT CAST(@mySchema AS xml);
CREATE XML SCHEMA COLLECTION ProductCategories AS @mySchema;
GO
-- Clean up the auxiliary tables.
DROP TABLE dbo.MobilePhones;
DROP TABLE dbo.FruitJuices;
GO
```

3. Check your schema collection by querying the sys.xml_schema_collections, sys.xml_schema_namespaces, and sys.xml_schema_components catalog views:

```
-- Retrieve information about the schema collection.
SELECT * FROM sys.xml_schema_collections
 WHERE name = 'ProductCategories';
-- Retrieve information about the namespaces in the schema collection.
SELECT n.*
  FROM sys.xml_schema_namespaces n
       INNER JOIN sys.xml_schema_collections c
         ON n.xml_collection_id = c.xml_collection_id
WHERE c.name = 'ProductCategories';
-- Retrieve information about the components in the schema collection.
SELECT cp.*
  FROM sys.xml_schema_components cp
       INNER JOIN sys.xml_schema_collections c
         ON cp.xml_collection_id = c.xml_collection_id
 WHERE c.name = 'ProductCategories';
GO
```

► **Exercise 2: Validate the XML Schema Collection**

1. Now that you have your schema collection, you need to create the Products table with *ProductId (int)*, *ProductName (nvarchar)*, *Category (nvarchar)*, and *DynamicAttributes (xml)* attributes. Verify that *Category* can accept the values *MobilePhones* and *FruitJuices* only and that the DynamicAttributes XML column is validated against the *Product-Categories* schema collection. The code should look like this:

```
CREATE TABLE dbo.Products
(ProductId int NOT NULL IDENTITY PRIMARY KEY,
 ProductName nvarchar(30) NOT NULL,
 Category nvarchar(30) NOT NULL
   CHECK(Category = N'MobilePhones' OR
         Category = N'FruitJuices'),
 DynamicAttributes xml(ProductCategories));
GO
```

2. You are not finished with your constraints yet. You need to ensure that you have the corresponding XML for each product category. SQL Server lets you insert XML data as long as it complies with any of the schemas in the schema collection. You need an additional *Check* constraint that checks whether you have the correct namespace in your XML, the namespace that belongs to the specific category. You can check the namespace by using the *value()* method of the *XML* data type; however, you cannot use *XML* data type methods in *Check* constraints. Therefore, you have to create a user-defined function (UDF) to retrieve the namespace first. Your code should look like this:

```
-- Function to retrieve the namespace.
CREATE FUNCTION dbo.ChkNamespace(@chkcol xml)
 RETURNS nvarchar(1000)
AS
BEGIN
 RETURN @chkcol.value('namespace-uri((/*)[1])','nvarchar(1000)')
END;
GO
-- Add the constraint.
ALTER TABLE dbo.Products ADD CONSTRAINT ck_Namespace
 CHECK (dbo.ChkNamespace(DynamicAttributes) = Category);
GO
```

3. Finally, test your solution by trying to insert a valid mobile phone, fruit juice, and one or more invalid rows:

```
-- Valid mobile phone
INSERT INTO dbo.Products
 (ProductName, Category, DynamicAttributes)
VALUES (N'Mobile phone 1', N'MobilePhones',
        N'<dbo.MobilePhones xmlns="MobilePhones">
           <HasCamera>1</HasCamera>
          </dbo.MobilePhones>');
-- Valid fruit juice
INSERT INTO dbo.Products
 (ProductName, Category, DynamicAttributes)
```

```
          VALUES (N'Orange juice', N'FruitJuices',
                 N'<dbo.FruitJuices xmlns="FruitJuices">
                     <RDA>50</RDA>
                     </dbo.FruitJuices>');
          -- Invalid insert - RDA for a mobile phone
          INSERT INTO dbo.Products
           (ProductName, Category, DynamicAttributes)
          VALUES (N'Mobile phone 1', N'MobilePhones',
                 N'<dbo.MobilePhones xmlns="MobilePhones">
                     <RDA>25</RDA>
                     </dbo.MobilePhones>');
          GO
          -- Check the data.
          SELECT *
            FROM dbo.Products;
          GO
```

Quick Check

1. Would you use the *XML* data type to store invoice details in your Invoices table?
2. You are using the *exist()* XML data type method in a WHERE clause for a single XML data type column in a table; however, you use the method in multiple SELECT statements. How can you improve the performance of those queries?

Quick Check Answers

1. This is a classic example of inappropriate use of the *XML* data type. Invoice details have a well-known structure that does not change much. Because you are dealing with money, take care to implement constraints strictly. In addition, invoice details are usually the starting point for sales analysis.
2. You have to create a Primary XML index and secondary for Path XML index on your XML data type column.

Lesson 2: Choosing Languages

Estimated lesson time: 15 minutes

In SQL Server 2005, you are not limited to using the T-SQL language only, as you are with earlier versions of the database system. Now in your database, you can use CLR languages, COM languages, the C family of languages, XQuery, and, through the *OPENQUERY* and *OPEN-ROWSET* functions, any other language that your remote OLE DB source supports. The decision about which language to use for your particular application scenario is not very complicated. Nevertheless, a wrong decision could lead to poor performance and security problems. In this lesson, you will learn the key guidelines about which language to use in which situation.

CLR vs. T-SQL

Remember: T-SQL is the primary language of SQL Server. CLR code cannot replace T-SQL code; CLR can only supplement it. T-SQL is still the only language for data manipulation. Even in CLR procedures, if you read or write data, you must do it with standard T-SQL data-modification language (DML) commands. To build solid applications, learn T-SQL fluently and use its set-oriented techniques to manipulate the data. For example, compared to T-SQL cursors, CLR code that moves row by row through a *DataReader* object might be a couple of times faster. However, if you can rewrite your cursor into a set-oriented command, this command will likely perform a hundred times better. Thus, the vast majority of code in your database should be T-SQL code.

That said, CLR code performs better for CPU-intensive operations such as string manipulations and intensive calculations. Therefore, it might be more appropriate for scalar UDFs. In addition, you can create in CLR two types of objects that you cannot create in T-SQL: user-defined aggregate functions and UDTs. CLR code also is not limited to SQL Server. By using CLR code, you can access other resources such as file system, registry, and network resources. However, consider security issues when your assemblies are not marked with the SAFE permission set, which allows database access only.

> **IMPORTANT** Set operations
>
> Row-by-row operations typically perform better in the CLR than in T-SQL code; however, if you manage to change the code to a set-based operation, T-SQL code performs magnitudes better.

T-SQL has another limitation in that you cannot consume Web services and query notifications from T-SQL. You might think that these tasks would be another reason to introduce CLR code in your database. First, however, think twice about why you want to consume Web services and query notifications in your database. These tasks are typically for middle-tier code.

Remember that your stored procedures should not be very complex and should deal mostly with data manipulation; your middle-tier code should deal with business logic such as workflow logic.

CLR and T-SQL vs. Other Languages

To browse XML in your database, you can use XQuery inside T-SQL statements. This is an additional language to learn. However, in some cases, you might be able to use CLR code instead of XQuery. If you are already familiar with CLR languages such as Microsoft Visual Basic .NET or C# .NET, you might consider using the ADO.NET *DataSet* object to handle your XML data type columns. The *DataSet* is represented in XML, and the transition from XML to tabular representation of the same data is seamless in CLR code. Reading XML data from a CLR database table-valued UDF that uses a T-SQL SELECT statement to retrieve the data and then return it in tabular format is far less efficient than simply using a SELECT statement with embedded XQuery directly on the data. Still, if performance is not an issue, you are familiar with CLR languages, and you have to do something quickly and do not have time to learn XQuery, this might be an option.

Another language you can use in your database is Component Object Model (COM). You can use *OLE Automation* objects in your database with the help of OLE automation procedures (sp_OA* procedures). For example, with the sp_OACreate system procedure, you can instantiate a COM object. However, this is not a good choice; COM code is not managed code. You need sysadmin permissions to instantiate an *OLE Automation* object. In addition, *OLE Automation* procedures are disabled in SQL Server 2005 by default. You can use the Surface Area Configuration tool to enable them. Nevertheless, if you are using *OLE Automation* procedures, consider replacing those components with managed-code CLR procedures immediately.

You can also extend the functionality of SQL Server through extended stored procedures. The Microsoft Extended Stored Procedure application programming interface (API) gives you a server-based interface that consists of C and C++ functions and macros used to build applications. Like the code of *OLE Automation* objects, the code of extended procedures is not managed. For example, extended procedures compete for the same memory space with SQL Server. Therefore, extended procedures are quite dangerous, so consider replacing them with CLR procedures immediately.

IMPORTANT   Extended stored procedures deprecated

Extended stored procedures are deprecated and will be removed in future versions of SQL Server.

You probably already know that, through the *OPENQUERY* and *OPENROWSET* functions, you can reach any OLE DB data source. You can use these functions in your T-SQL code. However, you should take care that you use them to retrieve only a rowset (that is, a tabular, two-dimensional form of the result). For example, SQL Server Analysis Services Unified Dimensional Model (UDM) cubes use the Multidimensional Expressions (MDX) language, and MDX can return multiple dimensions in the result. Thus, make sure you return two dimensions from the MDX statements that you use as parameters to the *OPENQUERY* and *OPENROWSET* functions. Analysis Services also uses the Data Mining Extensions (DMX) language for browsing data mining models. The DMX SELECT statement returns a table; however, this table can have one or more nested tables. Nested tables are not allowed in the relational model and are not supported within T-SQL. Instead, you can use the *DMX FLAT-TENED* keyword to return a relational table. To repeat: if you are accessing an external OLE DB source, take care to return data in relational format. As a final note, ad hoc distributed queries via the *OPENROWSET*, and *OPENDATASOURCE* functions are disabled in SQL Server 2005 by default.

Practice: Choosing Appropriate Languages

In this conceptual practice, select the appropriate language for specific tasks.

▶ **Exercise: Choose Appropriate Languages**

In the SQL Server 2005 Books Online topic, "CLR Stored Procedures," at *http://msdn2.microsoft.com/en-us/library/ms131094(SQL.90).aspx*, you will find the following CLR procedure example:

```
using System;
using System.Data.SqlTypes;
using System.Data.SqlClient;
using Microsoft.SqlServer.Server;

public class StoredProcedures
{
    [Microsoft.SqlServer.Server.SqlProcedure]
    public static void PriceSum(out SqlInt32 value)
    {
        using(SqlConnection connection =
            new SqlConnection("context connection=true"))
        {
            value = 0;
            connection.Open();
            SqlCommand command = new SqlCommand(
                "SELECT Price FROM Products", connection);
            SqlDataReader reader = command.ExecuteReader();

            using (reader)
            {
                while( reader.Read() )
                {
                    value += reader.GetSqlInt32(0);
                }
            }
        }
```

```
      }
    }
  }
```

If you are not familiar with C#, you can also find a Visual Basic example of the procedure in Books Online in the same topic, "CLR Stored Procedures," at *http://msdn2.microsoft.com/en-us/library/ms131094(SQL.90).aspx*. However, the code is quite simple, so you should be able to recognize the purpose of this procedure even if you are not familiar with CLR languages. Do you see any problems with this example?

Suggested Answer

This is an example of improper use of a CLR procedure. Why would you read the data and summarize the price by looping through a *DataReader* if you can do it directly by using a T-SQL SELECT statement with the *SUM* aggregate function? In addition, the SELECT statement inside the CLR procedure is referring to a table by a single-part name only, which is a bad practice. Finally, what business meaning does summing prices have? This example shows you how careful you have to be if you want to create solid applications. Note that the purpose of this example in Books Online is to show how to return output parameters from CLR procedures; it is not intended to show any kind of best practices.

Quick Check

1. You need to implement an aggregate function to perform a calculation in your database. Which language strategy would you use?
   A. XQuery
   B. CLR integration
   C. T-SQL UDF
   D. Extended procedure
2. In a T-SQL SELECT statement, you want to use the *OPENQUERY* function to browse data from the Analysis Services UDM cube. What issues should you consider for such a query?

Quick Check Answers

1. The correct answer is B. With T-SQL and XQuery, you cannot create user-defined aggregate functions. You could create an extended procedure to calculate the kurtosis; however, extended procedures are dangerous and deprecated. Therefore, you should use CLR integration.
2. For querying an AS UDM cube, you have to use MDX language; you have to use an MDX query inside your T-SQL query as a parameter for the *OPENQUERY* T-SQL function. Your MDX query has to return two dimensions only.

Lesson 3: Designing for Scalability

Estimated lesson time: 30 minutes

Scalability is a very broad term. Nearly everything you do has some impact on scalability. In short, scalability in the IT world means how well your solution can adapt to increased demands. Many times, scalability essentially means performance, although performance is not the only factor that affects the scalability of a system. Your solution should also be able to survive business changes, so a scalable system would include change-management procedures as well. This lesson focuses on designing for scalability from the SQL Server point of view. You will get an overview of technologies and methodologies for scaling up (that is, scaling a single SQL Server instance) and for scaling out (that is, scaling to additional SQL Server instances and other services shipped with SQL Server). In addition, because aggregations are an important point of scalability, you will learn guidelines for aggregation strategies.

Scaling Up

You begin scaling up by fortifying your hardware. SQL Server, depending on edition, can use any hardware you can afford. Commonly, you start strengthening your hardware by adding memory. You can also benefit from multiple CPUs, the appropriate redundant array of independent disks (RAID) configuration, and the proper operating system. For example, if you plan to use more than 16 GB of RAM, consider using the 64-bit edition of Microsoft Windows Server 2003.

One of the most important features of SQL Server is that it can grow with your needs through different editions. This means that when your business sees increased demand, you might be able to fulfill those demands by upgrading your current edition of SQL Server to a more scalable one. Table 5-1 summarizes the various SQL Server 2005 editions, describing their intended use.

Table 5-1 SQL Server 2005 Editions

Edition	Description
Express Edition	SQL Server Express Edition replaces Microsoft SQL Server Desktop Engine 2000 (MSDE). This edition is free for download, use, distribution, and embedding in applications. It is an easy-to-use, lightweight, and embeddable version of SQL Server. This edition is suitable for embedding with applications. You can download it from *http://www.microsoft.com/downloads/details.aspx?FamilyID= 220549b5-0b07-4448-8848-dcc397514b41&DisplayLang=en.*

Table 5-1   SQL Server 2005 Editions

Edition	Description
Express Edition with Advanced Services	Another free edition, this version of Express Edition includes Full-Text Search and Reporting Services. It is especially useful as a stan-dalone (not embedded) database management system for small busi-ness. You can download it from *http://www.microsoft.com/downloads/details.aspx?FamilyID=4c6ba9fd-319a-4887-bc75-3b02b5e48a40&DisplayLang=en.*
Workgroup Edition	SQL Server Workgroup Edition has no limits on database size or on concurrent user access. This edition is suitable for branch offices, Web servers, and smaller companies.
Standard Edition	SQL Server Standard Edition is probably the most widespread edi-tion. It is suitable for small, medium, and in particular cases, even enterprise-level business. It has integrated business intelligence and high-availability features. Standard Edition is also available on 64-bit platforms.
Enterprise Edition	SQL Server Enterprise Edition offers the highest level of perfor-mance and high availability features for transactional and BI applica-tions. It is suitable for companies of any size, especially for large enterprises. Similar to Standard Edition, if a 32-bit platform is not enough for your needs, you can obtain a 64-bit Enterprise Edition.
Compact Edition	SQL Server Compact Edition replaces SQL Server 2000 Mobile Edi-tion. This edition works on Microsoft Windows platforms for tablet PCs, mobile phones, pocket PCs, and desktops. It is free and intended for use with mobile applications.
Developer Edition	SQL Server Developer Edition includes the full set of features, just like Enterprise Edition. However, you can license it for development, test, and demo purposes only.

Database Design for Scalability

Neither hardware nor editions of SQL Server 2005 can help you if you select a poor database and application architecture. For OLTP applications, you should pursue as normalized a data-base design as possible, with few exceptions of denormalized aggregate data (for example, for levels and states). Poor logical design leads to poor performance and, thus, to poor scalability. For analytical applications, consider creating special analytical databases very early in the design process. You should also plan database indexes from the beginning. However, make checking your index schema a regular maintenance task in production. You can always drop, modify, or add indexes based on your data usage. SQL Server Profiler is the tool that helps you trace and analyze your workload, and Database Tuning Advisor helps you select appropriate indexes. For large tables, consider using table partitioning, which is especially useful with aligned indexes.

Physically, you can spread a database across multiple filegroups on multiple disk drives. Consider using filegroups for reducing the time you need for maintaining your database. You can store current, highly updateable data that needs frequent integrity checks and backups on a small filegroup and archive stale data that needs less maintenance on one or more filegroups. This way, you work with your frequent maintenance tasks on smaller subsets of your data. This strategy—using filegroups for administrative purposes—works well with large table partitioning. Through your partitioning scheme, you can move stale data onto partitions on archive filegroups. In addition, you can also use multiple filegroups to improve query performance. You can place a table on one filegroup on one disk and an index for that table on another filegroup on another disk to achieve better parallelism. However, for query performance reasons, consider using hardware RAID. SQL Server 2005 can perform parallel reads even on a single filegroup.

When designing for scalability, you also need to take special care when you decide to use CLR code in your database. If you build a performance problem into your user-defined type, for example, there's no technique for solving the problem. However, CLR code can speed up CPU-intensive operations, comparable to T-SQL code.

If you notice locking contention between read and update commands in your growing system, consider using snapshot isolation levels—either SNAPSHOT or READ_COMMITTED _SNAPSHOT isolation. When you use snapshot isolation levels, readers do not block writers because readers read the old version of the rows. Nevertheless, snapshot isolation levels are not a general solution because they also come with a price. SQL Server maintains old versions of rows in the *tempdb* system database, so you need to make sure you prevent *tempdb* from becoming a bottleneck.

To help reduce locking contention, you can also use Database Snapshots for some of your querying. As always, this technique has its price as well. SQL Server has to copy pages from the production database to the snapshot database before it writes the first time after the snapshot creation to a page in the production database. This could hurt the performance of updates. In addition, data in snapshots can become obsolete quickly.

Scaling Application Queries

From the database point of view, the most important part of the application design is queries that an application sends to the database management system. No index can help if your application sends a query such as SELECT * FROM table. For a query like this, SQL Server always performs a table scan. Your queries should follow at least this short list of best practices:

■ Always include a WHERE clause in your queries. Query optimization starts with the WHERE clause. Never return more rows than your end user actually needs.

- Always use an explicit column list; do not use SELECT * queries. With an explicit column list, the query has a better possibility of being covered with an index. In addition, such a query is less prone to errors.
- Always refer to an object by its two-part name. This way, you prevent ambiguity with schema name resolution and, thus, speed up the query.

Consider this list as a minimal (not exhaustive) set of best practices. In addition, consider using stored procedures as much as possible. If written correctly, stored procedures are the fastest way of working with SQL Server.

You can also scale performance when you import data from text files, which is common for data you collect automatically. For such imports, try to use minimally logged bulk insert instead of single-row INSERT statements. Besides using a recovery model other than Full for your database, to achieve minimally logged bulk insert, you need to make sure your table meets some strict prerequisites; namely, it has to be empty or have no indexes. This is easily achievable if you use table partitioning—just import data into a new table and then switch partitions to assign the new table data pages to your partitioned table. You can perform a bulk insert in a variety of ways, as the following list shows; it is up to you to select the one that best suits your needs:

- BULK INSERT T-SQL command
- INSERT . . . SELECT . . . FROM OPENROWSET(BULK . . .) command
- Bcp.exe command prompt utility
- SQL Server Integration Services Bulk Insert task

Scaling Out

When scaling up is not sufficient, you have plenty of possibilities for scaling out. You can scale out transactional and analytical data. In addition, you can scale out by using message queuing techniques.

For scaling out a transactional, normalized database, you can use distributed partitioned views. You can think of this technique as manual table partitioning. You can partition a table horizontally and create multiple tables on multiple instances of SQL Server, then UNION ALL data back together through distributed partitioned views. Your servers have to be connected through linked servers for this technique to work. Distributed partitioned views are especially useful if you can distribute your user connections on multiple servers in a way that most of the users use local data. However, you should be careful with this technique. If your users use mostly remote data, not the data from the SQL Server instance they connect to, you could actually slow down queries. In addition, do not forget that constraints cannot span databases and instances.

If your application needs to send many notifications, consider using SQL Server Notification Services (SSNS). SSNS enables digest and multicast deliveries. In a digest delivery, you can combine multiple similar notifications for a single subscriber into one digest message. In a multicast delivery, you send the same notification to a list of subscribers in a single notification, so the content formatter formats a notification only once. Both digest and multicast delivery are much more efficient than single notification delivery. An SSNS solution is thus much more efficient than using DatabaseMail, for example. Use DatabaseMail for administrative purposes only, such as informing database administrators (DBAs) about the outcome of scheduled jobs.

Although application data caching is not strictly a database solution, you should not forget that you can also use it to scale out. The Microsoft .NET *DataSet* object is designed for data caching on the middle or client tier. You can use it efficiently with ASP.NET applications, for example.

Message Queuing

If you spread your data across multiple SQL Server instances, or even across multiple database management systems, and if you can implement your transactions asynchronously, you can use message queuing instead of distributed transactions. This technology helps you finish the local part of a transaction quickly. Instead of performing the remote part of a transaction in real time, you can send it to a queue. The message system transfers messages to the remote queue, where a reader application reads the queue and executes the commands.

If you use multiple, different database platforms, you can use a general message system such as the Microsoft Message Queue (MSMQ) service. However, if you use SQL Server 2005 only, you can use SQL Server Service Broker (SSB). SSB is much more efficient than MSMQ because all message handling is done in SQL Server without crossing process boundaries. In addition, you can secure SSB objects by using regular T-SQL data control language elements because SSB objects are like any other database object. As noted, this chapter gives you a general overview of possible tools you can use for scalability; you will learn more about how to implement an SSB solution in Chapter 7, "Designing Objects That Extend Server Functionality."

Besides helping you scale out, message queuing solutions can also help you scale up. Instead of executing all commands synchronously, you can send some as messages to a queue in the same database and execute them later, during off-peak hours. This way, you can achieve load balancing over time.

Analytical Applications

You have so many different options for scaling out analytical applications that you should consider this scaling strategy in a very early stage of the design process. Options for scaling out for analysis include:

- **Report snapshots**   SQL Server Reporting Services can save datasets that you have read. This way, you have to read the data from the production database just once, and later multiple users can read from the report snapshot.

- **Replication**   You can use transactional replication to maintain a copy of selected data from your production database in nearly real time. You can move your queries to the subscription, or copy, database. This is especially useful if your queries are frequent but short. With long queries, you can experience locking contention between your queries and replication updates. In addition, you can replicate data to remote locations and, thus, bring the data closer to the users.

- **Data warehouses**   If you need to maintain historical data and merge data from multiple sources, consider using a data warehouse. In a data warehouse, you have merged, cleansed, historical data transformed in multiple star or snowflake schemas. Data in star schemas is very easy to use in reports.

- **UDM OLAP cubes**   If you want to enable your end users to perform online changes of how they are viewing the data in their reports and analysis, use Analysis Services to create UDM OLAP cubes. You typically build the cubes on top of your data warehouse. OLAP gives you lightning speed for analysis tasks that need large amounts of data. In fact, OLAP solutions are so efficient that you should consider using them with a data warehouse even for medium and small business applications.

Exam Tip   Know your data distribution options. Remember all the different possibilities for data distribution, not just techniques mentioned in this chapter. Other options include Bcp.exe (bulk copy utility), backup and restore, log shipping, distributed queries, and so on.

Developing Aggregation Strategies

Many analytical queries can benefit significantly from aggregations. You can prepare and maintain aggregations in production or analytical databases. Consider the following best practices:

- In a production database, you can maintain aggregations online. This is especially useful for maintaining levels and states, which are actually aggregates from events. You can maintain online aggregations in separate tables with the help of DML triggers on event tables. You can maintain aggregations with the help of indexed views as well. However, add aggregations to your production database deliberately because maintaining aggregations means slowing down updates. For analysis, use other options for aggregating data.

- In transactional systems, depending on your business problem, you could also introduce aggregations of old data. For example, in a specific business, you might not need to keep detailed transactions for more than six months. In such a case, you can move older data from production to archive tables and store it aggregated there. This way, you reduce the size of your database and speed up queries and administrative tasks.

- If you need aggregations for analytical purposes, consider creating them in the SQL Server Analysis Services (SSAS) UDM. SSAS is optimized for read-only access and for aggregate queries from star schemas. This optimization is incredibly efficient. Because SSAS ships with SQL Server, move toward implementing an SSAS solution as soon as possible.

- If you do not have the time, resources, or knowledge to design and implement an SSAS solution, you can still aggregate data once and store it for multiple users with the help of SQL Server Reporting Services (SSRS) report snapshots.

Practice: Using Bulk Insert

In this practice, you will compare the efficiency of a minimally logged bulk insert with a regular INSERT statement.

▶ Exercise 1: Export the Data

In this exercise, you export the data from the AdventureWorks.Person.Address table to a text file.

Export the data. For this task, you can use the Bcp.exe command prompt utility from the command prompt, or you can call it from SQL Server Management Studio (SSMS). The SSMS Query Editor lets you edit SQLCMD scripts. To learn how to turn the SQLCMD mode on, see the Books Online topic, "Editing SQLCMD Scripts with Query Editor," at *http://msdn2.microsoft.com/en-us/library/ms174187.aspx*. Your command should look like this, assuming you have copied code from this training kit to suggested folders such as C:\My Documents\Microsoft Press\TK70-441\Chapter05 for this chapter:

```
USE TK441Ch05;
GO
!!bcp AdventureWorks.Person.Address out C:\My Documents\Microsoft Press\TK70-
441\Chapter05\Ad.dat -c -T
```

Alternatively, execute the following from a command prompt:

```
bcp AdventureWorks.Person.Address out C:\My Documents\Microsoft Press\TK70-
441\Chapter05\Ad.dat -c -T
```

▶ Exercise 2: Import the Data by Using INSERT . . . SELECT

Now, you will try to import the data by using a regular T-SQL INSERT . . . SELECT statement. But first, re-create the chapter database to make sure you start with the same conditions for both the INSERT . . . SELECT and bulk insert techniques.

1. First, re-create a clean database and set the recovery model to BULK_LOGGED:

```
USE master;
DROP DATABASE TK441Ch05;
GO
```

```
IF DB_ID(N'TK441Ch05') IS NULL
   CREATE DATABASE TK441Ch05;
GO
ALTER DATABASE TK441Ch05
 SET RECOVERY BULK_LOGGED;
GO
```

2. Create the destination table. It should have the same structure as the original table from the *AdventureWorks* demo database:

```
USE TK441Ch05;
GO
CREATE TABLE dbo.Address
(AddressID int NOT NULL,
 AddressLine1 nvarchar(60) NOT NULL,
 AddressLine2 nvarchar(60) NULL,
 City nvarchar(30) NOT NULL,
 StateProvinceID int NOT NULL,
 PostalCode nvarchar(15) NOT NULL,
 rowguid uniqueidentifier,
 ModifiedDate datetime NOT NULL);
GO
```

3. Populate the table by using INSERT . . . SELECT:

```
INSERT INTO dbo.Address
SELECT *
   FROM AdventureWorks.Person.Address;
GO
```

4. Check the size of the transaction log. It should be more than 13 MB. Use the DBCC SQLPERF command to check the log size: *DBCC SQLPERF('Logspace'); GO*

▶ **Exercise 3: Import the Data by Using Bcp.exe**

Next, you will use Bcp.exe to repeat the same import task.

1. Again, start with a clean database:

```
USE master;
DROP DATABASE TK441Ch05;
GO
IF DB_ID(N'TK441Ch05') IS NULL
   CREATE DATABASE TK441Ch05;
GO
ALTER DATABASE TK441Ch05
 SET RECOVERY BULK_LOGGED;
GO
```

2. Create the destination table. It should have the same structure as the original table from the *AdventureWorks* demo database:

```
USE TK441Ch05;
GO
CREATE TABLE dbo.Address
(AddressID int NOT NULL,
```

```
AddressLine1 nvarchar(60) NOT NULL,
AddressLine2 nvarchar(60) NULL,
City nvarchar(30) NOT NULL,
StateProvinceID int NOT NULL,
PostalCode nvarchar(15) NOT NULL,
rowguid uniqueidentifier,
ModifiedDate datetime NOT NULL);
GO
```

3. Populate the table by using Bcp.exe:

```
!!bcp TK441Ch05.dbo.Address in C:\My Documents\Microsoft Press\TK70-
441\Chapter05\Ad.dat -T -c -hTABLOCK
```

4. Alternatively, execute the following from a command prompt:

```
bcp TK441Ch05.dbo.Address in C:\TK441\Chapter05\Ad.dat -T -c -hTABLOCK
```

5. Check the size of the transaction log. It should be about 0.5MB. Use the DBCC SQLP-ERF command to check the log size:

```
DBCC SQLPERF('LOGSPACE');
GO
```

Quick Check

1. Can you achieve load balancing over time?
2. What kinds of issues can you not correct with indexes?

Quick Check Answers

1. Yes, you can use a message queuing solution such as SQL Server Service Broker to achieve load balancing over time.
2. Although indexes are your primary tool for improving performance in a database, you cannot use them to solve all problems. For example, you cannot do anything if your application sends poor queries, if you have a performance problem built into your user-defined type, if you have a poor logical database design, and so on.

Lesson 4: Designing Interoperability with External Systems

Estimated lesson time: 20 minutes

Like scalability, interoperability is a broad term. SQL Server 2005 has many methods for implementing interoperability with external systems in synchronous and asynchronous ways. Interoperating can simply mean exporting data, or it can mean exposing procedures and functions as Web methods to external applications. In this lesson, you will learn about SQL Server tools and methods that you can use to connect SQL Server with external systems.

Synchronous Methods

When you interoperate with external systems synchronously, you exchange data and call methods in real time, without latency. For importing and exporting data in real time, you can use the following methods:

- With distributed queries, you can read and update data in and from heterogeneous data sources. All you need to interoperate with a specific source is the OLE DB provider for that source. OLE DB providers expose data in tabular format, which SQL Server can consume. You can implement distributed queries in the following ways:
    - ❑ You can create a permanent linked server. A linked server is a named connection string to the external source, with authentication information for that source stored on SQL Server. Then you can refer to linked objects with four-part names. In addition, you can use the *OPENQUERY* rowset function in the FROM clause for pass-through queries executed on the specified linked server.
    - ❑ You can use ad hoc distributed queries. By default, SQL Server does not allow ad hoc distributed queries. However, if a DBA allows them, you can use the *OPENROWSET* and *OPENDATASOURCE* rowset functions in the FROM clause for ad hoc access to the external data.
- You can also treat bulk import, which you learned about in the previous lesson, as an interoperability method. If you use the BULK INSERT or INSERT . . . SELECT . . . FROM OPENROWSET(BULK . . .) T-SQL commands from your application or stored procedures, then you can treat this as a synchronous method.

Besides exchanging data with other systems, you can interoperate with external systems by calling the methods the system exposes. SQL Server provides native XML Web services by supporting open standards such as Hypertext Transfer Protocol (HTTP), Simple Object Access Protocol (SOAP), and Web Services Definition Language (WSDL). HTTP is the core World Wide Web protocol and provides a platform-neutral way of exchanging data. SOAP defines how to use XML and HTTP to access Web services and objects. With a WSDL document, you describe Web services. Through native Web services, you can expose stored procedures and UDFs as Web methods and, thus, make them available to any application that can send a SOAP request. You will learn more about native Web services in Chapter 14, "Designing for Data Distribution."

Although SQL Server can expose Web methods, it cannot consume Web methods from other Web services through T-SQL expressions. However, you could consume Web methods from SQL Server through CLR integration, with the help of CLR procedures and UDFs. CLR integration is not limited to consuming Web services, however; you can treat it as a general tool for interoperability. However, be aware that using CLR objects outside SQL Server means giving the CLR assemblies at least the EXTERNAL_ACCESS permission set. Use anything other than the SAFE permission set extremely carefully.

Asynchronous Methods

If you interoperate with external systems asynchronously, SQL Server tools and services provide the following methods for data distribution:

- **Replication**   Transactional replication typically has very low latency and comes quite close to the latency of synchronous methods. SQL Server can serve as publisher or subscriber for replication.
- **SQL Server Integration Services (SSIS)**   With SSIS, you can use SQL Server as the source or destination of data movement. In addition, SSIS provides many built-in tasks and transformations you can use to transform the data on the way to its destination.
- **SQL Server Reporting Services (SSRS)**   End users can subscribe to reports, and you can deliver reports through different channels, rendering them in different formats, including XML.
- **Bcp.exe**   You can use the Bcp.exe bulk copy utility for asynchronous bulk import and export of data.

IMPORTANT   SSRS and data movement

Although you can use SSRS reports to export data, this is not the primary purpose of SSRS. If your task is just data movement, without any report rendering, choose SSIS instead.

You can also use message queuing for asynchronous interoperability with external systems. With message queuing, you are not limited to data exchange only; you can send and receive any kind of message. As you already know, SQL Server 2005 provides SSB as a message queuing system. However, for now, SSB is limited to communications between SQL Server 2005 instances only; thus, you cannot treat SSB as an interoperability tool yet.

Although you cannot use SSB to communicate with heterogeneous systems yet, SQL Server uses it internally for another kind of interoperability. SQL Server 2005 can notify applications that their data cache is obsolete. With ADO.NET 2.0, an application can subscribe to SQL Server 2005 Query Notifications through objects of the new *SqlDependency* or *SqlNotification-Request* classes. *SqlDependency* is a high-level abstraction class, which enables you to issue the *SqlCommand* object with a dependency. The *SqlDependency* object then watches for notifications of changes of the rows from the *SqlCommand* query definition. *SqlNotificationRequest* objects can use the internal query notifications Broker queue directly. SQL Server uses indexed-view technology for the change-detection mechanism.

Practice: Linking to Excel 2007

Later in this training kit, you will learn more about such interoperability methods as SSB and native Web services. In this practice, however, you will implement simple synchronous data interoperability with a Microsoft Office Excel 2007 worksheet through a linked server.

▶ **Exercise 1: Create a Linked Server**

To create a linked server to an Excel 2007 file, you cannot use the Microsoft Jet OLE DB provider anymore. You have to use the Microsoft Office 12.0 Access Database Engine OLE DB provider (Microsoft.ACE.OLEDB.12.0).

1. Create a linked server to the Excel 2007 file MyExcel2007.xlsx, which is provided on the CD in the folder for this chapter. The following code assumes you installed the file to the C:\My Documents\Microsoft Press\TK70-441\Chapter05folder:

```
USE TK441Ch05;
GO
EXEC master.dbo.sp_addlinkedserver
  @server = N'ExcelSource',
  @srvproduct=N'Excel',
  @provider=N'Microsoft.ACE.OLEDB.12.0',
  @datasrc=N'C:\My Documents\Microsoft Press\TK70-441\Chapter05\MyExcel2007.xlsx',
  @provstr=N'Excel 12.0';
GO
```

2. You have to provide the required security information. Because the Excel file is not protected, you must make connections without using a security context. You can use the sp_addlinkedsrvlogin system procedure for this task:

```
EXEC master.dbo.sp_addlinkedsrvlogin
  @rmtsrvname = N'ExcelSource',
  @locallogin = NULL ,
  @useself = N'False';
GO
```

▶ **Exercise 2: Browse the Linked Server**

After establishing the linked server, you need to browse the data stored on that server—that is, the data in your Excel 2007 file.

1. Before retrieving the data, you have to obtain information about table and column names exposed through the OLE DB provider. You can use the sp_table_ex and sp_columns_ex system stored procedures to find this information:

```
EXEC sp_tables_ex ExcelSource;
EXEC sp_columns_ex ExcelSource;
GO
```

2. Note that Excel does not use the catalog and schema part of the name for naming its objects. However, you still have to use the four-part name when you refer to linked objects in T-SQL queries. You need to have three dots in the name; however, you can omit the catalog and the schema part. You can refer to an Excel object by using the *linkedserver . . . sheet$* format. For browsing the Excel file, you can use the following query:

```
SELECT ProductCategoryID,
       Name,
       ModifiedDate
  FROM ExcelSource...Sheet1$;
GO
```

▶ **Exercise 3: Cleanup**

Because this is the last exercise for this chapter, clean up your SQL Server instance.

Drop the database for this chapter and remove the linked server information:

```
USE master;
DROP DATABASE TK441Ch05;
GO
EXEC sp_droplinkedsrvlogin 'ExcelSource', NULL;
EXEC sp_dropserver 'ExcelSource';
GO
```

Quick Check

1. Which of the following is not an interoperability tool?
    A. Distributed queries
    B. Native Web services
    C. Replication
    D. SQL Server Service Broker

2. You want to disseminate data asynchronously on your local area network. However, you need to achieve as small a latency as possible. Which technology would you use?

> **Quick Check Answers**
> 1. The correct answer is D. SQL Server Service Broker is limited to communication only between SQL Server 2005 instances for now.
> 2. Transactional replication on local area networks typically transfers the transactions to subscribers in just a few seconds. Therefore, you should use this technology.

Case Scenario: Implement Database Technologies and Techniques for Your Application

Tailspin Toys has implemented an ASP.NET application for ordering. The customers are generally pleased with this application. However, they occasionally complain that the list prices for the products in the ASP.NET application are not the same as they get on the invoices that Tailspin Toys sends to them. Obviously, the ASP.NET cache is not refreshed frequently enough.

The ASP.NET application is a big success. You realize this because the tables that support orders grow quickly, 24x7. However, you are concerned because your administrative tasks on the database, such as backups, take more and more time to complete.

1. How can you ensure current data in the ASP.NET cache?
2. What can you do to shorten the time that daily maintenance operations require?

Chapter Summary

- The *XML* data type is very useful for creating a dynamic schema.
- You can improve the performance of searches in an XML data type column by using XML indexes.
- CLR code is faster than T-SQL code for CPU-intensive operations.
- Use T-SQL for all operations on data.
- Design for scalability from the beginning of the design process.
- You can use tools and techniques to scale up within a single system and to scale out across multiple systems.
- SQL Server 2005 gives you many methods for implementing interoperability with external application and other database management systems.

Chapter 6
Designing Objects That Retrieve Data

Querying the database and retrieving data is possibly the most common activity executed against databases. Being a database developer involves defining tuned queries and applying Transact-SQL (T-SQL) constructions wisely to obtain the desired results in terms of the data being returned, the amount of time it takes for the database to process the query, data validation, and several other factors.

However, T-SQL code cannot exist by itself. It must be packaged in special objects that define the specific operations and context that the particular T-SQL code needs to retrieve data. There are three types of objects that retrieve data: views, stored procedures, and user-defined functions (UDFs).

In this chapter, you will learn the key design practices to apply when designing views, stored procedures, and UDFs to retrieve data. You will see when to use each of these different types of database objects, the implementation variations between them, and how to take advantage of what each has to offer. This chapter does not focus on how to design (or develop) the T-SQL code that those objects might contain. To learn how to design (or develop) the T-SQL code that views, stored procedures, and functions might contain, read *Inside Microsoft SQL Server 2005: T-SQL Querying* by Itzik Ben-Gan, Lubor Kollar, and Dejan Sarka (Microsoft Press, 2006).

Exam objectives in this chapter:
- Design objects that retrieve data.
- Design views.
- Design user-defined functions.
- Design stored procedures.

Before You Begin

To complete the lessons in this chapter, you must have:

- A general understanding of the different database objects supported in Microsoft SQL Server 2005.

- Knowledge about the T-SQL syntax required to write views, stored procedures, and user-defined functions.

- A SQL Server 2005 instance (any edition), with the sample *AdventureWorks* database installed. Sample databases are available with SQL Server 2005 Enterprise edition but are not a part of the default installation. Alternatively, you can install sample databases from *http://msdn2.microsoft.com/en-us/library/ms143739.aspx.*

IMPORTANT   Practices in this chapter build upon each other

All the lesson practices in this chapter build upon each other; to move to the next practice, you need to finish the previous one.

Lesson 1: Designing Views

Estimated lesson time: 40 minutes

Views are often called *virtual tables* because they can be referenced inside the T-SQL language whenever a table name is expected. This means that SQL Server 2005 enables you to encapsulate (or package) a specific T-SQL query inside a view and reference it anywhere else in the database without having to declare the T-SQL query again. For database developers, there are several scenarios in which this is valuable:

- Hiding implementation details as a matter of security
- Code maintainability
- Code reusability
- Backward compatibility when maintaining multiple versions of client applications not aware of changes in the database schema

In this lesson, you will look at the key design decisions to consider, depending on the scenario, when designing a view to retrieve data in SQL Server 2005.

Choosing Between the Different Types of Views

T-SQL offers the CREATE VIEW statement to define any type of view. Depending on certain implementation and deployment differences, views can be standard views, indexed views, or partitioned views. These implementation details are also used by the SQL Server query optimizer to decide the best strategy for executing the code contained in the view.

When designing views, you must have a clear understanding of the view's purpose, the scenario that it fulfills, where the data is located, and the security context under which it will execute. These details enable you to choose carefully the type of view that will provide the most benefit according to the requirements of the scenario that you are designing for.

Designing Standard Views

You use a standard view when you want to package a T-SQL query as a unit for security, deployment, and reusability. A standard view is the most common type of view, fitting most scenarios.

Standard views store only the encapsulated T-SQL query code instead of storing the resulting data. When referenced from another query, the view is expanded in place with the actual T-SQL query code it contains so that the SQL Server 2005 query processor compiles a single execution plan for the whole query. Because standard views are always materialized at run time, the execution cost is exactly the same as if the actual T-SQL query had been fed to the query engine.

The main benefits of encapsulating a query in a view are:

- Control over what you want to make visible outside of the database to protect the inner complexities of the database schema (this includes data structures as well as naming conventions). Acting as an abstraction layer, a view provides a public interface to the outside world, and you, as the designer, decide what is exposed and how.

- By hiding the database schema, the view protects outside data consumers and client applications from schema changes and gives database designers the ability to make changes to inner details without affecting consumers.

The following code example uses a standard view to filter the sales data by showing only the sales orders coming from the Northeast territory:

```
CREATE VIEW [Sales].[vNortheastSalesOrderHeader]
AS
SELECT  *
FROM  Sales.SalesOrderHeader
WHERE (TerritoryID IN
            (SELECT     TerritoryID
             FROM Sales.SalesTerritory
             WHERE (Name LIKE N'Northeast')))
```

On the Companion Disc   This chapter includes many code examples. You will find all the code from this chapter on the companion CD in the C:\My Documents\Microsoft Press\TK70-441 \Chapter06\Sql folder.

Because standard views do not occupy disk storage space, you can define as many views as needed without affecting system performance, so always design views that return just the right amount of data.

IMPORTANT   Maximum number of objects

The sum of the number of all objects in a database cannot exceed 2,147,483,647.

When designing a view, consider that it can provide different ways of looking at the data. You can use a view to pre-combine some values, pre-aggregate data, or consolidate multiple tables to provide a new perspective on the data.

A view represents an external interface that protects outsiders from schema changes and from understanding the inner complexity of the physical schema or abstracts such changes and complexity. This is an important concept and technology because it uncouples applications from the table's schema, which is harder to maintain and modify.

Designing Indexed Views

Because standard views store only the T-SQL query instead of the result set, a standard view might affect database performance in cases in which the T-SQL query in the view involves complex processing of large numbers of rows, multiple levels of joining and data aggregation, repeating patterns of queries, or repeated joins of the same tables on the same keys. In such cases, creating an indexed view might provide better performance than using standard views.

You convert a standard view into an indexed view when you define a unique clustered index (and optional nonclustered indexes) on the view to improve lookup performance. After you create the unique clustered index, the query's result set is materialized and stored in physical storage, so there is no overhead associated with executing this costly operation at run time. The query optimizer treats an indexed view referenced in the FROM clause as a standard view. However, if designed correctly, the indexed view will be the least expensive path, so SQL Server will use its index to execute the query.

IMPORTANT   **Clustered index on a view vs. a table**

There is a big difference between a clustered index on a view and a regular clustered index on a table. The clustered index on a view indexes a result set that might include pre-computed values, aggregates, and data coming from multiple tables.

As you learned in Chapter 4, "Designing a Database for Performance," adding indexes increases the overhead on the database because the indexes require ongoing maintenance. Therefore, give careful consideration to finding the right balance of indexes and maintenance overhead.

BEST PRACTICES   **Use indexed views for infrequently changing data**

Indexed views are recommended for querying infrequently changing data mostly used for read-only purposes. If you need to execute sporadic updates on the data, consider the possibility of dropping any indexed views before the update and re-creating the indexed views after the update to improve update performance.

When designing indexed views, you need to take into account the same factors as when designing table indexes. For example, the indexed view might not provide any significant performance gains if its size is similar to the size of the original table. In addition, when choosing the clustered index key, choose a key compact enough so that its size will not affect performance when creating multiple nonclustered indexes on the view or when doing key comparisons to find a row.

An important benefit of using indexed views in SQL Server 2005 is that the query optimizer might choose to reuse the index on any other query being executed even if the indexed view is not specified in the FROM clause. Database designers need to consider creating indexed views that can satisfy multiple queries, operations, or both.

The query optimizer might consider using the index of an indexed view only when certain conditions are met—for example, when several session options are set to ON (ANSI_NULLS, ANSI_WARNINGS, and others), when there is a match between the view index columns and elements in the query, and when the index is the least expensive execution path.

IMPORTANT   Using the NOEXPAND table hint to force index usage

In SQL Server 2005 Enterprise edition, indexed views are chosen automatically, even when not specified on the FROM clause. However, if you are using a different edition of SQL Server 2005, you need to specify the NOEXPAND table hint to force the use of an index. You might also choose to specify the EXPAND VIEWS hint so that the query optimizer will not use any view indexes.

The following code example uses an indexed view to materialize several aggregated sales data. Notice the different options that need to be set:

```
SET NUMERIC_ROUNDABORT OFF;
SET ANSI_PADDING, ANSI_WARNINGS, CONCAT_NULL_YIELDS_NULL, ARITHABORT,
    QUOTED_IDENTIFIER, ANSI_NULLS ON;
GO

CREATE VIEW [Sales].[vTotalSalesForAllRegions]
WITH SCHEMABINDING
AS
SELECT
    TerritoryID,
    SUM(SubTotal) AS SubTotal,
    SUM(TotalDue) AS TotalDue,
    COUNT_BIG(*) AS CountBig
FROM Sales.SalesOrderHeader
GROUP BY TerritoryID
GO

CREATE UNIQUE CLUSTERED INDEX IDX_V1
    ON [Sales].[vTotalSalesForAllRegions] (TerritoryID);
GO
```

There are other requirements that need to be fulfilled when designing indexed views. To learn about them, see the "Creating Indexed Views" topic in SQL Server 2005 Books Online at *http://msdn2.microsoft.com/en-us/library/ms191432(SQL.90).aspx*.

Designing Partitioned Views

A partitioned view consists of a T-SQL query that consolidates the data coming from multiple tables, called *member tables*. Each of these member tables has been designed to partition the data horizontally by storing certain ranges of data based on a *partitioning column*. A partitioned view provides a unified view of all the data stored in any number of member tables and hides the complexity of querying (local or remote) database servers to provide a single consolidated view of the data.

The partitioning column holds the values that specify where to look for a range of values. These ranges are enforced through CHECK constraints in the partitioning column. This column can be of any data type (usually numeric types and date types), but it must be part of the table primary key, it cannot accept nulls, and it cannot be an IDENTITY column.

The main difference—and benefit—of using a partitioned view is the declaration of CHECK constraints on each partitioning column to filter the values that can be inserted in each member table. (These values cannot overlap between tables.) When the view is queried, the SQL Server 2005 query optimizer first validates the CHECK constraints on each member table so that only the necessary tables are queried according to the lookup ranges required in the query, resulting in a performance improvement. If no CHECK constraints are defined, this would be the same as having a standard view.

The sample *AdventureWorks* database was designed to run on a single server, so all of the sales information is consolidated in one table called SalesOrderHeader, which has a foreign key constraint to the SalesTerritory table, as Figure 6-1 shows.

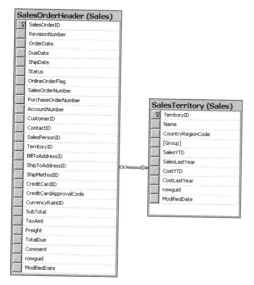

Figure 6-1   The SalesOrderHeader table and SalesTerritory table in *AdventureWorks*

Suppose that instead of consolidating the data in a centralized way like this, you want each of the territories to hold its own sales data. So, you create a SalesOrderHeader table for each territory, as Figure 6-2 shows. (This example creates a SalesOrderHeader table for the Central, Northwest, Northeast, Southwest, and Southeast territories.)

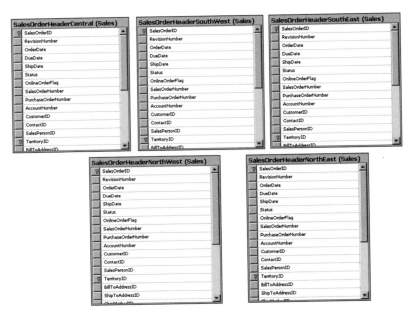

Figure 6-2   SalesOrderHeader tables for each territory

Each table has been designed as shown in the following code sample:

```
CREATE TABLE [Sales].[SalesOrderHeaderCentral](
[SalesOrderID] [int] IDENTITY(1,1) NOT FOR REPLICATION NOT NULL,
[RevisionNumber] [tinyint] NOT NULL
    CONSTRAINT [DF_SalesOrderHeaderCentral_RevisionNumber] DEFAULT ((0)),
[OrderDate] [datetime] NOT NULL
    CONSTRAINT [DF_SalesOrderHeaderCentral_OrderDate] DEFAULT (getdate()),
[DueDate] [datetime] NOT NULL,
[ShipDate] [datetime] NULL,
[Status] [tinyint] NOT NULL
    CONSTRAINT [DF_SalesOrderHeaderCentral_Status] DEFAULT ((1)),
[OnlineOrderFlag] [dbo].[Flag] NOT NULL
    CONSTRAINT [DF_SalesOrderHeaderCentral_OnlineOrderFlag] DEFAULT ((1)),
[SalesOrderNumber] AS
    (isnull(N'SO'+CONVERT([nvarchar](23),[SalesOrderID],0),N'*** ERROR ***')),
[PurchaseOrderNumber] [dbo].[OrderNumber] NULL,
[AccountNumber] [dbo].[AccountNumber] NULL,
[CustomerID] [int] NOT NULL,
[ContactID] [int] NOT NULL,
[SalesPersonID] [int] NULL,
```

```
[TerritoryID] [int] NOT NULL CHECK (TerritoryID BETWEEN 1 AND 10),
[BillToAddressID] [int] NOT NULL,
[ShipToAddressID] [int] NOT NULL,
[ShipMethodID] [int] NOT NULL,
[CreditCardID] [int] NULL,
[CreditCardApprovalCode] [varchar](15) NULL,
[CurrencyRateID] [int] NULL,
[SubTotal] [money] NOT NULL
    CONSTRAINT [DF_SalesOrderHeaderCentral_SubTotal] DEFAULT ((0.00)),
[TaxAmt] [money] NOT NULL
    CONSTRAINT [DF_SalesOrderHeaderCentral_TaxAmt] DEFAULT ((0.00)),
[Freight] [money] NOT NULL
    CONSTRAINT [DF_SalesOrderHeaderCentral_Freight] DEFAULT ((0.00)),
[TotalDue] AS (isnull(([SubTotal]+[TaxAmt])+[Freight],(0))),
[Comment] [nvarchar](128) NULL,
[rowguid] [uniqueidentifier] ROWGUIDCOL NOT NULL
    CONSTRAINT [DF_SalesOrderHeaderCentral_rowguid] DEFAULT (newid()),
[ModifiedDate] [datetime] NOT NULL
    CONSTRAINT [DF_SalesOrderHeaderCentral_ModifiedDate] DEFAULT (getdate()),
CONSTRAINT [PK_SalesOrderHeaderCentral_SalesOrderID] PRIMARY KEY CLUSTERED
(
    [SalesOrderID] ASC,
    [TerritoryID]
)
WITH
(
    PAD_INDEX = OFF,
    STATISTICS_NORECOMPUTE = OFF,
    IGNORE_DUP_KEY = OFF,
    ALLOW_ROW_LOCKS = ON,
    ALLOW_PAGE_LOCKS = ON
) ON [PRIMARY]
) ON [PRIMARY]
```

Notice that the TerritoryID column has been declared with a CHECK constraint that filters the values that this table can hold; this table will hold values only for territories with IDs between 1 and 10.

Then, you can create a partitioned view to consolidate the data coming from all the sales territories, as in the following code example:

```
CREATE VIEW [Sales].[vTotalSalesOrderHeaders]
AS
    SELECT * FROM [Sales].[SalesOrderHeaderCentral]
UNION ALL
    SELECT * FROM [Sales].[SalesOrderHeaderSouthWest]
UNION ALL
    SELECT * FROM [Sales].[SalesOrderHeaderSouthEast]
UNION ALL
    SELECT * FROM [Sales].[SalesOrderHeaderNorthWest]
UNION ALL
    SELECT * FROM [Sales].[SalesOrderHeaderNorthEast]
```

In case you want to look at all the sales order headers coming from all territories, you can query the partitioned view with a query such as this:

```
SELECT *
FROM [Sales].[vTotalSalesOrderHeaders]
```

When the view is executed without a WHERE clause, the query optimizer queries each of the member tables, as Figure 6-3 shows.

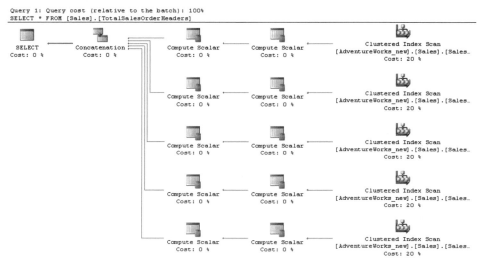

Figure 6-3   Estimated query plan for the execution of a partitioned view without a filter

However, if a WHERE clause is declared, the query optimizer validates the CHECK constraints in the partitioning column, so only the necessary tables are queried. For example, to look for the sales order header coming from the territory with ID 15, you would execute a query such as this:

```
SELECT *
FROM [Sales].[vTotalSalesOrderHeaders]
WHERE TerritoryID = 15
```

The query optimizer knows that Territory ID 15 is located in the range of values coming from the SalesOrderHeaderNortheast table.

Look at the difference in the estimated query plan for executing the partitioned view with a filter, which Figure 6-4 shows.

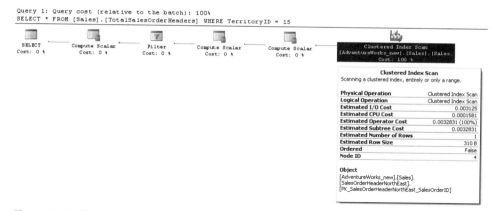

Figure 6-4 Estimated query plan for the execution of a partitioned view with a filter

When the member tables contained inside the partitioned view are all available inside the same database server, the partitioned view is called a *local partitioned view*. If at least one of the member tables is located on a remote server, it is called a *distributed partitioned view*.

Federated Database Servers with Partitioned Views   You can use partitioned views to enhance the performance of a system by horizontally partitioning and spreading the load through a set of remote servers that cooperate to share the processing load. This is a technique called *federated database servers*, which you use to *scale out* a set of servers to support the processing of large systems and Web sites.

IMPORTANT   Scaling out vs. scaling up

Scaling out is the technique of increasing the processing power of a system by adding one or more additional computers, or nodes, instead of strengthening the hardware of a single computer (to *scale up*).

In a set of federated database servers, no matter which server is queried, they all return the same data. This result is achieved by creating partitioned views in each of the servers that consolidate the local data plus the remote data from the other servers in the federation. Each federated server is known to one another through a linked server declaration.

IMPORTANT   Partitioned views vs. partitioned tables

As with any other view, partitioned views encapsulate only the T-SQL query used to consolidate the data. The partitioned view does not impose (or care about) any physical distribution of the data. This is the main difference between partitioned views and partitioned tables.

Going back to the previous example that extended the sample *AdventureWorks* database, you distributed the sales information in different member tables (one for each territory) to achieve location independence so that each territory can manage its own SalesOrderHeader table in its own database server. At the same time, however, you provided a consolidated view by declaring the other regions as linked servers and providing a partitioned view that unions all the data, thus creating a federation of database servers. Table 6-1 summarizes some key differences between the three types of views.

Table 6-1   Types of Views in SQL Server 2005

Standard View	Indexed View	Partitioned View
Stores T-SQL query only	Stores unique clustered index	Stores T-SQL query only
Can aggregate data from local and remote tables	Contains data from local tables	Can aggregate data from local and remote tables
Materializes query at run time	Materializes query during index creation	Materializes query at run time
Better for simpler queries and to encapsulate queries on frequently changing data	Better for complex queries and to encapsulate queries on infrequently changing data	Better for queries that aggregate data from multiple tables (local and remote)
Always queries all referenced objects in query	When well designed, the index provides the materialized result set	Intelligently chooses which tables to query, depending on partitioning column (when defined with a CHECK constraint)

Practice: Designing Views

In this practice, you must apply the concepts from Lesson 1, "Designing Views," to design a standard view and an indexed view. All the practices in this chapter refer to the Production set of tables from the *AdventureWorks* database, which the entity-relationship diagram (ERD) in Figure 6-5 shows.

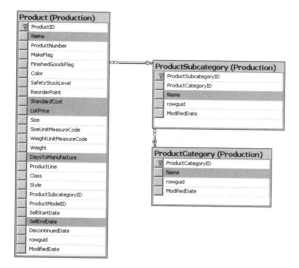

Figure 6-5   Entity-relationship diagram of the Production set of tables from the *AdventureWorks* database

The grayed rows in Figure 6-5 are the ones that will be needed in the following exercises.

IMPORTANT   **Practices build upon each other**

The practices in this chapter build upon each other. You should not delete your work after you finish this practice.

▶ **Exercise 1: Create a Standard View**

In this exercise, as the database designer for *AdventureWorks*, you must design a view that returns products that yield the most revenue in terms of the difference between the price and the cost to produce. The production department is looking for products sold at a higher price but produced at a lower cost. Make sure that the view also returns the Category and Subcategory names for the product. Design your own view before reading the suggested answer.

Suggested Answer

The following view satisfies the requirements:

```
USE [AdventureWorks]
GO
CREATE VIEW Get_Products_Estimated_Revenue
AS
SELECT
    Production.Product.ProductID,
    Production.ProductCategory.Name AS ProductCategory,
    Production.ProductSubcategory.Name AS ProductSubCategory,
```

```
    Production.Product.Name,
        Production.Product.ListPrice - Production.Product.StandardCost AS Revenue
    FROM Production.Product INNER JOIN Production.ProductSubcategory ON
    Production.Product.ProductSubcategoryID =
    Production.ProductSubcategory.ProductSubcategoryID
    INNER JOIN Production.ProductCategory ON
    Production.ProductSubcategory.ProductCategoryID =
    Production.ProductCategory.ProductCategoryID
    WHERE  (Production.Product.SellEndDate IS NULL)
```

▶ **Exercise 2: Create an Indexed View**

In this exercise, you decide to convert the preceding standard view into an indexed view to improve performance when reading the ProductID, the product revenue, and the days required to manufacture the product. You execute the following T-SQL declaration to generate the index on the view:

```
CREATE UNIQUE CLUSTERED INDEX IDX_V1
    ON dbo.Get_Products_Estimated_Revenue (ProductID, Revenue, DaysToManufacture);
```

What modifications are required in the view's T-SQL code declaration?

Suggested Answer

You need to make three key changes: mark the view declaration with the WITH SCHEMA-BINDING option, include an extra column in the SELECT list returning the COUNT_BIG(*) function, and include the DaysToManufacture column in the result set.

Quick Check

1. What type of view would you create if you needed to pre-aggregate data coming from multiple remote database servers?
2. What is the storage cost of defining a standard view?
3. What is the storage cost of defining an indexed view?

Quick Check Answers

1. Either a standard view or a partitioned view would work for pre-aggregating data from multiple remote database servers. Indexed views cannot be created when data is coming from remote tables.
2. There is no storage cost with standard views. Standard views store only the T-SQL query. This T-SQL query is executed every time the view is called, so the most up-to-date data is retrieved.
3. Indexed views materialize the results of the query by creating an index structure. As covered in Chapter 4, the size of the index depends on the type of index and the columns chosen to be part of the index.

Lesson 2: Designing Stored Procedures

Estimated lesson time: 30 minutes

Views can contain only a single SELECT statement and can be used only to retrieve data. Views are not suitable for situations in which the resulting result set (and, hence, the T-SQL query to be executed) depends on external values, on data that needs to be validated, on decisions that need to be made, or on conditions that need to be checked to construct the expected result set dynamically. Views also are not suitable for situations in which the expected result is not a result set but rather a scalar value. Instead, in these cases, you would use stored procedures.

Similar to views, stored procedures do not store data. Stored procedures store the T-SQL queries they contain, so they give designers the ability to package programming logic that is executed and that queries data in real time. Unlike with views, the T-SQL code inside a stored procedure is stored in pre-compiled format. So a query plan has already been calculated for the stored procedure, which translates into better execution performance.

IMPORTANT   Reusing programming logic

You can define as many stored procedures as you want without causing any toll on the system. Look for programming logic that can be packaged to be reused by multiple programs or by other stored procedures.

Even though stored procedures can contain any number and type of SQL statements (except some CREATE statements), in this lesson, you will focus on designing stored procedures to retrieve data. You will ignore, for now, stored procedures used to update data or for data-definition language (DDL) operations.

When designing stored procedures, you need to consider several design questions:

- What type of stored procedure do you need?
- What type of data will the stored procedure return?
- What input, output, and optional parameters do you need to define for the stored procedure?
- What status value do you need to define for the stored procedure to return?
- What error handling routines do you need to include?
- What security context should the stored procedure execute under?

What Type of Stored Procedure Do You Need?

The first stored procedure design decision you need to make is to choose the right technology for implementing the procedure. SQL Server 2005 supports three types of user-defined stored procedures that return data: T-SQL stored procedures, *common language runtime (CLR)* stored procedures, and extended stored procedures.

T-SQL Stored Procedures

This type of stored procedure is completely written in the T-SQL programming language, and as explained previously, it can contain any number and type of SQL statements. This type of stored procedure is usually used for set-based operations, for data-management language (DML) operations, and when necessary to manipulate heavy loads of data.

CLR Stored Procedures

This type of stored procedure is written in any Microsoft .NET programming language (usually Microsoft Visual Basic .NET or C# .NET). The main advantage of this type of procedure is that all the .NET base class libraries are available to use, so operations that are difficult to develop in T-SQL (such as XML manipulation, compression, encryption, string operations, complex mathematical calculations, and so on) are very easy to implement with .NET. This type of stored procedure is usually used to encapsulate reusable procedural code that must run inside the database server. It is not recommended for set-based operations or to manipulate heavy loads of data.

CLR stored procedures are outside the scope of this chapter; for more information about them, see the "CLR Stored Procedures" topic in SQL Server 2005 Books Online at *http:// msdn2.microsoft.com/en- us/library/ms131094.aspx.*

Extended Stored Procedures

This type of stored procedure is usually written in the C programming language. The main advantage of extended stored procedures is that they are compiled routines that run natively inside the SQL Server address space. They are usually used to encapsulate complex scientific or mathematical routines. CLR stored procedures provide a more robust and secure alternative to writing extended stored procedures.

IMPORTANT   Avoid extended stored procedures

Microsoft has announced that it will remove extended stored procedures in a future version of SQL Server and recommends that you avoid using them.

What Type of Data Will the Stored Procedure Return?

Stored procedures can return two types of data: tabular result sets and scalar values. Tabular result sets are returned when you include a SELECT statement inside the stored procedure code. The SELECT statement can be filtered by values coming from input parameters or from calculated local variables.

There are two ways to return scalar values out of a stored procedure: by using OUTPUT parameters and by setting the stored procedure return value. Remember that stored procedures do not return values in place of their names, and they cannot be used directly in an expression. You can run them only by using the EXECUTE statement.

Defining Input, Output, and Optional Parameters for the Stored Procedure

When designing the stored procedure's input and output parameters, take special care in choosing the appropriate number of parameters, their names, their data types, their default values, and their direction.

Choosing the Number of Parameters

Stored procedures are like an application programming interface (API) that the database exposes to external applications and callers. Each stored procedure defines an operation contract composed by the number of parameters that it exposes and their data types. It is called an operation contract because once set, it should not be broken (unless you are using optional parameters, as explained shortly). When designing a stored procedure, carefully choose how many input, output, and optional parameters are needed. If you find yourself having to add new input parameters (required parameters) in the life cycle of a stored procedure, consider creating a new version of the stored procedure so that earlier clients can still use the previous operation contract, while newer clients will support the new parameters.

Choosing the Name for a Parameter

Parameter names should be self-explanatory. The parameter name must transmit to the caller the parameter's intention. The recommendation is to avoid weird abbreviations and to be consistent. (The same word means the same thing throughout the database.) The maximum identifier size in SQL Server 2005 is 128 characters, so there is plenty of room for good naming practices!

Choosing the Data Type for a Parameter

The parameter's data type constrains the type of information that can be sent into that parameter. The recommendation is to use the data type that best fits the type and size of information the parameter will contain as well as providing filters to avoid overflow problems and security issues. For example, say you are considering whether to use the *integer* data type, which accepts values up to 32,000 characters long, or the *tinyint* data type, which accepts values up to 128 characters long. If you know that the parameter value should never be more than 128 characters long, select the *tinyint* data type.

Choosing Between Input, Output, and Optional Parameters

For all parameters declared in a stored procedure, the external caller can provide input values. These values can be consumed inside the stored procedure, but any modification to those values inside the procedure will not be reflected to the outside caller.

To pass values from inside the stored procedure to the outside caller, the parameter must be declared as OUTPUT and called with the OUTPUT modifier. By specifying the OUTPUT modifier, the parameter is passed by reference, meaning that any changes to the parameter's value inside the stored procedure will be copied back to the caller.

Default values can be specified for both input and output parameters. A default value indicates that the parameter is optional, so if the outside caller does not specify a value when calling the stored procedure, the default value will be used. Look at the following stored procedure parameter definition in this code example:

```
USE [AdventureWorks]
GO
CREATE PROCEDURE [Sales].[udpGetSalesByTerritory]
        @TerritoryID int,
        @SumTotalSubTotal money = 10000 OUTPUT,
        @SumTotalDue money OUTPUT
AS
SELECT
   @SumTotalSubTotal = SUM(SubTotal),
   @SumTotalDue = SUM(TotalDue)
FROM         Sales.SalesOrderHeader
WHERE     (TerritoryID = @TerritoryID) AND
               (SubTotal > @SumTotalSubTotal)
```

The @TerritoryID parameter is an input parameter, so the caller must supply an input value of type *int*. The @SumTotalSubTotal parameter is optional, so the caller can supply a new value of type *money* or use the default value of *10,000*. The @SumTotalDue parameter is an OUTPUT parameter, so the caller is not forced to supply an input value. If the caller declares the call by specifying the OUTPUT modifier, the value is copied back to the caller after the stored procedure execution.

The following code example shows how to call the preceding stored procedure:

```
USE [AdventureWorks]
GO
DECLARE @subTotal money, @TotalDue money;
SET @subTotal = 1
```

```
EXEC [Sales].[udpGetSalesByTerritory] 3, @subTotal OUTPUT, @TotalDue OUTPUT
PRINT @subTotal
PRINT @TotalDue
```

Database designers must carefully choose parameter direction to return only the necessary information. Optional parameters are more flexible in terms of maintainability when dealing with changes in the operation contract and having to maintain support to earlier calling applications.

Defining the Status Value the Stored Procedure Returns

Every stored procedure can return an integer value known as the execution status value or return code. By setting this return value, the stored procedure communicates any important result state to the caller.

SQL Server 2005 does not force stored procedures to return an execution status value, nor does it supply a list of possible values to return. When designing a stored procedure, the designer must decide what possible values will be returned as status by the stored procedure as well as their meaning. Outside callers must be aware of this information to understand the return codes.

BEST PRACTICES   Ensuring precision of return code

Pre-define a closed list of possible return codes that are consistent throughout all the stored procedures in the database to indicate different statuses and to ensure that the same return code means exactly the same in every stored procedure.

Designing Error Handling Routines

When an error is encountered inside a stored procedure, SQL Server tries to continue execution gracefully with the next statement in the T-SQL code. Thus, an error will not stop the execution of the stored procedure. However, this does not mean that the error has been handled or resolved.

T-SQL in SQL Server 2005 implements several error handling constructs, including the new TRY and CATCH technique. Explaining the new TRY and CATCH error handling technique is outside the scope of this chapter, but the topic, "Using TRY . . . CATCH in Transact-SQL," in SQL Server 2005 Books Online at *http://msdn2.microsoft.com/en-us/library/ms179296.aspx* offers a full explanation of this new feature.

When designing a stored procedure, you must always include error handling routines. The error handling must focus on errors that you expect could happen (because of data validation, for example) and errors that you do not expect to happen. (There is always a chance for something exceptional to happen, something you did not foresee or plan.)

The importance of including error handling is less focused on processing logic and more focused on making the application more manageable, reliable, and able to detect problems faster. Design an error handling strategy so that the database is capable of detecting errors, handling the errors so that it can continue execution gracefully, and logging and reporting error information to database administrators for monitoring and problem detection.

Executing Under the Right Security Context

The *security execution context* is the identity against which permissions to execute statements or perform actions are checked. Usually, this identity corresponds to the identity used to log on to the database.

In SQL Server 2005, the execution context of a session can be explicitly changed. This is called *impersonation*. When a user executes a stored procedure, the stored procedure can choose to impersonate a different identity to provide the user with more (or fewer) permissions than it currently holds under its own identity. This allows for the interesting scenario of denying users access to the database tables and instead granting only rights to execute stored procedures. Inside each stored procedure, the user is impersonated into a new identity with the proper rights to execute the operation and computations that the stored procedure is supposed to perform.

SQL Server 2005 introduces the EXECUTE AS clause for defining the execution context. Here is a code example of how you can apply the clause:

```
CREATE PROCEDURE
WITH EXECUTE AS 'user1'
AS SELECT * FROM
```

EXECUTE AS can be applied with four different options:

- **EXECUTE AS CALLER**   Executes the stored procedure by using the security context of the outside caller. This is the default.
- **EXECUTE AS** *user_name*   Executes the stored procedure by using the security context of the specified user.
- **EXECUTE AS SELF**   Executes the stored procedure by using the security context of the user that is creating or modifying the stored procedure.
- **EXECUTE AS OWNER**   Executes the stored procedure by using the security context of the user that owns the stored procedure.

For more information about EXECUTE AS, see the "Using EXECUTE AS in Modules" topic in SQL Server 2005 Books Online at *http://msdn2.microsoft.com/en-us/library/ms178106.aspx*.

Practice: Creating and Modifying a Stored Procedure

In this practice, which continues with the same scenario and tables from the practice in Lesson 1, you will create a stored procedure that retrieves a result set and then modify the stored procedure to add error handling.

IMPORTANT   **Practices build upon each other**

To work successfully with this practice, you need to have finished the practice from Lesson 1.

▶ **Exercise: Create and Modify a Stored Procedure**

In this exercise, you must create a stored procedure to return the product list, so the users can filter and sort the resultset.

1. The view you designed in Lesson 1 has been in production for a while, and now the end user needs the ability to filter and sort the products to conduct the proper analysis on the data more easily. You are given the task of designing a stored procedure that returns the product category name, product subcategory name, product name, revenue (difference between product price and product cost), and the number of days required to manufacture the product. The user wants to be able to filter the results by the category and subcategory as well as by the number of days required to manufacture the product. Design your own solution before reading the suggested answer.

2. Now, your task is to modify the Get_Products_Estimated_Revenue_By_Categories stored procedure definition to include TRY . . . CATCH error handling code. In case of an error, log an error into a Log table. Design your own solution before reading the suggested answer that follows.

    Suggested Answers

1. The following code satisfies the requirements:

```
USE [AdventureWorks]
GO
CREATE PROCEDURE Get_Products_Estimated_Revenue_By_Categories
(
    @ProductCategoryID INT,
    @ProductSubcategoryID INT,
    @DaysToManufacture INT
)
AS
SELECT    Production.ProductCategory.Name AS ProductCategory,
          Production.ProductSubcategory.Name AS ProductSubCategory,
          Production.Product.Name,
        Production.Product.ListPrice - Production.Product.StandardCost AS Revenue,
          Production.Product.DaysToManufacture
FROM      Production.Product INNER JOIN Production.ProductSubcategory ON
                Production.Product.ProductSubcategoryID =
Production.ProductSubcategory.ProductSubcategoryID
```

```
        INNER JOIN Production.ProductCategory ON
                Production.ProductSubcategory.ProductCategoryID =
    Production.ProductCategory.ProductCategoryID
    WHERE   (Production.Product.SellEndDate IS NULL) AND
            (Production.Product.DaysToManufacture < @DaysToManufacture) AND
            (Production.ProductCategory.ProductCategoryID = @ProductCategoryID) AND
            (Production.ProductSubcategory.ProductSubcategoryID = @ProductSubcategoryID)
    GROUP BY Production.ProductCategory.Name, Production.ProductSubcategory.Name,
    Production.Product.Name, Production.Product.ReorderPoint,
                Production.Product.DaysToManufacture,
    Production.Product.StandardCost, Production.Product.ListPrice
    ORDER BY Revenue DESC, DaysToManufacture DESC, ProductCategory, ProductSubCategory
```

2. Create a new table called Log that contains three columns: ID, [Error Number], and [Error Description]. Modify the stored procedure's code to include the SELECT statement inside a TRY . . . CATCH block. When the CATCH block is reached, execute an INSERT statement to insert the required details into the newly created Log table.

Quick Check

1. What happens if a parameter that is not defined as an output parameter is called with the OUTPUT modifier?
2. What happens if a parameter that is defined as an output parameter is not called with the OUTPUT modifier?
3. Consider the following scenario. Mark owns the SalesOrderHeaders table in the database. He does not grant SELECT access to anybody. John creates the GetSales-Headers stored procedure that needs to read from the SalesOrderHeaders table. Mary needs to execute the GetSalesHeaders stored procedure. What is the correct setting for the EXECUTE AS clause that lets all the users perform their required tasks?

Quick Check Answers

1. If a parameter that is not defined as an output parameter is called with the OUTPUT modifier, the database issues an error message.
2. If a parameter that is defined as an output parameter is not called with the OUTPUT modifier, there is no error message, and the procedure is called. However, the modified value of the parameter is not copied back into the outside caller stack frame.
3. The correct setting is EXECUTE AS OWNER because only Mark has SELECT access on the table. Under this scenario, anybody can execute the stored procedure without requiring specific permissions for the SalesOrderHeaders table.

Lesson 3: Designing User-Defined Functions

Estimated lesson time: 45 minutes

As you saw in the previous lesson, stored procedures provide the capability to include programming logic to generate a dynamic response—either a scalar value or a result set. In this lesson, you will learn how UDFs offer the same functionality with a twist: the possibility for this functionality to be called from different contexts than stored procedures.

Similar to views and stored procedures, UDFs do not store data. A UDF stores T-SQL queries that are executed when the function is called. As with stored procedures, the T-SQL code inside a function is stored in pre-compiled format, so a query plan has already been calculated, which translates into better execution performance.

However, unlike stored procedures, functions enable you to reuse their result in much more flexible ways than stored procedures do. A stored procedure is called by using the EXECUTE statement; it's impossible to call a stored procedure from a SELECT statement. In contrast, UDFs can be called from multiple contexts.

Table 6-2 summarizes some of the different contexts from which UDFs can be executed.

Table 6-2   Executing User-Defined Functions in SQL Server 2005

Context	Usage Example	Number of Executions
FROM clause of a SELECT statement	The result set returned by a user-defined function can be combined with result sets coming from other sources by using a JOIN condition or UNION operations.	The user-defined function is executed once.
Column list section of a SELECT statement	Computed and/or calculated values can be included as part of the returned result. Also, a user-defined function can be used to execute validation logic on each of the values from a column that is soon to be returned by the function.	The user-defined function is executed one time per row.
WHERE or HAVING clause of a SELECT statement	The number of rows returned by the SELECT statement can be filtered by a complex logic coded inside a user-defined function.	The user-defined function is executed one time per row.

Table 6-2   Executing User-Defined Functions in SQL Server 2005

Context	Usage Example	Number of Executions
GROUP BY clause in a SELECT statement	Output rows from a SELECT statement can be grouped according to the result of a user-defined function. The user-defined function must be present in both the SELECT list and GROUP BY clause.	The user-defined function is executed one time per row.
ORDER BY clause in a SELECT statement	Output rows from a SELECT statement can be ordered according to the result of a user-defined function. The user-defined function must be present in both the SELECT list and ORDER BY clause.	The user-defined function is executed one time per row.
SET clause in an UPDATE statement	The output value of a user-defined function can be stored in a column when calling the UPDATE statement.	The user-defined function is executed one time per row.
VALUES clause of an INSERT statement	The output value of a user-defined function can be stored in a column when calling the INSERT statement.	The user-defined function is executed one time per row.
CHECK constraint definition	Complex logic coded inside the user-defined function can validate and filter the allowed values to be stored in the column.	The user-defined function is executed one time per row.
DEFAULT definitions	A user-defined function can return the value to use as default value for a column in a table when inserting new records in the table and not providing a value for this column.	The user-defined function is executed one time per row.
Computed columns	A user-defined function can return the value to use to calculate the value for a computed column in a table when inserting new records in the table. Complex logic coded inside the user-defined function can aggregate or calculate values coming from multiple T-SQL queries inside the user-defined function.	The user-defined function is executed one time per row.

When designing UDFs, there are several design decisions you need to consider:

- What type of UDF do you need?
- What type of data will the UDF return?
- What kind of input parameters do you need to define for the UDF?
- What error handling routines do you need to include?
- What security context should the UDF execute under?

Exam Tip Unlike stored procedures, UDFs cannot be used to perform actions that modify the database state. The T-SQL code inside a UDF can modify its internal values (internal state) only. Hence, statements such as INSERT, UPDATE, and DELETE are not allowed inside a UDF unless they are used to modify local TABLE-type variables.

What Type of UDF Do You Need?

SQL Server 2005 supports UDFs written in T-SQL code or with the .NET programming languages (called CLR user-defined functions). Both programming environments support two types of UDFs: scalar UDFs and table-valued UDFs.

Scalar User-Defined Functions

Scalar UDFs enable you to return a single scalar value. This scalar value can be either a constant value or the result of a complex arithmetic calculation inside the UDF. Scalar UDFs can be written as *inline* scalar UDFs when just a single T-SQL statement is used or as *multistatement* scalar UDFs when multiple T-SQL statements are used inside a *BEGIN-END* block.

Some of the most common uses of this type of UDF are in the column list section of a SELECT statement and in the WHERE clause of a SELECT statement. If used in the column list, the UDF can execute validation logic on a column's values, calculations, or computations on a column's values or return calculated values not using a column value as input. If used in the WHERE clause, the UDF can execute validation and filtering logic.

The following code example shows how to define a scalar UDF that calculates the total amount of tax that a certain territory must pay:

```
CREATE FUNCTION Calculate_Tax_For_Territory
   (@TerritoryID INT, @TaxPercent FLOAT)
RETURNS MONEY
AS
BEGIN
   DECLARE @Tax MONEY

   SELECT  @Tax = SUM(Sales.SalesOrderDetail.LineTotal)
   FROM    Sales.SalesOrderDetail INNER JOIN Sales.SalesOrderHeader ON
           Sales.SalesOrderDetail.SalesOrderID = Sales.SalesOrderHeader.SalesOrderID
```

```
    WHERE    (Sales.SalesOrderHeader.TerritoryID = @TerritoryID)
    RETURN @Tax * @TaxPercent
END
```

You can call this scalar UDF in the SELECT's column list, as the following example shows; this example calculates the tax for all territories in *AdventureWorks*:

```
DECLARE @TaxPercentage FLOAT
SET @TaxPercentage = 0.13

SELECT  Sales.SalesTerritory.Name,
    dbo.Calculate_Tax_For_Territory(Sales.SalesTerritory.TerritoryID, @TaxPercentage) AS Tax
FROM    Sales.SalesOrderDetail INNER JOIN Sales.SalesOrderHeader ON
            Sales.SalesOrderDetail.SalesOrderID = Sales.SalesOrderHeader.SalesOrderID
        INNER JOIN Sales.SalesTerritory ON
  Sales.SalesOrderHeader.TerritoryID = Sales.SalesTerritory.TerritoryID
GROUP BY Sales.SalesTerritory.Name, Sales.SalesTerritory.TerritoryID
ORDER BY Tax DESC
```

Notice how the dbo.Calculate_Tax_For_Territory UDF is called from the SELECT for each of the Territory IDs.

Alternatively, you can call the UDF in the WHERE clause, as does the following code example, which returns the cost to date, the sales to date, and the sales from last year for all territories that pay more than $2 million in taxes:

```
DECLARE @TaxPercentage FLOAT
SET @TaxPercentage = 0.13

SELECT   Name, CostYTD, SalesYTD, SalesLastYear
FROM    Sales.SalesTerritory
WHERE
(dbo.Calculate_Tax_For_Territory(TerritoryID, @TaxPercentage) > 2000000)
```

Notice how the dbo.Calculate_Tax_For_Territory UDF is called from the WHERE for each of the Territory IDs to filter which rows are returned by the SELECT query.

Table-Valued User-Defined Functions

You use a table-valued UDF whenever a view or a table is expected. Because table-valued functions can be parameterized, they offer a very powerful replacement for views or stored procedures.

Table-valued UDFs can be written as an inline table-valued UDF when just a single T-SQL statement is needed or as a multistatement table-valued UDF when multiple T-SQL statements are used inside a *BEGIN-END* block. Multistatement table-valued UDFs are called multistatement because they do not directly return the result of executing a single SELECT statement (as inline table-valued UDFs do) but instead return a TABLE-type variable that needs to be defined and filled with data. Database designers must carefully define the format of the TABLE-type variable to be returned by the function in the RETURNS clause when creating the function. Inside the function, data must be inserted into this TABLE-type variable only.

Multistatement table-valued UDFs are used to encapsulate complex queries that can be pre-filtered by input parameters so that they can be called in the FROM clause of the SELECT statement. The following code example defines a multistatement table-valued UDF that calculates the total sales made by all sales employees in *AdventureWorks* and returns the TOP N best sellers:

```
CREATE FUNCTION BestSellingEmployees(@TerritoryID INT = 0, @Top INT)
RETURNS @Results TABLE
(
   [Name] nvarchar(160) NOT NULL,
   TotalSales money NOT NULL,
   Territory nvarchar(50) NOT NULL
)
AS
BEGIN
   IF (@TerritoryID = 0)
   BEGIN
     INSERT @Results
     SELECT TOP(@Top)
     Person.Contact.FirstName + ' ' + Person.Contact.LastName +
       '(' + Person.Contact.EmailAddress + ')',
     SUM(Sales.SalesOrderHeader.SubTotal) AS SalesTotal,
     Sales.SalesTerritory.Name AS Territory
     FROM Person.Contact
       INNER JOIN HumanResources.Employee ON
         Person.Contact.ContactID = HumanResources.Employee.ContactID
       INNER JOIN Sales.SalesPerson ON
         HumanResources.Employee.EmployeeID = Sales.SalesPerson.SalesPersonID
       INNER JOIN Sales.SalesOrderHeader ON
         Sales.SalesPerson.SalesPersonID = Sales.SalesOrderHeader.SalesPersonID
       AND
         Sales.SalesPerson.SalesPersonID = Sales.SalesOrderHeader.SalesPersonID
       INNER JOIN Sales.SalesTerritory ON
         Sales.SalesOrderHeader.TerritoryID = Sales.SalesTerritory.TerritoryID
     GROUP BY
       Person.Contact.FirstName,
       Person.Contact.LastName,
       Person.Contact.EmailAddress,
       Sales.SalesTerritory.Name
     ORDER BY SalesTotal DESC
   END
   ELSE
   BEGIN
     INSERT @Results
     SELECT TOP(@Top)
     Person.Contact.FirstName +''+ Person.Contact.LastName +
     '('+ Person.Contact.EmailAddress +')',
```

```
      SUM(Sales.SalesOrderHeader.SubTotal) AS SalesTotal,
      Sales.SalesTerritory.Name AS Territory
      FROM Person.Contact
        INNER JOIN HumanResources.Employee ON
          Person.Contact.ContactID = HumanResources.Employee.ContactID
        INNER JOIN Sales.SalesPerson ON
          HumanResources.Employee.EmployeeID = Sales.SalesPerson.SalesPersonID
        INNER JOIN Sales.SalesOrderHeader ON
          Sales.SalesPerson.SalesPersonID = Sales.SalesOrderHeader.SalesPersonID
        AND
          Sales.SalesPerson.SalesPersonID = Sales.SalesOrderHeader.SalesPersonID
        INNER JOIN Sales.SalesTerritory ON
          Sales.SalesOrderHeader.TerritoryID = Sales.SalesTerritory.TerritoryID
      WHERE Sales.SalesTerritory.TerritoryID = @TerritoryID
      GROUP BY
        Person.Contact.FirstName,
        Person.Contact.LastName,
        Person.Contact.EmailAddress,
        Sales.SalesTerritory.Name
      ORDER BY SalesTotal DESC
    END

    RETURN
END
```

Notice that the @TerritoryID parameter declares a default value. This multistatement table-valued UDF can be executed like this:

```
SELECT *
FROM dbo.BestSellingEmployees(5, 3)
```

In this example, the function returns the top three best-selling employees for the Southeast territory. If the caller is interested in overall results that evaluate all employees in the company, the function can be executed like this:

```
SELECT *
FROM dbo.BestSellingEmployees(DEFAULT, 3)
```

By specifying the *DEFAULT* keyword, the @TerritoryID parameter will use its default value of 0.

CLR User-Defined Functions

CLR UDFs are written in any .NET programming language (usually Visual Basic .NET or C# .NET). As with CLR stored procedures, the main advantage of this type of function is that all the .NET base class libraries are available for use. For example, CLR functions can be used to access external resources such as files, network resources, Web services, and other databases. As with T-SQL UDFs, CLR UDFs can be created as CLR scalar functions or CLR table-valued functions.

This type of function is usually used to encapsulate reusable procedural code that must run inside the database server. It is not recommended for set-based operations or to manipulate heavy loads of data.

CLR UDFs are outside the scope of this chapter; for more information about them, see the "CLR User-Defined Functions" topic in SQL Server 2005 Books Online at *http:// msdn2.microsoft.com/en-us/library/ms131077.aspx.*

What Type of Data Will the UDF Return?

UDFs must always return data, either as a scalar value or as a result set.

Scalar UDFs

When designing a scalar UDF, database designers should carefully choose the data type returned by the UDF:

- To minimize the need for casting to a different type to client callers.
- So that the data type is big enough to handle all possible results.

A scalar UDF can return any SQL Server 2005 native scalar types (except the *timestamp* data type) or any user-defined type created by using a .NET programming language.

Table-Valued UDFs

When designing a table-valued UDF, database designers must choose between creating it as an inline function or as a multistatement function.

For inline functions, you specify the function's return data type by using a *TABLE* return value, and, as explained previously, only one T-SQL statement is accepted. The following code example shows the *BestSellingEmployee* UDF written as an inline UDF:

```
CREATE FUNCTION BestSellingEmployees2(@TerritoryID INT, @Top INT)
RETURNS TABLE
AS
    RETURN SELECT TOP(@Top)
                Person.Contact.FirstName + ' ' + Person.Contact.LastName + ' (' +
Person.Contact.EmailAddress + ')' AS [Name],
                SUM(Sales.SalesOrderHeader.SubTotal) AS SalesTotal,
                Sales.SalesTerritory.Name AS Territory
    FROM    Person.Contact INNER JOIN HumanResources.Employee ON
                    Person.Contact.ContactID = HumanResources.Employee.ContactID
                INNER JOIN Sales.SalesPerson ON
                    HumanResources.Employee.EmployeeID = Sales.SalesPerson.SalesPersonID
                INNER JOIN Sales.SalesOrderHeader ON
                Sales.SalesPerson.SalesPersonID = Sales.SalesOrderHeader.SalesPersonID AND
                    Sales.SalesPerson.SalesPersonID = Sales.SalesOrderHeader.SalesPersonID
                INNER JOIN Sales.SalesTerritory ON
                    Sales.SalesOrderHeader.TerritoryID = Sales.SalesTerritory.TerritoryID
```

```
    WHERE Sales.SalesTerritory.TerritoryID = @TerritoryID
    GROUP BY Person.Contact.FirstName, Person.Contact.LastName, Person.Contact.EmailAddress,
Sales.SalesTerritory.Name
    ORDER BY SalesTotal DESC
```

For multistatement functions, you specify the function's return data type by using a TABLE variable defined as a return value. The structure of this TABLE variable must be defined inside the function declaration. Database designers should carefully define the returned table to:

- Include all expected columns in the result.
- Use a data type big enough to handle all possible results for each of the columns in the result.
- Correctly specify column settings such as DEFAULT values, column constraints (for instance, accept null values, primary keys, unique constraints), computed expressions for computed columns, and so on.

IMPORTANT   Defining a returned table

Make sure you take into consideration the same factors when defining a returned table from a table-valued UDF as when defining a database table.

Defining Input Parameters for the UDF

Unlike stored procedures, UDFs can declare only input parameters. This means that the only way to return more than one scalar value is to use a table-valued function. As noted earlier, parameters can be declared as any SQL Server 2005 native scalar types (except the *timestamp* data type) or as a user-defined type created with any .NET programming language.

In Lesson 2, "Designing Stored Procedures," several recommendations were presented for defining parameters for stored procedures, including choosing the right number of parameters, names, data types, default values, and direction. The same recommendations apply for UDFs, with some differences in the last two recommendations:

- **Default values**   UDF parameters can declare default values (as with stored procedure parameters). The difference is that when calling the function to execute, the *DEFAULT* keyword must be specified to retrieve the default value for the parameter. This behavior is different from using parameters with default values in stored procedures, in which omitting the parameter also implies the default value.
- **Parameter direction**   As specified previously, UDFs can have only input parameters.

Designing Error Handling Routines

Lesson 2 talked about error handling routines and stored procedures. When designing UDFs, error handling routines are even more important. In contrast to an error in a stored procedure, which does not stop execution, an error in a UDF causes the function to stop executing, which in turn causes the statement that called the function to be canceled.

Exam Tip   The new T-SQL TRY . . . CATCH statements in SQL Server 2005 do not apply to UDFs because they are not allowed in that context.

When using UDFs, if there is a computational error or a different type of error that needs to be handled, the calling context needs to handle the error and decide what the proper error handling action is.

Executing Under the Right Security Context

Lesson 2 explained security execution context for stored procedures, and the fact that UDFs cannot modify the internal database state does not mean that security context is not important. For example, UDFs can call other functions or stored procedures that do modify the database state. The same considerations for stored procedure security context discussed in Lesson 2 also apply to UDFs.

Practice: Designing User-Defined Functions

In this practice, you will design a scalar UDF, using the scenario and tables from this chapter's previous practices as a basis.

IMPORTANT   **Practices build upon each other**

To work successfully with this practice, you need to have finished the practices from Lessons 1 and 2.

▶ **Exercise: Design a Scalar User-Defined Function**

In this exercise, you must create a scalar UDF to validate whether a product should be discontinued. It is created as a UDF and not as a stored procedure so that it can be executed from different constructs and contexts.

The Product table contains a DiscontinuedDate column. This column indicates when the product will no longer be produced. Management wants to determine which products need to be discontinued. You are given the task to implement a UDF to validate whether a product should be discontinued. The required logic is that if the product price is 0, then the product should not be discontinued. Calculate the cost per day (dividing the product cost by the number of days to manufacture); calculate the number of units that need to be sold to reach the cost level (dividing the product sale price by the product cost). All products with a cost per day higher than 500 and with a handicap of having to sell at least 1.5 to make a profit should be marked as discontinued. Design your own scalar UDF to meet these requirements before reading the suggested answer.

Suggested Answer

The following T-SQL scalar UDF satisfies the business scenario requirements:

```
USE [AdventureWorks]
GO
CREATE FUNCTION SHOULD_SET_TO_DISCONTINUE
(
    @Cost MONEY,
    @Price MONEY,
    @DaysToManufacture INT
)
RETURNS BIT
AS
BEGIN
    IF (@Price = 0) RETURN 0

    DECLARE @CostPerDay MONEY, @UnitsToProfit MONEY

    IF (@DaysToManufacture = 0)
        SET @CostPerDay = @Cost
    ELSE
        SET @CostPerDay = (@Cost / @DaysToManufacture)

    SET @UnitsToProfit = (@Price / @Cost)

    IF (@CostPerDay > 500 AND @UnitsToProfit > 1.5)
        RETURN 1
    ELSE
        RETURN 0

    RETURN 0
END
```

Quick Check

1. What type of UDF is required to encapsulate logic to execute as a CHECK constraint definition?
2. List two facts that make UDFs much more agile than stored procedures.
3. What is the main difference between an inline UDF and a multistatement UDF?

Quick Check Answers

1. In this context, SQL Server 2005 supports scalar UDFs only. Usually, the returned value from the function is used to validate a CHECK condition to evaluate whether it's an allowed value.

2. There are many possible reasons UDFs can be more agile than stored procedures; for example, UDFs can be used in different contexts and integrated with the SELECT, INSERT, UPDATE, and DELETE syntax. In addition, table-valued UDFs permit the creation of parameterized result sets.

3. An inline UDF contains a single T-SQL block that must return a value to the caller. In a multistatement UDF, there could be several T-SQL blocks working together to generate a single scalar answer or result set.

Case Scenario: Designing Objects That Retrieve Data

The end of the fiscal year is coming, so the board of directors of Tailspin Toys needs to review the health and performance of the company throughout the year. They asked you to provide them with aggregated annual sales and expense data for the main factory. However, after you provided them with that information, they realized that they also needed information for the other factories, located in China, Costa Rica, and India. Based on the preliminary analysis that board members did, they realized that they also need to filter the information by territory and by date so that they can analyze and compare the data from different time perspectives—by halves, by quarters, and by individual months.

After discovering certain worrying flags in the numbers, the board of directors discovered that the sales for the factory in China were not as expected during the second quarter of the year. To understand the status of the situation fully, they decided to focus on specific product sales and combine that information with different factors that might have affected sales, such as external providers, the number of new employees hired, the number of employees leaving the company during the specific period, and the inventories of other factories for the same products.

1. To accomplish your first task—providing the board with aggregated annual sales and expense data for the main factory—you decided to use an indexed view. Why?

2. Describe the overall steps you took to provide the board with the sales and expense information it needed for all the other factories located in China, Costa Rica, and India.

3. To allow the board members to filter the information by territory and by date, what type of object would you use to retrieve this data and why?

4. To enable the board members to focus on specific product sales and combine that information with other factors such as external providers, the number of new employees hired, and so on, you decided to implement a table-valued UDF instead of using a stored procedure. Why?

Chapter Summary

- You can use views, stored procedures, and functions to retrieve data. Choose the proper type of object according to a particular situation's requirements and needs.
- Use a standard view when you want to package a T-SQL query as a unit for security, deployment, and reusability.
- Stored procedures are suitable for scenarios that require the input coming from external values and/or when the expected result might not be a result set but a scalar value.
- User-defined functions (UDFs) enable you to reuse their results in more flexible ways than stored procedures (for instance, in the FROM clause of a SELECT statement, in the Column list section of a SELECT statement, and in a WHERE or HAVING clause of a SELECT statement).
- UDFs cannot be used to perform actions that modify the database state, and they can only declare input parameters.

Chapter 7

Designing Objects That Extend Server Functionality

Developers and database administrators (DBAs) extend the functionality of Microsoft SQL Server by adding new database objects. These objects include user-defined types, stored procedures, user-defined functions (UDFs), triggers, and aggregates. Developers rely on these components to create modular database solutions with elements that can be easily interchanged, replaced, or combined.

In this chapter, you will learn how to create database objects that perform actions and extend the primary functionality of the database server. You will learn how to create Transact-SQL (T-SQL) stored procedures, UDFs, and triggers. You will also learn how to program stored procedures, UDFs, and aggregates by using the Microsoft Visual Basic .NET or C# .NET common language runtime (CLR) languages. Finally, you will see how to use Visual Basic .NET or C# .NET code to create your own aggregate function.

Exam objectives in this chapter:
- Design objects that extend the functionality of a server.
    - Design scalar user-defined functions to extend the functionality of the server.
    - Design CLR user-defined aggregates.
    - Design stored procedures to extend the functionality of the server.
- Design objects that perform actions.
    - Design data manipulation language (DML) triggers.
    - Design data definition language (DDL) triggers.
    - Design WMI triggers.
    - Design stored procedures to perform actions.

Before You Begin

To complete the lessons in this chapter, you must have:
- A computer that meets the hardware and software requirements for SQL Server 2005.
- SQL Server 2005 Developer Edition, Workgroup Edition, Standard Edition, or Enterprise Edition installed.

- The SQL Server 2005 *AdventureWorks* OLTP sample database installed. Sample databases are available with SQL Server 2005 Enterprise Edition but are not a part of the default installation. Alternatively, you can install the sample databases from *http://msdn2.microsoft.com/en-us/library/ms143739.aspx.*
- Microsoft Visual Studio 2005 or Visual Basic or C# 2005 Express Edition installed. You can download Visual Studio Express Editions from *http://msdn.microsoft.com/vstudio/express/.*

Lesson 1: Creating and Designing Stored Procedures

Estimated lesson time: 20 minutes

Stored procedures are subroutines or sets of instructions stored in the database. They are very similar to functions or procedures of standard programming languages. However, stored procedures are not stored with the rest of the application code; they are stored in the database.

Understanding Stored Procedures

Database developers use stored procedures for three main purposes. First, stored procedures provide access control, which enables developers to hide tables and views, providing a gateway to managing permissions. Second, stored procedures can help you provide data validation, which enables developers to add restrictions that would be too complex to implement with standard database constraints (*PRIMARY KEY, FOREIGN KEY, UNIQUE, CHECKS, NOT NULL*). Last, developers might use stored procedures to consolidate and centralize logic in an application.

Before SQL Server 2005, stored procedures could be written using only T-SQL code, but now you can also used managed code to create stored procedures and other database objects. Stored procedures created in managed code are also called CLR stored procedures. You use Visual Basic .NET, C# .NET, and Microsoft Visual C++ to create assemblies that are later registered in the database and used as regular T-SQL stored procedures.

Creating T-SQL Stored Procedures

In SQL Server 2005, there are three types of T-SQL stored procedures:

- **System stored procedures (sp_)**   System stored procedures perform administrative and informational activities. They are easily identified because they are named with the prefix sp_. Microsoft provides a collection of system stored procedures for a large number of activities, including security, database maintenance, and SQL Server Agent. Two examples of system stored procedures are sp_helpdb and sp_configure.
- **Local stored procedures**   Local stored procedures are stored in user databases. They are the most common type of stored procedure.

BEST PRACTICES   Naming local stored procedures

Microsoft recommends that you do not use the prefix sp_ to name local stored procedures. Local stored procedures with names that clash with system stored procedures cannot be run.

■ **Temporary stored procedures**   Temporary stored procedures are similar to local stored procedures; however, temporary stored procedures are automatically removed when the user session ends. Temporary stored procedures can be created locally by using the number character (#) before the name or globally by using two number characters (##).

T-SQL stored procedures in SQL Server 2005 can include any T-SQL statement except those included in the following list.

- ALTER FUNCTION
- ALTER VIEW
- CREATE DEFAULT
- CREATE TRIGGER
- SET PARSEONLY
- SET SHOWPLAN_XML
- ALTER TRIGGER
- CREATE AGGREGATE
- CREATE SCHEMA
- CREATE PROCEDURE
- SET SHOWPLAN_ALL
- USE
- ALTER PROCEDURE
- CREATE RULE
- CREATE FUNCTION
- CREATE VIEW
- SET SHOWPLAN_TEXT

Creating Procedure Syntax

To create a stored procedure, use the CREATE PROCEDURE statement. The statement defines the procedure name, parameters, and contents. The syntax to create a stored procedure follows:

```
CREATE { PROC | PROCEDURE } [schema_name.] procedure_name [ ; number ]
    [ { @parameter [ type_schema_name. ] data_type }
        [ VARYING ] [ = default ] [ [ OUT [ PUT ]
    ] [ ,...n ]
[ WITH <procedure_option> [ ,...n ]
[ FOR REPLICATION ]
AS { <sql_statement> [;][ ...n ] | <method_specifier> }
[;]
<procedure_option> ::=
    [ ENCRYPTION ]
    [ RECOMPILE ]
```

```
        [ EXECUTE_AS_Clause ]

<sql_statement> ::=
{ [ BEGIN ] statements [ END ] }

<method_specifier> ::=
EXTERNAL NAME assembly_name.class_name.method_name
```

The following code creates a stored procedure that provides a list price of AdventureWorks products:

```
CREATE PROC Sales.PriceList
AS
    SELECT ProductID
        , Name
        , ProductNumber
        , ListPrice
    FROM Production.Product
    WHERE FinishedGoodsFlag=1
      AND DiscontinuedDate IS NULL;
GO
```

After creating the procedure, you can run it by using the EXECUTE (or EXEC) statement. The syntax to execute a stored procedure follows:

```
[ { EXEC | EXECUTE } ]
  {
   [ @return_status = ]
   { module_name [ ;number ] | @module_name_var }
    [ [ @parameter = ] { value
                 | @variable [ OUTPUT ]
                 | [ DEFAULT ]
                 }
   ]
   [ ,...n ]
   [ WITH RECOMPILE ]
  }
[;]
```

An example of how to use the EXEC statement to execute the procedure that returns the price list of AdventureWorks products is:

```
EXEC Sales.PriceList;
```

Using Parameters

To extend the functionality of stored procedures, you can use parameters. Parameters enable you to reuse the code of the stored procedure with different variables. SQL Server supports two types of parameters: Input and Output. Input parameters allow the caller to pass information to the stored procedure. In contrast, output parameters allow stored procedures to pass information back to the procedure caller.

To define input parameters, use the syntax @Parameter Name Type. To define output parameters, use @Parameter Name Type OUT or @Parameter Name Type OUTPUT. You can also define a default value by using =VALUE syntax. The following code illustrates the use of input and output parameters:

```
CREATE PROCEDURE Sales.GetPriceAndInventory
    @ProductID       INT=NULL
  , @LocationID    SMALLINT=60
  , @ListPrice      MONEY OUTPUT
  , @Inventory      SMALLINT OUTPUT

AS
  SET NOCOUNT ON;
  SELECT @ListPrice=ListPrice
  FROM Production.Product
  WHERE ProductID=@ProductID;

  SELECT @Inventory=ISNULL(Quantity,0)
  FROM Production.ProductInventory
  WHERE ProductID=@ProductID
  AND LocationID=@LocationID;
GO
```

To execute the stored procedure and pass the parameters, you have two options:

■ **Passing values by parameter name** Use the syntax @Parameter = VALUE. For example, the following syntax executes the Sales.GetPriceAndInventory stored procedure by using parameter names.

```
DECLARE @Price MONEY
DECLARE @Stock SMALLINT

EXEC Sales.GetPriceAndInventory @LocationID=50
        , @ProductID=515
        , @Inventory=@Stock OUTPUT
        , @ListPrice=@Price OUTPUT
SELECT 515, 50, @Price, @Stock
```

■ **Passing values by position** List the parameter values in the same order in which they are defined in the CREATE PROCEDURE statement. The following example shows this method:

```
DECLARE @Price MONEY
DECLARE @Stock SMALLINT

EXEC Sales.GetPriceAndInventory 515, 50, @Price OUTPUT, @Stock OUTPUT
SELECT 515, 50, @Price, @Stock
```

Using Return Codes

Stored procedures can use return values to inform callers about the status of the execution. A return status is an optional integer that procedures use to help callers provide flow and error control. Stored procedures support integer values only as return values, and when no value is specified, the procedure returns 0.

IMPORTANT   Use 0 as return value to indicate success

In most programming languages, a return value of 1 means success and 0 means failure. This is not the case in T-SQL, in which the convention is to return a value of 0 when no errors are encountered; all other values indicate that an error has occurred. Follow this convention to facilitate the use of your stored procedures.

To return a status value, use the RETURN statement, as in the following code example:

```
CREATE PROCEDURE Sales.GetPriceAndInventory
      @ProductID    INT=NULL
    , @LocationID   SMALLINT=60
    , @ListPrice    MONEY OUTPUT
    , @Inventory    SMALLINT OUTPUT
AS
   SET NOCOUNT ON;
   IF (@ProductID IS NULL )
      OR (@LocationID IS NULL)
      BEGIN
      RETURN 1;
      END
   SELECT @ListPrice=ListPrice
   FROM Production.Product
   WHERE ProductID=@ProductID;
   IF (@@ROWCOUNT=0)
      BEGIN
      RETURN 2;
      END
   SELECT @Inventory=ISNULL(Quantity,0)
   FROM Production.ProductInventory
   WHERE ProductID=@ProductID
     AND LocationID=@LocationID;
GO
```

To get the return value of the procedure, create an integer variable and assign the procedure to it. Use the syntax @Result=StoredProcedure. The following code uses the return value defined previously in the stored procedure.

```
DECLARE @Price MONEY
DECLARE @Stock SMALLINT
DECLARE @Result INT
```

```
EXEC @Result=Sales.GetPriceAndInventory 1500, 50, @Price OUTPUT, @Stock OUTPUT
SELECT @Result

EXEC @Result=Sales.GetPriceAndInventory 515, NULL, @Price OUTPUT, @Stock OUTPUT
SELECT @Result
```

Changing and Deleting T-SQL Stored Procedures

Sometimes after a stored procedure is created, you need to change or delete the saved code. For that purpose, T-SQL offers the ALTER PROCEDURE and DROP PROCEDURE statements.

Changing Stored Procedures

When you want to replace the code stored in the database with new statements or change the parameters of the procedure, use the ALTER PROCEDURE statement. The syntax is very similar to the CREATE PROCEDURE statement, except that the procedure must exist in the database before the command is executed.

```
ALTER { PROC | PROCEDURE } [schema_name.] procedure_name [ ; number ]
    [ { @parameter [ type_schema_name. ] data_type }
    [ VARYING ] [ = default ] [ [ OUT [ PUT ] ]
    ] [ ,...n ]
[ WITH <procedure_option> [ ,...n ] ]
[ FOR REPLICATION ]
AS
    { <sql_statement> [ ...n ] | <method_specifier> }

<procedure_option> ::=
    [ ENCRYPTION ]
    [ RECOMPILE ]
    [ EXECUTE_AS_Clause ]

<sql_statement> ::=
{ [ BEGIN ] statements [ END ] }

<method_specifier> ::=
EXTERNAL NAME
assembly_name.class_name.method_name
```

The main advantage of using the ALTER statement, instead of using a DROP and CREATE statement, is that permissions assigned to the procedure before the ALTER statement will remain assigned to the procedure. Using DROP and CREATE to replace a procedure will remove all previously assigned permissions. The following code illustrates the ALTER statement:

```
ALTER PROC Sales.PriceList
AS
    SELECT ProductID
        , Name
        , ProductNumber
        , ListPrice
```

```
      , Class
  FROM Production.Product
  WHERE FinishedGoodsFlag=1
    AND DiscontinuedDate IS NULL;
GO
EXEC Sales.PriceList
```

Deleting Stored Procedures

When you do not need a procedure, you can drop it from the database. Dropping a store procedure deletes the code stored in the database. To delete stored procedures, use the DROP PROCEDURE statement:

```
DROP { PROC | PROCEDURE } { [ schema_name. ] procedure } [ ,...n ]
```

The following code uses the DROP PROCEDURE statement to delete the PriceList stored procedure:

```
DROP PROC Sales.PriceList
```

Designing T-SQL Stored Procedures

When designing stored procedures, consider the role they will play in the application and how they can help you enhance the reusability, performance, and maintainability of the application. Also consider that T-SQL is a computer language designed with a very limited purpose—to query and manipulate data in a relational database. The following guidelines will help you design effective stored procedures:

- **One procedure, one task**   Programmers with little or no experience often create do-it-all stored procedures. Do-it-all procedures reduce the performance and maintainability of the database. In contrast, if you create stored procedures with functional cohesion, you can greatly improve performance and maintainability. With functional cohesion, parts of a module (in this case, a stored procedure) are grouped together because they all contribute to a single well-defined task of the module.

- **Validating data before beginning transaction**   All input parameters should be checked at the beginning of the procedure to trap errors, eliminate unnecessary work, and reduce security risks.

  For example, assume that you want to write a stored procedure that allows name filtering only if the user provides three characters and no fewer. A clever user might try to override the limitation by using '%%%' as a value. The code to enforce the rule is:

```
CREATE PROCEDURE Sales.GetPriceAndInventoryByName
       @Filter          CHAR(3)
     , @LocationID      SMALLINT=60
     , @ListPrice       MONEY OUTPUT
     , @Inventory       SMALLINT OUTPUT
  AS
```

```
SET NOCOUNT ON;
IF (@Filter IS NULL)
    OR (@Filter NOT LIKE '[A-Z][A-Z][A-Z]')
    BEGIN
    RETURN 1
    END
```

BEST PRACTICES   Use CLR UDFs to create sophisticated *CHECK* constraints

With the help of CLR UDFs, you can implement very advanced checks if you use the regular expressions classes included in the Microsoft .NET Framework.

■   **Qualifying names inside stored procedures**   Object names used in DML SQL statements (INSERT, UPDATE, DELETE, and SELECT) that are not qualified with the schema use, by default, the same schema of the stored procedure. DDL SQL statements (CREATE, ALTER, and DROP) use the default schema of the procedure caller, not of the procedure schema. Use qualifying names to increase the maintainability of the procedure.

```
CREATE PROCEDURE Sales.Test
AS
    -- There is no Sales.Product table
    SELECT * FROM Product
GO
EXEC Sales.Test
-- The previous command fails
GO
CREATE TABLE Sales.Product(Test INT)
GO
-- The next command succeeds
GO
EXEC Sales.Test
```

■   **Using schemas to simplify stored procedure security**   Schemas enable simpler and cleaner permissions management. Grouping stored procedures in schemas enables DBAs to assign a single execute permission to the schema, which gives a user access to all stored procedures in the schema.

■   **Considering T-SQL stored procedures for all direct access to the database**   Using T-SQL stored procedures rather than directly querying the tables provides the flexibility of changing the schema of the database without modifying the application—a security mechanism to assign permissions at a very granular level and increase performance.

Creating CLR Stored Procedures

New in SQL Server 2005 is the ability to create stored procedures in other programming languages besides T-SQL. This feature enables programmers to take advantage of the .NET Framework inside the database engine. Now developers can use their favorite programming language to create static functions that are compiled and registered in the database as regular database objects.

IMPORTANT   Enabling the CLR

For security reasons, the CLR is disabled by default at the server level. To enable CLR integration, use the *clr enabled* option of the sp_configure stored procedure. You can also use the SQL Server Area Configuration (SAC) tool to enable CLR integration. For more information about enabling CLR, review Chapter 1, "Selecting and Designing SQL Server Services to Support Business Needs."

Three steps are required to create CLR store procedures:

- Programming the CLR stored procedure
- Debugging and testing the CLR stored procedure
- Deploying the CLR stored procedures

Programming a CLR Stored Procedure

To create a CLR stored procedure by using Visual Studio 2005, follow these steps:

1. Open Visual Studio 2005.
2. Create a new project. Click File, select New, and then click Project. In the New Project dialog box, select your preferred programming language and a SQL Server Project.

BEST PRACTICES   SQL Server project template

The SQL Server project template is included only when you install the SQL Server Client Tools. If you do not have the client tools installed, you still can create a class project and reference the appropriate namespaces.

---

3. Click OK to create the project.

    If the Add Database Reference dialog box is displayed, choose an available reference or click Add New Reference. If you click Add New Reference, Visual Studio will display the New Database Reference dialog box, as Figure 7-1 shows.

Figure 7-1   Configuration options in the New Database Reference dialog box

4. Configure server name, log in security configuration, and database name. Click OK to finish the connection string configuration required to access the database.

5. If prompted by Visual Studio, configure CLR Debugging. Click OK to continue.

6. In Solution Explorer, right-click the project and select Add Test Script.

7. Name your stored procedure. Click OK to create the class file.

8. Code the content of the procedure.

   The following code creates the equivalent of a Hello World message in a tabular format:

```csharp
//C#
[Microsoft.SqlServer.Server.SqlProcedure]
public static void HelloWorld()
    {
    // Create the record object
    SqlDataRecord record = new SqlDataRecord(new SqlMetaData("Message",
SqlDbType.VarChar, 32));
    // Populate the row
    record.SetSqlString(0, "Hello World!");
    // Return the row
    SqlContext.Pipe.Send(record);
    }
```

Testing and Debugging a CLR Stored Procedure

To test the CLR stored procedure, in Solution Explorer, expand the Test Scripts folder and double-click the SQL script you created and named. Add the required code to execute the stored procedure. For example, to test the HelloWorld CLR stored procedure, add the following statement:

```
EXEC HelloWorld
```

To debug the CLR stored procedure by using Visual Studio 2005, navigate to the CLR stored procedure code and set a breakpoint. To set a breakpoint, use one of the following methods:

- In the code window, click the left bar.
- Right-click the instruction and select Breakpoint-Insert Breakpoint.
- From the main menu, select Debug-Toggle Breakpoint.
- Press F9.

After setting one or more breakpoints, run your code by using one of the following methods:

- Press F5.
- Click Start Debugging from the Debug menu.
- Click the Start Debugging button from the Debug toolbar.

Figure 7-2 shows the debugging of a CLR stored procedure.

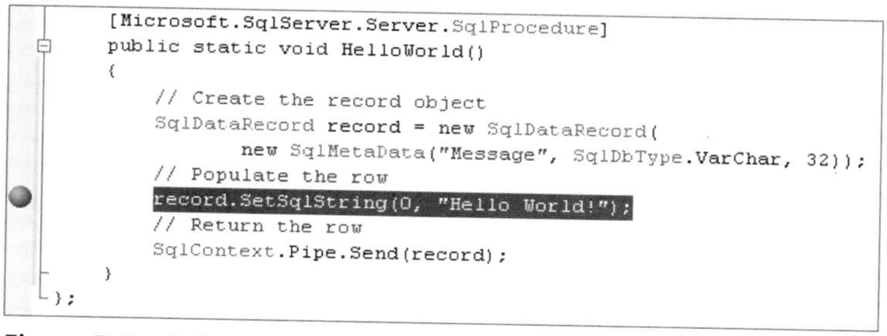

```
[Microsoft.SqlServer.Server.SqlProcedure]
public static void HelloWorld()
{
    // Create the record object
    SqlDataRecord record = new SqlDataRecord(
        new SqlMetaData("Message", SqlDbType.VarChar, 32));
    // Populate the row
    record.SetSqlString(0, "Hello World!");
    // Return the row
    SqlContext.Pipe.Send(record);
}
};
```

Figure 7-2   Debugging a CLR stored procedure

When debugging, use the step over (F10) command or step into (F9) command to continue running one line at a time.

Deploying a CLR Stored Procedure

The following steps will help you deploy a CLR stored procedure:

1. Using Visual Studio 2005, change the Solution configuration from Debug to Release. From the Project menu, select *projectname* Properties, click the Build tab, and then choose Release from the Configuration drop-down list.

2. Build the solution. From the Build menu, click Build *projectname.*

3. Find the compiled assembly path. By default, Visual Studio creates projects in C:\Documents and Settings\%*UserName*%\My Documents\Visual Studio 2005\Projects. The Release assembly is compiled in the subdirectory *SolutionName**ProjectName*\bin\Release.

4. Open SQL Server Management Studio (SSMS) and open a new database engine query. Create the assembly by using the CREATE ASSEMBLY statement. The statement will upload the dynamic-link library (DLL) into the database. If the assembly references other assemblies, the server will try to upload them also.

```
CREATE ASSEMBLY HelloWorld from 'C:\Documents and Settings\%UserName%\My
Documents\Visual Studio 2005\Projects\Demo\Demo\bin\Release\Demo.dll'
WITH PERMISSION_SET = SAFE
```

Limit developer access to the production servers

5. You can deploy the project directly from Visual Studio; however, you should learn how to deploy an assembly by using T-SQL code because most developing environments do not have direct access to production servers. Create the stored procedure by using the CREATE PROCEDURE statement. Use the EXTERNAL NAME option to reference the recently created assembly.

```
CREATE PROCEDURE HelloWorld
AS
EXTERNAL NAME Demo.StoredProcedures.HelloWorld
```

Assembly Permissions

The CREATE ASSEMBLY statement has the PERMISSION_SET option. The PERMISSION_SET option controls the level of access granted to the assembly on one of three levels. The first level, UNSAFE, is the most permissive. UNSAFE assemblies have access to all resources inside and outside the SQL Server instance. The UNSAFE permission set is the only level that supports running unmanaged code.

The second permission set level is EXTERNAL_ACCESS. Assemblies with EXTERNAL_ACCESS permission are able to access external system resources such as files, the registry, environmental variables, and the network.

Finally, the SAFE permission set level allows access only to the local database and restricts all other types of access. The SAFE level is applied by default.

On the Companion Disc   This chapter includes many code examples. You will find all the code from this chapter on the companion CD in the C:\My Documents\Microsoft Press\TK70-441 \Chapter07\ folder.

Practice: Creating a T-SQL Stored Procedure to Add Employees

In this practice, you create a simple stored procedure that follows the best practices learned in this lesson. The stored procedure will add a new salaried employee into the database.

▶ **Exercise 1: Add a New SSMS Project**

In this exercise, you create a new database scripts SSMS project. This project type enables you to track SQL scripts in a centralized manner.

1. Open SSMS and connect to the default instance of the database engine.
2. Click File, select New, and then click Project. This command enables you to create the file structure to maintain your SQL scripts.
3. Select SQL Server Scripts and name your project script **AdventureWorksStoredProcedures**. Click OK to create the project.
4. From Solution Explorer, right-click the Queries folder, and then click New Query. This will create a new SQL script file.
5. In Solution Explorer, rename the SQLQuery1.sql file to **InsertSalariedEmployee.SQL**. Press F2 or right-click and choose Rename to change the name of the file.

▶ **Exercise 2: Create the Stored Procedure**

In this exercise, you create the required code to insert a new employee into the database. The information about employees is stored in two tables: HumanResources.Employee and Person.Contact.

1. Select the Query Pane and change the database to AdventureWorks from the Available Databases drop-down list.
2. Write the CREATE PROC statement and the required parameters to populate the Employee and Contact tables. Each step in this exercise requires you to append the code in the query window to the code provided in the previous step.

```
CREATE PROC HumanResources.InsertSalariedEmployee(
      @NationalIDNumber        NVARCHAR(15)
    , @LoginID                 NVARCHAR(256)
    , @ManagerID               INT
    , @CompanyTitle            NVARCHAR(50)
    , @BirthDate               DATETIME
    , @MaritalStatus           NCHAR(1)
    , @Gender                  NCHAR(1)
    , @PersonalTitle           NVARCHAR(8)
    , @FirstName               NVARCHAR(50)
    , @MiddleName              NVARCHAR(50)
    , @LastName                NVARCHAR(50)
    , @PasswordHash            NVARCHAR(40)
    , @PasswordSalt            NVARCHAR(10)
```

```
        , @ContactID              INT OUTPUT
        , @EmployeeID             INT OUTPUT
    )
    AS
```

Notice that the ContactID and EmployeeID parameters are output parameters because they are IDs automatically assigned by the database.

3. Write a NOCOUNT statement to prevent the stored procedure from sending messages back to the client. The code should be:

```
SET NOCOUNT ON;
```

4. Declare an Email variable by using a 50-character-length NVARCHAR type.

```
-- Declare Variables
DECLARE @Email          NVARCHAR(50);
```

5. Validate that the following variables do not hold *NULL* values: NationalIDNumber, LoginID, BirthDate, MaritalStatus, Gender, FirstName, LastName, PasswordHash, and PasswordSalt. If one or more of the variables have a *NULL* value, return an error message and abort the procedure execution.

```
-- Validation
IF @NationalIDNumber IS NULL
    OR @LoginID IS NULL
    OR @BirthDate IS NULL
    OR @MaritalStatus IS NULL
    OR @Gender IS NULL
    OR @FirstName IS NULL
    OR @LastName IS NULL
    OR @PasswordHash IS NULL
    OR @PasswordSalt IS NULL
        BEGIN
        RAISERROR('Some of the required values are NULL', 16, 1)
        RETURN 1;
        END
```

6. Validate @Birthdate; make sure that no employee older than 100 years old is inserted.

```
IF @BirthDate<DATEADD(YEAR, -100, GETDATE())
    BEGIN
    RAISERROR('Birthdate may be wrong.', 16, 1)
    END;
```

7. Calculate the Email variable as the FirstName of the employee plus the adventure-works.com domain.

```
-- Other Operations
SELECT @Email=@FirstName+'@adventure-works.com';
```

8. Add the functional section of the stored procedure by first inserting the values into the Person.Contact and the HumanResources.Employees tables. Capture the ID for both tables and wrap the code in a single transaction, using the TRY statement to manage errors:

```
-- Insert Data
BEGIN TRY
    BEGIN TRAN
    INSERT Person.Contact(NameStyle, Title, FirstName, MiddleName
                , LastName, EmailAddress, EmailPromotion
                , PasswordHash, PasswordSalt)
    VALUES(0, @PersonalTitle, @FirstName, @MiddleName
            , @LastName, @Email, 0
            , @PasswordHash, @PasswordSalt);
    SET @ContactID=SCOPE_IDENTITY();

    INSERT HumanResources.Employee(NationalIDNumber, ContactID, LoginID
            , ManagerID, Title, MaritalStatus, Gender, HireDate, BirthDate
            , SalariedFlag, VacationHours, SickLeaveHours, CurrentFlag)
    VALUES(@NationalIDNumber, @ContactID, @LoginID
            , @ManagerID, @CompanyTitle, @MaritalStatus, @Gender
                , CAST(CONVERT(CHAR(10), GETDATE(),  112) AS DATETIME)
                , @BirthDate
            , 1, 0, 0,1)
    SET @EmployeeID=SCOPE_IDENTITY();
    COMMIT;
END TRY
```

9. Write the CATCH statement to return the error to the client, roll back any pending transaction and terminate the stored procedure.

```
BEGIN CATCH
    DECLARE @ErrorMessage NVARCHAR(4000);
    DECLARE @ErrorSeverity INT;
    DECLARE @ErrorState INT;
    SELECT @ErrorMessage = ERROR_MESSAGE()
            , @ErrorSeverity = ERROR_SEVERITY()
            , @ErrorState = ERROR_STATE();
    IF @@TRANCOUNT > 0 BEGIN
        ROLLBACK TRAN;
    END
        -- TODO: Add to the Log Table
        RAISERROR (@ErrorMessage, @ErrorSeverity, @ErrorState);
        RETURN 1;
END CATCH;
```

10. Return 0 if the stored procedure completes correctly.

```
RETURN 0;
```

11. Execute the code to create the stored procedure. Press F5 or click Execute on the SQL Editor toolbar to create the procedure.

12. Save and close the query window.

▶ **Exercise 3: Create the Code to Test the Stored Procedure**

In this exercise, you create the required code to test the InsertSalariedEmployee stored procedure.

1. In Object Explorer, navigate to SQL Server. Click Databases, select AdventureWorks, click Programmability, and then click Stored Procedures.

2. Right-click the HumanResources.InsertSalariedEmployee stored procedure and select Execute StoredProcedure.

3. Add values to each of the rows in the value column. Do not add values to the ContactID and EmployeeID rows.

4. Click OK to execute the test and create the T-SQL code required to execute the stored procedure.

Quick Check

1. You are designing a stored procedure. Which operation should be performed first?
   A. Begin the transaction.
   B. Validate input parameters.
   C. Execute error handling code.
   D. Set the default return value.

2. You want to use schemas to group stored procedures. Which of the following will be one of the benefits?
   A. Security: you can assign Execute permission to the schema object.
   B. Performance: stored procedures in user-defined schemas perform better.
   C. Development: it's easier to create stored procedures in a schema.
   D. None: there are no benefits in using schemas to group stored procedures.

3. You want to create a CLR stored procedure. Which tool offers better support for creating CLR stored procedures?
   A. SQL Server Management Studio
   B. SQL Server Profiler
   C. SQL Server Configuration Manager
   D. Visual Studio or Business Intelligence Development Studio (BIDS)

Quick Check Answers

1. The correct answer is B. Validation should be the first step in the stored procedure for security reasons and to avoid unnecessary work in the server.

2. The correct answer is A. You can assign Execute permission to the schema object, and schemas can be used to group database objects, including stored procedures. Because schemas are securable, database administrators can grant the Execute permission, and users will, consequently, have the Execute permission in the stored procedures defined in the schema.

3. The correct answer is D. Visual Studio is the preferred development tool in the Microsoft platform. Visual Studio is installed as part of the SQL Server 2005 client tools and is sometimes referred to as BIDS.

Lesson 2: Designing Scalar User-Defined Functions

Estimated lesson time: 20 minutes

One interesting feature of SQL Server is the ability to create UDFs. UDFs enable developers to create functions in SQL and CLR code; they can help by encapsulating functionality that later can be changed without modifying the rest of the application. UDFs also allow developers a higher degree of abstraction and ignore details of the implementation and focus only on the functionality.

SQL Server 2005 provides three different types of UDFs:

- **Multistatement table-valued functions**   Multistatement table-valued functions are similar to stored procedures; however, they are designed to return a single table. The advantage of multistatement table-valued functions is that they can be used in queries.
- **Inline table-valued functions**   SQL Server enables developers to create inline table-valued functions, which are very similar to views but provide the advantage of accepting parameters.
- **Scalar functions**   Scalar functions are routines that return a single value. They are similar to built-in functions such as DB_NAME or DATEPART.

Creating T-SQL Scalar Functions

To create a user-defined T-SQL scalar function, use the CREATE FUNCTION statement. The statement defines the name, parameters, return value, and contents of the function. The syntax to create a scalar UDF is:

```
CREATE FUNCTION [ schema_name. ] function_name
( [ { @parameter_name [ AS ][ type_schema_name. ] parameter_data_type
    [ = default ] }
    [ ,...n ]
  ]
)
RETURNS return_data_type
    [ WITH <function_option> [ ,...n ] ]
    [ AS ]
    BEGIN
                function_body
        RETURN scalar_expression
    END
[ ; ]
```

The following code creates a UDF to concatenate the first name, middle name, and last name into a full name *varchar* value.

```
CREATE FUNCTION Person.FullName(
      @FirstName          NVARCHAR(50)
    , @MiddleName      NVARCHAR(50)
    , @LastName          NVARCHAR(50)
    )
RETURNS NVARCHAR(150)
AS
    BEGIN
    RETURN @FirstName+ISNULL(' '+@MiddleName, '')+' '+@LastName;
    END
GO
```

After the function is created, you can use it in regular DML T-SQL commands such as *SELECT*, *INSERT*, *UPDATE*, and *DELETE*. You can also use it to create computed columns in CREATE TABLE statements and as columns in CREATE VIEW statements.

```
SELECT Person.FullName(FirstName, MiddleName, LastName)
FROM Person.Contact
WHERE LastName='Adams'
```

Creating CLR Scalar Functions

Creating CLR scalar functions is very similar to creating CLR stored procedures. You use Visual Studio to create a SQL Server Project; right-click the project and add a UDF. Notice that the difference between the previously generated code for the stored procedure and then for the function is the attribute in the method. The stored procedure uses *SqlStoredProcedure*, and the function uses *SqlFunction*. This attribute helps Visual Studio decide which type of object to register in the database when deploying the assembly.

The following code uses the power of regular expressions built in the .NET Framework to validate e-mails:

```
//C#
using System;
using System.Data;
using System.Data.SqlClient;
using System.Data.SqlTypes;
using Microsoft.SqlServer.Server;
// Added to use the Regex class
using System.Text.RegularExpressions;
public partial class UserDefinedFunctions
{
    [Microsoft.SqlServer.Server.SqlFunction]
    public static SqlInt16 IsEmail(SqlString expression)
    {
        if (Regex.IsMatch(expression.Value
            , @"^([\w-\.]+)@((\[[0-9]{1,3}\.[0-9]"
                + @"{1,3}\.[0-9]{1,3}\.)|(([\w-]+\.)+))"
                + @"([a-zA-Z]{2,4}|[0-9]{1,3})(\]?)$"))
        {
```

```
            return new SqlInt16(1);
        }
        else
        {
            return new SqlInt16(0);
        }
    }
}
```

UDF Properties

UDFs have some properties that affect how they can be used. These properties—determinism, precision, data access, system data access, and system verified—affect the ability of the database engine to create indexes over the results of the function.

Determinism is the ability of a function always to return the same value when called with the same parameter values. For instance, *COS* and *ISNULL* are deterministic functions. If you call *COS(10)*, it will always return the same value—0.839071529076452. In contrast, nondeterministic behavior happens when you call a function with the same collection of parameters, and every execution might return different values. For example, *GETDATE()* and *SYSTEM_USER* are nondeterministic functions.

When you create a UDF, the database engine parses the statements in the body of the function. If it finds any reference to a nondeterministic function, it marks your function as nondeterministic. This is an important concern because clustered indexes cannot be created over nondeterministic functions.

Precision is another property of functions. When a function is marked as precise, it does not involve any floating-point operation. Floating-point operations include inexact data types (real and float). Because float operations might result in rounding differences, the database engine is restrained from creating indexes over columns based on nonprecise functions. To create precise functions, avoid using float and real data types.

Data access and system data access properties report whether the function accesses the local database or the system catalog to provide its functionality. Computed columns cannot be defined based on functions that perform any data or system access.

The last function property is system verified, which determines whether the system can check that a function has determinism and precision. All T-SQL UDFs are system verified, and all CRL UDFs are not system verified.

Because CLR functions cannot be verified by the system, it is the developer's responsibility to set the properties in the code. The following code configures the properties of a CLR scalar function:

```
[Microsoft.SqlServer.Server.SqlFunction(DataAccess=DataAccessKind.None
    , IsDeterministic=true, IsPrecise=true)]
```

```
public static SqlInt16 IsEmail(SqlString expression)
{
...
```

Practice: Creating a CLR User-Defined Function to Extract E-Mail

In this practice, you create a UDF that uses regular expressions to extract e-mail information from a string value.

▶ **Exercise 1: Add a New Visual Studio Database Project**

Begin by creating a new Visual Studio project. This project template enables you to create, test, and deploy CLR stored procedures.

1. Open Visual Studio 2005.
2. Click File, and then click New Project.
3. From the Project Types list, select Visual C# Database.
4. From the Templates list, select SQL Server Project. Name the project **DataExtraction**. Click OK to create the solution and the project.
5. In the Add Database Connection Reference dialog box, select Add New Reference to create the connection string to the database.
6. Type **localhost** in the Server Name combo box. Select AdventureWorks in the database combo box, select Test Connection, and then click OK to create the connection reference.
7. Select the new reference in the Add Database Reference dialog box. Click OK to continue.
8. In the Enable CLR debugging window, click Yes to enable SQL/CLR debugging on this connection.

▶ **Exercise 2: Add the E-Mail Extraction Function**

In this exercise, you will create the required code to extract an e-mail using the regular expressions functionality of the .NET Framework.

1. In Solution Explorer, right-click the DataExtraction project and select Add; then select User-Defined Function. The Add New Item dialog box is displayed.
2. In the Name text box, type **ExtractFirstEmail** and click Add to produce the required code to create a UDF.
3. At the top of the C# file, before the class declaration, in the Using section, add the reference to the *RegularExpressions* namespace. This namespace contains a set of classes to access the regular expressions engine.

   //C#
   ```
   using System.Text.RegularExpressions;
   ```
4. Add property declarations to the *ExtractFirstEMail* UDF. Set the properties required to inform the database engine that the function does not access the database, is precise,

and is deterministic. The function should receive a SqlString as a parameter and return a SqlString.

```
//C#
[Microsoft.SqlServer.Server.SqlFunction(DataAccess=DataAccessKind.None
        , IsDeterministic=true, IsPrecise=true)]
    public static SqlString ExtractFirstEmail(SqlString Input)
    {
```

5. Write the functional section of the UDF. Use a regular expression constant to find a match in the input string and return the match.

```
//C#
string Result;
string EmailRegExpression = @"(\w+\.)*\w+@(\w+\.)+[A-Za-z]+";
Result=Regex.Match(Input.ToString(), EmailRegExpression ).ToString();
if (0==Result.ToString().Length)
    return new SqlString();
else
    return new SqlString(Result);
```

▶ **Exercise 3: Test the *ExtractFirstEmail* UDF**

In this exercise, you test the CLR UDF to extract e-mails from a string.

1. In Solution Exporer, navigate to the Test Scripts folder and double-click the Test.sql script file.

2. Comment on the last line of the provided SQL code and add your testing code. The code should test different scenarios in which the *ExtractFirstEmail* UDF can be used. The following code provides some examples:

```
SET NOCOUNT ON;
SELECT   dbo.ExtractFirstEmail('Test demo@demo.com');
SELECT   dbo.ExtractFirstEmail('Test No Email')
SELECT   dbo.ExtractFirstEmail('demo@demo.com demo2@demo2.com')
```

3. To run the tests, click Start Debugging or press F5.

Quick Check

1. Which of the following is not a type of user-defined function?

    A. Multistatement

    B. Multitable

    C. Inline

    D. Scalar

2. Which of the following is not a property of user-defined functions?
   A. Data access
   B. System data access
   C. Schema binding
   D. Precision

3. Why it is important to define a CLR user-defined function as deterministic?
   A. Deterministic functions can be used in UPDATE statements.
   B. Deterministic functions can be used in stored procedures.
   C. It is not important to define CRL user-defined functions as deterministic.
   D. Deterministic functions can be used in clustered indexes.

Quick Check Answers

1. The correct answer is B. SQL Server offers only three types of user-defined functions: multistatement, which are similar to stored procedures but return a single table; inline, which are similar to views except that they can be parameterized; and scalar, which return a single value.

2. The correct answer is C. Schema binding is an option of views that binds the view to the source tables. Schema binding is also an option of user-defined functions.

3. The correct answer is D. Deterministic functions can be used in clustered indexes. Because deterministic functions always return the same value when called with the same parameters, the database engine can store the result to create indexes.

Lesson 3: Designing DML and DDL Triggers

Estimated lesson time: 25 minutes

Triggers and stored procedures are very similar. They both are subroutines or sets of instructions stored in the database. The main difference between them is that triggers are automatically fired when data or objects change in the database. For example, you can create a trigger in a table so that every time someone inserts, updates, or deletes data in the table, the trigger fires and executes its code. You can also attach triggers to the database to be executed whenever someone creates, alters, or deletes a table.

In SQL Server 2005, you can create two different types of triggers:

■ **DML triggers**   DML triggers are stored procedures that are fired automatically when someone executes *INSERT*, *UPDATE*, or *DELETE* commands to a table.

■ **DDL triggers**   DDL triggers are stored procedures fired when objects change in a database. DDL triggers are fired when CREATE, ALTER, or DROP statements are used in a database.

Database developers use triggers for multiple reasons. Some of these reasons are:

■ **To maintain denormalized data**   Sometimes, for performance reasons, database designers choose to maintain redundant data in the database. Triggers provide an invaluable resource to keep redundancy synchronized in the database.

■ **To implement complex data constraints**   Constraints such as *CHECK*, *PRIMARY KEY*, and *UNIQUE* are powerful tools for maintaining valid data stored in the database, but they are also limited. You can use triggers to implement constraints that are too complex to implement through database constraints.

■ **To implement updateable views**   All views are not necessarily updateable in SQL Server 2005. For example, for a view that joins two or more tables to work UPDATE, INSERT, and DELETE statements must reference columns from only one of the base tables. Otherwise, the command will fail. Triggers can help you override this restriction.

■ **To implement database audit trails**   Triggers can help you monitor who changed sensitive data and when.

Creating DML Triggers

There are two types of DML triggers: AFTER triggers and INSTEAD OF triggers. After triggers fire after data has been changed in the table, which means that the *INSERT*, *DELETE*, or *UPDATE* operation has already occurred and data has already been modified. Keep in mind that AFTER triggers take place after all constraints (*Primary Key*, *Foreign Key*, *Unique*, *Not Null*, and *Check*) have validated the data. AFTER triggers are commonly used to keep audit trails and to maintain denormalized data. However, one limitation of AFTER triggers is that they cannot be applied to views.

INSTEAD OF triggers, however, happen before data is modified and act as a substitute for the original command. Take into account that INSTEAD OF triggers are responsible for implementing the change that was originally intended; in other words, the original statement will never be executed. For example, if you want to implement an updateable view, use an INSTEAD OF trigger and implement one INSERT statement per base table.

Inserted and Deleted Tables

Inserted and Deleted tables are logical tables that exist only during the execution of a trigger. The Inserted table holds copies of all rows that have been inserted in the statement. In an AFTER trigger, the Inserted table is a duplicate of the rows that were added to the table. For an INSTEAD OF trigger, the Inserted table holds a copy of the rows you intend to insert. The difference may seem semantic, but it is not. In an INSTEAD OF trigger, the data does not yet exist in the table.

Similarly, the Deleted table is a logical table that holds copies of rows deleted in a statement. In an AFTER trigger, the Deleted table has a copy of data that no longer exists in the table; in an INSTEAD OF trigger, the Deleted table has a copy of rows intended for deletion.

IMPORTANT   Trigger execution

Don't assume that only one row will be affected in a trigger. Use the Deleted and Inserted tables to work with the whole set of changes. Otherwise, the trigger will fail when a command that affects multiple rows executes.

SQL Server 2005 loads data into the Inserted and Deleted tables based on the executed statement. In an INSERT statement, the Inserted table has the new rows, and the Deleted table is empty. In a DELETE statement, the Inserted table is empty, and the Deleted table has the rows. In an UPDATE statement, the Inserted table contains the rows after the update, and the Deleted table contains the rows before the update. Table 7-1 summarizes how SQL Server manages the Inserted and Deleted tables.

Table 7-1   Inserted and Deleted Tables

Statement	Inserted	Deleted
INSERT	New Rows	Empty
DELETE	Empty	Deleted Rows
UPDATE	After Update	Before Update

Creating DML Trigger Syntax

To create a DML, use the CREATE TRIGGER statement. The statement defines the name of the trigger, the table on which the trigger is executed, and the contents. The syntax to create a trigger is:

```
CREATE TRIGGER [ schema_name . ]trigger_name
ON { table | view }
[ WITH <dml_trigger_option> [ ,...n ] ]
{ FOR | AFTER | INSTEAD OF }
{ [ INSERT ] [ , ] [ UPDATE ] [ , ] [ DELETE ] }
[ WITH APPEND ]
[ NOT FOR REPLICATION ]
AS { sql_statement  [ ; ] [ ...n ] | EXTERNAL NAME <method specifier [ ; ] > }

<dml_trigger_option> ::=
    [ ENCRYPTION ]
    [ EXECUTE AS Clause ]
```

An example of a DML trigger is:

```
CREATE TRIGGER dbo.Audit_Test
ON dbo.Test
AFTER UPDATE
AS
   BEGIN
   SET NOCOUNT ON;
   UPDATE Test
     SET AuditLoginName=SYSTEM_USER
        , AuditChangeDate=CURRENT_TIMESTAMP
   FROM Test
   JOIN INSERTED
   ON Test.Pk=INSERTED.Pk
   END
```

Creating DDL Triggers

New in SQL Server 2005 is the capability of creating DDL triggers. DDL triggers are like regular DML triggers except that they don't fire as a reaction to DML statements but rather in response to DDL statements. DDL statements include those that CREATE, DROP, and ALTER objects in the database. It is also possible to use DDL triggers to control data-control language (DCL) statements such as GRANT, REVOKE, and DENY.

The syntax to create a DDL trigger is very similar to that for creating a DML trigger. However, DDL triggers are not limited to *INSERT*, *DELETE*, or *UPDATE* statements.

```
CREATE TRIGGER trigger_name
ON { ALL SERVER | DATABASE }
[ WITH <ddl_trigger_option> [ ,...n ] ]
```

```
{ FOR | AFTER } { event_type | event_group } [ ,...n ]
AS { sql_statement  [ ; ] [ ...n ] | EXTERNAL NAME < method specifier >  [ ; ] }

<ddl_trigger_option> ::=
    [ ENCRYPTION ]
    [ EXECUTE AS Clause ]

<method_specifier> ::=
    assembly_name.class_name.method_name
```

The following code creates a DDL trigger that prevents CREATE TABLE statements in the master database.

```
USE Master
GO
CREATE TRIGGER Tr_NoNewTablesInMaster
ON DATABASE
FOR Create_Table
AS
    RAISERROR('No new tables in the Master Database', 10, 1)
    ROLLBACK
GO
```

Following is a list of the objects that you can monitor at the database level by using DDL triggers.

- Supported for CREATE, ALTER, and DROP actions:
    - APPLICATION_ROLE
    - FUNCTION
    - PARTITION_FUNCTION
    - QUEUE
    - ROUTE
    - STATISTICS
    - TRIGGER
    - VIEW
    - ASSEMBLY
    - INDEX
    - PARTITION_SCHEME
    - REMOTE_SERVICE_BINDING
    - SCHEMA
    - SYNONYM
    - TYPE
    - XML_SCHEMA_COLLECTION

- ❑ CERTIFICATE
- ❑ MESSAGE_TYPE
- ❑ PROCEDURE
- ❑ ROLE
- ❑ SERVICE
- ❑ TABLE
- ❑ USER

- ■ Supported for CREATE and DROP actions:
  - ❑ CONTRACT
  - ❑ NOTIFICATION
- ■ Supported for ALTER actions: AUTHORIZATION_DATABASE

Following is a list of server objects that you can monitor at the server level by using DDL triggers.

- ■ Supported for CREATE, ALTER, and DROP actions:
  - ❑ DATABASE
  - ❑ LOGIN
- ■ Supported for GRANT, DENY, and REVOKE: SERVER
- ■ Supported for CREATE and DROP Actions: ENDPOINT
- ■ Supported for ALTER actions: AUTHORIZATION_SERVER

Practice: Using a Trigger to Create a Deleted-Rows Table

In this practice, you create an audit trigger to populate a deleted rows table. A deleted rows table receives rows deleted from a transactional table for audit trail purposes. You will use the Sales.Currency table as the base table for the trigger.

▶ Exercise 1: Add a Deleted Table

1. Open SSMS and connect to the default instance of the database engine.
2. From the toolbar, click the New Query button.
3. If required, change the default database to the *AdventureWorks* database.
4. In the Query Editor, type the following code to create the table that will hold deleted values from the Currency Table. Also create an Audit schema to contain the Currency table.

```
CREATE SCHEMA Audit
CREATE TABLE Audit.CurrencyTomb(
    AuditID INT NOT NULL PRIMARY KEY
    , CurrencyCode  nchar(3) NOT NULL
    , Name          nvarchar(50) NOT NULL
    , DeletedDate   datetime    NOT NULL
```

```
                    DEFAULT(GETDATE())
      , DeletedBy         datetime     NOT NULL
                    DEFAULT(SYSTEM_USER)
      )
```

5. Click the Execute button on the SQL Editor toolbar or press F5 to create the schema and table.

▶ Exercise 2: Create the Audit Trail Trigger

1. Click New Query on the Standard toolbar.
2. In the QueryEditor, type the following code to create a trigger to populate the audit trail.

```
CREATE TRIGGER Sales.CurrencyDeletedTrail
    ON  Sales.Currency
    AFTER DELETE
AS
BEGIN
    SET NOCOUNT ON;
    INSERT Audit.CurrencyTomb(CurrencyCode, Name)
    SELECT CurrencyCode, Name
    FROM Deleted
END
```

3. Click Execute on the SQL Editor toolbar or press F5 to create the schema and table.

▶ Exercise 3: Test the Audit Trail Trigger

1. From the Standard toolbar, click the New Query button.
2. In the QueryEditor, type the following code to insert some test rows into the Sales.Currency table and delete other rows from it. Verify that the audit trail is working.

```
-- INSERT Some Test Values
INSERT Sales.Currency(CurrencyCode, Name)
SELECT 'TS1', 'Test 1' UNION ALL
SELECT 'TS2', 'Test 2' UNION ALL
SELECT 'TS3', 'Test 3'

-- Delete ONE ROW
DELETE Sales.Currency
    WHERE CurrencyCode='TS1'

-- Review the Trigger
SELECT * FROM Audit.CurrencyTomb

DELETE Sales.Currency
    WHERE CurrencyCode IN ('TS2' , 'TS3')

SELECT * FROM Audit.CurrencyTomb
```

3. Click Execute on the SQL Editor toolbar or press F5 to create the schema and table.

Quick Check

1. Which of the following is a valid reason to use triggers?
    A. To define a default value.
    B. To validate that a column does not store *NULL* values.
    C. To maintain denormalized data.
    D. There are no valid reasons to create triggers.
2. What is the main difference between AFTER and INSTEAD OF triggers?
    A. AFTER triggers are executed after the COMMIT command.
    B. AFTER triggers must be enabled at the database level.
    C. AFTER triggers offer better performance.
    D. AFTER triggers are fired after data is modified.
3. Which tables are dynamically created within a trigger?
    A. Inserted and Deleted
    B. Inserted, Deleted, and Updated
    C. Before and After
    D. Error and Log

Quick Check Answers

1. The correct answer is C. Triggers can be used to maintain denormalized data such as summary tables.
2. The correct answer is D. AFTER triggers are fired after data is modified and all constrains are validated.
3. The correct answer is A. The Inserted table holds the new records, and the Deleted table holds the old records.

Lesson 4: Designing CLR User-Defined Aggregates

Estimated lesson time: 20 minutes

In Lesson 2, "Designing Scalar User-Defined Functions," you learned how CLR UDFs help you extend the standard functionality provided by SQL functions. In the same way, CLR user-defined aggregate functions enable you to add to the built-in collection of aggregate functions provided by SQL Server 2005, such as *SUM*, *MIN*, and *MAX*.

Programming User-Defined Aggregates

Programming a user-defined aggregate function is similar to programming a UDF. You create a class or a structure by using any .NET language and then creating the code to perform the aggregation. After the class is compiled in a CLR assembly, the assembly is registered in the database, and a CREATE FUNCTION statement is issued to create the aggregate function.

However, user-defined aggregates are more complex than regular UDFs. In a UDF, you create only a single static method by using the *SqlFunction* attribute. In a user-defined aggregate function, you have to declare the aggregate class with the *SqlUserDefinedAggregate* attribute and implement four functions: *Init*, *Accumulate*, *Merge*, and *Terminate*. Table 7-2 describes these functions.

Table 7-2   Functions for User-Defined Aggregates

Function	Purpose
Init	To clean up the previous aggregate and start a new aggregate computation
Accumulate	To be responsible for the accumulation of the value passed as a parameter; invoked once for each aggregated value
Merge	To use when the query processor needs to aggregate to the previous calculation
Terminate	To return the result of the aggregation

The following example implements a user-defined *Concatenate* aggregate function:

```
//C#
using System;
using System.Data;
using System.Data.SqlClient;
using System.Data.SqlTypes;
using Microsoft.SqlServer.Server;
using System.Text;

[Serializable]
[Microsoft.SqlServer.Server.SqlUserDefinedAggregate(Format.UserDefined
        , MaxByteSize=8000
        , IsInvariantToDuplicates=false
```

```
          , IsInvariantToNulls=false
          , IsNullIfEmpty=true)]

public class Concatenate: IBinarySerialize
{
    private const int MaxSize = 8000;

    private StringBuilder RunningValue;
    private bool IsNull;

    public void Init()
    {
        RunningValue = new StringBuilder(100, MaxSize);
        IsNull = false;
    }

    public void Accumulate(SqlString Value)
    {
        if (Value.IsNull)
        {
            IsNull = true;
        }
        if ((!IsNull) && (RunningValue.Length<MaxSize))
        {
            try
            {
                RunningValue.Append(Value.Value);
            }
            catch (ArgumentOutOfRangeException)
            {
                if (MaxSize >= RunningValue.Length)
                {
                RunningValue.Append(Value.Value.Substring(0, MaxSize - RunningValue.Length));
                }
            }
        }
    }

    public void Merge(Concatenate Group)
    {
        if (Group.IsNull)
        {
            IsNull = true;
        }
        if ((!IsNull) && (RunningValue.Length<MaxSize))
        {
            try
            {
                RunningValue.Append(Group.RunningValue);
            }
            catch (ArgumentOutOfRangeException)
            {
                if (MaxSize >= Group.RunningValue.Length)
```

```
                {
                    RunningValue.Append(Group.RunningValue.ToString().Substring(0, MaxSize -
RunningValue.Length));
                }
            }
        }
    }

    public SqlString Terminate()
    {
        if (IsNull)
            return SqlString.Null;
        else
            return new SqlString(RunningValue.ToString());
    }

    #region IBinarySerialize Members
    void IBinarySerialize.Read(System.IO.BinaryReader r)
    {
        IsNull = r.ReadBoolean();
        RunningValue = new StringBuilder(r.ReadString());
    }

    void IBinarySerialize.Write(System.IO.BinaryWriter w)
    {
        w.Write(IsNull);
        w.Write(RunningValue.ToString());
    }
    #endregion
}
```

User-Defined Aggregate Attributes

An important step in programming user-defined aggregates is to define the attributes that indicate how the aggregate class or structure should be registered. Table 7-3 describes how to use the various attributes.

Table 7-3   User-Defined Aggregate Attributes

Attribute	Description
Format	Specifies how the class can be serialized. The *UserDefined* attribute demands that you use a class and implement the *IBinarySerialize* interface (read and write methods). The *Native* attribute enables you to use structures but limits the type of attributes you can use.
IsInvariantToDuplicates	When set to true, the engine will not call the method for duplicate values—for example, in a *MIN* or *MAX* function. When set to false, the engine will call the aggregate for each row, even when the value is repeated.

Table 7-3   User-Defined Aggregate Attributes

Attribute	Description
IsInvariantToNulls	Sets whether the aggregate ignores values. When set to true, the aggregate method won't be used with *Null* values.
IsInvariantToOrder	Reserved for future use.
IsNullIfEmpty	Sets the impact of empty sets in the aggregate. When set to true, the engine will return null. When set to false, the engine will return the result of the *Terminate* function.
MaxByteSize	Sets the maximum length of data serialized by the serialization methods.

Practice: Creating a User-Defined Aggregate

In this practice, you will create a user-defined aggregate that will calculate a special type of average; this average would not take into account the highest or the lowest value of the set.

▶ **Exercise 1: Add the AdjustedAverage Project**

In this exercise, you will create a new Visual Studio project. This project template enables you to create, test, and deploy CLR stored procedures.

1. Open Visual Studio 2005.
2. From the main menu, click File. Select New, and then click Project.
3. From Project Types, select Visual C#, and then click Database.
4. From the Templates list, select SQL Server Project. Name the project **AdjustedAverage**. Click OK to create the solution and the project.
5. If the *AdventureWorks* database is displayed, select it and click OK. This step will end this exercise.
6. If the *AdventureWorks* database is not displayed, select Add New Reference to create the connection string to the database. The new database reference window is displayed.
7. Type **localhost** in the Server Name combo box. Select AdventureWorks in the database combo box. Select Test Connection and click OK to create the connection reference. Select the new reference in the Add Database Reference dialog box. Click OK to continue.
8. In the Enable CLR debugging window, click Yes to enable SQL/CLR debugging on this connection.

▶ **Exercise 2: Add the *AdjustedAverage* Function**

In this exercise, you will create the required C# code to calculate the aggregated value.

1. In Solution Explorer, right-click the AdjustedAverage project and, on the shortcut menu, click Add, and then select Aggregate.

2. Verify that the Aggregate template is selected. Name the aggregate **AdjustedAverage** and click Add to create the C# code.

3. Before the *Init* method, declare the four variables required to calculate the average.

```C#
//C#
public SqlDecimal Terminate ()
{
    decimal Result = (Count < 3) ? 0 : ((decimal) (Sum - Max - Min) /
    (Count - 2 ));
    Result = decimal.Round(Result, 2);
    Return new SqlDecimal(Result)
```

4. In the *Init* method, replace the section Put Your Code Here and initialize the three variables.

```C#
//C#
public void Init()
    {
        Sum = 0;
        Count = 0;
        Min = Int32.MaxValue;
        Max = Int32.MinValue;
    }
```

5. The *init* function initializes the *Sum* and *Count* values to zero and sets the *Minimum* and *Maximum* values to a quantity that always will be assigned the first time the function runs.

6. In the *Accumulate* method, replace the section Put Your Code Here and write the required code to monitor all the variables. Change the parameter to accept a four-byte integer.

```C#
//C#
public void Accumulate(SqlInt32 Value)
    {
        Sum += Value.Value;
        Count++;
        Min = (Min <= Value.Value) ? Min : Value.Value;
        Max = (Max >= Value.Value) ? Max : Value.Value;
    }
```

7. In the *Merge* method, replace the section Put Your Code Here. The function should take the values from private variables in the Group parameter and accumulate them.

```C#
//C#
public void Merge(AdjustedAverage Group)
    {
        Sum += Group.Sum;
        Count += Group.Count;
        Min = (Min <= Group.Min) ? Min : Group.Min;
        Max = (Max >= Group.Max) ? Max : Group.Max;
    }
```

8. In the *Terminate* method, replace the section Put Your Code Here and calculate the return value. Change the type to return a SqlInt32 value.

```
//C#
public SqlInt32 Terminate()
    {
        int Result=(Count<3)?0:(Sum-Max-Min)/(Count-2);
        return new SqlInt32(Result);
    }
```

9. Delete the last section of the code generated by the assistant. You will not need this code.

```
//C#
// This is a place-holder member field
private int var1;
```

10. Build the project and examine and correct any syntax error.

▶ **Exercise 3: Test the *Aggregate* Function**

In this exercise, you will create a simple test to evaluate the aggregate user-defined function.

1. Double-click the Test.sql file in Solution Explorer. The Test.sql file is located in the Tests Scripts folder.

2. Write the following code to evaluate the AdjustedAverage user-defined aggregate.

```
//C#
; WITH Numbers AS
(
SELECT 0 AS Number
UNION ALL
SELECT Number+1
FROM Numbers
WHERE Number<50
)
SELECT dbo.AdjustedAverage(Number)
FROM Numbers
GROUP BY (Number/10)
```

3. From the Debug menu, click Start Debugging or press F5 to test the project.

4. Review the results pane to evaluate the function.

Quick Check

1. What is the purpose of the *Accumulate* function?

A. To prepare data for the summarize function

B. To inform the class of a new value that must be aggregated

C. To accumulate and clean up the previous value

D. To terminate the aggregation process and return the value

2. Which is one of the restrictions of a user-defined aggregate?
   A. You can define only 255 aggregates per database.
   B. You can use user-defined aggregates only on numeric data.
   C. User-defined aggregates can store only less than 8K of data during computation.
   D. User-defined aggregates can be defined only in T-SQL.

3. What will be the effect of setting the *IsInvariantToDuplicates* attribute to True?
   A. The database engine won't allow the aggregate to duplicate values.
   B. Multiple NULL values will cause the aggregate function to fail.
   C. The database engine will not call the method when duplicate values are provided.
   D. The database engine will be informed to serialize the function for every duplicate value.

Quick Check Answers

1. The correct answer is B. The *aggregate* method is called once per row in the statement to enable the *Accumulate* function to accumulate each value.

2. The correct answer is C. By design, SQL Server 2005 does not allow more than 8K in the aggregates state.

3. The correct answer is C. When set to true, the engine will not call the method for duplicate values, for example, in a *MIN* or *MAX* function. When set to false, the engine will call the aggregate for each row, even when the value is repeated.

Case Scenario: Adding an Audit Trail

AdventureWorks, a worldwide distributor of bicycles and accessories to small bicycle stores, has implemented an online ordering system on SQL Server 2005. The AdventureWorks accounting department has complained since the new database implementation that the department needs an audit trail to validate which users are changing information related to purchase orders. The AdventureWorks IT department wants to address the new auditing requirements without changing the application code. The accounting department needs to know only the last user who changed the order and the last updated date.

When analyzing the *AdventureWorks* database schema, you find that the sales orders information is stored in three tables: Sales.SalesOrderHeader, Sales.SalesOrderDetail, and Sales.SalesOrderHeaderReason. Each table already has a ModifiedDate column, which is used for the data warehousing extract, transform, and load (ETL) process but can also help you implement the audit trail functionality for accounting. You examine the database code to find default constraints that assign the current date to the ModifiedDate column. There are also AFTER UPDATE triggers that, among other things, keep the ModifiedDate column updated. The triggers are iduSalesOrderDetail on the Sales.SalesOrderDetail table; uSales-OrderHeader on the Sales.SalesOrderHeader table, and uSalesOrderHeaderSalesReason on the Sales.SalesOrderHeaderSalesReason table.

The audit trail must have the ModifiedDate column and the ModifiedBy column. The application uses Microsoft Windows authentication to validate users. Information about deleted rows is not preserved in the transactional tables, but the accounting department also wants to know whether a user deletes any order information and when the deletion occurred.

1. What changes will you implement to monitor which users change a purchase order?
2. After you implement the code to monitor users who change a row, the purchase orders application fails because it seems that some of the *INSERT* commands issued from the application are not specifying all the required columns. How will you fix the database and still provide the audit trail functionality?
3. What changes will you implement to monitor deleted rows for any of the tables related to purchase orders?

Chapter Summary

- Use stored procedures to extend the functionality of the server, to provide access control, to validate data, and to consolidate and centralize data-related logic.
- CLR stored procedures, user-defined functions, and aggregates enable you to use the advantages of the .NET Framework in the database and enable you to extend the functionality of SQL Server.
- DML and DDL triggers automatically execute code that can be used to validate commands, capture information for auditing purposes, or override the updateable view limitations.
- To create tables, defined parameters, and so on.

Chapter 8
Designing a Secure Application Solution

Security is one of the most important considerations when you design an application and a database to support your business processes. To secure your data, you must understand potential threats as well as the security mechanisms provided by Microsoft SQL Server and other components your application is using, including the operating system and programming language.

This chapter describes general and SQL Server–specific threats. You will see how you can develop a secure solution and mitigate those threats. You will learn about the security features of SQL Server 2005. You will also learn how to design a security strategy for components of a SQL Server solution.

Exam objectives in this chapter:

■ Design an application solution to support security.

    ❑ Design and implement application security.

    ❑ Design the database to enable auditing.

    ❑ Design data-level security that uses encryption.

Before You Begin

To complete the lessons in this chapter, you must have:

■ A general understanding of multi-tiered, asynchronous, and service-oriented architectures.

■ Knowledge about SQL Server components, including CLR integration, HTTP endpoints, replication, SQL Server Agent, DatabaseMail, Notification Services, Reporting Services, and Integration Services.

■ Knowledge of the Transact-SQL language elements that support security.

■ The SQL Server 2005 *AdventureWorks* sample database installed. Sample databases are available with SQL Server 2005 Enterprise edition but are not a part of the default installation. Alternatively, you can install the sample databases from *http://msdn2.microsoft.com/en-us/library/ms143739.aspx*.

■ Microsoft Visual Studio 2005 Express edition or Microsoft Visual Basic 2005 Express edition or Microsoft Visual C# 2005 Express edition installed. You can download Visual Studio Express edition from *http://msdn.microsoft.com/vstudio/express/*.

Lesson 1: Securing Components of a SQL Server Solution

Estimated lesson time: 30 minutes

When you talk about securing SQL Server, you are actually talking about defending data access to the database platform and guaranteeing the integrity of that access. In addition, you have to protect all SQL Server components included in your solution. Remember that your system is only as secure as the least secure component. As a defender, you have to close all holes, while an attacker has to find only a single hole.

To have a secure solution, you must secure all components in the solution. This lesson begins with a look at common threats and at the authentication and authorization options in SQL Server. Then, the lesson covers guidelines for securing different components of SQL Server 2005, including Hypertext Transfer Protocol (HTTP) endpoints, common language runtime (CLR) integration, replication, linked servers, SQL Server Agent, and DatabaseMail. This lesson also gives you best practices for designing security for Notification Services, SQL Server Reporting Services (SSRS), SQL Server Analysis Services (SSAS), and SQL Server Integration Services (SSIS) solutions.

The first step in securing your system is understanding who an attacker can be. The attacker can be either known or unknown to you. You need to be wary of disgruntled employees within your organization who could perform malicious updates in the database and intentional file deletions in the file system. Untrained and inexperienced users can also be a danger, unintentionally deleting or modifying files they shouldn't. Outside your organization, a casual hacker can attack your systems. These casual external attacks usually involve simple methods; to thwart these attacks, simply make sure you have not left any doors open to your system. More problematic can be an attack from a professional hacker, who might even be an industrial spy. Your system can also fall victim to a virus; there are new viruses every day.

There are many types of security threats. Microsoft uses the acronym STRIDE to describe the following taxonomy of security threats:

- **Spoofing identity** Using a valid user's credentials, an attacker can impersonate that user and gain access to the areas of the application and data to which the impersonated user typically has access.
- **Tampering** Data tampering is the deliberate destruction or manipulation of data.
- **Repudiation** Repudiation is the concept of denying that an action occurred.
- **Information disclosure** Information disclosure includes disclosing sensitive data and information about the application structure, such as path disclosure of a server-based application.
- **Denial of service** These attacks try to lower the application availability and reliability.

- **Elevation of privilege**   This threat occurs when a user obtains privileged access to portions of the application or data that are normally inaccessible to the user.

Many SQL Server attacks exploit insecure default configurations. In the relational database world, SQL injection is the most widely known attack. *SQL injection* tries to execute SQL code that the application was not intended to run by injecting the code where an application expects query parameter values. To prevent the injection attacks, you should always implement the *least-privilege* concept. If a user has no permissions to drop objects, the user cannot drop an object directly or through injection. Further, verify all user input and catch and log system error messages. In addition, do not concatenate strings to build SQL statements directly from user input; use parameters instead.

The structure of secure systems generally consists of three parts: authentication, authorization, and enforcement of rules. *Authentication* is the process of checking the identity of a principal by examining the credentials and validating those credentials against some authority. *Authorization* is the process of determining whether a principal is allowed to perform a requested action. Authorization occurs after authentication and uses information about the principal's identity and roles to determine which resources the principal can access. The *enforcement of rules* provides the mechanism to block direct access to resources. Blocking access is essential to securing any system. Figure 8-1 shows the structure of a secure system.

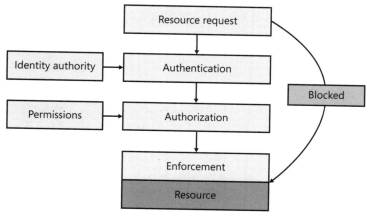

Figure 8-1   Structure of secure systems

SQL Server Authentication Modes

SQL Server supports two authentication modes: Microsoft Windows authentication mode and mixed mode (SQL Server and Windows authentication mode). In *Windows authentication mode*, when a user connects through a Windows user account, SQL Server validates the account name and password by using information from the operating system. In *mixed mode*, in addition to Windows authentication, a user can provide a SQL login and password to connect to SQL Server. SQL Server 2005 can use Windows password policy mechanisms but only if it runs on Microsoft Windows Server 2003 or Windows XP with Service Pack 2 (SP2) or later.

IMPORTANT   Mixed mode and brute-force attacks

If you use mixed mode authentication and SQL Server runs on Windows 2000, your SQL logins are vulnerable to brute-force attacks. Because there is no password and account policy, such as an account lockout policy, an attacker can continue trying to log in with different passwords until SQL Server accepts the connection. Because the SQL Server login name sa always exists and always has sysadmin permissions, it is the first target of brute-force attacks.

Always try to implement Windows authentication mode. In a domain, you should have strong account and password policies. If some of your SQL Server users are not members of the domain, you can implement mixed mode authentication. Apply mixed mode only if SQL Server runs on Windows Server 2003. In addition, audit failed logins. (You can set up auditing of logins in SQL Server Management Studio [SSMS] on the Security page of Server Properties.) You can open the Properties pages of an instance of SQL Server by right-clicking the instance in the Object Explorer window in SSMS and selecting the Properties option. In addition to implementing a regular password complexity policy, create an even more complex password for the sa login. Never use the sa login for your daily database administrator (DBA) tasks; reserve this login as a last resort for when you fail to connect with any other regular administrative login, such as if all other logins that have sysadmin permissions are accidentally dropped.

Authorization Strategy

SQL Server 2005 defines two fundamental terms for security: principals and securables. *Principals* are entities that can request SQL Server resources. They are arranged in a hierarchy in the principal's scope: you can have Windows-level, server-level, and database-level principals. A principal can be a Windows domain login, a Windows local login, a Windows group, a SQL Server login, a server role, a database user, a database role, or an application role in a database. In addition to having regular users, you can create a SQL Server login or a database user from a certificate or an asymmetric key.

Securables are the resources you are protecting. Some securables can be contained within others in nested hierarchies (scopes). You can secure a complete scope, and the objects in the scope inherit permissions from the upper level of the hierarchy. The securable scopes are server, database, and schema.

Your authorization strategy should include the following steps:

1. Identify the securables.
   - ❑ Identify all services and components of SQL Server 2005 that you are using in your solution, not just the database engine. Check the connecting endpoints for the services and interaction between the services.
   - ❑ List all databases and all objects in databases, such as schemas, tables, and procedures. Analyze those objects in terms of permissions.
   - ❑ Identify the scope of the securables.
2. Identify the principals. The principals are all users that need access to your complete solution or to parts of your solution. Check the authentication mode for each user.
3. Identify the permissions the principals need on the securables. Make a matrix of principals and securables and the kind of permissions the principals require on the securables.
4. Group the principals based on permissions they need.
   - ❑ If the principals are grouped based on similar permissions on the Windows level already, make Windows groups, create principals for them, create a database user for each group in every database they need access to, and then give permissions to the database users.
   - ❑ If you cannot group principals on the Windows level, you can group them on the database level by putting them in user-defined database roles. You cannot create a user-defined role on the server level. Reserve fixed roles on server and database levels for administrative purposes only.
   - ❑ An application role is a database principal that enables an application to run with its own, user-like privileges. An application role contains no members and is inactive by default. An application must activate the role. If an end user has no permissions in a database, and an application that the user is running activates an application role, the end user gets only permissions given to the application role and has no other means of accessing the securables. Before you close a connection that sets an application role by using sp_setapprole, you have to unset the role by using sp_unsetapprole; otherwise, application roles do not support connection pooling and thus have limited usability because they are not scalable. The sp_unsetapprole is new in SQL Server 2005; previous versions of SQL Server simply do not support application roles and connection pooling together.

Securing HTTP Endpoints

Exposing SQL Server over the Web can be a security threat. However, if you protect HTTP endpoints properly, the exposure is minimized. Follow these best practices when you use native Web services:

- Use Kerberos authentication. HTTP endpoints support the following authentication types: Basic, Digest, NTLM, Kerberos, and Integrated. Kerberos authentication is the most secure because it uses the strongest encryption algorithms and identifies both the server and the client. To use it, SQL Server must associate a service principal name (SPN) with the account it will run on.

- Limit endpoint connect permissions. You can use the GRANT CONNECT and DENY CONNECT statements to limit the endpoint connect permissions to specific users and groups only.

- Use Secure Sockets Layer (SSL) encryption to exchange sensitive data. The SSL protocol enables encryption of data over a secure TCP/IP socket interface. If you want to use the SSL encryption, you must first configure a certificate.

- Place SQL Server behind a firewall. You should never allow Internet clients direct access to your HTTP endpoints.

- Disable the Windows Guest account. The Guest account enables any user to access the local computer without providing a password. The Guest account is disabled by default in Windows Server 2003; however, in Windows 2000, it is enabled by default.

- Enable HTTP endpoints only when you need them. If you disable HTTP endpoints, you do not need to disable the Guest Windows account because you are minimizing the possible surface area for an attack.

- Disable ad hoc batches. You can expose stored procedures, user-defined functions, and ad hoc batches as Web methods. However, ad hoc batches are the hardest to control.

CLR Integration Security

The Transact-SQL (T-SQL) language has a limited set of expressions that allow risky actions. However, CLR integration gives you access to the richness of Microsoft .NET languages, and this richness can pose security threats. CLR integration is disabled by default in SQL Server 2005. Enable it only when you need it. You can enable it by using the Surface Area Configuration tool or the sp_configure system procedure.

CLR supports the code access security (CAS) model for managed code. CAS further tightens a current user's permissions for a specific assembly. Because CLR code can access not only SQL Server resources but also local computer, network, and Internet resources, setting the CAS can be an exacting piece of work. To mitigate this situation, SQL Server groups CAS permissions into three sets: SAFE, EXTERNAL_ACCESS, and UNSAFE. Table 8-1 summarizes these three CAS levels.

Table 8-1 CAS Security Sets

Security Set	Description
SAFE	This is the most restrictive permission set. With this permission set, CLR code can access only SQL Server internal data.
EXTERNAL_ACCESS	This permission set allows access to external resources such as the file system, network, and registry.
UNSAFE	As the name of this permission set tells you, this is the least safe permission set. It allows unrestricted access to resources.

Use the SAFE permission set unless you have strong, tested reasons to use either of the other two sets.

BEST PRACTICES   Use the SAFE permission set

Be sure you have a valid reason not to select the SAFE permission set.

Guidelines for Replication Security

When you secure your replication process, you are actually securing authentication and authorization, filtering replication, and performing specific measures for securing each piece of the replication environment, including the Distributor, Publisher, and Subscribers pieces and the snapshot folder.

Consider the following best practices for replication:

- Use the appropriate authentication mode. If your replication topology includes computers from the same domain only or from domains that have trust relationships with each other, use Windows authentication only. When some of the servers are not part of a trusted domain, use SQL Server authentication. Windows authentication is preferred.

- Enforce the new Replication Agent security model. In this model, you can specify a different account for each agent. Follow the principle of least privilege by allowing accounts only permissions they need for their tasks. You can set up different accounts for the following agents: Snapshot Agent, Log Reader Agent, Distribution Agent for a push or pull subscription, Merge Agent for a push or pull subscription, and Queue Reader Agent.

- Use the Publication Access List (PAL). PAL functions similarly to a Windows access control list (ACL). You can configure the PAL to contain a list of logins and groups that you want to grant access to the publication. All Merge Agent and Distribution Agent accounts must be in the PAL.

- Encrypt the connections between the computers in your replication topology by using virtual private networks (VPN), Secure Sockets Layer (SSL), or IP Security (IPSec).

- Give Merge and Distribution agents access to the snapshot share. If you use publications with parameterized filters, configure each folder to allow access only to the appropriate Merge agent.

- For pull subscriptions, use a network share rather than a local path for the snapshot folder.

Linked Servers Security

When you use a linked server connection, the sending server provides a login name and password to connect to the receiving server. You have to create login mappings between the linked servers by using the *sp_addlinkedsrvlogin* system procedure or SSMS.

The default mapping for a linked server is the current security credentials of the login. If security account delegation is available and the linked server supports Windows authentication, this self-mapping together with Windows authentication is the preferred security model. If self-mapping of a Windows account is not possible, you must set up a local login mapping from a login that uses Windows Authentication to a specific login on the linked server that is not a Windows-authenticated login. If the linked server is a SQL Server instance, the remote login uses SQL Server authentication. The linked server applies permissions for the distributed queries by using the permissions of the remote login at execution time.

SQL Server Agent and DatabaseMail

In SQL Server 2005, SQL Server Agent introduces three new database roles that control access to jobs for users who are not members of the sysadmin fixed server role. In addition, you can define a different security context for each job by using subsystems and proxy accounts. In addition, SQL Server 2005 introduces a new mail component, DatabaseMail, which uses Simple Mail Transport Protocol (SMTP) for sending e-mail notifications. You should use the new Database Mail instead of the old SQL Mail, which uses Microsoft Messaging Application Programming Interface (MAPI). Let us look at what is new in both components.

The following three new database roles for SQL Server Agent are part of the *msdb* database:

- SQLAgentUserRole is the least privileged of the new SQL Server Agent roles. Members of this role have permissions only on local jobs and job schedules that they own.

- SQLAgentReaderRole includes the SQLAgentUserRole permissions and adds permissions to multiserver jobs. Members of this role can also view all available jobs, not just jobs that they own.

- SQLAgentOperatorRole is the most privileged of the new SQL Server Agent roles. In addition to having permissions of the former two roles, members of this role can execute, stop, enable, or disable all local jobs; enable or disable all local schedules; and view and delete the history of all local jobs.

proxy accounts for replication subsystems, in SQL Server Agent, you can
accounts for the following subsystems: ActiveX Script, Operating System
Services Command, Analysis Services Query, and SQL Server Integra-
kage execution subsystem. There is no subsystem for T-SQL job steps.

the SQL Server Agent service account appropriately. It does not have to be a
of the local Windows Administrators group anymore. However, it must be a member
the sysadmin fixed SQL Server role and have the following Windows user rights:

- Adjust memory for quotas for a process
- Act as a part of the operating system
- Bypass traverse checking
- Log on as a batch job
- Log on as a service
- Replace a process level token

For DatabaseMail, follow these best practices:

- Enable DatabaseMail only if you need it. It is disabled by default.
- Use private profiles. With private profiles, you can select which database users have
  access to a profile.
- In the *msdb* database, SQL Server 2005 introduces the DatabaseMailUserRole fixed role.
  A user must be a member of this role to send SMTP mails.
- Restrict attachment sizes and make a list of prohibited extensions.

Designing Security for Notification Services

With Notification Services, you can implement security by using database roles and restricted
database user accounts. Notification Services consists of an engine that runs hosted event providers, generators, and distributors. In addition, you can have client applications for submitting events and managing subscriptions. The accounts that the engine and the clients use can
gain access to SQL Server through Windows or SQL Server authentication, then gain access to
databases through database user accounts, and, finally, obtain permissions through membership in Notification Services database roles.

For individual components, you can use the following database roles:

- NSEventProvider role gives permissions to accounts used by the hosted event that pro-
  viders use. Nonhosted event providers are independent applications.
- For accounts that the generators use, use the NSGenerator role.
- For accounts that the distributors use, use the NSDistributor role.
- Accounts that the subscription management interfaces use obtain permissions through
  the NSSubscriberAdmin role.

- Members of the NSReader role can execute stored procedures that read instance and application metadata.
- Members of the NSAnalysis role can execute stored procedures that produce reports for performance analysis and troubleshooting.
- For cleaning the obsolete data, you can use the NSVacuum role.
- If you are a member of the NSAdmin role, you can enable and disable instances, applications, and components.
- The NSRunService role combines the permissions of the NSEventProvider, NSGenerator, NSDistributor, NSReader, NSAnalysis, and NSVacuum roles.

In addition to using the fixed Notification Services roles, run the Notification Services engine under a low-privileged domain or local account. Do not use Local System, Local Service, or Network Service accounts. The account used to run the Notification Services engine must be a member of the SQLServer2005NotificationServicesUser$*ComputerName* Windows group. Use NTFS permissions to secure the files and folders Notification Services uses to store configuration information and application definition data.

Exam Tip   You need to understand only in general how to secure Reporting Services and Analysis Services. Details about securing these services are included in the Business Intelligence track exams. However, be sure to understand Notification Services and Integration Services security thoroughly.

Designing Security for Reporting Services

SQL Server Reporting Services (SSRS) uses two SQL Server databases for internal storage: *ReportServer* and *ReportServerTempdb*. The Report Server Web service and Report Server Windows service need access to these databases. You can use the Reporting Services Configuration tool to specify the connection. You can specify the service account, a domain account, or a SQL Server login. The account you use must be a member of the Public and RSExecRole roles for the report server databases. The RSExecRole provides services with permissions for accessing the database tables and for executing stored procedures.

For end users, SSRS does not provide its own authentication mechanism. It uses ASP.NET security, Microsoft Internet Information Services (IIS) security, and Windows security. Windows authentication (integrated security) is the most secure mechanism. You can use anonymous access only with custom extensions. Use basic authentication only for deployments that use SSL. Digest authentication is not supported. For extranet and intranet access, you can use a custom authentication scheme. You can still support Windows authentication if you meet the following conditions:

- Create a domain account with access to the computer hosting the report server. Create a custom Web form so that users can log on using this domain account.

- Define role assignments that map the user account to specific items in the SSRS folder hierarchy.
- Configure reports to use stored credentials to get data for the report.

For using the reports, SSRS uses role-based authorization. All users work with SSRS within the context of a role. In SSRS, tasks are pre-defined actions that a user or administrator can perform. There are two levels of tasks. Item-level tasks are performed on items managed by an SSRS instance, including reports, report models, resources, and shared schedules usage and folders. System-level tasks are actions that you perform at the system level, such as managing jobs or sharing schedules.

Role assignments determine access to stored items and to SSRS itself. A role assignment includes securable items such as reports, authenticated user or group accounts, and role definitions that define a set of managing or administrative tasks. To manage SSRS efficiently, use pre-defined role assignments, which Table 8-2 summarizes.

Table 8-2   SSRS Pre-Defined Roles

Role	Description
Browser	This role is enough to traverse folders and execute reports.
Content Manager	Members of this role can define a folder structure, set security at the item level, and view and manage the items.
Report Builder	Membership in this role enables you to use report models to build ad hoc reports with Report Builder.
Publisher	The Publisher role enables publishing content to a report server.
My Reports	Members of this role can build reports for personal use or store reports in a user-owned folder.
System Administrator	This administrative role gives users permissions to define features of an SSRS instance and set defaults, set site-wide security, create role definitions, and manage jobs.
System User	Users in this role can view system properties and shared schedules.

Security settings in SSRS follow the inheritance model. All items in a folder inherit security settings from that folder. You can override the inherited permissions by defining security for individual items.

Designing Security for Analysis Services

SQL Server 2005 Analysis Services (SSAS) does not have its own authentication mechanism; it relies on the operating system to authenticate users. After users connect, they get permissions through the SSAS roles they belong to. You can assign Windows users and groups to SSAS roles.

In SSAS, you have a single fixed-server role that grants members all permissions on the SSAS instance. By default, after installation, the Local Administrators group is the only member of this role.

You can put users in database roles. For each database role, you can define a customized set of permissions. These permissions include administrator permissions, process object permissions, view object metadata permissions, and permissions to view or modify data at multiple levels of an SSAS database. Security is inheritable; for example, all objects in a database inherit security settings from the database they belong to. A database role that has administrative permissions enables members to perform any task in the database. Inside a database, you can grant permissions to database roles for data sources, cubes, dimensions, and mining models. For dimensions, you can set permissions on a subset of data in a dimension only. For cubes, you can define permissions for a subset of data in that cube. You can set this cell-level security only through Multidimensional Expressions (MDX); because you have to deal with many—possibly millions or even billions of cells—there is no user interface for cell-level security.

In SSAS, a single cube can include multiple star and snowflake schemas, representing a complete data warehouse. Although this concept seems attractive, you have two problems with such a hypercube. You must direct your end users to their areas of interest; for example, you have to direct sales analysts to the sales part of the hypercube. In addition, you must secure the data; that is, you have to prevent the sales analysts from seeing human resources data. You can achieve the first task simply by using perspectives. A perspective serves like a view in a relational database, although it is a kind of multidimensional view. However, unlike a view in a relational database management system (RDBMS), a perspective is not a securable. You cannot set up permissions on perspectives; you have to grant permissions on underlying physical objects. Therefore, if you use a hypercube that has multiple measure groups, you end up with dimension and cell data security. The best practice is to create multiple smaller cubes from a single data warehouse. You can still take advantage of multiple measure groups per cube. For example, in your sales cube, you can combine the actual with the planned data as well as add some interesting data from the finance part of the data warehouse.

As with the database engine, SSAS 2005 supports CLR stored procedures. Similarly, you have three predefined CAS permission sets: SAFE, EXTERNAL_ACCESS, and UNSAFE. Use the SAFE set whenever possible.

For an SSAS service, use a domain or a local Windows account. The rights this account needs include:

- Bypass traverse checking.
- Token object creation.
- Security audit generation.
- Locking of pages in memory.
- Replacement of a process-level token permission.

The installation procedure grants the SSAS account these permissions. In addition, the SSAS account needs access to source data. All communication between clients and an SSAS instance is encrypted by default.

Designing Security for Integration Services

SQL Server Integration Services (SSIS) has a new multilayered security model. As a creator, you can digitally sign a package. By digitally signing a package, you prevent a malicious or inadvertent change. An SSIS package can include sensitive information such as usernames and passwords. You can protect this information by setting the ProtectionLevel property of a package. You have the following options:

- **Do Not Save Sensitive** Suppresses sensitive information in the package when you save it.
- **Encrypt All With Password** Encrypts the complete package with a password. To edit or run the package, the user must provide the package password.
- **Encrypt All With User Key** Encrypts the whole package by using a key based on the user profile.
- **Encrypt Sensitive With Password** Enables encryption of only the sensitive information by using a password.
- **Encrypt Sensitive With User Key** Enables encryption of only the sensitive information by using a key based on the user profile.
- **Rely On Server Storage For Encryption** Protects the whole package by using new SQL Server database roles when you save a package to the *msdb* database. When you store a package to SQL Server, you can add users to the following fixed *msdb* database roles to grant them permissions on a package:
  - ❑ db_dtsadmin, which allows all actions on saved packages.
  - ❑ db_dtsltduser, which allows importing packages; enumerating all packages; and viewing, executing, exporting, deleting, and changing package roles of your own packages only.
  - ❑ db_dtsoperator, which enables members to enumerate, view, execute, and export all packages. In addition, it allows the execution of packages in SQL Server Agent.

The package ProtectionLevel property does not protect packages stored in a file system from unintentional deletion or modification through the use of an incorrect tool such as Notepad. It also does not protect files that are stored outside the package such as configuration, checkpoint, and log files. You have to protect these files separately by using NTFS permissions.

In SSMS, you can use the SSIS service to list running packages. Members of the local Windows Administrators group can view and stop all currently running packages; other users can view and stop only packages that they started.

Practice: Securing a SQL Server Solution

In this conceptual practice, you will make some decisions about application security and about securing components of a SQL Server solution.

▶ **Exercise: Application Security**

In this conceptual exercise, you need to ensure that your SQL Server solution is safe from code injection attacks. In addition, you have to minimize the surface attack area.

1. How can you mitigate code-injection attacks? This is a broad question; think over all possibilities, and then compare your findings with the suggested answer.

2. How can you minimize the surface attack area for your SQL Server services and components quickly?

   Note your ideas, and then compare them against the suggested answer.

   Suggested Answers

1. Whenever you use string concatenation to build SQL code dynamically and accept user input as part of the concatenated string, treat your application as insecure. There are too many different techniques to exploit this vulnerability, and new techniques evolve all the time. You can mitigate the problem by using the minimal-privilege approach. Disable all unnecessary services and features, such as extended procedures, to minimize the attack surface area. You should not return SQL Server error messages to the client application directly because they can inform the attacker that your application is using string concatenation. Validate all user input, testing the size and type of the input. Validate XML input against XML schemas. Check and reject special characters that can be used to modify the intended execution of your SQL string, such as semicolons (command delimiter), apostrophes (string delimiter), and double hyphens (inline comments). Do not accept strings that an attacker can use to construct file names, such as AUX, CON, and so on.

2. Use the Surface Area Configuration tool to disable all services and features that you do not need.

Quick Check

1. How can you secure the sa login?

2. How would you implement the principle of least privilege for Notification Services, Reporting Services, and Analysis Services service accounts?

3. Your application uses the xp_cmdshell extended stored procedure. After you upgrade your database to SQL Server 2005, your application does not run anymore. What went wrong, and what can you do to mitigate the problem?

Quick Check Answers

1. Use Windows authentication mode. If you use mixed mode authentication, install SQL Server on Windows Server 2003 and use the Account Lockout policy. Set the account lockout threshold to five or fewer invalid login attempts. Give the sa login a very strong password, more than 10 characters long, including some non-alphanumerical characters. Store the password in a safe place and never use the sa login for your daily activities. In addition, audit failed login attempts on the SQL Server level.

2. Run all these services under a low-privileged domain or local account. Do not use Local System, Local Service, or Network Service accounts.

3. In SQL Server 2005, the xp_cmdshell extended procedure is disabled by default. You can enable it by using the SQL Server Surface Area Configuration tool as an intermediate solution. For a long-term solution, replace the procedure with one or more CLR stored procedures.

Lesson 2: Designing the Database to Enable Auditing and Encryption

---

Estimated lesson time: 30 minutes

Auditing is an important part of any security strategy. With auditing, you can prevent, resolve, or at least mitigate repudiation problems. You can protect the data by disallowing direct access and allowing data manipulation through programmable objects only. In addition, you can protect highly sensitive data by using encryption. SQL Server 2005 supports encryption through symmetric keys, asymmetric keys, certificates, and password phrases. In this lesson, you will learn about designing an auditing strategy and the different auditing techniques available. You will also learn about encryption support in SQL Server 2005.

Considerations for an Auditing Strategy

Auditing adds processing overhead to production servers. Therefore, it is important to choose carefully the auditing events you want to capture and appropriate storage for the audit information. You have to design a smart audit strategy that balances the amount of auditing information you collect with database performance. Of course, you need to catch all security breaches.

Exam Tip   Understand all the different possibilities you have for auditing. Do not forget that you can also use third-party tools for auditing.

The first thing you have to determine when you design an auditing strategy is the events you need to audit. You must decide whether to audit for successful, unsuccessful, or all events. You also have to determine the grain (that is, the level of detail) of each event you want to audit. You need to determine which resources you need to audit, such as servers, databases, or data. Audit only events that are relevant for your business. Follow these guidelines:

- Identify whether you have any regulatory requirements. These requirements, such as the Health Insurance Portability and Accountability Act (HIPAA) or General Principles for the Assessment of Certification Bodies for Product Certification (C2), already define the events you must audit. When you enable C2 auditing in SQL Server 2005 (by using sp_configure), SQL Server traces pre-defined events. SQL Server saves the files in the file system.

- If you use SQL Server logins that bypass Windows account policies, audit at least failed login attempts. SQL Server logins that bypass the account lockout policy are sensitive to brute-force attacks.

- You have to identify your business requirements. Some business processes require well-known auditing events. An online Web store, for example, might need to audit all orders to prevent repudiation. Banks might need to audit all money transfer operations. Interview all managers of each department to determine these business requirements.

- Besides business requirements, you might need to audit for additional security requirements. In your organization, for example, you might have a request to audit all login attempts, successful and unsuccessful.

- Obtain management support. People often think of auditing as an unnecessary control. Get approval for auditing from all stakeholders.

Auditing does not help your organization if nobody reviews the collected data. Your auditing strategy must include regular overview and examination of gathered information. Find out who is responsible for analyzing specific events and make sure the events are reviewed frequently enough to catch security breaches in a timely manner. Also, define the reporting process and possible countermeasures when a reviewer notices an incident. In addition, you need a way of preserving auditing logs. Define the retention period for collected data as well as the process for deleting auditing information after the retention period expires. Note that you might need to save some auditing data permanently. If you store auditing data on external devices such as tapes, find an appropriate location for saving these devices.

You have to secure the audit logs to prevent unauthorized access and possible modifications of the collected information. Implement a very restrictive policy; only authorized reviewers should have access to this information. You have to use regular security systems of the storage you use to protect your auditing information. For example, if you store auditing information in files in the file system, use NTFS permissions; if you store auditing information in SQL Server tables, grant permissions on these tables just as you grant permissions on production tables. Reviewers need read-only permissions on auditing data.

Make sure you support your auditing solution with documentation. Document how your strategy meets regulations and business and security requirements. Document events, resources, techniques, and storage of auditing information. In addition, clearly document the reviewing process.

Auditing Events, Techniques, Tools, and Storage

There are many different tools and techniques you can use for auditing. You can save the gathered information to different storage locations. In this lesson, you will learn which tools and storage are appropriate for selected events.

Security and DDL Events

For auditing security events, follow these guidelines:

- If you need to audit logins only, use SQL Server login audits. You can set up this auditing via SSMS, Server Properties, or Security, or by using the sp_configure system procedure. SQL Server writes auditing information to the Windows Application Log. The Windows Event Logs have limited size, and when full, new events overwrite old ones. Therefore, review this information frequently.

- SQL Server Profiler can trace a variety of security and data-definition language (DDL) events. You can save a trace to a file on the file system or to a SQL Server table.

- If you need to prevent security changes on DDL statements, such as creation of a login, besides auditing them, implement DDL triggers. DDL triggers are just like data manipulation language (DML) triggers and execute as part of the transaction, and you can use the ROLLBACK statement in the body of a DDL trigger. DDL triggers can have an all-server or specific database scope. You can access the audited information from DDL triggers by using the *EVENTDATA* function. This function returns data in XML format; you can use XQuery to parse this information and store it to a relational table.

- Event notifications are more lightweight than DDL triggers and are thus more appropriate if you just need to audit security and DDL events. However, event notifications use Service Broker, so you need to enable it in your database. Like DDL triggers, event notifications can have a server or database scope. The *EVENTDATA* function is called automatically when an event notification fires, and the results are returned to the specified Service Broker.

IMPORTANT   DDL triggers and event notifications caveats

Because DDL triggers and event notifications return data in XML format, they are prone to XML injection attacks. In SQL Server, you can create objects that have uncommon names. You can use special characters if you enclose the name in brackets. However, some special characters have special meanings in XML. The *EVENTDATA* function returns XML escape sequences instead of special characters; therefore, you cannot audit exact object names. The following practice shows this problem when a table with a name of [<] is created; the *EVENTDATA* function returns the name <.

Auditing DML Events

Users can modify (insert, update, or delete) data or read it (select). Depending on what you need to audit, you have the following options:

- Use DML triggers. You can use DML triggers to prevent modifications. DML triggers give you access to the state before and after the modification through Deleted and Inserted tables. You can access those tables in the body of a trigger. In addition, you can use system functions to get additional information, such as the name of the user who performed the DML statement. DML triggers can fire before (instead of) and after a DML statement. DML triggers do not fire for SELECT statements; therefore, you cannot use them to audit reads. You can store information from DML triggers in different places:

❑ If you need just information about who updated a row and when, you can add this information in additional columns of the production table itself. However, you cannot maintain a full history of events with this technique.

❑ You can write the auditing information to separate single or multiple audit tables. You can use SSRS to create reports on these tables.

❑ Triggers are part of a transaction; if the transaction is rolled back, then the auditing information you insert in SQL Server tables is rolled back as well. Therefore, you cannot use SQL Server tables to audit unsuccessful attempts. If you want to use a DML trigger to audit rolled back transactions, use nontransactional storage, such as a text file in the file system or the Windows Event Log, for your auditing information. Use CLR triggers to access storage outside SQL Server.

■ DML triggers can be very resource intensive; you can use Service Broker to send the auditing information to a queue and store it to your final storage asynchronously.

■ In SQL Server 2005, you can access the information from the Deleted and Inserted tables without using triggers through the new OUTPUT clause of INSERT, UPDATE, and DELETE statements. However, this technique might require changes in your application.

■ You can use SQL Server Profiler for DML events. With Profiler, you can trace SELECT statements as well. However, take care not to audit too many events because the impact on your production server could be too large. In addition, understand that Profiler can miss some events if the server is under heavy load.

■ Third-party solutions can be very useful for auditing. Some of them read the modification statements from the transaction log asynchronously and use SQL Server Profiler trace to catch SELECT statements. This way, the impact on your production server is minimal.

Auditing SQL Server Analysis Services (SSAS)

If you need to audit SSAS, you have the following options:

■ Use SQL Server Profiler. In SQL Server 2005, you can use Profiler to trace Analysis Services as well.

■ Use the SSAS query log. SSAS can save the query log; you can store it by using any OLE DB provider installed on your computer. You can define different query sampling. By default, SSAS logs every tenth query when you use query logging.

Data Protection

You can protect your data by disallowing direct access to it and allowing data manipulation only through programmable objects. In addition, you can protect highly sensitive data by using encryption. Let's first look at how you can protect your data by using views, stored procedures, and user-defined functions, and then look at SQL Server 2005 encryption support.

You can protect your data through views, stored procedures, and user-defined functions (UDFs). You do not have to give end users any permissions on base tables; instead, you can implement a strategy in which end users must work with data through the programmable objects that you control.

You can use views to implement column-level security; in the view definition query, simply include only columns that end users need to access. You can use views to implement row-level security through the WHERE clause of the SELECT statement in the view definition. However, for row-level security, include the WITH CHECK OPTION clause in your CREATE VIEW statement. When this option is enabled, a row must conform to the WHERE clause even after an update; therefore, this option prevents moving a row outside the view definition. Views can also help users preparing reports because the query in the view definition can join multiple tables and hide the complexity of database schema from users. You can use views to summarize data as well. Note that if you need parameterized views, you have to create inline table-valued, user-defined functions.

You do not have to use views for reading only; you can also allow data modification through views. However, stored procedures are more suitable for updating data, especially because they typically perform better than ad hoc queries. In addition, stored procedures accept parameters, and you can verify user input in the body of a stored procedure. You can also combine multiple statements in a stored procedure, thus performing complex updates.

You can protect the view, UDF, and stored procedure code by creating them, using the WITH ENCRYPTION option. You can digitally sign programmable objects and thus prevent unauthorized code changes. You can also specify any execution context you want for a stored procedure, function (except inline functions), queue, or trigger by using the EXECUTE AS clause.

Data Encryption

If you need to store confidential data in your database, you can use data encryption. SQL Server 2005 supports encryption with symmetric keys, asymmetric keys, certificates, and password phrases. Let's look at each of these encryption techniques.

When you use symmetric key encryption, the party that encrypts the data shares the same key with the party that decrypts the data. Because the same key is used for encryption and decryption, this is called *symmetric key encryption*. This encryption is very fast, but if an unauthorized party somehow acquires the key, that party can decrypt the data. Therefore, protecting symmetric keys is a challenge because they must remain secret. Symmetric encryption is also called *secret-key encryption.*

In *asymmetric-key encryption,* you use two different keys that are mathematically linked. You must keep one key secret and prevent unauthorized access to it; this is the private key. You make the other key public to anyone; this is the public key. If you encrypt the data with the public key, you can decrypt the data with the private key; if you encrypt the data with the private key, you can decrypt it with the public key. Asymmetric encryption is very strong; however, it is much slower than symmetric encryption. Asymmetric encryption is useful for digital signatures. A developer applies a hash algorithm to the code to create a message digest, which is a compact and unique representation of data. Then the developer encrypts the digest with the private key. Anybody with a public key from the same pair can decrypt the digest and use the same hash algorithm to calculate the digest from the code again. If the re-calculated and decrypted digests match, you can identify who created the code.

A *certificate* is a digitally signed statement that binds the value of a public key to the identity of the person, device, or service that holds the corresponding private key. It identifies the owner of the public and private keys. You can use certificates for authentication. A certificate can be issued by a trusted authority or by SQL Server. You can create a certificate from a file (if the certificate was issued by a trusted authority) or a digitally signed executable file (assembly), or you can create a self-signed certificate in SQL Server directly. You can use certificates to encrypt the data; of course, this way you are actually using asymmetric encryption.

Use symmetric keys to encrypt the data because secret-key encryption is much faster than public-key encryption. You can then use asymmetric encryption to protect symmetric keys and use certificates for authentication. You combine certificates and keys to encrypt data in the following manner:

- Server sends a certificate and public key to a client. The certificate identifies the server to the client.

- Client creates two symmetric keys. The client encrypts one symmetric key with the public key and sends it to the server.

- Server's private key can decrypt the symmetric key. The server and client encrypt and decrypt data with symmetric keys.

When encrypting data, consider all possible surface areas for an attack. For example, if you encrypt the data in SQL Server but send clear text over the network, an attacker could use a network monitor to intercept the clear text. Use IPSec or SSL on-the-wire encryption. An attacker can even sniff client computer memory to retrieve clear text. Therefore, use .NET encryption in client applications in addition to or instead of server encryption.

Consider the following tradeoffs when you design a solution that uses data encryption:

- Encrypted data is typically stored in a *varbinary(max)* data type column; space is not allocated according to the original data type like it is with unencrypted data. This means you need to change your database schema to support data encryption.

- Sorting of encrypted data is different from sorting of unencrypted data and makes no sense from the business point of view.

- Similarly, indexing and filtering operations on encrypted data are useless from a business point of view.

- You might need to change applications to support data encryption.

- Encryption is a processor-intensive process.

Practice: Using Event Notifications to Audit DDL Events

In this practice, you will create an event notification for any *CREATE TABLE* event. You test this notification by using an uncommon table name.

▶ Exercise 1: Create an Event Notification

You start this exercise by creating an event notification in the *tempdb* system database.

1. Use SSMS and open a new query window. Connect to an instance of SQL Server.
2. Event notifications use the Service Broker infrastructure. Enable Service Broker in the *tempdb* database:

```
USE tempdb;
GO
ALTER DATABASE tempdb SET ENABLE_BROKER;
```

3. Create a queue and a Service Broker service for the event notifications by using the following code:

```
CREATE QUEUE myEventQueue;
CREATE SERVICE myNotifications
    ON QUEUE myEventQueue
([http://schemas.microsoft.com/SQL/Notifications/PostEventNotification]);
```

4. Create an event notification for all CREATE TABLE statements with a database scope. You can use the following code:

```
CREATE EVENT NOTIFICATION myEvent
 ON DATABASE
 FOR CREATE_TABLE
 TO SERVICE 'myNotifications',
    'current database';
GO
```

▶ **Exercise 2: Testing the Event Notification**

In this exercise, you test the event notification that you created in Exercise 1, "Create an Event Notification."

1. Test your event notification by creating a table with an unusual name that includes one or more special XML characters, such as the less-than character (<) in this example:

```
CREATE TABLE [<] (id int);
GO
```

2. Check what you received in your queue by running the following SELECT statement:

```
SELECT CONVERT(xml,message_body), *
  FROM myEventQueue
GO
```

3. You can perform additional testing. For example, create an event notification for *ALTER TABLE* events.

4. After you finish your testing, clean up the *tempdb* database by using code similar to this:

```
DROP EVENT NOTIFICATION myEvent
 ON DATABASE;
DROP SERVICE myNotifications;
DROP QUEUE myEventQueue;
ALTER DATABASE tempdb SET DISABLE_BROKER;
DROP TABLE [<];
GO
```

Quick Check

1. Can you use query notifications for auditing?
2. You need to prevent changes of schema in a database. What can you do?
3. You defined an auditing strategy that uses SQL Server Profiler to gather auditing information and saves the information in a SQL Server table. What should you consider next?
4. If you encrypt data, can you skip the tiresome setting of user permissions?
5. How can you protect data without using data encryption?
6. When you encrypt large amounts of data, should you use symmetric, asymmetric, or certificate encryption?

Quick Check Answers

1. Query notifications are not suitable for auditing. You can consume them from client applications only by using the *SqlDependency* object; therefore, you cannot audit an application that does not subscribe to query notifications. In addition, query notifications just inform the client application that something has changed; it is up to the application to deal with the changes. Query notifications use the indexed views infrastructure on the SQL Server side; if you subscribe to many notifications, you can stress your production server heavily. Query notifications are suitable for middle-tier applications that maintain their own cache of the data they read from SQL Server, such as ASP.NET applications.

2. You can use DDL triggers on the database level. In a DDL trigger, you can roll back any DDL statement.

3. You should consider who is going to review the auditing information.

4. No, you cannot skip setting permissions. Treat encryption as the last resort, the final level of defense. Always use all other security layers, even when using encryption, including operating system, SQL Server, and .NET security mechanisms.

5. Instead of encryption, you can use programmable objects such as views, user-defined functions, and stored procedures to protect data.

6. For large amounts of data, use symmetric encryption.

Case Scenario: Design a Secure Application Solution

Your customers can use an ASP.NET application to place orders. However, customers do not have the capability to delete their own orders; if they change their mind, they must insert a new order containing negative quantities. Lately, your users who create purchase orders for suppliers have been complaining that purchase orders they have created for customers have mysteriously disappeared. In addition, rumors started that your company does not protect confidential data sufficiently in the human resources database. Of course, your employees are concerned about privacy.

1. What can you do to find out how a customer order disappeared?

2. How can you reassure employees that their data is private and protected?

Chapter Summary

- Security systems include enforcement, authentication, and authorization mechanisms.
- In your enterprise solution, you must protect all layers, components, and services. An attacker needs only a single hole to infiltrate your system; as the system defender, you must close all holes.
- Notification Services, Reporting Services, Analysis Services, and Integration Services have their own security mechanisms.
- With CLR code, you must deal with code access security.
- Auditing is an important part of a security strategy.
- Data encryption is the final level of defense.

Chapter 9
Designing a Secure Database

In Chapter 8, "Designing a Secure Application Solution," you learned how to secure different Microsoft SQL Server 2005 components and services to design and implement a secure application solution. This chapter deals more concretely with SQL Server databases and database objects, describing how to design a secure database. You will learn how to define a data-access strategy and how to use schemas, which are new in SQL Server 2005. Then, you will see how to secure specific database objects, including programmable objects that access data. Finally, the chapter covers how to define an execution-context strategy and implement module signing to handle ownership chains.

Exam objectives in this chapter:
- Design database security.
    - Define database access requirements.
    - Define schemas to manage object ownership.
    - Specify database object security permissions.
    - Specify database objects that will be used to maintain security.
    - Design an execution context strategy.
- Design an application solution to support security.
    - Design objects to manage user access.

Before You Begin

To complete the lessons in this chapter, you must have:

- A general understanding of how IT security works.
- Knowledge of SQL Server database objects and principals.
- Knowledge of the Transact-SQL language elements that support security.

IMPORTANT Practices build upon each other

Beginning with Lesson 2, "Managing Schemas," the lesson practices build upon each other; to move to the next practice, you need to finish the previous one.

Lesson 1: Designing a Database-Access Strategy

Estimated lesson time: 15 minutes

As you saw in the previous chapter, SQL Server 2005 introduces new security terminology. Resources that you can secure by using permissions are known as *securables*, and entities that can request SQL Server resources are *principals*. SQL Server organizes security in a hierarchical way. Table 9-1 shows the relationships among the permission hierarchies. Note that you can grant, revoke, and deny permissions on the server and database levels.

Table 9-1   Permission Hierarchies

Principals	Permissions	Securables
Windows level ■ Groups ■ Domain user accounts ■ Local user accounts	—	—
SQL Server level ■ Fixed server roles ■ SQL Server logins	**Grant–Deny–Revoke** ■ Control ■ Create ■ Alter ■ Drop ■ Select ■ Insert ■ Update ■ Delete ■ Execute ■ Connect ■ Reference ■ Take ownership ■ View definition	■ SQL Server logins ■ Endpoints ■ Databases

Table 9-1   Permission Hierarchies

Principals	Permissions	Securables
Database level ■ Fixed database roles ■ Database users ■ Application roles	**Grant—Deny—Revoke** ■ Control ■ Create ■ Alter ■ Drop ■ Select ■ Insert ■ Update ■ Delete ■ Execute ■ Connect ■ Reference ■ Take ownership ■ View definition	■ Users and roles ■ Assemblies ■ Keys and certificates ■ Full-text catalogs ■ Service Broker services, bindings, contracts, routes, and message types ■ Schemas ❑ Tables ❑ Views ❑ Functions ❑ Procedures ❑ Types ❑ XML schema collections ❑ Service Broker queues ❑ Synonyms

Chapter 8 also described how security systems consist of three parts: authentication, authorization, and the enforcement mechanism. Microsoft Windows and SQL Server–level principals are clearly part of the authentication process, while permissions on SQL Server objects are obviously part of the authorization process. However, database users and roles are sometimes confusing to database administrators: are they part of authentication or authorization? Because they are principals, they are part of authentication.

Managing Principals

In SQL Server 2005, you have new declarative data definition language (DDL) statements for managing principals. You create a principal as you do any other objects—by using the CREATE statement. You modify them by using the ALTER statement and delete them by using the DROP statement. Stored procedures such as sp_addlogin and sp_grantlogin are included for backward compatibility.

IMPORTANT   Use new declarative syntax

In future versions of SQL Server, Microsoft will remove the old syntax for managing principals by using system procedures. Therefore, use the new declarative syntax.

You can create SQL Server logins, or you can create logins from different sources such as from Windows, certificates, or asymmetric keys. When you create SQL Server logins, you can specify that you want to bypass password expiration and account policies. However, because these policies help secure your system, this option is not recommended. Regularly check the sys.sql_logins catalog view to see which SQL logins do not enforce the policies mentioned. The following code sample shows examples of how to create SQL logins and check whether the SQL logins enforce login policies.

```
-- Creating a SQL login.
-- Respecting policies is the default.
-- The password does not meet Windows policy requirements.
-- It is not complex enough because it is the same as login name.
-- This will not succeed.
CREATE LOGIN JankoCajhen WITH password='JankoCajhen';
GO
-- Bypassing policies
CREATE LOGIN JankoCajhen WITH password='JankoCajhen',
 CHECK_POLICY=OFF;
GO
-- Creating a login from Windows.
CREATE LOGIN [Builtin\Power Users] FROM WINDOWS;
GO
-- Check which SQL logins do not enforce policies.
SELECT name,
       type_desc,
       is_disabled,
       is_policy_checked,
       is_expiration_checked
  FROM sys.sql_logins;
GO
```

On the Companion Disc   This chapter includes many code examples. You will find all the code from this chapter on the companion CD in the C:\My Documents\Microsoft Press\TK70-441 \Chapter09\Sql folder.

As noted earlier, you can create database users from logins, certificates, or asymmetric keys. You can also create a database user without a login, which means the user is not mapped to any existing login. This user can gain access to other databases through the special principal called *guest*.

You can give login access to a database by putting the login directly in a database role. You add users to fixed server roles if you want them to perform server-level administrative tasks. You can add users to fixed database roles for database-level administrative tasks. In addition, some fixed database roles include permissions on data; you can use them to manage regular users efficiently. Note that you can create your own database roles; however, you cannot add server roles. For adding members to roles, you must use system procedures sp_addrolemember and sp_addsrvrolemember; SQL Server 2005 has no declarative statements for this task yet.

Special Principals

In SQL Server 2005, you have three special principals. On the server level, you have the sa SQL Server login, which is created when you install SQL Server. The default database for this login is master. This login has all permissions on the server, and you cannot revoke any permission from this login. Protect the sa login with a strong password. If you use Windows authentication only, you cannot use this login to connect to SQL Server.

In every database, you get the *public* fixed role and the guest user account. You cannot drop them. Any login without a directly mapped user in a database can access the database through the guest account. Application roles can also use this account to access the data in databases other than the database in which context they were invoked. Before you give any permission to the guest user account, make sure you consider all the ramifications. You can disable the guest account by using the REVOKE CONNECT FROM GUEST statement, which revokes its CONNECT permission. However, you cannot disable this user in the master or *tempdb* databases.

Exam Tip   Make sure you understand the special care you should take in using the sa login, the guest user, and the public role.

Every database user and every database role is a member of the public role. Therefore, any user or role—including an application role—inherits all permissions given to the public role.

BEST PRACTICES   Public role permissions

Be careful when giving any permission to the public role; the best practice is to never give any permission to it.

You can check permissions given to the guest user or the public role on user objects by using the following query on the sys.database_permissions catalog view:

```
SELECT class_desc,
       USER_NAME(grantee_principal_id) AS DbUser,
       OBJECT_NAME(major_id) AS DbObject,
       permission_name,
       state_desc
  FROM sys.database_permissions
 WHERE (USER_NAME(grantee_principal_id) = N'guest' OR
        USER_NAME(grantee_principal_id) = N'public') AND
       major_id > 0;
GO
```

The privileged database user dbo still exists in SQL Server 2005. This user is a member of the db_owner role and, therefore, has all permissions on the database. You cannot drop dbo from the db_owner role.

Every database includes two additional principals: INFORMATION_SCHEMA and sys. You cannot drop these principals because SQL Server needs them. They serve like schemas (namespaces) for ANSI-standard information schema views and for SQL Server catalog views. Finally, SQL Server provides four special logins based on certificates; these logins are for SQL Server internal use only:

- ##MS_SQLResourceSigningCertificate##
- ##MS_SQLReplicationSigningCertificate##
- ##MS_SQLAuthenticatorCertificate##
- ##MS_AgentSigningCertificate##

Securing Endpoints and Principals

In SQL Server 2005, you have a very granular level of control over principals. For logins, you can specify a set of server-level permissions when you are in the context of the master database. For example, you can secure the endpoints of your SQL Server. You already know that you have to create Hypertext Transfer Protocol (HTTP) endpoints manually and that you can secure them after creating them. After installation, SQL Server automatically creates an endpoint for each of the four protocols supported by SQL Server (Named Pipes, TCP/IP, Shared Memory, and Virtual Interface Architecture or VIA). By default, all logins have access to these endpoints when you enable the corresponding protocols. You can revoke the CONNECT permission or even deny it to some logins to prevent them from using one of the enabled protocols.

For example, if you want to be sure that a login cannot use Shared Memory to connect to SQL Server locally, you can do this by using the following command:

```
USE master;
DENY CONNECT ON ENDPOINT::[TSQL Local Machine] TO JankoCajhen;
GO
```

You can check endpoint access by querying the sys.server_permissions catalog view:

```
-- Checking endpoint access permissions
SELECT pr.principal_id,
       pr.name,
       pe.permission_name,
       pe.state_desc,
       pe.class_desc
  FROM sys.server_principals pr
       INNER JOIN sys.server_permissions pe
        ON pr.principal_id = pe.grantee_principal_id
 WHERE pr.name = 'JankoCajhen';
GO
```

You give database-level permissions to database users and roles when you are in the context of the database you want to secure. Earlier in this lesson, you saw how to disable the guest user by revoking its CONNECT permission. You have more granular control over permissions on the database level than you had in any previous version of SQL Server. You will learn about schema and object permissions in the next two lessons.

The principals are securables by themselves. You can control who can modify logins through membership in the sysadmin and securityadmin server-level roles and the ALTER ANY LOGIN server-level permission. You can control who can modify database users and roles by memberships in the db_owner and db_securityadmin roles and the ALTER ANY USER and ALTER ANY ROLE permissions.

For secure design and efficient management, your database-access strategy should use Windows groups as much as possible. For example, if you group your end users on the Windows level already, you can use a single statement to deny the CONNECT permission on a specific endpoint to an entire group. If you set up the strategy properly, you can control database access through Windows group membership only.

Metadata Visibility

In SQL Server 2005, the metadata is not visible to the public role (that is, everyone) by default. Applications that assume metadata access might break. You can control the metadata visibility by using two new permissions: VIEW ANY DATABASE and VIEW DEFINITION.

The VIEW ANY DATABASE permission is granted to the public role by default, so all logins can still see the list of all databases on a SQL Server instance unless you revoke this permission from the public role. You can check this server-level permission by querying the sys.server_permissions catalog view:

```
SELECT pr.name,
       pe.state_desc,
       pe.permission_name
  FROM sys.server_principals AS pr
       INNER JOIN sys.server_permissions AS pe
         ON pr.principal_id = pe.grantee_principal_id
 WHERE permission_name = 'VIEW ANY DATABASE';
GO
```

The VIEW DEFINITION permission enables a user to see the definition of a securable on which this permission is granted. However, this permission does not give the user access to the securable; you have to give other permissions to the user if the user must work with database objects. If the user has any other permission on an object, the user can see the metadata of the object as well. If you give a login VIEW ANY DEFINITION permission at the server scope, you actually negate the metadata visibility concept in SQL Server 2005, quickly simulating the behavior of previous versions of SQL Server. This is possible because SQL Server handles permissions hierarchically; permissions at a higher scope imply the same permissions at all enclosed scopes.

The rules for viewing a database object's source code are even stricter. If a user wants to see an object's code, the user must be the owner of the object or have one of the following permissions on the object: CONTROL, ALTER, TAKE OWNERSHIP, or VIEW DEFINITION.

Practice: Designing a Database-Access Strategy

In this practice, you must think through specific database-access issues.

Exam Tip   Remember that SQL Server is only a single part of an enterprise system that you are securing; you must also have a basic understanding of Windows and common language runtime (CLR) security to secure an application effectively.

▶ **Exercise 1: Explore Roles**

In this conceptual exercise, you need to ensure that your end users cannot perform any action other than actions that you explicitly allowed.

You are using application roles, and you invoke an application role that has only SELECT permissions on tables and views. However, you discover that some data has been changed. How could this happen? Write down your thoughts and compare them with the suggested answer.

Suggested Answer

Check the permissions of the public role. Even application roles are members of the public role, and a user could gain excessive permissions through the public role's permissions.

▶ **Exercise 2: Prevent Local Logins**

In this conceptual exercise, you need to ensure that nobody other than administrators can log in to SQL Server locally.

An employee uses a Windows login to access SQL Server. Besides revoking from this user the permission to use the Shared Memory protocol, how else could you prevent the user from logging in to SQL Server from a local computer on which SQL Server is installed? Compare your ideas with the suggested answer.

Suggested Answer

Users who try to log in at the local console of a computer running Windows must have local login privileges on the hosting computer. You can deny the Log On Locally Windows user right assignment to this user. The best practice is to allow only administrators local access to SQL Server.

Quick Check

1. Which login should you take special care in using, and which database user and database role should never get any permissions?
2. As a SQL Server database administrator (DBA), why would you prefer Microsoft Windows Server 2003 to Windows 2000 Server?

Quick Check Answers

1. You must take special care in using the sa login, which has all permissions on the server, and never give permissions to the guest database user or the public database role.
2. If for no other reason, as a SQL Server DBA, you should prefer Windows Server 2003 because, with this operating system, SQL Server can force account and password Windows policies for SQL logins as well as for Windows logins.

Lesson 2: Managing Schemas

Estimated lesson time: 20 minutes

SQL Server 2005 is the first version of SQL Server that properly implements schemas as namespaces or containers for database objects. Schemas can help you with logical grouping of objects and with efficient administration of security. This lesson gives you guidelines for managing schemas.

Defining Schemas

The complete name of a relational database management system (RDBMS) object consists of four parts. In previous versions of SQL Server, the form of this name was *server.database.owner.object*; the owner was the container for objects. With SQL Server 2005, however, the complete name form is *server.database.schema.object*. SQL Server 2005 separates users and schemas. Objects still have owners, and because a schema is a database object, it has an owner as well. Owners are database users and roles.

The way that SQL Server 2005 implements name resolution for objects that are referred to in applications by object name only has changed slightly compared with previous versions of SQL Server. In previous versions, when an application refers to an object by using object name only, SQL Server first checks whether an object with that name and owned by the calling user exists. If the object does not exist, SQL Server checks whether the dbo owns an object with that name. In SQL Server 2005, every user has a default schema. You can specify the default schema for a user when you create the user. You can change the default schema of a user anytime later. If you do not specify an explicit default schema for a user, the default schema is dbo. This schema exists in all SQL Server 2005 databases and is owned by the dbo user. In summary, SQL Server 2005 first checks for a partially specified object. If the object exists in the user's default schema, it checks the dbo schema. To understand this behavior fully, work through the practice at the end of this lesson.

Guidelines for Managing Schemas

The following are the best-practice guidelines for managing schemas:

■ Group objects in schemas based on application-access requirements. Classify applications by access requirements and then create appropriate schemas. For example, if an application module deals with sales data, create a sales schema to serve as a container for all database objects that pertain to sales.

■ Typically, you can map end users to application modules. Specify appropriate default schemas for database users and roles. For example, specify Sales as the default schema for users in the sales department.

- Because SQL Server 2005 uses a permissions hierarchy, you can manage permissions efficiently if you set up appropriate schemas. For example, you can give permissions on data to sales-department users quickly by giving them appropriate permissions on the Sales schema. Later, you can define exceptions by denying permissions to some users on the objects contained in the Sales schema.

- Use either the dbo user or database roles as owners of schemas and objects. This way, you can drop a database user without worrying about orphaned objects.

- Although you set appropriate default schemas for users, still always refer to database objects by using two-part names. With this strategy, you can avoid confusion in your application if the default schema for a user changes or if an object from the user's default schema is dropped, and an object with the same name exists in the dbo schema (as you saw in the code example).

- You can use schemas to control development environments as well. You can identify different developer groups based on application requirements and then map those groups to schemas.

- In SQL Server 2005, you can control permissions on schemas and objects with greater precision than you could in previous versions of SQL Server. For example, giving developers permission to create objects does not imply that they can create objects in all schemas. On the contrary, the developers must have ALTER or CONTROL schema permissions on every schema they want to modify by creating, altering, or dropping objects contained in that schema.

- You can move objects between schemas by using the ALTER SCHEMA command.

- Your documentation should include schema information.

- You cannot change the default schema from dbo for database users created for a Windows group login. You cannot change it for principals mapped to certificates or asymmetric keys. This restriction eliminates possible ambiguity. For example, if an end user were a member of two Windows groups, and both groups had logins and mapped database users with different default schemas, SQL Server wouldn't know which default schema to use for this end user.

Schemas and Database Roles

Schemas do not supersede database roles. Schemas make administering permissions easier; however, they are just containers, not principals. Database users and roles are the principals that need permissions on database objects.

Exam Tip Schemas are very important for good design, and they are new in SQL Server 2005—representing two good reasons to pay special attention to them as you prepare for the exam.

Classify your users in database roles synchronized with object schema classification. For efficient administration, always group users, and then give the permissions to a complete group. Group users as soon as possible. If you can use Windows groups, use them. Create a single login and a single database user for a complete Windows group, and then give permissions to this database user on complete schemas. If you cannot use Windows groups because you do not work with network administration, or if using Windows groups would lead to too many exceptions, then you can use database roles instead. Give permissions on schemas to database roles. You can create user-defined database roles and then map logins directly to these roles. If you have additional exceptions on the object-user granularity level, you can create database users for some logins and then revoke or deny permissions on objects to these users.

Note that you can also nest roles: you can create container roles for child roles. Nesting can help you implement even more efficient security administration. However, you cannot nest schemas.

Schemas and Object Ownership

Schemas do not replace object ownership. Every object in SQL Server, including schemas, has an owner. Objects that refer to other objects are still involved in ownership chains. The owner of an object has all permissions on that object.

In previous versions of SQL Server, you defined the owner of an object when you created an object. In the CREATE statement, you simply specified a two-part name for the object. In SQL Server 2005, a two-part name means schema name and object name. So how do you specify object ownership in SQL Server 2005?

When you create an object on the database level, you can use the new keyword *AUTHORIZATION* for specifying the object owner. When you create an object inside a schema, the owner of the object is the same as the owner of the schema in which the object is created. You can always change the object owner by using the new ALTER AUTHORIZATION statement. You can check the object ownership by using the *OBJECTPROPERTYEX* system function. You can check the owner of a schema by querying the *principal_id* attribute in the *sys.schemas* catalog view. The following code sample demonstrates this concept. In the code, you first create a schema with authorization LuborKollar and then create a table in this schema. The owner of the table is LuborKollar, as you can confirm by using the *OBJECTPROPERTYEX* function.

```
CREATE SCHEMA LuborSchema AUTHORIZATION LuborKollar;
GO
CREATE TABLE LuborSchema.Table2 --AUTHORIZATION LuborKollar
 (id int);
GO
SELECT OBJECTPROPERTYEX(OBJECT_ID(N'LuborSchema.Table2'), N'OwnerId'),
       USER_NAME(CAST((OBJECTPROPERTYEX
         (OBJECT_ID(N'LuborSchema.Table2'), N'OwnerId')) AS int));
GO
```

You can change the owner of this table by using the ALTER AUTHORIZATION statement. The following code changes the owner of LuborSchema.Table2 from LuborKollar to JankoCajhen.

```
ALTER AUTHORIZATION ON LuborSchema.Table2 TO JankoCajhen;
GO
SELECT OBJECTPROPERTYEX(OBJECT_ID(N'LuborSchema.Table2'), N'OwnerId'),
       USER_NAME(CAST((OBJECTPROPERTYEX
         (OBJECT_ID(N'LuborSchema.Table2'), N'OwnerId')) AS int))
GO
```

Objects could become orphaned if you drop the user who owns them. This is not allowed in SQL Server. As you already know, you can change the owner of an object. However, a better practice is to prevent orphaned objects. If the owner is a database role or a database user created for a Windows group, it is less likely the objects would be orphaned if you have to drop a single user.

Practice: Using Schemas and Name Resolution

This practice will help you understand how name resolution works with schemas for objects referred to by a single-part name.

IMPORTANT   dbo database user

This practice assumes you are working in the dbo database user context.

IMPORTANT   Practices build upon each other

The practices in this chapter, from this one onward, build upon each other. You should not delete your work after you finish this practice.

▶ **Exercise 1: Create Objects**

In this exercise, you prepare the infrastructure for this practice. You first need to create a test database. You must create two logins and two database users in the practice database. You need a user-defined schema and two tables with the same name: one in your new schema and one in the dbo schema.

1. Create a test database and two logins by using code similar to this:

```
-- Create a practice database.
IF DB_ID(N'TK441Ch09') IS NULL
   CREATE DATABASE TK441Ch09;
GO
-- Create logins.
-- Note that if you executed the demo code so far, you already have
-- login JankoCajhen.
CREATE LOGIN JankoCajhen WITH password='JankoCajhen',
 CHECK_POLICY=OFF;
```

```
GO
CREATE LOGIN LuborKollar WITH password='LK_ComplexPassword';
GO
```

2. Create the Sales schema and two tables with the same name: one in your new Sales schema and one in the dbo schema. You can use the following code as a template, or you can just copy it:

```
USE TK441Ch09;
GO
CREATE SCHEMA Sales;
GO
CREATE TABLE dbo.Table1
(id int,
 tableContainer char(5));
CREATE TABLE Sales.Table1
(id int,
 tableContainer char(5));
GO
```

3. Insert a row in each of the tables; these two rows will help you determine which table was used in the name resolution:

```
INSERT INTO dbo.Table1(id, tableContainer)
 VALUES(1,'dbo');
INSERT INTO Sales.Table1(id, tableContainer)
 VALUES(1,'Sales');
GO
```

4. Create two database users—one with the default schema dbo and one with the default schema Sales. Give both users SELECT permission on both tables:

```
-- JankoCajhen default schema is dbo.
CREATE USER JankoCajhen FOR LOGIN JankoCajhen;
GO
-- LuborKollar default schema is Sales.
CREATE USER LuborKollar FOR LOGIN LuborKollar
 WITH DEFAULT_SCHEMA = Sales;
GO
-- Grant Select to both users on both tables.
GRANT SELECT ON dbo.Table1 TO JankoCajhen;
GRANT SELECT ON Sales.Table1 TO JankoCajhen;
GRANT SELECT ON dbo.Table1 TO LuborKollar;
GRANT SELECT ON Sales.Table1 TO LuborKollar;
GO
```

▶ **Exercise 2: Test the Name Resolution**

Now that you have created the infrastructure, you can test the name resolution by using a single-part name of a table in your queries and by impersonating database users with different default schemas.

1. Impersonate JankoCajhen. You should get a row from dbo.Table1.

```
EXECUTE AS USER='JankoCajhen';
SELECT USER_NAME() AS WhoAmI,
       id,
       tableContainer
  FROM Table1;
REVERT;
GO
```

2. Impersonate LuborKollar. You should get a row from Sales.Table1.

```
EXECUTE AS USER='LuborKollar';
SELECT USER_NAME() AS WhoAmI,
       id,
       tableContainer
  FROM Table1;
REVERT;
GO
```

3. Now drop the Sales.Table1 table. Impersonate LuborKollar again. This time, you get a row from Sales.Table1.

```
DROP TABLE Sales.table1;
GO
EXECUTE AS USER='LuborKollar';
SELECT USER_NAME() AS WhoAmI,
       id,
       tableContainer
  FROM Table1;
-- You get row from the dbo.table1
REVERT;
GO
```

IMPORTANT   Using SETUSER to impersonate users

In this practice, you have already used the EXECUTE AS . . . REVERT commands to change the
execution context. You will learn more about changing the execution context in Lesson 5,
"Designing an Execution-Context Strategy." As a member of the db_owner role, you could use
the SETUSER command to impersonate another database user. However, the SETUSER command is included for backward compatibility only and might be removed in future releases of
SQL Server. In addition, you cannot use the SETUSER command to impersonate a user
mapped to a login that bypasses the account and password policies. Therefore, in the example, you would not be able to use SETUSER to impersonate user JankoCajhen.

Quick Check

1. You create a schema LuborSchema1 without an explicit owner. You are authenticated in the database as the dbo user. Who is the owner of the schema?
2. You are designing a data model for an application that supports sales, human resources, and warehouse departments. Should you create a single database with three schemas or three separate databases?

Quick Check Answers

1. The owner of the schema is dbo. When you do not specify an owner in the AUTHORIZATION clause when creating an object on the database level, the owner of that object is the current user. Remember that the default owner of objects inside the schema is the owner of the schema. You can check schema ownership when you create a schema without an explicit owner by using the following code:

```
CREATE SCHEMA LuborSchema1
GO
SELECT name, principal_id,
       USER_NAME(principal_id)
  FROM sys.schemas
 WHERE name = 'LuborSchema1';
GO
```

2. Design a single database with three schemas. You can maintain constraints and security more easily inside a single database. For example, foreign keys cannot span databases. However, you might encounter a rare situation in which you are dealing with a large amount of data with frequent changes; you might prefer the separate-databases approach in a situation like this. With three databases, you get three separate transaction logs; you can put them in different disks and thus achieve parallel writing to these logs.

Lesson 3: Specifying Database Object Security Permissions

Estimated lesson time: 25 minutes

In all practices and sample code so far, you were authorized inside a database as the dbo user. This user has all possible permissions inside a database. However, in real life, it might be necessary for other users to create and modify objects. These users can be developers or other DBAs. To modify objects, they need statement permissions. Statement permissions are on the server, database, schema, or object level, depending on which level you work. In addition, end users must use objects and, thus, need object permissions. Object permissions depend on the type of object you are working with.

Previous versions of SQL Server institute a strict boundary between statement and object permissions and provide only a couple of each type. In SQL Server 2005, you have much more granular control, and there are numerous additional permissions of both types. In SQL Server 2005 Books Online, the organization of chapters covering grant, revoke, and deny permissions is hierarchical because the permissions work hierarchically. However, there are tens of permissions at each level. For example, the "GRANT Database Permissions (Transact-SQL)" topic includes more than 60 distinct permissions.

This chapter uses the terminology *statement* and *object* permissions to give you a more logical approach to understanding these big groups of permissions. The statement permissions include permissions to use any DDL statements (for example, to create, alter, and drop objects). The object permissions include permissions to use the objects (for example, to use the data manipulation language [DML] statements). However, the two permissions classes slightly overlap, and you can treat a couple of permissions as both statement and object permissions.

You control permissions by using the data-control language (DCL) elements: GRANT, REVOKE, and DENY statements. You already know that without explicitly granted permission, a user cannot use an object. You give the permissions by using the GRANT statement. You explicitly prohibit usage of an object by using the DENY statement. You clear an explicit GRANT or an explicit DENY permission by using the REVOKE statement. You might wonder why you need an explicit DENY statement when without an explicit GRANT, a user cannot use an object. The DENY statement exists because all grants are cumulative. For example, if a user gets GRANT permission to select from table1 and the role that the user is a member of is granted permission to select from table2, the user can select from both tables. If you want to be sure that the user can never select from table2, deny the select permission from table2 to this user. A DENY statement always supersedes all GRANT statements.

You cannot grant, deny, or revoke permissions to or from special roles on the server or database level. For example, you cannot deny anything inside a database to the db_owner role. You cannot grant, deny, or revoke permissions to special logins and database users (for example, to sa, dbo, INFORMATION_SCHEMA, and sys). Finally, you cannot grant, deny, or revoke permissions to yourself.

Statement Permissions

Statement permissions enable users to create and alter objects or back up a database and transaction log. This chapter cannot cover all these permissions; refer to the "GRANT (Transact-SQL)" topic in SQL Server Books Online at *http://msdn2.microsoft.com/en-us /library/ms187965(SQL.90).aspx*, for detailed information. However, in this lesson, you will learn the key concepts regarding statement permissions.

Permissions granted on a higher level include implicit permissions on a lower level. For example, permissions granted on the schema level are implicitly granted on all objects in the schema. In addition, there is some hierarchy between permissions on the same level; some are stronger and implicitly include weaker permissions. The CONTROL permission is the strongest. For example, the CONTROL permission on the database level implies all other permissions on the same database. Therefore, you have two different kinds of hierarchy: hierarchy between securables and hierarchy between permissions. You can treat high-level permissions as *covering* the more detailed, low-level permissions that they *imply*.

This architecture can make maintaining security a very complicated task. Fortunately, you can get a lot of information through catalog views and system functions. For example, the "Covering/Implied Permissions" topic of SQL Server 2005 Books Online features code for a helpful function called *dbo.ImplyingPermissions* at *http://msdn2.microsoft.com/en-us/library /ms177450(SQL.90).aspx*. This takes as its arguments the name of the class of a securable and the name of permission. The function returns the list of permissions, including the specified permission by implication.

You can use this function to determine quickly which permissions imply the permission you want to control. For example, suppose you want to know which permissions imply the ALTER OBJECT permission. You can determine this by using the following call of the function:

```
SELECT * FROM dbo.ImplyingPermissions('object', 'alter');
```

You get the result shown in Table 9-2.

Table 9-2   Permissions That Imply ALTER OBJECT Permission

Permname	Class	Height	Rank
ALTER	OBJECT	0	0
CONTROL	OBJECT	0	1

Table 9-2   Permissions That Imply ALTER OBJECT Permission

Permname	Class	Height	Rank
ALTER	SCHEMA	1	1
CONTROL	SCHEMA	1	2
ALTER ANY SCHEMA	DATABASE	2	2
ALTER	DATABASE	2	3
CONTROL	DATABASE	2	4
ALTER ANY DATABASE	SERVER	3	4
CONTROL SERVER	SERVER	3	5

You can see from this output that if a user needs to alter an object, the user needs either ALTER OBJECT permission or any other higher permission, such as ALTER ANY SCHEMA permission. The Height column gives you information about the levels of hierarchy of securables, from the lowest to the highest: object, schema, database, and server. The Rank column shows you the hierarchy among permissions on the same hierarchy level of securables. For example, the CONTROL permission on the database level (class DATABASE in Table 9-2) has a rank of 4, the ALTER permission on the same level has a rank of 3, and the ALTER ANY SCHEMA permission on the same level has a rank of 2. This means that the CONTROL DATABASE permission implies the ALTER DATABASE permission, which in turn implies the ALTER ANY SCHEMA permission—all three on the database level.

Hierarchy of permissions does not work in the bottom-up direction. Although this sounds logical, it might be a little confusing sometimes. For example, in the "GRANT Database Permissions (Transact-SQL)" topic in SQL Server 2005 Books Online at *http://msdn2.microsoft.com/en-us/library/ms178569(SQL.90).aspx*, the CREATE TABLE permission is listed among other database permissions. This is because you grant this permission on the database level. However, this permission works on the object level (table); it does not imply any permission on the higher level of securables. By creating a table, you are altering a schema. A schema is on a higher level of hierarchy of securables than a table. Therefore, to create a table, a user needs not just the CREATE TABLE permission in the database, but also the ALTER SCHEMA permission on the schema in which the user is creating the table. You can twist this around. The ALTER SCHEMA permission by itself does not imply the CREATE TABLE permission; this is because you grant the CREATE TABLE permission on the database level. In summary, if a user wants to create a table, the user must have both the CREATE TABLE and the ALTER SCHEMA permissions. The practice at the end of this lesson demonstrates this concept.

Checking Object Permissions

Types of permissions depend on types of database objects. You can get a list of permissions applicable for an object or objects by using the *sys.fn_builtin_permissions* system function. For example, you can check which permissions are applicable for user-defined types by using the following function call:

```
SELECT * FROM sys.fn_builtin_permissions(N'TYPE');
```

Or, you can check for which objects the SELECT permission is applicable by using

```
SELECT * FROM sys.fn_builtin_permissions(DEFAULT)
  WHERE permission_name = N'SELECT';
```

Note that executing the code for checking applicable permissions does not give you very granular information. For example, it tells you that the SELECT permission is applicable for objects, schemas, and databases. You know that this permission makes sense for tables but not for stored procedures. Table 9-3 summarizes which object permissions are applicable for which objects on a more granular level.

Table 9-3 Permissions and Objects Mapping

Permission	Database Objects
ALTER	All database objects except DML triggers; for DML triggers, this permission implies from the ALTER TABLE permission
CONNECT	Endpoint
CONTROL	All database objects except DML triggers; for DML triggers, this permission implies from the CONTROL TABLE permission
DELETE	Tables, views, synonyms
EXECUTE	Stored procedures, scalar functions, aggregate functions, synonyms, user-defined types, XML schema collections, assemblies
INSERT	Tables, views, synonyms
RECEIVE	Service Broker queues
REFERENCES	Tables, views, table-valued functions, aggregate functions, Service Broker objects, keys and certificates, user-defined types, schemas, XML schema collections, assemblies; columns of tables, views, and table-valued functions; and aggregate functions
SELECT	Tables, views, table-valued functions, synonyms; and columns of tables, views, and table-valued functions
TAKE OWNERSHIP	All database objects except DML triggers; for DML triggers, this permission implies from the CONTROL TABLE permission

Table 9-3   Permissions and Objects Mapping

Permission	Database Objects
UPDATE	Tables, views, table-valued functions, synonyms; and columns of tables, views, and table-valued functions
VIEW DEFINITION	All database objects except DML triggers; for DML triggers, this permission implies from the CONTROL TABLE permission

In the statement permissions section, you already learned that the split between statement and object permissions is not strict anymore. The ALTER permission, for example, can be treated as a statement or object permission.

Exam Tip   SQL Server 2005 has many new object permissions. As you prepare for the exam, do not rely on your knowledge of object permissions from previous versions of SQL Server.

In addition, you can see that you can specify very detailed permissions. For example, you can specify that a user can select or update only some columns of a table. Specifying permissions on such a granular level means a lot of administrative work and is nearly impossible to do in a limited time with graphical tools such as SQL Server Management Studio. You should rarely go that far. Instead, specify permissions on higher levels of the object hierarchy, namely on the schema level, and then handle exceptions. If you need column-level permissions, use programmable objects such as views and stored procedures. Keep permissions as simple as possible.

Specifying Permissions by Using the GRANT, DENY, and REVOKE Options

When you specify permissions for an object by using GRANT, DENY, and REVOKE statements, some of the options that you will encounter might be confusing. For example, all three statements include the ALL [PRIVILEGES] option. The *PRIVILEGES* keyword is optional and does not change the behavior of the ALL option. You might think ALL means all possible permissions for an object. However, this means all ANSI-92 standard permissions; SQL Server 2005 has a richer permission set. In ANSI-92, ALL means:

- DELETE, INSERT, REFERENCES, SELECT, and UPDATE permissions for tables, views, and table-valued functions.
- EXECUTE permission for stored procedures.
- EXECUTE and REFERENCES permissions for scalar functions.

The GRANT statement includes the WITH GRANT OPTION. This option indicates that the principal to which you grant permission on an object can grant this permission on the same object to other principals.

The DENY statement comes with the CASCADE option. When you use this option with the DENY statement, you indicate that the permission you are denying is also denied to other principals to which it has been granted by this principal.

The REVOKE statement has the GRANT OPTION FOR and the CASCADE options. GRANT OPTION FOR means you are revoking permission to grant the same permission to other principals. (That is, you are revoking the WITH GRANT OPTION permission you gave to this principal by using the GRANT statement.) The CASCADE option means you are revoking permission not just from the principal you mention in the statement, but also from other principals to which it has been granted by this principal. Note that such a cascaded revocation revokes both GRANT and DENY of that permission.

Practice: Verifying Statement Permissions and Hierarchy

This practice helps you understand how the hierarchy among securables implies permissions from the top of the hierarchy to the bottom—but not from the bottom to the top.

IMPORTANT   Practices build upon each other

To work successfully with this practice, you should have finished the practice from Lesson 2, "Managing Schemas."

▶ **Exercise 1: Create a Top-Down Object Hierarchy**

Let's check the top-down approach first. When you worked through the previous practice, you created the *TK441Ch09* database and LuborKollar and JankoCajhen logins and database users. In this exercise, you will create a schema with LuborKollar as the owner and then give the ALTER SCHEMA permission to JankoCajhen. The JankoCajhen user cannot create a table.

1. Create a schema and give JankoCajhen permission to alter this schema:

```
USE TK441Ch09;
GO
CREATE SCHEMA LuborSchema2 AUTHORIZATION LuborKollar;
GO
GRANT ALTER ON SCHEMA::LuborSchema2 TO JankoCajhen;
GO
```

2. Try to create a table as JankoCajhen. The following code should give you an error stating that JankoCajhen has no CREATE TABLE permission in the *TK441Ch09* database:

```
EXECUTE AS USER = 'JankoCajhen';
CREATE TABLE LuborSchema2.JCTable1
  (id int);
GO
REVERT;
GO
```

3. Revoke the ALTER SCHEMA permission from JankoCajhen:

```
REVOKE ALTER ON SCHEMA::LuborSchema2 FROM JankoCajhen;
GO
```

▶ **Exercise 2: Create a Bottom-Up Object Hierarchy**

In this exercise, you will try the bottom-up approach. Although the CREATE TABLE permission is on the database level, the table objects are in a schema and, thus, a lower level in the object hierarchy.

1. Give JankoCajhen permission to create tables:

```
GRANT CREATE TABLE TO JankoCajhen;
GO
```

2. Try to create a table as JankoCajhen. The following code should give you an error stating that JankoCajhen has no ALTER SCHEMA permission on LuborSchema2:

```
EXECUTE AS USER = 'JankoCajhen';
CREATE TABLE LuborSchema2.JCTable1
  (id int);
GO
REVERT;
GO
```

3. Revoke the CREATE TABLE permission from JankoCajhen:

```
REVOKE CREATE TABLE FROM JankoCajhen;
GO
```

▶ **Exercise 3: Give All Permissions Needed to Create a Table**

Finally, give JankoCajhen all permissions needed to create a table.

1. Give JankoCajhen permissions to alter the schema and to create tables:

```
GRANT ALTER ON SCHEMA::LuborSchema2 TO JankoCajhen;
GO
GRANT CREATE TABLE TO JankoCajhen;
GO
```

2. Try to create a table as JankoCajhen. This time, you should get no error, and Janko-Cajhen should be able to create tables in LuborSchema2.

```
EXECUTE AS USER = 'JankoCajhen';
CREATE TABLE LuborSchema2.JCTable1
  (id int);
GO
REVERT;
GO
```

One of the lessons you can learn from this practice is that you can effectively manage multiple development teams by using schema and statement permissions. You can assign each team to a separate logical part of the application, which should map to a schema. You give permissions to each team to create objects in the database and to alter their schema.

Quick Check

1. You grant CONTROL permission on dbo.Table1 to database user LuborKollar. Later, you deny SELECT permission on the same table to LuborKollar. What are the effective permissions of LuborKollar on that table?

2. LuborKollar has CONTROL permission on dbo.Table1. Does this mean that LuborKollar can revoke the denied SELECT permission and thus bypass the limitations you defined as a DBA?

Quick Check Answers

1. The effective permissions of LuborKollar on dbo.Table1 are all but SELECT. You can check this by using the following code:

```
-- Grant CONTROL to LuborKollar.
GRANT CONTROL ON dbo.Table1 TO LuborKollar;
GO
-- LuborKollar can select.
EXECUTE AS USER = 'LuborKollar';
SELECT *
  FROM dbo.Table1;
REVERT;
GO
-- Deny SELECT to LuborKollar.
DENY SELECT ON dbo.Table1 TO LuborKollar;
GO
-- LuborKollar can insert, but not select.
EXECUTE AS USER = 'LuborKollar';
INSERT INTO dbo.Table1(id, tableContainer)
 VALUES (2, 'dbo');
REVERT;
GO
EXECUTE AS USER = 'LuborKollar';
SELECT *
  FROM dbo.Table1;
REVERT;
GO
```

2. No, LuborKollar cannot revoke the denied SELECT permission. You cannot grant, deny, or revoke permissions to yourself. You can check this by using the following code:

```
EXECUTE AS USER = 'LuborKollar';
REVOKE SELECT ON dbo.Table1 FROM LuborKollar;
REVERT;
GO
```

Lesson 4: Managing Objects That Access Data

Estimated lesson time: 20 minutes

You can completely protect your data from direct application access by allowing access only through programmable objects. In real-life scenarios, you typically combine direct access for responsible users, such as administrators, with indirect access through programmable objects for end users. In this lesson, you will learn how you can use programmable objects to develop and maintain a secure database.

Using Programmable Objects to Maintain Security

In Transact-SQL, you can write views, stored procedures, scalar and table-valued user-defined functions, and triggers. Views serve best as a layer for selecting data, although you can modify data through views as well. Views are especially useful for column-level and row-level security. You can grant column permissions directly; however, doing this incurs a lot of administrative work. You can create a view as a projection on the base table with selected columns only and then maintain permissions on a higher granularity level (that is, on the view instead of on the columns). In addition, you cannot give row-level permissions through a predicate in the GRANT statement. You can use the same predicate in the WHERE clause of the SELECT statement of the view you are using as a security layer. You can use table-valued functions as parameterized views.

Stored procedures are appropriate for all update activity. Maintaining security through stored procedures is the easiest form of administration; with stored procedures, you typically need to grant the EXECUTE permission only. You can use triggers and scalar functions for advanced security checking—for example, for validating users' input.

Exam Tip   Stored procedures are an important topic on the exam. Make sure you spend sufficient time understanding how to use them. You can review "Understanding Stored Procedures" in SQL Server 2005 Books Online at *http://msdn2.microsoft.com/en-us/library/ms191428.aspx*.

To minimize the attack surface area, the CLR integration in SQL Server 2005 is off by default. Turning it on does not mean necessarily exposing the database; on the contrary, with CLR code, you can enhance your security by writing validation code that is not possible with T-SQL. For example, you can use the function from Lesson 4, "Defining Domain Integrity and Business Rules" of Chapter 3, "Designing a Physical Database," which validates user input against a regular expression inside a check constraint for any string validation.

With the help of programmable objects, you can solve some advanced security problems. You already know the dangers of concatenating T-SQL code dynamically, especially combined with user input. For example, a common problem is how to build the list for the *IN* operator dynamically; you want to let end users create the list dynamically through the user interface. From the application, you get an array of values as a string with a delimiter such as a comma between different values. Many solutions simply create the SELECT statement dynamically and then concatenate this array of values with T-SQL code. However, this solution is prone to code-injection attacks. You can create a safer solution by using a table-valued function that parses the input string and returns separate elements from the array as rows of the output table. Then, you can use this function with *JOIN* or *APPLY* operators. This way, SQL Server always treats data (user input) as data and never as code. Such a solution is secure against code injection. You can find T-SQL and CLR solutions for a function that separates elements from an input string that represents an array in *Inside Microsoft SQL Server 2005: T-SQL Programming* by Itzik Ben-Gan, Dejan Sarka, and Roger Wolter (Microsoft Press, 2006).

What Are Ownership Chains?

Programmable objects refer to base tables and to each other in a kind of chain. For example, a stored procedure can use a view that selects from a base table. All the objects in SQL Server have owners. As long as there is a single owner of all the objects in the chain, you can manage permissions on the highest level only. Using the previous example, if the stored procedure, view, and base table have the same owner, you can manage permissions for the stored procedure only. SQL Server trusts that the owner of the procedure knows what the procedure is doing. This works for any DML statement (SELECT, INSERT, UPDATE, and DELETE).

Ownership chains are valid inside a single database only, although you can apply them across databases as well. However, cross-database ownership chains can present a security risk. A DBA of the target database in the ownership chain does not have control over the code of a procedure in the source database of the chain. Do not enable cross-database ownership chains unless you have control over all the databases involved in the chain and understand the implications. If you want to enable cross-database ownership chains, you have to start with enabling them on the server level by using the sp_configure system procedure: you must set the cross-db ownership chaining option to 1. Then you enable a specific database to serve as the source or the target of cross-database ownership chains by using ALTER DATABASE . . . SET DB_CHAINING ON.

If the chain of owners between dependent objects is broken, SQL Server must check the permissions for any objects where the chain is broken. For example, if the owner of the procedure from the previous example is different from the owner of the view, SQL Server would check the permissions on the view as well. If the owner of the table is different from the owner of the view, SQL Server would also check permissions on the base table. In addition, if you use dynamic T-SQL code and concatenate a T-SQL statement as a string and then use the EXECUTE command to execute them, SQL Server checks the permissions on all the objects the dynamic code is using. This is logical because SQL Server cannot know which objects the dynamic code is going to use until it actually executes the code, especially if you concatenate a part of the dynamic code from user input. Besides the threat of code injection, this extra checking is another reason not to use dynamic string concatenation in T-SQL code in production. The following practice helps you understand how ownership chaining works.

Practice: Using Ownership Chains

In this practice, you will learn how ownership chains work.

IMPORTANT   Practices build upon each other

To work successfully with this practice, you should have finished the practice from Lesson 3, "Verifying Statement Permissions and Hierarchy."

▶ Exercise 1: Create an Unbroken Chain

In this exercise, you first create a table and a procedure that selects data from the table with dbo as the owner. You will grant EXECUTE permission on the procedure to JankoCajhen. This user should have access to the table only through your stored procedure; because the owner of the procedure and the table is the same and the code in the procedure is not concatenated dynamically, JankoCajhen should be able to select from the base table without explicit SELECT permission. Note that if you followed the previous practices, you should already have the *TK441Ch09* database, LuborKollar and JankoCajhen logins and database users, and a schema named LuborSchema2 with LuborKollar as the owner.

1. Create a table and a procedure that selects from this table and give JankoCajhen permissions to execute the procedure:

    ```
    USE TK441Ch09;
    GO
    CREATE TABLE dbo.ChainTable
    (id int,
     strAttr nvarchar(25));
    GO
    INSERT INTO dbo.ChainTable(id, strAttr)
     VALUES(1, N'I can see the table!');
    GO
    CREATE PROCEDURE dbo.ReadChainTable
    AS
    SELECT id, strAttr
      FROM dbo.ChainTable;
    GO
    GRANT EXECUTE ON dbo.ReadChainTable TO JankoCajhen;
    GO
    ```

2. Try to read from the base table as JankoCajhen through the stored procedure. This code should work:

    ```
    EXECUTE AS USER = 'JankoCajhen';
    EXEC dbo.ReadChainTable;
    ```

```
REVERT;
GO
```

3. Try to read from the base table as JankoCajhen directly. You should get an error because JankoCajhen does not have SELECT permission on the base table.

```
EXECUTE AS USER = 'JankoCajhen';
SELECT id, strAttr
FROM dbo.ChainTable;
REVERT;
GO
```

▶ Exercise 2: Create a Broken Chain

In this exercise, you will create another procedure with dbo as the owner. This procedure will again read from the base table created in the previous exercise, only this time, you will have a dynamic T-SQL statement in the procedure. In addition, you will create a third procedure that selects from the base table; however, this procedure is going to have a different owner.

1. Create a procedure with dbo as the owner that selects from the base table by using dynamic code. Give JankoCajhen permission to execute this procedure. Give Lubor-Kollar permissions to create procedures and to select from the base table.

```
CREATE PROCEDURE dbo.ReadChainTableDynamic
AS
DECLARE @sqlstr nvarchar(100);
SET @sqlstr =
 'SELECT id, strAttr FROM dbo.ChainTable';
EXEC (@sqlstr);
GO
GRANT EXECUTE ON dbo.ReadChainTableDynamic TO JankoCajhen;
GO
-- Give LuborKollar permissions to create procedures
-- and to select from the base table.
GRANT CREATE PROCEDURE TO LuborKollar;
GRANT SELECT ON dbo.ChainTable TO LuborKollar;
GO
```

2. Impersonate LuborKollar to create a procedure that reads from the base table. Give EXECUTE permission on this procedure to JankoCajhen. Execute this procedure as LuborKollar; LuborKollar should be able to read from the base table.

```
EXECUTE AS USER = 'LuborKollar';
GO
CREATE PROCEDURE LuborSchema2.ReadChainTable
AS
SELECT id, strAttr
  FROM dbo.ChainTable;
GO
-- Give JankoCajhen permission to execute this procedure.
GRANT EXECUTE ON LuborSchema2.ReadChainTable TO JankoCajhen;
GO
-- Try to execute it as LuborKollar; it works.
```

```
EXEC LuborSchema2.ReadChainTable;
REVERT;
GO
```

3. Now impersonate JankoCajhen and execute the dynamic procedure with dbo as the owner. Try to execute the procedure with LuborKollar as the owner. You should get an error in both cases.

```
EXECUTE AS USER = 'JankoCajhen';
EXEC dbo.ReadChainTableDynamic;
GO
EXEC LuborSchema2.ReadChainTable;
GO
REVERT;
GO
```

Quick Check

1. You need to specify the SELECT permission for 20 users on the column level. You have to specify this permission for 10 tables, with seven columns on average per table. How can you speed up your administrative work?
2. Your DBA tells you to use a stored procedure to read from a table. You can execute the procedure; however, you get the Select Permission Denied error message when you execute it. What is wrong?

Quick Check Answers

1. You should create 10 views, one for each table, with projections on the base table including only the columns you want your users to see. Check also whether you could group these views in the same schema. Finally, check whether you could group the users in a single role. Ideally, if you could group objects and users, you could give all necessary permissions by using a single GRANT SELECT statement on the schema to the role.
2. You probably discovered a broken ownership chain problem. One possibility is that the owner of the procedure is different from the owner of the base table, and you do not have SELECT permission on the base table. The second possibility is that the procedure uses dynamic SQL, and, again, you do not have SELECT permission on the base table.

Lesson 5: Designing an Execution-Context Strategy

Estimated lesson time: 20 minutes

In previous versions of SQL Server, the only way you could use a programmable object to hide completely underlying tables was to use ownership chains carefully. In SQL Server 2005, you can help yourself by changing the execution context. In this lesson, you will learn how to use execution context.

What Is the Execution Context?

SQL Server determines the execution context by the login or user from the current session or by executing a module. A pair of security tokens identifies the user. The *login token* is used to check the server-level and database-level permissions; the *user token,* one per database, is used to check permissions on the database level only. A security token consists of a primary identifier, one or more secondary identifiers, zero or more authenticators, and the permissions of all identifiers. The primary identifier for a login token is the login that SQL Server used for authentication itself; the secondary identifiers are server roles and Windows groups of which the login is a member. For a user token, the primary identifier is the database user used to access the database, and the secondary identifiers are the roles of which the user is a member. Authenticators are principals, certificates, or asymmetric keys that vouch for the authenticity of the token; most of the time, the authenticator is the instance of SQL Server. You can check your current login and user token through the sys.login_token and sys.user_token catalog views.

Inside a database, SQL Server typically uses the user's token to check the necessary permissions for the action performed. You can change the execution context to solve a broken ownership chain problem, to test security, to give temporarily elevated privileges, or to build your custom permission set. When you execute a module in a different execution context, the original user still needs the EXECUTE permission on the module; during the module execution, SQL Server checks the initial user permissions and the additional permissions based on the impersonation in the module.

You can change execution context explicitly and implicitly. In this chapter, you explicitly changed the context interactively already by using the EXECUTE AS command. When you specify the EXECUTE AS statement in a module definition, you are using implicit context switching. You can switch the context on the server or database level. The impersonation remains in effect until the session is dropped, until the context is switched again, until you explicitly revert the context to the previous one by using the REVERT statement, or until the end of the execution of the module that is created with the EXECUTE AS clause. Modules in which you can define different execution contexts include DDL triggers on the server level or

DML triggers, stored procedures, user-defined functions, and queues on the database level. Note that you cannot change the execution context for inline user-defined functions.

When you define an execution context for a module, you can use the following options:

- **EXECUTE AS CALLER** This is the default execution context, and it means the context of the user who called the module. This is the same behavior as you had in previous versions of SQL Server. In this case, you are relying on unbroken ownership chains to bypass permission checks on underlying objects.
- **EXECUTE AS user_name** You can use this option to specify explicitly the user for the execution context of the module. You can use it to overcome broken ownership chains or to create a custom permission set.
- **EXECUTE AS OWNER** The execution context with this option is the owner of the module, and it changes if the owner changes. Use this option if you expect changes of ownership and do not want to deal with changing the execution context again.
- **EXECUTE AS SELF** This is just a shortcut for EXECUTE AS user_name, in which user_name is the user who is creating the module. Because this can result in some ambiguity about which context is used, use this option rarely. However, it can be useful when your application creates modules and you want to use impersonation, but you do not know at design time the user who is creating the module.

You can extend the scope of the impersonation from within a database, which is the default restriction, to other databases on the same instance or to other instances of SQL Server. The authenticator has to be trusted in the target scope, and the source database must be marked as trustworthy with the ALTER DATABASE statement. However, marking a database as trustworthy is potentially dangerous. In trustworthy databases, you can create assemblies with EXTERNAL_ACCESS and UNSAFE permission sets, and you can create modules that use the execution context of highly privileged users.

Module Signing

To prevent setting the TRUSTWORTHY database option to ON to allow the EXTERNAL_ACCESS or UNSAFE permission set for a CLR module, you can digitally sign the assembly by using Microsoft Visual Studio or the Microsoft .NET Framework Strong Name command prompt utility (*sn.exe*). Then, you can create inside the master database an asymmetric key pair from the assembly and a login mapped to this asymmetric key. You grant the login the EXTERNAL ACCESS ASSEMBLY or UNSAFE ASSEMBLY permission. This way, only the assembly with the signature used to create the asymmetric key can get the EXTERNAL_ACCESS or UNSAFE permission set; other assemblies can be created with the SAFE permission set only.

In SQL Server databases, you can sign modules by using the new ADD SIGNATURE TO statement. You can sign a module with a certificate or an asymmetric key. You create a database user for the certificate or asymmetric key you used to sign a procedure. You grant this user access to the underlying objects. You grant the EXECUTE permission on the signed procedure to end users. When an end user executes the module, SQL Server adds the user created from the certificate to the end user's user token. After the execution of the module finishes, SQL Server removes the certificate user from the end user's user token. This way, the end user can access the underlying data through the signed module only.

Practice: Defining the Execution Context

In this practice, you solve the problem of the broken ownership chains you experienced in the previous practice. This practice assumes you finished the previous practice.

IMPORTANT   Practices build upon each other

To work successfully with this practice, you should have finished the practice from Lesson 4, "Using Ownership Chains."

▶ **Exercise 1: Change the Execution Context of Modules**

In this exercise, you will change the execution context of two procedures to prevent a broken ownership chain.

1. Change the execution context of the dbo.ReadChainTableDynamic procedure. Check the login and user tokens inside the procedure. You can use the following code:

```
USE TK441Ch09;
GO
ALTER PROCEDURE dbo.ReadChainTableDynamic
WITH EXECUTE AS 'LuborKollar'
AS
DECLARE @sqlstr nvarchar(100);
SET @sqlstr =
 'SELECT id, strAttr FROM dbo.ChainTable';
EXEC (@sqlstr);
SELECT principal_id, sid, name, type, usage, 'SERVER' AS scope
  FROM sys.login_token
UNION
SELECT principal_id, sid, name, type, usage, 'DATABASE' AS scope
  FROM sys.user_token;
GO
```

2. Similarly, change the execution context of the LuborSchema2.ReadChainTable procedure:

```
EXECUTE AS USER = 'LuborKollar';
GO
ALTER PROCEDURE LuborSchema2.ReadChainTable
WITH EXECUTE AS OWNER
AS
SELECT id, strAttr
  FROM dbo.ChainTable;
```

```
SELECT principal_id, sid, name, type, usage, 'SERVER' AS scope
  FROM sys.login_token
UNION
SELECT principal_id, sid, name, type, usage, 'DATABASE' AS scope
  FROM sys.user_token;
GO
REVERT;
GO
```

▶ **Exercise 2: Test the Implicit Execution Context**

In this exercise, you will test the implicit execution context by executing the two procedures you altered in the previous exercise of this practice.

Test the new implicit execution context by switching the execution context to Janko-Cajhen explicitly and executing the procedures. The following code should now work without errors:

```
EXECUTE AS USER = 'JankoCajhen';
EXEC dbo.ReadChainTableDynamic;
EXEC LuborSchema2.ReadChainTable;
REVERT;
GO
```

▶ **Exercise 3: Check the Execution Context**

In this exercise, you will check the execution context of existing procedures.

1. You can check the schema, owner, and execution context of all modules in a database by using the sys.sql_modules, sys.objects, and sys.schemas catalog views. Try the following statement:

```
SELECT m.object_id, s.schema_id,
       o.name AS object_name,
       s.name AS schema_name,
       m.execute_as_principal_id,
       execute_as_principal_name =
       CASE
         WHEN m.execute_as_principal_id IS NULL THEN 'Caller'
         WHEN m.execute_as_principal_id = -2 THEN 'Owner'
         ELSE USER_NAME(m.execute_as_principal_id)
       END,
       OBJECTPROPERTYEX(OBJECT_ID
       (s.name + N'.' + o.name), N'OwnerId') AS owner_id,
       USER_NAME(CAST((OBJECTPROPERTYEX
       (OBJECT_ID(s.name + N'.' + o.name), N'OwnerId')) AS int)) AS owner_name
  FROM sys.sql_modules m
       INNER JOIN sys.objects o
        ON m.object_id = o.object_id
       INNER JOIN sys.schemas s
        ON o.schema_id = s.schema_id;
GO
```

▶ **Exercise 4: Cleanup**

In this exercise, you will clean your SQL Server instance.

Because this is the last practice in this chapter, you can use the following code to clean up your SQL Server instance:

```
USE master;
DROP DATABASE TK441Ch09;
DROP LOGIN [Builtin\Power Users];
DROP LOGIN JankoCajhen;
DROP LOGIN LuborKollar;
GO
```

Quick Check

1. As a DBA, how can you efficiently check an end user's permissions?
2. How can you find the execution context of a module?

Quick Check Answers

1. You can simply impersonate the end user by using the EXECUTE AS statement.
2. You can find the execution context of a module by examining the sys.sql_modules, sys.objects, and sys.schemas catalog views.

Case Scenario: Design a Secure Database

Tailspin Toys' human resources application uses stored procedures for all access to tables in the human resources database. However, in addition to permissions to execute the procedures, end users need permissions on base tables because the owners of the procedures are often different from the owners of the base tables. In addition, some end users use Microsoft Office Excel to create ad hoc reports from the base tables. You notice that end users frequently change the data in base tables directly, in an uncontrolled manner, instead of using the stored procedures and the application. You need to mitigate this situation.

1. How can you force end users to access the tables only through programmable objects?
2. If you revoke end users' permissions on base tables, how can you enable the users to create ad hoc reports in Excel?

Chapter Summary

- In SQL Server 2005, you can control security on a granular level.
- To administer security efficiently, group objects in schemas and group users in Windows groups and database roles.
- You can control metadata visibility.
- Use programmable objects to hide the underlying data from end users.
- Use a different execution context to bypass problems with ownership chains.

Chapter 10

Designing a Unit Test Plan for a Database

Throughout this book, you have learned how a database is really a complex group of objects—objects that retrieve data, objects that perform actions, objects that guard data, and so on—that work together to manage your data. As complex as they are, databases evolve. Applications connecting to the database will require additions and new features to address new business requirements. However, when you are making the changes, how can you be sure that you are not breaking compatibility with other client applications? How can you ensure that, by fixing some logic written in a stored procedure, you are not breaking the overall process that this single stored procedure was just a part of?

The answer is testing. Testing provides the solution for evaluating how the database will behave after a modification has been made on the database. You can execute different types of testing on a piece of software, such as a database, depending on what you want to evaluate or find out about its execution, such as whether it behaves as expected (functionality), performs as expected, is as secure as expected, scales as expected, and so on.

In this chapter, you will learn the key design practices for designing a *unit testing* plan for a database so that you can quickly pinpoint where to focus your attention when problems arise. A unit test plan is the building block for creating a performance baseline and a benchmark strategy, which you will study in Chapter 11, "Creating a Database Benchmarking Strategy."

Exam objectives in this chapter:
- Design a unit test plan for a database.
    - ❑ Assess which components should be unit tested.
    - ❑ Design tests for query performance.
    - ❑ Design tests for data consistency.
    - ❑ Design tests for application security.
    - ❑ Design tests for system resources utilization.
    - ❑ Design tests to ensure code coverage.

Before You Begin

To complete the lessons in this chapter, you must have:

- A general understanding of the different database objects supported in Microsoft SQL Server 2005.
- Knowledge about the Transact SQL syntax required to write views, stored procedures, user-defined functions, and triggers.
- A SQL Server 2005 instance (any edition) with the sample *AdventureWorks* sample database installed. Sample databases are available with SQL Server 2005 Enterprise edition but are not a part of the default installation. Alternatively, you can install the sample databases from *http://msdn2.microsoft.com/en-us/library/ms143739.aspx.*

Lesson 1: Assessing Which Components to Unit Test

Estimated lesson time: 40 minutes

Unit testing is usually defined as an automated way of testing individual components of a system in isolation to verify its behavior and to prove that it meets the expectations related to different requirements such as functionality, performance, integrity, security, and more. Let's further analyze this definition.

Automation implies that little human interaction is required, so when unit tests are executed, each test should:

- Set up its own execution environment and "before" conditions to measure.
- Execute a set of instructions or steps that exercise a specific database object.
- Reset the execution environment to its previous conditions.
- Return a result indicating the success or failure of the test.

From a database perspective, unit tests are usually run on database objects that can be isolated and measured independently. In a database, this usually involves stored procedures, user-defined functions (UDFs), views, constraints on tables, and triggers.

Exam Tip   In a database, create unit tests on stored procedures, user-defined functions (UDFs), views, constraints on tables, and triggers.

For each of these objects, the main goal of a unit test is to evaluate a certain expectation. Examples of some expectations are that:

- This view should return only 10 rows.
- This stored procedure's total execution time should be less than two seconds.
- This trigger should update the value in column X to the value of *100*.
- When the input parameters of this UDF are X and Y, it should return Z.

Unit tests are part of the deliverables of a programming project, so they should be included in the project scope and allocated enough time from the beginning of the project, when you are analyzing the requirements for the database. As with any other programming project, unit tests need to be designed, coded, tested, and executed—and they evolve as the database changes to fulfill new requirements.

Goals of Unit Testing

Unit testing might seem like a lot of work, and it is, but the benefits are worth it. The main goals of implementing a unit testing plan for a database are:

- To test each database object in isolation to determine the sources of bugs in your code and to evaluate whether the code executes as expected.
- To perform *regression testing* to evaluate the entire system after changes.
- To ensure that changes in one database object don't break another database object's functionality.

IMPORTANT   **What is a regression test?**

Regression testing is the process of running all the unit tests after a change or new requirement has been included in the database. Regression testing enables you to spot whether the specific change has caused any collateral damage that needs to be resolved.

Planning for Unit Testing

When designing a unit test, the following steps are recommended:

1. Create the testing script.
2. Create a setup testing script.
3. Create a teardown testing script.
4. Validate the testing, setup, and teardown testing scripts.
5. Create or set up a test database.
6. Set up testing data.
7. Execute the unit test.
8. Evaluate the test result.

IMPORTANT   **Types of database unit tests**

Unit tests can be categorized depending on what you want to evaluate or measure about a specific database object. There isn't a standard set of categories, but some common types of unit tests are:

- **Feature test**   Evaluates the database object functionality and verifies that expected results were returned or the appropriate behavior occurred after executing the database object.
- **Schema test**   Evaluates the database (or a resultset's) schema after execution. Some objects modify the database schema, for example, by adding a new table to the database or by verifying that a view returns the correct number of columns in the expected order.
- **Security test**   Validates both the security metadata (validates that a user or role exists in the database) and security execution context (validates that the executing user is allowed or not allowed to execute a set of operations).

Creating the Testing Script

A *testing script* is usually a Transact-SQL (T-SQL) script whose purpose is to exercise a database object. A testing script should be designed to be independent and complete so that no test depends on another test executed before or after it.

There are three possible result values after executing a unit test: success, failure, or *inconclusive*. Table 10-1 summarizes the different test result values.

Table 10-1   Possible Result Values for a Unit Test

Result Value	Description	Example
Success	Indicates that the unit test executed and finished successfully. "Successfully" means that the expected result was achieved.	The stored procedure returned an error (but this was expected behavior).
Failure	Indicates that the unit test was unable to finish its execution.	The stored procedure returned an error and could not finish execution (unexpected behavior).
Inconclusive	Indicates that the unit test executed and finished successfully but is unable to determine whether the result is positive.	The stored procedure returned an error (but this was expected behavior) but a different type of error than expected.

Example: How to Write Unit Testing Code with T-SQL

The following code samples provide a complete example of how to write a unit test with T-SQL. The example starts by providing a stored procedure to be unit tested.

The dbo.GetTop10SalesPeople stored procedure that follows returns the top 10 salespeople from the *AdventureWorks* sample database. This stored procedure will be the base for the following example unit tests:

```
CREATE PROCEDURE dbo.GetTop10SalesPeople
AS
  SELECT TOP (10)
    Person.Contact.FirstName,
    Person.Contact.LastName,
    SUM(Sales.SalesOrderHeader.SubTotal) AS TotalSales,
    Sales.SalesTerritory.Name
  FROM Sales.SalesOrderHeader INNER JOIN Sales.SalesPerson ON
Sales.SalesOrderHeader.SalesPersonID = Sales.SalesPerson.SalesPersonID
    INNER JOIN HumanResources.Employee ON
    Sales.SalesPerson.SalesPersonID = HumanResources.Employee.EmployeeID
    INNER JOIN Person.Contact ON
    HumanResources.Employee.ContactID = Person.Contact.ContactID
    INNER JOIN Sales.SalesTerritory ON
    Sales.SalesPerson.TerritoryID = Sales.SalesTerritory.TerritoryID
    GROUP BY Person.Contact.FirstName,
```

```
        Person.Contact.LastName,
        Sales.SalesTerritory.Name
ORDER BY TotalSales DESC
GO
```

The *dbo.GetTop10SalesPeople* stored procedure needs to be validated and tested to be sure that it provides the expected results.

If you are interested in validating that the stored procedure actually returns the expected number of rows, you can use the following T-SQL code to unit test the GetTop10SalesPeople stored procedure and validate that it returns only 10 rows:

```
PRINT 'TESTING STORED PROCEDURE [GetTop10SalesPeople]'

DECLARE @RC int
EXECUTE @RC = [dbo].[GetTop10SalesPeople]

IF (@@ROWCOUNT <> 10)
RAISERROR('Actual Rowcount not equal to expected 10',11,1)

PRINT '@RC = ' + CAST(@RC AS NCHAR(1))
GO
```

Validating a Scalar UDF

As stated, unit testing applies to any database object that executes an action. The next example creates a unit test around a scalar UDF.

In this case, the unit test will validate that the result returned by the UDF is the expected result. You can use this type of test to validate that the functionality implemented inside the database object calculates, computes, and/or updates that database state as expected.

In the code example that follows, the *dbo.ufnLeadingZeros* UDF adds as many leading zeroes to the input value as required, up to eight digits total. The unit test validates that the length of the returned value is actually eight characters:

```
PRINT 'TESTING SCALAR FUNCTION [ufnLeadingZeros]'
DECLARE @Value int, @RC varchar(8)

SET @Value = 150
SELECT @RC = [dbo].[ufnLeadingZeros] (@Value)

IF (LEN(@RC) <> 8)
    RAISERROR('Actual Len is not equal to expected 8',11,1)

PRINT '@RC = ' + CAST(@RC AS NCHAR(1))
GO
```

The *ufnLeadingZeros* function is part of the *AdventureWorks* sample database.

Validating a Table-Valued UDF

The same techniques for unit testing apply when you want to evaluate a table-valued UDF. You might be interested in validating the number of rows returned by the UDF, the number of columns returned in the resultset, the data types returned, or any other important attribute about the quality of the returned data.

The code example that follows writes a unit test for the *ufnGetContactInformation* table-valued function that is part of the *AdventureWorks* sample database. This UDF returns a single row with the specified @ContactID profile information. The unit test validates that this UDF actually returns just a single row:

```
PRINT 'TESTING TABLE VALUED FUNCTION [ufnGetContactInformation]'
DECLARE @ContactID int
SET @ContactID = 1

SELECT * FROM [dbo].[ufnGetContactInformation] (@ContactID)

IF (@@ROWCOUNT <> 1)
RAISERROR('Actual Rowcount not equal to expected 1',11,1)
```

Unit Testing a Trigger

Finally, here is a code sample that shows how to write a unit test for a trigger. In this case, the trigger is an UPDATE TRIGGER, but writing code to test a different type of trigger would be similar.

The [Production].[Product] table in the *AdventureWorks* sample database defines an ON UPDATE TRIGGER to update the value of the ModifiedDate column with the current date and time. The testing script compares the values obtained from ModifiedDate before and after the execution to validate whether the trigger actually ran and that it correctly updated the database.

Look at the code example:

```
PRINT 'TESTING UPDATE TRIGGER ON [Production].[Product]'

DECLARE
    @ReorderPoint smallint,
    @ProductID int,
    @Prev_ModifiedDate datetime,
    @Aft_ModifiedDate datetime

SET @ReorderPoint = 700
SET @ProductID = 1

SELECT @Prev_ModifiedDate = ModifiedDate
FROM [Production].[Product]
WHERE PRODUCTID = @ProductID
```

```
UPDATE [Production].[Product]
SET [Production].[Product].[ReorderPoint] = @ReorderPoint
WHERE [Production].[Product].[ProductID] = @ProductID;

SELECT @Aft_ModifiedDate = ModifiedDate
FROM [Production].[Product]
WHERE PRODUCTID = @ProductID

IF (@Prev_ModifiedDate = @Aft_ModifiedDate)
    RAISERROR('Trigger is not executing properly. Modified date was not changed',11,1)

PRINT '@Prev_ModifiedDate = ' + CAST(@Prev_ModifiedDate AS NCHAR(8))
PRINT '@Aft_ModifiedDate = ' + CAST(@Aft_ModifiedDate AS NCHAR(8))
GO
```

Notice that in the case of database triggers, you cannot execute it directly, but instead you must execute the action that causes the trigger to fire. Also, you must take a snapshot of the values before and after the trigger is executed to validate whether the values were updated correctly and as expected.

Creating a Setup Testing Script

Your testing script should not assume anything about the database but should evaluate whether all the conditions are met for it to execute. Before the execution of the actual unit test, a *setup testing script* must assert all the assumptions about the database—for example, to validate that all the required objects exist.

The setup testing script is executed before the testing script. The setup testing script can also be used to initialize the database state to the required state to execute the unit test. For example, when creating a unit test for a delete trigger on the Customers table, you need at least one customer record on that table to test the trigger.

Another important responsibility of the setup testing script is to begin a transaction. For unit tests to be repeatable, they should "clean" their state after execution. The easiest way to do this is to run all the unit test code inside a transaction. After test execution, roll back the transaction to return to the previous state. (The transaction is not rolled back in the setup script but rather in the teardown testing script, as you will see shortly.)

The following code example shows a setup script for a unit test. As stated, the testing script initiates a transaction so that test data can be returned to its initial state much faster after the test execution:

```
PRINT 'STARTING TEST EXECUTION AT ' + CAST(getdate() AS NVARCHAR(20))
USE AdventureWorks
GO

BEGIN TRANSACTION
```

Creating a Teardown Testing Script

A *teardown testing script* is executed after the testing script; it's used to return the database state to the initial state after executing the unit test. Just as the setup testing script begins a transaction, the teardown testing script should close the transaction by rolling it back.

The following code example shows a teardown script for a unit. The teardown script rolls back the transaction so that test data can be returned to its initial state much faster after the test execution:

```
ROLLBACK TRANSACTION
PRINT 'FINISHING TEST EXECUTION AT ' + CAST(getdate() AS NVARCHAR(20))
```

Validating the Testing, Setup, and Teardown Scripts

It is always possible that you inadvertently included an error in the scripts. The testing, setup, and teardown scripts should be validated and bug-free before clearing them as safe for executing unit tests.

Creating or Setting Up a Test Database

Unit testing might involve a lot of different operations on a database. It is usually recommended to have an independent testing environment to execute your unit tests in. When setting up a testing database, you have the following options:

- **Use a copy of a production database**   By restoring a database from backup or attaching an existing database, you do not have to re-create any database objects or set up testing data. However, there are some issues to take into account:
  - ❑ **Privacy**   Some of the data contained inside the database might be sensitive, so you might not have permissions to use it.
  - ❑ **Change management**   If the production database is constantly undergoing changes (to the database schema), you are forced to look continuously for the latest version of the database. You also need to update your unit tests to match the changes in the schema.
- **Create a new empty database by using the schema from a production database**   You do this by generating a CREATE DATABASE script (with all of its objects) and running it on a clean SQL server. The benefit of this approach is that it can be very easy to set up a new testing environment or to reset the database state after each test (by just running the CREATE DATABASE script again). Also, you are not forced to use the entire (usually complex) database; you re-create only the specific tables involved in the unit tests you are about to execute. The most important restriction of this approach is that you need to re-create the contained data every time after running the CREATE DATABASE script.

■ **Create a completely new database from the outset**   In this case, you are free to change the environment rules. This option is useful when you are interested in validating your database objects under different restrictions, different hardware, different configurations, and so on.

Setting Up Testing Data

The last step before you start executing your unit tests is to set up the initial data that the tests are going to be manipulating. In some cases, you might not care whether the database contains data. But in the cases in which you do require data, some common techniques for filling a database with testing data are:

■ To use a copy of a production database by restoring a database from backup or attaching an existing database. The main benefit of this approach is that you achieve 100 percent fidelity on the quality of the data because you are using real data. As stated previously, though, keep privacy issues in mind.

■ To use a data-generation tool to set the database state. Some generators enable you to customize the type of data being generated, for example, by using a regular expression for string values or for setting maximum and minimum constraints when generating integer values. Try to generate data that is as close as possible to the real data in terms of its fidelity and quality.

■ Import, bulk copy, or replicate data from a production database. You might use this approach when the testing database has a different schema than the production database, but you still want to use some of the database coming from the production database.

■ Have the unit test generate the required state in the setup script. This approach means that you do not worry about creating overall testing data but instead leave the responsibility to each of the unit tests to re-create the data that it needs to run. From a pragmatic point of view, this modularity might be seen as something better for maintenance, but depending on the amount of data involved, it can turn unit testing into a very long operation because each unit test needs to set up its own data.

Executing the Unit Test

The unit tests are plain T-SQL script files, so they can be executed in several ways and with several tools. The main idea behind the unit testing process is that it can be automated.

One approach to handling unit test execution is to use the SQL Server Command Line Utility (Sqlcmd.exe) that is part of SQL Server 2005. All the calls to execute each of the script files (setup, testing, and teardown) can be written into an operating system .cmd (batch) file. Finally, a SQL Server 2005 job step can be created to execute the test by using SQL Server Agent.

Exam Tip   Here is an example of the necessary command-line instruction to use the Sqlcmd.exe utility to execute the required scripts in the required order:

```
SQLCMD -S localhost -E -i SetupScript.sql -i TestScript.sql -i TeardownScript.sql -o
Output.txt
```

The –S indicates the server name to connect to. The –E option specifies the use of Microsoft Windows Authentication when connecting. With each –i option, a test script is added to the execution; notice the addition of the SetupScript.sql, TestScript.sql, and TeardownScript.sql files. The –o option lets you specify an output file, so any messages sent from the script file can be captured by this file.

Another possibility might be to have a user execute each unit test independently by using the SQL Server 2005 Management Studio (SSMS) console.

Evaluating the Test Result

Unit testing usually tries to compare the execution with a preset execution objective. The validation of whether the objective was successfully completed is called a *test condition*. Test conditions evaluate the test result. There are different types of test conditions, depending on what you are interested in evaluating; some examples might include:

- **Number of rows returned**   Validate the @@ROWCOUNT variable or the *ROWCOUNT _BIG ( )* function against a value comparing the expected number of returned rows with the actual number of returned rows.
- **Specific scalar values returned**   Especially when executing scalar UDFs, compare that the value returned by the UDF matches an expected scalar value.
- **Return of an empty resultset**   Especially when testing views, stored procedures, or table-valued functions, validate whether the database object actually returned an empty resultset.
- **Return of a non-empty resultset**   This is the same as the previous test condition except that this validates whether the database object actually returned rows.
- **Total execution time**   Validate that the total execution time is under a certain value.

You can create your own test conditions based on what you are interested in validating.

Practice: Creating a Unit Testing Script and a Testing Database

In this practice, you will apply the concepts from this lesson to assess which components should be unit tested and to create the necessary infrastructure to execute the tests. All the practices in this chapter refer to the Production set of tables from the *AdventureWorks* sample database.

On the Companion Disc This chapter includes many code examples. You will find all the code from this chapter on the companion CD in the C:\My Documents\Microsoft Press\TK70-441 \Chapter10\Sql folder.

▶ **Exercise 1: Create a View**

In this exercise, you will be given a business requirement. You must create the necessary database objects to fulfill the requirement. In the following exercises, you will be asked to unit test your code before deploying it.

> As the database designer for *AdventureWorks*, you must design a view that returns a list of all the products that need to be reordered. Validate from which products in stock you have less than the accepted amount for reordering. Design your own view before reading the suggested answer.

> **Suggested Answer**

> The following view satisfies the requirements:

```
CREATE VIEW dbo.ProductsToReorder AS
  SELECT Production.Product.ProductID,
     Production.Product.Name,
     Production.Product.ProductNumber,
     Production.ProductInventory.Quantity,
     Production.Product.ReorderPoint
FROM Production.Product INNER JOIN Production.ProductInventory ON
Production.Product.ProductID = Production.ProductInventory.ProductID AND
Production.Product.ReorderPoint > Production.ProductInventory.Quantity
WHERE (Production.Product.SellEndDate IS NOT NULL)
```

▶ **Exercise 2: Create a Unit Testing Script**

In this exercise, you will need to evaluate whether the view created in the previous exercise fulfills the business requirement. You will need to write a unit test for it.

> You decide to create a unit test on the ProductsToReorder view created in Exercise 1, "Create a View." The test condition that you want to evaluate is the return of a non-empty resultset. What modifications are required in the view's T-SQL code declaration? Write your own test script before reading the suggested answer.

> **Suggested Answer**

> The following view satisfies the requirements:

```
SELECT *
FROM dbo.ProductsToReorder

IF (@@ROWCOUNT = 0)
RAISERROR('View returned an empty resultset',11,1)
```

▶ **Exercise 3: Set Up a Test Database**

In this exercise, you will create a testing environment for the unit test created previously. Please answer the following question.

> You are ready to execute your newly created unit test. You need a testing database to run it. What possible options do you have?
>
> **Suggested Answer**
>
> The possible options to set up a testing database are:
>
> ❑ To use a copy of a production database.
>
> ❑ To create a new empty database that uses the same schema as the production database.
>
> ❑ To create a completely new database with a different database schema than the production database so that it models the business requirements to validate differently.

Quick Check

1. After applying some normalization rules in the database, you decide to split a table into two independent tables. After doing that, you need to modify the SELECT clause in all the existing stored procedures that retrieve data. When writing the unit tests to validate the change, which test conditions would you validate? (Choose all that apply.)

   A. Rows returned

   B. Scalar values

   C. Empty resultset

   D. Non-empty resultset

   E. Schema modification

2. You are designing a unit test on an AFTER DELETE trigger on the PurchaseOrder table. The trigger inserts a record into the Log table, storing the userid that executed the deletion. You created a setup script that inserts a new record into the PurchaseOrder table. What does the testing script code look like?

Quick Check Answers

1. Possible answers are rows returned, empty resultset, or non-empty resultset. These types of test conditions help you evaluate whether the resultset matches what is expected. You might want to compare the results of rows returned from before and after the change was made just to be sure that the same number of rows is returned.

2. The code of the unit test might look like this:

```
DECLARE @rc_before INT
SELECT @rc_before = COUNT(*)
FROM LOG

DELETE PurchaseOrder
WHERE ID = 100

DECLARE @rc_after INT
SELECT @rc_after = COUNT(*)
FROM LOG

IF ((@rc_before + 1) = @rc_after)
BEGIN
    PRINT 'Log registered 1 new record'
    RETURN
END
ELSE
BEGIN
    PRINT 'Log did not registered 1 new record'
    RETURN
END
```

Lesson 2: Designing Tests for Query Performance

Estimated lesson time: 25 minutes

The main objective of *performance testing* is to evaluate the response time when executing a specific database object. The response time is validated against a pre-defined set of performance objectives.

Performance testing assumes that the database object to test is functioning, stable, and robust, so any functionality should be validated with unit tests before you validate performance. To test performance correctly, you must maintain accurate and complete records of each test pass. Records should include:

- The exact system configuration.
- Both the raw data and the calculated results from performance monitoring tools.

During each test pass, run exactly the same set of performance tests; otherwise, it is not possible to discern whether different results are due to changes in the tests rather than to changes in the application. Automating as much of the performance test set as possible helps eliminate operator differences.

For automating the execution of a performance test, as discussed in the previous lesson, you must generate setup, testing, and teardown scripts. It might be interesting to consider adding *think time* to the scripts. Think time simulates the time spent by a user deciding what to do next. The following code example adds a think time of between 20 and 40 seconds:

```
DECLARE @RandomTime char(8)
SET @RandomTime = CONVERT(char(8), DATEADD ( ss , (RAND() * 10) + 10, '20000101' ), 108)

-- Execute user operations here...
PRINT 'Executing 1st operation'

WAITFOR DELAY @RandomTime

-- Execute user operations here...
PRINT 'Executing 2nd operation'
```

In Chapter 11, you will learn more about performance testing, how to set a performance baseline, and how to measure performance changes.

How to Design a Test

There are certain steps that need to be followed every time you design a test for performance. Remember that a test is always created to validate a certain condition.

In the case of performance tests, you must validate a condition related to a performance goal. A performance goal is expressed in terms of performance metrics that indicate how the code executed based on specific system resource, such as CPU consumption, memory usage, execution time, and more.

When designing a test for query performance, you need to:

1. Set performance goals.
2. Execute the test and measure performance metrics.
3. Evaluate the test results and document findings.
4. Test again and compare.

Setting Performance Goals

Before you can evaluate your solution for performance, you must have a detailed understanding of the expected production response times. Without a well-understood goal, you can't evaluate readiness. A well-formed set of performance goals is critical because it will drive your strategies related to system testing. Your performance goals should have the following elements:

- It should be measurable.
- It should indicate a maximum accepted value and/or minimum accepted value.

Executing the Test and Measuring Performance Metrics

When measuring performance metrics, you want to evaluate how close or far away the measurement is from your expected performance goals. The first time you execute the performance test, it is called a baseline. The baseline is used to compare further test passes and to see the results of any modifications you have included in your code.

Evaluating the Test Results and Documenting Findings

During the evaluation phase, compare the currently measured values with previous test passes. Evaluate the proper actions to take, depending on whether the measured value is above or below the performance goal and above or below the previous measurements.

It is very important that you document everything about each test pass. Typically, you would want to record test execution time and date, hardware details, software versions, test version, test input, test output, and measured response time.

Documentation maintains the history of the project in terms of execution performance.

Testing Again and Comparing Results

As noted previously, performance testing is an iterative practice. It is not enough to measure once and forget about it. Databases evolve, and many factors around them might affect performance. Performance testing is a continuous process, constantly comparing and validating performance metrics after each change in the database objects.

Writing a Test to Validate Query Performance

The following code example presents a modified version of the GetTop10SalesPeople stored procedure presented in Lesson 1. This modified stored procedure will simulate execution on a heavily used server:

```
ALTER PROCEDURE dbo.GetTop10SalesPeople
AS
  WAITFOR DELAY '00:00:08'

  SELECT TOP (10)
     Person.Contact.FirstName,
     Person.Contact.LastName,
     SUM(Sales.SalesOrderHeader.SubTotal) AS TotalSales,
     Sales.SalesTerritory.Name
  FROM Sales.SalesOrderHeader INNER JOIN Sales.SalesPerson ON
Sales.SalesOrderHeader.SalesPersonID = Sales.SalesPerson.SalesPersonID
     INNER JOIN HumanResources.Employee ON
     Sales.SalesPerson.SalesPersonID = HumanResources.Employee.EmployeeID
     INNER JOIN Person.Contact ON
     HumanResources.Employee.ContactID = Person.Contact.ContactID
     INNER JOIN Sales.SalesTerritory ON
     Sales.SalesPerson.TerritoryID = Sales.SalesTerritory.TerritoryID
     GROUP BY Person.Contact.FirstName,
          Person.Contact.LastName,
          Sales.SalesTerritory.Name
     ORDER BY TotalSales DESC
     GO
```

Notice that a WAITFOR DELAY has been added to stop execution for eight seconds. The following script can be used to test query performance, validating whether the stored procedure executes in less than four seconds:

```
DECLARE @s int, @maxSeconds int
SELECT@s = DATEPART(s, GETDATE())

SET @maxSeconds = 4
EXEC dbo.GetTop10SalesPeople

IF ((DATEPART(s, GETDATE()) - @s) > @maxSeconds)
RAISERROR('Execution time was longer than the expected 4 seconds',11,1)
```

Practice: Designing a Testing Script and Setting Performance Goals

In this practice, you will apply the concepts from this lesson. All the practices in this chapter refer to the *AdventureWorks* sample database.

▶ **Exercise 1: Design a Test Script**

In this exercise, you must decide how to design a testing script, based on a given business requirement.

As the database administrator for *AdventureWorks*, you receive a lot of complaints from users because the system is very slow when trying to determine which products need to be reordered. After investigating the problem, you find an old stored procedure that uses a cursor to fetch the Production.Product table, as shown in the following example:

```
CREATE PROC dbo.OldProductsToReorder AS
BEGIN
DECLARE @ProductID int, @ReorderPoint int

DECLARE ProductsToReorderCursor CURSOR FOR
  SELECT ProductID, ReorderPoint
  FROM Production.Product
  WHERE (Production.Product.SellEndDate IS NOT NULL)

OPEN ProductsToReorderCursor
FETCH NEXT FROM ProductsToReorderCursor
INTO @ProductID, @ReorderPoint

WHILE @@FETCH_STATUS = 0
BEGIN
  SELECT ProductID, Quantity
  FROM Production.ProductInventory
  WHERE Production.ProductInventory.ProductID = @ProductID AND
    Production.ProductInventory.Quantity < @ReorderPoint

  FETCH NEXT FROM ProductsToReorderCursor
  INTO @ProductID, @ReorderPoint
END
CLOSE ProductsToReorderCursor
DEALLOCATE ProductsToReorderCursor
END
```

To evaluate a possible database change, you decide to run some performance tests to evaluate the response time of the stored procedure. Design your own test script before reading the suggested answer.

Suggested Answer

The following test script satisfies the requirements:

```
DECLARE @s int, @maxSeconds int
SELECT @s = DATEPART(s, GETDATE())

SET @maxSeconds = 18
```

```
EXEC dbo.ProductsToReorder

IF ((DATEPART(s, GETDATE()) - @s) > @maxSeconds)
RAISERROR('Execution time was longer than the expected 18 seconds',11,1)
```

▶ **Exercise 2: Set Performance Goals**

In this exercise, you must set performance goals to validate the stored procedure reviewed in Exercise 1, "Design a Test Script." A performance goal enables you to validate that after every fix to the code, you are getting closer to or further from your expectations.

After executing the performance test, you now have a baseline to compare with when deciding on a possible solution to the performance issue raised by the users. You start first by setting a performance goal. Write your own performance goal for this scenario before looking at the suggested answer.

Suggested Answer

A possible performance goal could be that the ProductsToReorder stored procedure must return an answer to the calling process in no more than three seconds.

Quick Check

1. What should you do if you do not have a baseline? How do you set performance goals?
2. What are the steps to follow when designing a performance test?

Quick Check Answers

1. If you do not have a baseline to compare against, start by creating one. Run your tests and write down all the performance measurements. These first measurements will become your baseline and, hence, your performance goals. This gives you a head start so that you can start evaluating in which areas you want to improve performance.

2. When designing a performance test, you must start by deciding what your performance objectives are. Once the performance objectives are set, you need to decide what measurements you want to evaluate; this is usually straightforward, based on the chosen performance objectives. The next step is to start executing the tests and measuring performance metrics. When testing is done, you need to evaluate the test results and document the findings. With the results from the analysis, decide which database objects to fine-tune and start the process again.

Lesson 3: Designing Tests for Data Consistency

Estimated lesson time: 25 minutes

As explained in Chapter 3, "Designing a Physical Database," database designers typically define various constraints that all data should satisfy. These include constraints to ensure that the values of attributes are sensible (for instance, not NULL constraints or domain constraints), to ensure that certain attribute values (or combinations) appear only once in a table (uniqueness constraints), and to ensure that data in related tables are consistent with each another (foreign key constraints). If designed correctly, SQL Server will enforce these integrity constraints when the database state is modified.

You might also have other consistency constraints that are not coded in a declarative way but instead need to be coded inside stored procedures or UDFs. In this lesson, these constraints are called custom constraints.

When designing tests for data consistency, you want to evaluate whether constraints are enforced correctly (or if they are enforced at all). You might define different types of tests, depending on what you want to evaluate, such as:

- Testing values of attributes.
- Validating foreign key constraints.
- Validating custom constraints.

Testing Values of Attributes

Table attributes can be constrained by applying a *CHECK* constraint when defining the attribute. When testing for data consistency, you want to exercise the *CHECK* constraint by inserting allowable and prohibited values, depending on the rules enforced by the constraint.

BEST PRACTICES   Testing a *CHECK* constraint

When testing a *CHECK* constraint, try inserting maximum, minimum, just inside/outside boundary values (for example, +1 or -1), typical values, and error values.

Validating Foreign Key Constraints

Validating foreign key constraints means that you need to exercise the relationship created by the foreign key constraint and validate how the database reacts to referential integrity violations. This includes performing:

- Insertions in each participating table.
- Updates in each participating table, including evaluating CASCADING options.
- Deletions in each participating table, including evaluating CASCADING options.

Validating Custom Constraints

Custom constraints include any other integrity validation that is executed on the database but not enforced by the database management system (DBMS). Custom constraints are validated by code implemented, usually, inside a scalar UDF, for example, for calculated columns or for *DEFAULT* constraints. The main goal of testing these constraints is to validate that the logic coded inside the scalar UDF is correct.

Writing a Test to Validate Data Consistency

In the Person.Contact table in the *AdventureWorks* sample database, a *CHECK* constraint is defined on the *EmailPromotion* attribute. The constraint expression is:

([EmailPromotion]>=(0) AND [EmailPromotion]<=(2))

The following code example implements a data-consistency test that exercises this constraint:

```
DECLARE @NewValue int, @ContactID int
SET @NewValue = 10
SET @ContactID = 1

BEGIN TRY
    UPDATE Person.Contact
    SET EmailPromotion = @NewValue
    WHERE ContactID = @ContactID
END TRY
BEGIN CATCH
    IF (ERROR_NUMBER() <> 547)
    RAISERROR('Check constrained was not broken',11,1)
END CATCH
```

Another interesting example is a test to validate a foreign key constraint. In the *AdventureWorks* sample database, the Sales.Customer table declares a foreign key constraint with the Sales.Sales-Territory table, meaning that you cannot add a Customer to a territory that has not been defined yet in the database. To validate that constraint, you can define a test script such as the following:

```
DECLARE @TerritoryID int
SET @TerritoryID = 200

BEGIN TRY
  INSERT INTO [Sales].[Customer]
    ([TerritoryID],[CustomerType])
  VALUES (@TerritoryID,'s')
```

```
END TRY
BEGIN CATCH
   IF (ERROR_NUMBER() <> 547)
   RAISERROR('Foreign key constrained was not broken',11,1)
END CATCH
```

Practice: Validating Data Consistency in a UDF

In this practice, you will apply the concepts from this lesson. All the practices in this chapter refer to the Production set of tables from the *AdventureWorks* sample database.

▶ **Exercise 1: Validate a Default Value Set by a UDF**

In this exercise, you will design a strategy to validate that a default constraint defined on a table updates the table values as expected.

In the Sales.Customer table in the *AdventureWorks* sample database, a default constraint is defined on the AccountNumber column. If you check the table definition, you will find a declaration like this:

```
[AccountNumber]  AS (isnull('AW'+[dbo].[ufnLeadingZeros]([CustomerID]),''))
```

How can you design a test to evaluate such a condition? Design your own test script before reading the suggested answer.

Suggested Answer

There are two possible answers. One possibility is to test the *dbo.ufnLeadingZeros* UDF independently and make sure that it works as expected. (This example is implemented in Lesson 1 of this chapter.) The problem with this approach is that you are not testing the code written outside the UDF—for example, the string concatenation.

Another possibility is to validate that the *AccountNumber* value is set correctly when inserting a value inside the Sales.Customer table. What is interesting about this approach is that you need to use a teardown testing script to roll back the insertion of a new record in the table.

▶ **Exercise 2: Design a Test for Data Consistency in a Transactional Environment**

In this exercise, you must design a strategy for writing a test script to validate a ROLLBACK TRANSACTION statement without interfering with the transaction.

This chapter has explained that you should execute tests inside a transaction for correct data cleanup. How can you evaluate the transactional handling of your database? What if you want to evaluate whether a stored procedure can execute a ROLLBACK TRANS-ACTION statement without interfering with the external transaction from the test script? Can you come up with your own answer?

Suggested Answer

When designing tests for data consistency, you might be involved in a scenario in which you need to commit or roll back a transaction explicitly. In this type of scenario, the testing script cannot use a transaction because it will interfere with the internal transaction.

In previous lessons, you learned to use transactions because that method is a reliable, low-cost solution for cleaning up database state after test execution. However, if you cannot use transactions, you need to execute data cleanup directly. For example, if during the test you inserted a new record, then during the teardown script, you must call the DELETE statement to delete the record inserted by the test.

Quick Check

1. What type of data is validated during a data-consistency check?
2. When looking at the test code, what is the main difference when implementing this type of testing as compared to other testing?

Quick Check Answers

1. A consistency test evaluates the consistency constraints on the system. These constraints might be enforced directly by SQL Server or by a UDF or stored procedure. Consistency tests usually evaluate attribute constraints (*CHECK*, *DEFAULT*, or calculated columns), foreign key constraints, and custom constraints.
2. The main difference is that this type of test needs a TRY . . . CATCH construction to evaluate whether the constraint has been broken. You usually validate against the constraint being broken.

Lesson 4: Designing Tests for Application Security

Estimated lesson time: 25 minutes

In a database, testing application security involves validating that the required permissions, principals, and roles—at both the server and database levels—exist and validating that those permissions, principals, and roles are enforced by SQL Server.

Validating the Existence of Permissions, Principals, and Roles

SQL Server 2005 provides several system views that you can use to evaluate the existence of expected permissions, principals, and roles. Table 10-2 describes the most important views related to existence validation of security-related objects.

Table 10-2   System Views Related to Security in SQL Server 2005

View	Description
sys.database_permissions	Returns a row for every permission in the database
sys.database_principals	Returns a row for each principal in a database
sys.database_role_members	Returns one row for each member of each database role
sys.server_permissions	Returns one row for each server-level permission
sys.sql_logins	Returns one row for every SQL login
sys.server_principals	Returns a row for every server-level principal
sys.server_role_members	Returns one row for each member of each fixed server role

Validating the Execution Context for Specific Permissions, Principals, and Roles

By using the EXECUTE AS clause, you can validate multiple permissions, principals, and roles from within the same testing script. As explained in previous chapters, the EXECUTE AS clause enables you to change the execution context so that permissions are checked against a different user than the current user executing the script.

By using the EXECUTE AS clause, you can modify the execution context of certain testing scripts to validate how the script behaves when executed by different principals.

Writing a Test to Validate Application Security

Consider the following scenario. Suppose two users and two logins are defined in the SQL Server database (User1 and User2), but only User2 is granted the CREATE TABLE permission.

During the testing session (executed under the User1 identity), you need to insert data into the table, as shown in this code example:

```
CREATE LOGIN [User1] WITH PASSWORD=N'pass@word1'
GO
CREATE LOGIN [User2] WITH PASSWORD=N'pass@word1'
GO
CREATE USER [User1] FOR LOGIN [User1]
GO
CREATE USER [User2] FOR LOGIN [User2]
GO
ALTER LOGIN [User1] ENABLE
ALTER LOGIN [User2] ENABLE
GO
CREATE SCHEMA [MySchema] AUTHORIZATION [User2]
GO
GRANT CREATE TABLE TO [User2]
GO
EXECUTE AS USER = 'User2'
GO
CREATE TABLE MySchema.MyTable(Col1 int )
GO
REVERT
GO
```

The problem now is that if you try to insert new rows inside the MySchema.MyTable, using the User1 identity, you will not be allowed to do so. By using the EXECUTE AS clause, you can modify the execution context during certain portions of the testing script, like this:

```
BEGIN TRY
    EXECUTE AS USER = 'User2'
    INSERT INTO [MySchema].MyTable(Col1)VALUES(100)
    REVERT

    --CONTINUE WITH OTHER TESTS
END TRY
BEGIN CATCH
    IF (ERROR_NUMBER() <> 229)
    RAISERROR('Security was not broken',11,1)
END CATCH
```

Practice: Validating Whether a User Has Been Created

In this practice, you will apply the concepts from this lesson. All the practices in this chapter refer to the Production set of tables from the *AdventureWorks* sample database.

▶ **Exercise: Validate Security Metadata in a Database**

In this exercise, you will design a testing strategy to validate that certain security configurations are applied correctly and as expected.

The database administrator for *AdventureWorks* has automated the process of creating new logins and users for new users who need to work with the database. The code that implements this functionality is inside a stored procedure called dbo.CreateFull-NewUser.

You need to design a testing strategy to validate that the stored procedure actually creates all the necessary settings for the new user. Design your own test script before reading the suggested answer.

Suggested Answer

The following test script satisfies the requirements:

```
DECLARE @COUNT_LOGINS INT, @COUNT_PRINCIPALS INT

EXEC dbo.CreateFullNewUser 'User1'

SELECT @COUNT_LOGINS = COUNT(*) FROM sys.sql_logins
WHERE name = 'User1'
SELECT @COUNT_PRINCIPALS = COUNT(*) FROM sys.server_principals
WHERE name = 'User1'

IF (@COUNT_LOGINS <> 1 AND @COUNT_PRINCIPALS <> 1)
RAISERROR('Security logins and principals were not created as expected',11,1)
```

Quick Check

- Is it possible to use a unit test to evaluate a different type of security concern, such as a SQL injection attack?

Quick Check Answer

- A SQL injection attack is usually executed through a stored procedure that internally uses dynamic SQL. The main way this type of attack works is that the T-SQL code to execute is generated dynamically by concatenating pre-defined strings of code with values coming from input parameters. Hackers might take advantage of this by sending invalid strings through the input parameters, such as " *or '1 = 1 –'*. This type of string can be very dangerous. You can apply unit testing to validate SQL injection attacks but with some restrictions—specifically, that it is difficult to automate because the SQL injection attack requires the hacker to try different variations of the input string. You might develop a test script with some of the most common variations of input strings and evaluate how your stored procedures behave with this type of input.

Lesson 5: Designing Tests for System Resources Use

Estimated lesson time: 25 minutes

System resources are scarce commodities. Databases usually need to share system resources with other applications running on the same operating system and with the operating system itself.

System resources might include CPU, memory consumption, disk input/output (I/O) access, network access and data transmission, and any other operating system–controlled resources that your database interacts with. Testing for system resources usage enables you to find performance issues usually related to latency when accessing a system resource.

System usage metrics are recorded by different tools provided by SQL Server 2005 or by the Windows operating system.

IMPORTANT   System resource testing and load testing

System resource usage testing evaluates different system metrics and counters when executing a specific database object. These metrics are validated against a pre-defined set of performance objectives based on normally expected values. *Load testing* is the practice of evaluating the maximum load that a system can handle, so these are two different types of testing.

When designing a test for system resources use, you need to:

1. Set performance goals.
2. Evaluate and decide which performance counters and metrics to measure, according to performance goals.
3. Execute the test and measure the performance counters and metrics.
4. Evaluate the test results and document findings.
5. Test again and compare.

Notice that the steps are very similar to those discussed in Lesson 2, so only those that are different are expanded here.

Setting Performance Goals

In this type of testing, you need to have a detailed understanding of the expected production load in terms of transactions per second, number of concurrent users, amount of data being queried, or any other measurement that lets you determine the expected system use values. Some examples of system use metrics that you might be interested in are CPU use, locking time, locking mode, and number of page loads.

Using Performance Goals to Evaluate Performance Counters and Metrics

The performance goals will lead you to which counters and metrics you need to measure. For example, if you are interested in CPU use, you need to measure CPU use with Windows Performance Monitor. However, if you are interested in measuring table locking, you might want to validate the results of executing the SQL sp_lock system stored procedure.

T-SQL in SQL Server 2005 includes different commands for measuring performance. You need to choose which to use, depending on what you are interested in measuring. Table 10-3 summarizes some of the strategies to follow when choosing how to measure performance in T-SQL.

Table 10-3   Measuring Performance with T-SQL

Tool	When to Use It	More Information
Wait_Stats	To evaluate the waits encountered by threads that are in execution.	For an initial discussion about and usage of Wait_Stats, read about the sys.dm_os_wait_stats dynamic management view (DMV) in SQL Server 2005 Books Online at *http://msdn2.microsoft.com /en-us/library/ms179984.aspx.*
File_IO_Stats	To evaluate the input/output disk usage from a query.	For an initial discussion about and usage of File_IO_Stats, read about the sys.dm_io_virtual _file_stats DMV in SQL Server Books Online at *http://msdn2.microsoft.com/en-us/library /ms190326.aspx.*
SQL Server Profiler	To capture events from the database server. These events can then be replayed back to the server, so it is very easy to use SQL Server Profiler to generate testing scripts based on user executions.	See the SQL Server Profiler topic in SQL Server Books Online at *http://msdn2.microsoft.com /en-us/library/ms173757.aspx.* SQL Server Profiler can also be used from T-SQL code. Read the SQL Server Books Online topic about SQL Server Profiler Stored Procedures at *http://msdn2.microsoft.com/en-us/library /ms187346.aspx.*

Practice: Choosing Performance Counters and Metrics

In this practice, you will apply the concepts from this lesson to design tests for system resources use. All the practices in this chapter refer to the Production set of tables from the *AdventureWorks* sample database.

▶ **Exercise: Validate Performance with Performance Counters**

In this exercise, you will design a testing strategy to validate performance. You must decide which performance counters will provide the desired information to indicate whether your test was successful.

You have already set the following performance goals:

❑ Maximum CPU usage of 70 percent

❑ Maximum memory consumption of 1.5GB

❑ Maximum disk I/O waiting of 500 milliseconds

Now you need to evaluate and decide which performance counters and metrics to measure, based on these performance goals. Which performance counters from Windows Performance Monitor would fit your measurement needs?

Suggested Answer

There are many possible performance counters to evaluate, but the following items satisfy the requirements:

❑ CPU

- Processor\% Processor Time—This counter shows the percentage of time that the processor is working. It is the primary indicator of processor activity.

- System\Processor Queue Length—This counter shows the collection of threads waiting for the processor to free up.

❑ Memory

- Memory\Available Bytes—This counter shows the amount of RAM that is available to the operating system.

- Measure SQLServer:Buffer Manager\Buffer Cache Hit Ratio—This counter indicates that data is being retrieved from memory cache. The higher the value, the better.

❑ Disk I/O

- PhysicalDisk\Avg. Disk Queue Length—This counter indicates the average number of both read and write requests that were queued during the sampling interval.

- PhysicalDisk\Avg. Disk sec/Read—This counter indicates the average time dedicated to reading data from disk.

Quick Check

1. Describe how to set performance goals.
2. When designing tests for system resource use, what type of resources will be measured?

Quick Check Answers

1. The common practice when setting performance objectives is first to identify key scenarios that might require more resource consumption. From that list of key scenarios, prioritize them in terms of most significance to the end user. For each chosen scenario, adjust the expectations of the level of resource consumption required based on previous experience or simply common sense. Most performance objectives will modulate themselves after the first test runs.

2. The most important resources to measure are those scarce resources that are shared between multiple processes or multiple elements in the database. Usually, you want to focus on issues that do not allow your code to scale or perform better—for example, because there are a lot of requests waiting to enter the processor queue, a lot of requests waiting to enter the disk I/O read queue, and so on. CPU, memory use, disk I/O, and network I/O are the most common elements, but it is all right if you feel like your application might have different needs for other resources.

Lesson 6: Designing Tests to Ensure Code Coverage

Estimated lesson time: 25 minutes

Code coverage gives developers and testers information about areas of a program not exercised by a set of test cases, so code coverage actually ensures the quality of your set of tests, not the quality of the actual product being tested. By analyzing the results of a code-coverage test, testers can modify the conditions and input parameters to reach an accepted level of code executed during the testing exercise.

Setting a Goal for Code Coverage

The first step when designing tests to ensure that code coverage is adequate is to set a code-coverage percentage goal. The ideal would be to have 100 percent code coverage, but this is usually very expensive. You normally aim for 90 percent to 95 percent code coverage. The percentage goal indicates the amount of risk you are willing to take of delivering code to production that is not fully tested.

Code coverage is an iterative approach to code quality. Each test pass must modify the conditions, database state, and input parameters to try to reach 100 percent code coverage when executing unit tests.

Meeting Code-Coverage Test Requirements

Tests written to ensure code coverage must conform to the following requirements:

- Tests must report back on code coverage, somehow indicating which code was covered or not covered during the test execution.
- Tests could be parameterized to indicate the level of coverage measuring required. Code coverage can be measured at different levels, such as at each line of code, at each scope, at each batch, and so on.
- You must continuously validate your code-coverage result against your expected code-coverage metric. Varying the test conditions and running the test again will bring you closer to your code-coverage goal.

Writing a Test to Validate Code Coverage

The following code example shows one possible implementation of a code-coverage solution with T-SQL. First, set up a table in a testing database to store all the code-coverage information:

```
CREATE PROC CodeCoverageHelper(@TestRun int, @Message nvarchar(100))
AS
    INSERT INTO CodeCoverage([TestRun],[Message])
```

```
    VALUES (@TestRun, @Message)

CREATE TABLE CodeCoverage
(
    ID int IDENTITY(1,1),
    [TestRun] int,
    [TimeStamp] datetime DEFAULT GETDATE(),
    [Message] nvarchar(100)
)
```

Then, on each of the lines of code or batches that you want to execute as a whole, set up a code structure with the TRY . . . CATCH construct. This way, if the instruction fails, so will the insert to the code-coverage database. Here's an example of the TRY . . . CATCH constructs:

```
BEGIN TRY
CREATE LOGIN [User1] WITH PASSWORD=N'pass@word1'
EXEC CodeCoverageHelper 3, 'Create login User1'
END TRY
BEGIN CATCH
END CATCH

BEGIN TRY
CREATE LOGIN [User2] WITH PASSWORD=N'pass@word1'
EXEC CodeCoverageHelper 3, 'Create login User2'
END TRY
BEGIN CATCH
END CATCH

BEGIN TRY
CREATE USER [User1] FOR LOGIN [User1]
EXEC CodeCoverageHelper 3, 'Create user User1'
END TRY
BEGIN CATCH
END CATCH

BEGIN TRY
CREATE USER [User2] FOR LOGIN [User2]
EXEC CodeCoverageHelper 3, 'Create user User2'
END TRY
BEGIN CATCH
END CATCH
```

In this code example, the script is exercising the same security scripts you saw in this chapter's previous lessons but now with code coverage implemented. When finished executing, all of the successfully executed lines of code or batches will be stored on the *CodeCoverage* database:

```
SELECT *
FROM CodeCoverage
WHERE [TestRun] = 3
```

Finally, you can get metrics out of this data by knowing how many lines of code you were evaluating, for example:

```
DECLARE @totalLines int, @totalInCoverage int
SET @totalLines = 8

SELECT @totalInCoverage = count(*)
FROM CodeCoverage
WHERE [TestRun] = 3

PRINT @totalLines
PRINT @totalInCoverage
SELECT ((100 * @totalInCoverage) / @totalLines)
```

In this way, you can keep track of the percentage of code coverage that you have covered already.

Practice: Designing a Test to Ensure Code Coverage

In this practice, you will apply the concepts from this lesson. All the practices in this chapter refer to the Production set of tables from the *AdventureWorks* sample database.

▶ **Exercise 1: Set the Objectives for a Code-Coverage Test**

In this exercise, you must decide on a testing strategy for code coverage and provide an answer to key questions that evaluate whether your testing scripts really cover all of what is needed before shipping your code to production.

After following all the recommendations in this chapter, the designer for the *Adventure-Works* sample database created a set of unit tests on the most critical scenarios. The big questions raised now include: how much code is really covered by those unit tests? Were they worth the effort? How can you measure their success?

Explain the main objectives of a code-coverage test.

Suggested Answer

Code coverage measures the quality of a set of existing tests. Code coverage enables you to validate that all the code written inside unit tests is executed; hence, you look for the possibility of exercising 100 percent of the application code.

Code coverage is an iterative process as well, so if the first run did not cover more than 30 percent, try modifying some input parameters, change the conditions, and see whether you can get to 50 percent or more code coverage.

▶ **Exercise 2: Implement a Code-Coverage Strategy**

In this exercise, you must decide how to implement a code-coverage strategy when some of the T-SQL code is hard-coded in the application tier.

You are deciding how to implement a code-coverage strategy on the database objects, but some of the T-SQL code is also written in a data-access layer in ADO.NET. How can you implement a code-coverage strategy?

Suggested Answer

In cases in which the database code is distributed between the database and the data-access layers, you must create your code-coverage tests at the data-access layer (or at both layers). By having the code-coverage tests execute at the data-access layer, you can have a 360-degree view on the code execution path from the data-access layer all the way to your stored procedure.

Quick Check

1. What is the code-coverage metric?
2. On which occasions should you use a code-coverage test?

Quick Check Answers

1. The code-coverage metric indicates the percentage of exercised code that you are aiming for.
2. Always use code-coverage tests! Code-coverage tests apply to all the other test types reviewed in this chapter. Code coverage is about the quality of your tests.

Case Scenario: Design a Unit Test Plan for a Database

Tailspin Toys has never had a mature testing process. Testing is usually an afterthought because there is barely time to test before rolling out a solution. You are part of the team in charge of envisioning the next generation of applications inside the company.

Based on reviews coming from business partners and end users, database performance has always been a weak point, and your team is evaluating the opportunity to implement unit testing as part of the new project scope.

One of the most notable mistakes of the previous version of the database is that there weren't many primary keys defined and no foreign keys at all, so the database is unable to validate referential integrity.

Because you are upgrading to SQL Server 2005, you have already foreseen several scenarios in which you want to use the new EXECUTE AS clause, but you are not sure how it will affect the overall database stability.

1. Do you think that implementing unit testing could help improve Tailspin Toys' database applications? Why?
2. Given that the database is being upgraded, which components should be unit tested?
3. Database performance is a serious issue, and the problems go back a long time. Name some of the performance objectives that should be achieved.

4. You are really worried about data consistency. Currently, the database is full of data that is hard to handle because it is impossible to make sense of a lot of it. You design some tests for data consistency, but what is the benefit of those tests as compared to using the referential integrity of the database?

5. How can you evaluate the consequences of using the EXECUTE AS clause? Would code coverage testing help in this?

Chapter Summary

- Testing enables you to evaluate how well the database will behave, both functionally and nonfunctionally, after a certain modification has been made.

- In a database, create unit tests on stored procedures, user-defined functions (UDFs), views, constraints on tables, and triggers.

- The main objective of performance testing is to evaluate the response time when executing a specific database object. The response time is validated against a pre-defined set of performance objectives. You must have a detailed understanding of the expected production response times and load to set performance goals.

- When designing tests for data consistency, you want to evaluate whether constraints are enforced correctly (or if they are enforced at all).

- Testing application security involves validating that the required permissions, principals, and roles at the server and database levels exist and that they validate that those permissions, principals, and roles are enforced.

- Testing for system resources use enables you to find performance issues usually related to latency when accessing a system resource. System use metrics are recorded by different tools provided by SQL Server 2005 or by the Windows operating system.

- Code coverage gives developers and testers information about areas of a program not exercised by a set of test cases. Testers can then modify the conditions and input parameters to reach an accepted level of code executed during the testing exercise.

Chapter 11

Creating a Database Benchmarking Strategy

It is not unusual to find that a solution does not cover all proposed objectives, especially related to performance aspects such as the ability to scale properly or respond quickly when the volume of data to be managed exceeds certain thresholds. To avoid these types of issues, you must plan ahead and adopt a proactive way of thinking instead of trying to fix the problems once the solution is in production and difficult to fix.

You need to set a performance baseline and design a benchmarking strategy to guarantee that your database is ready to cope with changes in the execution environment. In this chapter, you will learn how to plan so you avoid many of the problems related to performance and system capacity that often arise when databases are already in production. This chapter proposes a proactive approach, suggests planning in advance for performance changes, and shows how to prepare a plan to keep performance and capacity growth issues under control.

Exam objectives in this chapter:
- Create a performance baseline and benchmarking strategy for a database.
  - Establish performance objectives and capacity planning.
  - Create a strategy for measuring performance changes.
  - Create a plan for responding to performance changes.
  - Create a plan for tracking benchmark statistics over time.

Before You Begin

- To complete the lessons in this chapter, you must have the SQL Server 2005 *Adventure-Works* sample database installed. Sample databases are available with SQL Server 2005 Enterprise Edition but are not a part of the default installation. You can also install the sample databases from *http://msdn2.microsoft.com/en-us/library/ms143739.aspx*.

Lesson 1: Establishing Performance Objectives and Capacity Planning

---

Estimated lesson time: 45 minutes

Performance objectives represent measurable criteria, such as response time, throughput (how much work the system can do in a given amount of time), and resource use (CPU, memory, disk I/O, and network I/O) that you want to attain.

Performance objectives should always be realistic and in accordance with the project's budget. Common sense will be your first guide when you are establishing performance objectives and planning for a suitable capacity that will enable your system to behave properly throughout its production lifetime. That stated, the goal is to achieve the best balance between effort and investment without compromising the maintainability, flexibility, and responsiveness of your database system.

Establishing Performance Objectives

To establish your performance objectives, you need to have a good understanding of your database and the environmental constraints placed on the system. Gather information about the levels of activity that the database is expected to meet, such as:

- The expected number of concurrent users.
- The number and size of data requests.
- The number of concurrent transactions.
- The length of each transaction.
- The amount of data and its consistency.
- The target central processing unit (CPU) utilization.

IMPORTANT   CPU utilization

It is essential both to determine a target CPU utilization based on your application needs, including CPU cycles for peak usage, and to avoid 100 percent CPU usage during normal hours, or peak loads will not be handled properly. High CPU usage (approaching 100 percent utilization) reduces response times while throughput stays constant or even increases because of work queuing up in the server. The general figure for the threshold limit for processor activity is 85 percent, but this might be different, depending on your own requirements.

Performance objectives might be limited by constraints such as:

- Hardware and software configuration.
- Ability to interoperate between domains—for example, interoperating with earlier systems and support for earlier data.
- Costs related to development, implementation, and maintenance of the plans and strategies to maintain a proactive approach.

Performance Modeling

Setting performance objectives is part of a bigger strategy known as performance modeling. *Performance modeling* is a structured and repeatable approach to modeling the performance of your software. It begins during the early phases of your application design and continues throughout the application life cycle. If you take a proactive approach to performance modeling, you might avoid certain problems that can arise later in production.

IMPORTANT Fight performance problems early

Performance problems are frequently introduced early in the design phase. Database tuning or more efficient coding later on cannot always fix design issues, and it is not always possible to fix architectural or design issues later in the software life cycle. If it is possible, it is often inefficient and expensive.

When you create performance models, you need to identify the critical application scenarios and set your performance objectives. You break down your critical scenarios into steps and assign *performance budgets*. Your budget defines the resources and constraints across your performance objectives.

The benefits of performance modeling are:

- Performance becomes part of your design and is not an afterthought.
- Modeling helps answer the question of whether the current design supports the performance objectives. By building and analyzing models, you can evaluate tradeoffs before you actually build the solution.
- You should know explicitly what design decisions are influenced by performance as well as the constraints that performance puts on future design decisions. Often, these decisions are not captured in the design, so they might lead to maintenance efforts contrary to your original goals.
- You can avoid performance surprises occurring after your application is released to production, and it is too late to fix them.

The main deliverable of performance modeling is a document with detailed scenarios that help you decide what is important. You will be able to identify quickly where to instrument, what to test, and whether you are on track for meeting your performance goals.

Another important recommendation of performance modeling is to build prototypes. The data obtained from prototypes can help you evaluate early design decisions before implementing something that will not meet your performance goals.

The time, effort, and money you invest at the outset in performance modeling should be proportional to your project risk. For a project with significant risk, when performance is critical, devote more time and energy at the beginning when developing your model.

For more information about performance modeling, read Chapter 2, "Performance Modeling" in the "Improving .NET Application Performance and Scalability" guide published by the Microsoft Patterns & Practices team, available at *http://msdn2.microsoft.com/en-us/library/ms998537.aspx*.

BEST PRACTICES   Setting performance objectives

Consider the following recommended best practices when creating performance objectives:

- Ensure that your design determines response time and resource usage budgets.
- Do your best to identify your target deployment environment.

IMPORTANT   Performance objectives and load testing

Do not replace scenario-based load testing with performance modeling:

- Performance modeling suggests which areas should be worked on but cannot predict the improvement caused by a change.
- Performance modeling feeds the scenario-based load testing by providing goals and useful measurements.
- Performance modeling might ignore many scenario-based load conditions that can have an enormous impact on overall performance.

Inputs Required for Establishing Performance Objectives

Before establishing performance objectives, analyze the following information:

- Relevant performance-related data—such as number of concurrent users, expected transaction load, and expected data load—for the most critical scenarios
- Communication patterns, query patterns, data filtering, and heavy data-processing operations by reviewing the client application logical and physical design
- Constraints imposed by the infrastructure environment by reviewing the infrastructure design
- The requirements and constraints derived from quality-of-service agreements
- Workload requirements and expectations

Establishing Performance Objectives

To establish your performance objectives, complete the following steps:

1. Identify scenarios in which performance is important and scenarios that pose the most risk to your performance objectives.

    IMPORTANT When key scenarios aren't documented

    In many cases, particularly with previous systems, use cases and scenarios are not documented. In those cases, the assessment team must work with the development team to identify the processing steps that are executed by the key scenarios.

    ---

2. Identify the expected workload, including total and concurrent users, amount of data and transaction volumes, or any other metric in which you are interested. For each of these metrics, identify how many or how much your system needs to support.

3. Define performance objectives for each of your key scenarios. Performance objectives reflect business requirements, and they usually include response time, throughput (for example, when the system must support a certain number of transactions per second), and resource utilization.

    When setting performance objectives, consider project growth and determine how long your expectations will be current. For example, take into account considerations for meeting expectations within six months or one year. In each case, the objective should be quantitative and measurable. Vague statements such as "should have a good performance" are not recommended.

    It is also important to specify the conditions under which the required performance is to be achieved for each combination of scenario and objective.

    Exam Tip   Performance objectives reflect business requirements and should be quantitative and measurable.

    ---

4. Identify budget and constraints. This includes the maximum execution time in which an operation must be completed and resource-utilization constraints such as CPU, memory, disk input/output (I/O), and network I/O. Don't forget that budgets are just constraints that you are willing to accept. An example of a budget is that on the production server, without installing the application, the CPU is already working at 40 percent; this is a constraint that you need to take into account.

5. Evaluate your design against the defined objectives and budget. You might need to modify your design or spread your response time and resource-utilization budget differently to meet your performance objectives. Ask yourself important questions such as: does the budget meet the objectives, and is it realistic? Should the current design or feature set be reduced or modified to achieve the performance objectives? Are there

any alternative patterns, designs, or deployment topologies available to achieve the performance objectives?

6. Validate your model and estimates. Performance tuning is an ongoing activity and includes prototyping, assessing, and measuring. So continue to create prototypes and measure the performance of the critical scenarios by capturing metrics. Continue performing validation checks until the performance goals are met.

Capacity Planning

Capacity planning is the process of estimating the computer resources required to meet an application's performance objectives over time. The main objective of capacity planning is to maintain a balanced computer system proactively.

Capacity planning uses input from multiple sources, such as measurement tools and feedback from business users, to understand the resource usage of the current workload and to understand future requirements as they relate to the expected growth in data and workload.

There are two main methodologies used for capacity planning: *transaction cost analysis* and *predictive analysis*. Both provide complementary approaches to the problem of planning required hardware capacity, and both should be taken into consideration for a good capacity-planning effort.

Transaction Cost Analysis

Transaction cost analysis (TCA) is a process for conducting a controlled estimate of application performance, based on key measurements for a single transaction through the application. Although TCA does not serve as a replacement for the complete and thorough performance testing of the entire system, it can be helpful in determining any obvious risks or serious underestimates related to the hardware required to support the system. Generally speaking, a TCA consists of six steps:

1. Compile a user profile, which is also known as workload characterization. Collect production traffic data or a transactional workload taken from your load test plan to be used as input for the analysis. This profile holds the most relevant operations executed by each user.

2. Execute discrete tests. Create a test script to execute discrete tests for each user operation identified in step 1 for a load at which your system reaches maximum throughput. For each test, identify the limiting resource against which the cost needs to be calculated for a given operation.

3. Calculate the cost of each operation. Measure the cost of each operation in terms of the measured limiting resource. Such measurement involves calculating the cost per request and then calculating the cost per operation.

4. Calculate the cost of an average user profile. Over time, variations in resource utilization between different users tend to even out statistically to average behavior. To estimate capacity, you need to assume an average user and then calculate the cost for that average user profile.

5. Calculate database capacity. This step involves knowing how many concurrent transactions your database can support on specific hardware and what your database's future resource requirements are. To estimate, consider measurements such as calculating how many simultaneous users are supported by using the average user profile and calculating the future resource estimates for your database, according to your growth expectations.

6. Verify site capacity. You can verify your calculated application capacity by running load tests with the same characteristics you used to calculate TCA. The verification script would be simply a collection of all TCA measurement scripts aggregated and run as a single script.

Predictive Analysis

In a similar way, predictive analysis predicts the future capacity requirements by extrapolating from historical and current data. With this approach, you analyze how computer resource usage relates to transaction volumes (or user operations). This can be done by analyzing log files to understand your database's usage and by recording performance data to understand resource utilization.

This type of analysis can be considered a four-step process.

1. Collect performance data over a period of time. The greater the time duration, the greater the accuracy with which you can predict a usage pattern and future resource requirements.

2. Query the collected performance data based on what you are trying to analyze. It is also possible to query segmented data from different, common points in the past, such as month-end processing over the past 12 months. The calculation is still useful to predict the future capacity of the system at future month-end processing dates.

3. Analyze the collected performance data. Analyze the data obtained by querying the database. The data obtained for a given time frame results in a pattern that can be defined by a trend line. The pattern can be as simple as a linear growth of the resource usage over a period of time.

4. Predict future requirements. By analyzing trend lines, you can predict the future requirements. The predicted resource requirements assume that the current trend would continue into the future.

When collecting performance data, cover all possible operations served by the server, not just for a single application but for all possible applications connecting to the server.

For examples of how to perform capacity planning, read the guide "How To: Perform Capacity Planning for .NET Applications" at *http://msdn2.microsoft.com/en-us/library/ms979198.aspx*. SQL Server 2005 Books Online includes a detailed analysis of capacity planning for *tempdb*, available at *http://msdn2.microsoft.com/en-us/library/ms345368.aspx*.

Practice: Setting Performance Objectives

In this conceptual practice, you will apply the concepts from this lesson to establish performance objectives for a fictitious company called City Power & Light, where you are working as a consultant to create a strategy to improve overall application performance.

► **Exercise 1: Set Performance Objectives**

In this exercise, you will justify why it is important to set the performance objectives prior to starting a project.

> In your first meeting with the database administrator (DBA), he complains that performance has been deteriorating recently—or at least, that is what the users have been complaining about lately. He hands you a graphic with the results of a System Monitor trace in which he measured CPU utilization. According to the graphic, CPU utilization is at an average of 60 percent.
>
> You explain to the DBA that there is no way to know whether 60 percent CPU utilization is a helpful metric. Why isn't this value enough?
>
> **Suggested Answers**
>
> You can answer this question in multiple ways, but there are two main issues to investigate:
>
> ❑ There is no way to determine accurately whether 60 percent CPU utilization is a valid metric. To make this determination accurately, you would need a baseline measurement from a point in time when the server was operating in a known "healthy" state.
>
> ❑ Although 60 percent isn't really high, the customer has concerns. You will need to determine what other applications might be running on the server or have a performance objective requiring that all applications be constrained to a certain CPU usage value. Either way, for some reason, the customer thinks that CPU is constrained on its installation.

▶ Exercise 2: Query Performance Information

In this exercise, you must indicate what information is useful for setting a performance objective by evaluating some of the current constraints in the production environment. This exercise continues from Exercise 1, "Set Performance Objectives."

You convince the database administrator that the best plan of action is to have a performance baseline for comparisons. But even if you had the performance baseline, it would be useless unless you have established performance objectives so that you know when you are closer to or further away from your goals.

You decide to meet with the person in charge of the production servers. She indicates that in the same database server, there are two other applications running; together, they might account for an average of 25 to 30 percent of CPU utilization. What other information might be useful to set a performance objective?

Suggested Answer

Answers can vary, but one of the most important pieces of information missing is the expected growth of each of the three applications. You might need more information about the type of operations that are executed by the application you are reviewing. For example, are they CPU-intensive operations? How many users will be using the application concurrently?

▶ Exercise 3: Establish Performance Objectives

In this exercise, you will set the current performance objectives based on the expected system growth. This exercise continues from Exercise 2, "Query Performance Information."

The customer indicates that the other two applications are not expected to grow, but the application's user base with which you are working is expected to grow by 10 percent per year, which translates to 20 percent more concurrent transactions per year. In the first year, only five users will be using the application.

The main scenario in this application executes a computing-intensive business logic.

Try to establish a performance objective for CPU usage with the given information.

Suggested Answer

Answers might vary, but a possible performance objective might say that CPU utilization should be under 50 percent (total between the three applications) in the first year, increasing to a maximum of 60 percent in the second year, with increases of 10 percent each year.

> **Quick Check**
>   1. What is the definition of a project budget?
>   2. What are the benefits of establishing performance objectives?
>
> **Quick Check Answers**
>   1. The project's budget is the set of available resources after subtracting any constraints that currently affect the system and that need to be taken into account by the performance objectives. These constraints might indicate actual load that the server must maintain.
>   2. Performance objectives represent measurable criteria, such as response time, throughput, and resource utilization that are intended to be attained. Performance objectives enable you to evaluate whether, by changing, modifying, or differently configuring your system, you are getting closer to or further from your expected goals.

Lesson 2: Creating a Strategy for Measuring Performance Changes

Estimated lesson time: 30 minutes

In the previous lesson, you learned about the importance of establishing performance objectives so that you know where to focus your available resources and energy. However, by setting performance objectives, you have not solved anything yet. After setting performance objectives, you need a strategy to detect whether there really are any performance changes.

The first step to being able to detect whether there are performance changes is to have something with which to compare current performance. This lesson explains how to create a performance baseline so that you can compare against it and detect any performance improvements—or performance reductions. Having a baseline is important, but it is also important to have the right toolset to measure performance. This lesson also evaluates different tools available with the Microsoft Windows operating system and Microsoft SQL Server.

Generating a Representative Baseline

To know whether you have achieved your objectives, first establish a baseline as a comparative pattern to check further measures, helping you identify trends and close gaps that show up in your project's life cycle.

Because baselines provide you with a comparison scheme, it is important to generate a representative baseline, including measuring on the same hardware (or as similar as possible) as the production server or trying to imitate the same constraints as in the production environment.

Baselines are ordinarily subject to configuration management audits. Audits can include an examination of specific actions performed against the baseline, an evaluation of change within the baseline, metric collection, comparison to another baseline, or all of these. In addition, you might have multiple baselines, each for a different scenario.

Measuring a Baseline

Testing is always a three-step process: defining, measuring, and improving. Let's look at some of the most important aspects of measuring.

Measuring is an ongoing activity, representing an investment that must be made before a dramatically higher level of performance can be reasonably expected or achieved. Measuring is essential to driving change in the right direction and then sustaining that change.

The most critical aspect of measuring is knowing what to measure. The choice of metrics is critical because what you measure is what you attend to.

The development and implementation of appropriate metrics should span the full process and reflect key values. Use multiple metrics to guide improvement on all dimensions of process performance: time, quality, and cost.

IMPORTANT   Measuring median performance

Improvement aims to reduce the variability in process performance; hence, metrics, as a rule, should measure median performance and variance, not only average performance.

Setting measurable targets for process objectives requires judgment and is not an exact science. To set process targets, planners should:

- Consider the current status (baseline) of the infrastructure.
- Seek input on the desired level of improvement.
- Make a realistic assessment of what can be accomplished.

In addition, keep in mind that to compare the results accurately from different performance test passes, the application must be working correctly.

Measuring Performance Changes

You must maintain accurate and complete records of each test pass. This record might include:

- The exact system configuration, especially changes from previous test executions.
- Both the raw data and the calculated results from performance monitoring tools.

Run exactly the same set of performance tests during each test pass; otherwise, it is not possible to discern whether different results are due to changes in the tests rather than to changes in the application or in the execution environment. To help eliminate operator differences, automate as much of the performance test set as possible.

Make sure that the database contains a realistic number of records and that tests use random (but valid) values for data entry, simulating the user input. If the number of records in use is too small, the effects of caching in the database server will yield unrealistic test results.

Monitoring the Test Environment

After you have defined performance goals and developed the performance test, run the test once to establish baseline values. Try to reproduce the situation as closely as possible to a real production environment to be sure it resembles the real scenario after deployment. If the collected information meets performance objectives, no tuning is necessary; however, chances are that, in a very first stage of testing, some changes will be necessary. Now that the baseline is set, perform the following activities:

- Keep track of all the changes and modifications on the testing environment. Documenting this process might help you in your future development and troubleshooting.
- Repeat testing walkthroughs periodically. Even seemingly small changes in a measure can change the information flow, sometimes in unexpected ways.
- Set testing targets to determine the desired amount of change over a given time interval.
- Monitor progress toward meeting the performance objectives by collecting and analyzing tracking data on a scheduled basis. Here are some hints that might help:
  - ❑ Address major data issues at the outset and be prepared to explain the impact of data changes.
  - ❑ Use a variety of sources for baseline measures.
  - ❑ Set realistic targets for your objectives.
  - ❑ Plan to track the progress of your objectives.

Implementing Performance Measuring Techniques

Metrics of particular interest tend to be response time, throughput, and resource utilization (how much CPU, memory, disk I/O, and network bandwidth your application consumes while performing its tasks). SQL Server 2005, as well as Windows Server, provides a set of tools to help in these tasks.

Measuring requires that you use the right tool, depending on what you want to measure. The following set of widely used tools and metrics help you focus on concrete performance goals:

- **SQL Server wait stats**   Used to analyze the causes behind waiting times in connection requests to the database.
- **Resource usage measured by the operating system**   Enables you to get information about the current utilization of basic resources, including I/O devices, memory, CPU, network, and system processes. This toolset also enables you to measure resources specific to SQL Server, such as compilations and recompilations per second, lifetime expectancy for pages, stored procedures caching, and more.
- **Employment of physical I/O devices by SQL Server**   Includes several important functions that inform you about these kinds of operations, which are critical to performance in SQL Server 2005.
- **Database consistency checker commands (and SQL Server 2005 correspondents)**   Provide detailed information about how memory caching, stored procedures, locks, and several other database objects are executing.
- **Dynamic management views (DMV)**   Specific to SQL Server 2005, DMVs provide administrative information about SQL Server, helping draw an accurate profile of the server performance. DMVs are an important complement to the information obtained through the previously mentioned methods.

Experience tells you how to choose between the different tools. You can use database consistency checker (DBCC) commands, the new DMVs, SQL Server Profiler, monitoring tools such as SysMon and PerfMon, and Windows Sysinternals availaible at *http://www.microsoft.com /technet/sysinternals/default.mspx.*

Wait Stats

Every request to the database server performs a series of internal steps that finally end up requiring some operating system resources. For example, some queries will require parallel processing in I/O devices, and others will require more CPU usage. In all cases, if the required resource is not available, requests will have to wait to be processed. SQL Server maintains an internal list, recording how much time and how many times connection requests have been waiting for the needed resource to be available.

In SQL Server 2005, wait stats are available through the DMV *sys.dm_os_wait_stats,* which exposes to the user the following information:

- **wait_type**   Name of the type of wait
- **waiting_tasks_count**   Number of times that the connection has been waiting
- **wait_time_ms**   Total time the connection has been waiting
- **max_wait_time_ms**   Maximum time connections have been waiting
- **signal_wait_time**   Total time elapsed since resource liberation (that is, until it started to be used)

If you need further information to complete your performance analysis, you can query DBCC WAITSTATS. SQL Server 2005 keeps track of 194 different types of waits (many more than in the previous SQL Server releases). Table 11-1 summarizes some of the most used wait stats.

Table 11-1   Most Used Wait Stats

Wait Type	Description
ASYNC_IO_COMPLETION	Waits for I/O asynchronous operations to finish.
CXPACKET	Waits for parallel processing of queries.
IO_COMPLETION	Waits for I/O operations to finalize.
LATCH_x	Waits due to latches on database objects. The difference between a latch and a lock is that locks are maintained all along the transaction time. Whereas locks protect the information during the transaction, latches manage physical access to data pages.
LCK_x	Waits for unlocking of objects (transactions).
LOGMGR	Waits for pending operations on the Transaction Register.

Table 11-1 **Most Used Wait Stats**

Wait Type	Description
NETWORKIO	Waits for pending I/O operations on network devices. Usually, this wait stat waits until the read or write operation has been terminated on the client.
OLEDB	Holds several types of waits, such as queries to linked servers, BULK INSERT operations, FULL-TEXT, or queries to system virtual tables.
PAGEIOLATCH_x	Waits due to latches on pages in which I/O operations are being processed.
PAGELATCH_x	Waits due to latches on pages in which no I/O operations are taking place.
WRITELOG	Waits due to finalization of operations on the Register of Transactions.

In many cases, wait stats analysis is an excellent starting point in getting to know how the client applications and the database server are working.

Operating System Resources Usage

Windows Server includes profiling tools to help you diagnose and evaluate operating system resource usage. One of the most important tools provided by the operating system is Performance Monitor, an extensible platform for measurement and analysis of performance counters. Each resource and application running in the operating system can alert Performance Monitor about changes in its state to modify the performance counters.

The collected information from Performance Monitor can be stored in counter logs. For detailed explanation of how to set up the Performance Monitor console to start monitoring and how to create counter logs, see *http://technet2.microsoft.com/WindowsServer/en/Library/8368dfd6-0d42-4fc7-b0ac-d331ee33be431033.mspx*. After you measure the set of performance counters in which you are interested, you need to analyze the collected data and make your conclusions about system performance.

Although SQL Server 2005 exposes some overlapping information through its own performance counters, SQL Server does not show any data related to memory, CPU, disks, network I/O, or any of the other operating system resources. By using Performance Monitor, you can compare what is going on at the database level with what is going on at the operating system level.

If you want to query SQL Server–specific performance counter information, you can query a system table called *sys.dm_os_performance_counters*, located in the master database. The following code example shows what your query might look like:

```
SELECT instance_name, cntr_value
FROM sys.dm_os_performance_counters
WHERE object_name = 'MSSQL$INSTANCE1:Plan Cache'
      AND counter_name = 'Cache Hit Ratio'
```

Exam Tip SQL Server 2005 includes the Dynamic Management View (DMV) sys.dm_io_virtual _file_stats, which lets you to monitor disk usage.

Using SQL Server Profiler

SQL Server Profiler captures events from a specific SQL Server instance. These events and their information can be stored in a trace file or a database table for later analysis. The information collected by the SQL Server Profiler enables you to reproduce (and replay) a series of past execution steps to identify or diagnose a problem.

The main purpose of the Profiler is to provide you with a complete view of requests arriving to the server in certain periods of time, but you can also use it to do the following:

- Debug stored procedures and Transact-SQL (T-SQL) statements.
- Perform load tests in multiple servers.
- Analyze query performance by keeping the execution plans in traces.
- Analyze the performance of the relational engine, SQL Server Analysis Services, or SQL Server Integration Services server instance.
- Measure the duration of events (in milliseconds) to detect latency in the database server.

IMPORTANT Executing SQL Server Profiler

Execute SQL Server Profiler from a different computer than your production server to avoid the extra workload at run time.

After a trace is collected, you have many possibilities for analyzing its information. For example, you can open the trace from the SQL Server Profiler user interface (UI), but you can also open the trace information directly by using T-SQL, as the following code example shows:

```
SELECT *
FROM ::fn_trace_gettable('C:\SQLHealth\Trace_1.trc', default)
```

The system function *fn_trace_gettable* returns the content of a trace file in tabular format. You can then use T-SQL queries to look for important tracing data.

This system function accepts as an argument the name of the trace file to be read and a second argument that specifies the number of rollover files to be read. (The *default* argument specifies the reading of all rollover files.)

Practice: Measuring Performance Changes

In this practice, you will apply the concepts from this lesson to help a fictitious company called City Power & Light create a strategy for measuring performance changes. This practice builds upon the scenario described in Lesson 1, "Establishing Performance Objectives and Capacity Planning."

▶ **Exercise 1: Measure a Baseline**

In this exercise, you will describe what is required to start measuring a baseline. Remember that a baseline is the starting point for performance comparisons, so you must take care that it is measured correctly.

Describe the steps required to start comparing and measuring against a baseline.

Suggested Answer

One of several answers might be correct, but the following shows the basic steps to follow:

1. Decide which performance counters and metrics are important for your measurements and for your baseline.
2. Set up performance tests that simulate user behavior and operation execution order.
3. Run a first set of performance tests. This is the baseline.
4. Compare the measured metrics against the performance objectives.
5. Modify the application, the database, and the server installation to move closer to the metric goal.
6. Document the environment and the results.
7. Start over from step 3.

This process continues until the performance objectives are attained.

▶ **Exercise 2: Identify Performance Changes**

In this exercise, you will evaluate and analyze the results provided by Performance Monitor. Based on these results, identify which metrics provide the best information to measure performance changes in this scenario.

You and the database administrator are ready to tackle the performance problems that the users are complaining about. You decide to look for metrics that might indicate contention on the database server. Which of the following metrics could be important in this case? (Choose all that apply.)

A. Deadlocks per second
B. Transactions per second
C. Total SQL Server memory
D. Number of user connections

Suggested Answer

A. True. Deadlocks per second is an important metric to take into account when you are measuring contention. This metric indicates only whether deadlocks are occurring. If deadlocks are occurring, different metrics and tools—for example, SQL Server Profiler—might tell you which T-SQL query is causing the deadlock, on which resource, and from which executing process.

B. False. Transactions per second by itself is not an important metric when evaluating contention.

C. False. Total SQL Server memory by itself is not an important metric when evaluating contention, although if you also measure total server memory (from the operating system), you might detect how much memory SQL Server is using in comparison to the total server memory.

D. True. Number of user connections is an important metric when evaluating contention. Because the end users are complaining about performance, this metric could indicate how many users are connected concurrently. You might consider complementing this metric with the number of timed-out requests.

Quick Check

1. Which SQL Server metrics indicate connection contention?
2. What are the benefits of establishing a strategy for measuring performance changes?

Quick Check Answers

1. Wait stats is an internal list that records how much time and how many times connection requests have been waiting for a resource to be available. Wait stats are available through the *sys.dm_os_wait_stats* DMV.

2. Some of the benefits of establishing a strategy for measuring performance changes are:

   ❑ You take a proactive approach, including performance as a requirement in your software development process.

   ❑ You can easily detect performance changes and have a way to decide whether the change is good for the system, depending on how close or how far it takes you from your performance objectives.

   ❑ Performance measuring becomes part of the software life cycle process, so that by maintaining historical records of the measurements and metrics, you can predict future behavior in the application performance.

Lesson 3: Creating a Plan for Responding to Performance Changes

Estimated lesson time: 40 minutes

In the previous lesson, you learned how to create a strategy for measuring performance changes. Continuous performance measuring is important when taking a proactive approach to performance tuning.

By comparing the current measurement with your baseline, you are able to detect changes in performance. Those changes could be positive or negative, depending on how close they get you to the performance objectives. Either way, you must decide what actions to take to respond to those changes in performance.

By taking a proactive approach, you can be ready when you detect unwanted behaviors. You will be able to determine what has changed, how this will affect the system, and which counter measures to apply.

Setting Goals

A plan for responding to performance changes should include possible actions to be taken for as many possible challenges affecting the performance goals. The main goal is to be able to react proactively and not to be surprised by the results. Concrete goals of such a plan will vary, depending on the system to be analyzed, its requirements and budgets, the performance expectations, and perhaps other user or corporate considerations.

Any plan for responding to performance change should follow at least three guidelines for the plan to be useful:

- It should be easy to determine what has changed.
- It should help estimate how changes could affect the system.
- It should state clearly what actions should be taken to respond to performance changes.

Determining What Has Changed

The first step in a plan for responding to performance changes is to determine what has changed. By using the tools and techniques described in previous lessons, you should be able to determine what has changed. Some of the potential causes for a performance change are:

- **Increment in the amount of data**   Something caused the amount of data being returned by normal queries to be incremented. This constrains the system execution environment because more resources are required to handle the queries.

- **Retrieval of too much data**   This is a common mistake, producing an unnecessary increase in network traffic and excessive use of resources. This could be a problem in two directions: vertically (too many columns) and horizontally (too many rows).

- **More users accessing information in a concurrent way**   Concurrency and scalability are closely related. The more users requesting a service at the same time, the bigger the queue that your system has to process.

- **An increase in the number of transactions per second**   As with concurrency, an increase in the number of transactions produces an increase in the number of resources needed by the system to execute the required operations.

- **Other types of transactional issues**   Beware of long-running transactions that depend on user input to commit or that never commit because of an error. Also, watch out for queries inside transactions that cause scalability and performance problems because they lock resources longer than needed.

- **An increase in I/O operations or in a deficient use of disk subsystems**   I/O operations are one of the most time-consuming resources. An increase in its number might have a negative impact on performance. Alternatively, disk subsystems should provide database servers with enough I/O processing power to allow servers to run without disk queuing or long waits.

- **Deadlocks**   These could be caused by choosing an inappropriate transaction isolation level, by executing the same operations but in a different order, or by having two threads lock a resource that each is requesting.

- **Outdated index statistics**   As the data in a column changes, index and column statistics can become out of date and cause the query optimizer to make less-than-optimal decisions about how to process a query.

- **Operating system failures**   This can happen due to bugs not yet corrected or, even worse, problems caused by an incorrect or inefficient upgrade policy.

- **Communications or network failures**   These convey unavailability of resources for clients and subsequent accumulation of potential requests to be processed in a narrower time slice.

- **General hardware failures**   If one server fails, it affects not only data but also additional servers in the cluster that take over the load.

- **Security issues**   Security issues are critical not just because they might lead to undesirable attacks or disclosure of information, but also for the impact that the introduction of new permissions or groups of users interacting with your system might have.

- **Other subtle bugs**   Sometimes they appear only when the application is under stress tests. (Stress tests are a special kind of test intended to produce a crash in the system, thus revealing subtle faults in code or deployment.)

Determining How Change Affects the System

The second step in a plan for responding to performance changes is to determine how the change in performance affects the system. These changes in performance might influence the system in a variety of ways. The common factor in most cases is that a process that has worked properly up to now experiences what is called a *bottleneck* or *latency*: a lack of responsiveness due to insufficient resources to complete a task. Those resources can be of many types: CPU resources (also called CPU starvation), memory resources (physical or virtual), I/O resources (indication of an insufficient channel to hold the amount of information flowing in both directions), and more.

To make things worse, sometimes these situations can lead to a total lack of response, including the abortion of the process, provoking a system failure, or even loss of information. Some typical effects on applications and systems due to lack of response are:

- **Resource starvation**   This is the most common of all. Every system process requires system resources. If one of those resources is used in a percentage far higher than expected, the rest of the processes using those resources will have to wait, causing what was called in the previous lesson a wait stat. These situations might also affect other processes not directly related—in a parallel way, affecting the behavior of the overall system under such conditions.

- **Larger amount of requests queued**   A request not being processed has to be queued for a later time. Queues need memory, and a system operating under such conditions could even deny acceptance of more requests until it has enough space to hold them. The larger the queue, the larger the amount of pending work to be processed.

- **Timeouts**   Many processes (especially the asynchronous ones) don't wait forever to get a response from the system. (A database connection is a typical example of this.) If there are not enough resources to attend to requests, many of them will time out, causing a state of unavailability for the application.

- **Errors and mistakes**   This is a common situation for users when the application is going through performance problems. In addition, because the number of possible errors is so large, chances are that it might show even unhandled exceptions and cause an unexpected crash with all the consequences that can incur.

- **System failure**   This is the worst possible case. The system is not only unresponsive but needs to restart; hence, there is downtime. Needless to say, you should try to avoid system failure by all means at your disposal.

Responding to Performance Changes

To respond to performance changes, compile a list of possible actions to take. By doing so, your system becomes more and more predictable. It is impossible to list everything, but depending on your system constraints, there is always going to be a scarce resource.

Two strategies for responding to performance changes are scaling up and scaling out. *Scaling up* means moving an application to a larger type of hardware with more powerful processors, more memory, and faster disk drives. *Scaling out* refers to an implementation of federated servers, adding standard computers and partitioning data or replicating it across them. An example of the latter would be when you create updateable partitioned views across multiple database servers (as explained in Chapter 6, "Designing Objects That Retrieve Data"). Both are typical solutions but, many times, are chosen due to an incomplete or absent analysis of other possible solutions.

Both types of scaling should be considered only when you are sure that you're getting the best performance that you can through application optimization.

Scaling up is usually recommended if your bottlenecks are processor related or memory related. Scaling up can also help resolve disk I/O–related bottlenecks. For online transactional processing (OLTP) applications, the I/O load can be spread by adding disk drives. Adding memory also helps reduce I/O load because the size of the SQL Server buffer cache increases.

Before deciding on a scale-up or scale-out growth strategy, consider the following (in this order):

1. Optimize the application.
2. Address historical and reporting data. Consider partitioning historical data, moving it offline, or implementing it in a separate data warehouse.
3. Scale up. Consider replacing slow hardware components with new, faster components or consider adding more hardware to your existing server.
4. If nothing else can be done or scaling up has a prohibitive cost, scale out.

Issues That Can Affect Performance and Scalability

To decide how to respond to performance changes, you must analyze what possible issues can affect your system performance and scalability. The recommendation is to make a list of the potential issues that could occur and plan accordingly for each of them.

Following is a list of possible (and typical) issues that could cause poor performance in database applications using SQL Server 2005.

- **Improper or inefficient use of indexes**   Lack of indexes to support queries issued against your server will lead to performance problems. However, don't fall into the opposite problem by having too many indexes, which affects insert and update operations. Find the appropriate balance for your application.
- **Incorrect mixture of OLTP, OLAP, and reporting workloads**   OLTP workloads are characterized by many small transactions and fast response, while online analytical processing (OLAP) and reporting workloads are based on a few long-running operations consuming more resources and causing more contention.

- **Inefficient schemas**   If table design is poor, this can lead to too many join operations or inefficient queries. Schema design is a key factor for performance improvement. An adequate schema gives the server information that can be used to optimize query plans. You must find the correct balance, depending on your application's budgets and goals: optimize for reading or optimize for writing. Denormalization helps the former; normalization helps the latter.

Practice: Responding to Performance Changes

In this practice, you apply the concepts from this lesson to help a fictitious company called City Power & Light create a plan to respond to performance changes. This practice builds upon the scenario described in Lessons 1 and 2.

▶ **Exercise 1: Respond to Performance Changes**

In this exercise, you must decide on a course of action based on the data collected by a monitoring tool. The monitoring tool provides performance counters and measurements that enable you to diagnose what the possible cause for the performance issues could be.

After creating a performance baseline, you start executing performance tests and tweaking the database. For each test pass, you evaluate the results of the test and the metrics you measured to determine the effect on performance. By reviewing the amount of free memory in the server and the SQL Server cache, you notice that physical memory is really a constraint in the server.

You first try to move the historical data to offline storage to try to reduce the resource burden placed on the server, but the performance issues continue.

Your IT manager decides to increase the physical memory in the server. At first, this seems to resolve the issue, but over time as the system scales, the performance issues resurface.

An external consultant recommends that you add a secondary server and create a cluster, but you are not completely sure of this solution because you are not looking for high availability but for a solution to address only the performance issues.

Why would optimizing the database schema and database objects be a viable solution?

Suggested Answer

Optimizing the database schema and database objects should always be the first course of action. In most cases, by adding more memory, you solve the issue, but you do not really resolve the problem. By trying to optimize first, you are really resolving the problem by looking for a different way to represent the data that fits the data growth and utilization model.

▶ **Exercise 2: Determine What Changed**

After the last optimization you tried, when compared with the performance baseline, your memory usage is now under the expected values according to the performance objectives. You decide to move the current improvements to the production environment.

After a while, City Power & Light's users are complaining that the application is timing out when working with the database during peak hours (from noon until 3 p.m.). Consider the graph in Figure 11-1.

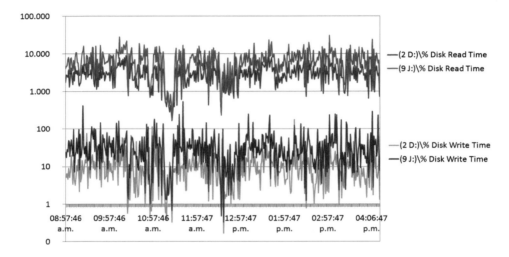

Figure 11-1   Performance graph

What do you think has changed from your testing environment to the production environment?

Suggested Answer

Answers can vary. The graphic indicates that there is I/O contention when reading data. Try to optimize all of the processes that are reading data. One hypothesis is that the amount of data is larger than expected, and the application is not tuned to read such a large amount of data. Another hypothesis is that instead of spreading the load across multiple disks, most of the data being read is always read from the same disk (drive D). There could be an issue with the SQL Server filegroups and how they are distributed across the different disk devices in the system.

Quick Check

1. What are the goals of a plan for responding to performance changes?
2. Name three types of impact that a performance change might cause in the system.

Quick Check Answers

1. The main goal of a plan for responding to performance changes is to provide a roadmap to follow when certain performance conditions are detected. This predictability allows you to respond faster to performance issues, which in turn enables you to minimize downtime and manage your maintenance budget better.
2. Answers can vary but might include resource starvation, timeouts, and system failure.

Lesson 4: Creating a Plan for Tracking Benchmark Statistics Over Time

Estimated lesson time: 25 minutes

Throughout this chapter, you have learned a proactive approach for tackling performance issues. By following these recommendations, you will get used to responding to trends and challenges in an effective way, thus improving your understanding of what needs to be done and allowing you to plan for the future—making your applications more predictable.

If you maintain the proper documentation and historical data about your performance testing measurements, you will have the essential data you need to know exactly how your system got to where it is. But, more important, it could help you decide where you are going. The basic concept in benchmarking is the ability to compare current data with statistics to obtain process improvements.

In this lesson, you will learn how to gain knowledge from benchmark statistics, how to plan a strategy that helps you go beyond a mere comparison of data, and how to find new ways to improve your application processes.

Setting Goals

Any plan for tracking benchmark statistics involves learning, sharing information, and adopting best practices to bring about changes in performance. In the preceding lessons, you learned about setting performance objectives and measuring performance. These measures would directly influence your future planning. The most important goals of a plan for tracking benchmark statistics over time are:

- **Improving productivity**   Predictability enables you to focus on what really matters and what really affects performance. Historical experience will help you approach the future based on lessons from the past.
- **Improving quality**   By comparing current performance measurements with historical data, you can find new ways to improve the quality of your design and code. As stated in Lesson 3, "Creating a Plan for Responding to Performance Changes," the first step to improving performance is always to try to improve the current application elements.
- **Gaining a complete picture of the application behavior**   After continuing with this plan for a while and by being proactive about performance, you will get to know the application in much more detail. You will be able to predict how a change or modification could affect application performance.

- **Opening your mind to new opportunities** By reviewing historical data and comparing current results with previous results, you might come up with newer and better solutions to solve technical issues. These new solutions might bring you better performance.

To implement a plan for tracking benchmark statistics, you must:

1. Select aspects of performance that can be improved and define them in a way that enables you to obtain relevant comparative data.
2. Choose relevant and proper performance metrics from which to obtain significant data.
3. Study the data to identify possible opportunities for improvement.
4. Examine the procedures of the best-performing processes to pick up ideas that can be adopted or adapted to achieve performance improvements.
5. Implement new processes by learning from previous experience.

IMPORTANT Benefits of tracking benchmark statistics

There are many benefits of tracking benchmark statistics, but two become more evident and desirable: predictability and lower business and maintenance costs.

Predictability is the extent to which future states of a system can be predicted, based on knowledge of current and past states of the system. Because knowledge of the system's past and current states is generally imperfect, as are the models that use this knowledge to produce a prediction, predictability is inherently limited. Even with arbitrarily accurate models and observations, there can still be limits to the predictability of a physical system, so take this into consideration. Knowing your objectives and keeping them achievable and realistic will be your best guidance.

Lowering business and maintenance costs are side effects of predictability. One of the predictable aspects is how much time and resources the system is expected to need, which leads to an anticipated plan and avoidance of unexpected requirements and fixes.

Continued Testing and Performance Measuring

A plan for tracking benchmark statistics is a continuous exercise similar to our instinctive way of learning. A benchmarking exercise can be used wherever a process can be identified. As with an application's development life cycle, benchmarking is a cyclical task that starts with testing the implementation and leading to the refinement of the model.

Exam Tip   It is important to repeat the benchmarking periodically. The frequency of tests will be dictated by the change rate you notice in your application's behavior.

When there is a change in the application requirements, the new situation might invalidate your previous baselines and make current statistics obsolete. In such cases, design and create a new baseline.

Nevertheless, if requirements are needed immediately—as often happens in real production—you just have to correct those aspects of your baseline affected by the changes and perhaps modify the baseline tests accordingly.

Once a new baseline is established, perform further baseline measurements as many times as necessary to produce valid information for comparison. Some empirical comparison can be done as well at this stage to make sure changes and new measures are as expected.

Generating and Documenting Best Practices

This set of performance guidelines, procedures, and collected data will lead to what is usually called *best practices*. A more formal definition of the term is: a best practice is a process or procedure that consistently produces superior results.

IMPORTANT   **Best practices**

Benchmarking leads to generating best practices. A best practice is a process or procedure that consistently produces superior results.

Benchmarking enables you to compare information to identify relative strengths and weaknesses and to learn how to make improvements. Thus, it is also a way of finding and adopting best practices. Use the following guidelines for implementing best practices:

- **Don't fix what's not broken.**   Balance the costs of doing nothing against implementing the best practice. Just because something is a good idea doesn't mean it is worth doing.
- **Consider context.**   Verify that the best practice has been successful for cases or situations similar to yours.
- **Validate the practice.**   Confirm that all best practices have been researched and have proven successful, using key performance indicators (KPIs). Make sure that the best practice improves a process that is aligned with the strategic objectives previously established.
- **Obtain concrete evidence before considering adoption of a practice.**   Confirm that it will be possible to duplicate the practice and prove a performance improvement, corroborating the success of the practice.
- **Try to find failures.**   Compare new metrics to metrics that were measured before the implementation, or find your own way of searching for failures until you are sure enough of the validity of that best practice.

Determining and implementing best practices is important for continuously improving any solution. As a last step, don't implement only the best practices you've determined on your own. Share and compare results with other people working on the same project, working in your company, or even working outside your environment. You will benefit from their experience without having to go through the whole set of processes yourself.

Practice: Creating a Plan

In this practice, you will apply the concepts from this lesson to help a fictitious company called City Power & Light create a plan for tracking benchmark statistics over time. This practice builds upon the scenario described in Lessons 1, 2, and 3.

▶ **Exercise 1: Identify the Benefits of Tracking Benchmark Statistics**

In this exercise, you must make a recommendation on how to compare your company's performance results with those of the competition or from other industries.

> During your meeting with the DBA from City Power & Light last week, he asked you whether there is a way to compare the company's performance results with those of other power companies in other cities or in other countries. You know the organization has a mature and proactive performance testing strategy. Why would you recommend creating a plan for tracking benchmark statistics?
>
> **Suggested Answer**
>
> Answers can vary, but in the case of City Power & Light, some of the benefits of implementing a plan for tracking benchmark statistics might include improving quality by comparing its systems performance with the performance of business partners or its competition. The company might as well come up with new solutions and opportunities to improve performance even more. Finally, the main objective is to generate intellectual property in the form of best practices—proven practices that can be applied to other systems to improve performance.

▶ **Exercise 2: Implement a Plan to Track Benchmark Statistics**

In this exercise, you must provide the steps required to implement a plan to track benchmark statistics. This plan must cover the necessary data that needs to be stored to be able to compare and validate your performance measurements with those from your competition or other industries.

> The DBA from City Power & Light follows your recommendation to implement a plan for tracking benchmark statistics. What steps should he follow?
>
> **Suggested Answer**
>
> The steps to implement a plan for tracking benchmark statistics are to document all performance-testing key scenarios, metrics, configurations, and results in a tool that allows comparisons and calculations over the tracking information; analyze the historical measured data to identify patterns and/or practices that prove to be reusable and that provide a benefit in performance; document the best practices to share them with others; and continue testing and improving the solution.

Quick Check

1. Explain why predictability lowers business and maintenance costs as claimed in this lesson.
2. One of the main benefits of implementing a plan for tracking benchmark statistics over time is to gain a complete picture of the application behavior. Why is this important?

Quick Check Answers

1. Predictability is reached once you have historical system performance data and knowledge, enabling you to foresee different aspects about how much time and resources the system is expected to need over time. This data and knowledge enable you to anticipate future requirements and fixes, which enables you to plan your budget according to the future needs of the system, hence lowering business and maintenance costs.
2. Answers can vary. A benchmarking strategy takes into account historical data to generate best practices. A best practice is a process or procedure that produces superior performance results. This knowledge can be generated only by knowing the application behavior at a deep level.

Case Scenario: Create a Performance Baseline and Benchmarking Strategy

You are part of the quality assurance team designing the new trading application for North-wind Traders. Management has been putting a lot of pressure on your team because this new version must provide better performance than the previous versions. The new application will be used nationwide across the Internet. It has to be available constantly, with nearly zero downtime.

You propose that performance should not be treated as an afterthought but, instead, should be included in the design phase as a nonfunctional requirement and that proper proactive plans should be implemented. Your manager asks you to help with the capacity planning for the production servers.

Before management commits the necessary investments, the managers ask you to provide more information about the performance objectives, your strategy for measuring performance changes, and your plan to respond to performance changes.

1. Which inputs would you need to generate the proper performance objectives?
2. Which techniques do you apply to perform capacity planning accurately? Explain them to management.

3. After creating the performance objectives, you start working on the strategy for measuring performance changes. You must ask for the necessary resources to implement a testing environment similar to the production environment. How will you justify this requirement?

Chapter Summary

- Performance objectives represent measurable criteria, such as response time, throughput (how much work is done in how much time), and resource usage (CPU, memory, disk I/O, and network I/O) that you intend to attain.
- There are two main methodologies used for capacity planning: transaction cost analysis and predictive analysis.
- A baseline will serve you as a comparative pattern to check further measures.
- Scaling up and scaling out should be considered only when you are sure that you're getting the best performance you can through application optimization.
- A plan for tracking benchmark statistics involves learning, sharing information, and adopting best practices to bring about changes in performance.

Chapter 12
Creating a Plan for Deploying a Database

Deployment planning reduces error and inefficiency during application deployment or update. Two key elements to consider when planning your deployment strategy are security and testing. You want to ensure that you or the person performing the deployment has permission to do so. You also need to know whether the deployment succeeded, hence the need for testing. Ignoring these and other related considerations can obstruct or delay deployment. Deployment planning can mitigate issues considerably and is a database design and development best practice. When deploying, you want to focus on following steps and document results from a carefully drawn plan. You do not want to make it up as you go along.

This chapter will discuss different deployment techniques and then proceed to practical considerations when deploying. You will learn about available mechanisms for deploying Microsoft SQL Server 2005 databases and how to use them to deploy databases, and you will examine the details of deployment, including security, object-change and data-change strategy, audit trails, change control, and project-management methodology.

Exam objectives in this chapter:
- Create a plan for deploying a database.
    - Select a deployment technique.
    - Design scripts to deploy the database as part of application setup.
    - Design database change scripts to apply application patches.
    - Design scripts to update database data and objects.

Before You Begin

To complete the lessons in this chapter, you must have:

- A general understanding of SQL Server 2005 and Transact-SQL.
- A general understanding of how to use SQL Server Management Studio, including how to connect to various SQL Server instances in a typical enterprise environment.
- SQL Server 2005 and SQL Server Management Studio installed on your computer.
- The SQL Server 2005 *AdventureWorks* and *AdventureWorksDW* sample databases installed. Sample databases are available with SQL Server 2005 Enterprise edition, although they are not a part of the default installation. You can also install the sample databases from *http://msdn2.microsoft.com/en-us/library/ms143739.aspx*.

Lesson 1: Selecting a Deployment Technique

Estimated lesson time: 30 minutes

There are several methods by which you can deploy a SQL Server 2005 database, including using:

■ The SQL Server Management Studio (SSMS) Copy Database Wizard.

■ A Transact-SQL (T-SQL) script.

■ The Import and Export Wizard.

■ A SQL Server Integration Services (SSIS) Package.

■ The SQLCmd utility.

Regardless of the method you choose, there are several questions to ask about the database you are deploying to before you begin:

■ Is the database published for replication? If so, you must remove replication before using any of the methods that detach the database.

■ Do database snapshots exist? If so, you must drop them before using any of the methods that detach the database.

■ Is the database being mirrored in a mirroring session? If so, the mirroring session must be terminated before using any of the methods that detach the database.

■ Is the database marked Suspect? If so, you must put the database in Emergency Mode before using any of the methods that detach the database. In addition, proceed with detaching the database only after identifying why the database is suspect and resolving these issues.

Also note that database snapshots and system databases cannot be detached. Now, let's look at each of the deployment methods to see which to use in different situations.

Deploying with the SSMS Copy Database Wizard

In SSMS, you can copy a database by using the Copy Database Wizard. Note that this feature is available only on servers with SQL Server Agent installed and running. The Copy Database Wizard creates an SSIS package based on options you select as you proceed through the wizard pages. You are prompted for source and destination database servers, transfer method, source and destination databases, and SSIS package configuration name and logging model. Let's look at how you use the Copy Database Wizard to deploy a database and then explore the considerations for when to use the wizard.

To copy a database by using the Copy Database Wizard, open SSMS. Right-click the database you want to copy, click Tasks, and then click Copy Database, as shown in Figure 12-1.

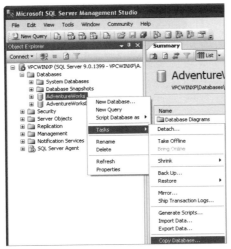

Figure 12-1   Right-click navigation to start the Copy Database Wizard

The Copy Database Wizard starts and displays a splash screen. By selecting the Do Not Show This Starting Page Again check box, you can hide the Welcome page in the future. Click Next to proceed.

The next two pages in the wizard, Select A Source Server (not shown) and Select A Destination Server (Figure 12-2), are nearly identical. As their names imply, here you configure the source and destination servers and define the connection authentication method of the database copy.

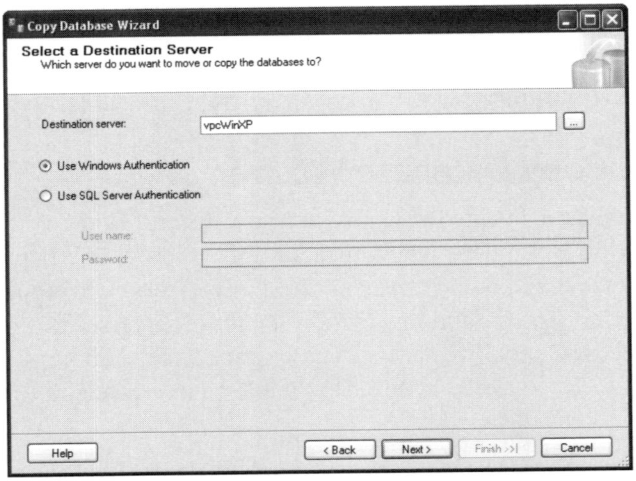

Figure 12-2   Copy Database Wizard Select A Destination Server page

Next, you choose a method of copying the database to the destination server on the Select The Transfer Method page.

Your options are to use the detach and attach method or to use the SQL Management Object (SMO) method. The detach and attach method automates detaching the database from the source server, copying the database files to the target server, and attaching the database files to the target server. The SMO option creates an SSIS project to accomplish the copy process. SMO is slower than the detach and attach method, but it allows the source database to remain online during the operation. (See the next section, "Customizing the SSIS Package Created by the Copy Database Wizard," for information about how to customize the SSIS package created by the SMO option.)

The next page in the wizard enables you to choose the database(s) you want to copy or move. You can select more than one database and operation, as shown in Figure 12-3.

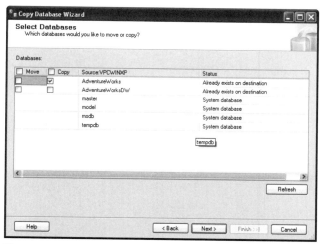

Figure 12-3 Copy Database Wizard Select Databases page

You configure the destination database by using the next step of the wizard, shown in Figure 12-4. Configuration options include the database name, data and log file locations, and how to respond if there is an existing database on the destination server with the same name.

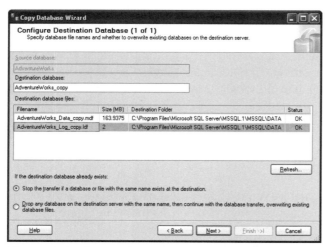

Figure 12-4 First Configure Destination Database page of the Copy Database Wizard

When you've configured these options, the Copy Database Wizard creates an SSIS package to accomplish the operation. In the next step of the wizard, you specify a name for the SSIS package and choose a logging option (Windows Event Log or a Text File).

The next page enables you to run the Copy Database Wizard immediately or schedule execution. The Copy Database Wizard is now complete and displays a summary of actions you have performed, as shown in Figure 12-5. Click Finish to begin the database copy or move process.

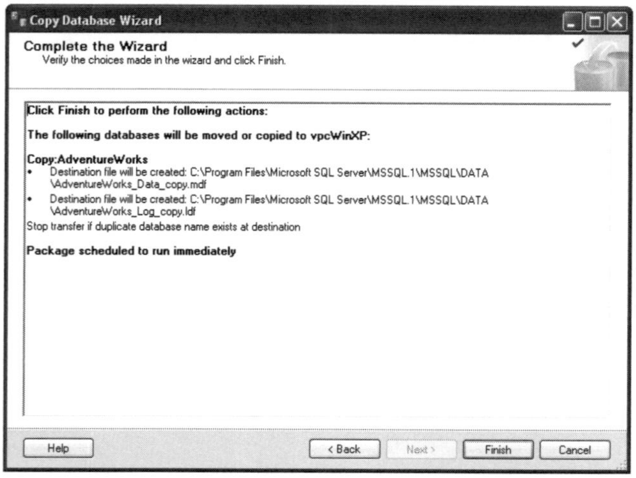

Figure 12-5 Completing the Copy Database Wizard

Use the Copy Database Wizard when deploying databases internally in an enterprise. It is ideal for quickly and easily moving databases around inside a domain or business organization. This makes it a powerful tool for deploying or updating single-instance databases.

Although the Copy Database Wizard can be automated (you can store the SSIS package and re-execute it manually or schedule it through a SQL Server Agent job), it is not well suited for distributed database application deployments or updates.

Customizing the SSIS Package Created by the Copy Database Wizard

You can customize the SSIS package created by the Copy Database Wizard, adding variables for source and destination servers, for example. The SSIS package is stored in the msdb database on the server where the Copy Database Wizard created it, usually on the source server.

Before editing the SSIS package, you must export it to a file. To accomplish this, you need to connect to the SSIS instance:

1. Open SSMS. Click Connect in Object Explorer and select Integration Services from the drop-down list.

2. The familiar Connect to Server login dialog box displays. Note that Server Type is disabled and Integration Services is selected. Select or type the server name. Note that "(local)" or similar aliasing will not work when connecting to SQL Server Integration Services. Click Connect.

3. In Object Explorer, navigate to the SSIS package. It should be under Stored Packages\MSDB\<Server name>\DTS Packages\Copy Database Wizard Packages\<Copy Database Wizard Package Name>. Right-click the package name and select Export Package from the context menu, as Figure 12-6 shows.

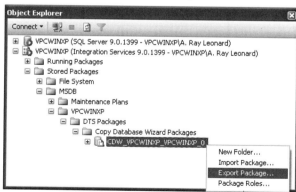

Figure 12-6   Exporting the SSIS package

The Export Package dialog box displays, as shown in Figure 12-7. To edit the package— for example, to make source and destination servers dynamic—you need to export it to the file system.

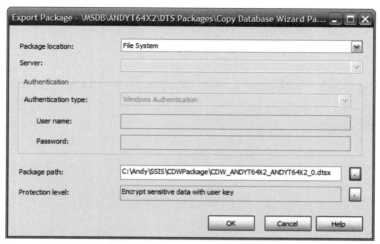

Figure 12-7   Selecting the file destination of the SSIS Package

4. Change the Package Location drop-down list value to File System. Click the ellipsis beside the Package Path text box and navigate to the file system target directory or enter the target directory and file name manually. Click OK to export the SSIS package.

5. Use Windows Explorer to navigate to the directory where you stored the exported SSIS package. Right-click the file and select Edit. By default, SQL Server Business Intelligence Development Studio (BIDS) opens and loads the package.

6. Click the Transfer Objects Task and press F4 to view properties.

    You can make detailed configuration changes to the transfer by adding, removing, and editing the DatabaseDetails and DatabaseObjects properties, as Figure 12-8 shows.

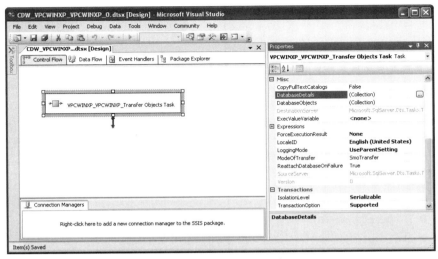

Figure 12-8   Properties for the Transfer Objects Task

7. After editing, save your changes and close BIDS. Return to SSMS Object Explorer. Right-click the package and select Import Package. The Import Package dialog box displays, as shown in Figure 12-9.

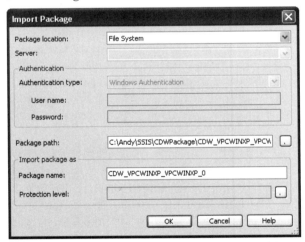

Figure 12-9   The Import Package dialog box enables you to navigate to the SSIS package file

8. Select File System in the Package Location drop-down list. Type the package path in the Package Path text box or click the ellipsis to navigate to the edited package file. Click the Package Name text box; the name of the package should auto-populate once this text box receives focus. Click OK to begin the import process.

Because you are overwriting an existing SSIS package, you will be prompted to confirm this action.

9. Click Yes to complete the import.

For more information about SSIS, see Chapter 17, "Developing Packages for Integration Services."

Deploying with T-SQL Scripts

There are several T-SQL script deployment options available, using either SSMS or manually created scripts. The three most common are:

- Detach and attach database files.
- Back up and restore database.
- Manually create a deployment script.
- Let's look at each of these options in turn.

IMPORTANT   Deploying with SSMS

Note that all database deployments can be accomplished by using SSMS.

Detach and Attach Database Files

Detaching and attaching database files is a two-step process that literally disconnects underlying database files from the SQL Server instance and then reconnects them to a SQL Server instance. This method is fast—as fast as a few clicks in SSMS to detach the file and copy it to a new location (if moving the database to a different server) and a few more clicks to reattach the file. Detaching and attaching databases takes the database offline, so you should use it only when database downtime is acceptable. An additional benefit of the detach and attach method of database deployment is that user activity ceases while the database is detached, so you don't have to worry about synchronizing with any changes that users make while you're deploying the new database.

To detach database files in SSMS, connect to the source server. Right-click the database, click Tasks, and then click Detach. Physically copy the database files to the target server by using Windows Explorer, a command prompt, FTP, or other method. Connect to the target server, right-click Databases, and select Attach. Click Add, and then navigate to a data file location and select it to begin the attachment process.

To detach a database by using T-SQL, execute the sp_detach_db stored system stored procedure. Use a command similar to the following:

```
sp_detach_db 'AdventureWorks'
```

After physically copying the database files to the target server, execute the T-SQL sp_attach_db stored system stored procedure. Use a command similar to the following:

```
sp_attach_db 'AdventureWorks', 'C:\Program Files\Microsoft SQL
Server\MSSQL.1\MSSQL\Data\AdventureWorks_Data.mdf'
```

Back Up and Restore Database

You can back up a database without taking it offline. This makes the backup and restore method more flexible than the detach and attach method of database deployment. One downside to this method, however, is that if users remain connected (or connect) to the database after the backup, their changes are not included in the restored version. You must take additional steps to resynchronize data in production databases.

To back up a database in SSMS, connect to the source server. Right-click the database, click Tasks, and then click Back Up. Configure backup options in the Back Up Database dialog box. Physically copy the database files to the target server by using Windows Explorer, a command prompt, FTP, or other method. Connect to the target server, right-click Databases, and select Restore Database. Navigate to the backup file or device, configure restore options, and click OK.

For more information about the backup and restore technique, see the topic "Backing Up and Restoring Databases in SQL Server" in SQL Server 2005 Books Online at *http:// msdn2.microsoft.com /en-us/library/ms187048(SQL.90).aspx.*

Manual Script Creation

You can also create your own T-SQL deployment scripts manually. This is the most flexible means to deploy databases and database upgrades. You can use T-SQL code to create, alter, or drop any object in a database.

Deploying with the Import and Export Wizard

You can import and export data tables by using the SQL Server Import and Export Wizard in SSMS. Similar to the Copy Database Wizard, the Import and Export Wizard creates an SSIS package that you can save at the end of the wizard. Also like the Copy Database Wizard, the Import and Export Wizard is better suited for deployments within the enterprise. There are three features unique to the Import and Export Wizard:

- You can select different source and destination types.
- You can use a query to select data from a source.
- You can select individual tables and views as sources.

These features make the Import and Export Wizard ideal for database updates.

To start the wizard, right-click either the source or destination database in SSMS. If you right-click the source database, click Tasks and click Export Data.

Complete the Source and Destination pages. On the Specify Table Copy or Query page, you decide whether you will select tables and views from a list or use a query as a data source. If you select the Copy Data From One Or More Tables Or Views option, the next page displays a list of tables and views, as shown in Figure 12-10.

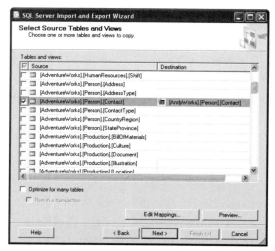

Figure 12-10   Selecting source tables and views in the Import and Export Wizard

After you select a table, click the Edit Mappings button for additional table-copy options such as Delete Existing Rows In Destination Table or Append New Rows To Destination Table. If you select the Write A Query To Specify The Data To Transfer option on the Specify Table Copy or Query page, the next page displays a text box for selecting the query, as shown in Figure 12-11.

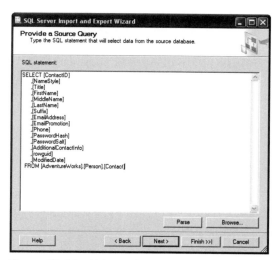

Figure 12-11   Using a Query as the Source in the Import and Export Wizard

You have the option of entering the query text manually or browsing to a file containing the query and loading it into the text box.

The next page enables you to save the SSIS package. You have the option here of saving it to a file or to SQL Server. Saving it to a file will enable you to edit the SSIS package directly, without needing to export it from Integration Services. If you select the Save Package check box, the next page prompts for a save location. The last page shows the status of the transfer as it executes. (For more information about the Import and Export Wizard, see the topic "Designing and Creating Packages Using the SQL Server Import and Export Wizard" at *http:// msdn2.microsoft.com/en-us/library/ms141091(SQL.90).aspx.*

Deploying with SSIS

You can deploy database objects by using the Transfer SQL Server Objects task in SSIS. The Transfer SQL Server Objects Task is very powerful and relatively fast. It enables you to transfer objects such as stored procedures, functions, schemas, and even users from one database to another. For these reasons, using SSIS to deploy databases is a recommended option when:

- Multiple databases make up the database solution.
- You seek a scriptless, repeatable mechanism to deploy stored procedures, functions, schemas, and users.

There is no wizard available in SMO to access this functionality; you must use BIDS to build an SSIS package.

Open BIDS. Click File, click New, and then select Project to open the New Project dialog box. Select Business Intelligence Projects from the Project Types list, and then select the Integration Services Project template. Enter a project name in the Name text box. Drag a Transfer SQL Server Objects task from the Toolbox onto the Control Flow and double-click it to open the Task Editor. Figure 12-12 shows the Transfer SQL Server Objects Task Editor.

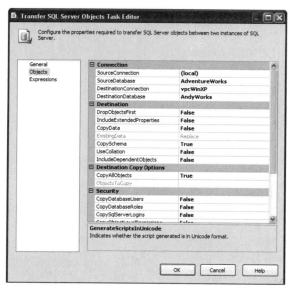

Figure 12-12   The SSIS Transfer SQL Server Objects Task Editor

You can use the Transfer SQL Server Objects task to copy database objects from a source to a destination. The ObjectsToCopy property contains a collection of SQL Server object collections. You can opt to copy all objects of a certain type or choose individual objects to copy. (See Chapter 17 for more information about creating SSIS packages.)

Deploying with the SQLCmd Utility

If you have experience with SQL Server 2000 or earlier releases of SQL Server, you might be familiar with the OSql utility, which uses the ODBC library to connect to and execute T-SQL statements from a command prompt. Although you can still use OSql in SQL Server 2005 to execute T-SQL statements for deployment and other operations, the utility will be removed in a future release. For this reason, it's a good idea to modify applications that currently use OSql and avoid using OSql in future releases.

The SQLCmd utility uses the OLE DB library to connect to and execute T-SQL statements against SQL Server. You can execute SQLCmd from a command prompt. You can also access it from the SSMS Query Editor, with the following caveat: When accessed from SSMS, SQL-Cmd uses the .Net SqlClient library.

SQLCmd is primarily a command-line utility that enables you to enter and execute T-SQL statements, call stored procedures, and execute scripts from the command prompt. You open a command prompt by clicking Start and then Run. Type **cmd** and then click OK to launch a command prompt. Type **SQLCmd /?** to view top-tier command-line options.

To deploy a database by using SQLCmd, you can type and execute each T-SQL statement manually, but generating the database script by using SSMS (as shown in Figure 12-13) or another scripting tool and then executing these scripts through SQLCmd is recommended. Why? SSMS contains valuable error-checking and syntax-checking utilities, saving you time and troubleshooting challenges later on.

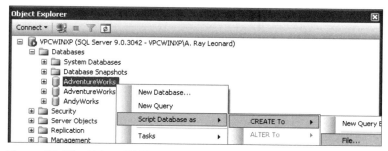

Figure 12-13 Using SSMS to generate T-SQL

Once SSMS has generated the T-SQL script file, you can execute it through SQLCmd by following these steps:

- Open a command prompt: Click Start, click Run, type **cmd** in the Open text box, and then click OK.

- To execute a script, type **SQLCmd –S** <servername\instance> **-i** <path\scriptfile>.

    If you append -o <*outputfilepath*> to the command, output generated by the script will be redirected to the specified file. This output file can then serve as a deployment log.

In practice, many application developers codify this process by combining several SQLCmd commands in a single batch file so that the commands can be executed as a group.

On the Companion Disc   This chapter includes many code examples. You will find all the code from this chapter on the companion CD in the C:\My Documents\Microsoft Press\TK70-441 \Chapter12\Sql folder.

Practice: Detaching and Attaching a Database

Detaching and attaching a database is a quick way to deploy a database. It's also a good way to move database files around your server. In this practice, you will detach and attach the *AdventureWorks* database.

▶ **Exercise: Detach and Attach the AdventureWorks Database**

In this exercise, you will detach the *AdventureWorks* database, physically relocate the data and log files, and then attach the files to the new location.

1. Open SSMS and connect to an instance of SQL Server 2005.
2. In Object Explorer, expand the Databases node.
3. Right-click the *AdventureWorks* database, click Tasks, and then click Detach. The Detach Database dialog box displays, as shown in Figure 12-14.

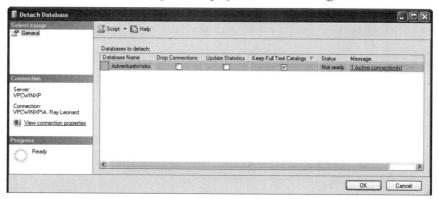

Figure 12-14   Detach Database dialog box

If connections to this database are currently open, you can drop them by selecting the Drop Connections check box. You can also choose to update statistics before detaching the database by selecting the Update Statistics check box. The Keep Full Text Catalogs check box is selected by default. The Status column declares whether the database is ready to be detached. Figure 12-14 shows that this database has 1 Active Connection(s) (see the Message column) and a Status of Not Ready.

4. To drop the database in the state shown in Figure 12-14, either close the active connection or select the Drop Connections check box.
5. Click OK to detach the database.
6. When the database is detached, open Windows Explorer and navigate to the location of your data files.

   The default location for data files will resemble C:\Program Files\Microsoft SQL Server\MSSQL.1\MSSQL\Data\.
7. Copy AdventureWorks_Data.mdf and AdventureWorks_Log.ldf to the clipboard and paste them in another location on your server.
8. Right-click the Databases node in the SSMS Object Explorer and select Attach.
9. Click Add in the Attach Databases dialog box and navigate to the location to which you moved the data and log files earlier.
10. Select the AdventureWorks_Data.mdf file and click OK. Note that the Current File Path now reflects the new data and log file path.

11. Click OK to attach the database to this instance of SQL Server.

You can use this same procedure to move databases between servers in an enterprise for deployment purposes.

Quick Check

1. What are some methods to deploy a SQL Server 2005 database?
2. Which method in the Copy Database Wizard allows the database to remain online?
3. According to Books Online, which SQL Server utility might not be available in future releases?

Quick Check Answers

1. The Import And Export Wizard, Backup and Restore, Copy Database Wizard, and Detach and Attach are some methods by which you can deploy a SQL Server 2005 database.
2. The correct answer is SMO. The only other method employed by the Copy Database Wizard is Detach and Attach, which takes the database offline.
3. OSql will be deprecated in future releases.

Lesson 2: Practical Deployment Considerations

Estimated lesson time: 30 minutes

Many applications require local database installation. In fact, any application that must use disconnected datasets needs to store data locally. Smart-client applications use local database caching to disconnected datasets for data sychronization and state management.

With the advent of the Microsoft .NET Framework came escape from dynamic-link library (DLL) versioning issues. Application databases, however, possessed no similar framework-managed mechanism to manage the schema, tables, or stored procedures of a database. Note the past-tense word "possessed." Team Edition for Database Professionals now nicely fills this void in the database development life cycle.

As a database developer, you must consider the impact of applying the change when you update a database to conform to application changes. Lesson 1, "Selecting a Deployment Technique," covered the mechanisms for deploying the database. This lesson will focus on applying these mechanisms. You will design scripts to deploy the database as part of application setup, to apply application updates, and to upgrade database data and objects.

Many organizations promote efficient database development by defining best practices documentation. This is a good thing—as long as this document remains fluid and flexible. Best practices and coding standards are a poor substitute for common sense and often hinder innovation when given an inordinate amount of importance.

Considerations for designing scripts for deployment as part of an application or upgrade include:

- Security.
- Object-change strategy.
- Data-change strategy.
- Audit trail.
- Change control.
- Project-management methodology.

Deploying Securely

Security should be one of the first considerations in any setup or upgrade deployment plan. Gone forever are the days when applications were designed and then secured. When deploying upgrades or application databases, data access security and object permissions should be a—if not the—main consideration. SQL Server 2005 boasts many security enhancements and new features. You can view built-in permissions by executing the following query against the master database:

```
SELECT * FROM sys.fn_builtin_permissions(DEFAULT)
```

This query returns 187 rows when executed on a server running SQL Server 2005 Developer Edition 9.00.2047.00 (Intel X86). That's a lot of permissions to manage!

Deployment security considerations can be described in two major categories: making sure the database administrator (DBA) performing the deployment has permission to deploy and deploying the permissions associated with the database.

Permission to Deploy

When deploying, the person performing the deployment (that is, the security principal) must have sufficient rights on the target server to make the desired changes. Microsoft recommends you use Microsoft Windows authentication whenever possible because it is integrated into Active Directory directory service domain security, providing an additional layer of security. Many enterprises configure Active Directory user accounts and groups specifically for use with SQL Server. This strategy has a couple of advantages:

- Active Directory security is generally considered more robust than SQL Server login security.
- It shifts maintenance of these accounts to the Network Administrative team, which often manages password expiration, history, and complexity via domain and group security policies.

If you cannot use Windows authentication, SQL Server logins will suffice. No matter which authentication method you use, the user needs permissions to accomplish whatever deployment tasks need to occur. For example, if the deployment consists of updates to data in a single table, the user needs permission to update the target table. If the deployment involves creating a database, the user needs to possess the CREATE DATABASE permission on the SQL Server instance.

Deploying Permissions

Synchronizing logins after moving a database is a painful process—or at least it was in previous releases of SQL Server. The reason? Security identifiers (SIDs). Before the discussion about SIDs, some background is appropriate.

An entity that can request SQL Server resources is known as a *principal*. Examples of principals include SQL Server logins, Windows logins, and database users. Principals possess a scope of influence described by the principal's definition. Deterministic properties include the type of login (Windows, SQL Server, Database) and whether the principal is indivisible or a collection. Windows logins and SQL Server logins are examples of indivisible principals; Windows groups and SQL Server database roles are examples of collections.

To view details about the principals with influence in a database, connect to the database and execute the following statement:

```
SELECT * FROM sys.database_principals
```

Note that each principal has a name, an SID, and a Principal_ID (called, simply, ID).

Deploying Permissions with Backup/Restore   When you create a SQL Server login on a local development instance, an ID and SID are generated and associated with that login. When you add a user (by name) to your database, those associated properties (ID and SID) are inserted into your database metadata.

So far, all is well. You are working in a local database on your local development instance of SQL Server. Problems arise when you deploy your database to another instance of SQL Server. Usually, the deployment goes something like this. You back up your local database, copy the .bak file to the target server, and restore it there. You conduct spot checks to ensure that your latest changes are now on the target server, checking for the latest schema and stored procedure changes as well as for new or altered users. You pronounce the database deployed and ready for testing and begin the next round of database development—until you're interrupted by developers and testers who inform you that they cannot connect to the database.

This is because SQL Server logins on your local instance have different IDs and SIDs than the target server. The names are the same, but all uniquely identifying metadata is different. What should you do now?

In SQL Server 2005, you can use the sp_change_users_login stored procedure to fix mismatched IDs and SIDs. Sp_change_users_login takes one or more parameters. The first parameter, @Action, defines the purpose of this execution of the stored procedure. There are three possible values:

- **Auto_Fix**   Auto_Fix requires you to specify a value for the @UserNamePattern parameter. The procedure attempts to map the value supplied to the @UserNamePattern parameter to an existing SQL Server login. If successful, the results include a description of the action taken. If not, results will indicate no orphaned users were updated. Auto_Fix can create the SQL Server login if it does not already exist.
- **Report**   Report returns a list of orphaned users (and their SIDs) for the current database.
- **Update_One**   Update_One requires you to specify the @UserNamePattern and @Login parameters. It effectively remaps an existing database user to another existing SQL Server login.

Deploying Permissions with the SSMS Copy Database Wizard   When using the Copy Database Wizard to copy databases that contain SQL Server logins, you will see the Select Database Objects page, similar to the one shown in Figure 12-15.

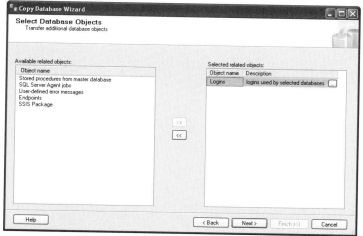

Figure 12-15   Deploying permissions with the Copy Database Wizard

Clicking the ellipsis beside the *Logins* object displays a dialog box that enables even more configuration, as Figure 12-16 shows.

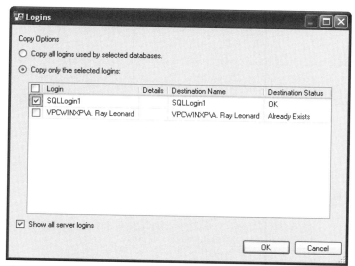

Figure 12-16   Configuring logins for the Copy Database Wizard

If you choose to copy SQL Server logins used by the database and they do not exist on the target server, the SQL Server logins will be created but disabled. You will need to enable them after the Copy Database Wizard completes.

Creating an Object-Change Strategy

Object changes are schema changes because database objects make up the database schema. When thinking about object changes, there are several considerations when deploying upgrades or application databases:

- What is the scope of the change?
- Is the database published for replication?
- Do snapshots of the database exist?
- What are the current database state, user access, and database update options?

The scope of the change refers to the objects affected by the change. Some examples are the database itself, files, filegroups, tables, views, stored procedures, and functions. Replication, snapshots, and database state also constrain the allowed types of object changes and affect the method used to implement the changes.

Replication and Object Changes

Replication allows changes to a SQL Server 2005 database schema, but restrictions apply. For instance, altering primary key columns is not permitted. Use the sp_replicationdboption stored procedure to create and drop replication system tables and security and manage replication metadata in the master.sysdatabases table.

It is possible to alter a table that is published for transactional replication by adding or removing a column, for example. The schema change will be propagated to the subscribers at the next update. If you want to drop a table that is being replicated, it's best to stop synchronization from Replication Monitor first. To reach Replication Monitor, open SSMS, connect to the replication distributor, right-click the Replication object in the Object Explorer, and click Launch Replication Monitor. Select the Publisher you want to monitor in the tree view at left, and then select the Subscription Watch List tab in the details portion on the right. Right-click the subscription you want to stop and click Stop Synchronizing, as shown in Figure 12-17.

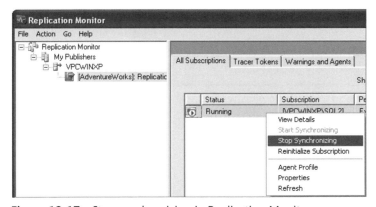

Figure 12-17   Stop synchronizing in Replication Monitor

In SSMS, expand the Replication object in Object Explorer and click the Local Publications logical folder. If the Summary page is not visible, press F7 to display a list of local publications configured on SQL Server. Right-click the publication from which you want to drop a table and click Properties. Click the Articles page from the list on the left, expand the Tables node in the Objects To Publish tree view, and deselect the table you want to drop. You will be warned that this action will invalidate the current snapshot (if a current snapshot is available) and asked to confirm this action.

Clicking Yes will remove the table from the published articles list. Click OK when finished.

As the warning dialog box foretold, you now have to reinitialize all subscriptions to this publication before proceeding. Reinitializing all subscriptions causes a new snapshot to be generated. In merge replication scenarios, this means all data contained in published tables will be retransmitted to the clients. To accomplish reinitialization, simply right-click the publication and click Reinitialize All Subscriptions, as shown in Figure 12-18.

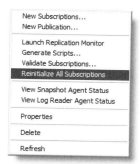

Figure 12-18   Reinitializing all subscriptions

When prompted, select the Generate The New Snapshot Now check box and click the Mark For Reinitialization button. Reinitialization might take a few seconds or a few minutes, depending on the number and size of the objects in the publication. When reinitialization completes, return to Replication Monitor, right-click the subscription, and click Start Synchronizing to restart replication of this publication.

You can now drop the table from the Publisher. It is a recommended best practice to drop the table from the Subscriber also, and SQL Server 2005 provides the sp_addscriptexec stored procedure to enable you to execute a script on all Subscribers to a publication. To use this stored procedure to drop your Subscriber table, create a DROP TABLE T-SQL statement and store it in a file with a .sql extension. Once the statement is saved, execute the following on the Publisher SQL Server:

```
exec sp_addscriptexec [@publication], [@scriptfile]
```

sp_addscriptexec enables you to log errors and continue using the optional @skiperrors bit parameter (1 to log and continue, 0 to stop the agent on error).

Object Changes and Database Snapshots

When a snapshot exists on a database, a stake is driven into the virtual ground and all differences from this point are recorded in log files. As long as a database snapshot exists, the source cannot be altered in a snapshot-breaking manner such as restoring over the existing source database or detaching or dropping the source. (For more information, see the topic "Limitations on Database Snapshots" in Books Online at *http://msdn2.microsoft.com/en-us/library /ms189940(SQL.90).aspx.*

Object Changes and Database State

SQL Server 2005 databases are always in one and only one state. Examples of database state include Online, Offline, Restoring, and Suspect. You can alter database objects while the database is in the Online state. However, you might need to take the database offline to perform some alterations, such as moving a file to a new disk.

Creating a Data-Change Strategy

Adding, removing, and updating data should be the simplest of all changes when deploying upgrades or application databases. The changes themselves might drastically alter application performance (for better or worse), functionality, or available lookup data, but the impact of the change is low.

BEST PRACTICES   Thorough change testing is essential

All changes should be thoroughly tested in a test database environment before deployment. Optimally, your test environment should be an exact duplicate of your production environment. The expense of maintaining an exact replica of the production environment for testing, however, is often cost-prohibitive–especially in very large database (VLDB) enterprises. Often, test environments are smaller and contain a representative sample of the data that is in the full production environment.

Creating an Audit Trail

Maintaining a record of database change activity is growing in popularity, largely due to regulations such as the Health Insurance Portability and Accountability Act (HIPAA) and the Sarbanes-Oxley Act in the United States. Although the threat of your supervisor's boss going to prison provides its own powerful and unique motivation, there are other good reasons to maintain a historical record of changes to the database schema.

For instance, sometimes you need to roll back a recently released application version. When you need to restore it to how it was before the release, it helps to have a list of the changes included in the release.

BEST PRACTICES   Change-control procedures

A tried and true change-control procedure (discussed next) can help you here. A pre-release backup should be a mandatory part of new releases.

Methods to audit SQL Server activity include SQL Server Profiler, C2 auditing, login auditing, Common Criteria Compliance, and data-definition language (DDL) triggers. These options are configured in SSMS on the Server Properties Security page.

SQL Server Profiler enables you to track most activity occurring in a SQL Server database. Traces of SQL Server activity are captured and displayed in the SQL Server Profiler interface. Users can fine-tune traces to record a minimal amount of information or to catch nearly all activity on the SQL Server. There are performance implications for capturing increasing amounts of activity. For details about using SQL Server Profiler, see the SQL Server 2005 Books Online topic "Introducing SQL Server Profiler" at *http://msdn2.microsoft.com/en-us /library/ms181091(SQL.90).aspx.*

C2 auditing tracks login and object access activities. C2 auditing has been superseded by Common Criteria Compliance. (See the following section.) For more information, see the SQL Server 2005 Books Online topic "C2 Audit Mode Option" at *http://msdn2.microsoft.com/en-us/library/ms187634(SQL.90).aspx.*

Login auditing can be configured to track failed logins, successful logins, both, or neither. By default, failed login attempts are tracked. Information is stored in the SQL Server error log. For more information, see the SQL Server 2005 Books Online topic "Auditing SQL Server Activity" at *http://msdn2.microsoft.com/en-us/library/aa905160(sql.80).aspx.*

Common Criteria Compliance supersedes C2 auditing and several other auditing standards. It tracks login attempts, both successful and unsuccessful. In addition, Common Criteria Compliance forces the principle of least privilege at the table level—that is, table-level DENY permissions take precedence over table-level GRANT permissions. Common Criteria Compliance also enforces Residual Information Protection (RIP), which overwrites memory buffers before releasing them for reallocation. However, as you might imagine, there are known performance issues with Common Criteria Compliance—most due to RIP functionality. For more information, see the SQL Server 2005 Books Online topic "Common Criteria Certification" at *http://msdn2.microsoft.com/en-us/library/bb153837(SQL.90).aspx.*

DDL triggers allow denial, tracking, or notification of attempts to alter the database schema. Similar to data-manipulation language (DML) triggers, which fire in response to UPDATE, INSERT, and DELETE statements, DDL triggers fire in response to CREATE, ALTER, and DROP statements. You can use DDL triggers to execute stored procedures that log date, time, and user information in an audit table. For more information, see the SQL Server 2005 Books Online topic "Understanding DDL Triggers" at *http://msdn2.microsoft.com/en-us/library /ms175941(SQL.90).aspx.*

Defining Change Control

Change control or change management is a process, procedure, or methodology to manage changes in an enterprise. The purpose of change control is to document communication to all affected by the proposed change, preferably before the change occurs. Change control has grown in importance as enterprises come to depend on stable application architectures to remain competitive.

Although change control might appear to be a bureaucratic nightmare, it is designed to ensure that everything has been done to deploy bug-free code. Change control procedures usually include reporting of test results, oversight (code review or peer review), and documentation.

Some institutions form Change Oversight Groups or Change Control Boards to monitor proposed changes. Most of these committees are composed of representatives from different departments within the enterprise. They are tasked with determining the impact of changes in one area on other areas of the enterprise. Some are empowered to decide which changes should and should not be deployed. For example, consider an application database schema change that adds a column to a table. The impact of this change might appear low to the application development group. But an extract, transform, and load (ETL) engine might be collecting new data from this application database regularly—perhaps nightly—and this seemingly innocuous change could cause the ETL operation to fail. The issue could be further complicated if a failure of this portion of the ETL process causes the enterprise data warehouse load to fail.

A thorough listing of change control tools and techniques is beyond the scope of this book. However, SQL Server 2005 database administrators and developers should refer to information about Microsoft Visual Studio 2005 Team Foundation Server products at *http://msdn2.microsoft.com/en-us/teamsystem/aa718825.aspx*.

Creating a Project-Management Methodology

Deploying upgrades or application databases in a modern enterprise of any size requires a project management (PM) methodology. Fortunately, almost all enterprises possess some form of PM. Some, such as the Capability Maturity Model Integration (CMMI), are formal, well-documented disciplines. Others are informal, such as "Go ask Earl; he's the DBA."

In practice, most enterprises operate somewhere between a formal and informal PM methodology. Either can be taken to an extreme, when more harm than necessary can be done. It's easy to see where an informal PM methodology falls short: There is a lack of documented procedures, so project proposals, status, and audits are subjective. However, poorly executed formal methodologies can kill creativity and hamper mobility in an enterprise, degrading business agility and, ultimately, profitability.

For project management, database developers can use SSMS to create database projects. Database projects provide a concise method of managing code because they maintain related SQL scripts in a single entity: the database project. To create a database project, open SSMS and click File, click New, and then click Project.

When the New Project dialog box displays, supply the name, type, and file system layout of the database project. Use SSMS Solution Explorer to manage database project files, as shown in Figure 12-19.

Figure 12-19   SSMS Solution Explorer

Once you've created a database project, you can protect and manage the database project source code by using a source control or version control engine. Microsoft Visual Studio Team System and Team Foundation Server provide integrated version control and project management. Project administrators create Team Projects, which contain one or more Solutions, which can each contain one or more Software Projects.

Microsoft Visual Studio 2005 Team Edition for Database Professionals takes database project management to the next level, including integrated unit testing, rename refactoring, data and schema comparison, and data generation.

Practice: Deploying to SQL Server Express by Using Backup and Restore

As you saw in this lesson, security is important when deploying databases. Deployment planning should start with plans to address object and access security, logins, and permissions.

IMPORTANT   Download SQL Server Express Edition

You will need an instance of SQL Server Express installed and running to complete this practice. You can download a free copy of SQL Server Express from the Microsoft Web site at *http:// msdn.microsoft.com/vstudio/express/sql/download/*.

▶ **Exercise: Manage Orphaned Logins**

In this exercise, you will create a simple database in SQL Server 2005. You will create a SQL Server login, add it to the users of *AdventureWorks*, and assign it permissions on the local *AdventureWorks* database. You will then back up and restore this database to an instance of SQL Server Express.

When you restore the database on SQL Server Express, your SQL Server login will be orphaned; the User object will be restored with the database, but there will be no corresponding SQL

Server login on the instance of SQL Server Express. You will need to address this situation before proceeding.

1. Open SSMS and, in a new query window, create a new database by using the following T-SQL script:

```
CREATE DATABASE [TestDB441] ON  PRIMARY
( NAME = N'TestDB441', FILENAME = N'C:\TestDB441.mdf' , SIZE = 2048KB , FILEGROWTH =
1024KB )
 LOG ON
( NAME = N'TestDB441_log', FILENAME = N'C:\TestDB441_log.ldf' , SIZE = 1024KB ,
FILEGROWTH = 10%)
GO
```

2. Execute the following T-SQL code to create a new login:

```
USE [master]
GO
CREATE LOGIN [TestLogin] WITH PASSWORD=N'TestLogin', DEFAULT_DATABASE=[TestDB441],
CHECK_EXPIRATION=OFF, CHECK_POLICY=OFF
GO
```

This creates the login TestLogin with a password of TestLogin and sets the default database to *TestDB441*.

3. To grant access to *TestDB441* and allow TestLogin to select from the Person schema, execute the following T-SQL script:

```
USE [TestDB441]
GO
CREATE USER [TestLogin] FOR LOGIN [TestLogin] WITH DEFAULT_SCHEMA=[dbo]
GO
ALTER AUTHORIZATION ON SCHEMA::[db_datareader] TO [TestLogin]
GO
GRANT SELECT ON SCHEMA::[dbo] TO [TestLogin]
GO
```

4. Back up the *TestDB441* database by using the following T-SQL script:

```
BACKUP DATABASE [TestDB441] TO DISK = N'c:\TestDB441.bak'
GO
```

5. In SSMS, connect to your instance of SQL Server Express and restore the database by using the following script:

```
RESTORE DATABASE [TestDB441] FROM  DISK = N'C:\TestDB441.bak' WITH  FILE = 1,   MOVE
N'TestDB441' TO N'C:\Program Files\Microsoft SQL
Server\MSSQL.4\MSSQL\Data\TestDB441.mdf',  MOVE N'TestDB441_log' TO N'C:\Program
Files\Microsoft SQL Server\MSSQL.4\MSSQL\Data\TestDB441_1.ldf',  NOUNLOAD,  REPLACE,
STATS = 10
GO
```

6. Verify that you have an orphaned user in the *TestDb441* database you just restored to SQL Server Express by using the sp_change_users_login stored procedure:

```
USE TestDB441
GO
EXEC sp_change_users_login 'Report'
```

The results pane should display the TestUser username and a UserSID. This indicates that an orphaned user, TestUser, exists in *TestDB441*.

7. Use the sp_change_users_login stored procedure to correct the orphaned user problem by executing the following script:

```
USE TestDB441
GO
EXEC sp_change_users_login 'Auto_Fix', 'TestLogin', NULL, 'TestLogin'
```

Barring a conflict, the row for user TestLogin will be fixed by updating its link to a new login. You should see a message similar to the following in the SQL Query Messages pane.

```
The number of orphaned users fixed by updating users was 0.
The number of orphaned users fixed by adding new logins and then updating users was 1.
```

Quick Check

1. You can use DDL triggers to audit database schema changes. True or false?
2. By default in SQL Server 2005, table-level DENY permissions take precedence over table-level GRANT permissions. True or false?
3. Suppose you work with a database that is modified daily. Modifications include inserts, updates, and deletes. The database is also replicated daily to several clients. A new application release requires dropping two tables. What must you do to deploy this update?

Quick Check Answers

1. The correct answer is True. DDL triggers fire when CREATE, ALTER, or DROP statements are executed, so you can use them to audit changes.
2. The correct answer is False. Table-level DENY permissions do not take precedence over table-level GRANT permissions by default. However, implementing Common Criteria Compliance will force table-level DENY permissions to take precedence over table-level GRANT permissions.
3. You must remove the tables from the publication articles and execute sp_addscriptexec at the publisher to call a DROP TABLE script on the clients. Any changes to the article list in a publication require you to reinitialize all subscriptions.

Case Scenario: Deploying a Database

IMPORTANT Download AdventureWorksLT

For this scenario, you will use the *AdventureWorksLT* database, detailed in the "Before You Begin" section of this chapter.

You are the database developer charged with supporting testing efforts for a new application release. Software quality assurance (SQA) follows a custom methodology for testing that uses a series of scripts (not to be confused with T-SQL scripts). Your manager has decided to deploy the database in concert with the SQA testing progress. SQA first tests for the existence of the database, tables, and views. Your manager asks you to deploy only the database, tables, and views to begin with. Answer the following questions:

1. Which deployment technique is suited for this type of deployment?
2. How would you implement this deployment technique?
3. SQA later completes this testing phase, and your manager tells you they're ready to populate the tables with data. What mechanisms can you use to push data into the tables on your SQL Server Express instance?

Chapter Summary

- Deployment planning reduces error and inefficiency during application deployment or update. SQL Server 2005 offers five different mechanisms for deploying databases: SQL Server Management Studio Copy Database Wizard, T-SQL scripts, the Import and Export Wizard, SQL Server Integration Services, and the SQLCmd utility.

- You can use SSMS to generate T-SQL scripts for all deployment tasks. The most common T-SQL script deployment options are detach and attach database files, backup and restore database, and manually create a deployment script.

- Like the Copy Database Wizard, the Import and Export Wizard creates an SSIS package that you can save at the end of the wizard and is best suited for deployments within the enterprise. However, three features are unique to the Import and Export Wizard: You can select different source and destination types, use a query to select data from a source, and select individual tables and views as sources.

- SQLCmd is primarily a command-line utility that enables you to enter and execute T-SQL statements, call stored procedures, and execute scripts from the command prompt. To deploy a database by using SQLCmd, you can type and execute each T-SQL statement manually, but generating the database script by using SSMS and then executing the scripts by using SQLCmd enables you to take advantage of the valuable error-checking and syntax-checking utilities of SSMS.

- Any comprehensive deployment plan takes into account the key elements of security, how to handle object changes, how to handle data changes, how to implement an audit trail, how to implement change control, and how to handle project management.

Chapter 13

Controlling Changes to Source Code

Source code version control is essential. As a database professional, you are well aware of the benefits of maintaining a single copy (or instance) of data. One primary benefit is that when you have a single instance of the data, you're always sure you're working with the current instance. The second main benefit is ease of maintenance—if a change is required, it is required in only one location.

Source code version control also facilitates:

- Developers working on new releases while maintaining current release versions.
- The ability to roll back to previous versions.

This chapter examines why and how you control changes to database source code. You will also explore the mechanisms for managing files and other code containers, including file permissions, encryption, full and partial version labeling (striping), and version comparison.

Exam objectives in this chapter:
- Control changes to source code.
  - ❑ Set file permissions.
  - ❑ Set and retrieve version information.
  - ❑ Detect differences between versions.
  - ❑ Encrypt source code.
  - ❑ Mark groups of objects, assign version numbers to them, and devise a method to track changes.

Before You Begin

To complete the lessons in this chapter, you must have:

- A general understanding of Microsoft SQL Server 2005 and Transact-SQL.
- A general understanding of SQL Server Management Studio, including how to connect to various SQL Server instances in a typical enterprise environment.

- SQL Server and SQL Server Management Studio installed.
- Access to source control applications. Ideally, you should have access to Microsoft Visual Studio 2005 Team Foundation Server. A trial version can be downloaded from *http://www.microsoft.com/downloads/details.aspx?FamilyID=d5c12289-f4e4-49a9-9235-ab2f6d4ca097&DisplayLang=en*.

You can also perform the exercises with Microsoft Visual SourceSafe if you have it. Optional instructions are included for this software, and Lesson 2, "Setting File Permissions," contains an optional practice for those who have administrative access to a Visual SourceSafe instance.

Lesson 1: Managing Source Code Changes

Estimated lesson time: 30 minutes

Database source code is composed of Transact-SQL (T-SQL) statements, or scripts, that define the schema of the database. Database source code can be (and usually is) extended to include at least some of the data contained in the database. You can maintain database source code by using an application designed solely to control source code. Such utilities are called source control or version control applications or servers.

In this lesson, you will look at key version control capabilities of Visual Studio 2005 Team Foundation Server and Visual SourceSafe 2005. SQL Server Management Studio (SSMS) enables you to create Database Projects, providing a way to manage related T-SQL statements. Visual Studio Team Foundation Server is designed to manage change and facilitate continuous improvement for teams of developers. Launched in March 2006, Visual Studio Team Foundation Server provides tools for every phase of the project and each member of the project team. This lesson will limit its examination to the roles of database developer and database administrator (DBA). Visual SourceSafe 2005 is the latest version of the popular source control application from Microsoft.

SQL Server Management Studio and Source Control

SQL Server Management Studio facilitates database project source control through:

- Database projects.
- Integrated Source Code Control Interface (SCCI).

Database projects enable database developers to group collections of scripts into logical units. The best way to understand an SSMS database project is to walk through the process of creating one.

Begin by opening SSMS. Click File, click New, and then click Project.

When the New Project dialog box displays, select the SQL Server Scripts template. Database projects are stored in the file system. Select a target directory and database project name, as Figure 13-1 shows.

The database project template loads into SSMS. You can view an empty database project by using Solution Explorer. Click View, and then click Solution Explorer to display Solution Explorer.

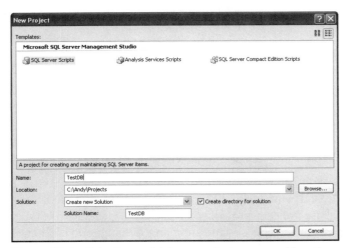

Figure 13-1   Selecting a database project name and location

At the top-most level in Solution Explorer, you will find the solution. By default, the solution and project are given the same name when you create the database project. (See Figure 13-1.) In this example, the solution is named TestDB and is represented in Figure 13-1 as Solution 'TestDB' (1 project). The solution maps to the solution folder in the file system, which is also defined when you create the project. The example solution is stored in C:\My Documents\Microsoft Press\TK70-441\Chapter13\Lesson1\TFS\TestDB. Because the Create Directory For Solution check box is selected, this path is a combination of the path specified in the Location text box and in the Solution Name text box (TestDB).

Inside the C:\My Documents\Microsoft Press\TK70-441\Chapter13\Lesson1\TFS\TestDB folder, you will find the solution definition files—in this case, TestDB.sqlsuo and TestDB.ssmssln. TestDB.sqlsuo contains user options in a proprietary (not humanly readable) format. TestDB.ssmssln is humanly readable and contains global solution properties and pointers to the project file or files.

In addition, this location contains a project folder, also named TestDB. The only file inside the TestDB project folder at this time is the project file, TestDB.ssmssqlproj. TestDB.ssmssqlproj contains Extensible Markup Language (XML) code that defines the project objects. Returning to Solution Explorer, your TestDB project is directly beneath the solution and contains three logical folders: Connections, Queries, and Miscellaneous. These logical folders are defined inside the TestDB.ssmssqlproj file.

The next step is to add a connection to the database project. In Solution Explorer, right-click the Connections logical folder and click New Connection. When the Connect To Server dialog box displays, provide instance location and credentials to connect to an instance of SQL Server. Once connected, Solution Explorer displays the connection similar to what Figure 13-2 shows.

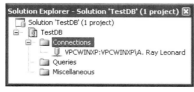

Figure 13-2 A connection in Solution Explorer

You can now add a query to the project. Right-click the Queries logical folder and click New Query. When prompted for connection information, supply a SQL Server instance name and login credentials. If you provide different connection credentials from those provided in your first connection, the new connection will be added to your Connections logical folder. If you do not supply connection information, you will be prompted the next time you open the query file.

Your query file is named SQLQuery1.sql by default. Open it by double-clicking SQLQuery.sql in Solution Explorer. In the query editor, enter the following T-SQL script to create a new database named TestDB:

```
use master;
CREATE DATABASE [TestDB]
```

Execute the script.

Adding the Project to Source Control

Now you are ready to add the project to source control. Before you do so, however, you need to configure SSMS to use source control. Click File, and then click Save All to save the project. Close SSMS before proceeding.

Visual Studio 2005 Team Foundation System provides project life cycle support, including version control. To use Visual Studio Team Foundation Server with SSMS, you must first install the Microsoft Source Code Control Interface (MSSCCI) provider for Visual Studio Team Foundation Server available at *http://www.microsoft.com/downloads/details.aspx?FamilyID=87e1ffbd-a484-4c3a-8776-d560ab1e6198&DisplayLang=en*.

Configuring the source control server—Visual Studio 2005 Team Foundation Server, in this case—is beyond the scope of this lesson. For information about how to configure Visual Studio Team Foundation Server, see the Microsoft Developer Network (MSDN) article "How to: Configure Visual Studio with Team Foundation Source Control" at *http://msdn2.microsoft.com/en-us/library/ms253064(VS.80).aspx*.

Download and install the Visual Studio Team Foundation Server MSSCCI Provider.msi file. After installation completes, open SSMS. Click Tools, and then click Options. When the Options dialog box displays, click Source Control and change the Current Source Control

Plug-in drop-down list of values from None to Team Foundation Server MSSCCI Provider, as Figure 13-3 shows.

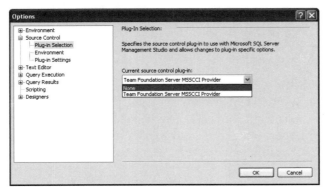

Figure 13-3   Configuring source control in SQL Server Management Studio

Click OK to exit the Options dialog box and save your changes.

Open SSMS and open your TestDB database project. (Click File, click Recent Projects, and then click the link to TestDB to open the file.) To add the solution to source control, open Solution Explorer and right-click the solution item. Click Add Solution To Source Control.

Figure 13-4 shows the Connect To A Team Foundation Server dialog box. If your enterprise has more than one Visual Studio Team Foundation Server configured, the servers should appear in the drop-down list. If they do not appear, click the Servers button to add servers to the drop-down list.

Figure 13-4   Connecting to a Team Foundation server

Click OK to connect to your Visual Studio Team Foundation Server. You will be prompted for Team Foundation login information; supply a valid user name and password to complete the connection process.

Once connected, you will be prompted to select a version control folder. By default, the Choose Folder In Team Foundation Server dialog box opens, showing the new version control folder under the root folder, designated by the dollar ($) symbol. You cannot use this folder to store your project's source code. To alter the default location, expand the root folder by clicking the plus (+) symbol to the left of $/. The items beneath the root folder are team projects.

IMPORTANT **Team projects**

Team projects in the Team Foundation Server are created and maintained by your Team Foundation Server administrator.

Select an existing folder in the Folder Location tree view or create a new folder by clicking the Make New Folder button. Figure 13-5 shows the selection of a team project named DatabaseProjects.

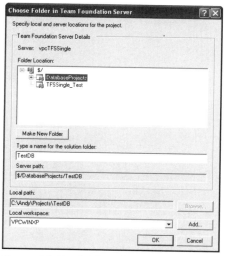

Figure 13-5   Adding the TestDB project to the DatabaseProjects team project

When you click OK, the Check In dialog box displays, as Figure 13-6 shows.

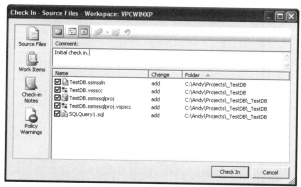

Figure 13-6   Checking in Source Files

To maintain communication during development efforts (and to remind you of what you were thinking when you look at the files in the future), it's a best practice to add a comment. Click the Check In button to add the selected files to your team project's source control.

Exam Tip   *Changeset* is the name for a collection of items that you check in together into Team Foundation Server version control.

Solution Explorer indicates items that are stored in Visual Studio Team Foundation Server with a blue padlock icon, as Figure 13-7 shows.

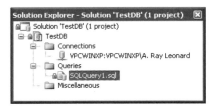

Figure 13-7   Source-controlled items in Solution Explorer

Items can be checked out for editing by right-clicking the item and clicking Check Out For Edit. If SSMS source control is set up using default behaviors, any change to items currently checked in will cause the item to be checked out automatically for editing. Checked out for edit status is indicated in Solution Explorer by a red checkmark icon, as 13-8 shows.

Figure 13-8   Checked out for edit

Several options, described as follows, are available after items are checked out from the file's context menu .

- **Open**   Opens the item in SSMS.
- **Cut**   Copies the item to the clipboard; the item is deleted once you've pasted it in its destination.
- **Copy**   Copies the item to the clipboard, and the item is unaffected by a paste.
- **Remove**   Removes the item from the database project. The user is prompted to remove the item, delete the item, or cancel the operation.
- **Rename**   Renames the item.

- **Check In**   Displays the Check In dialog box.
- **View Pending Checkins**   Displays the Pending Checkins dialog box.
- **Undo Checkout**   Removes the Checked Out For Edit status and restores the file-system version to the last checked-in version. If the item is open in SSMS, you might be prompted to reload.
- **Get Latest Version**   Gets the last checked-in version from Visual Studio Team Foundation Server.
- **Compare**   Starts the Compare dialog box, which enables you to compare versions of the file stored in Visual Studio Team Foundation Server and files stored in the file system.
- **Get**   Gets an item from Visual Studio Team Foundation Server.
- **View History**   Displays a check-in history of the item.
- **Properties Window**   Displays properties of the item.

Working with a Source-Controlled Database Project

After your database project is source-controlled or version-controlled, you can edit or add items as needed. To demonstrate, rename your existing script to something more descriptive. In Solution Explorer, right-click the SQLQuery1.sql item and click Rename. Change the name of the script to CreateDatabase.sql.

Renaming items checked out for editing is possible but tedious. For this reason, it's best to rename only checked-in items. After you click Rename, you are presented with the dialog box shown in Figure 13-9.

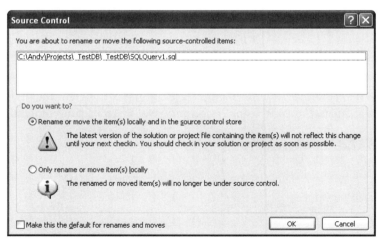

Figure 13-9   Renaming source-controlled items

The first option renames the local file and the item stored in source control. This is recommended to maintain consistency. The other option renames the file system object only. Click OK to rename the local file and item in Visual Studio Team Foundation Server version control. You will be prompted to check in the file with its new name. Once the file is checked in, Solution Explorer displays the file with its new name.

Now, let's add a new script to your database project and then to Visual Studio Team Foundation Server version control. In SSMS, click the New Query button. A new query window named SQLQuery1.sql opens. This item does not show up in Solution Explorer—yet. Add the following T-SQL to the query window:

```
use TestDB

CREATE TABLE dbo.TestTable
(ID int identity(1,1) NOT NULL,
Name varchar(25) NULL,
Value int NULL)
```

Execute the script to create the table.

To add the script to your TestDB solution, click File, click Move SQLQuery1.sql Into, and click TestDB. When the Save File As dialog box displays, change the name of the file to CreateTestTable.sql and click Save. In Solution Explorer, CreateTestTable.sql is added to the Queries logical folder with a plus sign (+) icon.

The plus sign indicates that the item is new to the solution and has not yet been added to source control. In SSMS, click View, and then click Pending Checkins. The Pending Checkins window displays changes to a source-controlled solution that have not been checked in. These changes represent the difference between the solution in its current state and its last checked-in state.

From the Pending Checkins window, you can add comments to this changeset by clicking the Comments button and typing text, as Figure 13-10 shows. Again, adding comments is a best practice because it serves to describe the change. After typing comments, click the Check In button to store the changeset in your Team Project in Visual Studio Team Foundation Server.

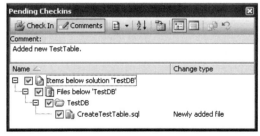

Figure 13-10 Pending Checkins dialog box

After the changeset is checked in, the Pending Checkins window is empty, and Solution Explorer displays all items with the blue padlock icon, indicating that all items in the current solution have been checked in.

Practice: Managing Changes to Source Code

In this practice, you use what you learned in Lesson 1, "Managing Source Code Changes," to add a new file to the TestDB project and check in your changes. If you need to review how to perform any of the following tasks, see the steps covered in Lesson 1.

On the Companion Disc   This chapter includes many code examples. You will find all the code from this chapter on the companion CD in the C:\My Documents\Microsoft Press\TK70-441 \Chapter13 folder.

▶ **Exercise: Create and Source-Control a New Stored Procedure**

In this exercise, you will add a new stored procedure to the TestDB project and then update the Team Project.

1. Add a new item, a stored procedure, to the TestDB project. Call the file **usp_GetTestNameAndValue**.

   Add the following T-SQL code to the file to create the stored procedure:

   ```
   use TestDB;
   GO

   CREATE PROCEDURE dbo.usp_GetTestNameAndValue
     @ID int
   AS
     select Name, Value
     from dbo.TestTable
     where id = @ID
   GO
   ```

2. Add the file to the TestDB solution.
3. Check in your changes.

Quick Check

1. Default behaviors for SQL Server Management Studio source control include which of the following? (Select all that apply.)
    A. Keep items checked out when checking in.
    B. On save, check out automatically.
    C. On edit, check out automatically.
    D. Allow checked-in items to be edited.
2. True or false: A changeset is a list of changes to source-controlled items.

Quick Check Answers

1. The correct answers are B and C: on save, check out automatically; and on edit, check out automatically. Keeping items checked out when checking in, and allowing checked-in items to be edited, are valid options but not default behaviors.
2. The correct answer is false. A changeset is a collection of items checked into Team Foundation Server together.

Lesson 2: Setting File Permissions

Estimated lesson time: 15 minutes

Source code access is controlled by file permissions. Some source control servers—Team Foundation Server, for instance—integrate with Microsoft Windows security and Active Directory directory service to manage user access. Other source control applications, such as Visual SourceSafe 2005, rely on internal users defined by application administrators in concert with file system permissions controlled by Windows integrated security. This lesson uses Visual SourceSafe 2005 to demonstrate principles of controlling database project source code.

Visual SourceSafe User Permissions and Rights

Visual SourceSafe users can be created with read-only rights, as Figure 13-11 shows.

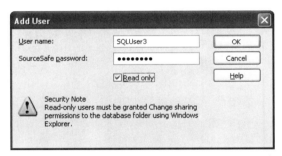

Figure 13-11   Creating a read-only user in Visual SourceSafe 2005

Visual SourceSafe 2005 allows even finer control over users. You can use the Visual SourceSafe Administrator utility to enable project rights and assignments. Once enabled, users can be granted specific rights on a database project. These rights include:

- **Read**   A user has read permissions for the items in a database project.
- **Check Out/Check In**   A user can check items into and out of source control.
- **Add/Rename/Delete**   Users with this right can add, modify, or delete items from a database project.
- **Destroy**   This includes purge and rollback permissions (usually reserved for source control administrators).

Folder Permissions

You can also maintain folder-level source control by using a combination of user groups and folder permissions. User groups are created on the computer running Visual SourceSafe or in the Active Directory domain. User groups can use local accounts or domain accounts. Permissions are then set on the Windows folder containing the Srcsafe.ini file and based upon the developer's (or user's) Windows security or Active Directory credentials.

Opening Visual SourceSafe–Controlled Projects

A Visual SourceSafe login dialog box, which Figure 13-12 shows, displays when you open a database project that uses Visual SourceSafe for source code control.

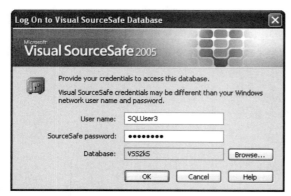

Figure 13-12   Logging on to Visual SourceSafe 2005

When a read-only user attempts to add to a database project, he or she is prohibited. A dialog box displays when a read-only user attempts to add an item to a database project, informing the user that he or she does not have access rights to the project source code.

Optional Practice: Setting Source Control File Permissions

This practice is optional. To perform the steps in the exercise, you will need administrative access to a Visual SourceSafe instance.

In this practice, you use what you learned in Lesson 2, "Setting File Permissions," and previous lessons to create two users in Visual SourceSafe; set one user as a read-only user, and then test the permissions by adding a project and trying to add an item as the read-only user.

▶ **Exercise: Use Visual SourceSafe 2005 with SSMS**

In this exercise, you will control an SSMS project with Visual SourceSafe 2005.

1. Configure SSMS to use Visual SourceSafe 2005.
2. Create two users in Visual SourceSafe 2005: SQLUser1 and SQLUser2.
3. Set SQLUser2 as a read-only user.
4. Create a new database project in SSMS.
5. Add the project to source control, connecting to Visual SourceSafe as SQLUser1.
6. Save changes and close SSMS.
7. Re-open SSMS and the database project, signing into source control as SQLUser2.
8. Test the read-only restriction by attempting to add a new item.

Quick Check

- True or false: A database project source-controlled with Visual SourceSafe 2005 can use Windows integrated security to control access to the Visual SourceSafe directory that contains the Srcsafe.ini file.

Quick Check Answer

- The correct answer is true. Visual SourceSafe 2005 can use a combination of internal (Visual SourceSafe) user accounts and Windows integrated security to control access and permissions to source control. Windows integrated security is used to control access to the Visual SourceSafe folder that contains the Srcsafe.ini file.

Lesson 3: Setting and Retrieving Version Information

Estimated lesson time: 20 minutes

Almost all source control products provide the ability to label, or stripe, versions of an application. Visual SourceSafe 2005 Explorer enables users to apply a label to a stored version. Labels are helpful progress markers for projects during development. Post-deployment, labels provide a means of tracking major and minor releases. This is important in the event that you need to roll back to a previous release.

In Visual SourceSafe 2005, you can apply labels to folders. To add a label in Visual SourceSafe 2005, open Visual SourceSafe 2005 Explorer and navigate to the desired folder. Right-click the folder and click Label.

When the Label dialog box displays, add label text in the Label text box, and then add an optional description, as Figure 13-13 shows. This is sometimes referred to as striping a version.

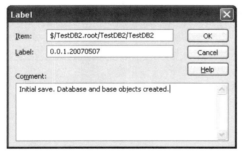

Figure 13-13   Applying a label (striping) in Visual SourceSafe 2005

To apply a label in Visual Studio 2005 Team Foundation Server, you need to use Team Explorer, the client for Team Foundation Server. Installing and configuring Team Explorer is beyond the scope of this chapter. For more information, see "Using Team Explorer" at *http://msdn2.microsoft.com/en-us/library/ms181304(VS.80).aspx*.

Team Explorer is an add-on for Microsoft Visual Studio 2005 Team Foundation Server, and SQL Server Business Intelligence Development Studio (BIDS) is actually Visual Studio 2005 with SQL Server development templates installed.

To access Team Explorer, open SQL Server BIDS, click Tools, and then click Connect To Team Foundation Server. When the Team Foundation Servers dialog box displays, select your Team Foundation Server and Team Project. When Team Explorer connects, as shown in Figure 13-14, double-click Source Control to open Source Control Explorer.

Figure 13-14   Team Explorer

Navigate to the item or folder you want to label. Note that, in Team Explorer, labels can be applied to individual items as well as to folders. Right-click the item or folder and click Apply Label, as Figure 13-15 shows.

Figure 13-15   Applying a label in the Team Foundation Server Source Control Explorer

Figure 13-16 shows the Choose Item Version dialog box. Using the Version drop-down list, you can select the latest version or a version by date, label, or changeset. Select a version and click OK.

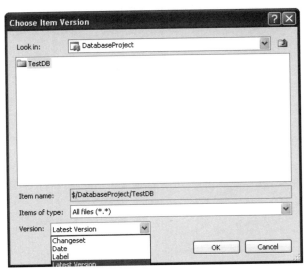

Figure 13-16 Selecting a version to label

The Apply Label dialog box displays, as Figure 13-17 shows. Enter the label text in the Name text box and an optional comment in the Comment text box. You can also add other items to this label or remove items listed by using the Add and Remove buttons in this dialog box.

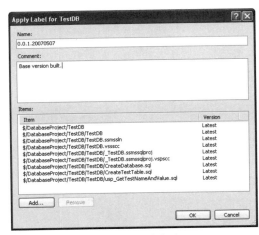

Figure 13-17 Applying a label

You use labels to manage versions. All major and minor database application releases should be labeled to facilitate application rollbacks and continued development.

Practice: Setting Version Information

In this practice, use what you learned in Lesson 3, "Setting and Retrieving Version Information," to apply descriptive labels with comments to individual items in your *TestDB* database project controlled by Visual Studio 2005 Team Foundation Server.

▶ **Exercise: Add Labels**

Add the labels as described in this lesson and give the items descriptions that would help you or another database developer or administrator clearly identify the items in case a rollback is required.

Quick Check

■ True or false: You can apply labels to individual items in Visual SourceSafe 2005.

Quick Check Answer

■ The correct answer is false. You can apply labels to folders in Visual SourceSafe 2005. You can apply labels to individual items in Visual Studio 2005 Team Foundation Server.

Lesson 4: Detecting Differences Between Versions

Estimated lesson time: 20 minutes

Most source control applications and servers provide comparison mechanisms. Visual Source-Safe 2005 and Visual Studio 2005 Team Foundation Server provide this functionality.

To see how the comparison utility in Team Foundation Server works, open your *TestDB* database project in SSMS. Log in to Team Foundation Server and open the usp_GetTestNameAndValue item from Solution Explorer. Edit the T-SQL code in the procedure to read as follows:

```
CREATE PROCEDURE dbo.usp_GetTestNameAndValue
  @ID int
AS
  select Name AS 'TestName'
       , Value AS 'TestValue'
  from dbo.TestTable
  where id = @ID
GO
```

Click File, and then click Save usp_GetTestNameAndValue to save your changes. Do not check the changes into source control.

In Solution Explorer, right-click the usp_GetTestNameAndValue item and click Compare. The Compare dialog box displays, as Figure 13-18 shows.

Figure 13-18   Selecting items to compare—Team Foundation Server

Click OK to compare the file you just saved to the last-saved version from source control. The Differences dialog box displays differences between the two versions, as Figure 13-19 shows. Differences are noted by color. Although the colors don't appear in the figure, blue text indicates text that has been altered (Changed Text), red text indicates text that has been deleted, and green text indicates text that has been added. Black text indicates no change.

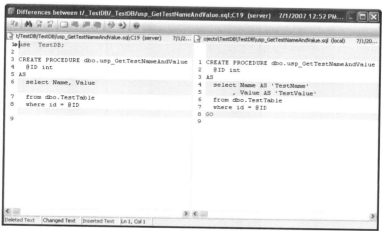

Figure 13-19   Differences dialog box—Team Foundation Server

Figure 13-20 and Figure 13-21 show the Visual SourceSafe 2005 counterparts to the Team Foundation Server Compare dialog box that was shown in Figure 13-18 and the Differences dialog box that was shown in Figure 13-19, respectively.

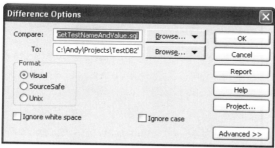

Figure 13-20   Difference Options dialog box—Visual SourceSafe 2005

Click OK in the Difference Options dialog box to compare the latest file version to the latest Visual SourceSafe 2005 version of the file.

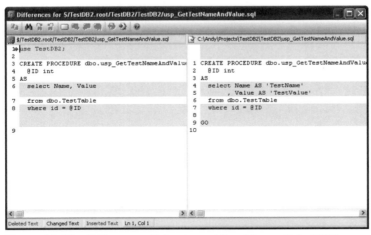

Figure 13-21   Differences dialog box—Visual SourceSafe 2005

The color code in the Visual Studio 2005 Team Foundation Server Difference dialog box is identical to the color code used in the Visual SourceSafe 2005 Difference dialog box.

Comparing source code in database projects can help you isolate the source of the problem between a version that functions as intended and a version that has a bug.

Practice: Detecting Version Differences

In this practice, use what you learned in Lesson 4, "Detecting Differences Between Versions."

▶ **Exercise: Compare Versions**

Store the current versions of usp_GetTestNameAndValue in Visual Studio 2005 Team Foundation Server and in Visual SourceSafe 2005 if you have access to it. Execute comparisons between source-controlled versions.

Quick Check

■ The Differences dialog box in Visual SourceSafe 2005 and in Visual Studio 2005 Team Foundation Server use the following color schemes to identify changes. (Select all that apply.)

- ❏ Red for deleted text.
- ❏ Brown for changed text.
- ❏ Green for changed text.
- ❏ Blue for changed text.
- ❏ Green for added text.
- ❏ Black indicates no change.

Quick Check Answer

■ The correct answers are A, D, E, and F. Red indicates deleted text, blue indicates changed text, green indicates added text, and black indicates no change.

Lesson 5: Encrypting Source Code

Estimated lesson time: 15 minutes

Encrypting database project source code is sometimes desired to protect intellectual property. At other times, it is required to protect sensitive industrial or government applications. In this lesson, you will walk through an example of adding encryption to the *TestDB* database project you created in previous lessons.

In this example, you will:

- Create a certificate and add it to the *TestDB* database.
- Create a SQL Server Login and add a User to the *TestDB* database.
- Create and sign a new stored procedure with the certificate.
- Create a certificate account and grant it sufficient database rights in the *TestDB* database.
- Display and test the access context.

IMPORTANT   Mixed Mode security

Your instance of SQL Server 2005 must use Mixed Mode security to execute the T-SQL code in this lesson.

Open SSMS and the TestDB project that you created earlier in this chapter. Log in to Team Foundation Server to access your database project source code. If the usp_GetTestNameAndValue item is still checked out for edit, right-click it and check this item in to source control.

Create a new query in SSMS and enter the following T-SQL code in the query window to create a login for a test user:

```
USE TestDB;
GO
-- Set up a login for the test user
CREATE LOGIN TestEncryptionUser
    WITH PASSWORD = 'QmJg&6zp0)'
GO
CREATE USER TestEncryptionUser
FOR LOGIN TestEncryptionUser;
GO
```

Save this script as CreateTestEncryptionUser and move it into the TestDB database project. Execute the script.

Certificates can be created in individual databases, in the master database, or in both. For a comprehensive look at the options for creating certifications, see the SQL Server 2005 Books

Online topic "CREATE CERTIFICATE (Transact-SQL)" at *http://msdn2.microsoft.com/en-us /library/ms187798(SQL.90).aspx*. Create a new query named CreateCertificate and insert the following T-SQL code:

```
CREATE CERTIFICATE TestDBCertificate
   ENCRYPTION BY PASSWORD = 'CJhorhins!@2258'
      WITH SUBJECT = 'Encryption for TestDB',
      EXPIRY_DATE = '07/10/2016';
GO
```

Move this script into the TestDB project and execute it.

Now, create a stored procedure to display information about the user and context to test your encryption method. Create a new stored procedure named usp_TestEncryption and add it to the TestDB database project:

```
USE TestDB
GO

CREATE PROCEDURE usp_TestEncryption
AS
   -- Show who is running the stored procedure
   SELECT SYSTEM_USER 'System User'
   , USER AS 'Database User'
   , NAME AS 'Context'
   , TYPE
   , USAGE
   FROM sys.user_token

   SELECT
     ID
     ,Name
     ,Value
   FROM dbo.TestTable;

GO

ADD SIGNATURE TO usp_TestEncryption
   BY CERTIFICATE TestDBCertificate
    WITH PASSWORD = 'CJhorhins!@2258';
GO
```

The stored procedure is created at the beginning of the T-SQL statement, beginning with the CREATE PROCEDURE statement. Two T-SQL statements are included: one that displays execution context information and another that displays all records in the dbo.TestTable table. The T-SQL code beginning with ADD SIGNATURE signs the stored procedure by using the certificate you created in the previous step. Execute this script.

The certificate requires a certificate account to control access to the underlying tables. Create a new query named CertificateUser and enter the following T-SQL code in the query editor window:

```
USE TestDB;
GO
CREATE USER TestDBEncryptionAccount
    FROM CERTIFICATE TestDBCertificate;
GO

GRANT SELECT
    ON dbo.TestTable
    TO TestDBEncryptionAccount;
GO

GRANT EXECUTE
    ON usp_TestEncryption
    TO TestDBEncryptionAccount;
GO

GRANT EXECUTE
    ON usp_TestEncryption
    TO TestEncryptionUser;
GO
```

Review the four T-SQL statements in this script. The first statement creates a user account from the certificate. The second grants select permission on the underlying table (dbo.TestTable) to the new user (TestDBEncryptionAccount). The third statement grants execute permission on your new stored procedure (usp_TestEncryption) to the new user (TestDBEncryptionAccount). The fourth T-SQL statement grants execute permission to the TestEncryptionUser account you created first, enabling you to display rights associated with the stored procedure access. Execute this script.

Now, test your work. First, open a new query window and copy the following T-SQL statement into the query editor window:

```
EXEC usp_TestEncryption;
```

Figure 13-22 shows the results you should receive when you run this query logged on as Administrator.

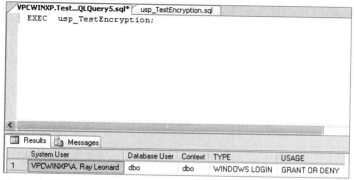

Figure 13-22   Executing a test query as Administrator

The results indicate that the Administrator account is running in its own security context as a Windows login.

Next, execute the following test query:

```
EXECUTE AS LOGIN = 'TestEncryptionUser';
GO
EXEC usp_TestEncryption;
```

Your results should resemble those shown in Figure 13-23.

```
EXECUTE   AS LOGIN = 'TestEncryptionUser';
GO
EXEC usp_TestEncryption;
```

	System User	Database User	Context	TYPE
1	TestEncryptionUser	TestEncryptionUser	TestEncryptionUser	SQL USER
2	TestEncryptionUser	TestEncryptionUser	public	ROLE
3	TestEncryptionUser	TestEncryptionUser	TestDBEncryptionAccount	USER MAPPED TO CERTIFICATE

Figure 13-23   Executing a test query as TestEncryptionUser

Note that the type column returns a SQL User, Role, and, finally, the certificate user account for the returned Contexts: TestEncryptionUser, public, and TestDBEncryptionAccount, respectively.

In addition to denying the user explicit permissions on the underlying database objects, using a certificate facilitates a high level of detailed auditing. Trace data can include user and context information.

Practice: Source Code Encryption

In this practice, use what you learned in Lesson 5, "Encrypting Source Code."

▶ **Exercise: Encrypt Source Code**

Create additional certificates, certificate user accounts, and SQL Server logins in TestDB. Alter the usp_GetTestNameAndValue procedure and sign it with your new certificate.

Quick Check

■ Certificates can be created in which objects? (Choose all that apply.)

❑ Stored procedures

❑ The master database

❑ Individual databases

❑ Tables

Quick Check Answer

■ The correct answers are B and C. Certificates can be created on the master database and individual databases but not on stored procedures or tables. Certificates are used to sign stored procedures. Certificate accounts are used to allow signed stored procedures to access data in underlying tables.

Lesson 6: Tracking Changes to Groups of Objects

Estimated lesson time: 10 minutes

Tracking changes to groups of objects and assigning version numbers are important parts of change control. Labels, discussed earlier in this chapter, provide some of this functionality. Source control folders, such as those you've observed in both Visual SourceSafe 2005 and Visual Studio 2005 Team Foundation Server, track changes on a group of objects. Visual Studio Team Foundation Server changesets take this concept to a more granular level, retaining information about when the developer checked a set of items into source control. Let's look more closely at marking a group of objects, assigning them version numbers, and devising a method to track changes to them.

There are several manual methods of maintaining a change history. Two popular methods are:

- Using extended properties.
- Creating a DBVersion table, such as the AdventureWorks.dbo.AWBuildVersion table.

Extended properties provide a mechanism for adding user-defined metadata to databases and database objects. To add an extended property to dbo.usp_GetTestNameAndValue, execute the following T-SQL script:

```
use TestDB;
GO
EXEC sys.sp_addextendedproperty
@name = N'MS_Description',
@value = N'Test Name and Value information by ID.',
@level0type = N'SCHEMA', @level0name = dbo,
@level1type = N'PROCEDURE',  @level1name = usp_GetTestNameAndValue;
GO
```

To view the extended property you just added, execute the following T-SQL query:

```
USE TestDB;
GO
SELECT objtype, objname, name, value
FROM fn_listextendedproperty (NULL, 'schema', 'dbo', 'procedure', 'usp_GetTestNameAndValue',
default, default);
GO
```

Your results should look like these:

```
objtype     objname                name              value
------------------------------------------------------------------------------------
PROCEDURE   usp_GetTestNameAndValue MS_Description  Test Name and Value information by ID.
```

Many database developers choose to implement custom database version mechanisms similar to the AWBuildVersion table included in the *AdventureWorks* sample database. These tables contain information about the database version and the date the version was implemented and/or last updated.

Figure 13-24 shows the AdventureWorks.dbo.AWBuildVersion table. It contains information about the database version, the version date, and the date the version was modified.

	SystemInformationID	Database Version	VersionDate	ModifiedDate
1	1	9.04.10.13.00	2004-10-13 16:43:14.583	2004-10-13 16:43:14.597

Figure 13-24 The AdventureWorks.dbo.AWBuildVersion table

In these examples, object version metadata must be maintained manually. The tradeoff between (somewhat) generic automated solutions provided by version-control servers such as Visual Studio Team Foundation Server and Visual SourceSafe must be weighed against manually maintaining a custom solution such as database tables and extended properties. In the end, you need to determine which solution is best for maintaining the database project source code in your enterprise.

Quick Check

Which are valid ways to track changes to groups of database objects? (Choose all that apply)

A. Use sp_add_job

B. Create a custom Version table

C. Use sp_adddistributor

D. Use sp_addextendedproperty

Quick Check Answers

The correct answers are B and D. Database developers can create a custom Version table to track changes to database objects. Database developers can also attach Extended Properties to individual database objects using the sp_addextendedproperty stored procedure.

Case Scenario: Controlling Changes to Source Code

You are tasked with specifying and implementing database source code control for your enterprise. You have the scenario of your dreams: an unlimited budget and enough time to complete this project properly. Your project sponsor, the director of Enterprise Application Development, asks that you do the following:

1. Choose a product, platform, and/or methodology that will serve your company for the next four to seven years.

2. Choose a technology that all members of the Enterprise Application Development Team can use—preferably integrated into the team's existing and future software development suites.

3. Consider in your selection that software engineers and testers are not the only users of the solution; project managers and sponsors will also be involved in the software life cycle.

Which choices would you make to fulfill these requirements? Why?

Chapter Summary

- Database source code control gives you a single instance of the data to ensure that it is the current instance and to ensure ease of maintenance. (If a change is required, it is required in only one location.)

- You maintain database source code by using an application designed for the sole purpose of controlling source code. Such utilities are called source control or version control applications or servers. Visual Studio 2005 Team Foundation Server is designed to manage change and facilitate continuous improvement for teams of developers. Visual Source-Safe 2005 is the latest version of the popular source control application from Microsoft.

- SQL Server Management Studio (SSMS) facilitates database project source control through database projects and Integrated Source Code Control Interface (SCCI). Database projects enable database developers to group collections of scripts into logical units.

- Source code access is controlled by file permissions.

- When you have an item checked out of the source control system for editing, you can perform a number of actions on the item, including cutting and pasting, copying, removing, renaming, comparing the item to another version, looking at the item history, and more.

- Visual SourceSafe 2005 enables you to apply a label to a stored version, a process also called striping. Labels are helpful progress markers for projects during development. Post-deployment, labels provide a means of tracking major and minor releases, which is important if you need to roll back to a previous release.

- Comparing source code in database projects can help you isolate the source of the problem between a version that functions as intended and a version that has a bug.

- In addition to using source-control applications and servers to compare and track code versions, there are several manual methods of maintaining a change history, including using extended properties and creating a DBVersion table such as the Adventure-Works.dbo.AWBuildVersion table.

Chapter 14
Designing for Data Distribution

In Microsoft SQL Server 2005, you have a number of options for distributing data to users and applications. The traditional way is to create and use custom applications such as Microsoft Windows and Web applications that query SQL Server databases. However, SQL Server includes several components and services for distributing data in a variety of scenarios without the need for custom applications. As you will see in this chapter, you can distribute data as reports by using SQL Server Reporting Services (SSRS), as e-mail messages by using DatabaseMail, as notifications by using Notification Services, and as operational information that you can send administrators by using *SQL Server Agent alerts*. As a database solutions developer, you should be familiar with all these options and be able to choose the most appropriate for different scenarios.

Exam objectives in this chapter:
- Design data distribution.
  - ❑ Design a DatabaseMail solution for distributing data.
  - ❑ Design SQL Server Agent alerts.
  - ❑ Specify a Web services solution for distributing data.
  - ❑ Specify a Reporting Services solution for distributing data.
  - ❑ Specify a Notification Services solution for distributing data.
- Design objects that perform actions.
  - ❑ Design WMI triggers.

Before You Begin

To complete the lessons in this chapter, you must have:
- A general understanding of multi-tiered, asynchronous, and service-oriented architectures.
- Knowledge about SQL Server components, including common language runtime (CLR) integration, hypertext transfer protocol (HTTP) endpoints, SQL Server Agent, DatabaseMail, SQL Server Notification Services, and SQL Server Reporting Services.

- Knowledge of the Transact-SQL (T-SQL) language elements that support security.
- The SQL Server 2005 *AdventureWorks* sample database installed. Sample databases are available with SQL Server 2005 Enterprise Edition but are not a part of the default installation. Alternatively, you can install the sample databases from *http://msdn2.microsoft.com /en-us/library/ms143739.aspx*.
- Microsoft Internet Information Services (IIS) with Simple Mail Transport Protocol (SMTP) virtual server installed.
- Microsoft Visual Studio 2005 or Microsoft Visual Basic or C# 2005 Express Edition installed. You can download Visual Studio Express Editions from *http://msdn.microsoft.com /vstudio/express/*.

Lesson 1: Designing a DatabaseMail Solution for Distributing Data

Estimated lesson time: 30 minutes

By sending e-mail, you can distribute data to users in a worldwide, standard, reliable, and proactive way. All users need to do is open their favorite mail client to get the information. No matter where users are, they will probably have an e-mail account by which you can likely reach them. Users do not need to stay connected all the time or have a very reliable Internet connection.

To send e-mails, you have two options: send from an external application or from a SQL Server application. SQL Server 2005 introduces *DatabaseMail*, a new component for sending e-mail by using SMTP as opposed to the obsolete SQL Mail feature, which uses Messaging Application Programming Interface (MAPI).

DatabaseMail enables you to send e-mail messages from T-SQL and CLR code. The messages can contain attached files and query results, and you can use either text or HTML format.

DatabaseMail operates asynchronously. It uses an external process that reads the messages from a SQL Server Service Broker queue and sends them to the SMTP server or servers. This infrastructure provides scalability and reliability.

DatabaseMail Architecture

The SQL Server *msdb* system database stores metadata for DatabaseMail. DatabaseMail is composed of the following components:

- **Configuration and security components** The *msdb* database contains objects to store and manage security and configuration information that DatabaseMail uses.
- **Messaging components** The *msdb* database also contains messaging components. These components include the sp_send_dbmail stored procedure and objects to store message information.
- **DatabaseMail executable** The external program DatabaseMail90.exe, which runs in the security context of the service account for SQL Server, reads the messages from a queue in the *msdb* database and sends them to SMTP servers. DatabaseMail uses Service Broker activation to start this external program.
- **Logging and auditing components** DatabaseMail logs information in the *msdb* database and the Windows Event Log.

Figure 14-1 illustrates the DatabaseMail architecture.

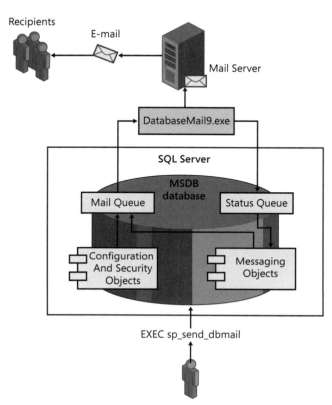

Figure 14-1   DatabaseMail architecture

When a user executes the sp_send_dbmail stored procedure to send an e-mail message, DatabaseMail adds the message to the mail queue. The DatabaseMail executable reads the mail queue, sends the e-mail messages to SMTP servers, and adds the outcome of the send operation to the status queue. An internal stored procedure reads the status queue and updates status information stored in the *msdb* database.

Enabling DatabaseMail

For security reasons, DatabaseMail is disabled by default. Before you can use it, a database administrator (DBA) must enable it and create at least one *DatabaseMail profile* with at least one DatabaseMail account. To enable DatabaseMail, you can use one of the following tools:

- DatabaseMail Configuration Wizard
- SQL Server Surface Area Configuration
- Sp_configure stored procedure with the DatabaseMail XP's configuration option

DatabaseMail Accounts, Profiles, and Security

A *DatabaseMail account* is a *DatabaseMail* object that contains information about an e-mail account. This information includes account name, e-mail address, SMTP server name, port number, and security information. A DatabaseMail account can be configured to use Secure Sockets Layer (SSL) and can also be configured to use Windows, basic, or anonymous authentication. When an account is configured to use Windows authentication, the DatabaseMail executable sends the credentials of the SQL Server service account to the SMTP server. You can associate a DatabaseMail account with one or more DatabaseMail profiles.

A DatabaseMail profile is a *DatabaseMail* object that contains DatabaseMail accounts. When you send an e-mail message by using sp_send_dbmail, you must specify a DatabaseMail profile in the information related to the message. To be usable, a DatabaseMail profile must have at least one DatabaseMail account. Each DatabaseMail account in a profile has an assigned priority (sequence number) in that profile. DatabaseMail uses the accounts in a profile based on priorities. DatabaseMail starts using the highest priority account (lowest sequence number). If the e-mail delivery operation fails when using that account, DatabaseMail uses the next account in the profile by priority order (next sequence number). To improve reliability, profiles should have more than one account. The second and following accounts are called failover accounts.

Profiles should be the same during the development, testing, and production phases, but the accounts can be different. A DBA can change the accounts in a profile without affecting the application.

Profiles are securable objects. To send a message, a user must be a member of the DatabaseMailUserRole database role in the *msdb* database and must have been granted permission to use at least one profile. From a security point of view, there are two profile types:

- **Public profiles**   All members of the DatabaseMail database role in the *msdb* database can use *public profiles*. To make a profile public, you must grant access permission on the profile to the public database role in the *msdb* database.
- **Private profiles**   Only the specified users and roles in the *msdb* database can use a *private profile*.

There are two configuration parameters related to security:

- **MaxFileSize**   The maximum attachment size
- **ProhibitedExtensions**   A list of prohibited file extensions for attachments

You can create and manage accounts and profiles and configure DatabaseMail by using one of the following methods:

- DatabaseMail Configuration Wizard
- DatabaseMail stored procedures
- SQL Server Management Objects (SMO)

Sending Messages

To send an e-mail message, you use the sp_send_dbmail stored procedure, specifying a DatabaseMail profile, one or more recipients, the subject, the body, and optionally attached files. You can format the message body in either text or HTML format. You can include query results in either the body or an attached file. To include query results, you have two options.

- Specify the @query parameter.

    DatabaseMail executes the query in another session in the security context of the caller, but synchronously. Because there is no way to specify parameters for the query, you have to concatenate values to simulate them. This is a security risk, so if you need parameters in the query, consider other options. You can specify only very basic formatting for the query result; therefore, if you need more complex formatting, consider other options.

- Manually execute queries.

    This is a more complex but flexible approach. You can execute parameterized queries and stored procedures, format the results, and include them in the @body parameter. To format the result, you can use the FOR XML clause and specify HTML tags as column aliases to get HTML. You can also use the FOR XML clause to get XML and transform it into HTML by using Extensible Stylesheet Language Transformations (XSLTs). You can write a CLR object that performs the transformation.

DatabaseMail delivers messages asynchronously, but the message preparation (query executions, formatting, and so on) is done synchronously by default. In some circumstances, such as when the message preparation cost is high, consider preparing the messages asynchronously by using Service Broker.

Practice: Sending E-mail Messages by Using DatabaseMail

In this practice, you will configure DatabaseMail and send e-mail messages by using the sp_send_dbmail stored procedure. Before beginning, you must set up SMTP.

On the Companion Disc   This chapter includes many code examples. You will find the lesson code from this chapter on the companion CD in the C:\My Documents\Microsoft Press\TK70-441 \Chapter14 folder.

▶ **Exercise 1: Set Up SMTP**

Before beginning the DatabaseMail exercises, you need to set up the required SMTP services by completing the following steps:

1. Verify that you have IIS 5.0 or later with the SMTP virtual server installed on your computer. The Windows setup program does not install IIS by default, and the default installation of IIS does not include SMTP services.

2. Open IIS Manager to create a domain alias for adventure-works.com.
3. Expand the local computer.
4. Expand the default virtual SMTP server.
5. Right-click Domains and select New Domain.
6. Select the Alias option and click Next.
7. Type **adventure-works.com** in the Name box and click Finish.
8. Close IIS Manager.

▶ **Exercise 2: Configure DatabaseMail**

In this exercise, you will enable DatabaseMail and create one public profile that contains one account.

1. Open SQL Server Management Studio (SSMS) and connect to the local Database Engine instance.
2. In Object Explorer, expand the Management node.
3. Right-click Database Mail and select Configure Database Mail.
4. The Database Mail Configuration Wizard dialog box appears. Select the Skip This Page In The Future check box and click Next.
5. On the Select Configuration Task page, select Setup Database Mail By Performing The Following Tasks and click Next.
6. A message box might appear, asking you to enable Database Mail. Click Yes if this message box appears.
7. On the New Profile page, type **AdventureWorksProfile** in the Profile Name box and click Add to add an account.
8. In the New Database Mail Account dialog box, type the following values in the appropriate text boxes, leave all other options at their defaults, and then click OK.

Text Box	Value
Account name	**AdventureWorksAccount**
E-mail address	**sqlserver@adventure-works.com**
Display name	**Adventure Works**
Server name	**localhost**

9. On the New Profile page, click Next.
10. On the Manage Profile Security page, select the Public Profiles tab, select the Adventure-Works Profile check box, and click Next.
11. On the Configure System Parameters page, review the parameters and click Next.
12. On the Complete The Wizard page, review the listed actions and click Finish.
13. When the wizard has completed configuring the account, click Close.

▶ **Exercise 3: Test DatabaseMail**

In this exercise, you will test DatabaseMail.

1. In Object Explorer, right-click Database Mail and select Send Test E-Mail.

2. In the Send Test Email From dialog box, in the To box, type **somebody@adventure-works.com** and click the Send Test E-Mail button.

3. In the Database Mail Test E-Mail dialog box, click OK.

4. Open Windows Explorer and navigate to C:\Inetpub\mailroot\Drop. There should be one .eml file. Double-click the .eml file to open it.

▶ **Exercise 4: Send an E-mail Message by Using sp_send_dbmail**

In this exercise, you will send an e-mail message by using the sp_send_dbmail stored procedure. The message will be formatted in HTML and will contain a query result.

1. In SSMS, open SendMail.sql, which is available on the companion CD in the C:\My Documents\Microsoft Press\TK70-441\Chapter14\Lesson1 folder.

2. Review the T-SQL code, and then execute the script by pressing F5 or the Execute button from the SQL Editor toolbar.

3. Open Windows Explorer.

4. Navigate to C:\Inetpub\mailroot\Drop. There should be a new .eml file in the folder.

5. Open the new .eml file by double-clicking it.

Quick Check

1. Which mail component would you use and why: SQL Mail or DatabaseMail?

2. Which profile type is more secure: public or private?

3. If you need to send a nonparametrized, basic-formatted query result, how would you do it?

Quick Check Answers

1. Use DatabaseMail because it uses SMTP instead of MAPI and because the send operation is performed by an external program. DatabaseMail is also more secure and reliable and easier to install than SQL Mail.

2. Private profiles give you more control over which users can use the profile.

3. Specifying the @query parameter and formatting information in the sp_send_dmail stored procedure would be the easiest way to meet the requirements.

Lesson 2: Designing SQL Server Agent Alerts

Estimated lesson time: 30 minutes

SQL Server Agent enables you to send notifications and run jobs in response to an event such as error messages from SQL Server, specific *performance conditions*, and *Windows Management Instrumentation* (WMI) events.

Alerts are automated responses to events. You can define an alert on one or more events to specify how you want SQL Server Agent to respond to their occurrence. An alert can respond to an event by notifying an administrator, running a job, or both.

The main use of alerts is to inform administrators about problems such as SQL Server errors and performance problems. A job configured as a response to an alert is typically intended to correct or further diagnose the problem. You can also use alerts for other purposes such as asynchronous processing, but you should probably use Service Broker for those cases instead.

Exam Tip   When there is more than one possible answer that meets the question requirements, choose the best one in terms of scalability, maintainability, ease of implementation, and cost.

Defining Alerts

To define an alert, you must specify the name of the alert, the event that triggers the alert, and the action to take in response to the event. The information required to define an alert depends on the selected event type. The event type can be one of the following:

- **SQL Server events**   SQL Server Agent can respond to messages logged in the Windows Application log. SQL Server logs error messages with severity 19 or higher, always-logged error messages, errors raised using RAISERROR WITH LOG, and messages logged by using the xp_logevent stored procedure. SQL Server Agent raises the alert when a message that meets the specified criteria is logged in the Windows Application log. You define the criteria by specifying the following information:
   - ❑ Either error number or error severity number.
   - ❑ An optional character string. SQL Server Agent checks whether the logged message contains this character string.
- **Performance condition**   In this case, SQL Server Agent monitors the *performance counter* you specify. It raises the alert when the performance counter value meets the condition you specify. This condition can be one of the following:
   - ❑ The performance counter value is equal to the specified value.
   - ❑ The performance counter value rises above the specified value.
   - ❑ The performance counter value falls below the specified value.

- **WMI event**   SQL Server Agent can respond to *WMI events*. In this case, you must specify the WMI namespace and the event notification query in Windows Management Instrumentation Query Language (WQL).

For more information about WQL, see the topic, "Using WQL with the WMI Provider for Server Events" in SQL Server 2005 Books Online at *http://msdn2.microsoft.com/en-us/library /ms180524.aspx.*

The action to take in response to an event can be one or both of the following:

- Execute a job.

  You can execute a job in response to an alert, and you can use tokens to get information about the event that triggered the alert. Typically, you use jobs as a response to an alert to try to solve a problem or register information about the event that triggered the alert.
- Notify operators.

  Operators are aliases for people who can be notified by e-mail, pager, or Net Send. You can specify one or more operators to be notified as well as the notification method (e-mail, pager, and/or Net Send).

Designing WMI Triggers

WMI triggers let you perform similar tasks that you do by using such SQL Server objects as DDL triggers and Event Notifications. With WMI triggers, which are SQL Server Agent alerts triggered by WMI events, you can define the action to take as a response to an event of the following types:

- **DDL events**   These types of events are raised when a DDL statement (such as CREATE TABLE or DROP TABLE) is issued.
- **Trace events**   These types of events are raised by specific activity in the SQL Server instance, such as when a deadlock occurs or when an object is created.

For a complete list of WMI events and properties, see "WMI Provider for Server Events Classes and Properties" at *http://msdn2.microsoft.com/en-us/library/ms186449.aspx.*

The difference between DDL triggers and WMI triggers is that DDL triggers are database objects that operate synchronously, whereas WMI triggers are SQL Server Agent objects that operate asynchronously.

Event Notifications are also database objects, but they operate asynchronously by using SQL Server Service Broker under the covers. In this sense, they are very similar to WMI triggers. In fact, WMI triggers use Event Notifications behind the scenes. The main difference between the two is where the event is managed: with WMI triggers, the response is managed by SQL Server Agent; with Event Notifications, the response is managed entirely in the Database Engine.

To define a WMI trigger, you first create a SQL Server Agent alert whose type must be a WMI event alert. You specify

\\.\root\Microsoft\SqlServer\ServerEvents\MSSQLSERVER

as the namespace. And you specify the WMI query in WQL—for example:

```
N'SELECT * FROM CREATE_DATABASE'
```

Then, you define the alert response. As with any SQL Server Agent alert, you can specify to run a SQL Server Agent job, to notify SQL Server Agent operators, or both. You can take advantage of token replacement so that you can access WMI event properties from within a T-SQL script job step. For example, you can use

```
'$(ESCAPE_SQUOTE(WMI(DatabaseName)))'
```

to access the DatabaseName WMI property. (For details about token replacement, see "Using Tokens in Job Steps" at *http://msdn2.microsoft.com/en-us/library/ms175575.aspx*.)

Defining and Notifying Operators

Operators are aliases for people or groups that can receive electronic notification when jobs have completed or alerts have been raised. SQL Server Agent can notify an operator by e-mail, pager, or Net Send. To define an operator, you must provide the operator name and contact information. The contact information consists of one or more of the following:

- **E-mail address**   SQL Server Agent can use either DatabaseMail or SQL Mail to send notifications by e-mail. The preferred way is using DatabaseMail. To enable SQL Server Agent for sending e-mail messages, you must set up DatabaseMail or SQL Mail and configure a profile for SQL Server Agent.
- **Net Send address (NetBIOS name for computer or user)**   SQL Server Agent uses the Windows Messenger service to send messages by Net Send. The Messenger service must be enabled on both sender and receiver computers.
- **Pager e-mail name**   For pager notification, you must have third-party pager-to-e-mail software and/or hardware.
- **Pager on duty schedule**   Defines when the operator is on duty and can be notified by pager.

You can configure a special operator, the fail-safe operator, who receives notifications when SQL Server Agent cannot notify the designed operators for an alert.

Creating User-Defined Events

With SQL Server Agent, you are not limited to pre-defined events; you can create user-defined events. To create user-defined events, you can do the following:

- Create logged user-defined error messages. You can create them by using the sp_addmessage stored procedure, specifying @*with_log* = 'TRUE'.
- Raise user-defined errors by using RAISERROR (msg_id, -1, -1). Users do not need special permissions to use RAISERROR in this way.

You can also use the xp_logevent stored procedure, but this requires being a member of the sysadmin role or being the owner of the master database. In addition, this stored procedure does not send a message to the client. Another alternative is using RAISERROR WITH LOG, but only sysadmin role members can execute this statement. You can embed xp_logevent or RAISERROR WITH LOG in stored procedures created with the EXECUTE AS clause and grant Execute permission on the stored procedures to users. In this way, you do not need to create always-logged messages available to all logins.

Practice: Creating a SQL Server Agent Alert

In this practice, you will create an alert to register drop-table WMI events for auditing purposes.

▶ **Exercise 1: Create Supporting Objects**

In this exercise, you create a table to store drop-table WMI event data.

1. In SSMS, open the CreateDropTableEventsTable.sql script, which is available on the companion CD in the C:\My Documents\Microsoft Press\TK70-441\Chapter14\Lesson2 folder.
2. Execute the script by pressing F5.

▶ **Exercise 2: Create the Alert and the Response Job**

In this exercise, you create one alert based on a WMI event and the job that will respond to the alert. The job will register drop-table WMI event data in the DropTableEvents table.

1. Ensure that SQL Server Agent is running. In Object Explorer, expand the local computer. If the SQL Server Agent icon is green, SQL Server Agent is running. If the icon is red, it is not running. If SQL Server Agent is not running, right-click it and select Start.
2. Enable token replacement by right-clicking SQL Server Agent and selecting Properties. Select the Alert System page, ensure that the Replace Tokens For All Job Responses To Alerts check box is selected, and click OK.
3. In SSMS, create the job and the alert by opening the CreateJobandAlert.sql script (from the C:\My Documents\Microsoft Press\TK70-441\Chapter14\Lesson2 folder).
4. Execute the script by pressing F5.

▶ **Exercise 3: Test the Alert**

In this exercise, you test the job and alert that you created in Exercise 2.

1. In SSMS, open the TestAlert.sql script from the TK441\Chapter14\Lesson2 folder.
2. Execute the script by pressing F5. A query result should appear in less than a minute.

Quick Check

1. Which methods can you use to send an alert to an operator?
2. What types of events can trigger an alert?
3. You are using user-defined error messages in your application to trigger alerts, and your application uses stored procedures extensively. How can you prevent users from directly raising and logging these messages?

Quick Check Answers

1. Alerts can be sent to operators by e-mail, pager, and Net Send.
2. SQL Server error messages, performance conditions, and WMI events can trigger an alert.
3. You can create non-always-logged messages, embed RAISERROR WITH LOG in your stored procedures and triggers, and specify the EXECUTE AS clause for the procedures and triggers.

Lesson 3: Specifying a Web Services Solution for Distributing Data

Estimated lesson time: 30 minutes

SQL Server 2005 introduces native support for XML Web services in the database engine by using open standards such as HTTP, *Simple Object Access Protocol* (SOAP), and *Web Services Description Language* (WSDL).

In earlier versions of SQL Server, the only available protocol was Tabular Data Stream (TDS). In SQL Server 2005, client applications can access database engine functionality by using other protocols such as HTTP. When using *SQL Server Web services*, clients no longer need Microsoft Data Access Components (MDAC) installed, and non-Windows clients can access the database engine directly.

SQL Server Web services requires and uses the HTTP listener http.sys, which is available in Microsoft Windows Server 2003, Windows XP Service Pack 2 (SP2), and Windows Vista. Http.sys is not available in earlier versions of Windows. Because SQL Server uses the http.sys driver directly, IIS is not required to support SQL Server Web services.

SQL Server Web services enables you to expose stored procedures and scalar user-defined functions (UDFs) as Web methods. You can also configure a SQL Server Web service to allow ad hoc queries. When ad hoc queries are enabled, clients can execute batches by calling the sqlbatch Web method.

Creating and Defining SQL Server Web Services

To define a SQL Server Web service, you basically specify the following:

- Stored procedures and scalar UDFs to be exposed as Web methods as well as their corresponding Web method names.
- Whether ad hoc queries (batches) are allowed.
- Security information, including the authentication type and whether to use SSL, clear HTTP, or both.
- Port information. You can specify the port for SSL, which defaults to 443, and the port for HTTP, which defaults to 80.
- Whether gzip compression is enabled or disabled. When gzip compression is enabled and the client accepts gzip encoding, SQL Server compresses the response.
- The location. You specify the location by using a Uniform Resource Locator (URL).
- Whether WSDL is returned.
- Whether an XML schema definition (XSD) schema is returned for SELECT statements.

To create a SQL Server Web service, you must create an *HTTP endpoint* by using the T-SQL CREATE ENDPOINT statement and specifying the preceding information.

SQL Server Web Services Security

SQL Server Web services supports the following authentication types:

- **Basic authentication** The client sends the credentials (username and password) in clear text. These credentials must map to a valid Windows account. You must use SSL with basic authentication because SQL Server does not allow basic authentication and clear HTTP at the same time.
- **Digest authentication** The client sends the credentials hashed by MD5 (a message digest algorithm). The credentials must map to a valid domain user account. Digest authentication requires a Windows Server 2003 domain controller.
- **NTLM authentication** This authentication mechanism is a challenge–response protocol that offers stronger authentication than either basic or digest. NTLM authentication is supported by Windows 95 and later.
- **Kerberos authentication** This is an Internet standard authentication mechanism. Kerberos authentication is supported in Windows 2000 and later.
- **Integrated authentication** This is a combination of NTLM and Kerberos; SQL Server permits both.

BEST PRACTICES **Kerberos or Integrated authentication**

Use Kerberos or Integrated authentication for optimum security.

SQL Server supports SSL for SQL Server Web services to secure the communication between client and server. SSL encrypts and signs the information on the wire and can be used for server authentication. To use SSL in SQL Server Web services, you must install a certificate in the server and register the certificate in http.sys.

BEST PRACTICES **SSL for sensitive data**

Use SSL to exchange sensitive data.

Endpoints are securable objects. To execute a Web method, a user must have CONNECT permission on the endpoint.

BEST PRACTICES **Limit endpoint connect permissions**

Limit endpoint connect permissions to specific users or groups.

Guidelines for Using SQL Server Web Services

SQL Server Web services are well suited for the following scenarios:

- Applications that send or receive XML data
- Applications conforming to the Service-Oriented Architecture (SOA)
- As a more performant replacement for SQLXML

SQL Server Web services are not well suited for the following scenarios:

- Applications with high concurrent access and short-duration transactions
- As a replacement for the middle tier
- Applications that use large object (LOB) data types

Practice: Creating a SQL Server Web Service

In this practice, you will create a SQL Server Web service and use a Windows application to access the Web service.

▶ **Exercise 1: Create Supporting Objects**

In this exercise, you create a stored procedure that will be exposed in the Web service as a Web method.

1. In SSMS, open the CreateSupportingObjects.sql script from the C:\My Documents \Microsoft Press\TK70-441\Chapter14\Lesson3 folder.
2. Execute the script by pressing F5.

▶ **Exercise 2: Create the HTTP Endpoint**

In this exercise, you create the HTTP endpoint that will expose the stored procedure you created in Exercise 1.

1. In SSMS, open the CreateHttpEndpoint.sql script from the C:\My Documents\Microsoft Press\TK70-441\Chapter14\Lesson3 folder.
2. Review the code and execute the script by pressing F5.

▶ **Exercise 3: Use a Client Application**

In this exercise, you use a Windows application to access the SQL Server Web service you created in Exercise 2.

1. With Visual Studio 2005, Visual C# Express, or Visual Basic Express, open either the CS\AWCatalog.csproj file or the VB\AWCatalog.vbproj file from the C:\My Documents \Microsoft Press\TK70-441\Chapter14\Lesson3 folder.
2. In Solution Explorer, right-click Web References and select Add Web Reference.
3. In the URL text box, type **http://localhost:8086/AdventureWorks/Catalog?WSDL** and click Go. The AWCatalog description should appear below.

4. In the Web Reference Name box, type SQLWebService and click Add Reference.
5. Right-click Form1.cs or Form1.vb and select View Code.
6. Review the code.
7. Execute the application by pressing F5.
8. In the Subcategory Name box, type **Mountain Bikes** and click Go. A list of mountain bikes should appear on the grid.
9. Close Form1 and close Visual Studio.

Quick Check

1. You want to use an HTTP endpoint to exchange sensitive data between SQL Server and mobile devices. Which protocol would you use?
2. Non-Windows clients need access to an HTTP endpoint. Which authentication mechanism would you use?
3. For security reasons, you do not want to expose WSDL to clients. What can you do?
4. Remote clients access your SQL Server Web service by using a low-speed connection. How can you improve the performance?

Quick Check Answers

1. HTTPS would provide appropriate privacy.
2. Kerberos is the best choice if clients support it. Because Kerberos is an Internet standard, it is supported by many operating systems. If clients do not support Kerberos or NTLM, digest is the preferred choice. Basic should be your last choice.
3. Disable WSDL generation on the HTTP endpoint.
4. Enabling gzip compression would improve the performance in this scenario if clients accept gzip encoding.

Lesson 4: Specifying a Reporting Services Solution for Distributing Data

---

Estimated lesson time: 30 minutes

There are many scenarios in which you need to distribute data to end users in a report format. You likely often need to send financial or sales reports to users on a given schedule, for example. SSRS enables you to meet these requirements to distribute data to end users in a scheduled way and in many report formats.

Reporting Services Delivery Options

When you implement an SSRS solution, you need to decide which delivery options you will give users so the users can subscribe to the reports they need. These options are:

- **Pull**   You can publish the reports to the Report Manager Web site so that users can go to the site and subscribe to the information they need.
- **Push**   You can publish the reports to the Report Manager and then configure subscriptions to deliver the reports to users by using a Delivery extension.

By default, SSRS SP2 provides four delivery extensions: E-mail, File Share, SharePoint, and NULL provider (used to fill the cache). However, you can extend this functionality by developing your own delivery extensions. For information about how to develop your own delivery extension, see the topic "Implementing a Delivery Extension" in SQL Server 2005 Books Online at *http://msdn2.microsoft.com/en-us/library/ms154050.aspx*.

Reporting Services Subscriptions

The component that SSRS uses to deliver a report on a specific schedule and to present the report in a given format is called a subscription. There are two types of subscriptions:

- **Standard subscriptions**   Created and managed by the end users. Standard subscriptions are created by end users to access the reports they need.

■ **Data-driven subscriptions**   Dynamic subscriptions that SSRS administrators create to distribute reports to a wide variety of users and in many different formats. With *data-driven subscriptions*, report delivery and parameters are dynamic and retrieved from a data source at run time.

Data-driven subscriptions are the most useful way to distribute data by using SSRS.

IMPORTANT   **SSRS features in SQL Server 2005 Express Edition**

Reporting Services subscriptions are not supported in SQL Server 2005 Express Edition with Advanced Services. For more information about the features in this edition, see the topic "Reporting Services in SQL Server 2005 Express Edition with Advanced Services" in SQL Server 2005 Books Online at *http://msdn2.microsoft.com/en-us/library/ms365166.aspx*.

Distributing Data by Using Data-Driven Subscriptions

SSRS data-driven subscriptions have some requirements:

■ Credentials for the report data source should be stored in the Report Server.

■ Use SQL Server 2005 Enterprise Edition.

■ You must be able to get dynamic information from a data source. You can use several data sources to get this information, such as SQL Server, Oracle, XML files, and a SQL Server Analysis Services (SSAS) database.

Creating a Data-Driven Subscription

To create a data-driven subscription, complete the following steps:

1. Open SQL Server Management Studio and connect to the Reporting Services instance. Navigate to the Report node, right click it, and choose New Data Driven Subscription.

2. Define the delivery data source to retrieve dynamic information, as Figure 14-2 shows.

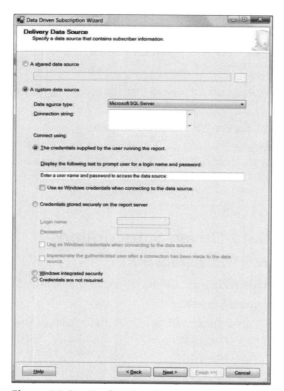

Figure 14-2   Configuring the data-driven delivery data source

3. After you have configured the delivery data source, specify the query to get the information from the data source.

4. Depending on the delivery method you select, you can map dynamic data to fields from the query or specify fixed values. For example, for an e-mail delivery, you can specify the To, CC, CCO, and Subject parameters.

5. If the selected report has parameters, you need to specify values for them. Again, you can map parameters to fields from the query.

6. Finally, you need to specify when the subscription will be executed: on a given schedule or when the report is updated in the Report Server.

You can create data-driven subscriptions from SSMS by connecting to the SSRS instance or in Report Manager.

Practice: Specifying SSRS Options for Distributing Data

In this practice, you will consider the best options for using SSRS to distribute data to end users.

▶ **Exercise 1: Delivery Extension**

In this conceptual exercise, you will think about the best scenario for each delivery extension so you can choose the best extension to meet user requirements.

Which delivery extension should you use to distribute data to end users? This is a broad question; you should think over all possibilities and then compare your solution with the suggested answer.

Suggested Answer

All delivery extensions could work to distribute data to end users, but data-driven subscriptions are the best way to maintain a distribution strategy in SSRS.

▶ **Exercise 2: Data-Driven Subscriptions**

Explain the advantages of using data-driven subscriptions for distributing data to end users.

Suggested Answer

Data-driven subscriptions enable you to configure dynamic subscriptions that retrieve information from an external data source so that you can specify format, delivery extension, destinations, and so on.

Quick Check

1. Which delivery extensions are provided by default with SSRS?
2. Can you use data-driven subscriptions with all SQL Server 2005 editions?

Quick Check Answers

1. By default, SSRS with SP2 provides four delivery extensions: E-mail, File Share, SharePoint, and Null providers.
2. No, data-driven subscriptions are available only in Enterprise edition.

Lesson 5: Specifying a Notification Services Solution for Distibuting Data

---

Estimated lesson time: 30 minutes

SQL Server *Notification Services* is a flexible and scalable platform and hosting environment for creating and deploying applications that generate and send notifications to subscribers (users and applications). Notification Services can send notifications when events occur or on a schedule and can deliver the notifications to a wide variety of devices. For example, you can use Notification Services to distribute weather data to users. As weather data arrives, the Notification Services application can send the weather data by e-mail to users. Or, your users might be stock market investors who are interested in specific stocks; when the stock price falls below a specified value on a stock, investors receive a notification.

Notification Services Architecture

Notification Services applications collect events, match events with subscriptions to generate notifications, and format and deliver the notifications to subscribers. Figure 14-3 illustrates the Notification Services architecture.

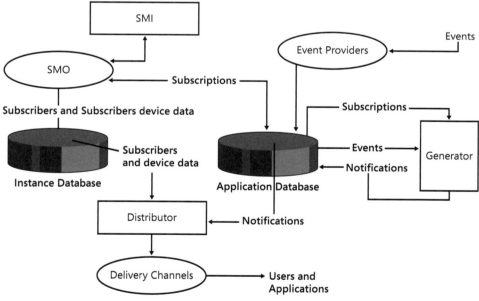

Figure 14-3   Notification Services architecture

Subscription management interfaces (SMI) are custom applications such as Web or Windows applications that manage subscribers and subscribers' device data and allow users to create subscriptions by using subscription management objects (SMOs).

Subscribers and subscriber device data is stored in the Notification Services instance database. There is only one instance database per instance. Subscription data is stored in the application database. There can be several applications running on an instance, and each application has its own application database.

Notification Services collects events by using event providers. Event providers collect events and use the event provider application programming interface (API) to store event data in the application database. You can use one of the pre-defined event providers, or you can create a custom event provider by using the event provider API. You can also use the event provider API to send event data directly.

The Notification Services generator, running at pre-defined intervals, matches event data with subscriptions to generate notifications. The generator stores notifications data in the application database.

After the generator creates a batch of notifications, the distributor formats the messages and sends them to users and applications through one or more delivery channels. Delivery channels use delivery protocols. You can use built-in delivery protocols or create and use custom delivery protocols. (Chapter 16, "Developing Applications for Notification Services," discusses designing applications for Notification Services.)

Scale-Out Options

Notification Services can be installed on the same server as the database engine that hosts Notification Services databases. This can be appropriate in some scenarios, such as for small applications, but when you need to manage a large number of notifications, you probably need to use one of the following scale-out options:

- Install the database engine and Notification Services on different servers. This frees up the database engine server from formatting and delivery operations.
- Install several instances of Notification Services on different servers and use multiple distributors for applications.
- Partition subscriptions in several instances of Notification Services installed on different servers.

Defining Notification Services Applications

To define Notification Services applications to distribute data, specify the following general information:

- The data to send. You define the data to send by defining notification classes.
- The recipients. The recipients are the subscribers. Subscribers have associated device data. You define which users and applications can receive notifications. You can manage subscribers and devices by using subscription management objects.
- When to send the data. Notification Services sends notifications to subscribers when events match subscriptions. You can define several event classes and subscription classes.
- The subscription management interface. You define the interface to manage subscribers, subscriber device data, and subscriptions. This interface is typically a Web application or a Windows application but can be any kind of application that uses subscription management objects.
- How to send the data. You can send the notifications by e-mail or by simply dropping a file on the file system. If you must send the notifications by other means, you need to create custom delivery protocols.
- Determine where events come from. Event data can come from a variety of sources. Notification Services has built-in support for event data that comes from XML files and SQL Server databases. If the events come from other sources, you can create custom event providers or use an external application that sends events to Notification Services.
- The message format. You can specify XSLT transformations to format messages.

Practice: Identifying When to Use a Notification Services Solution

In this practice, you will explore when you should use Notification Services as the best way to distribute data.

▶ **Exercise 1: Notification Services vs. Reporting Services**

In this conceptual exercise, you will learn when to use Notification Services instead of Reporting Services as a data distribution technology.

When should you use Notification Services instead of Reporting Services to distribute data? This is a broad question; think over all possibilities and then compare your findings with the suggested answer.

Suggested Answer

Both technologies enable you to distribute data by using different delivery channels. Reporting Services provides more flexibility for formatting data. However, Notification Services gives you more flexibility to respond to events instead of using a scheduled delivery, which is the most common scenario for Reporting Services.

▶ **Exercise 2: Notification Services vs. DatabaseMail**

In this exercise, you will learn when you should use Notification Services instead of Database-Mail as a data distribution technology.

When should you use Notification Services instead of DatabaseMail to distribute data? This is a broad question; think over all possibilities and then compare your findings with the suggested answer.

Suggested Answer

DatabaseMail enables you to distribute data only by e-mail. Use DatabaseMail only in scenarios in which you need to distribute data that does not need much formatting and that you can distribute through e-mail. Otherwise, Notification Services provides a more flexible solution.

Quick Check

1. You started with a small Notification Services application that managed a relatively small number of notifications. The number of subscribers and notifications has increased over time, and your system will soon be insufficient. How would you solve the problem?
2. An external application sends you event data by calling an HTTP endpoint that you are developing. How can you send event data to a notification application?
3. You need to deliver notifications to a Microsoft Message Queue (MSMQ). How can you do that?

Quick Check Answers

1. You can start by scaling up your system—adding more processors and memory could be a solution, at least for the short term. If this is not enough, you can scale out your Notification Services application. Start by moving Notification Services to a different server from the database engine server.
2. You can use the event provider API to send event data directly to a notification application. You would use SQL Server event provider API stored procedures.
3. You can create a custom delivery protocol to deliver notifications to an MSMQ.

Case Scenario: Design a Distributed Data Solution

You are the database solution developer for an airline that needs to distribute data about its flights to several travel agencies. The agencies need to access your data in real time, and they have different information systems to process your data. After examining the requirements, you think that data should be transmitted already formatted as XML, but you are not sure about what SQL Server technology you should use to distribute the data to the agencies. The travel agencies are requesting direct access to your systems, but your security policy does not allow it.

1. What data-distribution technology should you use to meet the scenario requirements?
2. What steps should you follow to implement the technology?
3. How can you protect transmitted data?

Chapter Summary

- DatabaseMail to send data as e-mail messages is a more reliable, scalable, and secure way than by the obsolete SQL Mail.

- SQL Server Web services give client applications access to database functionality through HTTP and SOAP protocols and enable the exchange of information in XML format.

- Notification Services create scalable applications that send notifications to subscribers based on events.

- Reporting Services distribute data as reports.

- SQL Server Agent alerts inform administrators about operational information such as application errors or performance problems.

Chapter 15

Designing Applications That Support Reporting and Use Reporting Services

Microsoft SQL Server 2005 includes SQL Server Reporting Services (SSRS), a server-based solution for building reports. Reporting tools such as SSRS query the relational engine and summarize information for users. This type of data access often loads the database with frequent and complex queries.

In this chapter, you will learn how to develop applications designed to support reporting activities. You will see how to configure different database options and technologies to increase the scalability of the reporting environment, and you will learn how to use indexes, views, and stored procedures to increase maintainability and performance of your solution. Finally, you will learn how to configure and optimize SSRS solutions.

Exam objectives in this chapter:

- Design an application solution that supports reporting.
  - ❏ Design a snapshot strategy.
  - ❏ Design the schema.
  - ❏ Design the data transformation.
  - ❏ Design indexes for reporting.
  - ❏ Choose programmatic interfaces.
  - ❏ Evaluate use of reporting services.
  - ❏ Decide which data access method to use.
- Develop applications that use Reporting Services.
  - ❏ Specify subscription models, testing reports, error handling, and server impact.
  - ❏ Design reports.
  - ❏ Specify data source configuration.
  - ❏ Optimize reports.

Before You Begin

To complete the lessons in this chapter, you must have:

■ A computer that meets the hardware and software requirements for SQL Server 2005.

■ SQL Server 2005 Developer Edition, Workgroup Edition, Standard Edition, or Enterprise Edition installed. Database Engine and Reporting Services components must be installed.

■ The SQL Server 2005 *AdventureWorks* sample database installed. Sample databases are available with SQL Server 2005 Enterprise Edition but are not a part of the default installation. Alternatively, you can install the sample databases from *http://msdn2.microsoft.com /en-us/library/ms143739.aspx.*

■ Microsoft Visual Studio 2005 or Microsoft Visual Basic or C# 2005 Express Edition installed. You can download Visual Studio Express Editions from *http://msdn.microsoft.com /vstudio/express/.*

Lesson 1: Evaluating the Use of Reporting Services and Designing Reports

Estimated lesson time: 20 minutes

One of the reasons companies and other organizations build databases is to share information among employees and business partners. SSRS enables organizations to transform their data into valuable information—information that can be shared and distributed at any level of the organization. In this lesson, you will learn the basics of building SSRS reports and different scenarios in which SSRS might be a useful tool.

Evaluating Reporting Services Uses

SSRS can be used in a wide set of scenarios. Based on its uses, it can be classified by audience, integration, or construction. Based on the audience, SSRS can deliver reports to departmental, corporate, or external audiences. Based on how reports are integrated with other applications, SSRS can distribute reports as a standalone application, in portal solutions, or embedded in business applications. Finally, based on construction, reporting solutions can be pre-defined or ad hoc reports.

Report Uses by Audience

One point to consider when designing solutions that use SSRS is the audience of the reports. You will have to take into account different factors based on which audience will consume the reports.

Departmental   When designing SSRS solutions for departmental audiences, consider the following factors:

- The solution usually needs to support only a small group of users. A typical departmental solution has between 5 and 50 users.
- Very rapid development is a frequent request.
- Often, data comes from a single data source. Combining and integrating data is unusual.
- Scalability is rarely an issue in these scenarios.
- Microsoft Windows authentication is adequate. In departmental solutions, Windows impersonation is frequently used.

Corporate   When designing SSRS solutions for corporate audiences, consider these characteristics:

- These solutions usually serve a large number of users. It is not extraordinary to support thousands of users.
- Scalability is a critical element when working with corporate audiences.

- Security is also an essential operational requirement.

- Often, data comes from multiple data sources. Combining and integrating data is a frequent request.

- Windows authentication is adequate. Corporate solutions mostly use delegation instead of impersonation.

Extranet   Extranet solutions, no matter how many users they support, are similar to corporate solutions, but the use of the Internet brings these additional considerations:

- Security is the most critical element for extranet reporting solutions. Expert knowledge in Web development and implementation is desirable.

- Development of custom extensions is often required. These custom extensions usually include proprietary-form Web authentication.

Reporting Services Integration

Another important consideration when designing SSRS solutions is how the reports will be delivered.

Standalone   When using SSRS as a standalone application, users interact with SSRS through a Web browser. To activate reports, users navigate to the Report Server virtual directory. By default, the URL for the Report Server is *http://ServerName/Reports*. You can change the default URL by using the Reporting Services Configuration Manager. When users navigate to the Report Server virtual directory, the home page will offer a Web interface for navigating through, displaying, and managing reports. Figure 15-1 shows a sample report.

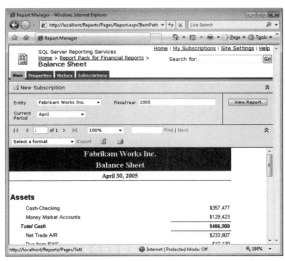

Figure 15-1   Report from a standalone Reporting Services implementation

Portal Integration   Another way of using SSRS is to integrate SSRS reports into a corporate or departmental portal. Including SSRS in a portal solution requires different software components that can interact with each other to generate a rich user experience. For example, you can use Windows SharePoint Services or Microsoft Office SharePoint Server with Microsoft Office Business Scorecard Manager 2005 and SSRS to provide business-critical information, as Figure 15-2 shows.

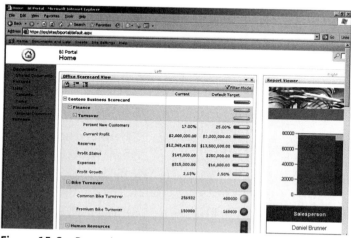

Figure 15-2   Reporting Services in a portal solution

Using SSRS in a portal solution requires a large number of very small reports with high performance requirements. Another element to consider in portal solutions is the need to access a wide variety of data sources.

Embedded Reporting   Finally, SSRS reports frequently are embedded in Web and Windows applications. In this scenario, developers use the SSRS infrastructure to extend the functionality of their applications with reporting capabilities. Figure 15-3 shows an example of what an embedded SSRS solution might look like.

When you use SSRS to extend a Windows or Web application, you will have to evaluate how the application will manage the metadata of the SSRS solution. Metadata management offers users the possibilities of navigating the Report Server folder structure, dynamically selecting reports, and managing report history and subscription elements.

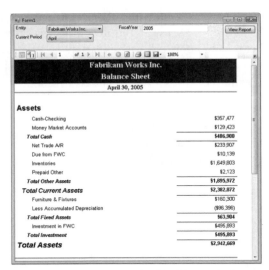

Figure 15-3   Report embedded in a Windows application

Reporting Services Construction

Finally, when designing an SSRS, consider how reports will be developed. SSRS offers two major report-building models. In the first model, professional developers create pre-defined reports in a standard development model. In the second model, developers create a framework for users to develop their own reports.

Pre-Defined Reports   The pre-defined reports model uses a standard development cycle. Users request certain reports, and someone evaluates the business need for the reports and ensures that all the functional and operational requirements are captured. A developer or development team then builds the reports, another developer or team tests the reports, and operations then deploys the reports.

In this scenario, reporting developers use SQL Server Business Intelligence Development Studio (BIDS) to create reports. BIDS extends Visual Studio 2005 with business intelligence (BI) project templates, including SSRS, SQL Server Analysis Services (SSAS), SQL Server Integration Services (SSIS), and Report Model project templates.

Ad Hoc Reporting   Ad hoc reporting requires a different approach to include users in the development cycle. Instead of using a single development cycle for building reports, ad hoc reporting breaks the development cycle into two phases. The first phase is the creation of a data model, and the second is the actual creation of the reports.

Developers lead the first stage of creating an ad hoc reporting solution. The objective of this phase is to create a report model. A report model is a metadata description of the data source, and it includes familiar names for database objects, denormalization of the database schema to mimic a more conceptual model, the definition of calculated elements, and so on. SSRS uses the report model to generate SQL statements automatically to the underlying data source.

After the model is created and deployed in a traditional development cycle, the second part of building the solution begins. In this phase, expert users navigate the model and select the data they want to use to create reports. Report Builder is a new tool that presents the report model and enables users to create reports in a straightforward interface. After users create and deploy the reports they need, the operations team is responsible for configuring and managing the reports.

Designing Reporting Services Reports

One of the main elements of SSRS is the data source. A data source is what developers define to configure how SSRS will get the data it needs for reports. A data source definition in SSRS requires a name, a data provider, a connection string, and a security configuration.

Configuring the Data Source

SQL Server 2005 reports can specify a data source in three different ways:

- **As a shared data source**   Shared data sources are individual items that can be reused in multiple reports.
- **As a fixed, embedded data source**   Fixed data sources are connections defined within the report. They are report-specific data sources.
- **As a dynamic expression**   A dynamic expression generates the connection information dynamically at run time.

▶ **Creating a Data Source from Report Manager**

You can use SQL Server Management Studio (SSMS) or Report Manager to create shared data sources. To create a new data source from Report Manager, follow these steps:

1. Using Microsoft Internet Explorer, navigate to the Report Server Manager. By default, the URL for Report Server is *http://ServerName/Reports*.
2. Navigate to the folder in which you want to create the data source.
3. Click the New Data Source button from the Report Server Manager to reach the New Data Source window.

4. In the *Name* field, type the data source name.

5. To use the *AdventureWorks* sample database, select Microsoft SQL Server in the Connection Type drop-down list.

6. In the *Connection String* field, type **Data Source=(local);Initial Catalog=AdventureWorks** to connect to the *AdventureWorks* sample database.

7. Select the type of connection that Reporting Services will use to connect to the database. To use impersonation, select Windows Integrated Security; to configure delegation, select Credentials Stored Securely In The Report Server and configure the username and password.

▶ **Creating a Shared Data Source from BIDS**

To create a shared data source using BIDS, perform the following steps:

1. From the main menu, click File, click New, and then choose Project.

2. In the New Project dialog box, for Project Types, select Business Intelligence Projects.

3. Select Report Server Project.

4. Name the project and click OK.

5. In Solution Explorer, right-click the Shared Data Source folder and select Add New Data Source.

6. In the Shared Data Source dialog box, name the data source.

7. Configure the connection type and the connection string.

8. Click the OK button to generate the connection string automatically.

Building Reporting Services Reports

SSRS supports two different ways of building reports. You can create reports by using Report Builder or by using the Report Designer built into BIDS. Report Builder enables users to create simple reports. Report Designer offers a wider range of report-authoring features.

When using Report Designer, you can create a report in three different ways:

- By using the Report Wizard
- By creating a blank report
- By importing an existing report from Microsoft Office Access

The Report Wizard takes you through a series of steps required to build the report. The report requires the following steps:

1. Select the data source.

   The wizard enables you to create a report data source. If the wizard is executed after the project is created, you can also select a previously created shared data source.

2. Design the query.

   Use the Query Designer to create the SQL or MDX statement that will provide the data to the report.

3. Select the report type.

   The wizard supports two types of reports: tabular and matrix. You cannot create chart and freeform reports in the wizard; you must use a blank report. You can choose, from a pre-defined set, template styles that configure default colors and fonts for the report.

4. Select the deployment destination (optional).

   When the wizard is run while creating the project, it will enable you to configure the server and folder to which the report will be deployed.

5. Configure the report name.

The following practice walks you through the steps required to create a report by using the Report Wizard.

Practice: Creating a Report with the Report Wizard

In this practice, you will create a simple report by using the Report Wizard included in BIDS. The report will summarize sales information by a salesperson.

On the Companion Disc   This chapter includes many code examples. You will find all the code from this chapter on the companion CD in the C:\My Documents\Microsoft Press\TK70-441 \Chapter15\ folder.

▶ Exercise 1: Add a New Report

In this exercise, you will use the Report template included in BIDS to create a new SSRS project. The template will automatically launch the Report Wizard to help you create a shared data source and an SSRS report.

1. Open BIDS.
2. From the main menu, click File, click New, and then choose Project.
3. Select Business Intelligence Projects from Project Types.
4. Select the Report Server Project Wizard template. Name the project **SalesReports** and click OK to begin the wizard.
5. The Welcome To The Report Wizard page appears. Click Next.
6. On the Select The Data Source page, create a new data source. Name the data source **AdventureWorks**.

7. Leave the default data source type as Microsoft SQL Server. Click Edit to configure the connection string.

8. The Connection Properties dialog box appears. In the *Server Name* field, type **localhost**. From the Database Name drop-down list, type or select **AdventureWorks**. Leave the security as Use Windows Authentication. Click Test Connection to validate the connection information, and then click OK to continue.

9. On the Select The Data Source page, select the Make This A Shared Data Source check box and click Next to continue.

10. On the Design The Query page, click Query Builder to create the SQL command to get the data.

11. In the Query Designer pane, type the following query, which selects sales from the SalesOrderHeader table and summarizes the information by salesperson name:

```
SELECT Person.Contact.FirstName + ' ' + Person.Contact.LastName
    AS FullName
    , SUM(Sales.SalesOrderHeader.SubTotal) AS SubTotal
FROM Sales.SalesOrderHeader
INNER JOIN Sales.SalesPerson
ON Sales.SalesOrderHeader.SalesPersonID = Sales.SalesPerson.SalesPersonID INNER JOIN
HumanResources.Employee
ON Sales.SalesPerson.SalesPersonID = HumanResources.Employee.EmployeeID
    AND Sales.SalesPerson.SalesPersonID = HumanResources.Employee.EmployeeID INNER JOIN
Person.Contact
ON HumanResources.Employee.ContactID = Person.Contact.ContactID
AND HumanResources.Employee.ContactID = Person.Contact.ContactID
GROUP BY Person.Contact.FirstName + ' ' + Person.Contact.LastName
```

12. Click OK to return to the wizard.

13. Click Next to accept the query and continue.

14. On the Select The Report Type page, select Tabular and click Next.

15. On the Design The Table page, add FullName and SubTotal as details. Click the Details button twice. Click Next to accept the table design and continue.

16. On the Choose The Table Style page, select Ocean and click Next.

17. On the Choose The Deployment Location page, review the default deployment options and click Next to continue.

18. On the Completing The Wizard page, name the report **SalesSummary** and click Finish to generate the report.

19. To preview the report in BIDS, in the Report Designer, select the Preview pane.

▶ **Exercise 2: Edit a Generated Report**

In this practice, you will make final changes to the report and use the Report Designer to edit some of the default attributes generated by the Report Wizard. You will make the Full Name column wider, add a general total amount, and set a currency format to the Sub Total column.

1. Select the layout pane of the Report Designer.

2. Select the Full Name column by first selecting the Full Name text box, in blue; when the table displays the handles, select the column header displayed over the Full Name text box, as Figure 15-4 shows.

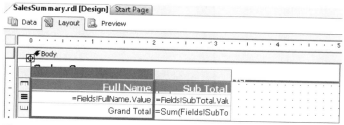

Figure 15-4 Selection of the column, not the field

3. In the Properties pane, select the Width property and set the value to 2in.

4. Change the TextAlign property to Right.

5. Right-click the handle in the last row of the table and, from the shortcut menu, select Table Footer.

   A footer is added to the table control.

6. From the View menu, select Datasets to display the Datasets pane.

7. Expand Report Datasets, and then AdventureWorks to display the columns. Drag and drop the *subtotal* field to the cell located in the new footer row and the Sub Total column. Notice that the value of the cell is =Sum(Fields!SubTotal.Value).

8. Select the Sub Total column by first selecting the Sub Total text box and, when the table handles are displayed, select the column header section over the Sub Total text box.

9. In the Properties pane, select the format property and type the letter **c**. The letter c will configure a currency format.

10. In the Properties pane, select the Width property and set the value to 1.25in.

11. Select the cell in the footer row and the FullName column. Type **Grand Total**.

12. Change the TextAlign property to Right in the Properties pane.

13. Select the Preview pane in the Report Designer to preview the report.

Quick Check

1. You have been working with SSRS in a departmental environment and have been asked to work with reports for a corporate solution. What new operational requirements challenges might you face at this new level?

2. Which is not an SSRS component?
   A. Report model
   B. Data source
   C. Data model
   D. Report

3. Which tool will you use to create an SSRS report?

Quick Check Answers

1. When working at a corporate level, scalability, security, and data integration are operational requirements to which you will have to give additional consideration to create effective reporting solutions.

2. The correct answer is C. SSRS uses three main files to provide its functionality: reports, data sources, and report models.

3. BIDS is the preferred development tool for the Microsoft platform and can be used to create SSRS Reports.

Lesson 2: Designing a Snapshot Strategy, Schema, Indexes, and Data Transformations

Estimated lesson time: 40 minutes

Solutions that use SSRS must take into account the types of queries that will be executed in the database. These queries frequently take a large number of rows and summarize information. Therefore, the SSRS architect should consider the burden of queries supporting the report and the impact the report will have on the server and other users. For example, some reports will block rows and tables in the database, preventing other users from modifying data. Other reports might use server resources so intensively that they will affect overall performance at the server level.

In this lesson, you will learn about four different design decisions that can help you build an effective SSRS solution. Those decisions involve the snapshot strategy, the database schema, the data transformation, and the indexes.

Reporting Services Real-Time Requirements

To have a better understanding of how different strategies affect the performance, availability, and scalability of the reporting services solutions, you also need to understand one of the most important business requirements of a report: how up to date reports need to be. Regarding time, there are three options to choose from: real-time, near real-time, or regularly refreshed. Reports that require real time will demand more from the database engine and will limit the options that you have as a designer; regularly refreshed reports will broaden your options.

Sometimes, reports need to provide real-time information. Real-time reports provide information about transactions that have been stored in the database as close as one microsecond ago. Real-time reports use transactional tables—the same tables that store the rows being modified by users.

Alternatively, reports can provide near real-time information. Near real-time reports provide information from a source that is usually just a few minutes away from real time. This type of report is similar to the real-time report except that it does not use the same transactional tables that users are modifying.

Further, reports might provide information that is refreshed on a scheduled basis. This type of report is usually based on tables that have been optimized for reporting purposes and are rarely modified by users.

Real-Time Reports

Because real-time reports query the same rows that users are modifying and use the same server resources, they are the most demanding on the SQL Server Database Engine. Optimizing real-time reports is a critical task because the report's performance not only affects report users but also the rest of the operational transactional users.

For real-time reports, consider using:

- SNAPSHOT and READ COMMITTED SNAPSHOT transaction isolation levels.
- Selective denormalization.
- Summary tables maintained by triggers.

Near Real-Time Reports

To support near real-time reports, consider using:

- Database snapshots.
- Database mirroring.
- Log shipping.
- Database replication.
- Summary tables maintained by SQL Server Agent jobs.

Scheduled Refresh Reports

To provide support to reports refreshed on a schedule, consider using:

- Star or snowflake schema.
- Online analytical processing (OLAP) reporting.

Designing the Snapshot Strategy

SQL Server 2005 offers a set of technologies and techniques—including transaction isolation levels, database snapshots, database mirroring, log shipping, and replication—that you can use to provide support for different types of reports. Let's look at which techniques might be useful in each type of report.

Transaction Isolation Levels: Snapshot and Read Committed Snapshot

A fundamental functionality of relational engines such as SQL Server is the use of transactions. Transactions in SQL Server support the four ACID properties: atomicity, consistency, isolation, and durability. Isolation is particularly interesting from the SSRS perspective because it controls how independent transactions are from each other. SQL Server 2005 supports six different isolation levels: read uncommitted, read committed, repeatable read, serializable, snapshot isolation, and read committed snapshot isolation.

Exam Tip   Questions about snapshot isolation and read committed snapshot isolation levels are more frequent because these are new in SQL Server 2005.

Snapshot isolation and the read committed snapshot isolation levels in SQL Server 2005 are additions that make the most sense for reporting purposes. These two types of isolation levels use row versioning to avoid conflicts and prevent readers from blocking writers. Other types of isolation levels use shared locks from readers, preventing other users from changing information until the transactions are committed.

To enable snapshot isolation, you need to take two steps. First, set the ALLOW_SNAPSHOT _ISOLATION option of the database to ON. Second, set the transaction isolation level to snapshot in each appropriate connection.

To enable snapshot isolation, use the following:

```
ALTER DATABASE DatabaseName SET ALLOW_SNAPSHOT_ISOLATION;
```

To use snapshot isolation, use the following:

```
SET TRANSACTION ISOLATION LEVELSNAPSHOT;
```

If reports or other database applications use snapshot isolation, each time they send a statement to the server, they will receive a copy of data before the start of the transaction. The main advantage of snapshot isolation is that database readers always get a consistent version of the data.

The other type of isolation level that uses row versioning is the read committed snapshot. You enable read committed snapshot isolation at the database level by using the *ALTER DATABASE* command. To enable read committed snapshot isolation, use the following:

```
ALTER DATABASE DatabaseName SET READ_COMMITTED_SNAPSHOT ON;
```

IMPORTANT   Changing to the read committed snapshot

When changing to the read committed snapshot isolation level, there must be no active connections to the database except for the connection executing the *ALTER DATABASE* command.

The read committed snapshot isolation level changes the behavior of the read committed isolation level. Because of that, there is no need to change the default isolation level in the connection. When the read committed snapshot isolation level is set, statements that reach the server will receive a copy of data before the beginning of the statement.

IMPORTANT Impact on *tempdb*

Because snapshot and read committed snapshot isolation levels use row versioning, they demand that the server keep copies of changed data in the *tempdb* database. Evaluate the impact on *tempdb* of using these technologies and make sure to optimize their implementation.

Use read committed snapshot isolation when readers frequently block writers and your reports require accuracy at the point at which the query starts. Use snapshot isolation when it is absolutely necessary to maintain transaction-level read consistency and when a snapshot of the same information must be provided in different queries that run in the same transaction. Snapshot isolation is always more demanding on *tempdb* than read committed snapshot isolation.

Database Snapshots

Also new in SQL Server 2005 is the ability to create database snapshots. A database snapshot is a read-only, static view of a database. To create a snapshot, you use the *CREATE DATABASE* command:

```
CREATE DATABASE AdventureWorks_Snap02April
ON ( NAME = AdventureWorks_Data
    , FILENAME = 'C:\Directory\AdventureWorks_Snap02April.ss' )
AS SNAPSHOT OF AdventureWorks;
```

Snapshots are useful for maintaining historical data. Because snapshots are transitionally consistent with the source database as of the moment of the snapshot's creation, they are useful for reporting purposes. Snapshots can also be combined with database mirroring to move information to another server.

Database Mirroring, Log Shipping, and Database Replication

Database mirroring, log shipping, and database replication are three technologies that you can use to move data from one server to another, offloading the reporting load from the transactional database.

Database mirroring is a new technology that, when used in high-performance mode (asynchronous mode) and in combination with database snapshots, enables you to delegate to another server the support for SSRS querying. The illustration in Figure 15-5 shows the database mirroring architecture.

Log shipping, which you can also use to distribute information to more than one server, uses backup and restore jobs to copy information from one primary server to one or more secondary servers. The main advantage of log shipping is that it allows distribution of multiple copies of the same database. However, the downside of log shipping is that it is more complex to manage and usually requires more time to deliver data than database mirroring. Use database mirroring when only a single copy of the database is required. Log shipping is a better solution when you need more than one copy of the database.

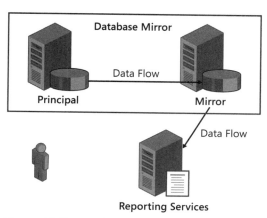

Figure 15-5 Database mirroring architecture

Alternatively, you can use replication to distribute data for reporting purposes. Replication is a set of technologies designed to distribute data geographically; you can use it to distribute data across multiple servers. Replication uses a publishing metaphor to assign different roles to the different servers in a replication topology. You can configure a server as Publisher, Distributor, and/or Subscriber. The Publisher is the original owner of the information that is published and is often the only place where data can be modified. The Distributor is responsible for storing replication status data, metadata, and in some replication scenarios, the actual replicated data. A Subscriber receives copies of published data. The same server can play all three roles in the same publication. Figure 15-6 illustrates the replication architecture.

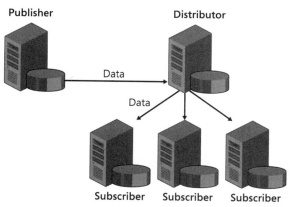

Figure 15-6 Replication architecture

Replication is far more complex to configure than database mirroring or log shipping, but it has some advantages:

- Replication allows multiple copies of data.
- Replication can be used to copy only some of the data in the database; you don't have to publish everything.
- Replication can be used to transform data. Replication doesn't require the schema to be the same at both ends of the replication.
- Replication allows different index strategies in the published and subscriber databases.

Designing the Schema

Database designers have several options when designing the database schema for reporting services purposes. Let's look at the options of using selective denormalization, summary tables, a star or snowflake schema, or OLAP reporting.

Selective Denormalization

In relational databases, one of the best practices is to normalize the database. A normalized database helps remove redundancy and increases the performance of changes (inserts, updates, and deletes) that the database supports. Because data is stored only once, normalization also reduces the amount of inconsistent data stored in the database.

However, sometimes after you normalize the database, you need to perform some of the opposing process: denormalization. Denormalization is the process of adding redundancy to the database. You use denormalization to increase the performance of reports and other database activities. The following code shows an example of how the *AdventureWorks* database uses denormalization:

```
SELECT ProductID, StandardCost from Production.Product
WHERE ProductID=707
SELECT ProductID, StartDate, EndDate, StandardCost
FROM Production.ProductCostHistory
WHERE ProductID=707
```

The StandardCost information stored in the ProductCostHistory table is, by design, normalized. Alternatively, the StandardCost information stored in the Product table is redundant because it can be obtained from the ProductCostHistory table simply by filtering where End-Date IS NULL. So, you can say that the StandardCost value has been denormalized.

After you denormalize certain data, you must decide how to maintain synchronized copies of the data. Data manipulation language (DML) triggers are frequently used to maintain the synchronization of denormalized information in the database. Later in this lesson, you will see an example of a trigger to maintain denormalized data.

Summary Tables

Summary tables are a special type of denormalization. A summary table aggregates data that is frequently queried and prevents reports from summing up the same information repeatedly. You can maintain summary tables by using triggers, business processes, or SQL Server Agent jobs.

The following code shows an example of a summary table's schema:

```
CREATE TABLE Sales.SummaryBySalesPerson(
      OrderPeriod    INT   NOT NULL
    , SalesPersonId  INT   NOT NULL
    , SubTotal       MONEY NOT NULL
    , TaxAmt         MONEY NOT NULL
    , Freight        MONEY NOT NULL
    , TotalDue       MONEY NOT NULL
    , PRIMARY KEY (SalesPersonId, OrderPeriod)
)
```

Notice that the schema does not capture details of the transactions. It is focused only on capturing summarized information—in this case, sales total amounts.

Star or Snowflake Schema

To facilitate data retrieval for reporting purposes, most data marts or data warehouses use star or snowflake schemas. The star schema is the simplest. It has a table in the center, named the fact table, and multiple points of the star, represented by dimension tables. The fact table stores all measures of a business event or process, and the dimensions store the context of the process. For example, a fact table might capture sales and include columns for quantity, price, sales amount, and sales cost. The dimensions associated with that schema might store information about the customer, the product, the date, the distributor, and so on.

As noted, the star schema has a center, represented by the fact table, and the points of the star, represented by the dimension tables. All dimension tables are directly linked to the fact table. The advantage of the star schema is that joins between the dimensions and the fact tables are simple and easy to understand by users and developers.

You can find an example of a star schema in the *AdventureWorksDW* database for the finance tables. The schema has the FactFinance fact table as a center of the star. This table is responsible for capturing all the measures of facts of the finance business process. It also has columns that link the measures with business entities or dimensions. The tables responsible for storing that information are always directly associated with the fact table. Figure 15-7 shows an example of a star schema.

The snowflake schema is a little more complex than the star schema. The snowflake schema also has a fact table in the center. However, in a snowflake schema, not all dimension tables are directly linked to the fact table. Dimension tables in a snowflake schema might be linked indirectly to the snowflake schema through other dimension tables. Figure 15-8 shows an example of a snowflake schema.

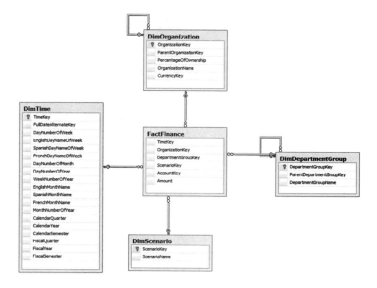

Figure 15-7   A star schema example

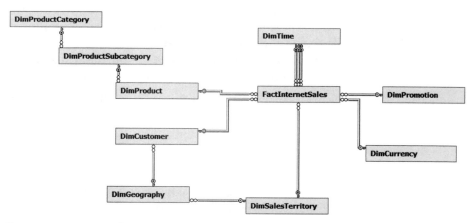

Figure 15-8   A snowflake schema example

In the snowflake schema example, as with the star schema example, the center of the schema is a fact table, FactInternetSales in this case. The columns (not shown in the illustration) store measures of Internet sales of AdventureWorks. The context of the sales is also stored in dimension tables, as it was in the star schema. However, in the snowflake schema, not all tables are directly linked to the fact table. For example, the DimProductCategory table requires three joins to link to the fact table.

OLAP Reporting

Finally, in reporting, there is always the possibility of completely replacing the source technology of reports. Instead of using a relational database as the source of your reports, you can use a multidimensional database. A multidimensional database is a special type of database optimized for data warehouses and OLAP applications. Multidimensional databases store detailed and aggregated data by using information extracted from existing relational databases.

Designing Indexes

Indexes are database structures that enable faster retrieval of rows. SQL Server 2005 supports two types of indexes: clustered and nonclustered. Clustered indexes sort and include the rows of a table, provided that the rows are the lowest (leaf) level of the index. Tables can have only one clustered index. In contrast, nonclustered indexes do not sort the rows of the table; they store keys and references to the clustered index. Tables can have more than one nonclustered index.

When designing indexes, keep in mind the following guidelines:

- Use the clustered index for queries that return a large number of contiguous rows.
- Avoid using wide columns as clustered indexes because the column width of columns participating in the clustered index have an effect on all indexes, clustered and nonclustered.
- Because nonclustered indexes reference clustered indexes, avoid clustered indexes on columns that experience frequent updates.
- Indexes over nonselective columns are rarely used; do not index columns with few distinct values.
- Evaluate the performance gain for indexes that are regularly used in JOINS and WHERE conditions. Foreign keys are normally evaluated as index candidates.

Computed Columns, Persisted Columns, and Indexes

A computed column is a special type of column that is calculated by using an expression based on other columns of the table. The following code is an example of a computed column:

```
CREATE TABLE Sales.Invoice(
    InvoiceNo      INT NOT NULL
      PRIMARY KEY
  , InvoiceDate    SMALLDATETIME NOT NULL
  , CreditDays    INT NOT NULL
  , DueDate    AS DATEADD(day, CreditDays, InvoiceDate)
)
```

By default, computed columns are virtual columns that are calculated when the user queries the table; they are never physically stored in the database. By default, computed columns are very similar to views.

New in SQL Server 2005 is the ability to persist the values of computed columns. Persisted computed columns are physically stored with the rest of the table columns. When a row is inserted or any of the referenced columns are updated, the persisted computed column is calculated and the results stored. Persisted computed columns are never calculated at query time. The following code is an example of a persisted computed column:

```
CREATE TABLE Sales.Invoice(
    InvoiceNo       INT NOT NULL
        PRIMARY KEY
  , InvoiceDate     SMALLDATETIME NOT NULL
  , CreditDays      INT NOT NULL
  , DueDate  AS DATEADD(day, CreditDays, InvoiceDate)
        PERSISTED
)
```

The only requirement for computed columns is that the expression must be deterministic. For example, a computed column based on the *GETDATE()* function or the *SYSTEM_USER* function cannot be persisted because these functions are not deterministic. Additionally, if you want to create an index by using a computed column, the expression must be precise. For more information about determinism and precision, see Chapter 4, "Designing a Database for Performance."

Use persisted computed columns to produce complex formulas based on columns that rarely change. Do not assume that, because a column is persisted, it will offer better performance than regular computed columns. However, persisted columns might help you denormalize a database without the burden of creating triggers to maintain redundancy.

IMPORTANT   Required persisted columns

Computed columns used to create constraints (*CHECK FOREIGN KEY* or *NOT NULL*) or used to create partitions must be persisted.

Covered Queries and Indexes with Included Columns

A covered query is a SELECT statement that uses a nonclustered index to answer the query without using the rows from the table or the clustered index. Covered queries can greatly increase the performance of reports. For example, the following query can benefit from a covered index:

```
SELECT SalesPersonID
   , SUM(SubTotal)
   , SUM(TotalDue)
```

```
FROM Sales.SalesOrderHeader
WHERE OrderDate BETWEEN '20040101' AND '20040131'
GROUP BY SalesPersonID
```

SQL Server 2005 required 703 logical page reads to answer this query. From the syntax, you know that the query uses only four columns of the SalesOrderHeader table: SalesPersonID, OrderDate, SubTotal, and TotalDue. Over the first two columns, SalesPersonID and Order-Date, it seems appropriate to create a nonclustered index. However, the last two columns, Sub-Total and TotalDue, would benefit from a new feature of SQL Server 2005: included columns.

Included columns are columns included in a nonclustered index at the lowest level of the index structure, the leaf level. With included columns, the performance of certain queries can increase dramatically. An example of a CREATE INDEX statement with the new INCLUDE option is:

```
CREATE NONCLUSTERED INDEX IDX_SalesHeaderSummary
ON Sales.SalesOrderHeader(OrderDate, SalesPersonID)
INCLUDE (SubTotal, TotalDue)
```

A quick comparison of the base query with and without the index will show that the query without the index required 703 logical reads to find the results, while the query with the index required only 12 logical reads to get the results.

Designing the Data Transformation

After you create the database schema in consideration of your reporting solution, you need to populate the tables designed to support reports. Based on how the transformation process is implemented, there are three methods for populating these tables. First, you can use data definition language (DDL) triggers. Triggers can populate and then keep the summary information updated in real time, but they have the greatest impact on the performance of the OLTP application. Second, you can integrate the process of transforming summary information into the business cycle. For example, in a Point of Sale (POS) system, you could summarize information when a cashier closes his or her cashier station. Finally, most designers choose a formal extract, transform, and load (ETL) process to perform transformations. ETL processes frequently use a fixed daily, weekly, or monthly schedule.

Using Triggers to Summarize Information

The following code will help you understand how to use triggers to maintain summary tables:

```
CREATE TRIGGER Sales.TrSummarySalesBySalesPerson
   ON  Sales.SalesOrderHeader
   AFTER INSERT,DELETE,UPDATE
AS
BEGIN
SET NOCOUNT ON;
-- DELETE Previous Amounts
```

```
DELETE Sales.SummaryBySalesPerson
FROM Sales.SummaryBySalesPerson
JOIN (SELECT YEAR(OrderDate)*100+MONTH(OrderDate) AS OrderPeriod
          , SalesPersonId
  FROM Deleted
      UNION-- Removes duplicates
  SELECT YEAR(OrderDate)*100+MONTH(OrderDate)
            , SalesPersonId
  FROM Inserted
      ) AS Changed
    ON SummaryBySalesPerson.OrderPeriod=Changed.OrderPeriod
AND SummaryBySalesPerson.SalesPersonId=Changed.SalesPersonId

  INSERT Sales.SummaryBySalesPerson( OrderPeriod, SalesPersonId, SubTotal,TaxAmt, Freight,
TotalDue)
  SELECT
 YEAR(OD.OrderDate)*100+MONTH(OD.OrderDate) AS OrderPeriod
, OD.SalesPersonId
, SUM(OD.SubTotal) AS SubTotal
, SUM(OD.TaxAmt) AS TaxAmt
, SUM(OD.Freight) AS Freight
, SUM(OD.TotalDue) AS TotalDue
  FROM Sales.SalesOrderHeader AS OD
  JOIN (SELECT YEAR(OrderDate)*100+MONTH(OrderDate) AS OrderPeriod
            , SalesPersonId
  FROM Deleted
      UNION-- Removes duplicates
  SELECT YEAR(OrderDate)*100+MONTH(OrderDate)
            , SalesPersonId
  FROM Inserted
      ) AS Changed
  ON YEAR(OD.OrderDate)*100+MONTH(OD.OrderDate)=Changed.OrderPeriod
 AND OD.SalesPersonId=Changed.SalesPersonId
  WHERE OD.SalesPersonID IS NOT NULL
  GROUP BY OD.SalesPersonId, YEAR(OD.OrderDate)*100+MONTH(OD.OrderDate)
END
```

Notice the following important facts about this trigger:

- The trigger is an AFTER trigger because you want to execute the code only after all validations have occurred.

- Because the code in the trigger is fired only once for all rows modified, it must work with the entire set of changes at the same time. The trigger must assume that multiple rows have been updated.

- The trigger must be optimized for performance. The code does not recalculate the entire summary table each time because that would severely affect the performance of each transaction that modifies the OrderHeader table. The trigger updates (deletes and inserts) only the rows that change their value.

Designing an ETL Process

ETL is the part of a data warehouse solution responsible for loading the information into the data warehouse. As its name suggests, it has three main tasks:

- Extracting data from different sources
- Transforming the data
- Loading the transformed data into the data warehouse

Exam Tip   Understanding the details of how to design an ETL process is beyond the scope of the certification exam and this training kit; however, you must have a general understanding of the ETL process.

Traditional ETL Architecture   Figure 15-9 illustrates the architecture of a traditional ETL process.

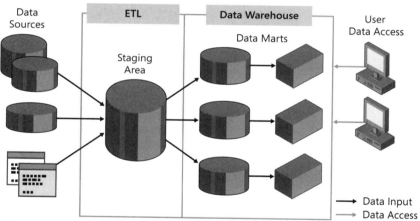

Figure 15-9   The traditional ETL architecture

The first step of the ETL process is extraction. Extraction is responsible for pulling information from multiple database sources and storing that information in a staging area. A critical requirement of the extraction process is to minimize the impact on the source, and because of that, the extraction process is always as simple as possible.

The second phase of the ETL process is the transformation, where most of the ETL process occurs. The transformation phase is responsible for cleaning bad data, joining information from multiple sources, summarizing rows, and changing the schema of the information to match the destination data warehouse schema.

Finally, the loading phase is responsible for storing the information in a relational database to maintain historical information and for populating the OLAP cubes when they exist.

SSIS In-Memory ETL   In some scenarios, the traditional ETL architecture might not be feasible. The traditional ETL process uses many tasks that produce numerous read and write operations. When the ETL process involves millions and millions of rows, the ETL process might not scale very well and can be hard to manage. SSIS offers an alternative.

SSIS was designed with the idea that a lot of the ETL tasks can be combined in a single in-memory process that performs much faster and can be easily managed. The illustration in Figure 15-10 outlines the SSIS ETL architecture.

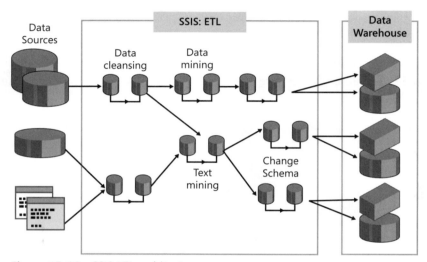

Figure 15-10   SSIS ETL architecture

In Chapter 17, "Developing Packages for Integration Services," you will learn more about how to build an ETL infrastructure by using SSIS.

Practice: Creating a Purchasing Summary Report

In this practice, you will create a report that summarizes purchases by vendor. The report will use a summary table to avoid using the transactional table as the report's data source. The summary table will be updated once a day by using a SQL Server Agent job.

▶ **Exercise 1: Create the Summary Table**

In this exercise, you will create a schema and summary table. The summary table will store rows that summarize the orders by month and by vendor.

1. Open SSMS and connect to the default database engine instance.
2. From the SQL Editor toolbar, click New Query.
3. From the Available Databases drop-down list, select AdventureWorks.

4. Write the required command to create a SummaryTables schema:

```
CREATE SCHEMA SummaryTables
```

5. Write the command required to create a summary table called PurchaseByVendor.

The summary table should be able to capture the order month and year, the VendorId, all purchase order amounts (SubTotal, TaxAmt, Freight, and TotalDue), and the number of order items:

```
CREATE TABLE SummaryTables.PurchasesByVendor(
    OrderMonth              INT   NOT NULL
    , VendorID              INT   NOT NULL
    , SubTotal              MONEY NOT NULL
    , TaxAmt                MONEY NOT NULL
    , Freight               MONEY NOT NULL
    , TotalDue              MONEY NOT NULL
    , NumberOrderedItems    INT   NOT NULL
    , CONSTRAINT PK_PurchasesByVendor
        PRIMARY KEY(OrderMonth, VendorID)
)
```

6. Click Execute or press F5 to create the database objects.

▶ **Exercise 2: Create the Job to Populate the Summary Table**

In this exercise, you will create a SQL Server Agent job to populate the summary table. The job should run once a day, deleting all previous information and filling the summary table from data collected from the PurchasingOrderHeader and PurchasingOrderDetail tables.

1. Open SSMS and connect to the default database engine instance.

2. Using Object Explorer, navigate to SQL Server Agent and then Jobs.

You might have to start SQL Server Agent to perform the following tasks. If the agent is stopped, right-click SQL Server Agent and select Start.

3. Right-click the Jobs folder and select New Job.

4. In the Name text box, type **PopulatePurchaseOrdersSummary** to name the job.

5. In the Select A Page pane, select Steps.

6. Click New to create a new job step.

7. In the *Step Name* field, type **PopulatePurchasesByVendor**.

8. From the Database drop-down list, select AdventureWorks.

9. Write the SQL statements required to delete the old information from the summary table and populate it with new information:

```
TRUNCATE TABLE SummaryTables.PurchasesByVendor;

INSERT SummaryTables.PurchasesByVendor(OrderMonth, VendorID
    , SubTotal, TaxAmt, Freight, TotalDue, NumberOrderedItems)
SELECT
    PurchaseOrderHeader.VendorID
    , YEAR(PurchaseOrderHeader.OrderDate) * 100
```

```
       + MONTH(PurchaseOrderHeader.OrderDate) AS OrderMonth
       , SUM(PurchaseOrderHeader.SubTotal) AS SubTotal
       , SUM(PurchaseOrderHeader.TaxAmt) AS TaxAmt
   , SUM(PurchaseOrderHeader.Freight) AS Freight
       , SUM(PurchaseOrderHeader.TotalDue) AS TotalDue
       , SUM(NumberOrderedItems) AS NumberOrderedItems
FROM Purchasing.PurchaseOrderHeader
JOIN (SELECT PurchaseOrderDetail.PurchaseOrderID AS PurchaseOrderID
        , COUNT(PurchaseOrderDetail.PurchaseOrderDetailID)
              AS NumberOrderedItems
     FROM Purchasing.PurchaseOrderDetail
      GROUP BY PurchaseOrderID) AS OrderedItems
on PurchaseOrderHeader.PurchaseOrderID = OrderedItems.PurchaseOrderID
GROUP BY PurchaseOrderHeader.VendorID
       , YEAR(PurchaseOrderHeader.OrderDate) * 100
       + MONTH(PurchaseOrderHeader.OrderDate);
```

10. Click OK to continue creating the job.

11. In the Select A Page pane, select Schedules.

12. Click New to create a new schedule.

13. In the *Name* field, type the name **Midnight**.

14. In the Frequency section, from the Occurs drop-down list, select Daily. Click OK to create the schedule.

15. Click OK to create the job, and then click OK to close the New Job dialog box.

▶ **Exercise 3: Execute and Validate the Job**

In this exercise, you will execute the job that populates the purchasing orders summary table.

1. In Object Explorer, navigate to SQL Server Agent and then to Jobs.

2. Right-click the PopulatePurchaseOrderSummary job and select Start Job At Step.

3. Wait for the job to execute and click Close after it reports success.

4. Click the New Query button to create a new window.

5. From the Available Databases drop-down list, select AdventureWorks.

6. Write a query to select all columns from the SummaryTables.PurchaseByVendor table:

```
SELECT * FROM SummaryTables.PurchasesByVendor
```

Quick Check

1. What is the main benefit of using the read committed snapshot isolation level?
2. What is the main difference between the star schema and the snowflake schema?
3. How do you create a covered index in SQL Server 2005?
    - A. With a clustered index
    - B. With a nonclustered index
    - C. With auto create statistics
    - D. With included columns in a nonclustered index

Quick Check Answers

1. Read committed snapshots use row versioning to avoid shared locks, preventing readers from blocking writers.
2. In the snowflake schema, not all dimension tables are directly linked to the fact table. In the snowflake schema, designers provide some normalization of dimension tables and divide the dimension information into two or more tables that might not be linked to the fact table.
3. The correct answer is D. A new feature of SQL Server 2005 is to allow the inclusion of non-key columns in a nonclustered index.

Lesson 3: Designing Programmatic Interfaces and the Data Access Method for Reporting

---

Estimated lesson time: 25 minutes

When designing reporting solutions, you must consider the type of data access and language and format message the reports will use to access the database. This consideration will affect the security, performance, scalability, and programmability of your solution. In this lesson, you will apply the knowledge learned in Chapter 8, "Designing a Secure Application Solution," about views, stored procedures, and user-defined functions (UDFs) and evaluate the impact they will have on your application.

Querying Tables Directly

When choosing which data access method to use for your reports, the first option to evaluate is querying the tables directly. Querying tables directly has the following advantages:

- **Programmability**   The Query Builder in BIDS, which Figure 15-11 shows, automatically detects primary, unique, and foreign keys, helping the developer create the SQL syntax.

Figure 15-11   Using the Query Builder in BIDS

For database developers, the SQL language is an easy and effective way to manage data.

- **Security**   When combined with impersonation, querying the tables directly can be managed from SQL Server and can be easily audited and traced with database tools.

However, querying the tables directly has the following disadvantages:

- **Programmability** Report designers might need to have advanced SQL abilities and profound knowledge of the database schema.
- **Maintainability** After the report is created and deployed, changes in the schema of the database might cause the report to stop working, thereby reducing the maintainability of the database.
- **Manageability** In corporate scenarios, managing the security of hundreds or thousands of users could be challenging for the IT department.
- **Security** When combined with impersonation, directly querying the tables requires permissions in every table that is included in the SQL command. It would be simple for a user to bypass SSRS and access the database directly.
- **Security** Denying access to detailed information is not possible.

Querying tables directly for SSRS reports is recommended only for small-group scenarios in which security and maintainability might be compromised to facilitate rapid development.

Using Views to Support Reports

Views are a data-access alternative to directly querying the tables. With views, database developers can hide some of the complexity of the database and offer reporting developers a simpler and more natural model to query. Views can also offer a good alternative for increasing security. With views, database developers can protect detailed information, hide sensitive columns, and use system functions to provide row security.

Hiding Detailed Information

To use views to protect detailed information, follow these steps:

1. Create a summary view.
2. Grant users access to the view.
3. Do not grant users access to the original tables.

SQL Server 2005 implements a concept called ownership chaining. When multiple database access objects access each other sequentially, SQL Server evaluates permissions only when the links belong to different users. This means that if a view references one or more tables and all the objects belong to the same user, users querying the view do not require access to the original tables. The following code shows an example of hiding detailed information:

```
CREATE TABLE Loans.Loan(
    LoanContractNumber   CHAR(12)    NOT NULL
        PRIMARY KEY
    , LoanApprovedDate    DATETIME   NOT NULL
    , CustomerCode        INT        NOT NULL
    , InterestRate        DECIMAL(5,2)   NOT NULL
```

```
    , LoanAmmount        MONEY       NOT NULL
    , AmmountDue         MONEY       NOT NULL
)
GO
CREATE VIEW Loans.SummaryApprovedLoans
AS
    SELECT LoanApprovedDate, SUM(LoanAmmount) AS ApprovedAmmout
    FROM Loan
    GROUP BY LoanApprovedDate
GO
-- Do not grant users access to the Loan Table
GRANT SELECT ON Loans.SummaryApprovedLoans TO User1
```

Hiding Sensitive Columns

Even when SQL Server 2005 allows security to grant or deny access at a column level, most database designers, for performance and maintainability reasons, choose to use views instead. The following code is an example of how you can use a view to hide sensitive columns:

```
CREATE SCHEMA HumanResources
CREATE TABLE HumanResources.Employees(
    EmployeeNumber    INT NOT NULL
        PRIMARY KEY
    , FirstName        VARCHAR(50) NOT NULL
    , MiddleName       VARCHAR(50) NOT NULL
    , LastName         VARCHAR(50) NOT NULL
    , Salary           MONEY       NOT NULL
)
GO
CREATE VIEW HumanResources.EmployeeList
AS
    SELECT     EmployeeNumber
    , FirstName
    , MiddleName
    , LastName
    FROM Employees
GO
-- Only users that need access to salary amounts must have access
-- to the HumanResources.Employees Table, Reports use EmployeeList
GRANT SELECT ON HumanResources.EmployeeList TO User1
```

Row Security Through Views

A final motive for using views is the ability to provide row security. Using views and system functions, database designers can filter rows and provide filtered views that give access only to appropriate users. A simple case of filtered views is when the table has a column that stores the owner's username. The following code is an example of filtering information through views:

```
CREATE TABLE Sales.CustomerBase(
    CustomerCode      INT NOT NULL
```

```
        PRIMARY KEY
    , CustomerName    VARCHAR(50) NOT NULL
-- ... other columns
    , SalesRep        VARCHAR(32) NOT NULL
      DEFAULT(SYSTEM_USER)
)
GO
CREATE VIEW Sales.Customers
AS
    SELECT CustomerCode
        , CustomerName
    FROM CustomerBase
    WHERE SalesRep=SYSTEM_USER
```

With this schema, database developers grant user access to the Customers view, and users are allowed to browse reports that display only their own customers.

A more complex scenario happens when you need to access more than one table to permit access to the rows. The following code builds on top of the previous example to create a more complex scenario:

```
CREATE TABLE Sales.SalesRegion(
    SalesRegionCode     CHAR(5)     NOT NULL
        PRIMARY KEY
    , SalesRegionName   VARCHAR(50) NOT NULL
    , SalesRep          VARCHAR(32) NOT NULL
      DEFAULT(SYSTEM_USER)
)
CREATE TABLE Sales.CustomerBase(
    CustomerCode        INT NOT NULL
        PRIMARY KEY
    , CustomerName      VARCHAR(50) NOT NULL
-- ... other columns
    , SalesRegionCode   CHAR(5)     NOT NULL
      FOREIGN KEY REFERENCES Sales.SalesRegion(SalesRegionCode)
)
GO
CREATE VIEW Sales.Customers
AS
    SELECT CustomerCode
        , CustomerName
    FROM CustomerBase
    WHERE SalesRegionCode IN (SELECT SalesRegionCode
                        FROM  Sales.SalesRegion
                        WHERE SalesRep=SYSTEM_USER)
```

As you can see from the example, the SalesRegion table is used to authorize access to the customer information. Naturally, you can repeat this technique with other tables to build a hierarchical permission structure. For example, you can use it to filter orders information, as follows:

```
CREATE VIEW Sales.Orders
AS
   SELECT OrderBase.OrderNumber
          , OrderBase.CustomerCode
          , OrderBase.OrderDate
          , OrderBase.OrderAmmount
FROM Sales.OrderBase
JOIN Sales.Customer
ON OrderBase.CustomerCode=Customer.CustomerCode
JOIN Sales.SalesRegion
ON SalesRegion.SalesRegionCode=Customer.SalesRegionCode
WHERE SalesRegion.SalesRep= SYSTEM_USER
```

IMPORTANT   Security reminder

If you plan to use filtered views, keep in mind that the reports must use impersonation to filter the information.

Using views is similar to querying the tables directly except for the following differences:

- **Programmability**   You can encapsulate some of the more complex queries from the reports, reducing the level of SQL knowledge developers require to create reports. You can use views to simplify some of the complexity introduced in the model by normalization.

- **Security**   Views add new alternatives for providing security. These security benefits can include hiding sensitive columns, hiding detailed information, and providing row-level security.

However, if you use filtered views, scalability is adversely affected because filtered views rely on system functions to filter rows; they work only when the reports use impersonation, which substantially reduces the scalability of the SSRS architecture.

Using Stored Procedures

Another approach when designing data access for reporting is to use stored procedures. The idea behind using stored procedures is to hide both the SQL language and the database schema from the report designers. Using stored procedures provides advantages in both security and maintainability at the expense of a more complex solution.

Filtered Rows Equivalent

The following code shows an example of how to create a stored procedure that provides row security without the need for impersonation:

```
CREATE PROCEDURE Sales.SalesSummary
(
   @SalesRep  CHAR(32)
)
```

```
AS
   SET NOCOUNT ON;
   SELECT Orders.OrderNumber
        , Orders.CustomerCode
        , Orders.OrderDate
        , Orders.OrderAmmount
   FROM Sales.Orders
   JOIN Sales.CustomerCode
   ON Orders.CustomerCode=Customer.CustomerCode
   JOIN Sales.SalesRegion
   ON SalesRegion.SalesRegion=Customer.SalesRegion
   WHERE SalesRegion.SalesRegion= @SalesRep;
GO
-- Do not grant users access to this stored procedure.
GRANT SELECT ON Sales.SalesSummary TO ReportServerServiceAccount
```

This procedure is designed on the assumption that only the Reporting Services account will use the procedure, and users won't have access to it. After the stored procedure is created, you need to create a report that uses the stored procedure. You do this by using the Report Wizard and entering the code to execute the stored procedure.

After finishing the Report Wizard, you need to perform two final steps to create the report. First, delete the parameter that the Report Wizard automatically creates and assign the *UserID* global variable to the SQL Parameter. To delete the parameter, follow these steps:

1. When editing the report, select Report from the main menu.
2. Select Report Parameters.
3. Click Remove to delete the parameter.

   After the report parameter is deleted, you must assign the *UserID* global variable to the SQL parameter. To map the *UserID*, follow these steps:

   a. In the Report Designer, select the Data pane.
   b. From the toolbar of the Data pane, click the Edit Selected Dataset button.
   c. Select the Parameters pane.
   d. Select the Value column of the parameter and configure the expression, using the UserID parameter.

Stored Procedure Advantages and Disadvantages

Using stored procedures to provide data access to reports has the following advantages:

■ **Programmability** Stored procedures encapsulate the complexity of the database schema and the SQL language from report designers.

■ **Security** Stored procedures offer a wide spectrum of security options, including denying users access to the database's underlying objects. The Report Server can be the only entity with database access.

- **Maintainability** Changing the schema of the database might not have a negative impact on the reports. Database administrators can tune the database without having to change the reports.
- **Manageability** Managing hundreds or thousands of users is simpler than with other methods; access to the database can be restricted.

Using stored procedures has the following disadvantages:

- **Programmability** The developer team requires a higher level of specialization and a clear definition of a programming interface to query the database. Further, ad hoc queries are not possible when using stored procedures unless you grant users permissions to the underlying database objects.

Practice: Creating a Row-Filtered Report

In this practice, you will create a report that uses a stored procedure and the identity captured in the SSRS interface to summarize filtered information for users. The users will be salespeople who need access to a sales quota report but are not allowed to see each other's information.

▶ **Exercise 1: Create the Stored Procedure**

In this exercise, you will create a stored procedure that receives a single parameter: the user running the report. This procedure is designed so that only a Reporting Services account is able to query the data.

1. Open SSMS and connect to the default database engine instance.
2. From the SQL Editor toolbar, click New Query.
3. From the Available Databases drop-down list, select AdventureWorks.
4. Write the required command to create the SalesReports schema:

   ```
   CREATE SCHEMA SalesReports
   Go
   ```

5. Write the command required to create the filtered stored procedure.

   The procedure should summarize Orders from the SalesOrderHeader table, filtered by LoginID and Group By quarter. The data should also include the Historic Quota for that quarter and salesperson:

   ```
   CREATE PROC SalesReports.SalesPersonHistoricQuota (
       @LoginID NVARCHAR(256)
   )
   AS
       SET NOCOUNT ON;
       SELECT
           CAST(YEAR(SalesPersonQuotaHistory.QuotaDate) AS CHAR(4))+' - Q'
           +CAST((MONTH(SalesPersonQuotaHistory.QuotaDate)/4)+1 AS CHAR(1))
               AS Quarter
         , SUM(SalesPersonQuotaHistory.SalesQuota) AS SalesQuota
         , SUM(SalesOrderHeader.SubTotal) AS Sales
   ```

```
FROM Sales.SalesPerson
INNER JOIN HumanResources.Employee
ON SalesPerson.SalesPersonID = Employee.EmployeeID
INNER JOIN Sales.SalesPersonQuotaHistory
ON SalesPerson.SalesPersonID = SalesPersonQuotaHistory.SalesPersonID
INNER JOIN Sales.SalesOrderHeader
ON SalesPerson.SalesPersonID = SalesOrderHeader.SalesPersonID
 AND YEAR(SalesPersonQuotaHistory.QuotaDate)
      = YEAR(SalesOrderHeader.OrderDate)
 AND MONTH(SalesPersonQuotaHistory.QuotaDate)/4
      = MONTH(SalesOrderHeader.OrderDate)/4
WHERE Employee.LoginID=@LoginID
GROUP BY CAST(YEAR(SalesPersonQuotaHistory.QuotaDate) AS CHAR(4))
      +' - Q'
      +CAST((MONTH(SalesPersonQuotaHistory.QuotaDate)/4)+1 AS CHAR(1))
GO
```

6. Click Execute or press F5 to create the database objects.

▶ **Exercise 2: Test the Stored Procedure and Prepare Data for the Report**

In this exercise, you will test the previously created report and prepare some data for testing purposes.

1. From the SQL Editor toolbar, click the New Query button.
2. In the Available Databases drop-down list, select AdventureWorks.
3. Write and execute the required command to test the SalesPersonHistoricQuota stored procedure:

```
EXEC SalesReports.SalesPersonHistoricQuota 'adventure-works\michael9'
```

The command should return 10 rows with the requested information.

4. Write and execute the command to find the login account you are using to connect to SQL Server:

```
SELECT system_user
```

The returned value is the login account you are using to connect to SQL Server.

5. Write and execute the command to replace the login adventure-works\michael9 account in the Employee table with your own login account.

In this practice, you will play the role of this salesperson:

```
UPDATE HumanResources.employee
   SET LoginId=SYSTEM_USER
WHERE loginId='adventure-works\michael9'
```

▶ **Exercise 3: Add a New Filtered Report**

In this exercise, you will use the recently created stored procedure to create a report that dynamically filters information based on the account accessing the Report Manager.

1. Open BIDS.
2. From the main menu, click File, click New, and then choose Project.

3. Select Business Intelligence Projects from Project Types.

4. Select the Report Server Project Wizard template. Name the project **SalesQuotaReports** and click OK to begin the wizard.

5. When the Welcome To The Report Wizard page appears, click Next to continue.

6. On the Select The Data Source page, create a new data source. Name the data source **AdventureWorks**.

7. Leave the default data source type as Microsoft SQL Server. Click Edit to configure the connection string.

8. When the Connection Properties dialog box is displayed, for server name, type **localhost**. For the database name, type or select **AdventureWorks**. Leave the security as Use Windows Authentication. Select Test Connection to validate the connection information and click OK to continue.

9. In the Select The Data Source page, select the Make This A Shared Data Source check box, and then click Next.

10. On the Design The Query page, type the following query to execute the SalesPerson-HistoricQuota stored procedure:

    ```
    EXEC SalesReports.SalesPersonHistoricQuota @UserID
    ```

    Using @UserID will create two parameters: one T-SQL parameter and one Reporting Services parameter.

11. Click Next.

12. Accept the default Tabular report type and click Next to continue.

13. Click the Details button three times to add all columns to the Details Displayed Fields. Click Next to continue creating the report.

14. Select Corporate Style to format the report and click Next.

15. Accept the default deployment locations on the Choose The Deployment Location page, and then click Next.

16. Name the report **Historic Quota Performance** and click Finish to create the report.

17. Select the Preview pane and notice the UserID report parameter.

    This is not the desired behavior; you do not want users to browse each other's information.

18. Select the Layout pane. From the Report menu, select Report Parameters.

    The Report Parameters dialog box will be displayed.

19. Select the UserID parameter and click Remove to delete the report parameter. Click OK to continue editing the report.

20. Select the Data pane. From the toolbar in the Data pane, click the Edit Selected Dataset button. The Dataset dialog box will appear.

21. Select the Parameters tab to change the value of the T-SQL parameter.

22. Select the @UserID row and, in the Value combo box, select <Expression>.

23. Enter the following expression to assign the UserID variable:

    =User!UserID

24. Click OK to accept the new expression and click OK to close the Dataset window.

25. Select the Preview pane again to preview the report.

    You should now see only your customers.

Quick Check

1. What is the main reporting advantage of directly querying database tables?

2. You want to give users access to summarized information and hide the detail items. Which is the simplest way to achieve this?

   A. Create a summary table and the required triggers.

   B. Create a summary table and a job to populate the table.

   C. Create a summarizing view.

   D. It cannot be achieved in SQL Server 2005.

3. You want to use SYSTEM_USER to filter information in a view. What will be the main constraint of using such a view from SSRS?

Quick Check Answers

1. The correct answer is programmability. The main advantage of directly querying the tables is how easily you can program a report.

2. The correct answer is C. A view with a GROUP BY statement will provide user access to the summarized information, and users do not need to have access to the base table to use the summarized view.

3. SSRS must use impersonation. In corporate and extranet scenarios, impersonation might not be desirable for scalability and security reasons.

Lesson 4: Optimizing Reports

Estimated lesson time: 15 minutes

In this lesson, you will learn about different options that can help you increase report performance. To optimize your reports' performance, you must understand how the reporting execution process works. The reporting execution process consists of the following phases:

- **Request**   The request phase initiates the process. It occurs when the client application makes a request to the SSRS Web service. Among other information, the request defines the target format type of the report.

- **Process**   The process step includes two major subphases. The first subphase is to read the configuration information. The configuration information includes the report layout, data source connection string, and report query command. The second subphase involves the process of reading data from the source and storing the information in an intermediate format. This format is independent of the target format type.

- **Render**   This process is responsible for creating the report. Rendering generates a formatted output from the intermediate format data.

- **Response**   The response phase sends the rendered output to the client application.

- **Display**   This optional phase is responsible for displaying the response from the Report Server to the client.

Report Caching

One option for increasing the performance of reports is to configure report caching. The report caching configuration changes the typical execution process. The goal of report caching is to reduce the number of times the Reporting Services has to read data from the source. Report caching reads data from the source once and then stores the information in the intermediate format for later use. After the intermediate format data is cached, executions use the intermediate format directly without pulling the information from the original data source.

To configure report caching by using Report Manager, follow these steps:

1. Navigate to the shared data source.
2. Configure the credentials required to access the source database.
   Credentials must be securely stored in the server.

IMPORTANT   Report caching

User impersonation and report caching are incompatible options. When caching reports, security must be configured by using delegation.

---

3. Apply your changes and navigate to the report.
4. Select the Properties tab of the report.
5. Select the Execution link of the report to configure caching.
6. Change the default option from Do Not Cache Temporary Copies Of This Report to any of the options that start with Cache A Temporary Copy Of The Report, as Figure 15-12 shows.

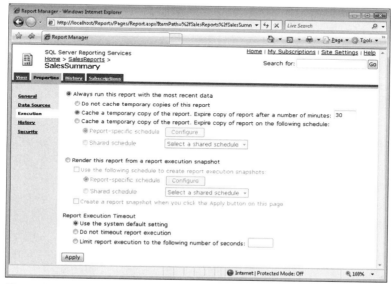

Figure 15-12   How to configure report caching

You can configure report caching for two different behaviors. The first option is to use users' navigation patterns to decide which reports are cached. Select the Expire Copy Of Report After A Number Of Minutes option if you want to use this option. Set the number of minutes based on users' requirements to report on real-time or near real-time data.

The second option enables the designer to use a fixed time pattern to cache reports. Select this option and configure a schedule for it. From the user's perspective, using a fixed time pattern to cache reports provides a better user experience because the user will not have to wait for the data to be generated. However, fixed time patterns usually consume more resources.

Report Snapshots

Another technique for increasing the performance of your reporting solutions is to generate report execution snapshots. Even more than report caching, report snapshots change the typical report execution process. The purpose of report snapshots is not only to avoid data access from the data source but also from the rendering process. Report snapshots execute on a pre-defined schedule that uses live data to generate the formatted output. Subsequent executions use the pre-rendered output.

To configure report snapshots:

1. Navigate to the shared data source.
2. Configure the credentials required to access the source database.
   Credentials must be securely stored in the server.

IMPORTANT   Report snapshots

Report snapshots are incompatible with user impersonation. Report snapshots require SQL Server Agent to work.

---

3. Apply your changes and navigate to the report.
4. Select the Properties tab of the report.
5. Select the Execution link of the report to configure rendering snapshots.
6. Select the Render This Report From A Report Execution Snapshot option.
7. Configure the rendering schedule and click Apply.

After you configure the schedule, you can navigate to the History tab, create a new snapshot, or view previous snapshot reports.

Specifying Subscription Models

You have already seen how SSRS enables users to generate reports. However, sometimes users require SSRS to distribute reports actively also. This implementation is called subscriptions. Subscriptions are configured in SSRS to send reports through e-mail or to store reports in a file share or directory in the file system. SSRS supports two different configurations for subscription models. Both models support e-mail and file share delivery.

▶ **Schedule Subscription**

To configure a scheduled Windows Shared File subscription:

1. Navigate to the report in Report Manager.
2. Select the report and navigate to the Subscriptions tab.
3. Click New Subscription.
4. From the Deliver drop-down list, select Windows Shared File.
5. Configure the path of the report, using UNC syntax (for instance, \\SERVER-NAME\Reports).
6. Select the preferred rendering format.
7. Configure the credentials to use the shared folder.

Configure whether you want the new versions to replace the old version, to fail if an old version exists, or to file names and numbers for version control.

8. Configure a schedule and click OK to configure the subscription.

Practice: Optimizing Report Performance

In this practice, you will create and optimize a report. The report will include a command that has a deliberate delay to simulate a complex query that generates a large database load.

▶ **Exercise 1: Create a Slow Report**

In this exercise, you will create a report that deliberately delays the query to simulate a large database load.

1. Open BIDS.
2. From the main menu, click File, click New, and then choose Project.
3. Select Business Intelligence Projects from Project Types.
4. Select the Report Server Project Wizard template. Name the project **SalesManagement-Reports** and click OK to begin the wizard.
5. When the Welcome To The Report Wizard page is displayed, click Next.
6. On the Select The Data Source page of the wizard, create a new data source and name it **AdventureWorksManagement**.
7. Accept the default data source type as Microsoft SQL Server. Click Edit to configure the connection string.
8. When the Connection Properties dialog box appears, for the server name, type **localhost**. For the database name, enter or select **AdventureWorks**. Accept the security as Use Windows Authentication. Select Test Connection to validate the connection information and click OK to continue and configure the connection string.
9. In the Select The Data Source dialog box, select the Make This A Shared Data Source check box and click Next.
10. On the Design The Query page, type the following command:

```
SET NOCOUNT ON;
WAITFOR DELAY '00:00:30'
SELECT
    Contact.FirstName + ' ' + Contact.LastName AS SalesPersonFullname
    , CAST(YEAR(SalesPersonQuotaHistory.QuotaDate) AS CHAR(4))+' - Q'
        +CAST((MONTH(SalesPersonQuotaHistory.QuotaDate)/4)+1 AS CHAR(1))
            AS Quarter
    , SUM(SalesPersonQuotaHistory.SalesQuota) AS SalesQuota
    , SUM(SalesOrderHeader.SubTotal) AS Sales
FROM Sales.SalesPerson
INNER JOIN HumanResources.Employee
ON SalesPerson.SalesPersonID = Employee.EmployeeID
INNER JOIN Person.Contact
```

```
ON Contact.ContactID = Employee.ContactID
INNER JOIN Sales.SalesPersonQuotaHistory
ON SalesPerson.SalesPersonID = SalesPersonQuotaHistory.SalesPersonID
INNER JOIN Sales.SalesOrderHeader
ON SalesPerson.SalesPersonID = SalesOrderHeader.SalesPersonID
    AND YEAR(SalesPersonQuotaHistory.QuotaDate)
        = YEAR(SalesOrderHeader.OrderDate)
    AND MONTH(SalesPersonQuotaHistory.QuotaDate)/4
        = MONTH(SalesOrderHeader.OrderDate)/4
GROUP BY Contact.FirstName + ' ' + Contact.LastName
    , CAST(YEAR(SalesPersonQuotaHistory.QuotaDate) AS CHAR(4))+' - Q'
    +CAST((MONTH(SalesPersonQuotaHistory.QuotaDate)/4)+1 AS CHAR(1))
```

The query uses the *DELAYFOR* command to slow down the query.

11. Click Next.

12. Change the default report type to Matrix and click Next.

13. Add SalesPersonFullName to the Columns Displayed Fields, add Quarter to the Rows Displayed Fields, and add the SalesQuota and Sales columns to the Details Displayed Fields. Click Next to continue creating the report.

14. Select Corporate Style to format the report and click Next.

15. Accept the default deployment locations on the Choose The Deployment Location page, and then click Next.

16. Name the report **Quota Performance by Sales Person** and click Finish to create the report.

17. Select the Preview pane and notice that the report takes a long time to generate (30 seconds).

▶ **Exercise 2: Deploy the Report**

In this exercise, you will deploy the report created in the previous exercise to the server. You will use BIDS to deploy the report; you can also use SSMS to deploy reports.

1. In Solution Explorer, right-click the SalesManagementReports project and select Deploy.

2. After the report is deployed, open Internet Explorer and navigate to the Report Manager. By default, the Report Manager URL is *http://localhost/Reports*.

3. From the main menu, click File, click New, and then select Project.

4. Navigate to the SalesManagementReports folder.

5. Open the Quota Performance By Sales Person report. Notice that it takes a long time to display the information.

6. Click the Refresh button a couple of times and notice that every time you click Refresh, the report takes 30 seconds to display information.

▶ **Exercise 3: Optimize the Report**

In this exercise, you will configure SSRS to cache the data and optimize the report generation in the deployed report.

1. In the Report Manager, click Home to return to the Home page.
2. Select the Data Sources folder.
3. Select the AdventureWorksManagement data source. You will need to change the connection string to allow SSRS to capture the source data with its own credentials.
4. Select Credentials Stored Securely In The Report Server.
5. Enter the required Windows credentials to access the server, configure the username and password, and select Use Windows Credentials When Connecting To The Data Source. Click Apply to save the changes.
6. Click Home to return to the Home page and select the SalesManagementReports folder.
7. Select the Quota Performance By Sales Person report and wait for the report to render.
8. To configure the cache, select the Properties tab and then the Execution link.
9. Select Cache A Temporary Copy Of The Report. Expire A Copy Of The Report After A Number Of Minutes.
10. Change the default value to 60 minutes and click Apply.
11. Select the View tab; notice that the report still takes a long time to display.
12. Click the Refresh button. Notice how fast the report is displayed. Navigate back to the Home page and again to the report. Notice the difference in performance. You can also create a scheduled report.

Quick Check

1. You want to optimize the performance of a report that provides information about last month's sales by product. How can you enhance the report performance?
   - A. Maximize the amount of memory the Report Server has.
   - B. Configure SSRS to cache a copy of the report.
   - C. Increase the CPU capacity of the Report Server.
   - D. Install an SSRS Web farm.
2. To configure a cached report, what changes do you need to make to the data source?
3. What is the difference between enabling report caching and configuring a report execution snapshot?

Quick Check Answers
1. The correct answer is B. Configuring report caching prevents SSRS from executing the query every time the report is browsed.
2. Change the data source to stored authentication credentials. When using a report cache, the data source must have the connection information required to connect to the database.
3. Report execution caches the result of the rendering process. Report caching stores data in a temporary intermediate format, and this data is used for the next report execution.

Case Scenario: Building a Reporting Services Infrastructure for a SharePoint Portal

Adventure Works, a worldwide distributor of bicycles and accessories, wants to build a corporate SharePoint intranet portal. You are responsible for building the SSRS infrastructure to support the portal. Adventure Works has only limited SSRS experience with small departmental portals.

Users are looking forward to using the SharePoint portal to integrate information that is scattered throughout the organization. The portal will gather information from multiple data sources, although most of the information will come from two line-of-business (LOB) applications: the customer relationship management (CRM) system and the Enterprise Resource Planning (ERP) system. The reports will be developed primarily by a few end users with the help of a small team of three developers. The end users have little or no experience with Transact-SQL (T-SQL), but they are skilled Microsoft Office Excel users.

The portal is being implemented with Windows 2003, SharePoint 2007, and SQL Server 2005. The company has built a data mart in SQL Server 2005 to integrate the information stored in the ERP and CRM databases. The LOB applications, which also use SQL Server 2005, were developed internally and are not linked to a data mart. The Adventure Works database administrators (DBAs) and software architects are concerned about how the SSRS infrastructure will manage security and how to design a solution that will scale well with thousands of users. You are responsible for answering their questions:

1. What tool or technology will enable end users to develop reports without having to learn T-SQL?
2. The DBAs responsible for the LOB applications are worried about the impact that real-time reports will have on other users updating data in the database. What new feature of SQL Server 2005 will prevent reports from blocking other transactional users?

3. Security is a main concern of the development team. For reports not using the report model, what approach will you propose to the development team for managing and filtering rows based on the authenticated users?

Chapter Summary

■ You have to make additional considerations when designing a database that provides information for SSRS purposes. You need to design a snapshot strategy and a programmatic interface with performance, scalability, programmability, and security in mind.

■ Create the strategy you need to evaluate the requirements for each report. For example, does it need to provide real-time, near real-time, or schedule-refreshed information? You can use different database objects and database technologies to provide the best user reporting experience without affecting other users. These objects and technologies include triggers, summary table, log shipping, replication, isolation levels, SSIS packages, SSAS databases, and so on.

■ To increase the performance of reports, evaluate the need to configure report caching and report execution snapshots.

Chapter 16

Developing Applications for Notification Services

SQL Server Notification Services is the Microsoft SQL Server technology to develop, host, and deploy applications that generate and send notification messages to users. Notification Services can send from thousands to millions of personalized notification messages to multiple subscribers, which enables you to improve communication with customers, partners, and employees.

The two main components of Notification Services are subscriptions and notifications. A *subscription* is a formal request for a specific event. Users subscribe to events. A notification subscription could be, for example, "Notify me when sales reach $100,000." *Notifications* are what the subscribers receive. A notification can contain a Web link, an acknowledgement of receipt, a personalized notification, and much more. A notification can be sent to a myriad of devices, including an e-mail account, cellular phone, PDA, Microsoft Windows Messenger, and so on. You specify in the subscription whether a notification is sent when a triggering event occurs or is sent on a schedule.

Notification Services is built on SQL Server 2005 and the Microsoft .NET Framework and provides a programming framework for easily developing and deploying notification applications. You can use Notification Services Management Objects (NMO) or XML to develop notification applications. In this chapter, you will first see how to create Notification Services configuration and application files and configure Notification Services instances. Then, you will learn how to define Notification Services events and event providers and configure the Notification Services generator and distributor. After looking at how to test your Notification Services application, you will see how to create subscriptions and how to optimize your notification solution.

Exam objectives in this chapter:

- Develop applications for Notification Services.
  - ❑ Create Notification Services configuration and application files.
  - ❑ Configure Notification Services instances.
  - ❑ Define Notification Services events and event providers.
  - ❑ Configure the Notification Services generator.

❏ Configure the Notification Services distributor.

❏ Test the Notification Services application.

❏ Create subscriptions.

❏ Optimize Notification Services.

Before You Begin

To complete the lessons in this chapter, you must have:

- A general understanding of SQL Server 2005 database concepts.
- A general understanding of Simple Mail Transfer Protocol (SMTP).
- Working experience with XML documents.
- Programming knowledge of either Microsoft Visual C# or Visual Basic.
- Knowledge of the Transact-SQL (T-SQL) and Multidimensional Expression (MDX) language syntaxes.
- A SQL Server 2005 instance (any edition) with Notification Services installed.
- Microsoft Visual Studio 2005 or Microsoft Visual Basic or C# 2005 Express Edition installed. You can download Visual Studio Express Edition from *http://msdn.microsoft .com/vstudio/express.*

On the Companion Disc   This chapter includes many code examples. You will find all the code from this chapter on the companion CD in the TK441\Chapter16 folder.

Lesson 1: Configuring Notification Services Instances and Applications

---

Estimated lesson time: 30 minutes

To build a Notification Services solution, you first develop the applications and then configure the host instance for the applications. This lesson gets you started by discussing how to define and configure instances for notification applications.

Configuring Notification Services Instances

A Notification Services instance hosts applications, with each instance managing its applications together. In other words, applications within the same instance share subscribers and delivery methods.

To create a Notification Services instance, you must first configure the instance. There are two ways of doing this. The first way is to create an XML file that contains the configuration of the instance. This file is called Instance Configuration File (ICF). The second way is to use NMO to create the configuration programmatically. In both cases, you need to configure the following information:

- Name of the Notification Services instance
- SQL Server instance that hosts the Notification Services instance and applications
- Name of the database and schema for the instance's database (optional)
- The applications that the instance hosts
- Custom delivery protocols
- All delivery channels
- Encryption information
- History and version information (optional)

Instance Name

An *instance name* is a unique name for an instance of Notification Services. If you do not specify a database name, Notification Services will name the database *instanceNameNSMain*. The instance name will also be the name of the instance's service.

The following code example shows how to define an instance name within an ICF file:

```
<!--XML-->
<InstanceName>My instance</InstanceName>
```

The following code example shows how to define an instance name by using NMO:

```
//C#
Instance myInstance = new Instance(notificationServices, instanceName);
```

IMPORTANT   Notification Services instance naming conventions

Notification Services instance names are not case-sensitive. There is no difference between the names ThisInstance and thisinstance. The name cannot contain quotation marks or be longer than 64 characters.

Database System

Notification Services instances contain metadata and subscriber data, and each application contains metadata and subscription, event, and notification data. This data is stored in SQL Server databases, while some Notification Services instance information is stored in the SQL Server *msdb* database. To specify the database engine for your configuration, you must provide the server and instance name—for example, MyServer/MyInstance. You cannot use an IP address or an alias such as localsystem. If your instance is on a remote server and you cannot use port 1433, you can specify the port. If your instance is in a failover cluster, use the SQL Server virtual server name.

The following code example shows how to define the database system within an ICF:

```
<!--XML-->
<InstanceName>MyInstance</InstanceName>
```

If you are defining the instance configuration programmatically, you need to connect to the SQL Server database. The most common option for doing this is by using the SQL Server Management Objects (SMO) namespace.

Instance Database and Schema

The instance database stores the hosted applications, protocols, delivery channels, and delivery protocols. It also stores subscriber data. You can define the name and schema for the instance database. If you are creating a new database, you can define the database specifications. If you do not specify a database, Notification Services creates a new database for the instance.

Here's how to specify a database and schema name within an ICF:

```
<!--XML-->
<DatabaseName>MyDatabase</DatabaseName>
<SchemaName>MySchema</SchemaName>
```

Here's how to specify a database and schema name by using NMO:

```
//C#
myInstance.DatabaseName = "MyDataBase";
myInstance.SchemaName = "MySchema";
```

List of Applications

To share subscribers, delivery protocols, and delivery channels between applications, Notification Services instances can host multiple applications. To host multiple applications in the same instance, you need to provide a list of applications when you configure the instance.

The following ICF code example shows how to define a list of applications by using the applications element, which specifies the application name, the base directory path, and the application definition file (ADF). (The ADF will be covered later in this lesson.) This example also shows how to pass parameters to the ADF, which can be specified here or in the command line.

```
<!--XML-->
<Applications>
    <Application>
        <ApplicationName>MyApplication</ApplicationName>
        <BaseDirectoryPath>%BaseDirectoryPath%</BaseDirectoryPath>
        <ApplicationDefinitionFilePath>
        appDefinition\MyApplicationADF.xml
        </ApplicationDefinitionFilePath>
        <Parameters>
            <Parameter>
                <Name>DBSystem</Name>
                <Value>%DBSystem%</Value>
            </Parameter>
        </Parameters>
    </Application>
</Applications>
```

You'll see later in this lesson how to configure Notification Services applications, but the following code shows how to add an application to an instance.

```
//C#
Application myApplication = ConfigureApplication(myInstance);
myInstance.Applications.Add(myApplication)
```

Custom Delivery Protocols

The instance's applications use custom delivery protocols. The built-in File and SMTP delivery protocols are already defined. The protocols implement communications between Notification Services and a delivery endpoint specified by a delivery channel. To create custom protocols, you use the *IDeliveryProtocol* interface.

You specify custom delivery protocols within an ICF as follows:

```xml
<!--XML-->
<Protocols>
    <Protocol>
        <ProtocolName>FAX</ProtocolName>
        <ClassName>Protocols.FAXProtocol</ClassName>
        <AssemblyName>%BaseDirPath%\FAX.dll</AssemblyName>
    </Protocol>
</Protocols>
```

Here's how to specify custom delivery protocols by using NMO:

```csharp
//C#
ProtocolDefinition customProtocol = new ProtocolDefinition(myInstance, "MyCustomProtocol");
customProtocol.ClassName = "MyNamespace.MyProtocolClass"; customProtocol.AssemblyName =
@"E:\MyCustomComponents.dll"; myInstance.ProtocolDefinitions.Add(customProtocol);
```

Delivery Channels

Delivery channels are the endpoints for notifications such as a Web server, e-mail, and so on. Devices, notifications, and subscriptions are all related. The following code example shows how to define delivery channels within an ICF.

```xml
<!--XML-->
<DeliveryChannels>
    <DeliveryChannel>
        <DeliveryChannelName>Filech</DeliveryChannelName>
        <ProtocolName>File</ProtocolName>
        <Arguments>
            <Argument>
                <Name>FileName</Name>
                <Value>C:\NSFolder\Notification.txt</Value>
            </Argument>
        </Arguments>
    </DeliveryChannel>
</DeliveryChannels>
```

You use NMO to define delivery channels as follows:

```csharp
//C#
DeliveryChannel fileCh = new DeliveryChannel(myInstance, "FileChannel"); fileCh.ProtocolName
= "File";
DeliveryChannelArgument fileNameArg = new DeliveryChannelArgument(fileCh, "FileName");
fileNameArg.Value ="C:\NSFolder\Notification.txt";
fileCh.DeliveryChannelArguments.Add(fileNameArg);
myInstance.DeliveryChannels.Add(fileCh);
```

Argument Encryption

Configuration arguments can be encrypted for security. You can encrypt delivery channels and host event provider arguments and instance and application databases. Encrypting arguments in the database protects sensitive information. You must provide a key when you create and register the instance, and you use the same key when updating.

IMPORTANT Encryption of XML configuration files

Be aware that XML configuration files are not encrypted.

The following code example shows how to define encryption within an ICF:

```
<!--XML-->
<EncryptArguments>true</EncryptArguments>
```

Here's how to implement argument encryption with NMO:

```
//C#
myInstance.EncryptArguments = true;
myInstance.ArgumentKey = "MyKey101010";
```

Instance Version and History

When you configure an instance of Notification Services, you can specify an instance version number. You can use your own version numbers. Notification Services adds the version number to the NSVersionInfo table in the instance database. When you update the instance, the version must be equal to or greater than the previous version.

You might also want to track history such as when the instance was created or last updated. This information is for your own use and is not stored in the instance database. You can provide this information in the ICF but not programmatically by using NMO. To track history programmatically, use comments. There are no instance history objects or properties available through NMO.

To add a version number within an ICF, use the following code:

```
<!--XML-->
<Version>
    <Major>1</Major>
    <Minor>0</Minor>
    <Build>1</Build>
    <Revision>1</Revision>
</Version>
<History>
    <CreationDate>2005-01-21</CreationDate>
```

```
<CreationTime>10:30:00</CreationTime>
<LastModifiedDate>2005-03-31</LastModifiedDate>
<LastModifiedTime>18:30:00</LastModifiedTime>
</History>
```

With NMO, you can implement version numbering by using:

```
//C#
myInstance.InstanceConfigurationFileVersion = new Version(1, 0, 1, 1);
```

Parameters in an ICF

You can use parameters in an ICF to make an instance more secure, portable, and easy to update. You can also use parameters to pass values to the application definition files. Configuring Notification Services programmatically doesn't provide parameter objects; instead, you can use variables. You can define a parameter value one time and use it multiple times in various elements.

The following ICF example shows how to set a parameter value and then use it in different elements:

```
<!--XML-->
<ParameterDefaults>
    <Parameter>
        <Name>BaseDirectoryPath</Name>
        <Value>C:\TestNot</Value>
    </Parameter>
</ParameterDefaults>
<BaseDirectoryPath>%BaseDirectoryPath%\Myapplication</BaseDirectoryPath>
<AssemblyName>%BaseDirectoryPath%\Myapplication.dll</AssemblyName>
```

Configuring Notification Services Applications

You also configure Notification Services applications through an XML file or programmatically by using NMO. Whether you use the XML ADF or NMO, you have to specify some of the following information:

- Application database definition (optional)
- Event class name, schema, rules, chronicles, and index properties
- Subscription class names, schemas, rules, chronicles, and index properties
- Notification class names, schemas, contents, protocols, and index properties
- Event provider specification
- Generator and distributor properties
- Operational settings
- History and version information (optional)

Application Database

Notification Services applications use a database to store event and subscription data and the results of notifications. It also stores application metadata. You can select an existing database or create a new database through Notification Services. If you specify an existing database, you need to provide the database name and schema name; any other information about the database, such as file names and file size, is ignored. If Notification Services creates a new database, you need to define the database properties such as file names, size, and locations. If you do not provide information about the application database, Notification Services creates a new database, using the model database as a template.

To specify the database and a schema name for an existing database by using an ADF, you use the following code:

```
<!--XML-->
<DatabaseName>myAppDatabase</DatabaseName>
<SchemaName>myAppDatabase</SchemaName>
```

To have Notification Services create a new database for the application by using an ADF, you use the following code:

```
<!--XML-->
<Database>
    <NamedFileGroup>
        <FileGroupName>Primary</FileGroupName>
        <FileSpec>
            <LogicalName>myAppPrimary</LogicalName>
            <FileName>E:\NS\myAppPrimary.mdf</FileName>
            <Size>2GB</Size>
            <MaxSize>5GB</MaxSize>
            <GrowthIncrement>500MB</GrowthIncrement>
        </FileSpec>
    </NamedFileGroup>
    <NamedFileGroup>
        <FileGroupName>Secondary</FileGroupName>
        <FileSpec>
            <LogicalName>myAppSecondary1</LogicalName>
            <FileName>E:\Data\myAppSecondary1.ndf</FileName>
            <Size>100MB</Size>
            <MaxSize>500MB</MaxSize>
            <GrowthIncrement>25%</GrowthIncrement>
        </FileSpec>
        <FileSpec>
            <LogicalName>myAppSecondary2</LogicalName>
            <FileName>E:\Data\myAppSecondary2.ndf</FileName>
        </FileSpec>
    </NamedFileGroup>
    <LogFile>
        <LogicalName>myAppLog</LogicalName>
```

```
        <FileName>D:\Logs\myAppLog.ldf</FileName>
    </LogFile>
    <DefaultFileGroup>Secondary</DefaultFileGroup>
    <CollationName>SQL_Latin1_General_Cp437_BIN</CollationName>
</Database>
```

IMPORTANT **Configuring applications with NMO**

Notification Services applications can also be configured by using NMO. See the SQL Server 2005 Books Online article "Defining Notification Services Applications" at *http://msdn2.microsoft.com/en-us/library/ms166506(SQL.90).aspx*.

Notification Classes

A notification class defines the type of notification you want to implement. When defining a Notification Services application, you have to create a notification class for each type of notification. Use a notification class to create tables, views, stored procedures, and functions to store and manage notification data. It also associates content formatters and delivery protocols.

You can define a notification class by using an ADF or by using NMO. The core elements of a notification class are:

- The name of the notification class and the SQL Server filegroup (optional).
- The notification class schema, which defines the notification data as well as how it is formatted and delivered to a subscriber; Notification Services creates a table that stores notification data.
- A content formatter, which takes the raw data and gives the format to notifications.
- The specification of digest or multicast delivery (optional).
- The notification batch size (optional).
- The delivery protocols for notification delivery.
- The notification expiration age (optional).

In the following code, you can see an example of a defining notification class using ADF:

```
<!--XML-->
<NotificationClass>
    <NotificationClassName>myApp</NotificationClassName>
    <Schema>
        <Fields>
            <Field>
                <FieldName>myAppField</FieldName>
                <FieldType>char(20)</FieldType>
            </Field>
        </Fields>
    </Schema>
```

```xml
            <FileGroup>Secondary</FileGroup>
            <ContentFormatter>
                <ClassName>myApp.myAppFormatter</ClassName>
                <AssemblyName>C:\NS\myAppFormatter.dll</AssemblyName>
                <Arguments>
                    <Argument>
                        <Name>OutputHTML</Name>
                        <Value>true</Value>
                    </Argument>
                </Arguments>
            </ContentFormatter>
            <DigestDelivery>true</DigestDelivery>
            <NotificationBatchSize>75</NotificationBatchSize>
            <Protocols>
                <Protocol>
                    <ProtocolName>SMTP</ProtocolName>
                    <Fields>
                        <Field>
                            <FieldName>Subject</FieldName>
                            <SqlExpression>%SubjectLine%</SqlExpression>
                        </Field>
                        <Field>
                            <FieldName>From</FieldName>
                            <SqlExpression>%fromAddress%</SqlExpression>
                        </Field>
                        <Field>
                            <FieldName>To</FieldName>
                            <FieldReference>DeviceAddress</FieldReference>
                        </Field>
                        <Field>
                            <FieldName>Priority</FieldName>
                            <SqlExpression>%mailPriority%</SqlExpression>
                        </Field>
                        <Field>
                            <FieldName>BodyFormat</FieldName>
                            <SqlExpression>&quot;html&quot;</SqlExpression>
                        </Field>
                    </Fields>
                    <ProtocolExecutionSettings>
                        <RetrySchedule>
                            <RetryDelay>P0DT00H20M00S</RetryDelay>
                        </RetrySchedule>
                        <FailuresBeforeAbort>15</FailuresBeforeAbort>
                        <MulticastRecipientLimit>12</MulticastRecipientLimit>
                        <WorkItemTimeout>P0DT00H35M00S</WorkItemTimeout>
                    </ProtocolExecutionSettings>
                </Protocol>
            </Protocols>
            <ExpirationAge>P0DT05H10M00S</ExpirationAge>
</NotificationClass>
```

Version and History

In the application configuration, you can also provide version and history information. The format of this information is similar to history and information stored in the instance configuration. The following code shows an example using ADF to define version and history information:

```
<!--XML-->
<Version>
    <Major>1</Major>
    <Minor>0</Minor>
    <Build>2</Build>
    <Revision>12</Revision>
</Version>
<History>
    <CreationDate>2004-02-10</CreationDate>
    <CreationTime>00:30:00</CreationTime>
    <LastModifiedDate>2006-03-31</LastModifiedDate>
    <LastModifiedTime>00:30:00</LastModifiedTime>
</History>
```

IMPORTANT More about application configuration

The event classes, event providers, generator settings, distributor settings, and execution setting are also defined in the application configuration. These elements of the application configuration are discussed later in this chapter.

Practice: Configuring Notification Services Applications and Instances

In this practice, you will apply the concepts from this lesson to configure Notification Services instances and applications.

▶ **Exercise 1: Configure a Notification Services Instance**

In this exercise, you will learn how to configure an instance of notification services using an ICF.

As a Notification Services solution designer, you need to configure an instance for hosting notification applications. Design your own ICF file, using parameters to configure the database system, file paths, and so on. Also, list an application and configure a delivery protocol for delivering notifications. Write your own solution before looking at the suggested answer.

Suggested Answer

The following ICF code satisfies the requirements:

```
<!--XML-->
<NotificationServicesInstance>
  <ParameterDefaults>
    <Parameter>
```

```
        <Name>_DBEngineInstance_</Name>
        <Value>%COMPUTERNAME%</Value>
      </Parameter>
      <Parameter>
        <Name>_ServerName_</Name>
        <Value>%COMPUTERNAME%</Value>
      </Parameter>
      <Parameter>
        <Name>_InstancePath_</Name>
        <Value>%ProgramFiles%\myInstance</Value>
      </Parameter>
    </ParameterDefaults>
    <InstanceName>myInstance</InstanceName>
    <SqlServerSystem>%_DBEngineInstance_%</SqlServerSystem>
    <Applications>
      <Application>
        <ApplicationName>myApp</ApplicationName>
        <BaseDirectoryPath>%_InstancePath_%</BaseDirectoryPath>
        <ApplicationDefinitionFilePath>%_InstancePath_%\myApp\appADF.xml
        </ApplicationDefinitionFilePath>
        <Parameters>
          <Parameter>
            <Name>_NSServer_</Name>
            <Value>%_ServerName_%</Value>
          </Parameter>
          <Parameter>
            <Name>_AppPath_</Name>
            <Value>%_InstancePath_%\myApp</Value>
          </Parameter>
        </Parameters>
      </Application>
    </Applications>
    <DeliveryChannels>
      <DeliveryChannel>
        <DeliveryChannelName>FileChannel</DeliveryChannelName>
        <ProtocolName>File</ProtocolName>
        <Arguments>
          <Argument>
            <Name>FileName</Name>
            <Value>%_InstancePath_%\myApp\Notifications.txt</Value>
          </Argument>
        </Arguments>
      </DeliveryChannel>
    </DeliveryChannels>
  </NotificationServicesInstance>
```

► **Exercise 2: Configure Notification Services Applications**

In this exercise, you will learn how to configure a notification service application using an ADF.

As a Notification Services solutions developer, design part of an ADF to configure the core elements of a Notification Services class. Write your own solution before looking at the suggested answer.

Suggested Answer

The following ADF code satisfies the requirements:

```
<!--XML-->
<NotificationClass>
    <NotificationClassName>myApp</NotificationClassName>
        <FileGroup>Secondary</FileGroup>
    <ContentFormatter>
        <ClassName>myApp.myAppFormatter</ClassName>
        <AssemblyName>C:\NS\myAppFormatter.dll</AssemblyName>
    </ContentFormatter>
    <DigestDelivery>true</DigestDelivery>
    <NotificationBatchSize>75</NotificationBatchSize>
    <Protocols>
        <Protocol>
            <ProtocolName>SMTP</ProtocolName>
            <Fields>
                <Field>
                    <FieldName>Subject</FieldName>
                    <SqlExpression>%SubjectLine%</SqlExpression>
                </Field>
                <Field>
                    <FieldName>From</FieldName>
                    <SqlExpression>%fromAddress%</SqlExpression>
                </Field>
                <Field>
                    <FieldName>To</FieldName>
                    <FieldReference>DeviceAddress</FieldReference>
                </Field>
                <Field>
                    <FieldName>BodyFormat</FieldName>
                    <SqlExpression>&quot;html&quot;</SqlExpression>
                </Field>
            </Fields>
            <ProtocolExecutionSettings>
                <RetrySchedule>
                    <RetryDelay>P0DT00H20M00S</RetryDelay>
                </RetrySchedule>
                <FailuresBeforeAbort>15</FailuresBeforeAbort>
                <MulticastRecipientLimit>12</MulticastRecipientLimit>
                <WorkItemTimeout>P0DT00H35M00S</WorkItemTimeout>
            </ProtocolExecutionSettings>
        </Protocol>
    </Protocols>
    <ExpirationAge>P0DT05H10M00S</ExpirationAge>
</NotificationClass>
```

Quick Check

1. How can you track history by using NMO?
2. What are the two ways to configure instances and applications?
3. What options are available when configuring the application database?

Quick Check Answers

1. Using NMO, you can specify a configuration to track only version information. To track history information, you must use comments instead.

2. You can configure Notification Services instances and applications by using XML files (ICF and ADF, respectively) or by using NMO to define the configurations programmatically.

3. When configuring the application database, you can choose to use an existing database; instruct Notification Services to create a new database by specifying the database properties; or, by not providing any database information, have Notification Services create a new database based on the model database template.

Lesson 2: Defining Notification Services Events and Event Providers

Estimated lesson time: 20 minutes

In this lesson, you will learn how to define Notification Services event classes and event providers. Notification Services applications can store data in the application database or retrieve it from other event sources such as an external database. You define event classes to store event data in an application database. An event provider retrieves data from sources and submits it to Notification Services.

Defining Event Classes

Notification Services stores event data in the application database or queries other event sources. To store data in the application database, you configure event classes. An *event class* defines name, fields, filegroup, indexes, additional event tables (chronicles), rules, and so on. You define a different event class for each type of event. When the notification application is created, Notification Services uses event classes to create SQL Server objects.

Event Class Properties

An event class represents a type of event. You have to define a different event class for each type of event. Notification Services creates tables, views, indexes, and procedures for each event class. The core elements of an event class are name, fields, and a filegroup, as shown in the following example:

```
<!--XML-->
<EventClass>
    <EventClassName>MyEvent</EventClassName>
    <Schema>
        <Field>
            <FieldName>MyEventField</FieldName>
            <FieldType>char(50)</FieldType>
            <FieldTypeMods>not null</FieldTypeMods>
        </Field>
    </Schema>
    <FileGroup>Primary</FileGroup>
</EventClass>
```

Chronicles

Chronicles are additional event tables in the application database. Events arrive in batches, so when Notification Services generates notifications, it uses the most recent batches and then marks them as completed. The marked event batch is never used again. Chronicle tables are used to store event data to be used for scheduled subscriptions or to track history. You can also use chronicles to archive all events for creating reports or to check for duplicate events and to store high and low values.

To define a chronicle, you have to define the table for the chronicles and the rules to maintain the tables. Chronicles and event classes are also implanted within the ADF file or by using NMO.

Defining Event Providers

Notification Services obtains data through event providers. *Event providers* collect an event and persist it as a single row in the application database or event table. Notification Services has three standard event providers that enable you to retrieve data from a file, through a T-SQL query, or by using an MDX query. You can also develop a custom event provider.

For information about developing custom providers, see the SQL Server 2005 Books Online topic "Developing a Custom Event Provider" at *http://msdn2.microsoft.com/en-us/library/ms171355.aspx*.

Hosted Event Providers

Event providers hosted by Notification Services are called hosted event providers. When Notification Services starts, it runs hosted event providers, of which there are two types: continuous and scheduled. A continuous event provider starts when Notification Services starts and ends when Notification Services stops. Notification Services starts a scheduled event provider when the engine starts and then checks for new events at defined intervals. Each application can have multiple hosted event providers.

To define a hosted event provider, you have to configure properties such as name, class, assembly, and arguments. You can define hosted event providers by using an ADF or with NMO.

The following example shows how to configure an event provider within the ADF:

```xml
<!--XML-->
<HostedProvider>
    <ProviderName>MyProvider</ProviderName>
    <ClassName>MyProvider </ClassName>
    <AssemblyName>
    C:\NS\EventProviders\MyProvider.dll
    </AssemblyName>
    <SystemName>%SYSNAME%</SystemName>
    <Schedule>
        <StartTime>10:00:00</StartTime>
        <Interval>P0DT00H10M00S</Interval>
     </Schedule>
    <ProviderTimeout>PT1M</ProviderTimeout>
    <Arguments>
        <Argument>
            <Name>getFile</Name>
```

```
            <Value>c:\data.txt</Value>
        </Argument>
    </Arguments>
</HostedProvider>
```

Nonhosted Event Provider

Notification Services does not control or manage nonhosted event providers. They are external applications that send event data to Notification Services. They use the *EventCollector* and *EventLoader* classes or the event collection stored procedures. To configure a nonhosted provider, you provide the name of the provider in the application definition.

The following example shows how to configure a nonhosted provider within the ADF:

```
<!--XML-->
<NonHostedProvider>
    <ProviderName>SalesProvider</ProviderName>
</NonHostedProvider>
```

IMPORTANT   Nonhosted provider name

The name provided in the ADF for a nonhosted provider is used only to track the source of events for administration and reporting purposes.

Notification Services Standard Event Providers

Notification Services comes with three standard event providers: the File System Watcher, SQL Server, and Analysis Services.

The File System Watcher event provider is a continuous event provider. It monitors directories for new event files. It is easy to configure when event data is provided in XML files; you need to specify the structure of the XML code only in an XML schema definition (XSD) file. It uses the *FileSystemWatcher* class of the .NET Framework and uses the *EventLoader* method provided by Notification Services to store the event information in the event table.

The SQL Server event provider is a scheduled event provider. It queries a database for events. You define T-SQL code to get the event data. You can also define a T-SQL query to be processed after the event data is gained. It is a hosted scheduled provider. The following example shows how to use the SQL Server event provider within an ADF:

```
<!--XML-->
<Providers>
    <HostedProvider>
        <ProviderName>SQLPrices</ProviderName>
        <ClassName>SQLProvider</ClassName>
        <SystemName>%SYSNAME%</SystemName>
        <Schedule>
            <Interval>P0DT00H00M30S</Interval>
```

```
    </Schedule>
    <ProviderTimeout>PT10M</ProviderTimeout>
    <Arguments>
        <Argument>
            <Name>EventsQuery</Name>
            <Value>
            SELECT PriceCode, Price
            FROM PriceTable
            </Value>
        </Argument>
        <Argument>
            <Name>EventClassName</Name>
            <Value>Prices</Value>
        </Argument>
    </Arguments>
  </HostedProvider>
</Providers>
```

The third standard event provider is the Analysis Services event provider, which enables you to monitor an Analysis Services cube. You use it to send event data based on an MDX query. It runs as a hosted scheduled event provider. With MDX, you can easily monitor key performance indicators (KPIs).

Exam Tip   Review all the configurations properties of the three standard event providers. For more information about standard event providers, see SQL Server 2005 Books Online.

Practice: Using Event Providers and Event Classes

In this practice, you apply the concepts from this lesson to configure Notification Services event providers and define event classes.

▶ **Exercise 1: Configure the File System Watcher Event Provider**

In this exercise, you will learn how to use the File System Watcher to get data from an XML file.

As a Notification Services solution developer, you need to retrieve data from an XML file stored in the c:\sales directory. Configure the File System Watcher event provider within your ADF to submit the event data to your sales event class. Write your own solution before looking at the suggested answer.

Suggested Answer

The following code satisfies the requirements:

```
<!--XML-->
<Providers>
    <HostedProvider>
        <ProviderName>myWatcher</ProviderName>
        <ClassName>FileSystemWatcherProvider</ClassName>
        <SystemName>%SYSNAME%</SystemName>
```

```
            <Arguments>
               <Argument>
                  <Name>WatchDirectory</Name>
                  <Value>C:\sales</Value>
               </Argument>
               <Argument>
                  <Name>EventClassName</Name>
                  <Value>sales</Value>
               </Argument>
               <Argument>
                  <Name>SchemaFile</Name>
                  <Value>C:\sales\sales.xsd</Value>
               </Argument>
               <Argument>
                  <Name>RetryAttempts</Name>
                  <Value>20</Value>
               </Argument>
               <Argument>
                  <Name>RetryQueueOccupancy</Name>
                  <Value>200</Value>
               </Argument>
               <Argument>
                  <Name>RetryPeriod</Name>
                  <Value>10000</Value>
               </Argument>
               <Argument>
                  <Name>RetryWorkload</Name>
                  <Value>1000</Value>
               </Argument>
            </Arguments>
         </HostedProvider>
      </Providers>
```

▶ **Exercise 2: Define an Event Class**

In this exercise, you will learn how to create an event class by using an ADF.

As a Notification Services solution developer, you need to define an event class within an ADF that will host two values: the price and the product code. Write your own solution before looking at the suggested answer.

Suggested Answer

The following code satisfies the requirements:

```
<!--XML-->
<EventClass>
   <EventClassName>MyEvent</EventClassName>
   <Schema>
      <Field>
         <FieldName>ProductCode</FieldName>
         <FieldType>char(50)</FieldType>
         <FieldTypeMods>not null</FieldTypeMods>
      </Field>
      <Field>
```

```
            <FieldName>price</FieldName>
            <FieldType>money</FieldType>
            <FieldTypeMods>not null</FieldTypeMods>
        </Field>
    </Schema>
    <FileGroup>Primary</FileGroup>
</EventClass>
```

Quick Check

1. Can you schedule a provider?
2. How does Notification Services manage nonhosted providers?
3. Can you use the Notification Services File System Watcher event provider to monitor non-XML files?

Quick Check Answers

1. Yes, there are two types of Notification Services event providers. Continuous providers start and stop when the Notification Services engine starts and stops. Scheduled providers can be scheduled to check for events at pre-defined intervals.
2. Notification Services does not manage nonhosted providers. It uses only the external provider for event source tracking.
3. Yes, you can monitor non-XML files by providing additional configuration information. XML files are easier to configure by using an XSD file.

Lesson 3: Configuring the Notification Services Generator and Distributor

Estimated lesson time: 20 minutes

The Notification Services generator manages the rule process for an application. The distributor or distributors manage notification formatting and delivery for an application. In this lesson, you will learn how to configure both the generator and the distributor.

Configuring the Notification Services Generator

A Notification Services instance can have only one generator. It is normally hosted by the Windows service of the Notification Services instance. The generator is specified when you define the application. The values to specify are the computer that hosts the generator and the number of threads that can be used.

The following code shows how to configure the generator by using an ADF:

```
<!--XML-->
<Generator>
    <SystemName>host123</SystemName>
    <ThreadPoolSize>20</ThreadPoolSize>
</Generator>
```

The following code shows how to configure the generator by using NMO:

```
//C#
Generator myGenerator = new Generator(myApplication, "Generator");
myGenerator.SystemName = "host123";
myGenerator.ThreadPoolSize = 20;
myApplication.Generator = myGenerator;
```

The number of threads, which determines the number of operations that can be performed in parallel, can improve application performance. When you define a number of threads, Notification Services decides the actual number to use, using an optimization algorithm. If you specify 0 as the number of threads, Notification Services will use as many threads as it can get from the system. In SQL Server 2005 Enterprise, SQL Server Developer, and SQL Server Evaluation editions, the maximum and default, if not specified, number of threads is 25. In SQL Server 2005 Standard Edition, the maximum number is 1.

IMPORTANT   Generator on a failover cluster

Use the virtual server name when the generator runs on a failover cluster.

Configuring the Notification Services Distributor

A distributor is run by the Windows service of a Notification Services instance. You can define multiple distributors for each application. The distributor formats and delivers notifications in a time interval called the quantum. A distributor polls for notifications, formats them, and delivers the notifications by using a delivery protocol. If a notification cannot be delivered, the distributor will retry, depending on the retry intervals and notification expiration information defined. The distributor attempts to retry in the next quantum. When you specify multiple distributors for the same application, all of the distributors perform the same function. Therefore, having two distributors in the same server does not improve performance. To improve performance, place multiple distributors among multiple physical servers.

The following code shows an example of a distribution configuration, using ADF:

```
<!--XML-->
<Distributors>
    <Distributor>
        <SystemName>host123</SystemName>
        <ThreadPoolSize>5</ThreadPoolSize>
        <QuantumDuration>P0DT00H00M10S</QuantumDuration>
    </Distributor>
    <Distributor>
        <SystemName>host124</SystemName>
        <ThreadPoolSize>1</ThreadPoolSize>
        <QuantumDuration>P0DT00H00M50S</QuantumDuration>
    </Distributor>
</Distributors>
```

The following code shows how to configure the distributor, using NMO:

```
//C#
Distributor myDistributor =
    new Distributor(myApplication, "Distributor");
myDistributor.SystemName = "host123";
myDistributor.QuantumDuration = new TimeSpan(0, 0, 30);
myDistributor.ThreadPoolSize = 10;
myApplication.Distributors.Add(myDistributor);
```

IMPORTANT Multiple distributors per application

SQL Server 2005 Enterprise, SQL Server Developer, and SQL Server Evaluation editions can have multiple distributors per application. SQL Server Standard Edition can have only one distributor per application.

Practice: Configuring the Generator and Distributor

In this practice, you will apply the concepts from this lesson to specify a generator and configure Notification Services distributors.

▶ **Exercise 1: Configure the Generator**

In this exercise, you will learn how to specify a generator for your Notification Services applications.

As a Notification Services solution developer, you have to configure the generator for your applications. Your Notification Services host is named SRV12, and your database system is running SQL Server 2005 Standard Edition. Define the distributor elements of an ADF configuration. Develop your own solution before looking at the suggested answer.

Suggested Answer

The following code satisfies the requirements:

```
Distributor myDistributor =
    new Distributor(myApplication, "Distributor");
myDistributor.SystemName = "host123";
myDistributor.QuantumDuration = new TimeSpan(0, 0, 30);
myDistributor.ThreadPoolSize = 10;
myApplication.Distributors.Add(myDistributor);
```

▶ **Exercise 2: Configure Multiple Distributors**

In this exercise, you will learn how to configure distributors for Notification Services Applications.

As a Notification Services solution developer, you need to define two distributors for your application. You want to host one distributor on server SRV14 and the other on server SRV15. You want to check for notifications every 20 seconds. Define your distributor configuration by using NMO. Write your own solution before looking at the suggested answer.

Suggested Answer

The following code satisfies the requirements:

```
//C#
Distributor myDistributor =
    new Distributor1(myApplication, "Distributor");
Distributor myDistributor =
    new Distributor2(myApplication, "Distributor");
myDistributor1.SystemName = "SRV14";
myDistributor1.QuantumDuration = new TimeSpan(0, 0, 20);
myDistributor1.ThreadPoolSize = 10;
myDistributor2.SystemName = "SRV15";
myDistributor2.QuantumDuration = new TimeSpan(0, 0, 20);
myDistributor2.ThreadPoolSize = 10;
myApplication.Distributors.Add(myDistributor1);
myApplication.Distributors.Add(myDistributor2);
```

Quick Check

1. Can you define two distributors for the same application on one server?
2. Can you set the number of threads value to 2 in a generator running SQL Server 2005 Standard Edition?
3. What happens if you set the threads value to 0 when configuring the generator?

Quick Check Answers

1. You can define two distributors on the same server, but doing so will not improve performance. Distribute your distributors among different servers to improve performance.
2. You can set the thread value to 2, but the Standard Edition of SQL Server 2005 uses only one thread for the generator.
3. When the threads value is set to 0, SQL Server can use the maximum number of threads available in the system, but only if the SQL Server edition allows it.

Lesson 4: Testing the Notification Services Application

Estimated lesson time: 20 minutes

In this lesson, you will learn how to test Notification Services applications. To test an application, you need to register, compile, and enable your Notification Services instance and applications.

Creating and Registering a New Instance and Compiling Your Application

To register a new Notification Services instance, complete the following:

1. Open SQL Server Management Studio (SSMS).
2. In the Object Explorer, connect to the database engine where you plan to install the instance. (If the Object Explorer pane is not visible, select Object Explorer from the View menu.)
3. In the Object Explorer tree, locate the Notification Services folder. It contains the already registered instances.
4. To create a new Notification Services instance, right-click in the Notification Services folder and select New Notification Services Instance.
5. Click Browse in the New Notification Services Instance dialog box and select your application Instance Configuration File.

6. In the Notification Services Instance dialog box pictured in Figure 16–1, you can see the application parameters from your ICF.

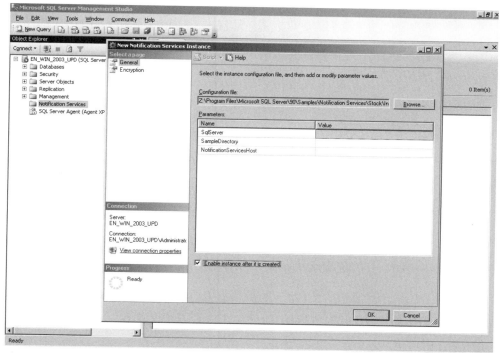

Figure 16-1   Creating a new Notification Instance in SQL Server Management Studio

7. Select the Enable Instance After It Is Created option.
8. Click OK to compile the instance and its associated application or applications. You will see a progress dialog box. When all the steps are completed successfully, click Close to close the progress dialog box.

9. You should see the instance just created in the Notification Services folder. Right-click that instance and select Register. This opens the Register dialog box.

10. Select the Create Windows Service check box and choose an authentication mode. Click OK to register your instance. After successful registration, close the dialog box.

Now that you have installed and registered your instance, you can start and stop it by selecting Start or Stop in the instance context menu. Your application is running now, and you can test your application by submitting subscriptions and events. (Subscriptions will be covered later in this chapter.)

Exploring Your Instance and Application Objects

You can see your Notification Services instance and application databases in the Object Explorer. You defined the database in the ICF and ADF. The Notification Services compiler created this database when it compiled the ICF. Notification Services stored objects associated with the instance and applications in the database just created.

The Notification Services compiler also stores the configuration information from the ADF in the database. This information includes the event providers, the generators, and the distributors. With all this information, the Windows service, created when the ICF was compiled, initializes all the components.

Removing the Instance and Application

After testing your Notification Services application, you might need to remove it from your test system. To remove the instance and application, complete the following steps:

1. In SSMS, locate the Object Explorer and stop the instance by right-clicking your instance in the Notification Services folder and selecting Stop. A dialog box asks you to confirm your request. After you have successfully stopped the instance, close the dialog box.

2. Unregister your instance by right-clicking it in the Notification Services folder and selecting Unregister. You have to confirm your request; after success, close the dialog box.

3. Right-click your instance name and select Delete. After success, all the instance and application objects are removed.

IMPORTANT Testing details

Chapter 10, "Designing a Unit Test Plan for a Database," covers testing theory and practices in detail. Use what you have learned from Chapter 10 to test your Notification Services applications.

Practice: Testing Your Application

In this practice, you will apply the concepts from this lesson and previous lessons to test your Notification Services instance and applications.

▶ **Exercise 1: Create an Instance and Compile Applications**

In this exercise, you will learn how to create an instance from an ICF and compile your Notification Services applications.

As a Notification Services solution developer, you have created your ICF and ADF to configure your Notification Services instance and applications. Create and register a new Notification Services instance and verify that the objects created in the database were specified in your configuration and definition files.

1. Connect to the database engine that will host your instance and applications.
2. Create a new instance in your Notification Services folder.
3. Select the ICF that configures the instance and specifies the application definition file.
4. Browse the objects created in the database that you specified in your configuration files and verify that they are the correct objects.

▶ **Exercise 2: Remove Your Instance and Application Objects**

Now that you have tested your instance and applications, you need to remove all the objects created when the ICF and ADF were compiled so you can get back to the state previous to testing.

1. Connect to the database engine that hosts your instance and applications.
2. In the Notification Services folder, stop your instance.
3. Unregister your instance.
4. Delete your instance.
5. After completion of these steps, verify that the objects have been removed.

Quick Check

1. How can you stop and start a Notification Services instance without using SSMS?
2. How can you test your application after the instance is started?
3. How do you delete all the instance and application objects without deleting the instance?

Quick Check Answers

1. A Windows service is created for each instance. You can start and stop the service as you would any other Windows service.

2. You can test your Notification Services application by submitting subscriptions and events.

3. You can delete the instance and application objects without deleting the instance by stopping and unregistering the instance but not deleting it.

Lesson 5: Creating Subscriptions

Estimated lesson time: 20 minutes

Subscriptions are a key component of a Notification Services solution. Subscribers specify the information they are interested in from the notification applications by creating subscriptions. Subscription data is stored in the application database. You use subscription classes to define the storage for this data and the rules to generate notifications. You can define a subscription class by using the ADF or, programmatically, by using NMO.

An application can have several subscription classes for multiple types of subscriptions. Notification Services uses the information from the subscription classes to generate the SQL Server objects that implement the notification solution, such as tables, views, and indexes.

Defining the Subscription Class

You create a subscription class for every type of subscription in your application. A subscription class has the following elements:

- A subscription class name
- A filegroup
- Subscription class schema (optional)
- Event rules (optional)
- Scheduled rules (optional)
- Custom indexes (optional)
- Subscription chronicles tables (optional)

Subscription Class Name and Filegroup

The following sample code shows how to specify the subscription class name and filegroup by using an ADF:

```
<!--XML-->
<SubscriptionClassName>mySubscriptions</SubscriptionClassName>
<FileGroup>Secondary</FileGroup>
```

The following sample code shows how to specify the subscription class name and filegroup by using NMO:

```
//C#
myApplication.SubscriptionClasses.Add(mySubscriptions);  mySubscriptions.FileGroup =
"SECONDARY";
```

Notification Services adds the following fields in the resulting subscription class table: *SubscriptionId*, *SubscriberId*, *Created*, *Updates*, and *Enable*. When a subscription class also has scheduled rules, Notification Services adds the *ScheduleId* field in the subscription class and an index on this field.

Subscription Schema

In most of the applications, you must specify the subscription fields that are used at notification generation. These fields are specified in the schema of the subscription class.

The following sample code shows how to specify the schema within an ADF:

```
<!--XML-->
<Schema>
    <Field>
        <FieldName>City</FieldName>
        <FieldType>nvarchar(255)</FieldType>
        <FieldTypeMods>NOT NULL</FieldTypeMods>
    </Field>
</Schema>
```

The following sample code shows how to specify the schema using NMO:

```
//C#
SubscriptionField city = new SubscriptionField(mySubscriptions, "city");
city.Type = "nvarchar(255)";
city.TypeModifier = "not null";
mySubscriptions.SubscriptionFields.Add(city);
```

Subscription Rules

Subscription rules join event data with subscription data to generate notifications. Subscription rules can be event-driven or scheduled.

The following code sample illustrates how to define rules to get information from chronicle tables and event tables:

```
<!--XML-->
<EventRule>
    <RuleName>PriceWatcherEventRule</RuleName>
    <Action>
    INSERT INTO PriceNotification
    ( SubscriberId, city,
      Product, Price )
    SELECT A.SubscriberId, A.city,
        B.Product, B.Price
    FROM PriceSubscriptions A JOIN PriceEvents B
    ON A.Product = B.Product
    JOIN PriceEventChron C
    ON A.Product = C.Product
    WHERE A.SaleTriggerPrice &lt;= B.Price
```

```
AND A.ProductTriggerPrice &gt; C.ProductHighPrice
INSERT ProductSubscriptionChron --
  (SubscriberId, Product, Price)
SELECT A.SubscriberId, A.Product, B.Price
FROM PriceSubscriptions A JOIN PriceEvents B
ON A.Product = B.Product
</Action>
<ActionTimeout>P0DT00H05M30S</ActionTimeout>
<EventClassName>PriceWatcher</EventClassName>
```

Indexes for Subscription Classes

You can improve Notification Services performance by creating indexes. In the next lesson, you will learn how to use indexes to increase performance. However, this example shows how to create an index on a subscription class by using ADF:

```
<!--XML-->
<IndexSqlSchema>
    <SqlStatement>
    CREATE INDEX SalesIndex
    ON SalesSubscriptions (SubscriberId)
    </SqlStatement>
</IndexSqlSchema>
```

The following sample shows how to create a subscription class index by using NMO:

```
//C#
mySubscriptions.IndexSqlStatements.Add(
    "CREATE INDEX SalesIndex ON " +
    "MyAppSchema.mySubscriptions ( SubscriberId )");
```

Subscription Class Chronicles

To store previous data about notifications, you can use chronicles. You can use previous notification information to determine whether a subscriber has received similar data or any notifications in the past hours. Subscription chronicles are tables. You can create as many chronicles as you want for a subscription.

For more information about subscription chronicles, see "Defining Chronicles for a Subscription Class" in SQL Server 2005 Books Online at *http://msdn2.microsoft.com/en-us/library/ms172554.aspx.*

Subscription Management Interfaces

To submit subscriber and subscription information to Notification Services, you need to use management interfaces. When developing management interfaces, you use the subscription management API. To learn more about developing custom subscription management interfaces, see "Developing Subscription Management Interfaces" in SQL Server 2005 Books Online at *http://msdn2.microsoft.com/en-us/library/ms166433.aspx.*

IMPORTANT Management views

SQL Server provides views to manage subscribers, subscriber devices, and basic subscriptions in Notification Services.

Practice: Subscription in Notification Services

In this practice, you will apply the concepts from Lesson 5, "Creating Subscriptions," and previous lessons to create Notification Services subscriptions.

▶ **Exercise 1: Define the Core Components of a Subscription**

In this exercise, you will learn how to create a complete subscription for your Notification Services application.

As a Notification Services solution developer, you must define the class name and the filegroup for a subscription within an ADF. Write your own solution before looking at the suggested answer.

Suggested Answer

The following code satisfies the requirements:

```
<!--XML-->
<SubscriptionClassName>mySubscriptions</SubscriptionClassName>
<FileGroup>Secondary</FileGroup>
```

▶ **Exercise 2: Create Indexes by Using NMO**

In this exercise, you will learn how use NMO to create indexes.

As a Notification Services solution developer, you have noticed poor performance when using SubscriberId in the Sales subscription. To improve performance, define an index by using NMO. Write your own solution before looking at the suggested answer.

Suggested Answer

The following code satisfies the requirements:

```
//C#
mySubscriptions.IndexSqlStatements.Add(
    "CREATE INDEX SalesIndex ON " +
    "MyAppSchema.mySubscriptions ( SubscriberId )");
```

Quick Check

1. How can you store information about previous notifications?
2. How would you improve performance within subscriptions?
3. How can you manipulate subscription and subscriber data without directly accessing the tables?

Quick Check Answers

1. You can use chronicles to store information about previous notifications.
2. Using the appropriate indexes within subscriptions can improve performance.
3. SQL Server provides views for managing subscribers, subscriber devices, and basic subscription information.

Lesson 6: Optimizing Notification Services

Estimated lesson time: 25 minutes

Notification Services can send thousands or millions of notifications. This means that the process for retrieving notification data, storing the data, and distributing notifications must be optimized for top performance. In this lesson, you will learn how to optimize Notification Services solutions.

Optimizing Event Data

Events are the triggers for notifications. An event can contain a little or a lot of data, and events can be sporadic or periodic. Each notification solution is different, so there are different aspects to consider when designing a notification solution. The different workloads generated by event management, notification generation, notification formatting, and notification delivery influence performance.

The event table stores event information. To design this table for optimum performance, you have to think of it as a regular table created in SQL Server. The event table is likely to have several indexes; work on identifying appropriate indexing candidates and the type of indexed fields.

IMPORTANT   Give *tempdb* enough capacity

Notification Services uses the *tempdb* database of SQL Server intensely, so you need to give *tempdb* a large initial capacity to avoid having to resize it later. Using the Full recovery model enables restore operations but also results in larger log files. Thus, set a large size for log files to avoid resizing. In addition, placing log files on a different physical spindle will reduce the amount of concurrent disk access and improve performance.

Event information is crucial for fulfilling business requirements. Events need to be processed quickly. Each event class becomes a table in the application database. Keep event information to the minimum size possible; consider storing a reference for extra information but note that the extra work looking up the additional information can reduce performance.

Indexes can improve performance when reading but can slow inserts, updates, and deletes. Therefore, it is critical to choose a good indexing strategy. Notification Services creates indexes on the EventID and EventBatchID columns.

BEST PRACTICES   Covering indexes

Using a covering index will force the query to run entirely against the index. This type of index can improve performance.

When using event chronicles tables, use a timestamp (or datetime value) for version control if time notification is required.

Optimizing Subscriptions

Notification Services uses database tables to store subscription data. It also uses rules to specify when a particular user or application should be notified. To plan an optimal subscription strategy, you must consider the subscription load, additional information, historical information, rules usage, indexing, subscription management, and whether notifications are scheduled or event driven. Consider whether your subscription allows user customization, specifying the locale and identifying devices.

Use chronicles when you need to maintain subscription history; use the timestamping of the last notification.

Rules are critical in a Notification Services solution; they determine when a subscriber needs to be notified. Subscription rules generate notifications by joining event data with subscription data. When you use rules, do not update event or subscription tables. Avoid the use of event-driven subscriptions unless it is essential to send notifications immediately.

Use indexing to improve performance when reading. Analyze column usage in JOIN and WHERE clauses to see whether indexing is needed. Consider using covering indexes.

BEST PRACTICES Using SQL Server tools

Use SQL Server tuning tools, particularly SQL Server Profiler and the Database Tuning Advisor, to determine the best indexing strategy for your Notification Services solution.

Optimizing Notifications

In a notification solution, accessing external information is a frequent task. It also has an impact on notification formatting. Notification generation and formatting generate heavy disk usage. Consider moving notification data to a specific filegroup or to a separate physical spindle. Also, consider using computed fields, which enable the distributor to compute notification data immediately before passing it to the content formatter. This might add more formatting processing, but it might also reduce processing at the client and reduce storage requirements. You can also improve performance in notifications by using the right indexing strategy. Consider indexing if your notification has computed values. These columns can be included in a covering index or with the *INCLUDE* keyword.

When designing notification delivery, remember that the file delivery protocol is primarily for testing purposes. If possible, use the SMTP delivery protocol. If you need to deliver files, and especially if you want to deliver several files, consider using custom delivery protocols. Multicast is the best way to send the same notification to several subscribers because the notification is formatted only one time. When only one system is distributing notifications, you can increase the batch size as much as your protocol allows. When multiple distributors are present, adjust the batch size to enable different distributors to work as equal partners.

Practice: Optimizing Notification Services Solutions

In this practice, you will apply the concepts learned in this lesson to optimize your Notification Services solution.

▶ **Exercise 1: Optimize Events**

In this exercise, you will learn a technique for optimizing events.

> As a Notification Services solution developer, you need to notify customers of changes to their contracts, including approval, rejection, and whether they need additional information. You need to send changes to their contracts once a day. Should you use event chronicles in this solution?

> **Suggested Answer**

> The best solution is to use a scheduled subscription that benefits from chronicles. Using chronicles is not a must.

▶ **Exercise 2: Optimize Notifications**

In this exercise, you will learn a technique for optimizing notifications.

> As a Notification Services solution developer, you notice that generating and formatting notification uses disks heavily. What optimization options can you implement to improve performance?

> **Suggested Answer**

> You can specify a different filegroup for notification data or move it to a separate physical spindle. You can also consider using computed values and indexing them.

> ## Quick Check
>
> 1. How is event data stored?
> 2. What should you know about *tempdb* and Notification Services?
> 3. How would you send the same notification to multiple subscribers?
>
> **Quick Check Answers**
>
> 1. Event data is stored as a traditional SQL Server table.
> 2. Notification Services uses *tempdb* heavily, so you need to set a large initial value to avoid the cost of resizing.
> 3. You can send the same notification to multiple subscribers by using multicast.

Case Scenario: Design a Notification Services Application

You are the database platform architect for an airline company. Your company wants to notify passengers about any issue regarding their flights via short message service (SMS) or e-mail. You are planning to implement a Notification Services application to accomplish this requirement. You need to maintain history for notification events, and performance is a must for the solution.

1. How should you create the Notification Services application so that you can track history?

2. To get the best performance, what do you need to configure in the SQL Server system databases?

3. What type of provider should you use for this scenario?

Chapter Summary

- Notification Services can send thousands to millions of notifications to subscribers.

- You can configure your Notification Services instance by using an XML instance configuration file (ICF) or by using Notification Services Management Objects (NMO). When configuring an instance, you specify the instance properties and a list of applications. You can also pass parameters to applications. You can configure Notification Services applications by using an XML application definition file (ADF) or by using Notification Services Management Objects (NMO). You can create and register a new Notification Services instance and compile your notification applications in SQL Server Management Studio (SSMS).

- Data is submitted to Notification Services via event classes and event providers. Event providers can be hosted or nonhosted. Subscription rules join event data with subscription data to generate notifications. Notification Services comes with three standard event providers: the File System Watcher, SQL Server, and Analysis Services.

- The generator manages rule processing for a notification application. A Notification Services instance can have only one generator. The Notification Services distributor formats and delivers notifications. You can define multiple distributors for each application.

- You can use database-tuning techniques to design Notification Services database tables. By designing the correct indexing strategy, you can improve notification performance.

Chapter 17

Developing Packages for Integration Services

SQL Server Integration Services (SSIS) is a new member of the Microsoft SQL Server 2005 family of technologies. SSIS, the successor to Data Transformation Services (DTS), is a platform for building extraction, transformation, and loading (ETL) solutions and data-integration applications. In this chapter, you will learn how to develop applications that benefit from SSIS technologies. After learning how to develop SSIS packages using SQL Server Business Intelligence Development Studio (BIDS), you will see how to debug and test SSIS packages. Finally, you will learn how to select which strategies and technologies to use in your ETL or integration projects.

Exam objectives in this chapter:

■ Develop packages for Integration Services.

❑ Select an appropriate Integration Services technology or strategy.

❑ Create Integration Services packages.

❑ Test Integration Services packages.

Before You Begin

To complete the lessons in this chapter, you must have:

■ A computer that meets the hardware and software requirements for SQL Server 2005.

■ SQL Server 2005 Developer Edition, Workgroup Edition, Standard Edition, or Enterprise Edition installed as well as the SQL Server Database Engine and Integration Services components installed.

■ The SQL Server 2005 *AdventureWorks* Online Transaction Processing (OLTP) and Online Analytical Processing (OLAP) sample databases installed. Sample databases are available with SQL Server 2005 Enterprise Edition but are not a part of the default installation. Alternatively, you can install the sample databases from *http://msdn2.microsoft.com/en-us /library/ms143739.aspx*.

- SQL Server 2005 Samples and SQL Server Client Tools. Both are selectable options during the SQL Server installation.
- Microsoft Visual Studio 2005 or Microsoft Visual Basic or C# 2005 Express Edition installed. You can download Visual Studio Express Editions from *http://msdn.microsoft.com/vstudio/express/*.

IMPORTANT   Practices in this chapter build upon each other

Beginning with Lesson 2, "Debugging and Testing SSIS Packages," the lesson practices build upon each other; to move to the next practice, you need to finish the previous one.

Lesson 1: Creating Integration Services Packages

Estimated lesson time: 40 minutes

In the database world, integrating data is a common requirement. You might need to use SSIS to build a data warehouse or data mart in an ETL process, or you might need to use it as a migration tool between application versions or to integrate data between applications at the database level. In this lesson, you will learn how to use Visual Studio to create SSIS packages. You will see how to configure the control flow of the package and how the package interacts with the environment, including the file system, databases, file transfer protocol (FTP) servers, and so on. You will also learn how to configure the data flow to create data transformation pipelines. Finally, you will see how to configure logging and package configurations to increase package manageability.

What Is a Package?

A package is the fundamental element of the SSIS platform. Packages are the central execution element and are a collection of different elements that can be configured to integrate data. Packages can contain tasks, containers, precedence constraints, variables, connections, data sources, transformations, destinations, event handlers, configurations, and other elements. You can design packages by using BIDS, or you can create them programmatically.

An SSIS package has two run-time engines: the control flow engine and the data flow engine. The control flow engine is where you configure the package's workflow. The workflow is responsible for interacting with the environment and has a distinct sequence of precedence constraints. The data flow engine is where you program data transformations. In contrast to control flow, the data flow does not have precedence constraints; instead, it defines data flow pipelines.

To create an SSIS package using BIDS, perform the following steps:

1. From the main menu, click File, click New, and then select Project.
2. From the Project Types pane, select Business Intelligence Projects.
3. Select the Integration Services Project template, name the project, and click OK.

Connection Managers

SSIS packages enable you to configure connections at the package level. Connection managers are the logical representation of a connection and describe the physical connection required to interact with a data source. Connection managers offer different properties that enable you to configure the connection; however, the central element of most connection managers is the connection string, in which most of the configuration takes place.

To configure a SQL Server 2005 connection, perform the following steps:

1. In the SSIS designer, right-click in any empty area of the Connection Managers pane. Select a New OLE DB connection.

2. If the connection has not been previously defined, click the New button to create a new connection.

3. In the Provider drop-down list, notice that by default it uses Native OLE DB\SQL Native Client, appropriate for SQL Server 2005 servers.

4. In the Server Name text box, type the server name.

5. Select the appropriate authentication method.

6. Select the appropriate database.

7. Click OK to confirm the configuration and click OK again to select the newly created connection manager.

Connection managers are used to connect not only to relational databases; they can also be used to connect to files and folders, FTP servers, and so on. Following is a list of the connection managers provided with SSIS.

- ADO
- FLATFILE
- MSOLAP90
- ODBC
- WMI
- ADO.NET
- FTP
- MULTIFILE
- SMOServer
- EXCEL
- HTTP
- MULTIFLATFILE
- SMTP
- FILE
- SMMQ
- OLEDB
- SQLMOBILE

After you create the connection manager, you can use it in multiple tasks and to configure multiple data sources.

SSIS Variables

SSIS variables are useful for maintaining the state during package execution. For example, you can define an SSIS variable to hold the name of a file being processed or the connection string of a database. SSIS variables can hold simple values such as integers, strings, or dates, and they can hold complex values such as recordsets or arrays.

To declare a variable in SSIS, follow these steps:

1. In the package designer, select the Control Flow Pane.
2. Right-click in an empty space of the design area.
3. Select Variables.
4. In the Variables pane, click the Add Variable button.

IMPORTANT   Variable scope

Later in this lesson, you will learn about containers. The scope of a variable is determined by which container you select when you right-click. If you want to define the variable at the package level, make sure that you are not selecting any area or object when you right-click. Adding a variable while in the data flow designer limits the scope of the variable to the Data Flow task.

Control Flow

Every SSIS package has one, and only one, control flow. The control flow is where developers define the workflow of the package, which is responsible for the orchestration of the package tasks and is where most of the traditional (not ETL) programming occurs. The control flow has three main components: tasks, containers, and precedence constraints.

Tasks

Tasks are the core control-flow elements; they are responsible for performing the specific tasks in an SSIS package. SSIS includes the following types:

- **Data flow task**   The data flow task is the foundation of the ETL process. It creates one data flow that you can use to read, change, and store data. You will learn more about data flow later in this lesson.

- **Data preparation tasks**   Data preparation tasks are designed to perform the groundwork necessary before the ETL process executes. These tasks usually perform the copying or downloading of files. The data preparation tasks include the File System Task, the FTP Task, the Web Service Task, and the XML Task, as Figure 17-1 shows.

Figure 17-1   SSIS data preparation tasks

■ **Workflow tasks**   Workflow tasks are responsible for communications with other processes. These tasks execute other packages, run other programs, read queues, send mail, and interact with Microsoft Windows Management Instrumentation (WMI). The workflow tasks consist of the Execute Package Task, the Execute DTS 2000 Package Task, the Execute Process Task, the Message Queue Task, the Send Mail Task, the WMI Data Reader Task, and the WMI Event Watcher Task, as Figure 17-2 shows.

Figure 17-2   SSIS workflow tasks

■ **SQL Server tasks**   These tasks are specifically designed to work with SQL Server 2005 and to manipulate SQL Server objects. The SQL Server tasks consist of the Bulk Insert Task, the Execute SQL Task, the Transfer Database Task, the Transfer Error Messages Task, the Transfer Jobs Task, the Transfer Logins Task, the Transfer Master Stored Procedures Task, and the Transfer SQL Server Objects Task, as Figure 17-3 shows.

Figure 17-3   SSIS SQL Server tasks

■ **Scripting tasks**   Scripting tasks enable you to use Microsoft Visual Basic .NET and scripting languages to extend the functionality of the package with custom code. The SSIS scripting tasks are the Script Task and the ActiveX Script Task, as Figure 17-4 shows.

Figure 17-4   SSIS scripting tasks

- **Analysis Services tasks**   Analysis Services tasks enable you to interact with SQL Server 2005 Analysis Services, enabling you to process cubes and dimensions, alter their schema, and query data mining models. Analysis Services tasks consist of the Analysis Services Processing Task, the Analysis Services Execute DDL Task, and the Data Mining Query Task, as Figure 17-5 shows.

Figure 17-5   SSIS Analysis Services tasks

- **Maintenance tasks**   Maintenance tasks are designed to work with SQL Server 2005 and SQL Server 2000 relational engines to perform administrative work to maintain the server and relational databases. These tasks include the Back Up Database Task, the Check Database Integrity Task, the Execute SQL Server Agent Job Task, the Execute T-SQL Statement Task, the History Cleanup Task, the Notify Operator Task, the Rebuild Index Task, the Reorganize Index Task, the Shrink Database Task, and the Update Statistics Task, as Figure 17-6 shows.

Figure 17-6   Maintenance tasks

Besides these tasks, which are shipped with SQL Server 2005, you can use Microsoft .NET programming languages to create your own custom tasks. In addition, you can buy or download custom tasks designed to work with SSIS.

To use any of the tasks, you can just drag and drop the task from a Toolbox category to the package designer and double-click the task or set the properties from the Properties window.

Containers

Containers are SSIS objects that enable you to group tasks and configure tasks that must be repeated. Containers can also be used to configure tasks that participate in a distributed transaction. SSIS, by default, provides three containers: the Sequence Container, the For Loop Container, and the Foreach Loop Container, as Figure 17-7 shows.

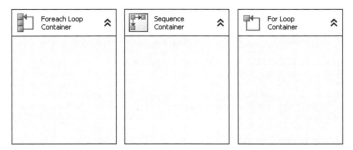

Figure 17-7   SSIS containers

Sequence Container   The sequence container is useful for grouping sets of tasks in a single container. With a sequence container, you can:

- Define a transaction boundary. You can set the transaction option of the sequence container so that all the tasks included in it will participate in the same transaction.

IMPORTANT   Using transactions in SSIS packages

If you want to require transactions at the package or container level, SSIS will demand a distributed transaction. Distributed transactions are coordinated through the Microsoft Distributed Transaction Coordinator (MSDTC). Make sure that the MSDTC is started when using transactions in SSIS packages.

- Define scope variables. You can define the scope of large variables that might consume scarce memory resources at the container level. Those variables will then exist within only the sequence container.
- Enable or disable a set of related tasks.

For Loop Container   You use the For Loop container to repeat a series of tasks. The For Loop container is similar to *For* or *While* commands in standard programming languages. The For Loop container has three main elements: initialization, evaluation, and iteration. The optional initialization element is used to configure the variables before the tasks are executed. The evaluation element is the condition at the end of the loop that determines whether the loop will run again. The iteration element, also optional, is used to increment or decrement the counter.

To configure a For Loop container to repeat the same group of tasks 10 times, for example, follow these steps:

1. In the package designer, select the Control Flow pane.
2. From the main menu, select SSIS, and then choose Variables.
3. On the Variables toolbar, click the Add Variable button to add the counter variable.
4. Name the variable **Counter**.

5. Select the Toolbox and, from the Control Flow Items category, drag and drop a For Loop container.

6. Double-click the For Loop container.

7. Define the InitExpression property as follows:

    ```
    @Counter=1
    ```

8. Set the EvalExpression property as follows:

    ```
    @Counter<=10
    ```

9. Configure the AssignExpression property as follows:

    ```
    @Counter=@Counter+1
    ```

Foreach Loop Container   The Foreach Loop container is similar to the For Loop container in that it can be used to repeat a series of tasks. However, instead of using a control variable to work through the tasks, the Foreach Loop executes once per element in a collection. For example, you can configure a Foreach Loop to execute a series of tasks once for each file in a folder, once for each table in a database, or once for each node in an XML document.

The following steps will help you configure a Foreach Loop container to execute a series of tasks for each file in a folder:

1. In the package designer, select the Control Flow pane.
2. From the main menu, select SSIS, and then choose Variables.
3. On the Variables toolbar, click the Add Variable button to add the counter variable.
4. Name the variable **FilePath** and change the data type to string.
5. Select the Toolbox and, from the Control Flow Items category, drag and drop a Foreach Loop container.
6. Double-click the Foreach Loop container.
7. Select the Collection Pane and, in the Enumerator drop-down list, review the optional collections that the Foreach Loop container offers. Accept the default of Foreach File Enumerator.
8. Select Browse to configure the folder or type the folder path in the Folder text box.
9. In the Files text box, using wildcards, configure which files will be added to the collection.
10. Select the Variable Mappings pane to assign the current loop value to a variable.
11. In the Variable drop-down list, select User:FilePath.

Precedence Constraints

Precedence constraints link different tasks in a control flow and define the order of execution of the tasks. In SSIS, you can link the objects and configure different conditions that determine whether the next task should run.

SSIS allows four different operations:

- **Constraint**   The next task execution depends on the result of the previous task. Constraints enable you to configure Success, Failure, or Completion.
- **Expression**   Expression enables you to create a Boolean expression. If the result is true, the next task will execute; if false, it will not execute.
- **Expression and constraint**   This operation combines the two previous values, and only when both conditions are present will the next task execute.
- **Expression or constraint**   This operation combines the two previous values, and only if any of the conditions is true will the next task execute.

To configure a Precedence constraint, follow these steps:

1. In the package designer, select the Control Flow pane.
2. Drag and drop two tasks. Select the first task, select the connection (green arrow), and then drag the connection (green arrow) on the other task.
3. Double-click the connection and configure the properties.

Data Flow

Unlike with the control flow, SSIS packages can have zero, one, or more data flows. A data flow is where most of the ETL process occurs. Data flows specialize in extracting data from different sources, applying diverse transformation to the data, and sending the transformed data to one or more destinations. Data flows are about creating high-performance data pipelines for the ETL process. Data flows have four components: data sources, data flow transformations, data destinations, and paths.

Data Sources

Data sources are data flow components responsible for providing data to the pipeline. Data sources supply the data pipeline with rows that can be transformed later and stored. SSIS includes the following data sources, shown in Figure 17-8: DataReader Source, OLE DB Source, Excel Source, Raw File Source, Flat File Source, XML Source, and Script Component.

Figure 17-8   Data sources

IMPORTANT Scripting data source

The only data source that is not available under the Data Flow Sources category in the Toolbox is Script Component. You will have to drag and drop a Script Component from the Data Flow transformations category and, when prompted, specify the data source as how the component will be used in the Data Flow.

Most data sources have two outputs: a regular output and an error output. Regular output sends all rows that do not generate an error when inserted into the data pipeline. An error output, when configured, sends rows that fail to enter the pipeline because they have an invalid type, because they need to be truncated, or simply because they generate an error.

To create a SQL Server 2005 data source from a SQL command:

1. Drag and drop an OLE DB Source to the Data Flow pane, and then double-click it.
2. Select a previously defined OLE DB Connection Manager or click New to create a new one.
3. In the Data Access Mode drop-down list, change the mode to SQL Command.
4. Write the SQL statement to select the information or click the Build Query button to use the query builder.

Data Paths

Data paths define the way the pipeline works in a data flow. A data path connects two components in a data flow; one component will output the rows that the other component will use as input. Some components have no output paths; others have one or more output paths. Additionally, other components don't allow input paths, and still others allow one or more. For example, the OLE DB Source does not allow any input paths, and it has two output paths: one regular path and one error path.

As an SSIS developer, the important element to remember about paths is that they enable you to configure the data pipeline, and that can be used to check the current state of the schema. To review the schema, double-click the path and select metadata.

Data Flow Transformations

Data flow transformations are data flow components responsible for changing data in the data pipeline. Data transformation can add columns, change column values, change data types, aggregate data, import and export images or large-object (LOB) columns, and so on. Data transformations can also transmit data to multiple destinations or merge data from multiple sources.

To work with a data transformation:

1. Drag and drop a transformation object to the Data Flow pane.
2. Select the data source or previous transformation.
3. Select the output path (the green arrow) from the data source or previous transformation and drag it to the new transformation.
4. Double-click the transformation.

Data transformations can be classified as row transformations, rowset transformations, split and join transformations, business intelligence transformations, and other transformations.

Row Transformations   Row transformation applies changes to each row in an independent manner. Row transformations include Character Map transformation, Copy Column transformation, Data Conversion transformation, Derived Column transformation, Script Component transformation, and OLE DB Command transformation, as shown in Figure 17-9.

Figure 17-9   Row transformations

IMPORTANT   OLE DB Command transformation

The OLE DB Command transformation is a data transformation that runs SQL commands to an OLE DB database. These commands include *SELECT*, *UPDATE*, *INSERT*, and *DELETE* commands as well as the execution of stored procedure of functions. In some ways, you can use the OLE DB Command transformation as a destination that does not insert rows; it updates or deletes information from the database.

Rowset Transformations   Instead of working with each row independently, rowset transformations work with groups of rows. The group can be all the rows in the pipeline or smaller groups. SSIS includes the following rowset transformations: Aggregate transformation, Sort transformation, Percentage Sampling transformation, Row sampling transformation, Pivot transformation, and Unpivot transformation, as illustrated in Figure 17-10.

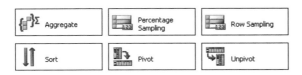

Figure 17-10   Rowset transformations

Split and Join Transformations   Split and join transformations have the ability to take in one input and send multiple outputs or the other way around. They are useful when joining data that comes from multiple sources or when sending data to multiple destinations. Split and join transformations include Multicast transformation, Union All transformation, Merge transformation, Merge Join transformation, and Lookup transformation, as illustrated in Figure 17-11.

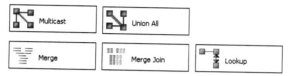

Figure 17-11   Split and join transformations

IMPORTANT   **Merge Join transformation vs. Lookup transformation**

The Merge Join transformation is the equivalent of the JOIN, LEFT JOIN, or FULL OUTER JOIN of SQL Server. However, SSIS requires the sets to be ordered before joining the rows; if ordering data is not feasible, use the Lookup transformation that does not require data to be sorted.

Business Intelligence Transformations   Business intelligence transformations enable you to add text and data mining transformations to your SSIS package. You can use these transformations to incorporate advanced data cleaning. The business intelligence transformations include Fuzzy Grouping transformation, Fuzzy Lookup transformation, Term Extraction transformation, Term Lookup transformation, and Data Mining Query transformation, as illustrated in Figure 17-12.

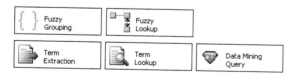

Figure 17-12   Business intelligence transformations

Other Transformations   Other transformations include tasks that can be classified in the previous categories. They include transformations to add audit columns, export and import data, and so on. The transformations included in this category are Audit transformation, Export Column transformation, Import Column transformation, Row Count transformation, and Slowly Changing Dimension transformation, as shown in Figure 17-13.

Figure 17-13   Other transformations

Exam Tip   The slowly changing dimension task is more than a transformation; it is also a wizard that helps you maintain dimension tables that generate other tasks. Familiarize yourself with this transformation because it is very likely you will face questions about it in the exam.

Data Flow Destinations

Data flow destinations are the counterpart of data sources; they take the rows from the pipeline and store the information in different destinations, including in memory datasets. Data flow destinations take one input path and have no outputs or one error output path only. SSIS includes the following data flow destinations: Data Mining Model Training Destination, DataReader Destination, Dimension Processing Destination, Excel Destination, Flat File Destination, OLE DB Destination, Partition Processing Destination, Raw File Destination, Recordset Destination, Script Component, SQL Server Mobile Destination, and SQL Server Destination, as shown in Figure 17-14.

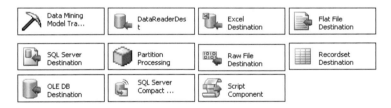

Figure 17-14   Data flow destinations

Practice: Creating an SSIS Package

In this practice, you will create an SSIS package that reads information from a file and from a relational database and then populates a dimension table in a data warehouse database.

On the Companion Disc   This chapter includes many code examples. You will find all the code from this chapter on the companion CD in the C:\My Documents\Microsoft Press\TK70-441 \Chapter17 folder.

▶ **Exercise 1: Create a New Database and Dimension Table**

In this exercise, you create a new database to support the *AdventureWorks* data warehouse. You also create a dimension table to store the geography.

1. Open SSMS and connect to the default database engine.
2. Right-click the databases folder and select New Database.
3. In the New Database dialog box, name the database **AdventureWorksDWPractice**. Click OK to create the database.
4. Click the New Query button on the SQL Editor toolbar to open a query window.
5. On the Standard toolbar, in the Available Databases drop-down list, change the default database to AdventureWorksDWPractice.
6. In the Query window, create the required code to create the Geography dimension table.

    The DimGeography table is a regular star-type dimension table, storing information about cities, postal codes, states, and countries. For countries, it will store the name in English, Spanish, and French. The following code creates the Geography dimension table:

```
CREATE TABLE dbo.DimGeography(
     GeographyKey                INT    IDENTITY(1,1) NOT NULL
      CONSTRAINT PK_DimGeography
        PRIMARY KEY
  , City                         NVARCHAR(30) NOT NULL
  , PostalCode                   NVARCHAR(15) NOT NULL
  , StateProvinceCode            NVARCHAR(3)  NOT NULL
  , StateProvinceName            NVARCHAR(50) NOT NULL
  , CountryRegionCode            NVARCHAR(3)  NOT NULL
  , EnglishCountryRegionName     NVARCHAR(50) NOT NULL
  , SpanishCountryRegionName     NVARCHAR(50) NOT NULL
  , FrenchCountryRegionName      NVARCHAR(50) NOT NULL
  , DimStart                     DATETIME     NOT NULL
     DEFAULT(GETDATE())
  , DimEnd                       DATETIME     NULL
)
```

7. Execute the query by clicking the Execute button on the SQL Editor toolbar or by pressing F5.

▶ **Exercise 2: Create a New SSIS Project and Package**

In this exercise, you use the SSIS Template project included in BIDS to create an SSIS project. The template creates the solution, the SSIS project, and the SSIS package.

1. Open BIDS.
2. From the main menu, click File, click New, and then select Project.
3. Select Business Intelligence Projects from Project Types.

4. Select the Integration Services Project template. Name the report **AdvWorksETL** and click OK to create the project.

5. In Solution Explorer, right-click the default package and select Rename. Rename the package **DimGeographyETL.dtsx**. When Visual Studio asks you if you want to rename the object as well, select Yes.

▶ **Exercise 3: Create the ETL Workflow**

In this exercise, you use the previously created package to generate the Geography dimension table. You will configure the package to read only modified rows from the source tables using a date variable.

1. Right-click the package designer and select Variables. This will enable you to create a new variable to hold the last date on which the package was executed.

2. From the Variables toolbar, click the Add Variable button.

3. In the column name, change the variable name to **LastExecutionDate**. Also, change the data type to Datetime and the default value to 1/1/2000.

4. From the Toolbox, under the Control Flow Item category, drag and drop an Execute SQL task to the Control Flow pane. This task will be responsible for reading the last datetime stored in the Geography table.

5. Right-click Execute SQL Task and select Rename. Type **Read Last Execution Time**. Double-click the task to configure its properties.

6. In the Connection property drop-down list, select New Connection to create a new connection object.

7. In the configure OLE DB Connection Manager dialog box, click the New button to create a new connection.

8. In the Server Name, type **localhost**; accept the default Windows Authentication method, and select the AdventureWorksDWPractice database from the Select Or Enter A Database Name drop-down list. Click Test Connection, and then click OK to create the connection string.

9. Click OK to create the connection.

10. In the SQL Statement property field, enter the following query to read the last execution date and time:

```
SELECT COALESCE(MAX(DimStart), '20000101') AS DimStart
FROM dbo.DimGeography
```

11. In the Result Set property drop-down list, change the value to Single Row.

12. Select Result Set in the left pane. Result Set will enable you to assign the returned value to the variable.

13. Click the Add button. In the Result Name column name, type **0** and make sure that the variable name is User::LastExecutionDate. The Result Name column enables you to select the column number you are mapping to the variable name.

14. Click OK to accept the changes.

15. Notice that, at the bottom of the package designer, the connection managers are displayed. There is a localhost.AdventureWorksDWPractice connection. Right-click the connection and rename it **DWConn**.

16. From the toolbox, drag and drop a Data Flow task to the Control Flow pane. Right-click the Data Flow task and select Rename. Name the data flow **Geography**.

17. Place the data flow task under Read Last Execution Time. Select the Read Last Execution Time object and drag and drop the Precedence constraint arrow to the Data Flow task. The precedence constraint enables you to define the workflow of the package.

▶ **Exercise 4: Create the ETL Dataflow**

In this exercise, you use the previously created package to generate the Geography dimension table. You first configure the transformation to read cities and ZIP codes from the Address table; the package then looks up countries and states from the *AdventureWorks* sample database. Finally, the package filters all the information that was previously stored in the data warehouse.

1. Double-click the Geography data flow to open the Data Flow editor. The Data Flow editor is where you configure the data pipeline to extract, transform, and load data.

2. Drag and drop an OLE DB Source from the toolbox Data Flow Sources category. Right-click the OLE DB source and select Rename. Name the object **Cities Source**. Double-click the Cities source to configure its properties.

3. Click the New button to create a new connection. The cities source will use the *Adventure-Works* sample database.

4. Click New to create a new connection string. In the Server Name text box, type **localhost**, accept the default Windows Authentication method, and select the Adventure-Works database from the Select Or Enter A Database Name drop-down list. Click Test Connection, and then click OK to create the connection string.

5. In the Data Access Mode drop-down list, select SQL Command.

6. In the SQL Command text box, enter the following command, which selects cities that were inserted or updated after the previous execution of the package:

```
SELECT DISTINCT City, PostalCode, StateProvinceID
FROM        Person.Address
WHERE       (ModifiedDate > ?)
```

You can also click the Build Query button to create the command in the Query Builder dialog box.

7. Click the Parameters button to map the variable to the parameter. In the Variables drop-down list, select User::LastExecutionDate. Click OK to configure the parameter and click OK again to configure the OLE DB source.

8. In the Connection Managers pane, right-click the localhost.AdventureWorks connection and select Rename. Name the connection **AdvWorksSource**.

9. To read the Region and Country information, drag and drop a Lookup transformation under the Cities source. Select the data flow path (green arrow) and drag it to Lookup.

10. Right-click the Lookup transformation and select Rename. Name the Lookup transformation **States and Countries**. Double-click States and Countries to configure the transformation.

    In the OLE DB Connection Manager drop-down list, select AdvWorkSource. Select the Use Results Of An SQL Query check box and type the following command to extract the state and country codes and names:

```
SELECT  StateProvince.StateProvinceID
      , StateProvince.StateProvinceCode
      , StateProvince.Name AS StateProvinceName
      , CountryRegion.CountryRegionCode
FROM Person.CountryRegion
INNER JOIN Person.StateProvince
ON CountryRegion.CountryRegionCode = StateProvince.CountryRegionCode
```

11. Click the Columns tab. The StateProvinceID is automatically mapped. In the Available Lookup columns, select StateProvinceCode, StateProvinceName, and CountryRegion-Code. Select OK to configure the task.

12. Even though the previous command filters cities by modified date, the city might exist from another record. To eliminate the row, you will use a Lookup task and remove cities that are already stored in the data warehouse.

13. Drag and drop a Lookup transformation under the States and Countries transformation. Select States And Countries; select the Success Data Flow arrow (green arrow) and drop it over the lookup transformation. Right-click the lookup and select Rename. Name the transformation **Filter Previous Rows**. Double-click the transformation to configure the lookup.

14. Select DWConn in the OLE DB Connection Manager drop-down list. Select the Use Results Of An SQL Query option and enter the following command:

```
SELECT City
     , PostalCode
     , StateProvinceCode
     , CountryRegionCode
FROM DimGeography
```

15. Select the Columns tab; all columns are automatically mapped. Do not add any Lookup columns.

16. Drag and drop a Sort transformation under the Filter Previous Rows. The Sort transformation will be used to order the results by country.

17. Select the Filter Previous Rows transformation and select Lookup Error Output (the red arrow); drag the red arrow to the Sort transformation. In this step, you will not use the green arrow because the rows that match the data warehouse should be removed. You want only to load new rows that do not match rows previously inserted in the data warehouse.

18. The Configure Error Output dialog box is displayed. In the Error column, select Redirect Row to send all new rows to the Sort transformation. Click OK to redirect the rows.

19. Right-click the Sort transformation and select Rename. Name the transformation **Sort By Country**. Double-click the transformation to configure the Sort column.

20. In the Input Column drop-down list, select CountryRegionCode to sort the data by Country code and then click OK. Data needs to be sorted for the Merge transformation to work.

▶ **Exercise 5: Merge Alternate Names**

In this exercise, you use the previous package to read information from a flat file and merge the information with the cities. The package then stores the information in the data warehouse.

1. Drag and drop a Flat File source. Place the Flat File source to the left of the States And Countries transformation. Right-click the Flat File source and select Rename. Name the task **Countries Alternate Names**. Double-click the task to edit its properties.

2. Click the New button to create a flat file connection. Name the connection **CountyNamesConn**. Click the Browse button to select the C:\Program Files\Microsoft SQL Server\90\Samples\Integration Services\Package Samples \AWDataWarehouseRefresh\AWDataWarehouseRefresh\Data\$$CountryRegion-ForeignNames.csv file. To display the file, you might have to change the file type to .csv.

3. Select the Preview pane to browse the file contents. After browsing the content, select the Advanced pane to configure column information. Use the following table to configure the CountryNames data source columns; these data types are consistent with the table's data types stored in the database:

Column	Name	OutputColumnWidth
Column 0	CountryRegionCode	3
Column 1	EnglishCountryRegionName	50
Column 2	SpanishCountryRegionName	50
Column 3	FrenchCountryRegionName	50

4. Click OK to create the connection and click OK again to configure the Flat File source.

5. Drag and drop a Derived Column transformation. Place the transformation under the Countries Alternate Names task and next to the Filter Previous Rows transformation. Right-click the transformation and select Rename. Rename the transformation **Remove Space**.

6. Select the Countries Alternate Names task, select the data flow path, and drag it to the Remove Space transformation. Double-click the transformation to configure its properties.

7. In the Derived Column drop-down list, select Replace CountryRegionCode. In the Expression text box, enter the following expression:

    ```
    RTRIM(CountryRegionCode)
    ```

8. Click OK to configure the transformation.

9. Drag and drop a Sort transformation; place the transformation under the Remove Space transformation and next to the Sort Alternate Names transformation. Rename the transformation **Sort Alternate Names**. Select the Remove Space transformation, and then select the data flow path (green arrow) and drop it on the Sort Alternate Names transformation.

10. Double-click the Sort Alternate Names transformation to configure the Sort column. In the Input Column combo box, select CountryRegionCode. Click OK to confirm the configuration.

11. Drag and drop a Merge Join transformation; place the transformation under the Sort By Country and Sort Alternate Names transformations.

12. Select the Sort By Country transformation, and then select the data flow path (green arrow) and drag it to the Merge Join task. The Input Output Selection dialog box is displayed. In the Input Column drop-down list, select Merge Join Left Input. Click OK to configure the data flow path.

13. Select the Sort Alternate Name transformation, and then select the data flow path (green arrow) and drag it to the Merge Join task.

    The data flow will be automatically assigned to the Merge Join Right Input.

14. Right-click the Merge Join transformation and select Rename. Name the transformation **Merge Alternate Country Names**. Double-click the task to edit its properties. Use the Input Grid to select the following columns:

Input	Input Column
Sort by Country	City
Sort by Country	Postal Code

Input	Input Column
Sort by Country	StateProvinceCode
Sort by Country	StateProvinceName
Sort Alternate Name	CountryRegionCode
Sort Alternate Name	EnglishCountyRegionName
Sort Alternate Name	SpanishCountyRegionName
Sort Alternate Name	FrenchCountryRegionName

Accept the default OutputAliases and click OK to configure the task.

15. Drag and drop an OLE DB Destination. Place the destination under the Merge Alternate Country Names transformation. Select Merge Alternate Country Names, and then select the data flow path (green arrow) and drag it to the OLE DB Destination. Right-click the OLE DB destination and select Rename. Name the destination **Geography Destination**. Double-click the destination to configure its properties.

16. In the the OLE DB Connection Manager drop-down list, select DWConn. Leave the Data Access Mode default selection, Table or View-fast load.

17. In the Name Of The Table Or The View drop-down list, select the dbo.DimGeography table.

18. Select the Mappings pane to configure column mappings between the SSIS data flow and the table. The columns are automatically mapped. Click OK to confirm the default mappings.

▶ **Exercise 6: Populate the Geography Dimension Table**

In this exercise, you execute the previously created package to populate the Geography dimension table. The first time you execute the package, all rows will be loaded into the data warehouse. If you run the package a second time, no rows will be stored.

1. In the package editor, select the Data Flow pane.

2. From the Menu, click Start Debugging. The package should start. Wait for all the tasks to become green. Notice how many rows flow in the data flow.

3. After the package is successfully executed, stop the debugger by clicking Stop Debugging from the Debug menu.

4. Execute the package again. Notice that no rows are read from the source database, and no data is loaded into the data warehouse.

Quick Check

1. What is the role of connection managers in SSIS packages?
2. Where do you define a data path in an SSIS package?
3. Which database engines are supported by maintenance tasks in SSIS packages?

Quick Check Answers

1. The correct answer is to maintain the connection configuration. The idea behind the connection manager is to centralize the connection string information for multiple data sources and give database developers and administrators a single management point.
2. The correct answer is Control flow pane. Data paths are responsible for the configuration of the data pipeline in the package data flow.
3. The correct answer is SQL Server 2005 and SQL Server 2000 Relational engines. Maintenance tasks support only the SQL Server Relational engine in SQL Server 2005 and SQL Server 2000.

Lesson 2: Debugging and Testing SSIS Packages

Estimated lesson time: 20 minutes

SSIS packages are susceptible to errors and failures, as are all software components. In this lesson, you will learn how to run, debug, and test SSIS packages, using BIDS.

Running SSIS Packages

After you have designed and developed your package, you can execute, debug, and test it. Unlike with DTS, you can run the SSIS package in the development environment before deploying the package to the server. There are two alternatives when running a package locally. The first option is to run the package without debugging; the second option is to debug the package.

There are several different ways of running an SSIS package without debugging. One way is by using BIDS, clicking Debug, and then selecting Start Without Debugging from the main menu. You can also press Ctrl + F5 to do the same thing. When using BIDS, if you have more than one package in the project, you can select which package to execute first by right-clicking the package in Solution Explorer and selecting Set As Startup Object.

You can also execute a package by using the SSIS execution utilities DTExec.exe and DTExecUI.exe. DTExec is a command-line utility that you can use to execute SSIS packages. It is useful for creating test scripts or batches. You can use DTSExec to execute packages stored locally in the file system, stored in a SQL Server database, or stored in the SSIS Package Store. An example of how to use DTExec is

```
Dtexec.exe /f "c:\DimGeography.dtsx"
```

DTExecUI offers a graphical interface to configure SSIS package execution. It is easier to configure than DTExec and can be used to generate the command required to execute packages without intervention. To generate a DTExec command by using DTExecUI, follow these steps:

1. Run DTExecUI from the command prompt or from the Run option in the Windows Start menu.
2. In the General pane, select the Package Source (File System, SQL Server, or SSIS Package Store). For SQL Server or SSIS Package Store packages, select the server name and authentication parameters.
3. Select the package name or path.
4. Configure the preferred execution parameters.

5. Select the Command Line pane. Select the text in the command line text box, right-click, and select Copy.

6. Paste the code into your script after a DTExec command.

The last option for running an SSIS package without debugging is to use a SQL Server Agent job. To execute a package in a job, you need to deploy the package in a testing or production server, use SQL Server Management Studio (SSMS) to add a SQL Server Agent job, and add an SSIS Integration Services Package job step to the job. For information about how to use SQL Server Agent jobs to execute SSIS packages, see the Books Online topic "Automating Administrative Tasks (SQL Server Agent)" at *http://msdn2.microsoft.com/en-us/library/ms187061.aspx*.

Debugging SSIS Packages

You use BIDS to debug an SSIS package. To debug an SSIS package, start the debugger by pressing F5, by clicking the Start Debugging button from the Debug toolbar, or by selecting Start Debugging from the Debug menu. To stop the debugger, press Shift + F5; click the Stop Debugging button from the Debug toolbar or select Stop Debugging from the Debug menu.

When the package is in debugging mode, BIDS informs you of the debugging progress in two ways. First, BIDS color codes the design area. Control flow tasks and data flow components will change color to let you know their execution status. Table 17-1 summarizes the color schema:

Table 17-1   SSIS Execution Color Schema

Color	Status
White	Waiting
Gray	Disabled
Green	Success
Yellow	Executing
Red	Error

You can also use the Execution Results pane to check the package execution results when debugging a package. One advantage of the Execution Results pane is that after the execution is stopped, the color status in the designer disappears, but the execution results remain until you close the package.

Debugging Control Flow

An important part of the development cycle is when developers observe the run-time behavior of the developed components. BIDS enables SSIS developers to observe the status of the control flow components. When debugging the control flow, you can evaluate variables, change their values, and advance to the next breakpoint. Debugging helps you locate errors and evaluate the logic of the package.

To debug the control flow, you need to define a breakpoint. A breakpoint is a deliberate pausing of the package for debugging purposes. The breakpoint does not affect the final package; it affects the package only when running in debug mode. To configure a breakpoint in the package designer, follow these steps:

1. Select the Control Flow pane.
2. Right-click the task at which you want the debugger to stop.
3. Select Edit Breakpoints.
4. Select the condition that determines the breakpoint at which to pause the package execution.

IMPORTANT   Break conditions

Two conditions are frequently used when defining a breakpoint: the *OnPreExecute* event that occurs just before executing the task and the *OnPostExecute* event that occurs just after executing the task. For more information about other conditions, see the SQL Server 2005 Books Online topic "Debugging Control Flow" at *http://msdn2.microsoft.com/en-us /library/ms140274.aspx*.

---

5. After defining the breakpoints, you can start debugging the package.

When running the package in debug mode, the package execution will stop at the first breakpoint it encounters. You will see a yellow arrow over the task at which the execution is paused. You will also see the Locals pane display, where you can evaluate the status of the variables. From the Locals pane, you can also add a watch. Here's how to add a watch:

1. In the Locals pane, expand the variables tree.
2. Select the variable you want to watch.
3. Right-click the variable and select Add Watch.
4. The Watch pane is displayed.

From the Watch pane, you can keep track of variable values and change them if you want.

To resume execution and advance to the next breakpoint, press F5 or click the Continue button in the Debug toolbar.

Debugging Data Flow

Debugging the data flow is similar to debugging the control flow. However, in the data flow, you configure data viewers rather than add breakpoints. Data viewers enable you to view data in the pipeline between data components. The package designer has four different data viewers: grid, histogram, scatter plot, and column chart.

Grids display information in a standard grid format. They are useful for examining each row in detail. Alternatively, histograms enable you to display distribution of a single numeric value. Histograms are useful for reviewing numeric values in all data records. Scatter plot enables you to analyze the relationship between two numeric values, such as between sales amount and sales tax, and you can use column charts with non-numeric data to report a list of occurrences.

To add a data viewer, follow these steps:

1. Select the data flow for which you want to add a data viewer.
2. Right-click the path between two data flow components.
3. Select Data Viewers.
4. Click Add.
5. In the Name text box, name the data viewer.
6. From the Type list, select the data viewer type, and then click OK.
7. Select Data Viewers, select the data viewer, and then click the Configure button.
8. On the Column Chart tab, select the appropriate column.
9. Click OK to configure the viewer, and then click OK again.

   Executing the package in debug mode will display the data viewer; click the Run button from the Viewer toolbar to continue the execution.

Debugging Script Code

You have three different script tasks or components for working with script code in SSIS packages. In the control flow, you have the Script Task and the ActiveX Script Task. Also, in the data flow, you can use the Script component.

The Script Task and the Script Component use Visual Basic .NET code, which is compiled and executed at run time. These tasks use the Visual Studio for Applications (VSA) environment to develop and debug the code.

The ActiveX Script task enables you to select the scripting language from the following options: Visual Basic Script, JScript Compact Profile (ECMA 327), or JScript. The ActiveX Script task does not offer a development environment because its primary use is to hold script that has been migrated from DTS packages. Keep in mind that the ActiveX Script task is provided only for backward compatibility with older code.

IMPORTANT   ActiveX code is deprecated

SQL Server 2005 offers the ability to execute ActiveX code only for backward compatibility; this capability will be removed in the next version of SQL Server. You should not use ActiveX in new development and should start planning how to remove or replace code written in ActiveX scripting languages.

Testing SSIS Packages

Testing is an essential process that helps you identify the quality of developed software. SSIS packages require the same process of investigation to expose quality-related problems in the development and operation of SSIS packages. Some of the attributes evaluated in package testing are functionability, reliability, performance, compatibility, and maintainability.

In software testing, there are four conventional testing levels:

- **Unit testing** Validates individual units of source code. A unit is the smallest testable part of an application. From the SSIS perspective, the unit you are testing is always a package.
- **Integration testing** Validates individual software modules combined and tested as a group. From the SSIS perspective, integration testing can refer to all SSIS packages in a solution or a smaller set of packages that are related by function. For example, you can test all ETL packages related to a particular star schema of the data warehouse.
- **System testing** Validates a complete and integrated system. System testing checks compliance with a specified set of requirements. System testing goes beyond testing SSIS packages. For example, in a data warehouse solution, system testing should include all elements, such as SSIS packages, SQL Server Analysis Services (SSAS) dimensions and cubes, SQL Server Reporting Services (SSRS) reports, and the intranet portal. System testing does not require knowledge of the inner design of the code and is frequently divided into functional and nonfunctional testing.
- **Acceptance testing** Performed directly by the customer or user before accepting the delivery of a system. After acceptance testing, the ownership of a system is transferred from the development team to the operations team.

IMPORTANT Regression testing

Another important type of software testing is regression testing. Regression testing tries to discover regression bugs. Regression bugs occur when some of the software functionality that used to work stops working, typically because a program changes. Maintenance code is usually more prone to errors. By applying the unit testing strategies reviewed in Chapter 10, "Designing a Unit Test Plan for a Database," you can diminish the effect of regression bugs.

Code Inspection

Before implementing a testing strategy, consider executing a technical review strategy. Technical reviews are extremely effective in detecting software defects in every type of software, including SSIS packages. A code inspection is a formal technical review in which code inspectors or reviewers examine SSIS packages and use checklists to detect software errors. In code inspections, you can evaluate not only the functional requirements compliance but also operational requirements. For example, you can review such things as: do all the tasks have descriptive names? Do all objects follow Pascal case convention? Are all the tasks enabled? And so on.

Unit Testing SSIS Packages

Unit testing can be manual or automated. Manual testing uses a step-by-step instructional document that enables testers to evaluate the correctness of a package. Unlike manual testing, automated testing uses software to control the execution of tests. Most development teams combine manual and automated testing.

Manual Testing   Manual tests start with a test case. The test case gives a testing engineer the steps to follow to test a software component. A test case consists of a series of steps with actions, inputs, and expected results. Table 17-2 shows an example of a test case.

Table 17-2   A Sample Test Case

Open C:\SSIS\ETL.dtsConfig in Notepad.	XML file displayed
Change the server name to the name of the testing server. Save the file.	File saved
Open a command prompt. Execute the command: dtexec /f "c:\DimGeography.dtsx".	DTExec: The package execution returned DTSER_SUCCESS (0) Started: x:xx:xx XM Finished: x:xx:xx XM Elapsed: 32.453 seconds

Test Automation   Unit testing is frequently automated, but automated testing is not a replacement for manual testing. One advantage of SSIS is that you can create SSIS packages to build a testing framework to test your own packages.

Here's an example of how to create a unit testing package:

1. Create a new SSIS project.
2. Add tasks to set up the environment. You can delete destination tables, set up testing tables, or restore databases.
3. Add an Execute Package task to launch the package you want to test.
4. Evaluate the package result, comparing rows and results of the package.
5. Store package execution results.

Practice: Debugging Control Flow and Data Flow

In this practice, you use the package you created in Lesson 1, "Creating Integration Services Packages," to practice how to debug the control flow and the data flow. You also create a test to evaluate your package.

► Exercise 1: Debug the Control Flow

In this exercise, you set up breakpoints, debug a package, and use the Watch pane to change variable values.

1. Open BIDS.
2. Open the AdvWorksETL solution.
3. Open the DimGeograpy package in the Control Flow designer.
4. Right-click the Read Execution Time task and select Edit Breakpoints.
   The Set Breakpoints dialog box appears.
5. Select the first two events: OnPreExecute and OnPostExecute. This will enable two breakpoints for the Read Execution Time task—one before the task is executed and the other after the task is executed.
6. Click OK to set the breakpoints.
7. To start debugging the package, right-click the package in Solution Explorer and click Execute Package or press F5.
8. The execution should be paused and a yellow arrow should be in the Read Last Execution Time.
9. In the Variables dialog box, expand the variables tree. Right-click the User:LastExecutionDate variable and select Add Watch. The watch 1 pane is displayed, and the variable is added to the watch.
10. Notice the value of the LastExecutionDate; it should be the default value of 1/1/2000.
11. From the Debug toolbar, click Continue or press F5 to resume execution.
12. Notice that the Read Last Execution Time is changed to yellow, and the LastExecutionDate variable has changed its value.
13. Expand the LastExecutionDate and change the value of the variable to 1/1/2001.
14. From the Debug toolbar, click Continue or press F5 to resume execution.
15. Select the Data Flow pane and notice that the Cities source has read some rows.
16. To stop debugging the package, click Stop from the Debug toolbar or press Shift + F5.
17. Select the Control Flow pane.
18. From the Debug menu select Delete All Breakpoints. Visual Studio prompts you to confirm that you want to delete all breakpoints. Click Yes.

► Exercise 2: Debug the Data Flow

In this exercise, you add a data viewer to debug a data flow.

1. In the DimGeography package, select the Data Flow pane.
2. Right-click the data path between the Countries Alternate Names transformation and the Remove Space transformation and select Data Viewers.

3. Click Add to configure a new data viewer.

4. Accept the default grid data viewer. Select the Grid tab to review the grid configuration. You can add or remove the columns in the data viewer. Accept the default and click OK to configure the viewer.

5. Click OK to close the Data Flow Path Editor.

6. Notice the eyeglasses icon next to the data path.

7. To debug the package, select Start Debugging from the Debug toolbar or press F5. The package execution is paused, and the data viewer is displayed.

8. From the viewer control, click Continue.

9. Close the data viewer.

10. To stop the debugger, click Stop Debugging from the Debug menu or press Shift + F5.

11. Right-click the data path between the Countries Alternate Names transformation and the Remove Space transformation and select Data Viewers.

12. Click OK to delete the data viewer.

▶ **Exercise 3: Test an SSIS Package**

In this exercise, you create an SSIS project to test your SSIS package. First, you set up the environment, in this case deleting the DimGeography data; later, you will configure the package to execute the package to be tested.

1. Open BIDS, and then open the AdvWorksETL project.

2. From the main menu, click File, click New, and then select Project. You will add a new project to the solution.

3. Select Business Intelligence Projects from Project Types. Select Integration Services Project. Name the report **TestAdvWorksETL**.

4. In the Solution drop-down list, select Add To Solution. Click OK to create the project.

5. In Solution Explorer, right-click the package and select Rename. Rename the package **TestDimGeographyETL.dtsx**. When Visual Studio asks whether you want to rename the object as well, click Yes.

6. From the Control Flow Items category in the toolbox, drag and drop a Sequence Container into the Control Flow pane. The Sequence Container will hold the DimGeography test. Right-click the container and select Rename. Name the container **DimGeographyTest**.

7. Drag and drop an Execute SQL Task on the DimGeography Test container.

8. Right-click an Execute SQL task and select Rename. Name the task **Delete DimGeography**. Double-click Delete DimGeography to configure the task.

9. In the Connection property drop-down list, select New Connection to create a new connection object.

10. In the Configure OLE DB Connection Manager dialog box, select localhost.Adventure-WorksDWPractice and click OK to create the connection manager.

11. In the SQL Statement property, enter the following query to delete the destination table:

    `DELETE dbo.DimGeography`

12. Click OK to configure the task.

13. In the Connection Managers pane, right-click the localhost.AdventureWorksDWPractice connection and select Rename. Name the connection **Destination**.

14. Drag and drop an Execute Package task into the DimGeography Test container under the Delete Geography task. The Execute Package task will be responsible for executing the package to be tested. Right-click the package and rename the task **ExecuteDimGeography**. Select the Delete Geography task and drag the precedence constraint (green arrow) to the ExecuteDimGeography task.

15. Double-click ExecuteDimGeography to configure the task.

16. Select the Package pane. Select File System in the Location drop-down list.

17. In the Connection property drop-down list, select New Connection to create a new connection object.

18. In the Usage Type drop-down list, accept the default option of Existing File. To configure the file name, click the Browse button and select the DimGeography.dtsx file from the projects bin folder. By default, the file is located in the My Documents\Visual Studio 2005\Projects\AdvWorksETL\ AdvWorksETL\bin folder.

19. Click OK to confirm the package and OK again to configure the task.

▶ **Exercise 4: Verify Package Execution and Use a Hash Value**

In this exercise, you verify that the package successfully executed and compare the rows in the source and destination data by using a hash value.

1. Click any empty area of the designer.

2. Select the Variables tab or right-click any empty area of the designer and select Variables.

3. Add four variables to the package. These variables will be used to compare the values in the data warehouse with the values in the relational source. The variables are:

Variable Name	Date Type	Default Value
DestinationHash	Int32	0
DestinationRows	Int32	0
SourceHash	Int32	0
SourceRows	Int32	0

4. Drag and drop a SQL task into the DimGeography container. Place the SQL task under the Execute DimGeography task. Right-click the SQL task and select Rename to name the task **Validate Source**. Select the Execute DimGeography task and drag the precedence constraint arrow to the Validate Source task.

5. Double-click the Validate Source task to configure its properties.

6. In the Connection drop-down list, select New Connection.

7. Select the localhost.AdventureWorks connection and click OK to configure the connection manager.

8. In the SQL Statement property field, enter the following command:

```
SELECT COUNT(*), CHECKSUM_AGG(CHECKSUM(City))
FROM (SELECT DISTINCT City, PostalCode, StateProvinceID
    FROM Person.Address) AS Source
```

The statement counts how many rows are stored in the Source table and generates a hash value based on the cities. In a production environment, you will probably want to validate other columns.

9. Click OK to accept the SQL statement.

10. In the ResultSet drop-down list, select Single Row. You will capture the values in two variables.

11. Select Result Set and click Add. In the Result Name column, enter 0 and, in the Variable Name combo box, select User::SourceRows.

12. Select Add and, in the new row, enter 1 as Result Name and select User::SourceHash in the Variable Name column. The SQL task will assign the first column to the *SourceRows* variable and the second column to the *SourceHash* variable. Click OK to configure the task.

13. In the Connection Managers pane, right-click the localhost.AdventureWorks connection and select Rename. Rename the connection **Source**.

14. Drag and drop a SQL task into the DimGeography container. Place the SQL task under the Validate Source task. Right-click the SQL task and select Rename to name the task **Validate Source**. Select the Execute DimGeography task and drag the precedence constraint arrow to the Validate Source task.

15. Double-click the Validate Source task to configure its properties.

16. In the Connection drop-down list, select New Connection.

17. Select the localhost.AdventureWorks connection and click OK to configure the connection manager.

18. In the SQL Statement property field, enter the following command:

```
SELECT COUNT(*), CHECKSUM_AGG(CHECKSUM(City))
FROM (SELECT DISTINCT City, PostalCode, StateProvinceID
    FROM Person.Address) AS Source
```

The statement counts how many rows are stored in the Source table and generates a hash value based on the cities. In a production environment, you will probably want to validate other columns.

19. Click OK to accept the SQL statement.

20. In the ResultSet drop-down list, select Single Row. You will capture the values in two variables.

21. Select Result Set and select Add. In the Result Name column, type **0** and, in the Variable Name combo box, select User::SourceRows.

22. Select Add and, in the new row, enter 1 as Result Name and select User::SourceHash in the Variable Name column. The SQL task will assign the first column to the *SourceRows* variable and the second column to the *DestinationHash* variable. Click OK to configure the task.

23. Drag and drop an Execute SQL task on the DimGeographyTest container under the Validate Source task.

24. Select the Validate Source task and drag the precedence constraint arrow to the Execute SQL task. Right-click the Execute SQL task and select Rename. Name the task **Validate Destination**. Double-click the task to edit its properties.

25. In the Connection property drop-down list, select Destination.

26. In the SQL Statement property field, enter the following statement:
```
SELECT COUNT(*), CHECKSUM_AGG(CHECKSUM(City))
FROM  dbo.DimGeography
```

27. In the ResultSet drop-down list, select Single Row.

28. Select the Result Set pane.

29. Select Result Set and select Add. In the Result Name column, type **0** and, in the Variable Name combo box, select User::DestinationRows.

30. Select Add and, in the new row, enter 1 as Result Name and select User::DestinationHash in the Variable Name column. The SQL task will assign the first column to the *SourceRows* variable and the second column to the *DestinationHash* variable. Click OK to configure the task.

31. Drag and drop a Script task outside the DimGeography Test container. Select DimGeography Test and drag the precedence constraint to the Script task. Right-click the Script task and select Rename. Name the task **Success**.

32. Double-click the precedence constraint between the DimGeography Test container and the Success task. In the Evaluation Operation drop-down list, select Expression and Constraint. In the Expression text box, enter the following expression:
```
(@SourceRows==@DestinationRows) && (@SourceHash==@DestinationHash)
```

33. Test the expression and click OK to configure the precedence constraint.

34. Drag and drop a Script task outside the DimGeography Test container, next to the Success task. Select DimGeography Test and drag the precedence constraint to the Script task. Right-click the Script task and select Rename. Name the task **Failure**.

35. Double-click the precedence constraint between the DimGeography Test container and the Failure task. In the Evaluation Operation drop-down list, select Expression Or Constraint. In the Value drop-down list, select Failure. In the Expression text box, enter the following expression:

    ```
    (@SourceRows!=@DestinationRows) || (@SourceHash!=@DestinationHash)
    ```

36. Execute the package to validate that the Success script is executed. In a real production environment, store the results in a log table or file.

Quick Check

1. You want to evaluate the value of a variable before a data flow task occurs; which event do you use to define the breakpoint on the task?

    A. OnProgress event

    B. OnVariableValueChange event

    C. OnPreExecute event

    D. OnPostExecute event

2. You want to debug a set of data that you are transforming in an SSIS package. Where do you define a data viewer?

    A. Data path

    B. Data flow pane

    C. Connection Manager pane

    D. Package Explorer

3. You want to debug an ActiveX Visual Basic script; how do you debug this code line by line?

    A. Use BIDS.

    B. Use Microsoft Visual Studio for Applications.

    C. Use SSMS.

    D. Debugging an ActiveX script in an SSIS package is not supported.

Quick Check Answers

1. The correct answer is C. The *OnPreExecute* event fires just before the execution of the task.

2. The correct answer is B. The data flow path enables you to configure data viewers to verify the status of data between data flow components.

3. The correct answer is D. The ActiveX Script task does not support debugging; it is offered only to maintain compatibility with earlier code.

Lesson 3: Selecting an Appropriate SSIS Technology or Strategy

Estimated lesson time: 25 minutes

In this lesson, you will learn about some of the design options you can consider when developing SSIS packages. First, the lesson looks at the various ways designers use SSIS technologies. Then you will see how to design your packages to optimize performance and how you can use SSIS technologies in projects that go beyond the traditional ETL process.

SSIS ETL Design Patterns

In computer science, a design pattern is a recommended, repeatable solution to common software design problems. A design pattern is a model or guide about how to create a solution. You find three typical design patterns in real-world ETL applications: SSIS packages as SQL placeholders, as conventional ETL, and as in-memory pipeline. Each of these solutions has advantages and disadvantages you must consider when using SSIS to design an ETL solution.

SSIS as a SQL Placeholder

The design pattern that uses SSIS as a placeholder for SQL code employs SQL to solve most of the ETL problems, including cleaning, transforming, formatting, integrating, and merging data. The role of the SSIS package is to provide a basic workflow for the tasks and, sometimes, to extract data from non-SQL sources.

A typical workflow diagram of a package that uses SSIS as a SQL placeholder looks like Figure 17-15.

You can see that control flow is primarily composed of SQL tasks. However, sometimes this type of package uses Bulk Insert or Data Flow tasks for the load segment of the ETL work. After the data is stored in a stage database, the rest of the process is performed through SQL tasks. The Bulk Insert task is used to gather data from files, and the data flow tasks in this pattern are very simple, using a single data source, no transformations, and single data flow destination.

SQL tasks in these packages are generally categorized by functionality, but this is not mandatory. Some designers use a single SQL task to do all the work, which provides all the required functionality in one or more statements.

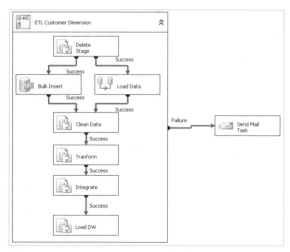

Figure 17-15   SSIS as a SQL placeholder

The SSIS task is used only to manage the workflow of the process and to provide minimum functionality, such as error control.

Advantages and Disadvantages   The main advantage of using SSIS as a SQL placeholder is that many developers are familiar with the SQL programming model. Database developers with ETL and integration experience likely also have deep knowledge of how to write efficient code to achieve the ETL goals.

Another important advantage is that, if programmed appropriately, this model can offer very good performance. Top performance is usually achieved because data might never have to leave the database server.

However, this design pattern also has limitations. The main limitation is that developers rarely have the required knowledge to solve ETL problems with Transact-SQL (T-SQL). Even when developers have the required experience, T-SQL is not always the appropriate language to solve these types of problems.

Another restriction of this pattern is that complex ETL tasks, such as text mining, data mining, and advanced transformations, might not be achievable by using SQL.

Conventional ETL with SSIS

The most common SSIS package design pattern is implementing conventional ETL with SSIS. Conventional ETL solutions feature very componentized packages with very narrow objectives. For example, a package's only purpose might be to extract data from a specific table, while another package might be responsible for cleaning wrong dates from a stage table.

A conventional ETL process can be organized into two elements: the ETL phase and the data warehouse object. In the ETL phase, you can design packages for the extraction phase, others for the transformation phase, and still others for the data loading phase. However, in most scenarios, one package per phase is not recommended; instead, you should create a set of packages for each object in the database (dimension or fact table) per phase. You then create a master package responsible for the overall control flow and orchestration of all packages. Figure 17-16 shows a sample master package that orchestrates other ETL packages.

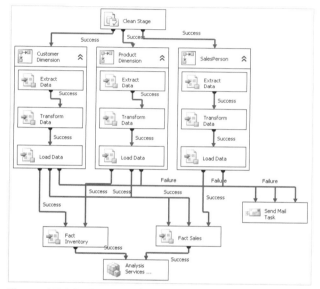

Figure 17-16   ETL Workflow master package

In the master package, you see that nearly all of the tasks are Execute Package tasks. In this case, the only exceptions are a SQL Command task to delete the stage database and an Analysis Services processing task to upload the information into the SSAS database. All other packages are responsible for a specific part of the ETL process in a particular database object.

Each package in the conventional ETL process has a different design pattern. The extraction package usually has a single simple data flow; its objective is to get data from the source as fast as possible, minimize the disruption of the OLTP systems, and store the data in a raw file or in a stage relational database, as Figure 17-17 shows.

Transformation packages in an ETL process are far more complex than extraction packages. Transformations are responsible for guaranteeing the quality of data stored in the database. Transformation packages clean, validate, change the format of, and merge data from different sources. Most of the time, these packages have a series of data flow tasks, each one responsible for one subtask. Figure 17-18 shows an example of a cleaning data flow task.

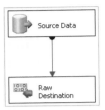

Figure 17-17 Conventional ETL extraction

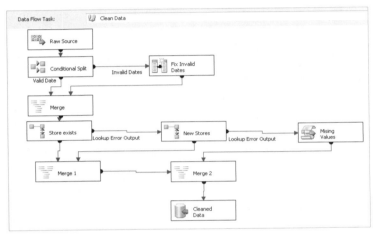

Figure 17-18 Cleaning data flow task

Finally, you have the loading tasks, which are similar to extraction tasks. They store the transformed data information in the data warehouse. Generally, a single data flow, containing a single data source and a single data destination component, does the job.

Advantages and Disadvantages   The main advantage of using conventional ETL with SSIS is that it is a mature model with proven results. The highly componentized solution breaks the complexity of the ETL into simple, easy-to-develop elements.

Another advantage of using this pattern is that it uses the power of SSIS, allowing rapid development of components that benefit from built-in components that solve standard ETL problems. Developers can use the best language or technology to solve the problem at hand.

One restriction of this SSIS pattern is performance. Because each component is a separate element of the process and each component reads and stores data in the database, it might need to read and store the same data numerous times. In large ETL processes, this model tends to deteriorate performance; it is not uncommon to have ETL processes that take more than 20 hours to process a data mart or data warehouse.

Another constraint of this design is maintainability. Because each package is responsible for only part of the processing, adding data attributes (columns) to the data warehouse requires changes in multiple packages.

ETL In-Memory Pipeline with SSIS

SQL Server 2005 introduced the ability to create in-memory ETL processes by using SSIS. An in-memory ETL solution uses the ability of SSIS packages to create fast in-memory pipelines that minimize the number of times data is stored in the database. These types of packages are designed with a one package–one object pattern. Furthermore, every step of the ETL process for a single data mart or data warehouse object happens in a single data flow task. The diagram in Figure 17-19 shows a simplified version of the in-memory ETL data flow responsible for extracting, transforming, and loading the customer dimension table.

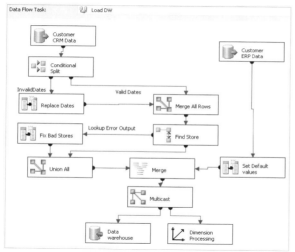

Figure 17-19   Data flow of an in-memory ETL

SSIS: Beyond ETL

Sometimes you use SSIS technologies to build solutions that go beyond the ETL process. The most common non-ETL scenarios include database maintenance, data or text mining, and application integration.

Database Maintenance

SSIS packages offer a set of tools designed to create maintenance plans. Maintenance plans use SSIS packages to personalize a workflow of tasks to manage databases. Database administrators can use maintenance plans to implement recovery plans for databases. Maintenance plans can also help administrators optimize database performance through the use of rebuild and reorganize index tasks.

You can create SSIS maintenance plans packages from BIDS or directly from SSMS. SSMS has a Maintenance Plan Wizard that helps automate the process of creating these packages. To create a maintenance plan from SSMS by using the Maintenance Plan Wizard, follow these steps:

1. Open SSMS.
2. In the Object Explorer, expand the Management folder.
3. Right-click the Maintenance Plans folder and select Maintenance Plan Wizard.

Data and Text Mining

Besides using data and text mining tasks in an ETL process, you can also create SSIS packages that support mining solutions. For example, if you attend an event and collect information about attendees, you can create a text mining package to import the data into your customer relationship management (CRM) system. The text mining tasks will help you determine whether the attendees are new customers or already exist in your CRM system. Data mining components might help you classify the new customers based on the likelihood that they will buy products.

Quick Check

1. What is the role of SSIS packages in an SSIS as SQL placeholder design pattern?
2. Which of the following is an advantage of creating a conventional ETL process?
   A. Performance
   B. Security
   C. Maintainability
   D. Mature and proven model
3. Which of the operational requirements is the main advantage of an in-memory ETL process?

Quick Check Answers

1. The correct answer is to orchestrate the SQL commands. The primary additional value of SSIS in this design pattern is to create the workflow to coordinate the SQL statements.
2. The correct answer is D. The main advantage of conventional ETL is that components are highly specialized and easy to develop, and the pattern is a mature and proven model.
3. The correct answer is performance. The primary benefit of an in-memory ETL design is to create transformations that do not read or store data between different ETL stages, increasing performance dramatically.

Case Scenario: Building an SSIS ETL Infrastructure

Adventure Works is a worldwide distributor of bicycles and accessories. The company's customers are primarily small bicycle stores that have a very limited technical infrastructure. You have been working with Adventure Works to help the company build an Internet Sales data mart, which will be used primarily by the sales and marketing departments. You are responsible for building the ETL infrastructure to populate an SSAS cube and dimensions.

Adventure Works users are looking forward to using the Internet Sales cube, and the sales manager wants to provide salespeople with a tool that enables them to track their sales and sales objectives. It will also help them choose when and how to launch promotional campaigns and other sales activities. The marketing manager is more interested in Internet Sales analysis, customer demographic information, and product profitability.

The cube will be implemented on a server running Windows 2003 and SQL Server 2005. The data mart needs to integrate information stored in the enterprise resource planning (ERP) and CRM databases. The LOB application was developed internally, and the CRM database is Microsoft Dynamics.

The IT department has some questions about the SSIS technologies you will be using in the ETL process. You are responsible for answering their questions.

1. Adventure Works database administrators (DBAs) are worried about the impact the ETL process will have on their OLTP databases. What are the performance advantages of using SSIS for ETL?

2. The Adventure Works development team wants to create the required infrastructure to test SSIS packages and provide the framework to practice regression testing. How would you suggest they achieve this goal?

3. The Sales department often receives copies of files, and salespeople want to import this data into the CRM application. What tasks or components would you use?

Chapter Summary

- SSIS is the new Microsoft SQL Server platform for creating ETL and data-integration solutions. SSIS offers new software development paradigms that help developers create ETL solutions faster than ever.

- SSIS has two main components: control flow and data flow. Control flow lets the designer orchestrate the ETL process and define how it interacts with the environment. Data flow is responsible for the actual ETL process.

- Debugging and testing SSIS packages is essential to ensuring their quality. BIDS provides a debug mode that lets you walk through your packages. You can set breakpoints to use in debugging control flow, and you can create data viewers to debug data flow.
- SSIS includes components for data mining, text mining, database management, and scripting that enable you to extend the functionality of your packages.

Case Scenario Answers

Chapter 1: Select SQL Server Services to Support Business Needs

1. Instead of creating a staging database every month, you can create a small data warehouse that you regularly populate by using Integration Services and then build an Analysis Services OLAP cube on the data warehouse. You can use Reporting Services to create the reports your customers need and build an extranet portal where you can post the reports for customers.

2. You cannot change your business application, but you can change the stored procedures that feed the application with data. You cannot consume Web services from T-SQL directly; however, you can create a CLR table-valued function that would use the supplier's Web service. Because you know exactly which Web service you are going to use, you can maintain security appropriately.

Chapter 2: Design a Logical Database

1. The first task you must perform to generate the needed report would be quite simple if there was no data in the database yet. You just need a supertype table called Partners that has a common identification schema and other attributes in common. You would use the Partners table for unique identification of a partner, and the Customers and Suppliers tables would become subtypes. They would need to use the same identification schema (that is, the same primary key), which you get from the Partners table. The problem is that you have existing data with no connection between the primary key of the Customers table and the primary key of the Suppliers table. Given the existing data, you must merge and cleanse the Customers and Suppliers tables into a Partners table; during the merge, you must create a new, common primary key. Add this primary key to both subtype tables, and then drop all the columns that you transferred to the supertype table. You have to add a foreign key from the Customers and Suppliers tables to the Partners table. However, you need to keep old identifications from Customers and Suppliers to maintain history, or you must update all historical data in the events tables with new identifications. In addition, you have to change the application to reflect the new schema. If you cannot change the application, you could have the application access views of the Customers and Suppliers tables instead of the tables themselves. As you can see, this is not an easy task. This example shows how important it is to identify supertypes at database design time.

2. Speeding up maintenance tasks is easier. You can store old data in historical tables or historical partitions of existing tables in a separate read-only filegroup. This filegroup needs less maintenance and, because the original filegroup is now smaller, the maintenance tasks run faster.

Chapter 3: Design a Physical Database

1. You can implement a partner hierarchy by using the adjacency model. Besides a PartnerId column, you can add a ParentId column and associate the columns with a *Foreign Key* constraint.

2. Your second task is somewhat tricky. Because you can have multiple *NULL* properties in the TaxId column, you cannot use a *Unique* constraint. You can enforce uniqueness for known tax IDs by using a trigger. In addition, you could create a view on the Partners table that includes only rows with known tax IDs. Then, you could create a unique index on that view. The unique index would reject duplite tax IDs; however, the index would not react to unknown values. You will learn more about indexed views in Chapter 4, "Designing a Database for Performance."

Chapter 4: Design a Database for Performance

1. You can create a view that aggregates the sales data and groups the data over the EmployeeId. You can index that view. Because you have SQL Server 2005 Enterprise Edition, the query optimizer will redirect the aggregate queries to the indexed view.

2. Include the SSID column in the nonclustered index on the EmployeeName column. This way, the query will be covered with the index.

Chapter 5: Implement Database Technologies and Techniques for Your Application

1. Your ASP.NET application can subscribe to query notifications for changes on the Products table. Thus, whenever a change is made, the application can update its cache with the latest data.

2. You can spread your database across multiple filegroups to reduce the time it takes to perform daily maintenance operations. You can use table partitioning to partition orders tables and have the current partition (the one that is updated frequently) on a small filegroup, while putting archive orders on a separate partition on another filegroup. Then, you can implement different administrative schedules for different partitions. For example, you can back up the filegroup with the current partition a couple of times per day, while backing up other, larger filegroups only once per week.

Chapter 6: Designing Objects That Retrieve Data

1. Because this query will be called from different analytical applications from different security contexts and environments, you want to protect the external applications from any changes in the data source by packaging the query into a view. The aggregated data is historical data. By defining an indexed view, you ensure that the aggregated values are materialized to disk, so there is no need for them to be recalculated on each call.
2. To accomplish this task, you decide to change the indexed view to a partitioned view. This way, data coming from all factories can be consolidated into a single view. The overall steps to achieve this are:
    A. Drop the index(es) on the view.
    B. Create the linked server connections to all the remote servers.
    C. Alter the view and change the query into a query that uses UNION ALL to combine the results coming from the multiple factories.
    D. Set up security on the view.
3. To allow filtering on the result set returned by the partitioned view created in the preceding task, you could take one of two approaches:
    A. Apply a filter to the SELECT statement that calls the view and apply the filter externally. The downside is that the applied filter will not be shared by all users because it is happening outside the view.
    B. Modify the partitioned view and change it into a stored procedure. Declare the territory and date as INPUT parameters for the stored procedure.
4. The need to join (or merge) the data with different factors, such as external providers, suggests that the query filter and join tables would vary, depending on input parameters. If you used a stored procedure, you could end up with a solution that uses dynamic T-SQL (executed with the sp_executesql system stored procedure), and it would be difficult to call the procedure with the EXECUTE statement instead of having the ability to analyze the results further and explore newer queries (possibly through subqueries).

Chapter 7: Adding an Audit Trail

1. You should add a ChangedBy column to each of the three tables related to purchase orders: Sales.SalesOrderHeader, Sales.SalesOrderDetail, and Sales.SalesOrderHeaderReason. The columns should have a *Default* constraint defined as *SYSTEM_USER*. You will also need to change the triggers to update the column when a row is updated.
2. The problem is that the earlier purchase order application is using the INSERT INTO statement without specifying the new column you added to the tables. You can rename the original table and create a view that has the original table name. The view will

include only the original columns and hide the recently added column so the application can successfully query the view.

3. Create three different Tomb tables, one each for DeletedOrderHeaders, DeletedOrder-Details, and DeletedOrderHeaderReasons. Copy the schema from the original tables and add an AuditID integer column as *Primary Key*. Create DELETE AFTER triggers in the source tables to copy the rows from the virtual Deleted tables into the Tomb tables.

Chapter 8: Design a Secure Application Solution

1. Implement auditing. SQL Server Profiler is shipped with SQL Server, so you can start using it immediately to trace events and find out what happened to certain transactions.

2. To reassure employees about the security of their personal data, encrypt all sensitive data.

Chapter 9: Design a Secure Database

1. You can force end users to access tables through the stored procedures by eliminating the broken ownership chains problem in the human resources database. You can do this by changing the owner of the objects to a single owner or by altering the procedures to use a different execution context and, for example, impersonate a single fictitious user who has permissions to access the base tables. Then, you can revoke all permissions on base tables from end users.

2. If you revoke all permissions on base tables from end users, they will no longer be able to create ad hoc reports. You can create views that have the same owner as the base tables and then grant SELECT permission only to your end users. However, when you create a view, you cannot specify a different execution context. Therefore, you can use views if there is a single owner of all base tables only; otherwise, you would encounter the same broken ownership chain problem as soon as your view joins data from two base tables with different owners. In such a case, you could use stored procedures and multistatement table-valued functions instead of views as the intermediate data access layer.

Chapter 10: Design a Unit Test Plan for a Database

1. Unit testing would definitely help improve the quality of applications. Currently, no testing is being executed, not even at the application level. However, because the database is accesed from multiple applications, you want to make sure that the database is fine-tuned. The main benefit of implementing unit testing is the ability to evaluate, in an independent testing environment, the effects of implementing a specific modification to the database.

2. You need to prioritize which are the most critical scenarios that require your attention. It is impossible to fix everything, and it is impossible to fine-tune everything. You need to focus on the top scenarios that, through optimization, will provide the greatest benefits by increasing the database performance and scalability. For each of these critical scenarios, you need to define performance goals so that you know how far from or close to your goal you are.

3. After revisiting the critical scenarios, you must decide which performance objectives you are going to aim for. This could involve objectives such as:

    A. Increasing CPU use by 20 percent to maximize the investment in the new database server, up to a high of 80 percent CPU use overall.

    B. Ensuring that the critical scenarios are served at least by 90 percent from the memory cache to decrease disk I/O.

    C. Ensuring that the response time is less than one second for the longest queries and 0.5 second for the average queries.

4. Data consistency tests and referential integrity are two different tools that database developers can use to maintain data integrity. Referential integrity is enforced by the relational database management system (RDMS) as defined by the database designer in a declarative approach that sets up the integrity validations the database should be maintaining. Some of those integrity enforcement rules cannot be easily written in a declarative form. Therefore, in other cases, the database designer implements validators in the form of stored procedures and functions. Data consistency testing enables you to validate data consistency enforcement overall, either by the RDMS or by your own custom constraint implementations.

5. The best way to evaluate a single feature independent of the whole is by using unit testing. When designing tests for application security, you could isolate all of the security features and evaluate them independently. Code coverage could always help. In this specific case, code coverage could help you discover that, because of a security context modification, a certain piece of software is not being executed.

Chapter 11: Create a Performance Baseline and Benchmarking Strategy

1. You must ask for the following documentation:

    ❑ The client application logical and physical design

    ❑ The infrastructure design

    ❑ Quality-of-service agreements with end users

    ❑ Expected workload metrics for the present and for the future (expected growth)

2. You decide to apply only transaction cost analysis. This technique enables you to estimate the computer resources required to meet an application's performance objectives over time. Transaction cost analysis estimates based on a single transaction. This transaction should be compiled based on the most common critical scenarios the end user will be executing. For this scenario, you must calculate the cost of each operation and the cost of executing the complete transaction. These costs are used to extrapolate the values based on the expected number of concurrent users and concurrent transactions and to estimate the required resources needed to execute them. You decide that predictive analysis is not a proper technique because the requirements for the new application differ from the requirements of the previous version of the application. Thus, the log files and historical data of the application cannot be used to predict the future capacity requirements.

3. Performance tuning and performance testing are iterative processes that usually include setting objectives, testing, tuning, and starting again. Testing must be executed in an environment with the same constraints, budgets, and capacity as the production environment for the tests to be as realistic as possible.

Chapter 12: Deploying a Database

1. The Copy Database Wizard copies data and doesn't give you the granular option to select tables and views only. The Import and Export Wizard also copies data. That leaves T-SQL scripts, SSIS, and SQLCmd as possible deployment techniques. The *Adventure-WorksLT* database is rather small at 7 MB total, so using SSIS seems excessive. If you choose SQLCmd, you will be executing T-SQL scripts, so they need to be generated anyway, and you can use the scripting functionality built into SSMS to generate the T-SQL scripts automatically.

2. To script the database deployment, in SSMS, expand Databases. Right-click *Adventure-WorksLT*, click Script Database As, and then click CREATE To. Click New Query Editor Window, as shown here.

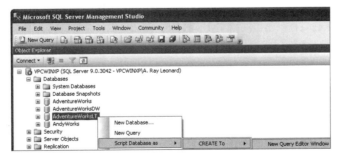

IMPORTANT   Test environment simulation

Use SQL Server Express to simulate the test environment server.

   A.   Change the current connection of the query window. Right-click in the query
window, click Connection, and then click Change Connection, as shown here.

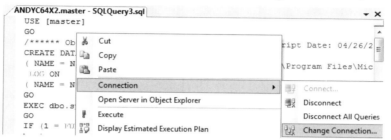

   B.   Login to SQL Server Express.
   C.   Before executing the script, edit the paths in the FILENAME statements.
   D.   Execute the script. Upon successful completion, you should see a statement simi-
lar to the following:

```
DBCC execution completed. If DBCC printed error messages, contact your system
administrator.
```

You have now deployed an empty database and are ready to deploy the tables to it.
Before you begin, you know that some of the tables exist within schemas. Also,
some of the columns use user-defined data types, which must be created first.
   E.   In SSMS, expand the *AdventureWorksLT* database, expand the Security folder, and
click the Schemas folder.
   F.   On the SSMS menu, click View, and then click Object Explorer Details. A list of
AdventureWorksLT schemas displays in the Object Explorer Details pane.
   G.   Right-click the SalesLT schema, click Script Schema As, click CREATE To, and then
click New Query Editor Window.
   H.   Change the connection to SQL Server Express and execute the script.
   I.   Repeat this procedure for user-defined data types and XML Schema Collections
(located in the AdventureWorksLT\Programmability\Types folder).
   J.   Next, navigate to the Tables folder in the *AdventureWorksLT* database. Ignore the
System Tables folder in the Object Explorer Details pane. Click the first table
(BuildVersion). Hold down the Shift key and click the last table (SalesOrder-
Header). This should select all tables displayed.

K. Right-click the selection, click Script Table As, click CREATE To, and then click New Query Editor Window.

L. In the Query window, change the connection to SQL Server Express and execute the script.

You have successfully deployed the tables and associated objects. Views are next.

M. In SSMS, navigate to \Databases\AdventureWorksLT\Views. In Object Explorer Details, select the three views and generate CREATE scripts to a new query window. Change the connection and execute the scripts to deploy the views to SQL Server Express.

3. The Import and Export Wizard is an excellent choice to accomplish data migration to the tables you've deployed. Here's how you plan to do it:

    A. In SSMS, navigate to the *AdventureWorksLT* database. Right-click the database, click Tasks, and then click Export Data.

    B. Click Next when the Welcome page displays.

    C. Click Next on the Source Selection page.

    D. When the Destination Selection page displays, set the Server Name to your instance of SQL Server Express and the Database to *AdventureWorksLT*.

    E. On the next page, select the Copy Data From One Or More Tables Or Views option. Click Next.

    F. On the Select Source Tables and Views screen, select the tables.

    G. Click Next.

    H. Accept the defaults on the Save and Execute page and click Finish to execute the package. The Import and Export Wizard should succeed, as shown here.

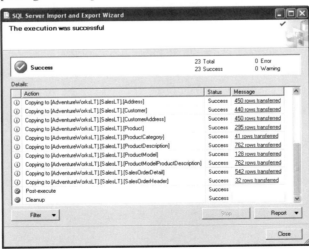

Chapter 13: Controlling Changes to Source Code

1. The first requirement requests a source control application or server that will be supported for the next four to seven years. Visual SourceSafe 2005 might or might not survive the next four to seven years. Visual SourceSafe is certainly integrated into database and application development environments, but it falls short of supporting the full software development life cycle. So, you continue your search.

2. The second requirement refers to an application or server with an integrated client for database and application development. There are several third-party and open-source tools available that accomplish all the component requirements to support the full software development life cycle. There will likely always be third-party and open-source tools available. Although the tools integrate into development environments, there are multiple tools to manage and no guarantee that they will continue to work well together. You think there must be a better solution.

3. The third requirement seeks an application or server that supports the full software development life cycle and all project roles. Visual Studio Team Foundation Server, released in 2006, is a core component of the Microsoft Visual Studio 2005 Team System and will survive four to seven years. It integrates seamlessly into database and application development environments. Visual Studio Team Foundation Server supports all project roles throughout the full software development life cycle. Visual Studio Team Foundation Server meets all your requirements.

Chapter 14: Design a Distributed Data Solution

1. In this case, the technology that meets the requirements is HTTP endpoints.

2. You could create stored procedures that retrieve the data to be distributed and then create HTTP endpoints that publish the stored procedures as Web methods. Use the stored procedure sp_reserve_http_namespace to reserve the namespace in http.sys.

3. Use SSL to protect the data transmitted between your databases and the travel agencies.

Chapter 15: Building a Reporting Services Infrastructure for a SharePoint Portal

1. Report Model will enable your development team to create a report model that enables users to create reports without learning T-SQL or the complex normalized schema of relational databases.

2. The READ COMMITTED SNAPSHOT isolation level uses row versioning to prevent readers from blocking writers.

3. You can recommend that the development team create a set of stored procedures that have a LoginID input parameter, group this stored procedure in one or more schemas, and grant a Reporting Services account Execute right to the schemas. No other end users should have access to these schemas or stored procedures. Use the UserID captured in SSRS to assign the value of the parameter.

Chapter 16: Design a Notification Services Application

1. Use ICF and ADF files instead of NMO. NMO does not enable you to track history information.
2. Notification Services uses the SQL Server *tempdb* system database intensely. Implement common *tempdb* optimization techniques such as sizing *tempdb* appropriately, using as many files as processors, and so on.
3. In this case, implement a continuous provider, which starts and stops when Notification Services does.

Chapter 17: Building an SSIS ETL Infrastructure

1. You can assure the Adventure Works DBAs that SSIS enables you to design packages that do a lot of the work required in the ETL process without affecting the performance of the source dataset.
2. For each SSIS package the developers build, they can create one or more test SSIS packages that evaluate the performance and functionality of a package.
3. With SSIS, you can use the File data source to extract the information. Fuzzy Grouping and other transformations can help you clean the data, and you can specify an OLE DB destination to incorporate the data into the CRM application.

Index

Symbols and Numerics

Additional SQL Server Resources for Administrators
Published and Forthcoming Titles from Microsoft Press

Microsoft® SQL Server™ 2005 Reporting Services *Step by Step*
Hitachi Consulting Services • ISBN 0-7356-2250-7

SQL Server Reporting Services (SRS) is Microsoft's customizable reporting solution for business data analysis. It is one of the key value features of SQL Server 2005: functionality more advanced and much less expensive than its competition. SRS is powerful, so an understanding of how to architect a report, as well as how to install and program SRS, is key to harnessing the full functionality of SQL

Server. This procedural tutorial shows how to use the Report Project Wizard, how to think about and access data, and how to build queries. It also walks the reader through the creation of charts and visual layouts to enable maximum visual understanding of the data analysis. Interactivity (enhanced in SQL Server 2005) and security are also covered in detail.

Microsoft SQL Server 2005 Administrator's Pocket Consultant
William R. Stanek • ISBN 0-7356-2107-1

Here's the utterly practical, pocket-sized reference for IT professionals who need to administer, optimize, and maintain SQL Server 2005 in their organizations. This unique guide provides essential details for using SQL Server 2005 to help protect and manage your company's data—whether automating tasks; creating indexes and views; performing backups and recovery; replicating transactions; tuning performance; managing server

activity; importing and exporting data; or performing other key tasks. Featuring quick-reference tables, lists, and step-by-step instructions, this handy, one-stop guide provides fast, accurate answers on the spot, whether you're at your desk or in the field!

Microsoft SQL Server 2005 Administrator's Companion
Marci Frohock Garcia, Edward Whalen, and Mitchell Schroeter • ISBN 0-7356-2198-5

Microsoft SQL Server 2005 Administrator's Companion is the comprehensive, in-depth guide that saves time by providing all the technical information you need to deploy, administer, optimize, and support SQL Server 2005. Using a hands-on, example-rich approach, this authoritative, one-volume reference book provides expert advice, product information, detailed solutions, procedures, and real-world troubleshooting tips from experienced SQL Server 2005 professionals. This expert guide shows you how to design high-availability database systems, prepare for installation, install and configure SQL Server 2005, administer services and features, and maintain and troubleshoot your database system. It covers how to configure your system for your I/O system and model and optimize system capacity. The expert authors provide details on how to create and use defaults, constraints, rules, indexes, views, functions, stored procedures, and triggers. This guide shows you how to administer reporting services, analysis services, notification services, and integration services. It also provides a wealth of information on replication and the specifics of snapshot, transactional, and merge replication. Finally, there is expansive coverage of how to manage and tune your SQL Server system, including automating tasks, backup and restoration of databases, and management of users and security.

Microsoft SQL Server 2005 Analysis Services *Step by Step*
Hitachi Consulting Services • ISBN 0-7356-2199-3

One of the key features of SQL Server 2005 is SQL Server Analysis Services—Microsoft's customizable analysis solution for business data modeling and interpretation. Just compare SQL Server Analysis Services to its competition to understand/grasp the great value of its enhanced features. One of the keys to harnessing the full functionality of SQL Server will be leveraging Analysis Services for the powerful tool that it is—including creating a cube, and deploying, customizing, and extending the basic calculations. This step-by-step tutorial discusses how to get started, how to build scalable analytical applications, and how to use and administer advanced features. Interactivity (which is enhanced in SQL Server 2005), data translation, and security are also covered in detail.

Microsoft SQL Server 2005 Express Edition
Step by Step
Jackie Goldstein • ISBN 0-7356-2184-5

Inside Microsoft SQL Server 2005:
The Storage Engine
Kalen Delaney • ISBN 0-7356-2105-5

Inside Microsoft SQL Server 2005:
T-SQL Programming
Itzik Ben-Gan • ISBN 0-7356-2197-7

Inside Microsoft SQL Server 2005:
Query Processing and Optimization
Kalen Delaney • ISBN 0-7356-2196-9

For more information about Microsoft Press® books and other learning products,
visit: **www.microsoft.com/mspress** *and* **www.microsoft.com/learning**

Additional SQL Server Resources for Developers
Published and Forthcoming Titles from Microsoft Press

Microsoft® SQL Server™ 2005 Express Edition
Step by Step
Jackie Goldstein • ISBN 0-7356-2184-5

Teach yourself how to get database projects up and running quickly with SQL Server Express Edition—a free, easy-to-use database product that is based on SQL Server 2005 technology. It's designed for building simple, dynamic applications, with all the rich functionality of the SQL Server database engine and using the same data access APIs, such as Microsoft ADO.NET, SQL Native Client, and T-SQL. Whether you're new to database programming or new to SQL Server, you'll learn how, when, and why to use specific features of this simple but powerful database development environment. Each chapter puts you to work, building your knowledge of core capabilities and guiding you as you create actual components and working applications.

Microsoft SQL Server 2005 Programming
Step by Step
Fernando Guerrero • ISBN 0-7356-2207-8

SQL Server 2005 is Microsoft's next-generation data management and analysis solution that delivers enhanced scalability, availability, and security features to enterprise data and analytical applications while making them easier to create, deploy, and manage. Now you can teach yourself how to design, build, test, deploy, and maintain SQL Server databases—one step at a time. Instead of merely focusing on describing new features, this book shows new database programmers and administrators how to use specific features within typical business scenarios. Each chapter provides a highly practical learning experience that demonstrates how to build database solutions to solve common business problems.

Microsoft SQL Server 2005 Analysis Services
Step by Step
Hitachi Consulting Services • ISBN 0-7356-2199-3

One of the key features of SQL Server 2005 is SQL Server Analysis Services—Microsoft's customizable analysis solution for business data modeling and interpretation. Just compare SQL Server Analysis Services to its competition to understand the great value of its enhanced features. One of the keys to harnessing the full functionality of SQL Server will be leveraging Analysis Services for the powerful tool that it is—including creating a cube, and deploying, customizing, and extending the basic calculations. This step-by-step tutorial discusses how to get started, how to build scalable analytical applications, and how to use and administer advanced features. Interactivity (enhanced in SQL Server 2005), data translation, and security are also covered in detail.

Microsoft SQL Server 2005 Reporting Services
Step by Step
Hitachi Consulting Services • ISBN 0-7356-2250-7

SQL Server Reporting Services (SRS) is Microsoft's customizable reporting solution for business data analysis. It is one of the key value features of SQL Server 2005: functionality more advanced and much less expensive than its competition. SRS is powerful, so an understanding of how to architect a report, as well as how to install and program SRS, is key to harnessing the full functionality of SQL Server. This procedural tutorial shows how to use the Report Project Wizard, how to think about and access data, and how to build queries. It also walks through the creation of charts and visual layouts for maximum visual understanding of data analysis. Interactivity (enhanced in SQL Server 2005) and security are also covered in detail.

Programming Microsoft SQL Server 2005
Andrew J. Brust, Stephen Forte, and William H. Zack
ISBN 0-7356-1923-9

This thorough, hands-on reference for developers and database administrators teaches the basics of programming custom applications with SQL Server 2005. You will learn the fundamentals of creating database applications—including coverage of T-SQL, Microsoft .NET Framework, and Microsoft ADO.NET. In addition to practical guidance on database architecture and design, application development, and reporting and data analysis, this essential reference guide covers performance, tuning, and availability of SQL Server 2005.

Inside Microsoft SQL Server 2005:
The Storage Engine
Kalen Delaney • ISBN 0-7356-2105-5

Inside Microsoft SQL Server 2005:
T-SQL Programming
Itzik Ben-Gan • ISBN 0-7356-2197-7

Inside Microsoft SQL Server 2005:
Query Processing and Optimization
Kalen Delaney • ISBN 0-7356-2196-9

Programming Microsoft ADO.NET 2.0 Core Reference
David Sceppa • ISBN 0-7356-2206-X

For more information about Microsoft Press® books and other learning products,
visit: **www.microsoft.com/mspress** *and* **www.microsoft.com/learning**

Microsoft
Press

Additional Resources for Developers: Advanced Topics and Best Practices

Published and Forthcoming Titles from Microsoft Press

Code Complete, Second Edition
Steve McConnell • ISBN 0-7356-1967-0

For more than a decade, Steve McConnell, one of the premier authors and voices in the software community, has helped change the way developers write code—and produce better software. Now his classic book, *Code Complete*, has been fully updated and revised with best practices in the art and science of constructing software. Topics include design, applying good techniques to construction, eliminating errors, planning, managing construction activities, and relating personal character to superior software. This new edition features fully updated information on programming techniques, including the emergence of Web-style programming, and integrated coverage of object-oriented design. You'll also find new code examples—both good and bad—in C++, Microsoft® Visual Basic®, C#, and Java, although the focus is squarely on techniques and practices.

More About Software Requirements: Thorny Issues and Practical Advice
Karl E. Wiegers • ISBN 0-7356-2267-1

Have you ever delivered software that satisfied all of the project specifications, but failed to meet any of the customers expectations? Without formal, verifiable requirements—and a system for managing them—the result is often a gap between what developers think they're supposed to build and what customers think they're going to get. Too often, lessons about software requirements engineering processes are formal or academic, and not of value to real-world, professional development teams. In this follow-up guide to *Software Requirements*, Second Edition, you will discover even more practical techniques for gathering and managing software requirements that help you deliver software that meets project and customer specifications. Succinct and immediately useful, this book is a must-have for developers and architects.

Software Estimation: Demystifying the Black Art
Steve McConnell • ISBN 0-7356-0535-1

Often referred to as the "black art" because of its complexity and uncertainty, software estimation is not as hard or mysterious as people think. However, the art of how to create effective cost and schedule estimates has not been very well publicized. *Software Estimation* provides a proven set of procedures and heuristics that software developers, technical leads, and project managers can apply to their projects. Instead of arcane treatises and rigid modeling techniques, award-winning author Steve McConnell gives practical guidance to help organizations achieve basic estimation proficiency and lay the groundwork to continue improving project cost estimates. This book does not avoid the more complex mathematical estimation approaches, but the non-mathematical reader will find plenty of useful guidelines without getting bogged down in complex formulas.

Debugging, Tuning, and Testing Microsoft .NET 2.0 Applications
John Robbins • ISBN 0-7356-2202-7

Making an application the best it can be has long been a time-consuming task best accomplished with specialized and costly tools. With Microsoft Visual Studio® 2005, developers have available a new range of built-in functionality that enables them to debug their code quickly and efficiently, tune it to optimum performance, and test applications to ensure compatibility and trouble-free operation. In this accessible and hands-on book, debugging expert John Robbins shows developers how to use the tools and functions in Visual Studio to their full advantage to ensure high-quality applications.

The Security Development Lifecycle
Michael Howard and Steve Lipner • ISBN 0-7356-2214-0

Adapted from Microsoft's standard development process, the Security Development Lifecycle (SDL) is a methodology that helps reduce the number of security defects in code at every stage of the development process, from design to release. This book details each stage of the SDL methodology and discusses its implementation across a range of Microsoft software, including Microsoft Windows Server™ 2003, Microsoft SQL Server™ 2000 Service Pack 3, and Microsoft Exchange Server 2003 Service Pack 1, to help measurably improve security features. You get direct access to insights from Microsoft's security team and lessons that are applicable to software development processes worldwide, whether on a small-scale or a large-scale. This book includes a CD featuring videos of developer training classes.

Software Requirements, Second Edition
Karl E. Wiegers • ISBN 0-7356-1879-8

Writing Secure Code, Second Edition
Michael Howard and David LeBlanc • ISBN 0-7356-1722-8

CLR via C#, Second Edition
Jeffrey Richter • ISBN 0-7356-2163-2

For more information about Microsoft Press® books and other learning products, visit: **www.microsoft.com/mspress** *and* **www.microsoft.com/learning**

Microsoft®
Press

Additional Windows (R2) Resources for Administrators
Published and Forthcoming Titles from Microsoft Press

Microsoft® Windows Server™ 2003 Administrator's Pocket Consultant, Second Edition
William R. Stanek • ISBN 0-7356-2245-0

Here's the practical, pocket-sized reference for IT professionals supporting Microsoft Windows Server 2003—fully updated for Service Pack 1 and Release 2. Designed for quick referencing, this portable guide covers all the essentials for performing everyday system administration tasks. Topics include managing workstations and servers, using Active Directory® directory service, creating and administering user and group accounts, managing files and directories, performing data security and auditing tasks, handling data back-up and recovery, and administering networks using TCP/IP, WINS, and DNS, and more.

MCSE Self-Paced Training Kit (Exams 70-290, 70-291, 70-293, 70-294): Microsoft Windows Server 2003 Core Requirements, Second Edition
Holme, Thomas, Mackin, McLean, Zacker, Spealman, Hudson, and Craft • ISBN 0-7356-2290-6

The Microsoft Certified Systems Engineer (MCSE) credential is the premier certification for professionals who analyze the business requirements and design and implement the infrastructure for business solutions based on the Microsoft Windows Server 2003 platform and Microsoft Windows Server System—now updated for Windows Server 2003 Service Pack 1 and R2. This all-in-one set provides in-depth preparation for the four required networking system exams. Work at your own pace through the lessons, hands-on exercises, troubleshooting labs, and review questions. You get expert exam tips plus a full review section covering all objectives and sub-objectives in each study guide. Then use the Microsoft Practice Tests on the CD to challenge yourself with more than 1500 questions for self-assessment and practice!

Microsoft Windows® Small Business Server 2003 R2 Administrator's Companion
Charlie Russel, Sharon Crawford, and Jason Gerend • ISBN 0-7356-2280-9

Get your small-business network, messaging, and collaboration systems up and running quickly with the essential guide to administering Windows Small Business Server 2003 R2. This reference details the features, capabilities, and technologies for both the standard and premium editions—including Microsoft Windows Server 2003 R2, Exchange Server 2003 with Service Pack 1, Windows SharePoint® Services, SQL Server™ 2005 Workgroup Edition, and Internet Information Services. Discover how to install, upgrade, or migrate to Windows Small Business Server 2003 R2; plan and implement your network, Internet access, and security services; customize Microsoft Exchange Server for your e-mail needs; and administer user rights, shares, permissions, and Group Policy.

Microsoft Windows Small Business Server 2003 R2 Administrator's Companion
Charlie Russel, Sharon Crawford, and Jason Gerend • ISBN 0-7356-2280-9

Here's the ideal one-volume guide for the IT professional administering Windows Server 2003. Now fully updated for Windows Server 2003 Service Pack 1 and R2, this *Administrator's Companion* offers up-to-date information on core system administration topics for Microsoft Windows, including Active Directory services, security, scripting, disaster planning and recovery, and interoperability with UNIX. It also includes all-new sections on Service Pack 1 security updates and new features for R2. Featuring easy-to-use procedures and handy work-arounds, this book provides ready answers for on-the-job results.

MCSA/MCSE Self-Paced Training Kit (Exam 70-290): Managing and Maintaining a Microsoft Windows Server 2003 Environment, Second Edition
Dan Holme and Orin Thomas • ISBN 0-7356-2289-2

MCSA/MCSE Self-Paced Training Kit (Exam 70-291): Implementing, Managing, and Maintaining a Microsoft Windows Server 2003 Network Infrastructure, Second Edition
J.C. Mackin and Ian McLean • ISBN 0-7356-2288-4

MCSE Self-Paced Training Kit (Exam 70-293): Planning and Maintaining a Microsoft Windows Server 2003 Network Infrastructure, Second Edition
Craig Zacker • ISBN 0-7356-2287-6

MCSE Self-Paced Training Kit (Exam 70-294): Planning, Implementing, and Maintaining a Microsoft Windows Server 2003 Active Directory® Infrastructure, Second Ed.
Jill Spealman, Kurt Hudson, and Melissa Craft • ISBN 0-7356-2286-8

For more information about Microsoft Press® books and other learning products,
visit: **www.microsoft.com/mspress** *and* **www.microsoft.com/learning**

Microsoft Press products are available worldwide wherever quality computer books are sold. For more information, contact your book or computer retailer, software reseller, or local Microsoft Sales Office, or visit our Web site at **www.microsoft.com/mspress**. To locate your nearest source for Microsoft Press products, or to order directly, call 1-800-MSPRESS in the United States. (In Canada, call **1-800-268-2222**.)

System Requirements

We recommend that you use a test workstation, test server, or staging server to complete the exercises in each lab. The following are the minimum system requirements your computer needs to meet to complete the practice exercises in this book. For more information, see the "Introduction."

Hardware Requirements

The following hardware is required to complete the lab exercises:

- Personal computer with a 600 MHz Pentium III compatible or faster processor
- 512 MB of RAM or more (1 GB or more recommended)
- 350 MB free hard disk space for the Microsoft SQL Server installation
- 450 MB additional free hard disk space if you plan to install SQL Server Books Online and sample databases
- 3 GB additional free hard disk space for Microsoft Visual Studio 2005
- CD-ROM drive or DVD-ROM drive
- Super VGA (1,024 x 768) or higher resolution video adapter and monitor
- Keyboard and Microsoft mouse or compatible pointing device

Software Requirements

The following software is required to complete the lab exercises:

- One of the following operating systems:
  - Microsoft Windows Server 2003, Standard Edition SP1
  - Windows Server 2003, Enterprise Edition SP1
  - Windows Server 2003, Datacenter Edition SP1
  - Windows XP Professional SP2
  - Windows Vista Business edition
  - Windows Vista Ultimate
  - Windows Vista Enterprise
- SQL Server 2005. A 180-day evaluation of SQL Server Enterprise Edition is included on companion DVD with this book and is available as a free download from the MSDN Web site at *http://www.microsoft.com/sql/downloads/trial-software.mspx*.
- The *AdventureWorks* database; available as a separate download with the SQL Server 2005 samples from the Microsoft Downloads site at *http://www.microsoft.com/downloads/*.

- Visual Studio 2005 or Visual Studio 2005 SP1. A free 90-day evaluation of Visual Studio 2005 Professional Edition is available for download from the MSDN Web site at *http://msdn2.microsoft.com/en-us/vstudio/bb188238.aspx*. Visual Studio 2005 SP1 works with Visual Studio 2005 Standard Edition, Professional Edition, and Team Edition and is available from the Microsoft Download site.
- Microsoft Office Visio or, if you do not have Office 2007, Visio 2007 Viewer, available for download from *http://www.microsoft.com/downloads/details.aspx?FamilyID=d88e4542-b174-4198-ae31-6884e9edd524&DisplayLang=en*.
- Microsoft Internet Explorer 6.0 SP1 or later.
- Internet Information Services (IIS) 5.0 or later with Simple Mail Transport Protocol (SMTP) virtual server installed.

What do you think of this book?

We want to hear from you!

Do you have a few minutes to participate in a brief online survey?

Microsoft is interested in hearing your feedback so we can continually improve our books and learning resources for you.

To participate in our survey, please visit:

www.microsoft.com/learning/booksurvey/

...and enter this book's ISBN-10 number (appears above barcode on back cover*). As a thank-you to survey participants in the United States and Canada, each month we'll randomly select five respondents to win one of five $100 gift certificates from a leading online merchant. At the conclusion of the survey, you can enter the drawing by providing your e-mail address, which will be used for prize notification only.

Thanks in advance for your input. Your opinion counts!

* Where to find the ISBN-10 on back cover

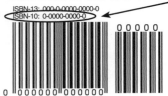

Example only. Each book has unique ISBN.

Microsoft Press